An Asian American Ancient
Historian and Biblical Scholar

All rights reserved. Illustration of Dr. Edwin Yamauchi
by Alex Waldo © Museum of the Bible, 2017

An Asian American Ancient Historian and Biblical Scholar

Edwin M. Yamauchi

FOREWORD BY
Stephen B. Kellough

RESOURCE *Publications* · Eugene, Oregon

AN ASIAN AMERICAN ANCIENT HISTORIAN AND BIBLICAL SCHOLAR

Copyright © 2024 Edwin M. Yamauchi. All rights reserved. Except for brief quotations in critical publications or reviews, no part of this book may be reproduced in any manner without prior written permission from the publisher. Write: Permissions, Wipf and Stock Publishers, 199 W. 8th Ave., Suite 3, Eugene, OR 97401.

Resource Publications
An Imprint of Wipf and Stock Publishers
199 W. 8th Ave., Suite 3
Eugene, OR 97401

www.wipfandstock.com

PAPERBACK ISBN: 979-8-3852-1160-9
HARDCOVER ISBN: 979-8-3852-1161-6
EBOOK ISBN: 979-8-3852-1162-3

VERSION NUMBER 06/10/24

To
Gail a.k.a. Haruko
Our "Daughter of Spring"

Contents

List of Figures and Maps | x
Foreword by Stephen B. Kellough | xv
Preface | xvii

1. Hawaiian Royalty and Missionaries | 1
2. Pineapples, Sugar, and Immigrants | 7
3. Ancestors, Relatives, and Parents | 29
4. World War II | 39
5. Elementary Years | 56
6. Iolani and the Episcopal Church | 61
7. Conversion | 70
8. A New Father and a New City | 74
9. C.Y.C. and C.B.C. | 84
10. U.H. and *Ka Leo* | 92
11. Shelton College | 97
12. Brandeis University | 111
13. Rutgers University | 126
14. Israel and a Final Year | 134
15. Miami University | 152
16. An Eventful Year | 168
17. The Next Three Years | 175

CONTENTS

18. Near East Travels | 186
19. The Rest of the 1970s | 206
20. The First Half of the 1980s | 214
21. The United Kingdom | 231
22. The Rest of the 1980s | 241
23. The First Half of the 1990s | 252
24. The Second Half of the 1990s | 266
25. The First Two Years of the 2000s | 284
26. The E. T. S. | 294
27. Retirement | 313
28. Switzerland and Scotland | 327
29. Japan and Okinawa | 333
30. The Year 2009 | 345
31. Glaciers and the Canadian Rockies | 350
32. Hawaii | 357
33. A Wedding | 366
34. The Year 2013 | 374
35. The Year 2014 | 381
36. New England | 385
37. The Year 2016 | 392
38. Family Reunion | 399
39. The Year 2018 | 407
40. Downsizing and a Move | 411
41. The Year of the Pandemic | 418
42. The I.B.R. | 425
43. The D.D.L. | 442
44. The Scriptorium | 453
45. T.M.O.B. | 470
46. O.B.F. | 493

Excursus List

A. Barack Obama in Hawaii | 537
B. The MIS in Okinawa | 542
C. Japan's Imperial Family | 546
D. The Higa Boarding House | 548
E. Carmen Higa Mochizuki | 551
F. Kimie Honda | 553
G. Gordon's PhD Students | 555
H. Tributes to Cyrus Gordon | 562
I. A Public Ivy | 563
J. The Cradle of Coaches | 566
K. Signers of The Gentle Revolution | 569
L. Bible Interpreters of the Twentieth Century | 571
M. Schools, States, and Countries Where My Students Have Taught | 573
N. Annual History Lectures | 575
O. Near East Archaeological Society Honors | 577
P. Colleges and Universities Where I Have Lectured | 579
Q. Seminaries Where I Have Lectured | 583
R. Chapters Contributed to Festschriften | 585
S. Mary Stout | 586
T. Notable OBF Alumni | 588
U. List of Publications | 618
V. Biographical Listings | 644

List of Figures

Figure 1. Shingon Buddhist temple | 22

Figure 2. Makiki Christian Church | 26

Figure 3. Owan Family: front row: Chogi (Jim), Choken (Tom), Babasan, Jijisan. Behind: Yoshie (Kaytie), Shizuko (Beryl), Chosei (Bob). Missing are the two oldest children, Haruko and Choko. | 31

Figure 4. Yamauchi Family: front row: Shojin, Ojisan, Mithcan, Kiyochan, Masanobu, Obasan; back row: Shoyei, Shokyo (my father), Hatsue | 34

Figure 5. Shokyo and Haruko Yamauchi, wedding portrait | 36

Figure 6. My parents with their newborn son | 37

Figure 7. With a toy samurai sword | 38

Figure 8. With Ronald Tsuchiya | 44

Figure 9. Sentry tower at Manzanar (courtesy Jon Yamashiro) | 46

Figure 10. Albert Nakama, receiving a military award from France | 53

Figure 11. With my mother | 57

Figure 12. Judo class. I am at the left in the top row. | 59

Figure 13. With Harry Fujiwara | 60

Figure 14. Iolani, class of 1954 | 62

Figure 15. Dick Lum | 71

Figure 16. Renyu and Haruko Higa | 73

LIST OF FIGURES

Figure 17. Yamauchi Family: Shoan standing second from left | 81

Figure 18. Renyu and Haruko with Akiko | 83

Figure 19. CYC group: EMY and Claude Curtis standing on right | 86

Figure 20. At the CYC ranch | 88

Figure 21. At Columbia Bible College | 90

Figure 22. *Ka Leo* on the Golden Rule Debate | 96

Figure 23. At the Shelton College library | 103

Figure 24. Ralph Beich | 109

Figure 25. Arabic class: kneeling EMY and Gordon Newby; back row: George Giacumakis, Joseph DeSomogyi, Jack Sasson, Fred Bush, and Harry Hoffner | 115

Figure 26. With Cyrus Gordon | 119

Figure 27. Mandaic Magic Bowl published in *Berytus* | 121

Figure 28. Ed and Kimi, wedding portrait | 123

Figure 29. With Eugene Genovese | 131

Figure 30. IVCF chapter at Rutgers | 132

Figure 31. Benjamin Mazar at the Temple Mount | 142

Figure 32. Walter Farmer and the bust of Nefertiti (courtesy of *The Miamian*) | 161

Figure 33. With Alan Millard | 172

Figure 34. With John Warwick Montgomery | 178

Figure 35. NT panel at Wheaton College chaired by Merrill Tenney: from left to right: Bill Lane, F. F. Bruce, Howard Marshall, EMY, and George Ladd | 184

Figure 36. By the Sphinx | 195

Figure 37. Mithraic Congress at Tehran: the empress is flanked on her right by Harold Bailey and on her left by Roman Ghirshman; I am in the front row, the fourth from the right. | 202

Figure 38. History faculty: I am fourth from the left; Dr. Shriver is at the far right. | 217

LIST OF FIGURES

Figure 39. ASA council: Ann Hunt, Russ Heddendorf, and Don Munro, Tom Olson, and EMY | 223

Figure 40. With David Stronach | 226

Figure 41. As president of the ASA, I congratulated Dick Bube, the editor of the *Journal of the ASA.* | 227

Figure 42. With Kenneth Kitchen | 230

Figure 43. With Donald Wiseman | 240

Figure 44. With Mickey Maudlin | 259

Figure 45. With Kelly Monroe | 264

Figure 46. With Lee Strobel | 269

Figure 47. With John Polkinghorne | 273

Figure 48. With Samuel Moffett, Scott Luley, and Bruce Metzger | 277

Figure 49. With Mandeans at the Charles River | 281

Figure 50. Mandean Conference at Harvard | 282

Figure 51. Wedding in Hawaii: Brian, Gail, Kimi, Alicia, Heinz, EMY, my mother, Tama from Taiwan, and Tom Owan | 285

Figure 52. With Daniel Master and Larry Stager | 296

Figure 53. Officers of the CFH congratulate Dick and Charlene Pierard. From left to right: Tom Askew, Bob Linder, Ron Wells, Chuck Webber, and EMY | 298

Figure 54. With Harold Mare | 300

Figure 55. With Ward Gasque | 303

Figure 56. With Eugene Merrill | 308

Figure 57. Louisville Conference: from left to right: Harry Hoffner, Simon Sherwin, John Walton, Lawson Younger, Rick Hess, Alan Millard, Jerry Mattingly, Daniel Fleming, Daniel Block, Jim Hoffmeier, Joel Drinkard, and EMY | 311

Figure 58. With Dr. Philip Shriver at my retirement | 314

Figure 59. With Nicholas Perrin | 318

Figure 60. Venture for Victory Team | 323

Figure 61. With doctoral students at the ETS conference: From left to right: Bob Smith, John DeFelice, John Wineland, Jerry Pattengale, Steve Stannish, Adam Chambers, and Carl Smith | 325

Figure 62. Mark Noll | 351

Figure 63. With Dennis Kinlaw | 363

Figure 64. With Dot Chappell | 364

Figure 65. With Paul Maier | 368

Figure 66. With William Lane Craig | 379

Figure 67. With Daniel Wallace | 387

Figure 68. With Paul Gould | 391

Figure 69. With Santa Ono | 394

Figure 70. With Jim Hoffmeier | 405

Figure 71. With Ben Witherington III | 409

Figure 72. With Deirdre Fulton | 420

Figure 73. Ed and Kimi at the Knolls | 415

Figure 74. Poster for Jennifer Wiseman's lecture | 416

Figure 75. With Darlene Brooks Hedstrom | 422

Figure 76. With Earle Ellis | 430

Figure 77. With Jerry Hawthorne | 433

Figure 78. With Bas Van Elderen | 435

Figure 79. With Craig Evans | 439

Figure 80. With Peter Machinist | 450

Figure 81. With Marvin Wilson | 452

Figure 82. With Scott Carroll at the Van Kampen home | 457

Figure 83. Walt and Marge Kaiser | 458

Figure 84. Portrait of Bob and Judith Van Kampen | 461

Figure 85. Kimi at Hampton Court, Hereford | 462

Figure 86. Hereford Conference 1995. In the center, I am flanked by Scott Carroll on my right and Jerry Pattengale on my left. | 463

LIST OF FIGURES

Figure 87. Hereford Conference 2000. I am kneeling in the front row on the left. | 467

Figure 88. With Géza Vermes | 468

Figure 89. With Jerry Pattengale on my right and Steve Green on my left | 481

Figure 90. With David Trobisch, Rick Warren, and Jerry Pattengale | 485

Figure 91. Bill and Enid Wilson | 495

Figure 92. Portrait of Herb and Winnie Kane | 502

Figure 93. Bill Wilson at the groundbreaking at 800 S. Maple Street | 505

Figure 94. With Ralph Winter and Herb Kane | 507

List of Maps

Map 1. The Hawaiian Islands | 2

Map 2. The Big Island of Hawaii | 3

Map 3. The Island of Oahu | 5

Map 4. Japan | 13

Map 5. Okinawa | 16

Map 6. Pearl Harbor | 42

Map 7. The Internment Camps | 47

Map 8. Jerusalem | 140

Foreword

I CAME TO KNOW Dr. Edwin Yamauchi in the fall of 1969 during his first year on the faculty of Miami University. It was my senior year at Miami, recently married to Linda Burgess, who had just completed her degree from the Wheaton College Conservatory in Illinois and was teaching music in Ohio public schools.

As a college senior, I was seriously exploring grad school and vocational options. While attending meetings of the InterVarsity Christian Fellowship, I met an engaging, spiritually sensitive, personable history professor, Dr. Yamauchi. Beyond IVCF, I recall meeting Professor Yamauchi in his campus office where I shared concerns about my future. Although brief and seemingly inconsequential at the moment, I'm confident that Dr. Yamauchi's counsel was used of the Lord to give direction to my path. A seminary degree, ordination, pastoral ministry, and a twenty-five-year chaplaincy at Wheaton College have been part of what God has ordained for my life.

What a delight it has been to pour over Dr. Yamauchi's recently completed personal memoir. It was of interest to learn how a boy born into a Buddhist home came to faith in Christ as a teenager. His formative years of high school and college gave significant evidence of successful academic achievement that was sure to come. Learning of Edwin's early life experiences and educational opportunities is a help in understanding the man and the career revealed in this memoir.

As we follow the details of Dr. Yamauchi's life experiences, we are reading words of a skilled historian and a careful researcher. We are left with an account that is more than facts and figures. In this memoir we discover a man who respects the past but lives in the present. Always the consummate academic, Dr. Yamauchi leaves us with meticulous details and precise descriptions of people and places. He chronicles much of what has been left behind so that we might have lessons for today. Beyond writing about history, Dr. Yamauchi communicates the subtle but evident truth that there's a living Lord who is above and behind all of that history.

In my reading of this memoir, I cannot help but commend Dr. Yamauchi for his profound career and corpus of academic production. His professorial work before and after retirement has been packed with travels, lectures, conferences, publications, visits, friendships, and consultations with scholars at institutions around the world. Dr. Yamauchi is a lifelong learner and a lifelong teacher. His significant interactions with other Christian leaders are also noteworthy, as well as his ongoing interest in teaching the Bible to students of any age who are willing to learn.

Finally, I want to share some of my personal, lasting impressions of Dr. Yamauchi revealed in this memoir:

- the breadth of his academic interests
- the humility of his leadership roles
- the servant mentality in his relationships
- the priority of faithfulness to Scripture and the gospel
- the personal friendships he has maintained over time.

I trust that readers of this book will discover at least a bit of what I have learned from and about Professor Ed Yamauchi. If so, you will agree that this memoir is a treasure!

Rev. Stephen B. Kellough, D.Min.

Chaplain Emeritus
Wheaton College

Preface

PAUL L. MAIER, THE Russell H. Seibert Professor of Ancient History at Western Michigan University, begins the foreword to *The Light of Discovery*, a Festschrift of essays presented to me by my students,[1] by this statement: "A Japanese Buddhist, born in Hawaii, moves to Ohio and becomes an internationally known historian and one of the most influential scholars of our time. What are the odds? No publisher on earth would buy such a plot, but welcome to the world of Edwin M. Yamauchi."

I have been inspired by reading the memoirs of scholars I have known and admired (F. F. Bruce,[2] Richard H. Bube,[3] Richard N. Frye,[4] Cyrus H. Gordon,[5] Kenneth A. Kitchen,[6] Bruce M. Metzger,[7] and Donald J. Wiseman[8]). These reveal fascinating features of their lives, which one would not learn from their scholarly publications.

I am a descendant of Japanese (Okinawan) immigrants who came to work on the sugar plantations in Hawaii. After my father's suicide

---

1. Edited by John D. Wineland (Eugene, Oregon: Pickwick Publishers, 2007).

2. F. F. Bruce, *In Retrospect: Remembrance of Things Past* (Grand Rapids, Michigan: Baker Book House, 1980).

3. Richard H. Bube, *Putting It All Together* (Lanham, Maryland: University Press of America, 1995).

4. Richard N. Frye, *Greater Iran: A 20th-Century Odyssey* (Costa Mesa, California: Mazda Publishers, 2011).

5. Cyrus H. Gordon, *A Scholar's Odyssey* (Atlanta, Georgia: Society of Biblical Literature, 2000).

6. Kenneth A. Kitchen, *In Sunshine & Shadow: An Autobiographical Sketch in a Family Context* (Wallasey, United Kingdom: Abercromby Press, 2016).

7. Bruce Manning Metzger, *Reminiscences of an Octogenarian* (Peabody: Hendrickson, 1997).

8. Donald J. Wiseman, *Life Above and Below: Memoirs* (privately published, 2003).

when I was three, my mother, who knew little English, raised me by working as a maid. We moved a dozen times in a dozen years. I went to three elementary schools, three high schools, and three colleges. Though I graduated from a very small college with underqualified teachers, I was able to study under Cyrus H. Gordon, the foremost Jewish scholar of his day.

I wrote a dissertation on an obscure language (Mandaic), which I had to learn on my own. Not knowing any better, I finished all my doctoral courses and the dissertation in two years. As I finished the PhD in 1964, I received letters of interest from six Christian colleges and offers of a teaching position from three universities.

Without a single graduate course in science, I became the president of the American Scientific Affiliation. With but a single graduate course in history, I became a history professor and the president of the Conference on Faith and History. With but a single graduate course in the Hebrew Bible, I became the president of the Institute for Biblical Research. Without a single graduate course in theology, I became the president of the Evangelical Theological Society. With but a single graduate course in archaeology, I became the president of the Near East Archaeological Society. But how was this possible, one might rightly ask. It was because I was an autodidact who read a lot and who presented many papers and published many reviews, articles, and books.

Before graduate school, it was my stated goal to become a missionary to the Japanese in Brazil. Though sidetracked into academia, I have never lost my interest in sharing the Good News of Christ's death and resurrection for all who will come to Him. To Him be all the glory.

I am indebted to two graduate students in geography for the maps: Teng Keng Vang and Zoey Armstrong. Steve Gifford has provided invaluable aid in addressing my computer and printing problems. I thank Sarah Pechan Driver for copyediting the manuscript. I am also indebted to Don Fairburn for several suggestions he made. I am greatly indebted to Stephen Compton for further improvements of this manuscript including the placement of notes and the scanning of photos.

Finally, I owe everything to the unfailing support of my dear wife Kimi.

Chapter 1

Hawaiian Royalty and Missionaries

The Hawaiian Islands

HAWAII, THE FIFTIETH STATE, consists of a chain of islands 2,000 miles from the California coast. Mark Twain called them, "The loveliest fleet of islands anchored in the seven seas." The islands range from the northwest to the southeast, with the geologically oldest island in the west and the newest island in the east. As the prevailing trade winds come from the east, rain falls on the eastern or windward side of the mountains.

There are only four islands that have significant populations: 1) Kauai, the Garden Island, which is noted for its "Grand Canyon"; 2) Oahu, with the capital city of Honolulu, Pearl Harbor, and Waikiki beach; 3) Maui, a popular tourist destination; and 4) Hawaii or "The Big Island" with its constantly erupting volcano, Kilauea, on the slopes of Mauna Loa.

The native Hawaiians were Polynesians who traversed the vast Pacific Ocean from the region of Tahiti 2500 miles away around AD 600. The islands were first discovered in 1778 by the British explorer Captain James Cook, who first landed on Kauai. He named them "The Sandwich Islands" after his patron, the Earl of Sandwich, who was the First Lord of the Admiralty. On a return voyage, he docked at the western bay of Kealakekua on the Kona coast of the Big Island.[1] He and his crew were at

---

1. The Kona coast, which is dry and sunny, has become a mecca for tourists. It is famed for its coffee. Coffee beans from Brazil were first planted on Oahu in 1825 by John Wilkinson, a British agriculturist. Three years later cuttings from Oahu were

first feted with honors and feasts, but then, when the British took some wooden idols for firewood and the Hawaiians stole some metal tools, armed conflict ensued. The Hawaiians surrounded Captain Cook and clubbed him to death on February 14, 1779.

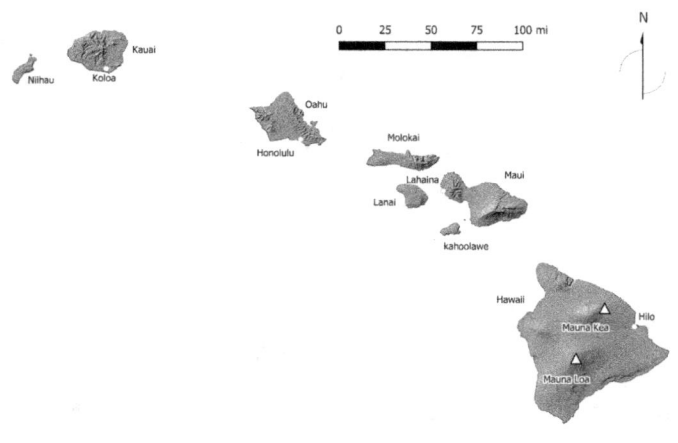

Map 1. The Hawaiian Islands

The Kamehamehas

Kamehameha I (c. 1758 to 1819), who came from Kohala in the northern part of the Big Island, fought rival chiefs from the other islands. He won the decisive battle at the Pali, a cliff on Oahu in 1784. He was aided by two captive British sailors, Isaac Davis and John Young, who became his trusted military advisors on the use of firearms and cannons. Kamehameha made his capital at Kailua, Kona. His statue is visible in the opening scene of the Hawaii Five-O television series.

---

planted in Kona by a missionary, Samuel Ruggles. My history colleague, Robert W. Thurston, is the author of *Coffee: From Bean to Barista* (Lanham, Maryland: Rowman & Littlefield, 2018). He may be related to the original Thurston missionaries.

The other unique Big Island product, the macadamia nut, was introduced to Honokaa, north of Hilo, in 1879 by William Purvis from Australia, where it had been known as the Queensland nut. The tree takes fifteen years to mature.

His son Liholiho (Kamehameha II), in 1820, six months after his accession, broke the ancient kapu (taboo) system by eating with his stepmother, the queen regent Kaahumanu. The king ordered the destruction of the temples and the disbanding of the priesthood.

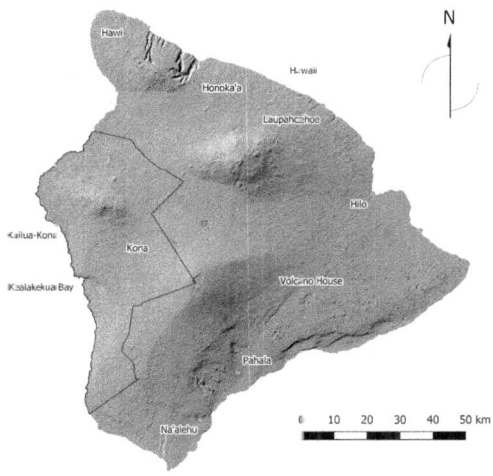

Map 2. The Big Island of Hawaii

The Missionaries

Opukahaia, a young Hawaiian boy, whose father had been killed by Kamehameha, escaped the islands by boarding an American ship. After converting to Christianity, he attended classes at Yale and at Andover Academy. He learned Latin, Greek, and Hebrew, and translated Genesis from Hebrew into Hawaiian. Before he died of typhus in 1818, he wrote his memoir, lamenting the paganism of the Hawaiians. This inspired the Congregational churches of New England to form a missionary board to evangelize the Hawaiians in the Sandwich Islands.[2] The first two missionary couples, Hiram and Sybil Bingham and Asa and Lucy Thurston,

---

2. For details of his remarkable life, see Gary Y. Okihiro, *Island World: A History of Hawai'i and the United States* (Berkeley, California: University of California Press, 2008), ch. 3.

were sent out by Park Street Church in Boston. After an arduous 157-day voyage around Cape Horn, they arrived in Hawaii on April 19, 1823. In addition to the two missionary couples there were thirteen others on board, including a physician, a carpenter, a farmer, and three converted Hawaiians. Hiram served as the first pastor of the Kawaihao Church in Honolulu. Asa and Lucy established the first church at Kailua, Kona, on land given to them across from the palace. The large stone structure of the Mokuaikaua Church with its tall steeple was made in part from stones taken from the *heiaus*, the abandoned pagan sites.[3] Asa also translated the Bible into Hawaiian.[4] The missionaries had brought with them from New England a Ramage press, which they used to print the Bible and other Christian literature.[5] Over the next thirty years, eleven more companies of missionaries would arrive.

Landing in 1835 in Hilo on the Big Island in the seventh company was Titus Coan (d. 1882). As he was preaching in 1837, a tsunami struck Hilo, which he interpreted as a warning from God.[6] He witnessed the conversion of seven thousand Hawaiians in a great revival that lasted until 1839.

The missionaries succeeded in converting some of the members of the royal family, including Queen Kaahumanu. Kamehameha II, however, did not wish to give up his five wives or his alcohol and was not

---

3. In a fitting coda to the story of missions in Hawaii, Dr. Paul E. Toms, who served as the pastor of this historic church, returned to the mainland to become the pastor of Park Street Church (1965–1989).

4. Hawaiian is a very simple language with only eight consonants (b, h, k, l, m, n, r, and w) and five vowels (a, e, i, o and u). It also has a glottal stop represented by a reversed apostrophe and often used between two vowels (e.g., Hawai'i, Nu'uanu). In English the glottal stop is non phonemic; it is the sound between the two "o's" in "cooperate."

5. The original printing house, 28 by 17 feet and built in 1823, still stands on the grounds of the Kawaihao Church.

6. An earthquake in Alaska triggered a massive *tsunami* (popularly misnamed "a tidal wave"), which reached Hawaii 2300 miles away on the morning of April 1, 1946. The waves reached a height of over thirty feet in places, killing seventeen on Kauai, six on Oahu, and fourteen on Maui. The tsunami took its greatest toll on the Big Island, devastating Hilo and taking 120 lives. Among those killed were twenty-four from the beach town of Laupahoehoe ("Leaf of Lava") north of Hilo, four residents, sixteen students, and four teachers. Among the latter were two recent graduates of Miami University in Ohio; a third alumna was spotted floating on a piece of wood after several hours. I owe this information to Donna Boen, the editor of *The Miamian*. See Walt Dudley and Scott C. S. Stone, *Tsunami or 1946 and 1960* (Hilo, Hawaii: The Pacific Tsunami Museum, 2000).

converted. On a trip to England, he contracted measles and died there in 1824.

He was succeeded by his brother Kamehameha III (1814 to 1854) when he was but nine years old. Advised by his *haole* (white) counselors, he instituted a constitutional monarchy. Haoles occupied twenty-eight of the thirty-four cabinet seats though they constituted but 7 percent of the population. Kamehameha III proclaimed the Great Mahele ("division") in 1848, which allowed the sale of land to non-Hawaiians. Within two generations of the arrival of the missionaries, 80 percent of the private land was in the hands of the haoles. As James Michener in his sprawling novel *Hawaii* (1959) depicted, the missionaries came to do good, their descendants did well.

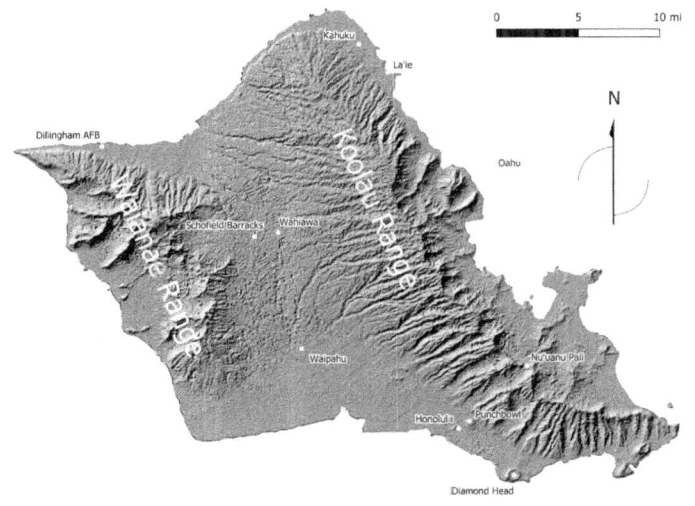

Map 3. The Island of Oahu

The king's adopted nephew, Liholiho, succeeded him in 1854 as Kamehameha IV. He courted European powers to counterbalance the growing American influence. He translated the Book of Common Prayer into Hawaiian.

When Kamehameha V died without a successor, Kalakaua was elected by the legislature as the new king in 1874. He was nicknamed the "Merry Monarch." He built Iolani Palace in Honolulu, the only royal palace in the United States.

A key leader in the business community was the publisher of the Commercial Advertiser, Lorin A. Thurston, the grandson of one of the original missionary couples. He was a leader of the "Missionary Party," which was renamed the Reform Party in 1887. He devised the so-called "Bayonet Constitution," which limited the powers of Kalakaua. Voting rights were reserved to property owners, who were mainly the white wealthy class.

On Kalakaua's death in 1891 in San Francisco, he was succeeded by his sister, Liliuokalani. In 1893, Thurston and his co-conspirators, with the support of US marines who arrived in January, overthrew Lilliuokalani and established the Republic of Hawaii.[7] The queen was rendered a virtual prisoner in the Iolani Palace. A gifted musician, she composed the beloved song "Aloha Oe."

The annexation of Hawaii was opposed by both Benjamin Harrison and Grover Cleveland, but in 1898, William McKinley gladly responded to the invitation of the American leaders in the Islands and annexed Hawaii as America was extending the Spanish American War across the Pacific to the Philippines. Hawaii became a territory of the United States in 1900.[8]

Punahou

The missionaries established schools for the Hawaiians, including a Royal School in 1839 for the monarch's family. For their own children, they established in 1841 Punahou (earlier called Oahu College). When I was in high school in the 1950s, Punahou was known as the school for the children of wealthy haole families. It later became more racially diverse. It has an impressive list of alumni who have excelled in academia, the arts, athletics, and politics. Barack "Barry" Obama (class of '79) was a reserve on Punahou's champion basketball team (see Excursus A).

---

7. A century later in 1993, the United States apologized for the use of the marines to overthrow a legitimate kingdom. Some Hawaiians have tried unsuccessfully to achieve the status of a sovereign nation like Native American tribes on the mainland.

8. As is the case today with Puerto Rico, those born in a territory become US citizens.

Chapter 2

Pineapples, Sugar Cane and Immigrants

Pineapples

THE WARM SUNNY DAYS, abundant rains, and fertile soil of the islands were perfect for the growing of certain crops, such as pineapples (*Ananus comosus*). Christopher Columbus first saw them in 1493 and brought back with him pineapples from Guadeloupe, which greatly impressed King Ferdinand. Cultivated in hot houses, especially in England, the pineapple became a symbol of prosperity and pineapple designs appeared on furniture and on ceramic and glass vessels.

We do not know how pineapples were introduced into Hawaii. Captain Cook took with him pineapples from Kew Gardens in London and recorded that he had planted them in Tahiti and Tonga but not in Hawaii. Perhaps his records were not complete. The first recorded reference to the pineapple in Hawaii was made in 1813 by a Spaniard, Francisco de Paula.

The gold rush in California created a wealthy class who were willing to pay the high prices involved in importing fresh pineapples from Hawaii. But the fruits were often bruised and overripe when they arrived. An Englishman, John Kidwell, imported the sweet Smooth Cayenne[1] variety of pineapples from Kew Gardens and opened the first cannery

---

1. Cayenne was the capital of French Guiana in South America. This superior pineapple spread from Hawaii to Haiti (1921), Taiwan (1923), Philippines (1926), Fiji and Kenya (1930), Mexico (1946), and Cuba (1947). See Gary Y. Okihiro, *Pineapple Culture* (Berkeley, California: University of California Press, 2009), 90–91.

in Hawaii in 1892. However, the tariff of 35 percent imposed on foods processed for export—such as canned pineapples—made the industry economically problematic until the annexation of the islands in 1898 removed this barrier.

Daniel Dole (1808 to 1878) came to Hawaii in 1841 to serve as the principal of Punahou School. Although it had been created for the children of missionaries, he allowed the children of other white families to enroll. His son Sanford B. Dole (1844 to 1926) became the first president of the Republic of Hawaii and then the first governor of the Territory of Hawaii.

A young cousin from New England, James Dole, the son of a Unitarian minister, arrived in Hawaii in 1899. In 1900, he bought sixty-one acres of land in Wahiawa in central Oahu and planted 75,000 pineapple plants on this farm.[2] He also opened a small cannery in Wahiawa. The Dole Food corporation, which is now the world's largest producer of processed fruits and vegetables, traces its roots back to 1851 with the formation of Castle & Cooke, one of the so-called "Big Five" companies that were to dominate Hawaii's economy.[3] This was formed by missionaries Samuel Castle and Amos Cooke. Castle & Cooke acquired Dole's Hawaiian Pineapple Company. Dole established a large pineapple cannery in the Iwilei district of Honolulu. Henry Ginacka, an employee, invented a machine in 1911, which could peel, core, and slice thirty-five pineapples per minute. The pineapple slices would then be placed in cans by women along an assembly line.[4] Because of the ripening of the pineapples during the summer, work at the canneries reached its height from June to August, employing many high-school women, like my wife.

The island of Lanai was purchased by Dole and planted entirely with pineapples. Hawaii once provided 80 percent of the world's pineapples. Competition from countries with lower labor costs, such as the Philippines and Costa Rica, have now drastically affected the industry. There is still a display pineapple farm for tourists in Wahiawa.

---

2. Fran Bauman, *The Pineapple: King of Fruits* (London, United Kingdom: Chatto & Windus, 2005), 220.

3. The other four are: Alexander & Baldwin, C. Brewer & Co., American Factors, and Theo H. Davies & Co.

4. According to Bauman (2005, 222), by 1928, 23 percent of the women in Hawaii were employed in the twelve pineapple canneries in the Islands. While in high school, my wife worked the Ginacka machine during the summer.

Sugar Cane

But it was not pineapple but sugar cane that transformed not only the economy but also the society of Hawaii. Sugar cane (*Saccharum officinarum*) is a grass that was indigenous to New Guinea. Growing to a height of 15 feet, its stalks are rich with sucrose.

Its cultivation spread westward in stages to India c. 500 BC, to Persia c. AD 500, and after the spread of Islam c. AD 700 to Egypt, Palestine, Syria, Cyprus, Crete, Sicily, North Africa, Spain, then to the islands off the northwest coast of Africa.

It was Christopher Columbus who brought sugar cane from the Canary Islands to Hispaniola (Haiti and the Dominican Republic) on his second voyage in 1493.[5] Sugar cane was then introduced into the other Caribbean islands (Barbados, Jamaica, Puerto Rico, Cuba, Haiti, etc.), Brazil, and Louisiana.[6]

The cultivation of sugar cane demanded back breaking labor. The sharp leaves of the cane require workers to wear heavy protective clothing even in hot, humid conditions. In the New World the labor demands of sugar plantations were the major driver of the slave trade from Africa.[7] A world history textbook states: "Above all, the use of enslaved labor made sugar cultivation fantastically profitable, fueling economic growth

---

5. Also on that same voyage, Columbus introduced pigs from Europe into the New World.

6. Andrew Dial, a Miami University MA grad who wrote his PhD dissertation at McGill University on an aspect of the sugar industry in the Caribbean, supplied me with this historical summary:

> The short story of sugar cane production is that the Portuguese brought it west from the Mediterranean to the Atlantic Islands (Cape Verde and Canary) in the 1450s and Brazil in the 1500s. Columbus did bring sugar canes to Hispaniola, but Spanish output was minor compared to Portuguese Brazil. Brazil was the center of sugar production for much of the sixteenth and seventeenth centuries. In the 1640s, Jewish planter refugees from Brazil brought sugar production to the nascent English and French Caribbean. From the 1670s Barbados and Martinique were the major sugar producers in the Caribbean until Jamaica and Saint Dominique overtook them in the eighteenth century. With the Haitian Revolution in the 1790s and British emancipation in the 1830s, the center of sugar production shifted to Cuba and back to Brazil where it remained for most of the nineteenth century.

7. Sidney W. Mintz, *Sweetness and Power: The Place of Sugar in Modern History* (Baltimore, Maryland: Penguin Books, 1986); Dale Tomich, *Through the Prism of Slavery* (Lanham, Maryland: Rowman and Littlefield, 2004)

and political instability around the world."[8] The textbook adds: "Between 1690 and 1790 Europe imported 12 million tons of sugar, approximately 1 ton for every African enslaved in the Americas."[9]

After Britain abolished slavery in 1833,[10] plantation owners sought cheap labor in the form of indentured workers from Portugal, India, and China. These were required to work for a contracted number of years.

Sugar in Hawaii

Sugar cane may have been brought to the Islands by the original Polynesians. On the other hand, Dennis M. Ogawa speculates: "Early Japanese castaways probably even brought the first sugar cane to Hawaii."[11] In any case when westerners arrived, they found it growing abundantly.

Soon after Captain Cook's discovery of Hawaii, Chinese began importing fragrant sandalwood from Hawaii. The Chinese had been milling sugar cane for centuries. The earliest sugar mill was set up by Wong Tze Chun in 1802 in Lanai, but he gave up after a year and returned to China. In 1820, Hung Tai opened a small mill in Wailuku, Maui.

A missionary, Joseph Goodrich, built a mill in Hilo in 1829 to grind the sugar cane.[12] In 1830 the first large scale plantation was established in Koloa on Kauai by P. A. Brinsmade, William Ladd, and William Hooper, who leased a thousand-acre tract. By 1846, there were eleven plantations, two run by Chinese.

By this time, the original *kanaka* population of Hawaii had been decimated by measles, smallpox, and venereal diseases introduced by Westerners, for example, by seamen from whaling ships that docked at Lahaina on the southern coast of Maui.

---

8. J. Adelman, E. Pollard, C. Rosenberg and R. Tignor, *Worlds Together, Worlds Apart* (New York, New York: Norton & Company, 2021), 463–464.

9. Ibid., 488.

10. After the Revolution, France abolished slavery in 1794. But then with Napoleon's rise to power, he reinstituted slavery in 1802. France then abolished slavery in its colonies in 1848.

11. Dennis M. Ogawa, *Kodomo no tame ni: For the Sake of the Children, the Japanese-American Experience in Hawaii* (Honolulu, Hawaii: University of Hawaii Press, 1978), 2.

12. Sophia V. Schweitzer and Bennet Hymer, *Big Island Journey* (Honolulu, Hawaii: Mutual Publishing, 2009), 64.

Estimates of the native population when Captain James Cook discovered the Hawaiian Islands, or Sandwich Islands as he christened them in 1778, vary anywhere from 220,000 to 400,000.... The first official census in 1832 showed the figure at 130,313, which had dwindled to 57,000 in 1866, and by 1872 it had declined to less than 50,000.[13]

Accustomed to an easy-going lifestyle, most Hawaiians were averse to working under the demanding conditions of the plantation system. The first attempt to solve this labor gap was to import Chinese men to do the work, starting in 1851, then the Japanese in 1868, the Portuguese from the Madeira and Azores Islands in 1878, and finally the Filipinos in 1906.[14]

Chinese Immigration

The earliest group of two hundred coolies or contract laborers from China came to Hawaii in 1851. They were under contract for five years for $3 per month. A large group came from Amoy in Fujian (or Fukien) province on the coast west of Taiwan. Most then came from the provinces near Canton (Guangdong) at the mouth of the Pearl River near Macao and Hong Kong. Between 1852 and 1876 some 1,800 Chinese laborers came to Hawaii.[15] In 1882, Chinese laborers were banned from entering Hawaii. At that time Chinese constituted 50 percent of the laborers on the sugar plantation. Because of their exclusion their place on

---

13. James H. Okahata, *A History of Japanese in Hawaii* (Honolulu, Hawaii: The United Japanese Society of Hawaii, 1971), 69. The 1900 census listed 32,000 Hawaiians and 10,000 part-Hawaiians.

14. According to Ronald Takaki, *Strangers from a Different Shore: A History of Asian Americans* (Baltimore, Maryland: Penguin Books, 2012), 132: "The sugar industry required the constant importation of workers whose increasing numbers led to the ethnic diversification of society in the islands. For example, in 1853, Hawaiians and part-Hawaiians represented 97 percent of the population of 73,137 inhabitants, while Caucasians constituted only 2 percent and Chinese only half a percent. Seventy years later, Hawaiians and part-Hawaiians made up only 16.3 percent of the population, while Caucasians represented 7.7 percent, Chinese 9.2 percent, Japanese 42.7 percent, Portuguese 10.5, Puerto Ricans 2.2 percent, Koreans 1.9 percent and Filipinos 8.2 percent." The first group of seven thousand Koreans was brought to Hawaii in 1903 as strikebreakers when Japanese laborers went on strike. The first group of Filipinos was brought to Hawaii in 1907.

15. Relatively few Chinese women were fit for plantation labor because of the ancient practice of foot binding, which bound the feet of little girls so they were only three to four inches long.

the plantations was replaced by the Japanese. Consequently, by 1902, Chinese constituted less than 10 percent of the plantation workers. The Chinese gained a monopoly on rice production, and many became successful merchants.[16]

Japan

After numerous wars the Tokugawa clan defeated its main rivals in 1600 and established their Shogun as the supreme military leader, resident in Edo. The emperor, who resided in Kyoto, remained a mere figurehead. All of the feudal lords (*daimyo*) and their armed retainers (*samurai*) pledged fealty to the Shogun. Members of their families were required to reside as hostages in Edo.

Francis Xavier, the Spanish Jesuit, had introduced Catholic Christianity to Japan after arriving in 1549 on the southern island of Kyushu. Many of the people who inhabited the Shimabara peninsula of Kyushu became Christians. Led by a charismatic sixteen-year-old noble, Amakusa Shiro, they rebelled against the excessive taxation of the shogunate in 1637 and 1638. The huge army of the Shogun aided by Dutch gunboats finally captured the castle of Hara. The army beheaded 37,000 rebels.[17] Christianity was then strictly banned and the Catholic Portuguese expelled from Japan. Some Christians went underground as *Kakurei Khristian* "Hidden Christians," who maintained their secret faith for centuries.[18] The shogunate maintained a strict policy of isolation, except for a Dutch merchant enclave in the port city of Nagasaki. Japanese were not allowed to travel abroad.

---

16. See Arlene Lum, ed., *Sailing to the Sun: The Chinese in Hawaii 1789–1989* (Honolulu, Hawaii: University of Hawaii Press, 1988).

17. There is a church in Tomioko, not far from where Xavier first landed, which has the remains of about ten-thousand Christians.

18. In 2008, I joined a tour of sites associated with these Hidden Christians, led by Rev. Sam Tonomura of the Japanese Evangelistic Missionary Society. See ch. 29.

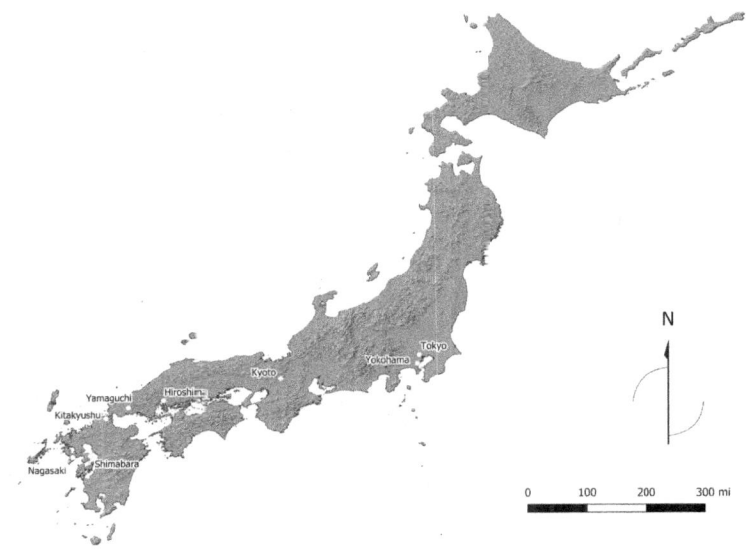

Map 4. Japan

This policy of "Seclusion" was finally broken by the arrival of Commodore Matthew C. Perry's fleet of four warships in Edo Bay on July 8, 1853, and the forced signing of the Treaty of Kanagawa in March 1854, granting American ships access to Japan's harbors. The Tokugawa shogunate soon gave way in 1868 to the ascension of the Meiji Emperor, who moved his residence to Edo (better known as Tokyo "The Eastern Capital"). He pursued a deliberate policy of inviting Western specialists and of sending Japanese abroad.

Okinawa

Okinawa ("Big Rope"), 350 miles south of Kyushu, is the largest island in the archipelago of Ryukyu Islands, which stretch from just south of Kyushu to just east of Taiwan. The island is seventy miles long, and averages seven miles in width. Okinawa is subject to periodic droughts and is buffeted by frequent typhoons. Less than 30 percent of the land is arable. Farms were very small, averaging less than half an acre. The main crops were rice, sweet potatoes, sugar cane, and soybeans. Resources to feed the population, estimated to be about 200,000 in the eighteenth century and 400,000 in the nineteenth century, were quite inadequate.[19]

The *Uchinanchu* (Okinawans) were originally from Japan, but by the sixth century developed their own dialect *Uchināguchi*, which became incomprehensible to the Japanese. Whereas Japanese has five vowels (a, e, i, o, u), Okinawan has but three (a, i, u). Okinawan also has a "wu" sound not found in Japanese. Even on such a small island distinct sub-dialects developed so that people in the Shuri/Naha area would understand **kūn** as "he is not coming," whereas those in Itoman to the south would understand the word to mean "he is coming."

Official and literary works were not written in this language but in Chinese or Japanese. In appearance Okinawans were in general darker and hairier and had eyes that were more round than slanted. They were also shorter than the Japanese.[20]

Okinawa is first noted as *Liu-chi'iu* in records of the Chinese Sui Dynasty (AD 589–618). It is first noted in Japanese records in the eighth century AD. The first reference to Ryukyu appears in Korean records in 1389. Diplomatic relations were established with the Ming Dynasty in 1372. Thereafter ambassadors and tribute were sent periodically from Naha to Peking (Beijing). Chinese envoys were also sent to Ryukyu, known at this time as Chuzan. The Ryukyuan embassy would land in Fujian and then travel by river and canal north to Beijing. The Ryukyuans would perform the act of submission to the emperor and offer tributes of sulfur, copper, and horses. They were in turn showered with gifts including silk garments and were given the opportunity to trade. In 1392 Kumemura, a site adjacent to Shuri, was designated as a place for Chinese immigrants and for Okinawans to study the Chinese language and culture.

Ryukyu was unified as a single kingdom in 1429 with its capital at Shuri in the south. Okinawan seamen developed a prosperous trade with neighboring countries.

---

19. Yukiko Kimura, "Social-Historical Background of Okinawans in Hawaii," *Romanzo Adams Social Research Laboratory Report* (1962), no. 36, 3. Prior to World War II the population stood at 742,174.

20. As my wife noted that my father and I were tall and fair, she repeatedly asked if we might have had some European blood in our ancestry. So, I took a genetic test that proved that I had no European DNA from some castaway Portuguese or Spanish sailor in Itoman but that indicated that I did have a sliver of Chinese DNA!

In 1374, sugar cane and, in 1605, the sweet potato were introduced from China.[21] Many other Chinese elements influenced aspects of the Okinawan culture, including Buddhism, which was introduced in 1603. Thereafter Buddhist priests came from Japan chiefly of the Shingon and Rinzai Zen sects. Confucianist ideals were embraced by the kings.

The intrusion of Europeans into the seas of Southeast Asia greatly diminished opportunities for the Ryukyuan trading ships in the region. In 1511, Malacca fell to the Portuguese. In 1571, the Spanish conquered the Philippines.

By 1590, Toyotomi Hideyoshi had defeated all of the rival *daimyōs* in Japan. He conceived a mad scheme to conquer China by invading Korea. Okinawans traveling to Beijing in 1591 warned the Chinese of his invasion, which proved to be disastrous for the Japanese.

In 1609, an army from the Satsuma domain, ruled by the Shimazu family and based at Kagoshima in Kyushu invaded Okinawa and captured the king Sho Nei (r. 1587 to 1620) at Shuri. They held him for two years and then returned him to Okinawa after he had agreed to submit to their terms. Deprived of arms, the Okinawans developed their own unique form of martial arts, *kara-te* "empty hand."[22]

Under the reign of the shogun Tokugawa Iemitsu (r. 1623 to 1651), Japan imposed the restriction of *Sakoku* ("closed country") or isolation. But the Shimazu clan of Satsuma was allowed to use Ryukyu for continued trade with China. Satsuma's control of this trade was hidden from the Chinese. In 1624, some Christians were discovered on the southern island of Yaeyama. The king wanted them to be exiled, but Satsuma ordered them to be burned at the stake.

---

21. My mother recalls that when she was sent back to Okinawa from Hawaii about all she and her grandparents had to eat daily was the sweet potato! In spite of (or because of) their very spare diet, Okinawans have more centenarians than almost any other society today.

22. Karate was popularized by the movie *The Karate Kid* (1984), which featured Ralph Macchio and Pat Morita.

AN ASIAN AMERICAN ANCIENT HISTORIAN AND BIBLICAL SCHOLAR

Map 5. Okinawa

In 1853, before visiting Japan, Commodore Perry forced Okinawa to sign a treaty granting American ships the right to obtain provisions at Naha. France, Britain, the Netherlands, Spain, and Portugal also demanded similar privileges.

After the Meiji Restoration, the emperor asserted exclusive Japanese sovereignty over Okinawa in 1872. In 1879, the Okinawan kingdom was abolished, and Okinawa was made a province of Japan. Though officially a province, Okinawa was treated more like a colony. The teaching of the Okinawan language was banned in favor of the teaching of Japanese.[23] The Japanese colonizers established large sugar cane farms which dispossessed many Okinawan farmers.[24] The poll tax imposed on Okinawans was so heavy it led some pregnant women to commit infanticide.

---

23. For a general history, see George H. Kerr, *Okinawa: The History of an Island People* (Rutland, Vermont: Charles E. Tuttle Co., 1958). For detailed scholarly studies of early Ryukyuan history, see Gregory Smits, *Visions of Ryukyu* (Honolulu, Hawaii: University of Hawaii Press, 2017); idem, *Maritime Ryukyu 1050–1650* (Honolulu, Hawaii: University of Hawaii Press, 2020).

24. During World War II, the "Battle for Okinawa" (April 1 to June 21, 1945) was the costliest battle for both sides. See Excursus B.

The *Gannen-mono*

Following Kamehameha IV's request for Japanese laborers, an American recruiter, Eugene Van Reed, came to Japan. With promises of wealth, he assembled a motley group from the streets of Yokohama as laborers for Hawaii. This was in the critical year of 1868 when the Shogun gave up his power to the Meiji Emperor.

After he had gathered his 153 recruits and hired a ship, the Scioto, Van Reed was denied permission to depart with his passengers by the new Meiji government. Defying these commands, Van Reed ordered the Scioto to sail under cover of darkness. The ship landed in Hawaii in June 1868.

The *Gannen-mono* (The first year [of the Meiji Era] People) were under contract for three years at a monthly wage of $4.00 per month. They were for the most part unfit for the hard labor that awaited them. Some tried to escape their contracts; three committed suicide.

In 1881 Kalakaua, the last monarch of Hawaii, during a world tour, paid a state visit to Emperor Meiji. He was pleased by the warm reception he received, with the Japanese band playing the Hawaiian national anthem, *Hawai'i Pono'i*. His appeal for Japanese laborers met with more success than Van Reed's attempt in 1868. After a voyage of fourteen days the ship, the *City of Tokyo*, arrived in Honolulu in February 1885, with its load of 944 immigrants, mainly farm workers from the economically depressed southern provinces of Hiroshima-ken, Kumamoto-ken, and Yamaguchi-ken. These workers were contracted to work for three years, twenty-six days of the month, working ten hours a day in the fields.

From 1885 to 1900, it has been estimated that 86,000 Japanese emigrated to Hawaii. By 1901, 69 percent of the sugar plantation workers were Japanese.[25]

The first group of immigrants from Okinawa was assembled by Toyama Kyuzo, a highly educated leader who knew English. Twenty-six young men first sailed to Yokohama, and then on a British ship, the S. S. City of China to Hawaii, arriving in Honolulu in January 1900. They were all sent to the Ewa Plantation on Oahu.

One of the pioneers gave a vivid picture of his harrowing experiences when he returned to Okinawa:

---

25. Roland Kotani, *The Japanese in Hawaii: A Century of Struggle* (Honolulu, Hawaii: Hawaii Hochi, 1985), 33.

> The life on Ewa Plantation was very hard; getting up at 4 A.M., breakfast at 5, starting to work at 6, and working all day under the blazing sun. We worked like horses, moving mechanically under the whipping hands of the luna.[26] Because of the perpetual fear of this unbearable whipping, some other workers committed suicide by hanging or jumping in front of the on-coming train. Fortunately, we Okinawans had been trained through ages to endure hardships caused by terrible typhoons, so no one among us committed suicide. There was no one who wasn't whipped. Once when the luna whipped me . . . I was really mad . . . and challenged him with Karate. Since the luna was a big man, a six-footer, it wasn't easy for me. But finally, I threw him to the ground. I could have kicked him to unconsciousness.[27]

Despite this negative report, the sums the returnees earned sparked a Hawaii *netsu* "fever" among the Okinawans, who were earning only the equivalent of 10 cents a day. The workers were greatly encouraged by the development that contract labor was abolished after 1900, as the US laws did not allow indentured service. They would enter Hawaii as *jiyu-imin* "free immigrants," and could earn 60 cents a day. In 1903, a second group of thirty young Okinawan men accompanied by Toyama arrived in Honolulu.

> In Okinawa, the enthusiasm for emigration to Hawaii picked up momentum, with more than 260 young men in the third group going to Hawaii in 1904, followed by 1,200 in 1905 . . . In 1906 the number increased to nearly 4,500 and in 1907 about 2,500 came. The number of Okinawan immigrants constituted about one-fifth of the total Japanese immigration of more than 44,000 during this period.[28]

The Gentleman's Agreement

Responding to growing anti-Asian sentiment, President Theodore Roosevelt in 1907 persuaded the Japanese government to sign the so-called "Gentleman's Agreement," as follows:

---

26. A luna was a Portuguese foreman on horseback.
27. As quoted in Kimura, 5–6.
28. Kimura, 8.

> This understanding contemplates that the Japanese government shall issue passports to continental United States only to such of its subjects as are non-laborers or are laborers who, in coming to the continent, seek to resume a formerly acquired domicile, to join a parent, wife or children residing there or assume active control of an already possessed interest in a farming enterprise in this country so that the three classes of laborers entitled to receive passports have come to be designated: "former residents," "parents, wives, or children of residents," and "settled agriculturists."[29]

This agreement not only meant no more laborers could emigrate to Hawaii, but it also stopped the movement of Japanese from Hawaii to the mainland. It did allow for so-called "chain migration" of relatives, what the Japanese called *yobiyose* "called for." This opening was to last only until 1924 when all Asian immigration was halted. By that date, more than 200,000 had emigrated to Hawaii from the prefectures of Okinawa, Hiroshima, Yamaguchi, Fukuoka, Kumamoto, and Wakayama.

The *Shashin* "Picture" Brides[30]

As most of the immigrants to Hawaii had been single men, they took opportunity of the Gentlemen's Agreement to arrange for *baishakunin* or matchmakers to choose brides for them, offering to pay for their passage to the Islands. Both prospective grooms and brides exchanged photographs beforehand, but these were sometimes misleading.

> Less than 700 arrived in 1908, and in 1909 and 1910 only 200 came each year. However, the number increased to nearly 600 in 1911, and in 1912, which was the peak of Yobiyose immigration, 1700 came. For ten years from that time until July 1924 an

---

29. Paul Spickard, *Japanese Americans* (New Brunswick, New Jersey: Rutgers University Press, 1991), 32. Students were allowed to come to the US. In 1872, Matsudaira Tadatsu graduated from Rutgers University in New Jersey, according to Robert A. Wilson and Bill Hosokawa, *East to America: A History of the Japanese in the United States* (New York, New York: William Morrow, 1980), 30.

30. A movie "The Picture Bride," featuring Tamlyn Tomita produced in 1995 won awards at the Cannes Film Festival and the Sundance Film Festival. Though generally accurate, there are some minor discrepancies which would only be recognized by those familiar with Hawaii. The bride Riyo lands in Honolulu and is then transported immediately to a plantation in Oahu in 1918. But in a scene where she is contemplating suicide at a beach, there is a reference to an eruption on Kilauea which was on another island!

average of 500 to 600 came to Hawaii each year. A total of about 20,000 came from Okinawa from 1900 to 1924.[31]

The brides were generally between eighteen and twenty-five, whereas their grooms were often forty to fifty. Upon actually seeing their husbands, many women were dismayed at the sight of the sun-burned and wizened men who looked nothing like their photographs!

Although their marriages were legalized in Japan before the women's departure, American authorities in Honolulu at first insisted upon a dockside "Christian" wedding, though the immigrants were not Christians. Due to a misunderstanding one father was even married to his daughter! After a protest to US authorities in 1917 by Fred Makino or the *Hawaii* Hochi, this ill-conceived practice was discontinued.[32] After this, marriages were performed by Shinto priests.

Buddhism in Hawaii

Gautama (567 to 487 BC) was born in Kapilavastu, now in southern Nepal. After six years of seeking peace as a wandering Hindu monk he found enlightenment under a Bodhi tree and became a Buddha or "Enlightened One." He realized that the way to Nirvana was to eliminate desire through a "Middle Way" between asceticism and self-indulgence. He advocated an eight-fold path of: 1) right views, 2) aspirations, 3) speech, 4) conduct, 5) livelihood, 6) effort, 7) mindfulness, and 8) concentration.

He succeeded in converting his ascetic companions, then his parents and wife, and then king Bimbisara. In his eightieth year he became mortally ill after eating some pork. The last words of Buddha, who did not appeal to the gods (*devas*), was for his disciples to be lamps unto themselves.

For many centuries Buddha's teachings were handed down orally. It was in the first century BC that his teachings were first put down in

---

31. Kimura, 10. My maternal grandmother, Tsuru Owan, my paternal aunt, Tsuru Yamauchi, and my mother-in-law, Sen Honda, were picture brides.

32. Roger Daniels, *Asian American: Chinese and Japanese in the United States Since 1850* (Seattle, Washington: University of Washington Press, 1988), 126, observes: "The Gentlemen's Agreement changed drastically the nature of the Japanese American population in the United States. Female immigration began to predominate. As a result, the sex ratio among Japanese in America began to change from one that was overwhelmingly male to one that by 1924 was beginning to approach a balance."

writing in Ceylon. The earliest texts are the Pali canon of the Theravada or Hinayana school, which spread to southeast Asia.

The Sanskrit canon of the Mahayana School, which spread north to Tibet, China, Korea, and Japan, dates at its earliest to the first or secnd century AD. By the second and third century AD Mahayana Buddhism developed a doctrine of Bodhisattvas, innumerable perfected Buddhas distributed through space and time who help mankind by their merits.

Buddhism reached Japan in the sixth century AD.[33] There it attained a symbiosis with Shintoism, which was Japan's native religion. Weddings tended to be Shinto ceremonies, funerals Buddhist ones.

Before World War II there were in Hawaii 180 Buddhist temples from a dozen different sects. The Jōdo Shin (The True Pure Land) sect was established by Shinran (1173 to 1263). It stresses the repetition of the prayer *Namu Amida Butsu* "I take refuge in Amida," a practice known as *Nembutsu*, to achieve salvation in the Pure Land through the merits of the Buddha Amida. Prayer beads are used to keep count; some have prayed this prayer thousands of times in a day. As the simplest and least demanding denomination it became the most popular branch of Buddhism both in Japan and in Hawaii.

Sōryū Kagahi, one of its priests, established the first Buddhist temple at Hilo in 1889. Yemyō Imamura, the second bishop of Honolulu's Honpa Hongwanji temple, built in 1900 at Fort Street,[34] adapted Buddhism to appeal to Nisei by creating the Young Men's Buddhist Association. A pulpit, pews, hymnals and an organ were introduced. Children were taught in Sunday School to sing "Buddha Loves Me, This I know". Like other temples it sponsored a school in the Japanese language for children.[35] Such schools were originally intended to prepare students to be able to study in schools in Japan. I went to the Japanese language school and judo classes sponsored by this temple.

Another important denomination in Hawaii was Shingon "True Word" Buddhism. This was established by Kukai (774 to 835), who traveled to China to obtain secret lore. It is an esoteric branch of Buddhism which emphasizes mysteries passed down from a teacher to his disciple. Shingon holds that there were thirteen Buddhas manifested through history, Gautama being the second in this series. The Shingon

---

33. Elizabeth Lyons and Heather Peters, *Buddhism* (Philadelphia, Pennsylvania: University of Pennsylvania Press, 1985).

34. My aunt Yoshie Cwan was married to Eiso Yamada, a Naichi, in this temple.

35. I attended the Japanese school sponsored by this temple for one year.

temple on Sheridan Street in Honolulu, established in 1915, is an artistic and architectural marvel.³⁶ My father stayed at the temple as he attended high school.

Figure 1. Shingon Buddhist temple

Japanese Virtues

Several key virtues of Japanese culture enabled immigrants of the Issei (first generation) to persevere—certain traits which they tried to inculcate in their Nisei (second generation) descendants. ³⁷ These include:

36. On the anniversary of my father's death, my mother and I would come to this temple to light a *senkō*, an incense stick in his memory.

37. For a vivid fictional account of the clash between Issei and Nisei values set in a small plantation on Maui, where the parents stress filial obligation especially from

oyakōko "filial piety," *or* "an attitude of obligation and respect," *giri* "a sense of duty," *sekinin* "responsibility," *kansha* "gratitude," *enryo* "modesty, restraint," *haji* "shame," and *gaman* "perseverance." In the course of setbacks, the Japanese were fatalistic, saying *shikata ga nai* "it can't be helped." As a result of these values, in contrast to Caucasians who were outgoing, assertive, and expedient, the Nisei were reserved, humble, and conscientious.

Sugar Plantations

With the influx of cheap laborers, especially from Japan (including Okinawa), the growth of sugar cane became a hugely profitable enterprise for the owners of plantations and mills. In 1876, in exchange for the use of Pearl Harbor, the United States signed a Treaty of Reciprocity that removed tariffs from sugar imported from Hawaii into the United States.

The plantations provided medical services and supported the ministry of Buddhist temples and Christian churches. The workers were housed in camps grouped according to their origins, for example, Okinawans in their own camp. At first workers were housed in long houses, 18 by 30 feet. Couples lived in rooms 6 by 6 feet, single men in rooms 6 by 3 feet. Later after the strikes families were given individual houses.

By 1920, there were forty-four sugar mills employing fifty-thousand Japanese laborers. In 1895, the Hawaii Sugar Plantation Association had been formed. Due to collusion among all the owners the wages had not risen at all in thirty years.[38] Workers were being paid 77 cents for a ten-hour day for men, and 58 cents for women! As early as 1890, workers protested by marching off the plantations, including 400 on the Big Island, and 200 from Ewa to Honolulu. About 150 marched all the way from Kahuku and up the steep Pali Road to Honolulu, but the workers who did so were fined $5 each and taken back to Kahuku! Only after a three-month long strike in 1909 by Japanese workers did they obtain slightly better wages. The Japanese joined the Filipinos in a five-month-long strike in 1920. Strikebreakers were hired, including Portuguese and

---

the oldest son and the avoidance of shaming the family, see Milton Murayama *All I Asking for is my Body* (Honolulu, Hawaii: University of Hawaii Press, 1975). The classic anthropological study of Japan's shame culture is Ruth Benedict, *The Chrysanthemum and the Sword* (New York: New York: Houghton Mifflin 1946).

38. By 1910, the "Big Five" controlled 75% of Hawaii's sugar plantations; by 1933 96%.

Puerto Ricans who were paid four dollars a day, and Chinese and Koreans who were paid three dollars per day. During these strikes the families of strikers were expelled from their plantation homes. Many of the Japanese left the plantations as soon as they were able to do so.[39]

The changing proportions of the ethnic groups working on the plantations may be seen in the following statistics:

> By 1890, Japanese workers exceeded Chinese. The Japanese constituted 42.2 percent of the plantation workers and reached a high of 73.5 percent in 1902. Twenty years later, Filipinos made up 41 percent of plantation laborers. In 1932, when the Japanese were a mere 18.8 percent of the plantation workforce, Filipinos supplied 69.9 percent of the laborers.[40]

Rev. Okamura and Makiki Church

The most influential Christian to minister to the Japanese in Hawaii was Rev. Takie Okamura (1865–1951).[41] He came from a samurai family. His father was the governor at Kochi in Shikoku province. He tried various business ventures which failed and then became a political activist in 1887. He believed that it was his patriotic duty to disrupt Christian gatherings, but he was then converted in 1889. He graduated from Doshisha English School[42] and heeded the call to evangelize the Japanese in Hawaii in 1894.

---

39. For an autobiographical account of a Japanese Nisei, who was born on a plantation north of Hilo and worked there all his life, see Yasushi "Scotch" Kurisu, *Sugar Town: Hawaii Plantation Days Remembered* (Honolulu, Hawaii: Watermark Publishing, 1995). For a scholarly study, see Ronald Takaki, *Pau Hana: Plantation Life and Labor in Hawaii 1835 1920* (Honolulu, Hawaii: University of Hawaii Press, 1983). By coincidence, Ronald's mother and my mother were born in the same plantation, Hawi in the Kohala region of the Big Island. Ron (class of '57) and I both attended Iolani High School. In a *New York Times* editorial (January 16, 2017, A20), "The Sun Sets on Sugar Cane in Hawaii," Lawrence Downes announced the closing of the last sugar plantation in the Islands at Puunene, Maui. Downes' maternal grandparents came from Okinawa to live on the Pepeekeo plantation on the Big Island.

40. Gary Y. Okihiro, *The Cane Fires: The Anti-Japanese Movement in Hawaii, 1865–1945* (Philadelphia, Pennsylvania: Temple University Press, 1991), 59.

41. See Fusa Nakaawa, *From Tosa to Hawaii: The Footsteps of Takie Okamura*, tr. from Japanese by Paul Reddington (Tokyo, Japan: Ozorasha, 2015).

42. This first Christian school in Japan was founded at Kyoto by Niijima Jō, also known as Joseph Neesima, in 1875. Despite the travel ban, he had managed to get to America in 1864 and studied at Amherst College in Massachusetts. Granted university

He was dismayed by the drinking and gambling of single Japanese men, who jeered at his moral admonitions. He crusaded against Japanese gangs who controlled prostitutes and had his life threatened.

He played a major role in politics, urging the Japanese not to strike in 1909 and not to cooperate with the Filipinos in 1920. He received funding from owners to spread Christianity on their plantations.[43] He gained the financial support of white Christians, including Governor Sanford Dole and Mary Castle, the widow of the co-founder of Castle & Cooke. He promoted the Americanization of the Japanese in Hawaii and was a great admirer of Abraham Lincoln. In 1896, he established *Chuo* Gakuin, the first Japanese language school in Hawaii. He worked to revise the texts from Japan which promoted loyalty to the emperor. In 1917, he began a chapter of the Young Men's Christian Association in Nuuanu.

Rev. Okamura served at first at a church in Nuuanu and then began a fresh start in a more central district of Honolulu. He began the Makiki Christian Church in 1904 in a shed with twenty-four members on Kinau Street not far from McKinley High School. By 1906, church membership reached 111; by 1914 it had grown to 500. Up until 1918, all services were conducted in Japanese.[44]

In 1930, in the midst of the Depression, Rev. Okamura launched an audacious building program to build a new church in the form of a *shiro* or medieval castle. This unique building was completed in November 1932; 143 new members were received at the same time. Rev. Okamura also built dormitories for young men and women near the church.[45]

---

status in 1920, Doshisha Daigaku is one of the most prestigious universities in Japan today.

43. Buddhist priests such as Bishop Imamura supported the demands of the Japanese workers.

44. *Makiki Christian Church: A Brief History (Centennial Anniversary)*, (Honolulu, Hawaii: Makiki Christian Church, 2004), 22.

45. I attended a nursery at this church. My wife lived in the Okamura dormitory for women while attending McKinley High School; after her conversion she became a member of this church. Mildred Kiyuna, a missionary from Makiki Christian Church to Okinawa, was most helpful to me on my visit to the island in 2008.

Figure 2. Makiki Christian Church

Naichi vs. Uchinanchu

The Japanese immigrants were segregated from other ethnic groups (Chinese, Filipinos) in the plantation camps. They also tended to adhere to people from their own provinces in societies called *kenjin-kai*. Moreover, the *Naichi*, immigrants from the main Japanese islands, were disdainful of the *Uchinanchu*, those from Okinawa. Dennis Ogawa has commented: "The relationship between the Okinawans and the Naichi in Hawaii is somewhat like that between the Irish and the English: the one group feeling superior to the other, and the other having a defensive pride."⁴⁶ In addition to their different appearance and incomprehensible dialect, the Okinawans had peculiar customs, such as married women tattooing their hands, and above all their predilection for raising pigs, which required the collecting of garbage to feed them. This smelly and dirty work was practiced in Japan only by the lowly caste of the *eta* "filth," now euphemistically called *burakumin* "hamlet people."

Naichi children in Hawaii would taunt Okinawan children by calling out *Okinawa ken ken, buta kau kau*, combining the Japanese word for pig (buta) with the Hawaiian words for food (kau kau). The antipathy between the two groups of Issei immigrants made it impossible for any of their Nisei children to get married to mates from the other group until after World War II, when men of both groups fought together in the US army.⁴⁷

Pidgin English

To communicate in a polyglot situation on plantations a Creole type of language, Hawaiian Pidgin, evolved. This combined the Hawaiian pronunciation of English and incorporated words from Hawaiian, Japanese, and other languages.⁴⁸ As there are still some in Hawaii, especially in the Leeward side of Oahu, who are more comfortable with Pidgin than with standard English, the Wycliffe Bible Translators, Joe and Barbara Grimes,⁴⁹ with the help of native speakers, produced in 2000 a Hawaiian Pidgin translation of the New Testament, *Da Jesus Book*.⁵⁰ The Lord's Prayer is rendered:

---

46. Dennis M. Ogawa, *Kodomo no tame ni: For the Sake of the Children: The Japanese American Experience in Hawaii* (Honolulu, Hawaii: University of Hawaii Press, 1978), 241.

47. For three plays by Jon Shirota on Okinawans in Hawaii, see *Voices from Okinawa*, ed. Frank Stewart and Katsumori Yamazato (Honolulu, Hawaii: University of Hawaii Press, 2009).

48. Myra Sachiko Ikeda, *A Harvest of Hawai'i Plantation Pidgin: The Japanese Way* (Honolulu, Hawaii: Mutual Publishing, 2016). When I was growing up, schoolmates spoke pidgin outside of the class. If one tried to speak good English, he would be accused of trying to act like a "haole."

49. I first met the Grimes in 1960 at the Summer Institute of Linguistics in Norman, Oklahoma. After teaching Linguistics at Cornell University, Joe and his wife retired to Hawaii.

50. (Orlando, Florida: Wycliffe Bible Translators, 2000).

God, you our Fadda.
You stay inside da sky.
We like all da peopo know fo shua how you stay,
An dat you stay good an spesho,
An we like dem give you plenny respeck,
We like you come King fo everybody now,
We like everybody make jalike you like,
Ova hea inside da world,
Jalike da angel guys up inside da sky make jalike you like.
Give us da food we need fo today an every day.
Hemo our shame, an let us go
Fo all da kine bad stuff we do to you,
Jalike us guys let da odda guys go awready,
An we no stay huhu wit dem
Fo all da kine bad stuff dey do to us.
No let us get chance fo do bad kine stuff,
But take us outa dea, so da Bad Guy no can hurt us.
[Cuz you our King
You get da real power,
An you stay awesome foeva.]
Dass it![51]

---

51. *Da Jesus Book*, 16. The familiar doxology is in brackets, as these verses are not in our earliest Greek manuscripts.

Chapter 3

Ancestors, Relatives, and Parents

The Last Samurai

THE SAMURAI OF JAPAN'S feudal period, who were armed with long, sharp swords (*katana*) as well as short swords (*wakizashi*), were the retainers of the lords of clans. Peasant farmers cowered before them as anyone who showed disrespect to the samurai could be summarily beheaded by them. In battle they wore armor and were armed with spears, bows, and arrows. In the sixteenth century the Portuguese introduced the arquebus, a matchlock rifle, and later cannons.

A samurai whose lord (*daimyō*) was defeated could become a *rōnin* "a vagrant samurai," who was impoverished and who sometimes became a mercenary. Such *rōnin* were the favorite subject of the famed director, Akira Kurosawa. His masterpiece, *Seven Samurai* (1954), has been hailed as one of the greatest films ever made.[1] The samurai code of honor (*bushidō*) at times required a defeated or disgraced samurai to commit ritual suicide (*seppuku* or *harakiri*) by stabbing himself to death.[2]

With the rise of the Meiji Emperor in 1868 and the development of a conscript army, some of the samurai, who were highly educated,

---

1. It inspired the western film, *The Magnificent Seven* (1960).
2. In Puccini's opera, *Madame Butterfly*, set in Nagasaki, Cio ciosan lives with the American Lieutenant Pinkerton and bears him a son. He departs to America, promising to return for his son. But Butterfly is shocked when he returns with an American wife. In the last scene, she goes behind a screen and kills herself with a dagger inscribed "Die with honor, when it is impossible to live with honor."

became bureaucrats and diplomats. The last samurai conflict in 1877 was the Satsuma Rebellion, which was the basis for the acclaimed movie, *The Last Samurai*, starring Tom Cruise and Ken Watanabe (2005). In Okinawa, samurai stipends ended in 1876.

The male descendants of samurai had the right to prefix their first names with the honorific *Sho* or *Cho*. Both my father's and my mother's families from Okinawa claim descent from the samurai who once lived at the Shuri castle.[3] My father and my paternal cousins have names prefixed by Sho, and my mother's brothers all have names prefixed by Cho. My mother recalls that a samurai sword was displayed in the inn owned by her grandparents in Okinawa.

The Owan Ancestors

The *kanji* (Chinese characters) for the name Owan (my mother's family) signifies "Big Bay." Genealogical records originally kept at Shuri trace the family's ancestors for 15 generations. In the first generation Chori Owan, served as the head clerk for the Okinawan delegation to Beijing in 1795. On his return from a trip to China in 1802 he was lost in a typhoon. In the second generation Choho Owan went on a delegation to Beijing in 1820.[4]

The Owan Family

The Owans came from Makabe village now incorporated into the city of Itoman on the southern tip of Okinawa. My maternal grandfather (*Jijisan*) was Chiyoko (Choki) Owan (1882 to 1964). Choki emigrated from Okinawa to Hawaii in 1906. My grandmother (*Babasan*) was Tsuru (Kuniyoshi) Owan (1891 to 1983). Tsuru came to Hawaii as a picture bride in 1912.

They first worked at the sugar plantation of Hawi in Kohala in the northern part of the Big Island, where my mother, Haruko, was born on June 24, 1913. They had three daughters: Haruko, Yoshie (Katie),

---

3. The castle, which was destroyed in World War II, was rebuilt in 1992. It was destroyed again by a fire in October 2019.

4. I owe this information to my cousin Hiromi Nagasawa, the daughter of my uncle Choko in Tokyo.

Shizuko (Beryl), and four sons: Choko, Chose (Bob), Chogi (Jimmy), and Choken (Tom).

Figure 3. Owan Family: front row: Chogi (Jim), Choken (Tom), Babasan, Jijisan. Behind: Yoshie (Kaytie), Shizuko (Beryl), Chosei (Bob). Missing are the two oldest children, Haruko and Choko.

My Mother

As women were expected to work with their husbands in the plantation, my grandparents made the decision in 1917 to take their three oldest children (Haruko, Choko, Yoshie) back to live with relatives in Okinawa. When my mother saw Babasan leaving on the boat she almost threw herself into the ocean. She lived with grandparents, Choko and Yoshie lived with other relatives. It was not until nine years later that their parents were able to bring them back to Hawaii. By this time the Owans had moved to the plantation at Kahuku on the northern tip of Oahu.

Not knowing any English, the thirteen-year-old Haruko balked at being placed in a class with six-year-olds.[5] On the other hand, Choko

5. As a result my mother did not have an English education. Late in life, by attending night school in Los Angeles, she earned the equivalent of a junior high diploma. Her numerous letters to me were always half in English and half in Japanese. While I

learned English and graduated from Mid-Pacific High School. He went on to medical school in Japan, where Okinawans were regarded as outsiders like Koreans and Taiwanese. He became a successful eye, ear, and nose surgeon in Tokyo.

Babasan was a kindly mother, who as a devout Buddhist, prayed daily before the image of Kannon, the goddess of mercy.[6] Jijisan, a short energetic man, was a hardworking father. They raised and butchered pigs, as well as chickens. They peddled pork and eggs as well as fish throughout the plantation camps. Most plantations had a company store. Jijisan built his own store which also had a restaurant.

My mother as the *nēsan* or oldest daughter had a lot of responsibility thrust upon her. There were days, she said, when she crept in the crawl space under their home to weep. Then one day to her surprise her father said to her *Mire* "Look," there was a notice in the Japanese paper that girls who could pass a *shiken* "test," could stay in a dormitory in Honolulu to study sewing. When she passed the test, she was overjoyed that she could escape her onerous duties in Kahuku, but her sister Shizuko was dismayed that she now had to undertake those tasks.

My mother was quite beautiful and had a number of suitors, including a wealthy Okinawan named Mr. Tonaki who owned a service station. When she turned him down in favor of my father, who though poor was tall and handsome, Jijisan called her *baka* "a fool," because she had regard to his *kao dake* "face only."

The Yamauchi Family

The kanji characters for Yamauchi signify "mountain" and "interior." The Yamauchis came from Kanegusuku, a village north of Itoman. My uncle (*Ojisan*) Shokin (1888 to 1960), the oldest member of his family emigrated to Hawaii probably in 1906. My father, Shokyo was seventeen years younger than Shokin. He was born in 1905 and came to Hawaii when he was thirteen. He learned English and graduated from McKinley High School, whose students were almost entirely Japanese.

---

understood Japanese as a child, it was only after I studied *kaiwa* ("conversation") at the University of Hawaii that I could speak to her in Japanese.

6. The Owans followed the Jodo Shu sect of Buddhism, which was related to the Jodo Shin sect. The main difference was that the recitation of the Nembutsu was not a means of gaining merit, but simply an affirmation of gratitude to Buddha.

My aunt (*Obasan*), Tsuru Kamigawa (1890 to 1990), has given a detailed oral history of her life.[7] Tsuru, who was from Itoman, recalls:

> We had never seen Shokin Yamauchi, because his family was living far away from Itoman … in Kanegusku. They were samurai from Shuri who had moved out there earlier when they were able to buy country land cheap. They farmed on a large scale growing cane.[8]

As for her own family's background, Tsuru relates: "My parents, whose name was Kamigawa, were of samurai lineage and moved from Shuri to Itoman when I was three years old (in 1893)."[9]

Tsuru came to Hawaii as a picture bride in 1910, when she was twenty; her husband was twenty-two. She joined her husband on the sugar plantation in Waipahu on Oahu, where they lived in a windowless cottage in Camp 35, which was exclusively Okinawan. There was no furniture; they slept on a *futon*.

As she had one child after another, four sons (Shoan, Shoyei, Shojin, Masanobu) and three daughters (Hatsuye, Mitchan, Kiyochan), she could not work out in the fields but worked as a launderer, washing by hand clothes stained with red dirt and ironing them with a coal iron.

In 1919, she took her four oldest children (Hatsuye, Shoan, Shoyei, and Shojin) back to Okinawa to stay with relatives. Ojisan and Obasan left the plantation to work in Honolulu, he as a gardener and she as a cook and launderer. She also toiled in the pineapple cannery for 30 cents an hour and the tuna processing plant for 20 cents an hour. She walked rather than spending five cents on the trolley.

---

7. Tsuru Yamauchi, in *Uchinanchu: A History of Okinawans in Hawaii* (Honolulu, Hawaii: University of Hawaii, 1981), 488–509.

8. Op. cit., 490.

9. Ibid., 491.

Figure 4. Yamauchi Family: front row: Shojin, Ojisan, Mithcan, Kiyochan, Masanobu, Obasan; back row: Shoyei, Shokyo (my father), Hatsue

The Aala Tofuya

In 1940 the Yamauchis were able to buy a *tofuya*, named the Aala Tofu Factory, which was the oldest in the Islands.[10] This was located in an alley across from the Japanese theater, which not only showed Japanese movies but also live entertainment at one time.[11] The Aala area was once the center of the Japanese community with many stores on King Street offering produce, fish, and dry goods.[12] Later Aala Park became a gathering place for single Filipino men.

---

10. It was started in 1923 by H. Iwanaga according to William Shurtleff and Akiko Aoyagi, compilers, *How Japanese and Japanese Americans Brought Soyfoods to the United States and the Hawaiian Islands: A History (1851 to 2011)* (Lafayette, California: The Soy Institute, 2011), 4.

11. I learned later that my wife's sister, Jane Honda, had worked in the ticket booth of this theater.

12. Michael M. Okihiro, *Aʻala: The Story of a Japanese Community in Hawaii* (Honolulu, Hawaii: Japanese Cultural Center of Hawaii, 2003).

Tofu, a white cake made of soybean curds, is a staple among Chinese, Japanese, and other Asians. Preparing tofu required getting to work at 2 or 3 a.m. at the latest. To process soybeans into bean curd, they must be soaked overnight, mashed, boiled, strained, and mixed with *nigari*, a coagulant of magnesium chloride derived from seawater. After being pressed between cheesecloth, the pressed curds are soaked in cold water and then sliced into cubes. The waste, *okara*, can be fed to pigs. *Age* is deep fried tofu. Tsuru's oldest son, Shoan, came back from Okinawa in 1939 and helped her make the tofu. When he left for California in 1947, Shojin or Jin took over.[13]

A Wedding, a Birth, and a Death

After my parents were wed, Jijisan wanted his new son-in-law to help him on the farm in Kahuku.[14] Shokyo had a better idea. He took his bride to Hilo, where he found work as a clerk and salesman at Kitagawa Automobile, a firm which is still in business in Hilo today.

---

13. As I worked at the Aala Tofu Factory on Saturday mornings between 1948 and 1952, it was Jin who taught me how to drive and to back into the alley, as well as to carry hundred-pound sacks of soybeans on my shoulder. I helped him deliver tofu to Japanese groceries and restaurants.

14. I owe some of the information about my father to Roy Yamauchi, the son of my cousin Shoyei, who was a great admirer of Shokyo.

Figure 5. Shokyo and Haruko Yamauchi, wedding portrait

That is how I, Edwin Masao Yamauchi, came to be born in Hilo on February 1, 1937. Alas, I was never to know my father. He went into debt and suffered from an excruciating ear infection. He could not afford to be flown to the mainland for specialist treatment. He received care at the Japanese Kuakini Hospital in Honolulu. On July 16, 1940, he threw himself from the Kuakini Bridge down to the Nuuanu River below, leaving my desolate mother a widow.[15]

---

15. I know at least three occasions when my mother sought to take her own life, including after the death of her second husband.

Figure 6. My parents with their newborn son

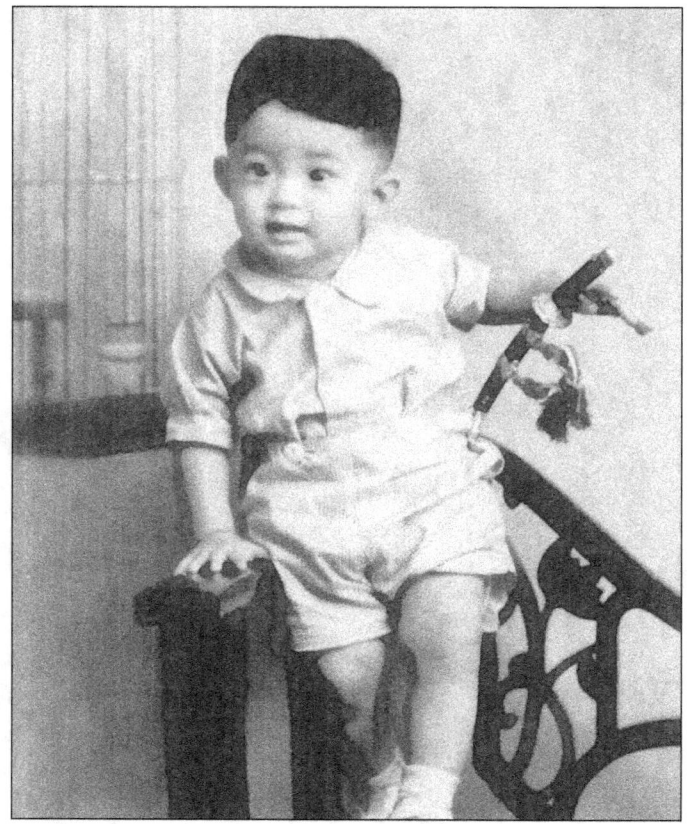

Figure 7. With a toy samurai sword

Chapter 4

World War II

(1941 to 1945)

A Working Widow

STARTING IN 1940, FOR the next dozen years, to raise her son, my mother worked a variety of jobs, primarily as a maid and cook and occasionally as a dressmaker. Many of these jobs lasted less than a year. She at first worked as a dressmaker at the Style Center on King Street near Makiki Christian Church, where I attended a nursery class. She worked for two young women but then quit when she realized they were prostitutes. She worked for an elderly Mrs. Cox, who scolded her for throwing away some overripe guava fruit.

Most of her employers were haoles, but some were Japanese. Once while employed by an elderly dressmaker who had a crippled wife, she reported that her employer tried at night to sneak into the room she and I were sharing. She also worked at Dixie Dazel dressmakers on Kalakaua Avenue., and for about a year had her own dressmaking business in a house on Fort Street across from the Honpa Hongwanji Temple.

She worked briefly at the cafeteria of Roosevelt High School. She served as a cook and maid for Ross Sutherland, the owner of a men's clothing store, as well as for his sister. She worked in Manoa Valley for a haole family, whose young son called me a "Jap." She was cleaning their living room window when she saw smoke arising in the distance. It was Sunday, December 7, 1941.

Pearl Harbor and Mitsuo Fuchida

The pilot who led the first wave of attack was Mitsuo Fuchida, who signaled *Tora, Tora, Tora* "Tiger, Tiger, Tiger," to indicate the success of the surprise attack.[1] The attack, which involved 360 planes launched from six aircraft carriers positioned undetected, north of Hawaii, began at 7:57 a.m. Three waves of planes destroyed or severely damaged eight battleships at Pearl Harbor and 188 planes at Hickam Airfield, inflicting 2,335 military deaths.[2] Only sixty-four Japanese were killed. One sailor from a minisub, Kazuo Sakamaki, who lost the use of his compass and went aground, was captured. He felt disgraced and wanted to commit suicide.[3] A map on the sub revealed that Japan had excellent information about the ships in Pearl Harbor compiled by spies working for Japan's consulate on 1742 Nuuanu Street. They also employed a German, Otto Kuehn, who had a beach house.

Fuchida fought in numerous battles and escaped death on several occasions. His admiral, Kakuji Kakuta, committed seppuku when he failed to stop the Americans at Guam. Fuchida would have been in Hiroshima when the atom bomb was dropped there on August 6, 1945, but he had been ordered to another location on August 5.[4] After the war, he was a bitter and broken man. But then in 1949, when he learned of the testimony of Jacob DeShazer, Fuchida became a Christian and then an evangelist.[5]

---

1. In 1970 a movie titled *Tora, Tora, Tora*, narrated the story of the attack. Akira Kurosawa, who wrote the Japanese dialogue, was so displeased with the result, that he had his name removed from the credits.

2. Of these deaths half (1,177) came from the crew of the Arizona, whose sunken remains are the centerpiece of the memorial in Pearl Harbor today. Among the 180 Miami University alumni who perished in World War II was Ensign William Lawrence who died on the Arizona. On December 7, 2018, only twenty survivors of the attack were able to attend the anniversary in Hawaii.

3. See Mark Harmon and Leon Carroll, Jr., *Ghosts of Honolulu* (San Francisco, California: Harper Select, 2023).

4. A second atomic bomb was dropped on Nagasaki on August 9; Nagasaki had not been the primary target, but clouds obscured Okura, the primary target. In 2008 I was able to visit the museums at Hiroshima and Nagasaki. The bomb on Hiroshima killed and maimed relatives of the many Japanese in Hawaii who had originally come from Hiroshima-ken.

5. I heard Fuchida's testimony twice, once in Los Angeles and then at M.I.T. I gave a copy of his autobiography, *From Pearl Harbor to Calvary* (Escondido, California: Christian, 2011) to my barber in Oxford, Ohio, Harold Jones, who had been a sailor at Pearl Harbor. As it was a Sunday, he had been on shore leave that fateful day.

Jacob (Jake) DeShazer had been a bombardier on one of sixteen B-25 bombers led by General James Doolittle on April 18, 1942, to bomb Japan. When his plane ditched in China, its five-member crew was captured by the Japanese. They were beaten, starved, and shuttled from prison to prison. He spent forty months in prison, all but six in solitary confinement. Jake was able to obtain a copy of a Bible for three weeks. On June 8, 1944, he gave his life to Christ and found that his hatred of the Japanese had been replaced with love for them.

Jake studied at Seattle Pacific College and returned with his wife Florence to Japan as missionaries. His testimony, "I Was a Prisoner of Japan," was published in a tract which was given to Mitsuo Fuchida. When both Fuchida and Jake spoke at an evangelistic meeting, three hundred responded to the invitation to accept Christ. Fuchida was later to give his testimony at Annapolis and to meet General Doolittle.[6]

Children's Memories

My mother remembers that she and others burned their Japanese books in the aftermath of Pearl Harbor. I was too young to have any memories of that day or of the war. But Gordon Sakamoto, who later became the Associated Press's bureau chief in Hawaii, recounts some of his memories:

> The scattered patches of brown-black puffs against the sparkling blue sky should have been an indication that something was wrong that Sunday morning. But, as a 6-year-old, I was more eager to get in a full day of "pee-wee"—a game using different lengths of an old broomstick—not knowing the enormity of events taking place 8 miles away. As we went to bed, my father placed the radio under a table draped with a sheet so there would be no visible light outside. That was when it struck me that something was seriously wrong.... (Though the next day was Monday) there was no school for students at Lunalilo Elementary. There was good reason: a shell had landed on the two-story building and burned down the second level... Martial law was in effect with a strictly enforced 8 p.m. curfew. There was rationing of food, especially fresh meat, probably the reason Hawaii remains the biggest consumer of Spam.... All windows

---

6. Janet and Geoff Benge, *Jacob DeShazer: Forgive Your Enemies* (Seattle, Washington: YWAM Publishers, 2009).

AN ASIAN AMERICAN ANCIENT HISTORIAN AND BIBLICAL SCHOLAR

had to be painted over so no light should show outside.... The war also meant backyard shelters.⁷

My wife, who is seven years older and was living on the Big Island, recalls food rationing, the planting of vegetable gardens, and the digging of underground shelters. Children had to learn how to wear gas masks. She chuckles as she recalls blacking out the windows, while the volcano goddess Pele defied government orders by lighting up the skies with eruptions from Kilauea on the slopes of Mauna Loa.⁸

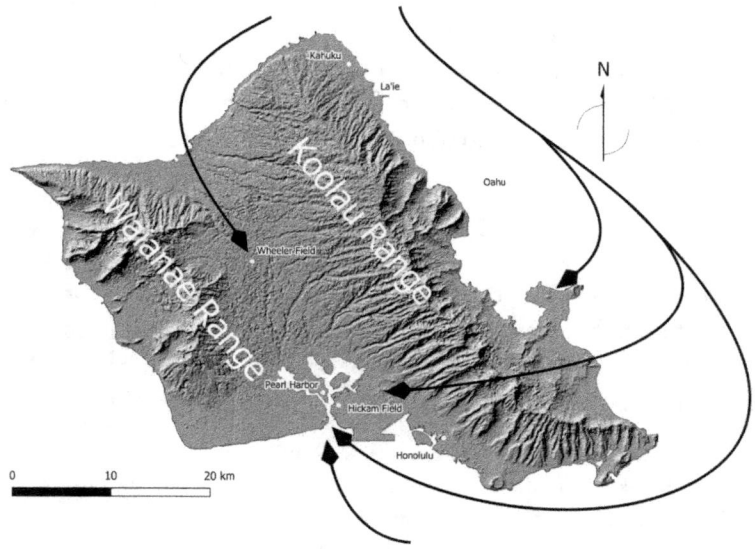

Map 6. Pearl Harbor

Seichi Tsuchiya

By the 1940s, 37 percent or about 158,000 of Hawaii's total population of 423.330 were of Japanese descent, 73 percent of these were American

---

7. Gordon Sakamoto, "Pearl Harbor Changed a Young Boy's World," *Rafu Shimpo* (Dec. 8, 1998), 1–2.

8. In 2018 continuous lava flowing down to the sea in the district of Puna, south of Hilo, destroyed 700 homes. Because of previous eruptions people are well aware of the potential danger, but build in this area because it is the cheapest land available.

citizens.⁹ Prior to Pearl Harbor the FBI had compiled a list of Japanese, primarily *Issei* (first generation immigrants), *Kibei* (those born in the US but raised in Japan like my mother), and a few *Nisei* (second generation descendants) who would be subject to arrest if war broke out between Japan and the US. These included fishermen, veterans of the Russo-Japan War, those who had traveled to Japan or who had sent money there, Buddhist priests,¹⁰ Japanese language teachers,¹¹ diplomats, businessmen, and journalists.

By the evening of December 7, the FBI had seized about 1,300 on this list; by March 1942, they had arrested more than 5,000. Fathers and husbands were taken away from families without any explanation. After interrogation they were placed in detention on Sand Island, a five-acre site in Pearl Harbor. A few European aliens were also held there. Some would later be held at the 160-acre Honouliuli Prison near Ewa, but many would be shipped to various internment camps on the mainland.¹²

In 1942 my mother served as the cook and maid for Seiichi Tsuchiya, in a home in the Manoa Valley just above Punahou High School. He had a son, Ronald, who was the same age as I. Mr. Tsuchiya was the president of the *Shōgyō Jihō*, a monthly business periodical.¹³ He was the half-brother of Fred Makino, the editor of the most important Japanese newspaper, the *Hawaii Hochi*. Makino had vigorously criticized the plantation owners and had supported the Japanese strike of 1909.

---

9. *Judgment without Trial: Japanese American Imprisonment during World War II* (Seattle, Washington: University of Washington Press, 2003), 67.

10. The removal of all Buddhists priests from Hawaii had a crippling effect upon Buddhism in the Islands. In 1941, there were in Hawaii sixty-five priests of the three branches of the Jōdo or Pure Land sects, thirty priests of the Shingon sect, forty-six Shinto priests, and forty-one priests of minor sects. Suzanne Falgout and Linda Nishigaya, *Breaking the Silence; Social Process in Hawai'i* vol. 45 (Honolulu, Hwaii: University of Hawaii, 2014), 175.

11. Okamura, who had begun one of the first Japanese language schools in the Islands, opposed the re-establishment of such schools after the War.

12. For a detailed autobiographical account of a Japanese leader, who was arrested and then moved from camp to camp on the mainland, see Suikei Furuya, *An Internment Odyssey*, tr. Tatsumi Hayashi (Honolulu, Hawaii Japanese Cultural Center of Hawai'i, 2017).

13. This was "A monthly journal on political, social, economic, and cultural eventsin and outside of Hawaii published since August 1921, (temporarily ceased publication from December 1941 to November 1946). Published and edited by Tsuchiya Seiichi." *A Buried Past: An Annotated Bibliography of the Japanese American Research Project Collection*, Compiled by Y. Ichioka, Y. Sakata, N. A. Tsuchida, and E. Yasuhara (Berkeley, California: University of California Press, 1987), 144.

Mr. Tsuchiya was playing golf on December 7. His wife passed away soon afterwards. He had escaped the first dragnet, but was then arrested by the FBI in 1942, imprisoned for the duration at the prison near Ewa. His son Ronald was cared for by an aunt in Aiea. The next Japanese owner of the property made improper advances to my mother, which caused her to quit this job.

Figure 8. With Ronald Tsuchiya

The Internment Camps[14]

Whereas in Hawaii only a few thousand Japanese, mainly Issei, were arrested, this was not to be the case with the Japanese on the West Coast, where, by hard work, they had developed a prosperous life establishing farms, nurseries, and businesses, especially in California. The 1940 census listed about 94,000 in California, with about 18,000 in Oregon and

---

14. See Alice Young Murray, ed., *What Did the Internment of Japanese Americans Mean?* (Boston, Massachusetts: St, Martin's, 2000).

Washington.[15] Sizeable "Japanese towns" were to be found in Los Angeles, San Francisco, Portland, and Seattle.[16]

Prompted by racist anti-Japanese hysteria promoted by politicians and newspapers, President Franklin Roosevelt signed the infamous Executive Order 9066 in February 1942, ordering the removal of all Japanese from the West Coast to the interior for reasons of military necessity.[17] An egregious example of how strictly this order was carried out was the removal of orphans from the Japanese Children's Home in Los Angeles to Mananar.

Ten euphemistically called "relocation" camps were created. In reality, these were incarceration camps, ringed with barbed wire fences, and guarded by sentries armed with machine guns on towers, prepared to shoot anyone who sought to leave.

Harold Ickes, who oversaw the camps for President Roosevelt, later wrote: "Crowded into (railway) cars like cattle, these hapless people were hurried away to hastily constructed and thoroughly inadequate concentration camps, with soldiers with nervous muskets on guard, in the great American desert. We gave the fancy name of 'relocation centers' to these dust bowls, but they were concentration camps nonetheless."[18]

---

15. Roger M. Daniels, *Prisoners Without Trial: Japanese Americans in World War II* (New York, New York: Hill & Wang, 2004), 8.

16. Before World War II there were about 7,000 Japanese in Seattle.

17. In 1942, Japanese from the west coast of Canada were also removed into the interior but were not placed in concentration camps. They were transported to Slocan Valley where they were placed in three-room houses, with Royal Canadian Mounted Police patrolling the edge of the town.

18. Harold Ickes, "Man to Man: Wartime abuse of American Japanese should now be corrected by US," *Washington Evening Star* (September 23, 1946), A-9.

Figure 9. Sentry tower at Manzanar (courtesy of Jon Yamashiro)

The order affected 110,723 persons, about 70,000 of whom were *Niseis* (second generation children) who were American citizens. They were given only two weeks to sell their holdings for a pittance or in a few cases to entrust them to non-Japanese friends. Each person was allowed only what could be carried in a single suitcase. The Japanese American Citizens League [19] counseled compliance and the Japanese cooperated by gathering at assembly points at designated times. One of these was the Santa Anita racetrack, where they were housed in smelly stables. They were then transported in buses or in trains, with the shades lowered so they could not see where they were going.

There were ten camps in seven states: 1) California (Manzanar, Tule Lake), 2) Arizona (Poston, Gila River), 3) Idaho (Minidoka), 4)

---

19. The JACL, founded in 1930, was an organization dedicated to promoting Americanization among Nisei and also to protecting their civil rights.

WORLD WAR II

Wyoming (Heart Mountain), 5) Colorado (Amache), 6) Utah (Topaz), and 7) Arkansas (Rohwer, Jerome). Most housed about 10,000, Amache held only 7,318, Poston had 17,814, and Tule Lake 18,789 at their maximum.[20] The camps were placed in remote and desolate places; for example, those in Arkansas were located in a swampy forested area, whereas Manzanar was placed at the edge of the Mojave Desert. Families were separated among different camps.

Poston[21]

Poston was situated in western Arizona on the grounds of an Indian Reservation. Winds blew sandstorms. It reached over 100 degrees in the summer and was bitterly cold in the winter. There were three camps separated by a mile or two from each other. Each camp was sectioned into blocks, with ten barracks, containing about three hundred persons in each block.

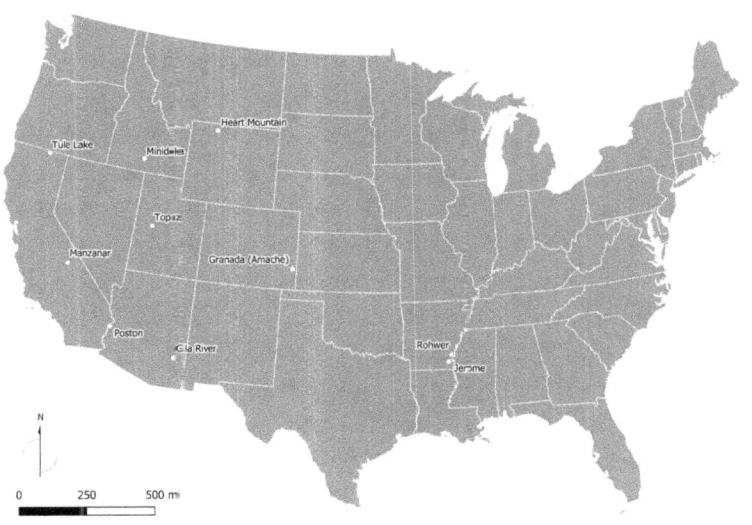

Map 7. The Internment Camps

20. Roger Daniels, Sandra C. Taylor, and Harry H. L. Kitano. ed., *From Relocation to Redress* (Seattle, Washington: University of Washington Press, 1991), i.

21. Frances Iida, who married my uncle Tom Owan was transported with her family to Poston when she was fifteen.

Those interned were housed in flimsy wooden buildings covered with tarpaper, which did not prevent sand from seeping in through the cracks. There was no air conditioning or electrical appliances such as refrigerators, stoves, or washing machines. Everyone ate in a common mess hall and used communal facilities. Separate latrines for men and women consisted of a row of seats without any separation; shower facilities likewise had no separate stalls. The living quarters were rooms that were 25 feet by 25 feet, accommodating six or seven people. At first, the only furniture were army cots and mattresses stuffed with straw.

The camps were self-governed. After the internees were able to make some improvements themselves—planting gardens, making furniture from scrap wood, etc., conditions became more livable. Jobs paying $16 to $19 per month or about 10 cents an hour became available. Items could be ordered from Sears and Roebuck catalogues. Caucasian friends such as Dr. Ralph Mayberry and Rev. Herbert Nicholson, a former Quaker missionary to Japan, brought truckloads of goods, and other Christians served as pen pals for the youth.

Organized recreational activities such as sports, dances, parties, and movies served as temporary distractions. Especially important at Poston was a thriving church, which at Christmas had a two-hundred-member choir singing the Hallelujah Chorus!

At Poston, a dynamic Baptist evangelist, Dr. Jitsuo Morikawa, and his assistant Paul M. Nagano, inspired numerous young men who became prominent ministers and educators, such as Hideo Aoki, Akira Kuroda,[22] Mas Toyotome, and Art Tsuneishi.[23] Paul Nagano attended Bethel Theological Seminary and pastored churches in Minneapolis, Los Angeles, and Hawaii.[24] In 1950, Paul was instrumental in establishing the Japanese Evangelistic Missionary Society (JEMS) in Los Angeles, an organization which sponsors missionaries to Japan and Brazil, and also supports ministries to the numerous Asian American students at

---

22. Rev. Kuroda attended Wheaton College and began Lakeside Japanese Church near Wrigley field, a church my wife attended when she was a student in Chicago. He later he became the pastor of the LA Holiness Church.

23. For the inspiring testimonies of 52 men and women who endured the internment camps, see Victor N. Okada, *Triumphs of Faith: Stories of Japanese-American Christians During World War II* (Los Angeles, California: Japanese-American Internment Project, 1998).

24. Paul Nagano served as the pastor of Makiki Christian Church from 1957 to 1962, a church my wife attended.

universities in California.²⁵ JEMS also sponsors an annual conference at the Mount Hermon campgrounds in northern California.²⁶

Displaced young people were able to complete their high school degrees by correspondence courses. A National Japanese American Student Relocation Council began in July 1942, soliciting college scholarships from schools in the interior. By June 1946, close to four thousand students had been allowed to leave the camps for universities in the east. One of these was Peter Hironaka, who left in June 1945, for a college in southwestern Ohio. Pete, who became a cartoonist for the *Dayton Daily News*, described his first impression as he came to the town of Oxford in southwestern Ohio

> I headed down High Street towards the university. It was only a couple of blocks til I sighted what Robert Frost, the beloved poet, was said to have described as "the prettiest college there is." In describing my transference from the Poston camp to Miami U. to my Jayhawker friend Dick Simms, I said, "Dick, it was like Dorothy leaving Kansas in black and white and arriving in Oz in technicolor."²⁷

The 100th and the 442nd

There was another way for young Nisei to leave the internment camps— that was to enlist in the army. There were two separate all Nisei units, commanded by Caucasian commanding officers, which were eventually merged together: the 100th Infantry Battalion and the 442nd Regimental Combat Team.²⁸

---

25. Even before Proposition 209 was passed in 1996 banning considerations of race in admissions, the proportion of Asian Americans at the University of California campuses had spiked in the 1970s and 1980s. In 2006 they constituted 38.5% of students at UCLA, the largest ethnic group there according to Julie J. Park, *When Diversity Drops* (New Brunswick, New Jersey: Rutgers University Press, 2013), 9. Moreover, according to Julie J. Park, *Race on Campus* (Philadelphia, Pennsylvania: Temple University Press, 2018), 42, "69.2% of Asian Americans active in student groups participated in one that was majority Asian American . . . "

26. I was one of the speakers at the 25th Mt. Hermon Conference in June 1974, along with Paul Nagano and Josh McDowell.

27. Pete Hironaka, *Report from Round-Eye Country* (Dayton, Ohio: Graphic Concept Center, 1981), 7. Earlham College, a Quaker school in nearby Richmond, Indiana, accepted 24 Niseis.

28. The average Nisei soldier was 5'6" tall and weighed 130 pounds.

The 100th was formed in June 1942 with 1,432 Nisei members of the Hawaii National Guard. They trained at Camp McCoy in Wisconsin and then at Camp Shelby in Mississippi. The 100th first saw combat in Italy in September 1943. The Germans occupied many mountain tops, including Monte Cassino, which held the monastery of St. Francis on its summit. After an unsuccessful attempt to take this summit, the unit was down to 512 men.[29] They suffered so many casualties that they were nicknamed "The Purple Heart" battalion.

The 442nd was created by order of President Franklin D. Roosevelt on February 1, 1943, with volunteers from Hawaii and from the internment camps. About 2,700 volunteers came from Hawaii and 800 from the mainland. There was initial friction between these two groups as the mainlanders could not understand the Hawaiian Pidgin English. The Army selected mainland Nisei who spoke better English to serve as non-commissioned officers, which rankled those from Hawaii. Fights broke out between the "Buddhaheads"[30] from the Islands and the "Kotonks"[31] from the mainland. The unit arrived in May 1943 at Ft. Shelby and as they were excluded from the white USO, they socialized with women from the internment camps in Arkansas.

The 442nd arrived in Naples in June 1944 and were combined with the 100th as a single unit. In fighting up the west coast of Italy to Rome, the 100th/442nd suffered 1,300 casualties, almost a fourth of their roster.[32] The Nisei were the first soldiers to reach the outskirts of Rome but were halted there so other Americans could be hailed as the liberators of Rome.[33]

The combined unit was then transported to southeastern France, where they fought the Germans there. In October the so-called "Lost Battalion" of 275 Texans became surrounded by Germans in the Vosges Mountains. When other American troops failed to break through to the Texans who were short of ammunition, food, and water, Major General

---

29. C. Douglas Sterner, *Go for Broke: The Nisei Warriors of World War II Who Conquered Germany, Japan and American Bigotry* (Clearfield, Utah: American Legacy Historical Press, 2015), 29.

30. A derisive term given them either because some of them were Buddhists, or as a term derived from the Japanese word *buta*, "pig."

31. Explained as the sound made when two mainlander's heads were knocked together!

32. Sterner, 54.

33. Thomas D. Murphy, *Ambassadors in Arms: The Story of Hawaii's 100th Battalion* (Honolulu, Hawaii: University of Hawaii Press, 1955), 190.

Dahlquist ordered the badly depleted and weary 442nd to rescue the Texans. After furious fighting in the forests the Nisei fighters succeeded in rescuing the 211 surviving Texans but at a terrible cost to themselves.

> When the 442nd had entered the Vosges a month or so before, its strength was 2,943 men. Of those 161 had died in battle, 43 were missing, and about 2,000 were wounded (882 of them with serious wounds). Of the dead 13 were medics. The regiment had dwindled to less than a third of its authorized strength.[34]

A Jewish scholar at the University of Cincinnati, Roger Daniels, who is the foremost historian of the Japanese Americans during World War II, has commented:

> In what may have been the supreme irony of their service, the men of the 442nd helped to liberate the Nazi concentration camp at Dachau even while their parents and other relatives were still held in American concentration camps.[35]

Mathew R. Sgan, another Jewish author, adds: "Near Waakirchen, they saved Jews on a death march. . . . Members of the 100th helped the prisoners stay alive until transferred to a medical detachment."[36]

The motto of the 100th/442nd was "Go for Broke!" a phrase used in gambling, which meant to risk everything to win.[37] They fought recklessly to demonstrate their patriotism. The 100th/442nd became the most highly decorated unit in US Army history.

Both my uncle, Bob Owan and Albert Nakama, who married my aunt, Shizuko Owan, fought with the 442nd. They both earned purple heart and bronze star medals. I can recall seeing Bob's displayed in a glass case in my grandmother's house in Kahuku.

My uncle Bob, who was 5'5" tall and weighed 130 pounds, enlisted on March 23rd, 1943. He left Hawaii on the S. S. Lurline on April 4 for the mainland. He and other members of the 442nd trained for a year at Camp Shelby in Mississippi. His unit arrived in Naples on May 22.

---

34. Masayo Umezawa Duus. *Unlikely Liberators: The Men of the 100th and 442nd*. Tr. from the Japanese by Peter Duus (Honolulu, Hawaii: University of Hawaii Press, 1983), 217.

35. Daniels, 64. According to Daniels, Taylor, and Kitano, 74, 2,355 Nisei from the camps eventually volunteered for the armed services.

36. Mathew R. Sgan, *Torah and Taro: Jewish Contributions to Hawaii* (n.p.: Xlibris.com, 2020), 55.

37. In 1951 a movie about the Niseis in combat titled "Go for Broke!" featured Van Johnson as the commanding officer.

Bob served in the following campaigns: Rome–Arno in Italy, Rhineland Vosges in France, and the Po Valley back in Italy. He was wounded twice. Bob and another soldier braved heavy artillery fire, snipers, and mine fields to evacuate wounded comrades in the Vosges mountains in October 1944. He was awarded the Purple Heart, the Bronze Star medal, and other medals. On October 5, 2010, along with other 442nd veterans he received the Congressional Gold Medal on October 5, 2010. Bob passed away on September15, 2011.

The *Honolulu Star Advertiser* on September 1, 2019, published an article by William Cole titled, "Jacket Found in France Tracked Back to World War II Vet in Hawaii."

> Albert Nakama remembers the Vosges Mountains and how cold it was in late 1944 when his unit, L Company of the 442nd Regimental Combat Team, reached northeastern France in World War II. "It was winter time," Nakama, now 96, says... He remembers Italy in the spring of 1945 and soldiers climbing up steep Mount Folgorito at night on hands and knees to surprise sleeping Germans at the top to help break the "Gothic Line." That's where Nakama was shot in the buttocks, "right on the right cheek," he said with a laugh. Somewhere along the way, Nakama was struck in the forehead by a glancing bullet. He was wearing his helmet at the time, which protected him. "All I know is I got shot here," he said, pointing to his head. "But I never fall down." The former infantryman doesn't remember the long green Army trench coat handwritten on the back that was bought from an old farmer in more recent years near Bruyeres, France a town that the 442nd and 100th Infantry Battalion liberated. When a French farmer in his 90s was spotted wearing an old GI coat with "A Nakama" on the back, it spurred immediate interest. The jacket was purchased for $15 and ended up with the Seattle Nisei Vets Hall. Chris Sketchley, museum curator with the Nisei Veterans Committee Memorial Hall in Seattle, who brought the trench coat to Hawaii for Nakama to examine, said that in Bruyeres, "they have the 442nd unit patch painted along the streets and walls" as part of a tour route. Sketchley said Nakama served in four campaigns in France and Italy, earning two Bronze Stars: one for fighting near Pisa, Italy, and another in France—a few more pieces of the puzzle about a nisei vet who never talked much about his service. "He said things were flying at them and they went under heavy fire to save one of their men."

Sergeant Albert Nakama commanded thirty riflemen, who took part in the rescue of the Texas "lost battalion." Only ten survived the war. In 2020 the 98-year-old Nakama was inducted into the French Legion of Honor. On November 8, 2021, at a ceremony at the Punchbowl Military Cemetery he was one of six veterans honored by the French consul with the awarding of the Croix de Guerre. As he was bedridden in a nursing home, his daughter Iris Chang, holding a photo of her father in uniform, accepted the medal for him.

Figure 10. Albert Nakama, receiving a military award from France

Daniel K. Inouye

On April 24, 1945. shortly before the end of the war in Europe Second Lieutenant Daniel K. Inouye, a graduate of McKinley High School, commanded a unit attacking a German position on a ridge in Terenzo, Italy. As he advanced forward throwing grenades a German shot him in his gut and then hit his right arm while he held a grenade. Dan managed to remove the armed grenade from his useless right arm with his left hand and threw it against the Germans. He continued to shoot his Tommy Gun with his left arm. For this valiant action he was awarded the Distinguished Service Cross, which was later upgraded to the Congressional Medal of Honor.[38]

Just a week before, Second Lieutenant Robert J. Dole of Kansas on a nearby hill had been wounded. Dole received two Purple Hearts and a Bronze Star for his heroism. Dole recounts:

> We first met weeks later in Percy Jones Army Hospital in Battle Creek, Michigan. Danny arrived there ahead of me. He weighed just 93 pounds and was now missing his arm, but he was upbeat and optimistic. His surgeries were complete, and he was rehabilitating. I was laying on a stretcher. My surgeries were yet to come. Danny and I spoke shortly before his release from the hospital. His injuries would keep him from fulfilling his dream of becoming a doctor, so he asked what I intended to do when I was released. I shared my intention to run for political office, starting locally in Kansas and working my way up to the Senate, and hopefully higher. (AARP Nov. 8. 2018)

After returning to Hawaii, Dan became prominent in the Democratic party. He was a leader in gaining statehood for Hawaii as the 50th state in August 1959 after Alaska became the 49th state earlier that year. He credited his friendship with Lyndon Johnson to the gratitude the Texans had for the 442nd's role in rescuing their lost battalion.

Dan became the first Japanese American to be elected to the House of Representatives (1959 to 1963) and then served as a distinguished Senator (1963 to 2012), who at his death on December 17, 2012 was given the honor of lying in the rotunda of the Capitol.[39] On this occasion

---

38. After a review, twenty-one other Nisei who had received the Distinguished Service Cross also had their medals upgraded to the Medal of Honor.

39. Daniel K. Inouye with Lawrence Elliottt, *Journey to Washington* (Englewood Cliffs, New Jersey: Prentice-Hall, 1967). In 2013 President Barack Obama awarded Daniel Inouye a posthumous Presidential Medal of Freedom. The international airport

Dole commented: "When Danny passed away, I paid my respects as he lay in state in the US Capitol's rotunda. Both injuries and time had begun to get the best of me, so I spent much of my time seated. But I made sure to walk up to Danny's casket. He dedicated and nearly gave his life to our nation. He deserved one more standing salute."

---

in Honolulu is named in his honor.

Chapter 5

Elementary Years

(1943 to 1949)

Elementary Schools

HAWAII'S DEPARTMENT OF INSTRUCTION in 1924 established a kind of de facto segregation by designating three schools: Lincoln Elementary, Robert Louis Stevenson Intermediate, and Roosevelt High School as "English Standard Schools." Admission to these schools was determined by written and oral tests to see if students were able to speak and write standard English rather than Pidgin. In the beginning this would have favored the haoles and wealthier Asians. This form of discrimination was not abolished until 1955.

It was not surprising that I failed the English Standard tests when I entered the first grade. I enrolled at Manoa Elementary School. It was more surprising when the teachers there recommended that I skip the second grade, so I entered Pauoa Elementary School for the third grade at the age of seven. My only memories of this school are of walking down and up the steep road of Pacific Heights to attend the school. I recall the soy sauce factory at the bottom of the hill with its tall smokestack emitting a distinctive odor. My mother made me a lunch of *musubi* a "rice ball" enclosing a red *umeboshi*, a pickled apricot. I also remember that we were given a holiday on the day that Franklin D. Roosevelt died—April 12, 1945.

ELEMENTARY YEARS

I did pass the tests the next year and attended Lincoln Elementary School for the fourth, fifth, and sixth grades. This was located near McKinley High School and was next to the Honolulu Academy of Arts. My report cards indicate that I did well in all subjects except for manual arts. They also reveal that I was living at a different address each year. To get to school from different areas I always took the buses of the Honolulu Rapid Transit system.

A Peripatetic Childhood

Because of my mother's short-term jobs, we moved to a dozen places in a dozen years: Woodlawn, Moilili, Kapiolani, Pacific Heights (three places), Manoa Valley (two places), Nuuanu Valley (two places), Emerson Avenue, School Street, and Fort Street.

Figure 11. With my mother

At the time, I did not realize that this was not normal, but I now see that I was missing what many other children would have taken for granted. I did not have a father or siblings, or pets and few neighborhood friends. I did not have a room to myself but shared cramped maid's quarters with my mother. We did not have a car, a phone, a radio, or a television. I did have a 45-rpm record player, a few illustrated children's books, and access to the Nuuanu YMCA.[1] My mother also paid for a subscription to *Classic Comics*. In retrospect the lack of distractions may have been a boon as I immersed myself in books. Beginning in the fourth grade I would spend hours in the public Honolulu Library[2] and read shelves of books about Indians and ship captains. When I had read all there was to read in the juvenile section, I was allowed to borrow from the adult section. The first adult novel I read was Rafael Sabatini's *Scaramouche*.

Charles M. Hite

The one exception to our constant moving was the three happy years (1946 to 1949) my mother was employed by Charles Maner Hite at his home at 3833 Old Pali Road. Hite had served as the Secretary of the Territory of Hawaii from 1936 to 1942. He also served as the chairman of the central committee of the Democratic Party. He and his wife Alice had three children, including twins Alice and Maner, who were attending Punahou.

Mr. Hite was an extraordinarily kind man. My mother reported that when she served dinner, he would admonish his children not to eat everything she had cooked, so she could give some leftovers to her son. One day he said to her, "Haruko, why don't you learn to drive?" She took up his challenge and secretly took driving lessons. When she showed Mr. Hite her license, he told her that she could use his car, a convertible, on Sundays. It was the only car, so this offer may have been received with dismay by his teenagers!

---

1. This multi-ethnic YMCA was established through the efforts of Rev. Okamura and Dr. Syngman Rhee, the future president of Korea. After receiving his PhD from Princeton University, Rhee returned to Japanese-occupied Korea as a YMCA missionary. He then spent many years in Hawaii. In 1917, Rhee established the Korean Christian Church in Honolulu.

2. This library was built in 1909 with a gift of $100,000 from Andrew Carnegie.

Harry M. Fujiwara

This was the one time that I lived at the same place long enough to develop a friend from the neighborhood. Harry Fujiwara's parents also worked for a haole family on Old Pali Road. He was three years older than I. We rode the bus to see movies and sporting events. We went to judo classes sponsored by the Honpa Hongwanji temple. I only achieved the third or yellow belt rank. I also went to the Japanese school sponsored by this temple for one year.

Figure 12. Judo class. I am at the left in the top row.

While I enjoy watching football, basketball, and tennis on television, I never watch professional wrestling. But my wife's father was a fan. Once in his home in Hilo as he was watching wrestling, I recognized a name from the past, "Mr. Fuji from Japan," as he was billed was none other than my old friend Harry Fujiwara! But it was not until I read his obituary in the *New York Times* (August 28, 2016) that I learned how famous (or infamous) Harry had become. He was known for concealing salt which he would throw into his opponent's eyes to blind them. He wrestled from 1965 to 1985, winning many championships and then enjoyed a successful managerial career. He was inducted into the Professional Wrestling Hall of Fame.

AN ASIAN AMERICAN ANCIENT HISTORIAN AND BIBLICAL SCHOLAR

Figure 13. With Harry Fujiwara

The Marks Estate

The residence of the Hites was a modest bungalow on the right side of Old Pali Road as you walked up the hill. Almost immediately across the road but a little farther up was a gate, which I never noticed. This was at the entrance of the Marks Estate. It guarded an 18-acre property which reached up to the mountains. On its grounds in 1924 a famed architect, Hardie Phillip, who designed the Honolulu Academy of Arts, built a mansion for Clarence H. Cooke, a descendant of the missionary who had founded Castle & Cooke, one of the Big Five Companies of Hawaii. On the grounds were three guest cottages, a swimming pool, a garage for four cars with quarters for servants above, and a gatehouse for the gatekeeper. The property was acquired by Lester Marks, a land commissioner for the Territory. He resigned when Governor Stainback decided in 1949 to build the new Pali highway which was to run through the middle of the estate. I later learned that while I was living across the street, my future wife, Kimie Honda, was working as an upstairs maid for the Marks in 1948 while she attended McKinley High School!

Chapter 6

Iolani and the Episcopal Church

(1948 to 1952)

The Anglican Mission

KAMEHAMEHA IV MARRIED QUEEN Emma, a descendant of John Young, Kamehameha I's British advisor. In the course of visiting Queen Victoria, the king who was averse to the stern Calvinism of the original Congregationalist missionaries, asked Victoria to send an Anglican mission to the Sandwich Islands. The queen sent Bishop Thomas N. Staley to Hawaii in 1862.

The cornerstone of St. Andrews Cathedral on Beretania Street was laid on March 5, 1867. The cruciform building in the French Gothic style, built with stones imported from England, is 160 ft. long and 60 ft. wide. Its stained-glass window depicts the encounter between the Europeans and the Hawaiians. The cathedral was dedicated to the memory of Kamehameha IV, who had died on Nov. 30, 1863, St. Andrews Day.

Iolani School

In 1863 St. Alban's School was established in the Pauoa Valley in Honolulu. It was Queen Emma who renamed the school *Iolani* "Royal

AN ASIAN AMERICAN ANCIENT HISTORIAN AND BIBLICAL SCHOLAR

Hawk," in honor of her husband's birth name. Iolani was an Anglican college prep school for boys.[1]

It was in 1927 that Iolani raised $50,000 to purchase the five-acre Davies property at Nuuanu and Judd Streets across from the Nuuanu Cemetery. The relatively small campus had wooden classrooms, and St. Alban's Chapel. Initially 278 boys, including 32 boarders, were enrolled at this campus.

Exercising great foresight, the Headmaster Albert H. Stone purchased a twenty-five-acre plot along the Ala Wai Canal. In 1946, a school for grades one to six was established at this site. In the fall of 1983, the entire junior and senior high school moved from Nuuanu to the Ala Wai site.

Since I had done well in elementary school, my aunt, Tsuru Yamauchi, decided to pay for my tuition at Iolani in the 7th grade in 1948. I was to study at Iolani until the 10th grade in 1952 as a member of the class of 1954. Tuition in the 1950s cost $600.[2] My mother could not on her maid's salary have afforded to send me to such a private school.

Figure 14. Iolani, class of 1954

1. An all-girls school, St. Andrews Priory, was established near the Cathedral in 1867. The girls wore uniforms. Iolani boys and Priory girls practiced dancing in Davies Hall next to the cathedral.

2. Iolani became co-educational in 1979 and has become an elite and expensive school with students from kindergarten to high school. Tuition rose to $23,450!

Sun Yat-sen

The most important alumnus of Iolani's early years was Sun Yat-sen, the founder of the Republic of China. Sun was born in 1866 in Kwantung Province. His older brother, Sun Mei, had emigrated to Hawaii in 1871 and had succeeded as a rice planter. He opened up a store in Ewa and invited his younger brother to Hawaii.

Sun, who knew no English, enrolled at Iolani in 1879 and graduated in 1882. He was awarded the second prize for achievement in English by King Kalakaua. He also spent a semester at Oahu College (i.e. Punahou). Sun's conversion to Christianity at first angered his older brother. But they were later reconciled, and Sun Mei paid for Sun's medical education in Hong Kong. He was baptized in Hong Kong and practiced medicine there.

Returning to Hawaii, from 1896 to 1908 Sun organized The Hsing Chung Hui (Revive China Society), a society of similar minded Chinese to overthrow the last Manchurian[3] emperor of China in 1910. His Tung Meng Hui Society became the basis of Chiang Kai-shek's Kuomintang Party. On January 1, 1912, in Nanking Dr. Sun Yat-sen was named the first president of the Republic of China, the first democratic country in Asia. Sun Yat-sen declared: "This is *my* Hawaii . . . here I was brought up and educated; and it was here I came to know what modern civilized

---

3. The last dynasty of Imperial China was the Qing Dynasty which had been established by Manchus from Manchuria to the north of China in 1644. In the nineteenth century China was beset by internal rebellions and by external attacks, which greatly weakened it as a world power. In attempting to ban the importation of opium from British India, the Chinese seized from British merchant ships their cargo of opium. This led to the First Opium War (1839-1842). Superior British ships vanquished the Chinese navy. As a result Hong Kong was acquired by the British. In a Second Opium War (1856-1860) the Chinese lost to the British and French and were forced to make further concessions, including the opening of more ports such as Shanghai. The Taiping (Heavenly Kingdom) Rebellion (1850-1864) was begun in south China by a leader Hong Xinquan, who claimed to be the younger brother of Jesus. As the result of a war with Japan (1894-1895), China lost control of Korea and Taiwan. In 1901 the so called "Boxers" with the support of the Dowager Empress besieged foreign delegations in Peking and Tientsin for 55 days. Armed forces from eight foreign nations suppressed the revolt and demanded reparations from China as the result of their victory. The Dowager Empress Cixi, who had originally been the emperor's concubine, was the power behind the throne from 1861 to 1908, serving as the regent for a series of young ineffectual emperors. Upon her death, a child Puyi ascended the throne. His life is portrayed in the acclaimed movie, The Last Emperor, which won the Oscar for the best movie of 1987.

governments are like and what they mean."[4] Sun died in 1925 and was succeeded by Chiang Kai-shek as the leader of the Kuomintang party.

High School Football

Hawaii has no major professional sports teams. It has only one major university, the University of Hawaii. As its teams must compete on the mainland, their travel budget is enormous. This helps to explain why the rivalry between high school football teams was "the only game in town," so to speak. The annual Thanksgiving doubleheader attracted twenty-four thousand fans to the stadium on King Street.

As the population of the islands apart from Oahu is relatively sparse, high school teams from those islands cannot compete, although elite athletes from these islands have come to play on Oahu.

The overwhelming proportion of the island of Oahu lives in Honolulu on the south shore. But one rural team from the north shore at the former sugar plantation town of Kahuku has been able to compete.[5] That is because it is five minutes away from Laie, a town where the Latter-Day Saints have a temple and the Hawaii branch of Brigham Young University. The Mormons have attracted a large population of their converts from Polynesia (Fiji, Samoa, Tahiti, Tonga, etc.), who perform native dances at the Polynesian Cultural Center established in 1963, one of the most popular tourist destinations.

My uncle Tom Owan served as the student body president of Kahuku High School and though slight in build played on the line for the Red Raiders. My cousin Gary Owan, son of my uncle Bob Owan, played quarterback for Kahuku. His younger brother, Bobby, served as the Director of Procurement of Brigham Young-Hawaii.

During the 1940s and 1950s the Interscholastic League of Honolulu (ILH) included four public high schools and four private high schools. The public schools were: 1) McKinley High School[6] (The Tigers), located on King Street in the center of the city. It was founded in 1865. 2) Roosevelt High School[7] (The Rough Riders), founded in 1930, is

---

4. Yansheng Ma Lum and Raymond Mun Kong Lum, *Sun Yatsen in Hawaii* (Honolulu, Hawaii: Hawaii: Chinese History Center, 1999), 5.

5. Since the inception of the Hawaii High school Athletic Association (HHSAA) State Championship in 1999, Kahuku has won the most in Division I (eight).

6. Named after President William McKinley.

7. Named after President Theodore Roosevelt.

located on the slopes of Punchbowl, an extinct crater which is home to the National Military Cemetery. 3) Farrington High School [8] (The Governors), founded in 1936, is located in Kalihi on the west (Ewa) side of the city. 4) Kaimuki High School (The Bulldogs), founded in 1944, is located on the east (Diamond Head) side of the city.

The four private schools were: 1) Punahou (The Buff and Blue), founded in 1841, is located at the base of Manoa Valley. 2) Kamehamea High School (The Warriors) is situated on the Kapalama Heights above Kalihi. Founded in 1887, it has been funded by the Bishop Estate,[9] which has an endowment estimated at ten billion dollars. It offers free education to anyone who has a degree of Hawaiian ancestry. 3) St. Louis High School (The Crusaders) is located on the heights above Kaimuki.[10] It is a Catholic school, founded in 1846.[11] 4) Iolani High School (The Raiders), founded in 1863, was the smallest and poorest of the private schools. Yet because of the arrival and influence of a legendary coach, Iolani had unexpected success.[12]

Father Kenneth A. Bray

Kenneth Augustine Bray was born on May 26, 1879, in England. He was the descendant of Thomas Gray, who had founded the Society for the Promotion of Christian Knowledge in 1698 and the Society for the

---

8. Named after Governor Joseph R. Farrington.

9. The Bishop Estate, which is the largest landowner in Hawaii, was established by the will of Bernice Pauahi Bishop, the great granddaughter of Kamehameha I.

10. St. Louis has produced a 2014 Heisman Trophy winner in Marcus Mariota, who starred at the University of Oregon. He has played for the Tennessee Titans, Las Vegas Raiders, and Atlanta Falcons. Another St. Louis graduate, Tua Tagovailoa, who was the quarterback of the champion Alabama Crimson Tide, was the runner-up in the Heisman race in 2019. Tua plays for the Miami Dolphins. Both are of Samoan descent. Tua's younger brother Taulia played one season with him at Alabama, and then became an outstanding quarterback at the University of Maryland. Another notable Hawaiian of Samoan descent is coach Ken Niumatalolo, who has led Navy to nine victories over Army since he became the head coach in 2008. He came from Laie and played for the University of Hawaii.

11. Between 1973 and 1998 the state champion was decided at the Oahu Prep Bowl, which pitted the leading high school from the Interscholastic League of Honolulu against the leading school from the Oahu Interscholastic Association. St. Louis was dominant in this series, winning 14 championships.

12. Iolani has won the most HH SAA championships in Division II (eight).

Propagation of the Gospel in Foreign Parts in 1701. His father Thomas Gray, an Anglican priest, died when Kenneth was eight.

Bray emigrated to the US and graduated from the General Theological Seminary in New York City. He then served as a teacher of Latin and Greek, as well as an athletic coach at several schools, including a stint at St. Stephen's College (later renamed Bard College) in Annandale-on-Hudson.

Bray was sent out to Hawaii in 1932 as a missionary of the Episcopal Church to serve as the pastor at St. Andrews Cathedral and also as the vicar of St. Mark's Church in Kapahulu. He also taught and coached all major sports at Iolani for twenty years.

Father Bray was a demanding and idiosyncratic coach who required extreme conditioning and precise execution of plays. Once when a player did not seem to know the play, Father Bray kicked him! He ran his players in practice to exhaustion without allowing them to drink any water. In desperation some players developed a ruse, kicking the ball down the hill to the Nuuanu Stream. While pretending to look for the ball they would slake their thirst at the stream![13]

Father Bray went out of his way to recruit athletes in the slums of Honolulu and even went to Laie. He was the first Honolulu coach to recruit Samoans. Iolani's Al Lolatai, who went to the Washington Redskins in 1945, became the first Samoan from Hawaii to play in the NFL.[14]

Though 40 out of about 240 students made the football team, only 11 to 14 actually played because Father Bray did not believe in substitution! If an Iolani football player was injured, unless he had to be carried out on a stretcher, he was to walk off the field on his own without any aid. His extreme methods seemed to work in developing competitive teams. In 1936 in their first games in the Interscholastic League of Honolulu Iolani upset highly favored St. Louis 12–0 and Punahou 13–0.

During World War II Iolani shut down its athletic programs as many of the faculty and senior students volunteered for the war effort.

In 1951 and 1952, just before his retirement and his death (January 9, 1953), Iolani won the ILH championships in football, basketball, and

---

13. During the 7th grade I lived on School Street (near the intersection with Fort Street) and during the 8th grade I lived on Fort Street opposite the Honp Hongwanji Temple. I walked the about a mile up Fort Street, and entered Iolani by a back route, down the valley and across the stream on a wooden bridge located next to a Buddhist temple. I would then climb up from the practice field to the campus.

14. Rob Buck, *The Tropics of Football: The Long and Perilous Journey of Samoans to the NFL* (New York, New York: New Press, 2018).

baseball. True to Father Bray's convictions in the football championship game Iolani played only eleven men and in the championship basketball game only five men.[15] It is ironic that Father Bray, who emphasized the One Team concept and who did not recognize individual stars, at the same time used only his star players and not the reserves.

Yet his boys, who affectionately called Father Bray "The Ol' Man," revered him. Many of his players such as Eddie Hamada, who coached at Iolani, followed his principles. One of my classmates, Lawrence (Lary) Ginoza had success at Waianae High School.[15] Mervin Lopes, a member of the championship basketball team, later coached at Chaminade College, affiliated with St. Louis High School. In 1982 his basketball team upset the University of Virginia, which had 7-foot All American Ralph Samson and was ranked number one in the nation then.

I did not appreciate the magnitude of the success of Iolani's athletic teams at the time I was there (1948 to 1952). Their success was all the more remarkable because the Nuuanu campus did not have a football stadium, a baseball field, a running track, a gymnasium or tennis courts. We had only the football practice field and one outdoor basketball court. Iolani never enjoyed home field or home court advantage, as we did not have a home field or home court!

I made the sophomore tennis team which practiced at the Ala Moana courts. I was also on the freshmen track team, which was coached by Moses Ome, Father Bray's first recruit. We practiced at the University of Hawaii. I ran one memorable half mile race at the Punahou track. I was leading coming into the second lap, but as we neared the end, much to my chagrin I was passed by several runners. I then learned by experience the adage that it is not how one starts, but how one finishes which counts!

Students, Teachers, and Subjects

The student bodies of the high schools in Honolulu varied greatly as to ethnic backgrounds. Kamehameha's students were understandably all part Hawaiian. McKinley's students were almost all Japanese. Punahou's students as late as 1975 were 60 percent haole and 15 percent children of wealthy Japanese families.

---

15. There were thirteen boys on the basketball team.
16. Don Johnson and Ronald Oba, *The Ol' Man: Father Kenneth A. Bray* (Honolulu, Hawaii: Iolani Raiders Booster Club, 1994), 184.

As to Iolani the 83 members of the class of 1954[17] consisted almost entirely of the sons of the immigrants who had come to Hawaii to work on the plantations: nearly 60 percent (49) were Japanese, 28 percent (23) were Chinese;[18] there were a few partHawaiians, Koreans, and Portuguese. There were only two haoles, most conspicuously Roger Wiley, a tall, pale, and popular student who commuted from the plantation town of Ewa, where his father was the Mill Superintendent. In his senior year Roger became the student body president.

My closest friend at Iolani was Raymond Fujii, class of 1955. Ray and I would play tennis together. His parents owned the Kanraku Tea House and had a boarding house on Emerson Avenue on the slopes of Punchbowl, where my mother and I stayed in 1952. Among the interesting guests from Japan was a xylophonist who performed for us and some gargantuan sumo wrestlers. Ray eventually became a reference librarian at the Honolulu Library.

All of our teachers were haoles, who had been recruited from the mainland. I especially appreciated Charles Halter, a graduate of Ohio University, who taught US history and geography. At Father Bray's request, Mr. Halter coached the athletic teams of the seventh and eighth grades. Between 1952 and 1959 his football teams won seven championships, his basketball teams won nine championships, and his baseball teams won seven championships!

Another favorite teacher was Valerie Haas, a graduate of Hunter College who taught Latin. I also took French from Elton Cathcart, a graduate of Holy Cross. Other teachers included: Lorraine McCarthy, a graduate of Emmanuel College, who taught English; Paul Simpson, a graduate of Colorado University, who taught Algebra; Mary Whitten, a graduate of the University of Pennsylvania, who taught Music Appreciation, and Edna Winnie, a graduate of Iowa State Teachers College, who taught World History.

I was chosen the outstanding student for each of the four years I was at Iolani. I harbored an ambition to go to Harvard University as a few of the Iolani alumni had done. In the ninth grade, I was chosen class president. I was a member of the Dramatic Club, the Projectionists Club,

---

17. Though I did not get to graduate with my class, my classmates graciously invited me to join them for the 50th class reunion in 2004.

18. Reuben Wong, a classmate, attended the University of Hawaii and obtained a J.D. from the University of Illinois. When he returned to the Islands, he was one of the very few lawyers of Asian descent to practice there.

and most significantly on the staff of the school paper, *Imua Iolani*, an experience which stood me in good stead in the future.

The Episcopal Church

I was baptized as an Episcopalian by Rev. John Moulton on December 13, 1950, along with a number of other Iolani boys including Thomas Yoshida, who had been a classmate at Lincoln Elementary School. Tom later became the chaplain at Iolani.

I served as an acolyte, dressed in white and red vestments at St. Andrews Cathedral under Father Bray. I recall with pleasure marching in the procession while singing "O Come Emmanuel." I was given the privilege once of speaking from the high pulpit on the Episcopalian mission to Micronesia.

I was an officer of the Episcopal Youth Fellowship and was its representative to the Oahu Youth Council. I took part in the presentation which our fellowship presented of South Pacific. Paul, the son of Bishop Harry S. Kennedy was the star; I was one of the sailors. But though I had taken Religious Education classes at Iolani under Rev. Moulton, a Harvard University graduate, these were presented from a liberal theological perspective which explained away the miracles in the Bible—a viewpoint which Father Bray also shared. In short, whereas previously I had been a *nabakkari Bukkyō shinja* "a name only Buddhist," I had become a *nabakkari Kirisuto shinja* "a nominal Christian."

Reading

In the four years while at Iolani I read Hugo's *Les Miserables*, Reade's *The Cloister and the Hearth*, and Eliot's *Adam Bede*. I also read novels by Dostoevsky, Maugham, Shalakov, Steinbeck, and Stendahl. I read works by Aristotle and Plato, which I did not understand. But with all my love for reading I had not read a single page of the Bible up until 1952. But that was all to change.

Chapter 7

Conversion

(1952)

Kalihi Union Church

My Iolani classmate Dick Lum engaged me in conversations about science and Christianity. He is the younger brother of Ada Lum, a well-known Bible teacher and missionary to southeast Asia. Dick invited me to his young people's fellowship at Kalihi Union Church,[1] an evangelical Congregational church.

---

1. After a fire in 1900 devastated China Town in Honolulu, many Chinese, Japanese, and Filipino families were forced to settle in Kalihi, at that time on the westernmost outskirts of the city.

Figure 15. Dick Lum

I was warmly welcomed to the games and activities of this group of about 30 young people, including another classmate from Iolani. I was impressed by the gusto with which they sang hymns such as "He Lives," but most of all I was amazed by the intimacy and confidence with which they offered spontaneous prayers. The only prayers I knew were the ones from the Episcopalian Common Book of Prayer.

Venture for Victory

Then at a service at Kalihi Union Church on May 25, 1952, a basketball player from the mainland gave a powerful evangelistic sermon, at the end of which I raised my hand at the invitation to accept Christ as my savior. After this I spoke briefly to Pastor Herbert Eggleston.[2]

2. Rev. Eggleston was the speaker at the Youth for Christ meeting four years earlier when my wife, Kimie Honda, who was at McKinley High School, made her decision

The speaker was one of a group of seven basketball players (six from Taylor University in Upland Indiana, one from Wheaton College). They were on their first mission trip for Venture for Victory, organized by coach Don Odle of Taylor University.[3] They had stopped in Honolulu on their way to play against national teams in Asia. The team also received a personal invitation from Madame Chiang Kai Shek. They played eighty-seven games in Formosa (later known as Taiwan), Hong Kong and the Philippines. Their mission was historically significant as it was the first attempt to use athletics as a platform for the Gospel, later followed with great success by Campus Crusade's Athletes in Action and other organizations.

Robert W. Hambrook

It was, however, only after a few months that I fully understood what commitment to Christ really means. I became acquainted with Rev. Theodore Yeh, the vicar of St. Luke's Episcopal Church who had been converted in China. Through Rev. Yeh I met Dr. Robert W. Hambrook.

Dr. Hambrook, who was born in England in 1887, had served in the US Office of Education, writing booklets on such subjects as *Aviation in Public Schools* and *Light Frame House Construction*. At one time he had served the US Office of Education as an advisor to Emperor Haile Selassie of Ethiopia.

He was a man of ample girth, a twinkle in his eye, and firm and rather narrow Christian convictions. He had been a member of Carl McIntire's controversial Bible Presbyterian Church in Collingswood, New Jersey. In Hawaii he spoke at numerous churches and served as the president of the so-called Honolulu Bible College & Seminary, which was more of a dream rather than a reality.

On October 2, Dr. Hambrook invited me to his home in the Nuuanu Valley. He patiently explained key Scriptures: 1) Isaiah 53 which prophesied the coming of the Suffering Messiah; 2) Romans 3:23 which declared that all men are sinners; 3) Romans 6:23 which stated the penalty for sin; 4) John 3:16 which declared that God so loved the world that He gave His only Son, Jesus, to die in our stead; 5) 1 John

---

for Christ.

3. Jessica and Alan H. Winquist, *Coach Odle's Full Court Press* (Upland, Indiana: Taylor University Press, 2001).

CONVERSION

1:9 which promised to forgive our sins, if we confessed them; and 6) Revelation 3:20 which revealed that Jesus was standing and knocking, inviting us to let Him into our lives. As I knelt and prayed to commit my life wholly to Christ, I became a "born-again" Christian, committed to do His will and follow His leading, which I thought meant staying in Hawaii to be trained as a missionary.

On September 6, 1952, after twelve years of widowhood, my mother married Renyu Higa, an Okinawan who had emigrated to Peru, and moved to Los Angeles. I was not at their wedding. Relatives persuaded me to leave Hawaii and to spend at least a year with my mother and new stepfather in Los Angeles.

Figure 16. Renyu and Haruko Higa

Chapter 8

A New Father and a New City

(1951 to 1952)

Japanese in South America

IN BRAZIL IN ADDITION to sugar plantations, coffee growers required laborers. When the Brazilian slave trade was abolished in 1853, the Portuguese who ruled Brazil attempted at first to import Italian laborers, but they could not cope with the harsh and demanding conditions of plantation labor.

The first immigrants from Japan to Brazil arrived at Santos in 1908. This first group consisted of 781 Japanese, 190 of whom were females.[1] The difficulty of making a living on the coffee plantations of São Paulo led many of these first immigrants to abandon their six-month contracts and even led to the separation of families. Despite this initial failure, immigrants subsidized by the Japanese government kept on arriving in Brazil.

By 1927 5,464 Okinawans had emigrated to Brazil. By 1934, when restrictive laws were passed, 142,457 Japanese had settled in Brazil. Before World War II 180,175 Japanese had emigrated to Brazil.[2] More than 90 percent settled around São Paulo. Many succeeded in establishing vegetable farms. Today Brazil has about a million and a half

---

1. Daniel M. Masterson and Sayaka Funada-Classen, *The Japanese in Latin America* (Urbana, Illinois: University of Illinois Press, 2004), 44.
2. Ibid., 74.

descendants of the Japanese immigrants, the largest population of Japanese outside of Japan.³

The other Latin American country with a sizable Japanese population is Peru. In 1873 Peru became the first Latin American country to establish diplomatic relations with Japan.⁴ In 1899 the Sakura Maru transported 790 Japanese men to the Peruvian port city of Callao. These men came from Yamaguchi, Hiroshima, Okayama and Niigata prefectures. This first contingent came to disastrous results with 143 dying from tropical diseases such as malaria and yellow fever.⁵ Because of the harsh work conditions 93 fled to Bolivia. Despite this discouraging beginning emigration to Peru continued unabated because immigrants could earn twice what they could in their homeland. Between 1898 and 1923 four emigration companies recruited 17,764 men from the prefectures of Gifu, Hiroshima, Kanagawa, Osaka and especially Okinawa.⁵ By 1941 about 30,000 Japanese, including 10,300 from Okinawa, were living in Peru.⁷ Most of the Japanese left the plantations and became small business owners in Lima and other cities, or worked small farms.⁸

---

3. The Sixth Worldwide Uchinanchu Festival was held in Okinawa from October 22 to November 4, 2016. The numerous programs included Okinawan dance and music, karate, and *Shinakutuba*, "the Okinawan dialect." The official guide has a tabulation of the Okinawan diaspora: 1) in the US 105,670 (including about 45,000 in Hawaii); 2) in Brazil 162,892; and 3) in Peru 71,831. Of the more than 7,000 participants from more than 25 countries, the largest delegations were from: 1) the USA 4,274 (including 1,864 from Hawaii); 2) Brazil 1,131; and 3) Peru 620. I gathered this information from materials provided me by the parents of Selena Tutino.

4. There were smaller Japanese communities in Argentina, Bolivia, Colombia, Ecuador, Mexico, and Paraguay.

5. C. Harvey Gardner, *The Japanese and Peru 1873-1973* (Albuquerque, New Mexico: University of New Mexico Press, 1975), 25.

6. Ibid, 33.

7. James C. Carey, *Peru and the United States 1900-1962* (Notre Dame, Indiana: University of Notre Dame Press, 1964), 107, n. 20.

8. Alberto Fujimori, whose parents had emigrated from Kumamoto, Japan to Peru in 1934, became the rector of the Universidad Nacional Agraria, and was elected president of Peru in 1990. Serving until 2000, Fujimori succeeded in crushing the "Shining Path" rebels and establishing trade relations with Japan. But he was then arrested on charges of bribery and human rights abuses and imprisoned.

Renyu Higa

Renyu Higa was born on May 28, 1909, to Rensuke and Kamado Higa in Nago, a northern city of Okinawa.[9] His father emigrated to Peru in 1913 and established a small dairy farm. Rensuke was an accomplished horseman who performed before the president of Peru. After completing his studies at an agricultural school, Renyu was called by his parents to join them in Peru in 1930, where he found work as a journalist for a Japanese newspaper. The family grew to have ten children (five boys and five girls) and enjoyed modest prosperity until the outbreak of World War II.

Crystal City and Seabrook Farms

The US Alien Enemy Act of 1798 authorized the seizure of enemy aliens, including those living in South America. From Peru, the US transported to the US 288 Italians, 4,058 Germans, and 2,264 Japanese.[10] The initial prospect was that some of these prisoners could be exchanged for Americans held in the Axis countries.[11]

In April 1942, a group of 141 Japanese men were shipped from Peru to San Francisco. En route their passports and visas were confiscated and when they entered US jurisdiction, they were declared illegal immigrants! They were then transported to Kenedy, Texas.

Their families were then gathered and placed on a ship that went through the Panama Canal, arriving twenty-one days later in the US. The women and children were placed as many as ten in a cabin, while the men and boys were crammed into the hold below. They were allowed up on the deck for only ten minutes twice a day and were not allowed to see their families. Upon docking at New Orleans, the women and girls were ordered to take off all their clothes so they could be sprayed with disinfectant in the presence of the men and boys who were then ordered to do the same. As they traveled in a train with the

---

9. *History of the Okinawans in North America (Hokubei Okinawajin Shi)*, tr. Ben Kobashigawa (Los Angeles, California: The Okinawa Club of America, 1988), 444.

10. Jan Jarboe Russell, *The Train to Crystal City* (New York, New York: Scribner, 2015), xix. As was the case in Hawaii, only the leading members of the Japanese community were deported. Many others were allowed to remain. Renyu's nephew, Ricardo Higa Mitsuya became the first Japanese-Peruvian toreador.

11. C. Harvey Gardiner, *Pawns in a Triangle of Hate: The Peruvian Japanese and the United States* (Seattle, Washington: University of Washington Press, 1981).

shades drawn, some thought that they were going to be executed. This group arrived at Seagoville, Texas.

In March 1943, the two groups were joined in a family camp set up at Crystal City, 120 miles southwest of San Antonio, under the supervision of the Immigration and Naturalization Service. Some of the internees came from the West Coast and others from Hawaii. Of about 1,500 Japanese from South America, 80 percent were from Peru. Crystal City also held about 800 German internees who lived in their own separate area.

Schools in English, Japanese and German were provided the youth. One could work a job but the pay was but ten cents an hour. Unlike the internment camp for the West Coast Japanese, families were able to live in separate homes with their own kitchen facilities.[12]

In December 1945, when at last the internees were released, those from the West Coast and Hawaii returned to their homes. Peru, however, refused to readmit most of their Japanese,[13] who were then faced with a difficult choice. Some 660 Peruvian Japanese chose repatriation to Japan, including Rensuke and nine of his ten children. He believed that Japan had won the war. His source of information was the propagandistic Radio Tokyo. He and other similar minded Japanese belonged to the *Kachigumi* (victory group) as opposed to the *Makegumi* (defeatist group). The truth became clear when they arrived in Japan to be met with cries of *Sumimasen, makemashita* "We are sorry, we were defeated!"[14]

Renyu, who had been a journalist, refused to go back to Okinawa and along with a few others sought to remain in the US. Due to a successful suit on their behalf by ACLU attorneys Wayne M. Collins and A. L. Wirin, 364 of the internees were allowed to stay if they could find sponsorship. This was provided by Seabrook Farms in southern New Jersey, the largest vegetable farm in the world.[15] Between 1944 and 1945

12. Thomas K. Walls, *The Japanese Texans* (San Antonio, Texas: Institute of Texan Cultures, 1996).

13. According to Daniel M. Masterson and Sayaka Funada-Classen, *The Japanese in Latin America* (Urbana, Illinois: University of Illinois Press, 2004), 168, Peru accepted only 79 of those deported.

14. Rensuke, his wife, and their nine children were forced to live with his sister in Nago. Food, even sweet potatoes, was scarce and expensive.

15. According to Cheryl L. Baisden, *Seabrook Farms* (Charleston, South Carolina: Arcadia Publishing, 2007) Seabrook Farms, which was originally begun in 1893, grew to 20,000 acres in the twentieth century. Seabrook introduced many innovations into farming including overhead irrigation systems, scientific and climatological data,

over 2,000 Japanese Americans had been released from internment camps to work at Seabrook. When the war ended, these went back to Hawaii and to the West Coast. In desperate need of laborers, Seabrook recruited workers from Crystal City. Renyu was one of 209 Peruvian Japanese who responded.[16]

The work was hard, and the hours were long. During the peak harvest season workers were expected to toil for twelve hours a day, seven days a week. The pay was very meager, from 50 to 75 cents an hour. As illegal aliens this pay was subject to a 30 percent tax!

In order to stay in the US, Renyu wanted to marry an American citizen. Through the Oganekus, an Okinawan family in Hawaii, he learned of a widow, Haruko Yamauchi, who was an American citizen. When he came to court her in the fallof 1952, he showed her a suitcase full of cash which he had massed by his diligent labor at Seabrook.[17] My mother told me that she hoped to use that money to send me to college. That proved to be a vain hope as Renyu's salary of $275 per month as a journalist and columnist for a minor Japanese paper, the *Shin Nichi Bei Shimbun* ("The New Japanese American Newspaper"[18]) located in "Little Tokyo"[19] in Los Angeles proved to be quite insufficient for even their basic needs.

---

factory assembly plants, and the fast freezing of vegetables. Seabrook Farms welcomed workers from twenty-five nations who spoke over thirty languages. In 1947, there were 2,500 Japanese living at Seabrook.

16. *Pawns*, 155.

17. In order to remain in the US, Renyu wanted to marry an American citizen. After the 1924 Immigration Act until 1952, the only Japanese permitted into the US were the so-called "war brides," Japanese women who had married US soldiers. In June 1952 Congress passed The Immigration and Nationality Act (known as the McCarran-Walter Act), which for the first time allowed a limited number of Asians to become citizens, if they had legally been in the US for five years.

18. The major Japanese newspaper, which was begun in 1903, is the *Rafu Shimpo* "The Los Angeles Newspaper." It also has an English section and is still publishing today.

19. "Little Tokyo" is a section of Los Angeles, with a cluster of Japanese shops, restaurants, and boarding houses located on First and Second Avenue, between San Pedro and Alameda Streets, south of City Hall. In 1880 there were no Japanese in Los Angeles, a city of 11,000. By 1890 there were about 70 Japanese. *Nihon Machi*, "Japan Town," as this area was called in 1903, developed as thousands of Japanese laborers came to LA from San Francisco. The great earthquake which devastated that city in 1906, sent even more Japanese southward, so that by 1907 there were 6,300 Japanese in LA See William M. Mason and John A. McKinstry, *The Japanese of Los Angeles* (Los Angeles, California: The Museum of Natural History, 1969), 1–16.

A New Home

I had not appreciated Hawaii's beauty and warmth until I came to Los Angeles. My parents rented a two-story house on Fedora Drive between Olympic Boulevard and Pico Avenue. Though there were radiators, they could not afford to pay for heat, so even in the mild winter of southern California I felt cold outdoors and indoors.

Renyu was fluent in Japanese and in Spanish but limited in English. Though I could understand Japanese, I was not able to converse until I studied *kaiwa* "conversation" later at the University of Hawaii. I began to study Spanish only in the second semester of high school in LA, so our conversations were quite limited.

I enjoyed outings with my parents such as viewing the Rose Parade in Pasadena on January 1, 1953, and then later examining the floats after the parade. Renyu's friend drove us up to Yosemite National Park, where I saw snow for the first time, albeit on the ground.

Renyu was an avid golfer who began a golf program with the Okinawa Club of Los Angeles.[20] He had played softball in Peru. After the Brooklyn Dodgers moved to Los Angeles in 1958, he became their devoted fan.

J. H. Francis Polytechnic High School

I caught the bus to attend John H. Francis Polytechnic High School, which was located in downtown LA at the corner of Washington Boulevard and Flower Street.[21] The urban school consisted of multistoried buildings, lacking a campus with trees or a lawn. I did not realize that, founded in 1897, it was the second oldest high school in LA or that its numerous alumni included Tom Bradley, who became mayor of LA, and J. Paul Getty, who became one of the richest men in the world.[22]

I did well in a number of subjects, the most useful of which turned out to be typing. I enjoyed singing *La Cucaracha* "The Cockroach" in

---

20. Renyu was the president of this club at the time of his death on December 26, 1968.

21. In 1957 Poly moved to the San Fernando Valley.

22. He is noted for the Getty Museum of Greek and Roman Art, housed at Malibu in a reconstruction of the Villa of Papyri from Herculaneum, and a later and larger museum on a hill west of the University of California at Los Angeles.

Spanish. My chemistry teacher informed me that he could get me a job paying $4,000 if I wanted it.

This was the first time that I met Black and Latino students. I noted a number of Chinese, but no Japanese students. I did not engage in extracurricular activities, as I was otherwise occupied on weekends.

Shoan Yamauchi

Tofu, a cake of soybean curd, which was first invented by the Chinese in 965, is essential to the diet of Japanese, as well as *shoyou*, Japanese soy sauce.[23] It was a shipwrecked Japanese picked up by an American ship and taken to San Francisco in 1851 who brought the first soybeans to the US.[24] These were given to Dr. Benjamin F. Edward, who took them to Illinois.[25] And what an important crop they have become![26]

The earliest tofu company was a Chinese one in San Francisco in 1878; the earliest Japanese tofuya was one in Sacramento in 1895. Tofu was made by Japanese women in the sugar plantations of Hawaii; it was made by them in the internment camps. By 1950 over four hundred tofu shops were in business in the US.

When my cousin Shoan Yamauchi went to the mainland, it was for a vacation. But in 1947, he and his wife Shizuko seized the opportunity to buy the Matsuda Tofuya in Central LA. Later branded the Hinode ("Rising Sun") company, it became the largest tofu company in the US.

---

23. Though the Japanese in Hawaii and US began making shoyou themselves, millions of gallons of Kikkoman shoyou were imported from Japan. Probably the oldest continuing company in the world, Kikkoman started making its superior brand of shoyou for the Shogun in 1790! The labels on its bottles boast: "300 YEARS OF EXCELLENCE."

24. In 1908, Frank Meyer, an official of the Department of Agriculture, brought soybeans back from China, according to Daniel Stone, *The Food Explorer* (New York, New York: *Penguin Random House, 2018*).

25. William Shurtleff and Akiko Aoyagi, *How Japanese and Japanese-Americans Brought Soyfooods to the United States and the Hawaiian Islands: A History (1851–2011)* (Lafayette, California: The Soy Institute, 2011), 5.

26. According to William Shurtleff and Akiko Aoyagi, *The Book of Tofu: Protein Source of the Future . . . Now!* (New York, New York: Ballantine Books, 1979), 1: "Not only is the protein yield of soybeans high in terms of quantity-soybeans contain about 35 percent protein, more than any other unprocessed plant or animal food-it is also excellent in terms of quality. Soy protein includes all of the eight essential amino acids in a configuration readily usable by the human body."

I worked on weekends at Shoan's tofu factory, which was housed in a very large building and employed numerous employees, including relatives from Okinawa. He also employed a number of machines, including conveyor belts[27].

Figure 17. Yamauchi Family: Shoan standing second from left

27. It was Shoan who in 1966 secured the plastic containers used for the shipping and sale of tofu today. In 1983 Hinoichi House Food Industrial Co. of Japan purchased 50% of Shoan's business; in 1993, they purchased the remainder. By 1984, Shoan's factory was producing 130,000 pounds of tofu each week. According to Shurtleff and Aoyagi, 392, Shoan became a very wealthy man, purchasing the Kono Hawaii Restaurant in Santa Ana in the 1970s. He became a generous supporter of the Okinawa Club's scholarship program. His name is engraved on the building of the National Japanese American Museum on Second Street as the result of a generous donation. The museum includes a Shoan & Shizuko Yamauchi Gallery . . . Shoan and Shizuko were honored along with other major donors such as the actor George Takei on the tenth anniversary celebration of the museum at a gala held at the Hyatt Regency Plaza Hotel on April 25, 2009. The museum was founded by a Sansei (third generation) Japanese American, Irene Hirano, who served as its director for 20 years. In 2008, she married the widowed Senator Daniel Inouye, who had served as the president of the museum's board.

Christian Ministries

On Sundays, I had the time to explore different Christian ministries and churches. When I worked there, Shoan's tofu factory was located on Sixth Street near "Skid Row," an area where numerous alcoholics and homeless people lived on the streets. Also in the same area on Towne Avenue was the American Soul Clinic, a ministry founded by television evangelist Fred Jordan to minister to those in this area. I took classes at the center and was baptized by immersion there.

I once visited the large Foursquare Church founded by the famous Pentecostal female preacher, Aimee Semple MacPherson. I was urged to receive "the baptism of the Holy Spirit" so I could speak in tongues, but I failed to do so. I visited the Church of the Open Door, founded by Reuben A. Torrey, next to the Bible Institute of Los Angeles, near the city's library.[28]

The one church that was recommended to me by Dr. Hambrook was the University Bible Church pastored by Rev. Milo Jamison in Westwood, near the campus of UCLA. It took me an hour and a half by bus to get to that church. Coming home I would sometimes take a short cut by walking through the grounds of the Ambassador Hotel, where Bobby Kennedy was shot.

In 1951, a former candy maker, Bill Bright, had begun a parachurch organization, Campus Crusade for Christ (now simply called Cru), which sought to convert student leaders at UCLA. I heard the testimony of his star convert, Don Moomaw, an All-American football player, who later became the pastor of the Bel Air Presbyterian Church, which was attended by Ronald and Nancy Reagan.

In July, I returned to Hawaii to begin my training to become a missionary under the tutelage of a minister Dr. Hambrook had recommended—Rev. Claude H. Curtis.

A New Sister

On February 7, 1954, in Los Angeles my mother gave birth to Alicia Akiko HIga. Because of very limited finances, Renyu wanted my mother to have an abortion. But she refused. The birth of a child did complicate and challenge their lives. (See Excursus D.)

28. BIOLA University along with Talbot School of Theology is now located on a spacious campus in La Mirada southeast of LA, near Disneyland in Anaheim.

Figure 18. Renyu and Haruko with Akiko

Chapter 9

C.Y.C. and C.B.C.

(1953 to 1957)

FOR THREE YEARS (1953 to 1955, 1956 to 1957) with a year (1955 to 1956) off to attend a Bible college, I worked as a missionary in training for the Christian Youth Center (C.Y.C.) in rural Wahiawa, where I finished my high school education in 1954.

Claude H. Curtis

Claude H. Curtis had been born in 1913 in Brockton, Massachusetts. Because his father was an abusive alcoholic, Claude was sent away to live with grandparents in Prince Edward Island. When he returned to Massachusetts, he was teased by his fellow students for his Canadian accent. He was sent to China as a marine in 1932 during the Sino-Japanese conflict. Upon his discharge he worked for a Chinese publisher in Shanghai. He was offended when a missionary asked him if he was a Christian, since he had been baptized as an Episcopalian. But then he was radically converted at an evangelistic service in July 1933 and became a passionate proclaimer of the Gospel. He nurtured a lifelong admiration for the Republic of China, Sun Yat-Sen, Chiang Kai Shek and his wife,[1] and an equally deep dislike of the Chinese Communists.

---

1. Curtis first met them in 1933 and was invited by them to Taiwan in 1955. Curtis led public protests against the policies of Presidents Nixon and Carter, who favored

He returned to the States in 1935 to witness to his family and to speak about his experiences in China. He wrote about his testimony in his first book, *A Marine among the Idols* (published by Zondervan in 1939 and later translated into Chinese). Though fervent, he lacked formal training. He was not admitted to Gordon College because he lacked a high school diploma. For a short time, he attended a liberal seminary, but was dismayed at the dismissive attitude toward the Bible assumed by his professors. Curtis was ordained by a group of fundamentalist ministers.

After a successful ministry of evangelism in many states with the support of prominent leaders like Harry Ironside of Moody Church, John Rice and Jack Wyrtzen, Curtis then served for nine years as an assistant minister of a prominent Methodist church in San Francisco which he does not name.[2]

He came with his wife, Kathleen (Kay) whom he had met in San Francisco and three of his children to Hawaii in 1948. Under the rubric of Gospel Missions he established in Wahiawa at the junction of Kamehameha Highway and California Avenue the Christian Youth Center (C.Y.C.), which was to sponsor the Oriental Bible Church[3] and a servicemen's center for soldiers from the nearby Schofield Barracks.[4] He had a weekly radio broadcast which was beamed to the mainland as well as the Islands. To support his ministry, he had a staff of three women (Alice Araki, Nora Handa, Chieko Komata) who cared for about thirty nursery children during the week.[5]

---

detente with Communist China. Curtis would make more than fifty trips to Taiwan and also trips to Japan, Korea, Hong Kong, and, finally, China itself. It became his mission to bring Chinese Bibles into that country, a mission which has been continued by his son Philip.

2. This was the Glide Memorial Methodist Church. Founded in 1930, it was at first conservative theologically. Julian C. McPheeters, who was the pastor from 1942 to 1948, served as the president of Asbury Theological Seminary, commuting between San Francisco and Wilmore, Kentucky. Then in the 1960s the church became a flagship for gay rights.

3. Though he was an effective evangelist, Rev. Curtis's brusque personality did not make him an attractive pastor.

4. Very few servicemen attended the church, which had a congregation of no more than fifteen on Sundays. One service couple with whom I developed a lifelong friendship are Arthur and Peggy Hill. Art later became the head of a Christian school and the chair of the trustees of Eastern University.

5. Alice and Nora were to serve as missionaries to Japan.

Figure 19. CYC group: EMY and Claude Curtis standing on right

Leilehua High School

As I already had acquired sufficient credits, I took only English, social studies, and algebra to graduate in 1954 from Leilehua High School in Wahiawa. Before my conversion my favorite subjects had been fiction, science, and math, but now my interest was in the Bible. Once during an algebra class, the teacher noted that I had an open Bible on my desk and came by to slam the Bible shut. When I later wrote to apologize for my action, she responded that it was rude for me not to pay attention. Despite getting a B in algebra, upon graduation I received the Reader's Digest award as the senior with "the highest scholastic rank." Apart from the Christian Fellowship, I had little time for extracurricular activities because of my chores at the "ranch."

The "Ranch"

To support his ministry Rev. Curtis had leased about two acres of land where he raised a number of animals, who became my charges. They included horses[6], heifers,[7] goats, sheep[8], chickens,[9] ducks, geese,[10] rabbits, and a turkey.[11] It was my responsibility to feed the animals, to milk the goats, to cut grass for feed, to slaughter rabbits,[12] to collect eggs, to gather up the manure in a wheelbarrow and to dump it on a hillside. In retrospect this was not a very good location as it was above the reservoir that provided water for Wahiawa!

---

6. I had the experience of seeing the birth of a colt and its struggle to stand.

7. We took the heifers to a slaughterhouse on the Sunday School bus, which I had to clean up later.

8. Whereas the sheep were docile, the goats were frisky, escaping the electric fence to nibble at the neighbor's papaya trees.

9. In a letter dated April 19, 1956, Curtis wrote to me as follows: "Now for the inventory on the ranch. 131 rabbits, 70 good layers, 70 just beginning, 25 due to start laying, the end of next month, 88 one month old pullets. 175 fryers and broilers, and 100 baby chicks due today or tomorrow."

10. When Mrs. Curtis went out to hang the laundry, it was my duty to keep our geese, Winston Church and Lady Astor, from nipping at her.

11. The turkey was very difficult to kill.

12. Curtis in *By Faith* (Wahiawa, Hawaii: Gospel Missions, 1985), 255, comments: "I found that it was much easier to raise rabbits than to kill and dress them. Nearly every time I picked out a bunny for the dinner table, it had to be when the children were away or else I would hear one of them crying, 'Not that one, Daddy. Please don't kill it.'"

Figure 20. At the CYC ranch

Rev. Curtis was my spiritual "father." At the same time, he was a very demanding taskmaster. He called my attention to a few blades of grass I had missed when mowing his lawn. Once when he was not satisfied with the job, I had done in cleaning out a chicken coop, he sent me back out at night to clean it more thoroughly with a flashlight. But instead of resenting this rebuke, I experienced an epiphany of God's presence as I walked back in the shadow of tall mango trees on a moonlit night.

Bible Studies

Doing hours of farm chores gave me time to meditate on the Scriptures. Inspired by a Christian officer from Taiwan who testified that he would read a New Testament passage a hundred times, by using a small King James Version of the New Testament I began memorizing the New Testament books, chapter by chapter until I had memorized all except the Synoptic Gospels (Matthew, Mark, Luke). I was able, for example, to meditate on the book of Hebrews while moving the heifers from one pasture to another. I also memorized hymns while washing the eggs, though this led to a few cracked eggs!

At our church there was a very small selection of books for sale. One in particular, J. B. Lightfoot's classic commentary on the Greek text of Philippians, inspired me to learn Koine Greek by using J. G. Machen's basic grammar of New Testament Greek. Rev. Curtis asked me to teach in our evening Bible Institute, which was unaccredited and had very few students. I taught courses on the Minor Prophets, using E. B. Pusey's classic commentary and the book of Ezra. My first article, an exposition of James 1, was published in 1957 as "The Blessings of Trials" in *His Magazine*, a publication of InterVarsity Press, along with my photo with a class of fifteen young boys.[13]

Columbia Bible College[14]

Rev. Curtis had come to know Robertson McQuilkin, the president of Columbia Bible College in South Carolina, a school known for its emphasis upon missions. In the fall of 1955, he paid for my travel expenses to go there for my freshman year in college. I would work in the library to pay for my tuition, room, and board.

For the first and only time in my life, I went to California by boat on the Lurline. On board I led a discussion of the Gospel of John, which I had been memorizing. The trip went smoothly until we got closer to California, when the motion of the ship made most of the passengers seasick.

After a brief visit with my parents in LA, I boarded a Greyhound bus for a non-stop seventy-two-hour trip to Columbia. When I was in Hawaii, I thought that the hour and a half trip to Kahuku was too long! This was my first experience with segregated public bathrooms. I asked Dr. Fleece, the president of C.B.C, why there were no Blacks at the college. He responded that it was against state law, and that the faculty taught in a separate Bible school for Blacks.

I did not realize it then but our dormitory with silver doorknobs and creaking floors was quite a historic building.[15] Our dorm was about two

13. This was published as a tract, along with another essay, "Hawaii—Paradise or Prison of the Pacific?" by the American Tract Society.

14. The school began in a hotel in 1923 as the Columbia Bible School; it became Columbia Bible College in 1929. It moved to its present location on Monticello Road on the outskirts of Columbia in in 1960 and changed its name to Columbia International University in 1994.

15. The building was designed in 1823 for Ansley Hall by Robert Mills, a South Carolinian who was the national architect under seven presidents. It was Mills who designed the Washington Monument. The building was used for nearly a century by the Presbyterian Columbia Theological Seminary. It then served as a dormitory for

blocks away from the main building with its cafeteria. Along the way I passed the home of Woodrow Wilson, which I did not visit until many years later. Coming from Hawaii I associated blue skies with warm weather and at first went out that winter with only a thin Aloha shirt!

Among the teachers I enjoyed were Dr. George Dollar[16] who taught history, and Frank Sells, who taught a survey of the Bible.[17] One popular teacher I did not get to study with was "Buck" Hatch, who taught psychology.[18]

Figure 21. At Columbia Bible College

C.B.C. from 1937 to 1960.

16. Dollar wrote a history of Fundamentalism, and later taught at Dallas Theological Seminary.

17. Sells provided prepared outlines, a method that I later adopted in teaching large Western Civilization classes at Miami University.

18. His son Nathan Hatch became a prominent historian of US religion and served as the provost of Notre Dame, and then as the president of Wake Forest University.

I served as the freshman class's representative and led a group of them to help clear the ground on what was to become the future campus on Monticello Road. I enjoyed singing in the choir. Nobu Ayabe from Kauai, who had been a classmate of my wife at Fort Wayne Bible College, was quite diminutive but had a booming voice as our soloist.[19] There were two other Nisei at CBC. Mildred (Milly) Kiyuna from Makiki Christian Church was a senior.[20] Kathy Omaye, a grad student, was a tall Floridian with a distinctive southern accent.[21]

I worked on the school newspaper and wrote extensive articles on the powerful messages of Alan Redpath, the pastor of Moody Church. I was the only male on the large staff of 15 students at the library under Shirley Wood. I had learned to speed read, so I read shelves of books, mainly missionary biographies. I was also involved in a Foreign Missions Fellowship prayer group.

For Christian service, I witnessed to and invited servicemen from Fort Jackson to attend church services in Columbia. Once, I went with a group of students to the Catawba Indian Reservation near the North Carolina border. During the winter break I drove a laundry truck in the rural Black districts. I did not have much time for leisure, but once played tennis on the school's clay courts with Grace Hancox, who later became the wife of the noted theologian Harold O. J. Brown.

---

19. Nobu became a pastor in Hawaii.

20. Milly became a missionary to Okinawa.

21. Kathy and her husband Hitoshi were to serve as missionaries to the Japanese in the Amazon region of Brazil.

Chapter 10

U.H. and *Ka Leo*

(1957 to 1958)

Tuition, Room, and Board

IN THE SPRING OF 1956, I was recalled back to Hawaii because of the urgent need for my services both for the ministry and for work on the ranch. Rev. Curtis sent me the fare for the flight home. I finished my first year in college without any funds left, but also without any debt. After another year at the C.Y.C., I became interested in studying anthropology and languages at the University of Hawaii in Honolulu.

In addition to free room and board at the Christian Youth Center I had received $.75 an hour for the 60 hours I worked each week at the Ranch as an "allowance." This provided me with a little spending money but with no savings. In a letter to the University of Hawaii on my behalf, Rev. Curtis wrote: "At the time of this letter (February 17, 1956) Edwin has but $4.00 in the Bank of Hawaii, Wahiawa Branch." From time to time my mother would send me a check for $50, always with the apology that she could not send me more.

To study at the University of Hawaii I stayed at the home of Dr. Hambrook on Harding Avenue in Kaimuki. I did twenty hours a week of housework and also served as the secretary for a Bible correspondence course he was directing. With recommendations from Charles Hite and Representative Steve Noda I received the Fushinomiya Memorial Scholarship from the University of Hawaii to pay for two semesters of my tuition. I took twenty-one hours the first semester and twenty-three the second semester.

Anthropology and Languages[1]

As an aspiring missionary, I chose anthropology as my major, which included the study of Samoan from an informant.[2] I also took a course in biology and the required physical ed (swimming, gymnastics) and joined the Air Force R.O.T.C.

During the first semester I took Greek,[3] Japanese, French, Spanish, and German. During the second semester for some unknown reason, I switched from German to Russian.[4] In retrospect, it is odd that as one who intended to minister to the Japanese in Brazil, I never considered studying Portuguese.[5]

Kaleo O Hawaii

I led Bible studies twice a week for students at a building owned by the Hawaii School of Religion. I was a finalist in the Territorial Oratorical Contest and joined the Oriental Literature Club. Most of my time outside of classes was consumed by my work on *Kaleo O Hawaii* "The Voice of (the University) of Hawaii," the school paper which came out twice a week. Based on my prior experience on school papers at Iolani High School and at Columbia Bible College, I was given the position of feature editor.

This allowed me the opportunity to interview visiting scholars such as Dr. Genshu Asato, the president of the University of Ryukus, built near the site of the ancient capital of Shuri in Okinawa. Another visiting scholar was Professor Herbert Feigl of the University of

---

1. After my conversion, I developed a lifelong fascination with languages. During my years teaching at Miami University (1969 to 2005) I audited courses in Latin, Italian, French, German, Russian, Spanish, Japanese, and Chinese.

2. The most valuable lesson I learned from this major was the existence of the Human Relations Area Files, which categorizes all human behavior and culture under 150 rubrics. I was to later use this as a framework for a unique dictionary of daily life in the Bible (see chapter 43).

3. My professor, Dr. Ruth Pavlantos, had received her PhD from the Classics Department at the University of Cincinnati.

4. As a result, it took me three tries to pass my German exam in graduate school!

5. A church history text that I co-authored has been translated into Portuguese in Brazil.

Minnesota, a leading proponent of Logical Positivism. When I shared my Christian faith with him, he mentioned a colleague in Psychology, Paul Meehl, who had been converted to Christ upon reading Augustine. Meehl served as the president of the American Psychological Association. Feigl, who was an atheist, reported that Meehl, who had become a Lutheran, attempted to convert him.

"He That Hath Ears . . . "[6]

In a regular column titled "He That Hath Ears . . . " I discussed books such as C. W. Ceram's *Gods, Graves and Scholars*, Arnold Toynbee's *A Study of History*, Andres Nygren's *Agape and Eros*, William James's *Varieties of Religious Experience*, Albert Schweitzer's *The Quest of the Historical Jesus*, André Dupont-Sommer's *The Dead Sea Scrolls*, William Dampier's *A History of Science*, Karl Heim's *The Transformation of the Scientific World View*, and William Hordern's *Christianity, Communism, and History*.

In one column, I quoted from an article, "Religion in the Life of the College Professor," written by Walter C. Langsam, president of the University of Cincinnati, who wrote: "The professor who has faith will guide these restless boys and girls in a fruitful search for the truth. The professor who has no faith will feed his vanity by making irresponsible remarks for the sake of laughter and a transient and shallow popularity."[7] In another article I noted that the familiar translation of the Christmas angel's message, "Peace on earth, and good will to men," from the King James Version was based on a defective Greek text.[8]

Though my essays were appreciated by Professor Aoki, the chair of the religion department, they drew sarcastic scorn from two graduate students in sociology, Harold R. Weaver and Darrow L. Aiona,[9] who addressed two letters to the editor. In a brief letter they wrote: "Hallelujah! Praise the Lord! Brother Yamauchi has been saved. Now who is going to save US from Brother Yamauchi?" In a longer letter, they wrote in part:

---

6. Taken from a frequently used phrase, by Jesus, "He that hath ears, let him hear," Matthew 11:15 (KJV).

7. From *The Association of the American Colleges Bulletin* (MAY 1957), 349–55. The main library at the University of Cincinnati is named after President Langsam.

8. I was to reprise this subject many years later when I served as one of the senior editors of *Christianity Today*.

9. I was at Iolani with Darrow, who became an Episcopalian priest and also a strong advocate for the claims of those descended from the native Hawaiians.

"Since the term's beginning, the Feature Editor ... has spouted his fundamentalist para-Christian dogma and pseudo-profundities supported, occasionally by quotes from other 'thinkers.'" To their suggestion that I invite other viewpoints, I informed them that I pursued students who wished to write on such topics as "Too Many Religious Organizations on Campus?" but that such articles were never actually submitted.

The Golden Rule Controversy

A thirty-foot ketch called "The Golden Rule," carrying a crew of four Quaker pacifists docked in Hawaii on April 19, 1958, on their way toward the Marshall Islands, where they hoped to disrupt the US nuclear test "Operation Hardtack" at the Enewetak atoll. In addition to captain Albert Bigelow, the crew included William R. Huntington, Orlon Sherwood, and George Willoughby. They were greeted with leis by Patsy Mink and invited to speak about their mission at the University of Hawaii. While everyone conceded that they were quite sincere, others including myself and students such a Janos Virag from Hungary considered their views about the danger of Communism naive. In response to a student's question Willoughby declared, "The communists have not expanded by military might. In the countries they have gone into, there was something wrong there."

I persuaded Frank Forbes, a UH senator, to propose a resolution before the Associated Students of the University of Hawaii (A.S.U.H.) condemning the mission of the Golden Rule and supporting the government's right to continue nuclear testing in view of the threat of Communism.

This ignited a firestorm of debate which led to a panel discussion on May 19. I defended the proposition which was opposed by Patsy Mink[10] and by Ben Norris, a Quaker professor. After rejecting the wording of the original proposal as too inflammatory, on May 20 the A.S.U.H. did pass a resolution to "express support of the nuclear tests as long as the United

---

10. Patsy Takemoto Mink (1927 to 2002) was to become one of the most important Asian American Democrats in Washington, DC, serving twelve terms in the House of Representatives, and even seeking the Democratic nomination for president. At the time of the Golden Rule debate she was a member of Hawaii's territorial congress. Hawaii became a state only in 1959. Patsy Mink was the primary person responsible for the passage of Title IX, which has been renamed the Patsy T. Mink Equal Opportunity in Education Act. She was named "Woman of the Year" in 1972 by *Time Magazine* and was posthumously awarded the Presidential Medal of Freedom.

States government feels that it is necessary." Furthermore, the resolution was to be presented at the national meeting of student governments convening at Ohio Wesleyan University in August 1958. My involvement was reported in the *Honolulu Star Bulletin* by Elsie Loo, the editor of *Kaleo*, who noted that I had been influenced by Dr. Hambrook. The crew of the Golden Rule were arrested, but their example inspired a number of other attempts to disrupt nuclear testing.[11]

Figure 22. *Ka Leo* on the Golden Rule Debate

After this eventful year at the U.H., I was ready to move on to learn more about biblical languages (Hebrew, Koine Greek). When I asked Dr. Hambrook for recommendations, he suggested two small Christian colleges, both aligned with the American Council of Christian Churches: Highland College in Pasadena, California, and Shelton College in Ringwood, New Jersey.

---

11. The US was to continue nuclear bomb tests at Enewetak for a dozen years. Moreover, the US shipped 1300 tons of irradiated soil from the Nevada testing site to the atoll. My uncle, James Owan, who took part in Operation Ivy in 1952 at Enewetak developed cancer as did other soldiers and many Marshallese who lived in the area.

Chapter 11

Shelton College

(1958 to 1961)

Shelton College

IN 1907, DR. DON O. Shelton started the National Bible Institute in Brooklyn. He later moved the school to 55th Street in Manhattan.[1] Shelton remained president until his death in 1941.[2] The new president was J. Oliver Buswell, who had been a very successful president at Wheaton

---

1. A notable graduate of N.B.I. was Spiros Zodhiates from Greece. Spiros founded the American Mission to Greece, hosted a popular Bible broadcast and published many books.

2. William W. Borden (1887 to 1913) was the heir of a fortune gained by his father from the silver mines of Colorado. He was an extraordinary young man whose evangelistic zeal impressed his classmates and teachers at Yale University. He founded a rescue mission in New Haven, the Yale Hope House. He attended Princeton Theological Seminary as he prepared to go out as a missionary of the China Inland Mission to evangelize the Muslim Uighurs of northwest China. While still a student at Princeton, Borden served as a member of the council of the China Inland Mission, as a trustee of Moody Bible Institute, and as a board member of the National Bible Institute. He found a kindred spirit in Don Shelton, who was an evangelist and a founder of rescue missions in New York City. Borden played a key role in the early development of N.B.I., drafting the "principles and practices" of the school, lecturing to its students, and giving generously of his time and money. Just as he was graduating from Princeton, Shelton suffered a breakdown and Borden took over the complete operations of the school and rescue missions. His exemplary life was tragically cut short when he contracted meningitis in Cairo and died at the age of twenty-six. His will bequeathed $900,000 to the China Inland Mission. See Mrs. Howard Taylor, *Borden of Yale '09* (Oxford, United Kingdom: Benediction Classics, 2017 repr. of the 1913 ed.).

College but who had just been dismissed because of his strong separationist views. The school was renamed Shelton College in 1950. In 1953 the college acquired Skylands, a 1,075-acre estate first established by Francis L. Stetson, a lawyer for J. P. Morgan. The estate was then bought by Clarence Lewis, who built Skylands Manor in 1924.[3] This 51-room mansion became the administration building of the school. A later wing housed the chapel above and a cafeteria below.

The campus was located in the borough of Ringwood in Passaic County in northern New Jersey.[4] When I first arrived at Shelton College in the fall of 1958 as a transfer junior, I was disappointed that the two professors under whom I wished to study, Dr. Elmer Smick[5] and Dr, Wilber Wallis,[6] were no longer there. Gone also was the president, Dr. Buswell. Dr. Hambrook had shown me an outdated catalogue.

Carl C. McIntire

As a new Christian with limited knowledge of denominations and coming from far off Hawaii, I had no inkling of what had transpired among the Bible Presbyterians in the east. To understand the situation, one has to review the pivotal role played in the US and abroad by a towering figure in church politics, Carl McIntire, the influential pastor of a thriving twelve-hundred-member church in Collingswood, New Jersey, near Philadelphia.

Carl had been a student at Princeton Theological Seminary, which was once the bastion of conservative orthodoxy with scholars such as A. A. Hodge and B. B. Warfield. The seminary reached a crisis with the hiring of liberal scholars who accepted the higher criticism of the Bible.

J. Gresham Machen, an outstanding professor of New Testament, and three Old Testament scholars. Robert Dick Wilson, Oswald T. Allis and Allan A, MacRae left Princeton in 1928 to establish Westminster Theological Seminary in Philadelphia. The school later moved to Chestnut

---

3. My history colleague at Miami University Judith Zinsser, who grew up in Manhattan, recalls visiting the manor when it was still occupied by the Lewis family.

4. In 1966, the state of New Jersey purchased Skylands. With its beautiful trees and many flowering plants, Skylands is now the State Botanical Garden of New Jersey.

5. Smick earned his PhD in 1951 with a study of third millennium B.C. cuneiform tablets in the Philadelphia Free Library.

6. Wallis earned his PhD in 1956, writing his dissertation on "Aramaic and Mandean Magic and Their Demonology."

Hills, a suburb of the city.[7] Machen, MacRae, McIntire, and Buswell in 1937 began a new denomination, the Orthodox Presbyterian Church.

Then a dispute between faculty members at Westminster over eschatology and Christian conduct led to the departure of MacRae and McIntire from Westminster. Those who remained held to amillennialism (interpreting the millennium as symbolic), while those who left held to premillennialism (the belief that Christ would return before a literal millennium). Those who left objected to some faculty who considered it permissible to smoke and drink alcoholic beverages.

The new school Faith Theological Seminary began in Delaware in 1937 with MacRae as its president. Its first graduate was Francis Schaeffer,[8] who would establish L'Abri near Lausanne, Switzerland and become a noted author.[9] In 1952 McIntire was able to purchase the mansion of a wealthy railroad magnate, A. B. Widener[10] in Elkins Park, a suburb of Philadelphia. He moved Faith Theological Seminary there.[11]

McIntire had mounted a very public campaign against liberalism and ecumenicalism. In opposition to the Federal Council of Churches founded in 1908, which became the National Council of Churches in 1950, he had formed the American Council of Christian Churches (A.C.C.C.) in 1941. In opposition to the World Council of Churches formed in 1948, he formed the International Council of Christian Churches (I.C.C.C.) also in 1948.

---

7. Westminster later acquired a faculty of outstanding scholars such as Edward J. Young (Old Testament), Ned B. Stonehouse (New Testament) and Cornelius Van Til (Theology and Apologetics). Meredith G. Kline, who taught Old Testament there and later at Gordon Conwell Theological Seminary, earned his PhD in 1956 under Cyrus H. Gordon.

8. Other notable graduates of Faith Theological Seminary include Arthur Glasser, Vernon Grounds, R. Laird Harris, Gordon R. Lewis, Kenneth Kantzer, W. Harold Mare, Elmer Smick, Samuel Schultz, and Wilber Wallis.

9. InterVarsity Press published many of Schaeffer's books, e.g., *Art in the Bible, Back to Freedom and Dignity, The Church at the End of the Twentieth Century, Death in the City, Escape from Reason, Genesis in Space and Time, The God Who Is There,* and *Joshua and the Flow of Biblical History.*

10. The main library at Harvard University is named after this benefactor.

11. In 1971, in a revolt against the domineering influence of McIntire, MacRae, and almost the entire faculty with the exception of the registrar left Faith Theological Seminary to establish Biblical Seminary in Hatfield outside of Philadelphia. The school which survived, lost its Elkins Park property and moved back to Delaware. Many of its faculty and students are drawn from I.C.C.C. churches in Korea and India.

McIntire believed in second-degree separation,[12] that is, separation not only from liberals but from evangelicals like Billy Graham who cooperated with liberals and Catholics in his crusades.[13] He denounced the new Revised Standard Version for replacing "virgin" with "young maiden" in Isaiah 7:14, a verse that is cited in Matthew 1:23.

McIntire promoted his views in a newspaper, *The Christian Beacon*[14] and in daily radio broadcasts of the Twentieth Century Reformation on 620 radio stations, reaching an audience estimated at 20 million. He also played an important role in the Independent Board for Presbyterian Foreign Missions.

He did not take kindly to those who disagreed with his decisions. This was a character flaw which even his admiring biographers acknowledged. "He was CONTROLLING . . . If anyone did oppose his decisions, if any questioned his methods, that man would be distrusted."[15]

Discontent with McIntire's leadership resulted in a revolt led by Francis Schaeffer and Robert Rayburn at the 1955 synod meeting of the Bible Presbyterians in St. Louis. The rebels wanted the various institutions to be controlled by the synod rather than by any individual.[16] This led to the formation of Covenant College[17] and Covenant Theological Seminary based at Creve Coeur, a western suburb of St. Louis. These schools were staffed by former professors at Shelton College (J. Oliver Buswell, Elmer Smick, Wilbur Wallis) and Faith Theological Seminary (R. Laird Harris, Peter Stam, William Sanderson).

---

12. In addition to the Bible Presbyterians the General Association of Regular Baptists held this position.

13. In opposition to McIntire's militant fundamentalism his erstwhile friend at Princeton Seminary Harold J. Ockenga, the pastor of Boston's Park Street Church, established the National Association of Evangelicals in 1942 and promoted a New Evangelicalism as exemplified by Billy Graham, Fuller Theological Seminary in Pasadena and *Christianity Today*.

14. The paper reached 130,000 subscribers.

15. Gladys Titzek Rhoads and Nancy Titzek Anderson, *McIntire: Defender of Faith and Fredom* (n.p.: Xulon Press, 2012), 513.

16. The initial split in 1955 was between the Columbus Synod of the Bible Presbyterians and the Collingswood Synod loyal to McIntire. By mergers the former evolved as the Reformed Presbyterian Church in 1965 and then became the Presbyterian Church in America in 1982, now the second largest Presbyterian denomination in the US.

17. The college relocated to the top of Lookout Mountain, Tennessee, near the border of Georgia on the grounds of a resort hotel, where Elizabeth Taylor once honeymooned.

Faculty

The new president of Shelton College Dr. John (Jack) W. Murray in 1957 was not an academic but an evangelist who was the pastor of the Church of the Open Door in Philadelphia. His wife Eleanor, who accompanied him occasionally on his visits to the campus, was a gifted pianist and composer. His new secretary was Olive Fleming, a recently widowed missionary, whose husband Peter had been one of the five murdered by the Auca Indians in Ecuador in January 1956.[18]

Of the twenty faculty who were left only Dean Banta had an earned doctorate (DEd). William Paul, my professor of philosophy and theology, was to gain his PhD from Columbia University, writing on Paul Tillich's philosophy of history, in the second semester that I was there.[19]

Though lacking in academic credentials, my instructors were dedicated and well informed such as Allan Bleecker in Biology, who was a grad student at Rutgers. Gordon Tweeten, my instructor in Greek, was studying for a master's degree at Columbia University. He commuted from Brooklyn and worked at a bank at night. He had his class memorize the opening lines of Homer's *Iliad* in Greek.

My most important teacher was Melvin Dahl, who taught the Semitic languages. He was unfailingly enthusiastic even when there were only two of us, Nita Somerville and I, in his Aramaic and Arabic classes.[20] Rev. Dahl, who pastored a church an hour west of the campus, had taken 60 hours of graduate credits studying under Cyrus H. Gordon

---

18. In January 1956 five missionaries were speared to death in the Amazon area of Ecuador by the "Aucas," a Quechua term meaning "savage" given to the Guarani tribe. Their martyrdom and the mission of two of the widows to reach members of this tribe are memorably recounted by Elisabeth Elliot, *Through Gates of Spendor* (New York, New York: Harper, 1957) and *The Savage My Kinsman* (New York, New York: Harper, 1961). See also, Steve Saint, *The End of a Spear* (Carol Stream, Illinois: Tyndale House, 2005), Olive married Walter Liefeld, a graduate of Shelton who served on the staff of InterVarsity Christian Fellowship. Walt earned his PhD in Classics from Columbia University and became a New Testament professor at Trinity Evangelical Divinity School. They both came from the (Plymouth) Brethren tradition.

19. Dr. Paul attended a special seminar at the University of Minnesota, where he heard Dr. Feigl, the logical positivist whom I had interviewed at the University of Hawaii, declare that religious language is meaningless.

20. Relying on my rudimentary Arabic, I played a mischievous joke at a conference of international students at Washington, DC. I asked a boy from Hong Kong if he wanted to learn an Arabic phrase, which would make a big impression on a beautiful Egyptian girl. He memorized the Arabic I taught him, "*Anti akbaru wa asmanu min fili*" and did make quite an impression. Translated it meant, "You are bigger and fatter than my elephant!"

and others at the Dropsie College for Hebrew and Cognate Studies in Philadelphia. My voice instructor Manly Price Boone had been the first teacher of George Beverly Shea. One of the teachers whose courses I did not take was Virginia Mollenkott, an English instructor who gained considerable influence and notoriety after she left Shelton.[21]

Students and Work

There were only 114 students, fifty from New Jersey, twenty-four from Pennsylvania, the rest from a number of states, and two from the territory of Hawaii, Annie Chow and I. The following year, the student body expanded to 157 students.[22]

As I had only $50 to my name, I needed a work scholarship for tuition, room, and board. Tuition cost $600 per semester. To earn my tuition during the first semester I cleaned Gatewood, a converted sheep shed which served as the men's dormitory. Later I cleaned and waxed the dining hall with the help of Philip Heng,[23] a student from Singapore. I would often finish at 1 a.m., and when waxing at 3 a.m., after which I would have to trudge a mile down an unlit and unpaved road to the dormitory.

---

21. Virginia Rainey Mollenkott (1932 to 2020) was a graduate of Bob Jones University. She married Fred Mollenkott, a fellow BJU student. She earned an MA at Temple University and worked on her PhD in English at New York University while teaching at Shelton. She and her husband divorced in 1973. After teaching at Nyack Missionary College, she gained a position at William Paterson University in Wayne, N.J. She and Letha Scanzoni published a landmark book, *Is the Homosexual My Neighbor?* in 1978. As a lesbian Christian, she supported gay rights and was honored by the LGBTQ community.

22. The outstanding student leader at Shelton was Dr. McIntire's son, Carl Thomas. At Shelton he was known as Carl, but later to distance himself from his famous father he preferred to be called Thomas or C. T. He was tall and athletic, an outstanding tennis and basketball player. In a memorable victory over Nyack College, Carl who was recently stricken with chicken pox scored forty points to break a conference record! He and his close friends Albert Gedraitis and Deborah Steel were involved in Young Americans for Freedom, the movement begun by William Buckley. They invited to campus the noted conservative writer, Russell Kirk. C. T. later attended Faith Theological Seminary and taught at Shelton. He then earned a PhD in history from the University of Pennsylvania. An admirer of the Dutch theologian Herman Dooyeweerd, C. T. taught at the Institute for Christian Studies located across the street from the University of Toronto. He then became a professor of history at the University of Toronto, and an authority on the Christian historian, Herbert Butterfield.

23. Philip would transfer to Moody Bible Institute and return to Singapore to pastor a Bible Presbyterian Church.

I also had to walk uphill in the morning to get to breakfast, which I sometimes missed when the gate was closed if I did not get there in time. My mom from time to time would send me some Japanese delicacies such as *tsukemono* (pickles) and *unagi* (broiled eel).

Figure 23. At the Shelton College library

Christian Service

On weekends, I worked with other students in three areas, Ramapo[24] and Sloatsburg, ten miles north of the campus in southern New York, and at Ringwood just west of the campus. Work in the New York areas was among poor white teenagers, whom we sometimes brought up to the campus. Among those with whom I worked there were Barbara Hughes[25] and Carole Ross. A knife wielding fifteen-year-old girl was

---

24. The village has been absorbed by the large town of Ramapo, which has been noted recently for the large influx of the so-called Ultra-Orthodox Jews from New York City.

25. Barb went with her husband Don Borgman to work among the Sanuma Indians of northern Brazil.

converted. But life with an abusive alcoholic mother caused her to ask us one day for a ride to the campus. We did not realize that she was running away until the police came to seek her. Since we had taken her across state lines, we could have been accused of kidnapping her.

Work in Ringwood was among the "Jackson Whites," whom legend had it were descended from native Americans, Blacks, and runaway Hessian soldiers. Steven Cohen, a scholar who lived among this small and poor enclave, has debunked such stories. Cohen prefers to call them "Ramapo Mountain People."[26] They are a unique population descended from Indians, Blacks, and some mulattoes, with many having Dutch names. They lived as tenants in two-story houses built by the Ringwood Iron Mine company. The mines once produced important supplies of iron for the revolutionary army. The love of Sally Sharp[27] for their children inspired me as I worked with her and others to teach Sunday School and hold services in their home.

I was also the president of the Foreign Missions Fellowship and was responsible for sending two students on a summer missions trip to Jamaica, Nancy Knopf[28] and Elaine Ortowski.[29]

---

26. David Steven Cohen, *The Ramapo Mountain People* (New Brunswick, New Jersey: Rutgers University Press, 1986).

27. Sally and her husband Ed Koehn worked among the Apalai Indians of northern Brazil.

28. Nancy served as a missionary in Chad and the Central African Republic. On her return to the US she held Bible classes for women and children in the Cleveland area.

29. Elaine married Chuck Moore, the brother of Sam Moore, whose remarkable "rags to riches" life is recounted in his autobiography, *American by Choice* (Nashville, Tennessee: Thomas Nelson, 1998). Sam was born in Beirut as Sam Ziady, a name which in Arabic means "more." When he wanted an English equivalent for his American name, the court clerk misspelled his name as "Moore" instead of "More." Sam was befriended by famed American missionary doctor, Thomas Lambie, who was related by marriage to Robert McQuilkin, the president of Columbia Bible College. In 1949, Dr. Lambie enabled Sam to attend C.B.C. While fluent in Arabic and French Sam knew limited English. During two summers, he earned money for his tuition by selling Bibles as a door to door salesman. After graduating from the University of South Carolina, Sam began the National Book Company in Tennessee, in 1958. This became quite successful. The American branch of the venerable Thomas Nelson Publishers, founded in 1798, had floundered when their exclusive right to publish the Revised Standard Bible was ended by the National Council of Churches. Sam was invited to manage Thomas Nelson. Instead, he made a counteroffer to buy the company outright for $2,640,000. Sam transformed Thomas Nelson into one of the largest evangelical publishing houses, printing various versions of the Bible such as the New King James Version and best-selling authors such as Robert Schuller. Among the company's achievements was the printing of one million Bibles for distribution in China. To run the Bible division Sam

The Gospel Team

The college planned to send out a "Gospel Team," in the summer of 1959 which consisted of a group of women musicians, a male song leader and a male speaker, accompanied by a chaperone. The musical group called the Skyland-Heirs consisted of Sarah Murray[30] as pianist and the trio of Carole Ross, Mary Monroe, and Bonnie Rigg.[31] The chaperone was Mrs. Monroe. The speaker was to be George Giacumakis, the exuberant student body president. I was to be the song leader, though with little experience in this practice. But then George's parents, who were immigrants from Greece who ran a bakery in New Castle, Pennsylvania needed his help. So, I was then enlisted to be the speaker, with John Hibbard, a gifted trumpeter as the song leader.

I do not know how we all managed to squeeze into a Buick, as only Bonnie, Mrs. Monroe, and I were undersized. John did most of the driving. Bonnie and I sat in the front with the other four women somehow squeezed into the back seat. We traveled through the states of Connecticut, Massachusetts, New Jersey, Maryland, Pennsylvania, Ohio, and Michigan, visiting camps and churches to promote both the Gospel and Shelton College. It proved to be a most rewarding and enjoyable adventure. I experienced a number of firsts with the team such as my first roller coaster ride at the Euclid Beach amusement park.

Graduation

During my junior year, I received A's in all of my courses; during my senior year I slipped a bit, getting a B one semester in Hebrew and another B in an Arabic course. I graduated *summa cum laude* with a GPA of 3.94 plus additional honor points for Christian service. There were only 22 other students graduating with me. I was pleased that my mother and six-year old sister, Alice, were able to attend the ceremonies.

---

recruited his brother Chuck, who with a PhD in chemistry was working for Bristol Myers.

30. Sarah, the daughter of Dr. Murray, served with her husband Michael Eremic, planting churches in Germany. After his death, she served as the Dean of Women at Columbia International University (1997 to 2001). Her brother George after serving as a missionary, became president of Columbia International University (2000 to 2007).

31. Bonnie married Howard Carlson, a graduate of Highland College and Faith Theological Seminary. He served as a pastor in various cities in the US, including Paradise, California. They also served overseas in Kenya and Israel.

Despite a rather unconventional education and studying with underqualified teachers,[32] I did well enough in my graduate record exams[33] to apply for graduate studies at Wheaton College. I was accepted and was assigned to assist Samuel Schultz, a noted Old Testament professor who had just published *The Old Testament Speaks*. I was to work for ten hours a week at $1.50 per hour.

Summer Institute of Archaeology

During the summer of 1960 I was able to attend a six-week Institute of Archaeology at Brandeis University. Joining me from Shelton College was Roy Honeywell and also Bob Vannoy, a Shelton grad who had gone to Faith Theological Seminary. Among the other students were Jewish rabbis, a Catholic priest, Walter Kaiser, Frederic Bush, and Donald Madvig. Fred and Don were from Fuller Theological Seminary, where they had been students of William Sanford Lasor, who in 1941 became Cyrus Gordon's second PhD student.[34]

Besides the stimulating course offered by Gordon, there was a course on Sumerian literature taught by Samuel Noah Kramer of the University of Pennsylvania. Sam and Cyrus had been fellow students at Penn.[35] Kramer had just translated an important Sumerian tablet on the death of Dumuzi (Akkadian Tammuz), which proved that instead of Inanna (Ishtar) raising him from the dead as most scholars believed, the goddess had sent her ungrateful consort as her substitute to the Netherworld. Kramer was so pleased with my paper on "Cultic Clues in Canticles" that he encouraged me to have it published.

A Neophyte Instructor (1960 to 1961)

I was prepared to go to Wheaton College where I hoped to be with a young lady from Hawaii whom I had met through mutual friends on my

---

32. I was quite unaware that the New Jersey Board of Education had in 1954 declared that Shelton's faculty was "underpaid and undertrained."

33. I scored 97.5 percentile on the quantitative test and 99+ percentile on the verbal test; I scored 89.5 in the natural sciences, 92.5 in the humanities, and 95 in social sciences.

34. Cyrus Gordon's first PhD student in 1948 had been G. Douglas Young.

35. Cyrus H. Gordon, *The Pennsylvania Tradition of Semitics* (Atlanta, Georgia: Scholars Press, 1986).

way to Shelton College on Labor Day weekend in 1958 (see Excursus F), when a crisis arose at Shelton College. Not only had the president Dr. Murray resigned, but Dr. Banta, the dean was moving on to Tennessee Temple Schools. Then Dr. Paul, who had succeeded him as the dean, accepted an offer to head the Philosophy Department at Central College in Pella, Iowa. Moreover Gordon Tweeten, my Greek instructor, had resigned. This did not surprise me as he had often complained about not receiving his paycheck from the college.[36]

At this juncture Dr. Paul asked me to return to the college to teach in Mr. Tweeten's stead, an offer that other faculty members advised me to decline. But I was led to accept the challenge. Though there were other instructors who also had only a bachelor's degree, I would be the only one who had not had any graduate work. This would often mean staying up all night to prepare, sometimes for two nights in a row, and once for three nights in a row!

To distance myself from former classmates who were now my students I asked them in public to address me from now on as "Mr. Yamauchi" instead of as "Ed." I was to be paid $1,404 per semester plus free room and board. I had a choice bedroom on the second floor of the manor facing the entrance.

I was asked to teach the following classes: New Testament Survey (2 hours), Beginning Classical Greek (4 hours), Intermediate Greek (3 hours) and the Greek text of Herodotus (2 hours). I aimed to challenge the best students, but also gave help to those who struggled. I had students not only translate from Greek to English but also from English to Greek. I had but two students in the class on Herodotus, but the study of this Greek historian began my interest in the Persians and the

---

36. Shelton College had been operating at a loss. In 1959, a lifeline appeared in the offer of a developer who wished to buy 1,000 acres of Skylands for a million dollars, but the borough vetoed the sale. In 1964 McIntire moved Shelton College from Ringwood into the Admiral Hotel in Cape May, a resort town on the south Jersey shore. In 1965 the state of New Jersey revoked Shelton's right to grant degrees. In 1971, McIntire purchased a resort property at Cape Canaveral for a million dollars and moved Shelton College there. He acquired permission from the state of Florida to grant degrees. Then in 1979 McIntire moved the college back to Cape May, but the state ruled that Florida's approval could not overrule New Jersey's denial of Shelton's right to grant degrees. McIntire appealed this verdict in lower courts but lost. In 1985 the Supreme Court refused to hear his appeal. In 1992 Shelton College finally closed.

Dr. Arthur Steele, a graduate of Faith Theological Seminary, who was president of Shelton College from 1962 to 1965 started Clearwater Christian College in 1966 near Tampa, Florida. Among its faculty was Dr. Ralph Beich, who had taught at Shelton. Because of a decline in enrollment, the college closed in 2015.

Scythians. I had 41 freshmen in the New Testament Survey class. By assigning them seats, I learned all of their names.

Once I gave this class a quiz of 87 completion questions. A young Chinese student from Malaysia Bob Chua finished first in thirteen minutes and got all but three answers correct![37] Another outstanding student in this class was Swee Hwa Quek, the son of a prominent Bible Presbyterian pastor in Singapore.[38] Other exceptional students were Richard Eldred[39] and Robert Hassert.[40]

During 1960 to1961 while Mel Dahl took a leave of absence, Ralph Beich who had been studying at Brandeis came to Shelton to teach the Semitics and Old Testament courses. He had a heavy load of seventeen hours per semester. He left his wife and children back on their farm in Wisconsin. Ralph eventually earned his PhD at Brandeis in 1963.

---

37. Bob Chua transferred to Brandeis University while I was in grad school there. He earned his PhD from Harvard and returned to Malaysia to teach there. But he found his status as a Christian teacher untenable in the Muslim environment there, so he returned to the US and went into banking.

38. Swee Hwa Quek went on to Faith Theological Seminary and earned his PhD under F. F. Bruce at Manchester University. His dissertation was on "Adam and Christ, An Exegetical Study of the Pauline Analogy in the Light of the History of Interpretation." He returned to pastor the Zion Bible Presbyterian Church in Singapore. He also served as the Dean of the Biblical Graduate School of Theology where I taught for a week in 1996.

39. Dick Eldred became a beloved professor of world history at Nyack College.

40. Bob Hassert earned an MA at Brandeis University, then a PhD at the University of Chicago, writing a dissertation on the Late Bronze pottery of Palestine and Syria. He participated in Chicago's expeditions to Iran. Others from Shelton with whom I had contact in later years include Lin Crowe who served on the ministerial staff of the Tenth Presbyterian Church in Philadelphia and Janet Rohler who worked at *Christianity Today* when it was based in Washington, DC.

Figure 24. Ralph Beich

S.I.L.

In the summer of 1961, I studied at the Summer Institute of Linguistics, sponsored by Wycliffe Bible Translators[41] at the University of Oklahoma in Norman. I took courses in anthropology, phonetics and phonemics, the study of which sounds are significant in any given language. The aim of Wycliffe has been to analyze all the unwritten languages in the world and to translate the Bible into them.

---

41. Wycliffe Bible Translators was founded by W. Cameron Townsend, a missionary to Guatemala in 1942. He had founded S.I.L. in 1934 to train missionaries in linguistics. Their missionaries completed the 500th translation in 2000.

I worked with a Comanche informant and was able to correctly identify the phonemes in this language. One very useful technique I learned for recording the data was the use of Remington Rand punch cards.[42] These cards had holes punched around their periphery. By assigning values such as parts of speech or consonants to each hole, one could then notch the marked hole and by running a knitting needle through the desired category cause all the cards with that value to drop out of a stack.[43]

We had the privilege of having Kenneth Pike, the great linguist at the University of Michigan demonstrate how he could learn an unknown language. It was at this session that I got to know Robert Longacre, a graduate of Faith Theological Seminary who would use discourse analysis to analyze the biblical story of Joseph. And it was here that I got to know Joe and Barbara Grimes, who after teaching at Cornell University, would translate the Bible into Hawaiian Pidgin.

While at this institute, I received two important letters. The first was from my draft board, directing me to get a physical. I was judged to be fit for the military draft. I was fortunate that my number did not turn up during the years that I was eligible for the draft. The second letter informed me that I had been accepted for graduate studies at Brandeis University.

---

42. The cards were 3 1/2 inches by 7 1/2 inches with 110 holes around the periphery.

43. I used this technique later in writing my PhD dissertation. I taught this to Fred Bush, who in turn taught it to Jack Sasson.

Chapter 12

Brandeis University

(1961 to 1964)

Brandeis University

BRANDEIS UNIVERSITY IS A unique institution. It was funded by the Jewish community, including Albert Einstein, as a nonsectarian undergraduate and graduate university in 1948 in Waltham, nine miles west of Boston. Because of the infusion of funds and talented professors, it soon achieved a distinguished rank with many notable faculty and alumni.[1]

The school was named after Louis Brandeis, the first Jewish Supreme Court justice. A bronze statue of the justice is located in the middle of the campus. Signifying its ecumenical openness are three chapels, one for Jews, one for Catholics and one for Protestants. Kosher and non-Kosher meals are served. Its Department of Near Eastern and Judaic Studies was one of the first graduate programs in Jewish studies. The university's Rose Art Museum is a small building which has displayed many priceless masterpieces.[2]

---

1. Among the former, were the psychologist Abraham Maslow and the political philosopher Herbert Marcuse, whose student Angela Davis (class of 1965) became a prominent activist. Among current faculty, Anita Hill has been very much in public view. Leonard Bernstein and Elizabeth Roosevelt served as visiting faculty.

2. To earn additional funds I worked as an attendant at the Rose Museum, opening and closing the museum and counting the number of visitors.

AN ASIAN AMERICAN ANCIENT HISTORIAN AND BIBLICAL SCHOLAR

Cyrus H. Gordon

Cyrus Herzl Gordon, who has been called a "Giant among Scholars,"[3] was born in 1908 in Philadelphia. His father Benjamin L. Gordon, who came from Lithuania, was a physician. Cyrus was a linguistic prodigy. He learned Hebrew at the age of five. He studied Greek and Latin in high school and continued his studies in Hebrew at the Jewish Gratz College. He entered the University of Pennsylvania at the age of sixteen and earned his PhD shortly before his twenty-second birthday![4] His dissertation was on "The Rabbinic Exegesis in the Vulgate of Proverbs."

At Penn, he was especially indebted to James A. Montgomery, an Episcopalian priest, who had written the definitive work on the Aramaic incantation bowls from Nippur.[5] He studied Assyriology under Ephraim Speiser, a Jewish scholar who was later to become Gordon's academic enemy. He studied Sumerian with George Barton, Old Persian with Roland G. Kent and Sanskrit with W. Norman Browne.

Gordon also took classes at Dropsie College. There he studied the Talmud under Solomon Zeitlin. His most important teacher was the demanding Max Margolis. On his first day in class where different versions of the Old Testament were to be discussed, Margolis assigned Gordon the Peshitta. But Gordon protested that he did not know Syriac. Margolis growled, "Where do you think you are? In kindergarten? Go home and learn Syriac."[6] Gordon recalled, "He would fire a half verse of the Hebrew Bible at a student. If the student could not tell in which book of the Bible it occurred, Margolis would bark at the student, 'Go to hell!' If the next student could not locate it either, Margolis would say, 'There's room for you there, too.'"

Gordon recounts, "One summer I decided to learn French, Italian, Spanish, Portuguese, Dutch, and Dano-Norwegian by myself, through studying each one of them one hour per day during the three-month

---

3. Gary A. Rendsburg, "Cyrus H. Gordon (1908–2001): A Giant among Scholars," *Jewish Quarterly Review* 92 (2001), 137–143.

4. Gordon published his first scholarly article at the age of twenty-one.

5. Nippur in southern Iraq was the site of the earliest excavation by the University of Pennsylvania in 1888 of an ancient Mesopotamian city.

6. Cyrus H. Gordon, *Forgotten Scripts:* (New York, New York: Basic Books, 1968), 142.

vacation."⁷ Gordon felt that if he could learn a language without an instructor, so could his students also.⁸

From 1931 to 1935 Gordon travelled in the Near East as a fellow of the American Schools of Oriental Research. He worked with all the noted archaeologists in the field, including J. D. S. Pendlebury at Amarna in Egypt, Flinders Petrie at Tell elAjjul in Palestine, Leonard Woolley at Ur and with Speiser at Tepe Gawra in Iraq and W. F. Albright at Tell Beit Mirsim in Palestine. He accompanied Nelson Glueck on his surveys in Jordan.

He lived among the Yezidis, the maligned and persecuted "Devil Worshippers" in northern Iraq.⁹ He became acquainted with the Mandaeans, a unique Gnostic sect in southern Iraq and with Lady E. S. Drower, the wife of a British diplomat, who learned Mandaic and translated many of the religious texts of the Mandaeans.¹⁰

From 1936 to 1939 Gordon taught as Albright's assistant at Johns Hopkins University. But when Albright tried to discourage the younger scholar from writing a grammar of Ugaritic, Gordon moved on to Smith College where he copied cuneiform texts and taught the Hebrew Bible to the women of the college.

During World War II, Gordon served as a cryptographer for the army, a skill which he later used in deciphering ancient texts. He also taught soldiers colloquial Arabic and Farsi (modern Persian). Upon his discharge he began teaching for a decade (1946 to 1956) at Dropsie College, where he began to attract evangelical students because of his rejection of the regnant Documentary Hypothesis of the Pentateuch.¹¹

---

7. Cyrus H. Gordon, *A Scholar's Odyssey* (Atlanta, Georgia: Society of Biblical Literature, 2000), 18. Gordon adopted Margolis's inductive manner but not his abrasive style. One had to be prepared to translate and to comment on a text in class. Once when a student, who shall not be named, was not prepared, Gordon dismissed the class in disgust. I would have nightmares of coming to class unprepared!

8. Gordon, *Forgotten Scripts*, 137.

9. Cyrus H. Gordon, *Lands of the Cross and Crescent* (Ventnor, New Jersey: Ventnor Publications, 1948), 103, reports: "The Yezidis consider God as the good principle, and since He is incapable of evil, there is no point in worshipping Him. Harm comes from Satan, who must therefore be propitiated." They believe that at the Day of Judgment Satan will be restored to his original position as the chief of the angels.

10. I met Lady Drower in England and got her to autograph the Mandaic dictionary she had co-authored with Rudolph Macuch.

11. Cyrus H. Gordon, "Higher Critics and Forbidden Fruit," *Christianity Today* 4.4 (November 23, 1959), 3–6.

Then in 1956, he was able to move to Brandeis University,[12] where he was allowed to establish a unique Mediterranean Studies Department which incorporated both the Near Eastern and Aegean worlds.[13] Gordon's genius lay in his ability to draw attention to striking parallels between Homer and the Old Testament.[14] This was a small department which featured faculty who were his own students and also distinguished visiting professors. From Gordon himself I took courses on the Hebrew Bible, the monastic sayings in Coptic[15] and Ugaritic, a language written in a unique alphabetic cuneiform script. The texts written between 1400–1200 BC were found at Ugarit.[16] They provide both literary parallels with the Psalms and illuminate the Canaanite myths of Baal and Astarte mentioned in the Old Testament.[17] Gordon was the foremost authority on this important corpus.[18]

---

12. Gordon was the first American-born, American-trained Jewish Bible scholar to gain a tenured position at a university, albeit a Jewish-sponsored school. Other Jewish scholars, such as Nelson Glueck, H. L. Ginsberg, Robert Gordis, and Harry Orlinsky, taught at rabbinical seminaries, namely Hebrew Union College and the Jewish Theological Seminary.

13. Near Eastern and Classical studies are usually taught in separate departments. An exception is the department at Penn State University which combines Near Eastern, Biblical, and Classical studies.

14. Cyrus H. Gordon, *Homer and the Bible* (Ventnor, New Jersey: Ventnor Publications, 1961).

15. Coptic is the Egyptian language used by the early Christians. It is written in Greek letters with a few additional letters derived from the late Demotic script. It was Gordon's student, Loren Fisher (Brandeis, 1969), who at Claremont taught Coptic to James Robinson, the editor of the Coptic Nag Hammadi Library.

16. In 1928, a peasant's plow uncovered a Late Bronze tomb at Minet el-Beida on the Syrian coast across from Cyprus. Excavations at the nearby Ras Shamra uncovered the ancient city of Ugarit.

17. See Peter C. Craigie, *Ugarit and the Old Testament* (Grand Rapids, Michigan: Eerdmans, 1982).

18. Gordon's *Ugaritic Grammar* was written while he was in Uppsala, and despite the outbreak of war in Europe in 1939, he managed to send the manuscript by the Vatican's diplomatic pouch to Rome, where it was published in 1940 by the Pontifical Biblical Institute. Albright and many others praised its publication. See Mark S. Smith, *Untold Stories: The Bible and Ugaritic Studies in the Twentieth Century* (Peabody, Massachusetts: Hendrickson, 2001), 33. See also Cyrus H. Gordon, *Ugaritic Literature: A Comprehensive Translation of the Poetic and Prose Texts* (Rome, Italy: Pontificium Institutum Biblicum, 1949), idem, Ugaritic Textbook (Rome, Italy: Pontificium Institutum Biblicum, 1965).

Faculty

Many of the grad students in this department, including myself, took advantage of the National Defense Foreign Language Act, which provided us with free tuition and a stipend of $1500 if we took six hours of Arabic per semester.[19] Our Arabic teacher was Joseph de Somogyi of Harvard University, a Hungarian Lutheran scholar, who never tired of reminding our class that he was the disciple of the Hungarian Jewish scholar, Ignace Goldziher, considered to be the founder of modern Islamic studies. De Somogyi was a short man who said that he knew T. E. Lawrence (of Arabia) at Oxford, who was shorter than he was. Lawrence was only 5 ft. 5 in, unlike Peter O'Toole who portrayed him in the film "Lawrence of Arabia," who was 6 ft 2 in. tall! We studied the Arabic texts of the Qur'ān the Hadith Traditions and *Alf Layla wa Laylatun* "The Thousand and One Nights."

Figure 25. Arabic class: kneeling EMY and Gordon Newby; back row: George Giacumakis, Joseph DeSomogyi, Jack Sasson, Fred Bush, and Harry Hoffner

19. During the summer of 1962 George Giacumakis and I took a Colloquial Arabic class at Harvard, taught jointly by an Israeli and a Jordanian. One of the members of the class was Dr. Calvin Plimpton, the president of the American University of Beirut. I unwisely stayed up late at night cramming for the final exam, with the result that sleepiness overcame me during the exam, so I got a rather disgraceful C for the course!

Many of the basic courses were taught by Dwight Young,[20] a graduate of Dallas Theological Seminary. We studied the Akkadian cuneiform texts of Hammurabi's law code and his letters and the Egyptian hieroglyphic tales of Sinuhe and the Shipwrecked Sailor with Young.[21] He was a specialist in the Coptic texts of the famous monk Shenoute.[22] A course on Ancient Egyptian History taught by Young was the only history course I had in graduate school.

We studied the Mishnah, the rabbinic compilation which preceded the Talmud, with Baruch Levine,[23] a rabbi, who later taught at New York University and wrote the Jewish Publication Society's commentary on Leviticus. I also studied Aramaic and Syriac [24] under Levine.

Among visiting scholars was Benjamin Mazar, the foremost Israeli archaeologist and president of Hebrew University. I wrote a research paper on the Philistines for him. We were privileged to learn from Shemaryahu Talmon, the leading Israeli scholar on the Dead Sea Scrolls. Ernest Lacheman of Wellesley College taught a course on the Nuzi texts, which some of the other students took.

One visiting professor was Erwin Goodenough of Yale University, who was an authority on Philo. who was famed for his thirteen-volume study of Jewish artistic symbols which indicated borrowing of pagan

---

20. As a young Marine, Dwight Young took part in the battle for Okinawa.

21. Later Young felt he was not given the freedom to teach the courses he wanted to teach and was not being compensated as he deserved. He left for a few years to teach at Cornell University but did come back to Brandeis to teach—not in the Mediterranean Studies Department—but in the Department of Near Eastern and Judaic Studies Department. There must have eventually been a reconciliation, because Gordon contributed an essay to the Festschrift in Young's honor.

Students from the Near Eastern and Judaic Studies Department (N.E.J.S.) took courses in the Mediterranean Department, and vice versa. One student in our Akkadian class was Tzvi Abusch, a graduate of Yeshiva University, who later earned his PhD at Harvard. Abusch, who returned to teach at Brandeis, became the foremost authority on Assyrian magical texts. Another N.E.J.S. student in our Ugaritic class Barry Margolis later Hebraized his name as Baruch Margalit. An evangelical student in N.E.J.S. was Thomas E. McComiskey, who taught the Old Testament at Trinity Evangelical Divinity School and wrote commentaries on the Minor Prophets.

22. My doctoral student, Darlene Brooks Hedstrom, took part in Yale University's excavation of this monk's famous monastery.

23. Levine had just received his PhD at Brandeis in 1962, writing on Ugaritic survivals in the Mishnah.

24. Syriac was a late Aramaic dialect written in a distinctive script. It was used by the Christians in Mesopotamia. Roy Hayden, who had his own offset printing press, took out of print German grammars of Coptic and Syriac, and printed copies, which he sold to his fellow students at bargain prices.

motifs even by rabbis.²⁵ He was the teacher of Samuel Sandmel, the Jewish New Testament scholar at Hebrew Union College. Gordon in his memoir mentions an incident in this class which I do not recall but which Walt Kaiser remembers: "Goodenough loved to shock 'true believers,' both Christian and Jewish. The conservative Jewish students put up with his provocative antics, albeit not gladly. Their Christian counterparts proved not as tolerant, and one of them (Edwin Yamauchi, who has turned out to be a very productive and versatile scholar) walked out of class in a huff. I did not understand Goodenough's abrasive attitude until he told me one day that he had been raised as a fundamentalist but had subsequently achieved secular enlightenment. Thereafter, his pleasure in life was tormenting 'true believers.'"²⁶ I do remember Goodenough one day in class expressing his chagrin that his M.I.T. trained son had become an evangelical believer!

Linear A and Linear B

In 1900, Arthur Evans began excavating at Knossos in north central Crete. He uncovered a splendid palace which revealed a new civilization which he dubbed "Minoan," after the legendary King Minos of Greek myth. He also found two sets of clay tablets written in syllabic scripts, which he called Linear A and Linear B. The former was used by the Minoans between 1800 to 1450 BC. The largest cache of Linear A tablets was found at Hagia Triada ("Holy Trinity"), a villa in south central Crete. Linear B tablets, which are dated 1450 to 1200 BC were also found on the Greek mainland, most notably at Pylos in the southwestern Peloponnese. Carl Blegen of the University of Cincinnati uncovered a palace there which he named after the Homeric king Nestor.²⁷

In 1952, Michael Ventris, a British architect, deciphered Linear B as the earliest form of Greek, a decipherment which has been universally accepted. The texts primarily relate to commodities of the palace

---

25. I received a set of these folio volumes from Eleanor Vogel, the secretary of Nelson Glueck.

26. Gordon, *A Scholar's Odyssey*, 98.

27. In 2015, Jack Davis and his wife Sharon Stocker from the University of Cincinnati returned to Pylos. They have made spectacular discoveries including an intact warrior's grave and two collapsed *tholoi* ("beehive tombs"), which confirm strong Minoan influence upon the Mycenaeans.

economy, but there are also a few religious texts. Many proper names are similar to those found in the Homeric epics, the Iliad and the Odyssey.

Since similar signs are used in both Linear A and Linear B, there was little doubt that two different languages were involved. Some scholars guessed that Linear A represented Hittite, but Gordon began to recognize some groups of signs as revealing Semitic words. His first identification of a few words appeared in an article published in *Antiquity* in 1957, followed by a series of other articles in various journals. Then the publication in 1961 of photographs of Linear A inscriptions on clay tablets and stone objections by W. C. Brice led to a breakthrough. Late bilingual Eteocretan inscriptions in Greek letters also indicated the survival of a Semitic dialect in eastern Crete. In April 1962, Gordon released to the public his decipherment of Linear A, as a Semitic language, an achievement which was heralded in the *New York Times* and other papers. That decipherment, while accepted by his students and others, has been questioned by other scholars. One of his severest critics was Emmett Bennett, the scholar who published the Pylos Linear B tablets.

Now, it seemed that Gordon had shown particular favor to two of the sixteen graduate students in the department, to Harry Hoffner and to myself. We were the two who were asked to give lectures to the class, and we were the two who were asked to write to *Christianity Today* in response to an article by W. F. Albright. Harry knew the Hebrew Bible better than others. I may have been favored because I knew Homer better than others. Gordon asked me to speak on Greek Letters Day at the Orthodox Greek Cathedral in Boston on "Homer and the Bible."

In December 1962, as I was finishing my first semester as a master's student, Gordon asked me to teach during the next semester a course on Linear A and Linear B. There would be no monetary compensation, only the honor of being listed as an instructor. This was no easy task as there was no textbook on these scripts. A major reference book on Linear B had been published by John Chadwick and Michael Ventris. But I had to rely on Gordon's class notes and articles for Linear A.[28] I had to copy the texts by hand and have them mimeographed. Among the nine students I had were David Owen, Jack Sasson and Daphne Andronikos, a graduate of the University of Athens, who knew far more about Aegean art and archaeology than I did.

---

28. Gordon later published *Evidence for the Minoan Language* (Ventnor, New Jersey: Ventnor Publications, 1965).

Figure 26. With Cyrus Gordon

Mandaic Incantation Texts

Following the example of his mentor James Montgomery at Penn, Gordon had from the beginning of his career copied and translated magic bowls in Aramaic and Mandaic which he found in museums in Istanbul, Baghdad and Tehran. These bowls, which were inscribed in Aramaic for Jews[29], in Syriac for Christians[30] and in Mandaic for Mandaeans have been found in numerous sites in Iraq and southwestern Iran. They are generally dated c. AD 600. They were meant to protect the families from demons, some of which like Lilith are portrayed as bound in chains. Before the discovery of the Dead Sea Scrolls in 1947 and apart from the Nash papyrus, the Aramaic bowls preserved the earliest known citations of Hebrew Scriptures.

I chose to write my dissertation on the Mandaic bowls, which are the earliest texts of the Mandaeans, the sole surviving Gnostic sect in the world. Mandaic, which is written in a unique script which somewhat resembles Syriac, is a late Aramaic dialect which most closely

---

29. Charles Isbell wrote his dissertation (1973) on the Aramaic bowls.
30. Victor Hamilton wrote his dissertation (1970) on the Syriac bowls.

resembles the Aramaic of the Babylonian Talmud. As there was no course given in Mandaic, I had to learn the language on my own, using Theodor Nöldeke's *Mandäische Grammatik* (1875), which had been printed in archaic Germanic font.[31]

The Mandaeans had earlier in the twentieth century been the subject of great interest, as their texts had been used by the great German New Testament scholar Rudolf Bultmann as a basis for a presumed pre-Christian Gnosticism which had influenced John and Paul. But interest in these texts had waned with the discovery of the Nag Hammadi Coptic texts in 1945 and of the Dead Sea Scrolls in 1947.

My dissertation reproduced all the 51 known Mandaic bowl texts which had been published, many of them with French and German translations. Gordon himself had published ten of these bowls. I also included a long lead amulet, which M. Lidzbarski had dated to AD 400. I reproduced the Mandaic text by using a Hebrew typewriter and added English translations. I analyzed the grammar and phonology of Mandaic and compiled a glossary of words. I provided an extensive bibliography of ancient magic and a few illustrations. Members of my dissertation committee were Gordon, de Somogyi, and Carleton Hodge, a linguist. I completed the 500-page dissertation in April 1964.

William W. Hallo, the curator of the Yale Babylonian Collection, who allowed me to copy and translate a large Mandaic bowl, which I published in *Berytus*,[32] encouraged me to have my dissertation published in the monograph series of the American Oriental Society,[33] which at that time was housed at Yale's Sterling Library.[34] *Mandaic Incantation Texts* has been used as a textbook at Harvard University and Hebrew University, and has been reprinted by Gorgias Press. While

---

31. This was a very rare book which had originally been owned by James Montgomery and which was kindly loaned to me by William H. Rossell, Gordon's third PhD student at Dropsie (1949). Rossell wrote *A Handbook of Aramaic Magical Texts* (Ringwood, New Jersey: Shelton College, 1953).

32. Harald Ingholt of Yale University invited me to have this Mandaic bowl text published in *Berytus* in 1967.

33. This series includes monographs by W. F. Albright, Millar Burrows, Albrecht Goetze, Moshe Greenburg, Roland G. Kent, and Franz Rosenthal. After the publication of *Mandaic Incantation Texts*, I received congratulatory letters from Lady Drower and from Rudolf Macuch (Berlin). Jacob Neusner wrote that his mentor, Morton Smith of Columbia University, was interested in seeing a copy. Smith later wrote a review of the volume.

34. In the printed version of the dissertation (1967) I included the Yale Mandaic bowl, which I published in 1966.

I was writing my dissertation, G. Ernest Wright of Harvard notified Gordon of an unpublished Aramaic bowl, which Gordon entrusted to me to copy and translate.[35]

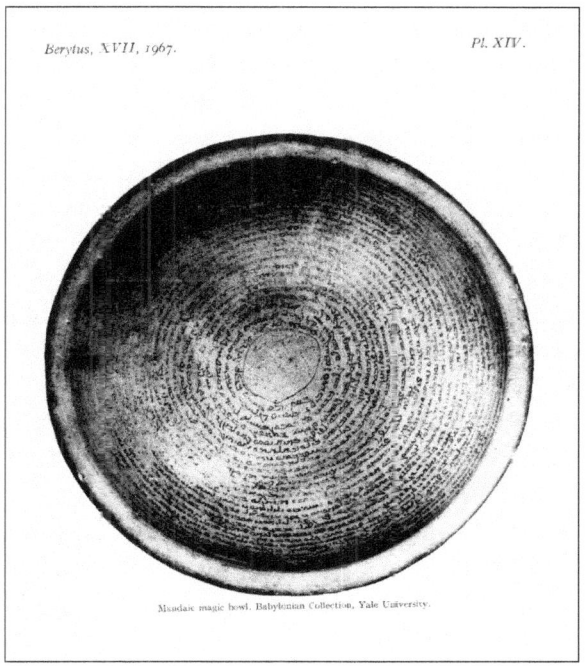

Figure 27. Mandaic Magic Bowl published in *Berytus*

A Companion for Life

In the fall of 1958, I had taken the train from Los Angeles to get to Shelton College in New Jersey. En route I stopped at Chicago on the Labor Day weekend to meet an old friend from the Christian Youth Center, Alice Araki, who was now married to Leonard Tanishima, a graduate of Asbury Theological Seminary from Japan. I was met at the Dearborn Station by Alice's friend at Wheaton College, Kimie Honda, who was unknown to me (see Excursus E).

---

35. I published the Aramaic bowl text in the *Journal of the American Oriental Society* in 1965. The chair of the Hebraic Studies Department at Rutgers University persuaded a wealthy donor, Sol Feldman, to purchase the bowl for Rutgers in 1967.

She recognized me as someone from Hawaii as I was wearing a colorful blue Aloha shirt. She had heard good things about me from Alice and had read my article in *His* magazine.[36] She offered to take me around Chicago that weekend. We went from north to south, starting at Moody Church, the Art Institute, and then the museums in the south. I was impressed with her stamina and was captivated by her smile.

Her Japanese name Ki-mi-e, with the accent on the second syllable means "princess"; she does not have an English first name. After marriage she often jokes when signing her married name, that her maiden name Honda, was a simple two-syllable name, but now her new name is a four-syllable name Yamauchi, with the accent on the third syllable.

Kimi and I fell in love at our first encounter, but our continued romance over the next four years was largely by correspondence as we were far apart in New Jersey and in Illinois. We corresponded weekly, she in handwritten letters and I in typed letters. It is from the carbon copies of my letters that I have been able to reconstruct my years at Shelton College. I did keep a diary but my sparse hand-written entries provided little information.

In 1961 to 1962, while I was pursuing my master's degree at Brandeis, she completed a master's degree in education at Columbia University's Teachers College. She student taught in the Bronx, where her students said to her amusement, "Miss Honda, you have a funny accent." Kimi worked in the office of the president, Dwight Eisenhower, helping him send out his Christmas cards. She was able to help at the famed Riverside Church on Sundays.

During this year (1961 to 1962) I stayed in Auburndale with two older bachelors, Wally Sims and Dr. Marlin Kreider, who were members of Park Street Church. I paid only $50 per month and did a few hours of housework for room and board.

Kimi and I were finally wed on August 31, 1962, at the College Church in Wheaton. Presiding over the ceremony was her teacher, Dr. Kenneth Kantzer. His message was so inspiring that I forgot the marriage vows I had memorized! Kimi had not been able to afford the costs of travel back to Hawaii since she left the Islands in 1952 and none of her family could travel to attend the wedding. But she had many friends from the college and Scripture Press, where she had worked in attendance. Kimi had bought an inexpensive wedding dress from the

---

36. "When Trouble Comes: A Study in James," *His* (March, 1958), was my first published article. It was later reprinted by the American Tract Society.

bargain basement of Macy's in Herald Square. Her bridesmaid was June Fujimoto, a Wheaton student from Hawaii who had attended Makiki Christian Church with her.

My mother was able to come to the wedding and my eight-year old sister Alice served as a junior bridesmaid. My only friends who attended were from Shelton College. They included Ralph Beich as my best man, and Philip Heng and Bill Broadwick (who had married Carole Ross) as my groomsmen. Bonnie Rigg from the Gospel Team was the soloist.

After the wedding, my mother and sister accompanied us as far as Niagara Falls. We spent our honeymoon at Sandwich on Cape Cod. We lived in a small apartment over a liquor store in West Newton. Kimi found work at the Brandeis bookstore.

Figure 28. Ed and Kimi, wedding portrait

Ministries and Presentations

We attended a small Presbyterian church in Waltham, pastored by Dr. Wyeth Willard, who had once served as the assistant to the president of Wheaton College. I taught an adult Sunday School class and we helped with the young people at the church. In addition, I led a home Bible study in Waltham and another Bible study for students from Japan in Cambridge. I spoke at a banquet for international students at M.I.T.

There were also many opportunities to speak at other area churches especially on the subject of "The Dead Sea Scrolls." I spoke to the collegiate and young adult groups at Park Street on three occasions. Once I accompanied them on a winter retreat to a ski resort near the border between Vermont and New Hampshire. They paid for a free skiing lesson. Skiing seemed like a lot of fun, but I forgot how to stop and twisted my ankle as I fell!

I spoke at the Ruggles Street Church, and at a Presbyterian church in Newburyport, where the famed British evangelist George Whitefield's remains were buried. Once I appeared at a Presbyterian church in Whitinsville, where I was not expected until the following week. That Sunday I was supposed to be at the Cornerstone Baptist Church in Boston 30 miles away!

Academics

I presented papers on "Slaves of God" and "Qumran, Colosse, and Nag Hammadi" at meetings of the Evangelical Theological Society. These papers were later published.[37] In January 1964 I presented a paper, "Tammuz and the Bible"[38] at Union Theological Seminary before the Society of Biblical Literature. Just before I spoke, I had a brief chat with W. F. Albright about a paper he had written on this subject years before. After I had delivered my paper, I received a positive comment from Moshe Greenberg. H. L. Ginsberg thanked me for the paper. I had ridden to New York City with three professors from Gordon Conwell Theological Seminary. When we got into the car which had been parked on the street, it would not start. An inspection revealed the problem: during the night, thieves had stolen the battery!

---

37. The former was published in the *Bulletin of the Evangelical Theological Society*, the latter in *Bibliotheca Sacra*.

38. This paper, which was reviewed for me by Samuel Noah Kramer, was published in the *Journal of Biblical Literature*.

Job Offers[39]

Even before finishing my course work or my dissertation, I had received a letter from Dean Leonard W. Levy informing me that I had been appointed as an Instructor in the Mediterranean Studies Department for $7,000. I would teach courses in Homer, Hellenistic subjects, the New Testament, and Gnostic texts.

As I neared the completion of my PhD, I received letters about teaching positions from Wheaton College[40] and a number of other Christian colleges.[41] In December 1963 I attended the Archaeological Institute of America conference at Pittsburgh. I had sent in my credentials but had not arranged for any interviews. In a casual encounter at breakfast I met William A. MacDonald, the noted authority on Mycenaean archaeology, who taught at at the University of Minnesota. MacDonald had studied under Gordon at Johns Hopkins University. He had asked Gordon for graduates who could teach Hebrew at Minnesota. He remarked that the university had about a hundred pre-ministerial students, some of whom needed Hebrew. He said that it was "ridiculous" that the University had to use professors from Bethel Seminary to teach such courses. After receiving my c.v., he had his school offer me a one-year contract for $8,200 to teach Hebrew, Greek, and also Japanese.

Then I was approached at the same conference in Pittsburgh by Professor Peter Charanis of Rutgers the State University of New Jersey. He was interested in my teaching courses on the ancient Near East and Greece. The offer from Rutgers was for a three-year term which would be renewable for another three years. After I had obtained a release from the contract I had signed with Brandeis,[42] I accepted the position at Rutgers. My initial salary was $7,700 with the possibility of applying for a $1,000 summer research grant. I would have to teach but two courses or six hours per semester.

---

39. Graduates of the Mediterranean Studies with our knowledge of Arabic could apply for positions with the CIA and the NSA which paid $8500 per year.

40. Harry Hoffner who had been teaching at Wheaton College had just received a three-year appointment to teach at Brandeis.

41. The other colleges from which I received tentative job offers were Ashland in Ohio, Barrington in Rhode Island, Central in Iowa, Eastern Nazarene in Massachusetts, Huntington in Indiana, Tennessee Temple, and Japan Christian College.

42. The one-year position at Brandeis I had relinquished was given to Fred Bush.

Chapter 13

Rutgers University

(1964 to 1967)

Queens College and New Brunswick Seminary

THE MAIN CAMPUS OF Rutgers University is located in New Brunswick in the center of New Jersey midway between New York City and Philadelphia. Rutgers has two large branch campuses, one in the north at Newark and one in the south at Camden.

Founded as Queen's College in 1766 in honor of King George III's consort, Rutgers is one of only nine schools established before the Revolution. The others include in order of their charters:

1. Harvard University (1636)
2. William and Mary College (1693)
3. Yale University (1701)
4. University of Pennsylvania (1740)
5. Princeton University (1746)
6. Brown University (1764)
7. Columbia University (1764)
8. Dartmouth College (1769)

With the exception of William and Mary, now a Virginia supported public university, the others are private schools renowned for their excellence as "Ivy League" schools.[1]

Queen's College was originally born out of the desire of Dutch Reformed leaders in New Jersey to have their own school rather than merge with the Anglican King's College (which became Columbia University) in New York City. They were led by the energetic Theodore Freylinghausen, a leader of the Great Awakening. Applicants to Queens College had to be able to translate the Latin of Caesar's commentary on the Gallic Wars and Virgil's Aeneid as well as the Greek text of the Gospels into English. Students were strictly forbidden "to frequent taverns, keep cards, dice, or gaming fowls, or liquor in their lodgings, or engage in fighting or riots."[2]

The desire to train American ministers rather than to import Dutch ministers led to the establishment of a seminary in 1784 in New York City.[3] The seminary moved to New Brunswick in 1810. At first all the classes for Queens College and the seminary were held in one building known as Old Queens.

Because of financial problems Queens College closed twice (1795 to 1807, 1816 to 1824). It was the synod of the Dutch churches which enabled the college to reopen, in particular the generosity of Colonel Henry Rutgers, a revolutionary officer after whom the college was renamed in 1825. It was in 1856 that the seminary and the college developed separately with new buildings provided for the former on a hill in the middle of the campus.

Rutgers became the state university of New Jersey in 1945. Like many other early universities, it had an all-male student body until in 1955 it acquired the New Jersey College for Women, which was renamed Douglass College. In 1964 when I was hired Rutgers had 20,000 students, making it the twentieth-largest university in the country.

---

1. This is a term which in the 1930s originally designated a football league, which included Cornell University, founded as a land-grant school in 1865.

2. Richard P. McCormick, *Rutgers: A Bicentennial History* (New Brunswick, New Jersey: Rutgers University Press, 1966), 20.

3. Now affiliated with the Reformed Church in America, it is the oldest Protestant seminary in the United States.

Courses

At Rutgers I was hired for an initial term of three years, with the possibility of a renewal for three additional years. At first, I was given a light load of six hours or two courses per semester, allowing me time to do research. While the library holdings at Rutgers and at the New Brunswick Theological Seminary were limited, the Speer Library at Princeton Theological Seminary was only a half hour drive south.

The upper division history courses I taught were: Near Eastern History, Persian History, Greek and Hellenistic History, and Religions in the Roman Empire. The graduate courses I taught were Problems in Greek History and Topics in Ancient History. I would have 40 to 50 students in the undergraduate courses and only three or less in the graduate courses. As the only graduate history course which I had taken at Brandeis was in Egyptian history, this meant a lot of new course preparation. Often after taking a nap after supper, I would work until 4 or 5 a.m. preparing for classes.

The History Department

The History Department, with sixteen faculty members was the largest department at Rutgers. It was chaired by three distinguished historians while I was there. My first chair was Henry R. Winkler, a British diplomatic historian, who was the editor of *The American Historical Review*. Henry was promoted to the post of provost at Rutgers. A graduate of the University of Cincinnati, he became U.C.'s president in 1977 and saw its transformation from a struggling municipal college into the second largest state university in Ohio.

My second chair was Peter Charanis, who was an outstanding scholar of the Byzantine Empire. He trained about a dozen PhDs in Byzantine studies. Peter, who was born in Lemnos, a Greek island off the west coast of Turkey, understood the "ch" in my name as the Greek letter *chi* as in *Christos* and kept pronouncing my name as Ya-ma-u-ki![4]

My last chair was Richard P. McCormick an outstanding American historian who specialized in the history of New Jersey. He wrote a history of the university as we celebrated its bicentennial in 1966.

---

4. It was the Rutgers IV students who began the practice of calling me "Dr. Y," as they were not sure how to pronounce my name.

Among others in the department were Sidney Ratner an authority on American taxation, Traian Stoianovich a historian of the Balkans, Sam Bailey a Latin American historian with a focus on Argentina, and John Lenaghan who taught the Roman history courses. The Classics Department, which was housed at Douglass College, had Anna Benjamin who had excavated at the Athenian Agora.

Marxist Historians

A decade before I arrived at Rutgers during the Joseph McCarthy hearings a historian at the Newark branch invoked his Fifth Amendment right to refuse to answer whether he had ever been a Communist.[5] His name was Moses Finley (born Finkelstein). Though the university did not wish to fire him, the Trustees intervened and forced him to resign. Finley emigrated to Britain in 1955 and taught at Jesus College at the University of Cambridge. He became such a distinguished historian of the economics of the ancient world that he was knighted![6]

When I was in the department we had three notable Marxist historians. I shared a third-story office under the eaves of Bishop House with Lloyd Gardner, a diplomatic historian. A graduate of the University of Wisconsin, Lloyd published numerous books which were highly critical of American foreign policy. A second Marxist was Warren Susman, a cultural historian, who died in 1985 of a heart attack while addressing the convention of the Organization of American Historians in Minneapolis.

Eugene D. Genovese

By far the most famous (or infamous) Marxist historian in our department was Eugene D. Genovese. A colorful figure with his silk suits and ever-present cigarillo, Gene was proud of his Sicilian heritage and was fiercely independent, not caring a whit for his critics left or right. At the age of fifteen he had joined the Communist Party, but they kicked him out as a nonconformist. He earned his BA at Brooklyn College and his

---

5. In his history of Rutgers, McCormick discusses this controversy in great detail (295–300) without, however, naming Finley.

6. When I was in Cambridge in 1985, I phoned to see if I could meet professor Finley. But he was not available because his wife was ill at that time.

PhD at Columbia University. He had joined the department in 1963, a year before I came.

Then, in the midst of a gubernatorial election in New Jersey, Gene ignited a furious firestorm when in a teach in against the Vietnam War he declared on April 25, 1965, "I do not fear or regret the impending Viet Cong victory in Vietnam, I welcome it." There were many calls for the university to fire him. Cars displayed bumper stickers which read "Rid Rutgers of Reds." But president Mason Gross refused to fire Genovese.

Gene's 1974 book *Roll, Jordan Roll: The World the Slaveholders Made* won the Bancroft Prize, the highest honor given to American historians. After teaching in Canada and at the University of Rochester, Gene moved to Emory University where his wife Elizabeth Fox-Genovese served as the director of Women's Studies. Betsy, a leading feminist scholar, became critical of other feminists. Then she converted to Catholicism. Even more surprising Gene who had been an atheist, also converted. My colleague Michael O'Brien told me that Gene had tried to convert him! Gene gave the McClellan History Lecture at Miami University in February 1989.

In opposition to the traditional scholarly historical associations, which they deemed too dominated by leftwing ideology, the Genoveses formed a new Historical Society in 1998 and published *The Journal of Historical Studies*, which Betsy edited. In a brief post card inviting me to join the society, Gene wrote: "O.K.—you were right, I wrong." He invited me to organize a session at a conference in 2002 on "Reconstruction" in Atlanta. I invited David Weisberg of Hebrew Union College to present a paper in this session. My paper was published in their journal. For their magnum opus (828 pages), *The Mind of the Master* (2005), Gene consulted me concerning biblical references to slavery. The book was dedicated to: Msgr. Richard Lopez, Catholic Archdiocese of Atlanta. Gene and Betsy spoke at a conference a Wheaton College in 1994. Gene became a friend of Mark Noll, an evangelical historian who occupied an endowed chair at the University of Notre Dame.

Figure 29. With Eugene Genovese

I.V.C.F.

I served as the faculty advisor for the InterVarsity Christian Fellowship for Rutgers and Douglass. IV, for short, is an evangelical student movement which began at the University of Cambridge in 1877. After IV was introduced to Canada, it was then brought to the US by Stacey Woods in 1938. The Rutgers and Douglass chapter was a large and active one. I have kept in touch with a number of its alumni.[7]

I went with the students to IV's Hudson House at Nyack on the Palisades cliff for retreats. Once Christian faculty met there to hear Kenneth S. Latourette, the Yale historian who wrote the definitive history of Christian missions.

At a time when the national IV did not yet sponsor work with graduate students, I organized a regular meeting of grads at our home.

---

7. These include Steve Hoffmann who became a professor of Political Science at Taylor University, James Patterson who became the associate dean of the School of Theology and Missions of Union University, and William and Aida Spencer, who became professors at GordonConwell Theological Seminary. The Spencers became leaders in the egalitarian Christians for Biblical Equality organization. Edwina Wright became the first African American woman to earn a PhD in Near Eastern Languages from Harvard University. She went on to teach at Union Theological Seminary in New York City.

This graduate fellowship eventually numbered over forty and developed its own officers.

In 1965 I spoke in April and in November at the graduate forum sponsored by I.V. at Yale University. One of the students I met was a history major, Ron Sider, who would write the influential book, *Rich Christians in an Age of Hunger* (1977) and would begin Evangelicals for Social Action.

Figure 30. IVCF chapter at Rutgers

A New Home and a Son

When we first arrived at Rutgers we rented an apartment on Eleventh Avenue in Highland Park across the Raritan River from New Brunswick. Highland Park was a lovely small town noted for numerous Jewish families and synagogues.

Kimi initially taught a fourth-grade class in New Brunswick. To establish discipline in a rowdy class, she made their ringleader the one in charge of the class when she had to leave it. Later she worked as a secretary for Waldron Hartig, a company in Highland Park. The smoke-filled office was quite uncomfortable for her.

We were then able to buy a brand-new Levitt style Cape Cod house in the suburb of Somerset for $22,000 with the aid of a loan of $2,000 from my mother. On May 2, 1966, we were blessed with the birth of a son Brian Masao Yamauchi at the New Brunswick Hospital.

Ministries and Presentations

When we were in Highland Park, we attended the First Baptist Church, which was pastored by Roger Palms. Roger later became the editor of Billy Graham's *Decision Magazine*.[8] In addition to teaching Sunday School classes, we occasionally sang at the services. The one time Kimi and I sang a duet, I went flat, and she vowed never to sing with me again in public! After moving to Somerset, we attended the New Brunswick Bible Church.

I spoke at the university's Kirkpatrick Chapel and also arranged to bring down from Harvard Law School, Sir Norman Anderson, a British authority on Islamic Law, who spoke on the Resurrection of Jesus. I was invited to give a lecture on Mandaic magic incantations at the Oriental Institute of the University of Chicago.[9] I gave a talk at the New Brunswick Theological Seminary on "The Origins of Gnosticism." I also spoke on the Dead Sea Scrolls to the Princeton "Old Guard." I delivered the John W. Ritter lecture at the Evangelical School of Theology in Myerstown, Pennsylvania and gave lectures at Calvin College and Calvin Theological Seminary.

The New Testament scholar Earle Ellis, who was then teaching at New Brunswick Theological Seminary, helped me start a weekly Bible discussion for a small group of faculty that included William Fortenbaugh of Classics. Bill was an authority on Aristotle.

I spoke at the Calvary Baptist Church and at the Marble Collegiate Church in New York City. Earle Ellis attended the latter, which was pastored by Rev. Norman Vincent Peale noted for his *Power of Positive Thinking*. I also had the opportunity to speak to a synagogue, to the Jewish faculty group, to a Jewish Community Center, and to a chapter of Hadassah, the Jewish women's group.

---

8. My article on the Bible and Archaeology in the October 1977 issue of *Decision Magazine* was the most widely distributed of any of my publications as this periodical had a circulation of three million at this time!

9. I was an unsuccessful candidate to replace Raymond Bowman, the professor of Aramaic at Chicago. The position was filled by a far greater Aramaic specialist than I, Joseph Fitzmyer, SJ. I am grateful for his articles on the Dead Sea Scrolls that Father Fitzmyer would later share with me.

Chapter 14

Israel and a Final Year

(1968 to 1969)

Israel

AFTER WORLD WAR I Britain was given a mandate over Palestine. Before the extermination of millions of Jews by the Nazis, Theodore Herzl (d. 1904) led the Zionist movement which sought Palestine as a homeland for the persecuted Jews. The United Nations in 1947 under British prodding allocated 57 percent of Palestine for a new nation of Israel. In 1948 Jewish forces defeated the Arabs who fiercely resisted with hundreds of thousands fleeing to neighboring Arab countries. When a truce was finally achieved, the Jews held the West Bank, the former areas of Samaria and Judea. Jerusalem itself was divided, with the Arabs holding on to the Old City with its sacred sites.

The Six-Day War

Then in June 1967 in less than a week, the political geography was completely transformed.[1] When Egypt closed the Straits of Tiran at the

---

1. According to Simon Sebag Montefiore, *Jerusalem: The Biography* (New York, New York: Vintage Books, 2011), 594, before the outbreak of the war: "The Arab world, now fielding 500,000 men, 5,000 tanks, and 900 planes, had never been so united. 'Our basic aim will be the destruction of Israel,' said Nasser. 'Our goal', explained President Aref of Iraq, 'is to wipe Israel off the face of the map.' The Israelis fielded 275,000 men,

entrance to the Gulf of Suez against Israeli shipping on June 5, the Israeli air force launched a preemptive strike and destroyed almost all of the Egyptian war planes. The Israelis then launched a land offensive led by tanks that seized the Sinai Peninsula and reached the Suez Canal. The Israelis were also able to defeat decisively the Jordanians and the Syrians. They seized the Golan Heights above the Sea of Galilee from Syria.

By the morning of June 7 members of the IDF (Israeli Defense Forces) after street-to-street fighting had captured the Rockefeller Museum near the Damascus Gate just outside the walled Old City. Their forces entered St. Stephen's Gate (also known as the Lion Gate) in the northeast section. Other forces entered through the Dung Gate and soon secured the Herodian platform called by the Arabs the *Ḥaram al-Sharif* "The Noble Sanctuary," which is known to the Israelis as *Har ha-Bayit* "The Temple Mount." With great joy Israeli paratroopers who led the attack reached the Western Wall (also known as the "Wailing" Wall, as Jews have prayed there and mourned the destruction of their temple in AD 70). Shlomo Goren, the Chief Rabbi, urged: "In preparation for the imminent Messianic era, the IDF should utilize the explosives it had on hand and demolish the Temple Mount's mosques."[2] Much to the chagrin of Orthodox Jews, Moshe Dayan, the commander of the Israeli forces, made the decision to allow the Muslim Waqf to retain its jurisdiction over the Ḥaram al-Sharif where they had built the golden Dome of the Rock, and the silver domed al-Aqsah Mosque.[3]

1,100 tanks and 200 planes."

2. Michael B. Oren, *Six Days of War, June 1967 and the Making of the Modern Middle East* (New York, New York: Ballantine Books, 2017), 246.

3. The name al-Aqsah is derived from the Qur'ān 17:1, which states "Blessed is He who transported his servant (i.e. Muhammad) by night from the sacred mosque to the farthest (al-Aqsah) mosque." It is clear that the sacred mosque was in Mecca. Two centuries after Muhammad the interpretation developed that the farthest mosque was in Jerusalem, and that the prophet was miraculously transported there on a winged horse, ascended from the rock covered by the Golden Dome to heaven to converse with Allah, and returned to Mecca in one night. Muslims deny that there ever was a Jewish temple there. The Jewish occupation of Jerusalem was one of the motivations behind Usama bin Laden's formation of al-Qaeda "The Foundation."

The Institute of Holy Land Studies

For the spring of 1968 I had managed to secure a leave from Rutgers,[4] having received a National Endowment for the Humanities Younger Scholars grant and also a fellowship from the American Institute of Holy Land Studies which paid for my travel. The institute had been started by G. Douglas Young, Cyrus Gordon's first PhD.student (1948). Young had begun the school in 1956 on the Street of the Prophets. In the spring of 1967, the school had just moved into the former Anglican Bishop Gobat School with 55 rooms.[5] This was located on Mount Zion just south of the southwest corner of the Old City. Because it was right on the border between the Israeli and the Arab section of Jerusalem, no one else had wanted to use that property.[6] The tower of the Dormition Abbey which looms above was pockmarked with bullet holes in the fighting which broke out in June. During that week Young served as a reserve ambulance driver for the Israelis. Mrs. Young commented, "It was interesting to get dinner in the kitchen with the rattle of machine guns and bombs in the distance and airplanes swooping overhead."

En Route

En route to Israel, we stopped in Paris where we saw the Swan Lake ballet at the Opera. I was interested in visiting the Louvre Museum, not so much to see the Mona Lisa but to view frescoes from Mari and the glazed reliefs of Persian archers from Susa. I spoke on Biblical Archaeology at the European Bible Institute at Lamorlaye and lectured on "Mandean Gnosticism," at the Faculté Évangélique Protestante.

We then traveled to Rome where we saw the ruins of the forum. We took a tour bus south to Naples, where we viewed the ruins of Pompeii, a city that had been buried by the eruption of Mt. Vesuvius in AD 79. We were able to spend only an hour and a half at the site, but I overheard a tourist from Japan asking, "Why are we spending so much time here?"

---

4. The professor who took my place while I was on leave was Robert Littman, who later became the chair of the Classics Department at the University of Hawaii.

5. The grounds of the school include the old Protestant cemetery, which contained the body of the great archaeologist, Sir Flinders Petrie minus his head which had been sent back to Liverpool.

6. The Anglican bishop allowed the Institute to use the building rent free for 15 years if the Institute undertook the renovation of the building and for a modest fee thereafter.

Lodgings in Israel

We arrived in Israel on February 4 after a rare snowstorm had toppled trees. Burned out tanks from the recent war still littered the sides of the highway from the Lod airport to Jerusalem. For the first part of our five-month stay we were able to use the home of G. Douglas Young while he and his wife were away. It was a stone house within a walled court in Talpiot.[7] It required four keys to enter. The temperature in the house dipped into the 50s, so we used an electric blanket to keep ourselves warm at night.

When the Youngs returned in April, we moved to the former Arab section to a third-floor apartment halfway up on the Mount of Olives with a panoramic view of the temple area. This building had been strafed by an Israeli plane. We had to heat our apartment by buying kerosene from a donkey peddler. Kimi had to wash clothes by hand. Sheep grazed on the lawn below.

As we had no television, we entertained ourselves by playing scrabble and a Hebrew version of Monopoly. Kimi taught Brian the alphabet. He learned about two hundred English words, and a word in Hebrew and one in Arabic. The Israelis celebrated the twentieth anniversary of their establishment on May 2, 1968, Brian's second birthday. He enjoyed the sight of planes and helicopters, tanks and captured Egyptian vehicles. A crowd of 600,000 Israelis gathered to view the spectacle.

Classes

I took an Israeli bus from Talpiot to get to classes at the Institute on Mount Zion. Once as I was on my way to a class, I was invited to join some Jews in a service as they needed a tenth man to form a *minyan* or the necessary quorum for such a service. It did not matter that I was not Jewish.

---

7. Talpiot is the district of Jerusalem where an Israeli archaeologist Amos Kloner found a tomb with ossuaries (limestone boxes for bones) which were inscribed with such names as Jesus son of Joseph, Maria, Judah and others as reported in his publication in 1996. But it remained for a Jewish television producer, Simcha Jacobovici, with financing from James Cameron to produce a TV documentary on the Discovery Channel on March 4, 2007, to make the sensational claim that this was the tomb of Jesus, his wife Mary, and his son Judas. Jacobovici also wrote a book, *The Jesus Family Tomb*. For an examination and rebuttal of these claims, see René A. López, *The Jesus Family Tomb Examined* (Springfield, Missouri: 21st Century Press, 2008).

Our classes included Historical Geography, which was taught by Anson Rainey.[8] Anson led about thirty of the students on a *tiyyul*, a tour as we traveled seated in an open truck. We visited the following sites: Gezer, Megiddo, Mount Gilboa, Ein Harod, Jezreel, Capernaum, Tabgha, Hazor, Dan, Golan Heights, Banias, Samaria and Shechem. At Mount Gerizim we witnessed Samaritans preparing sheep for their Passover sacrifices. On another tour in the south, Anson guessed correctly that the unexcavated mound of Tell es-Safi contained the Philistine city of Gath.

A number of lecturers came from the Hebrew University including David Flusser, Moshe Kochavi, Ami Mazar, and Michael Stone. In addition to these classes, I studied modern Hebrew and did research at the École Biblique, Hebrew Union College and Hebrew University.

Touring the Country

As Israel is a very small country, it is easy to see a lot in a short period of time. Our friends Howard and Bonnie (Rigg) Carlson were serving the Baraka Presbyterian Church in Bethlehem. We saw a number of sites with them, including Qumran by the Dead Sea. Howard introduced me to Abu Daoud, one of the Ta'amireh Bedouin who had made the initial find of the Dead Sea Scrolls from Cave I in 1947. When he came to Howard with news of another cave northeast of Ramallah, I accompanied Howard as he reported this to Yigael Yadin. Their inspection of this cave, however, did not yield any scrolls. Coins from Bar Kochba's Revolt were found.[9]

The Carlsons babysat our son when we went to visit Herod's fortress at Masada to the west of the Dead Sea. It was a day when the temperature reached close to 100 degrees. Kimi barely made the climb up to the top as we walked up the steep path near the siege ramp. In later years the Israelis installed a lift on the other side of Masada for tourists.

We were able to visit Samaria where I sampled water from the well at Sychar (John 4:4–6), a site which can authentically be connected with Jesus. We visited Nazareth with its massive Catholic cathedral. More

---

8. Anson translated from Hebrew into English Yohanan Aharoni's *The Land of the Bible: A Historical Geography* (Philadelphia, Pennsylvania: Westminster Press, 1979). He co-authored with R, Steven Notley, *Carta's New Century Handbook and Atlas of the Bible* (Jerusalem, Israel: Carta, 2007).

9. Howard Carlson reported that the roof of this cave had collapsed, making further exploration difficult.

authentic is the spring in the Greek Orthodox shrine as a source of water that Mary must have used.

In Jerusalem, I enjoyed the experience of wading through the tunnel which Hezekiah had carved out by two gangs of workers who met in the middle, a feat which was commemorated by an inscription found just before the Siloam entrance. The water was just knee high. But when unexpected rainstorms have occurred tourists have been drowned while wading through the tunnel. I flew to the south to visit Elath, where Dr. Hambrook had retired. I went snorkeling in the Red Sea and viewed "Solomon's Pillars," where remains of ancient copper mining were visible.

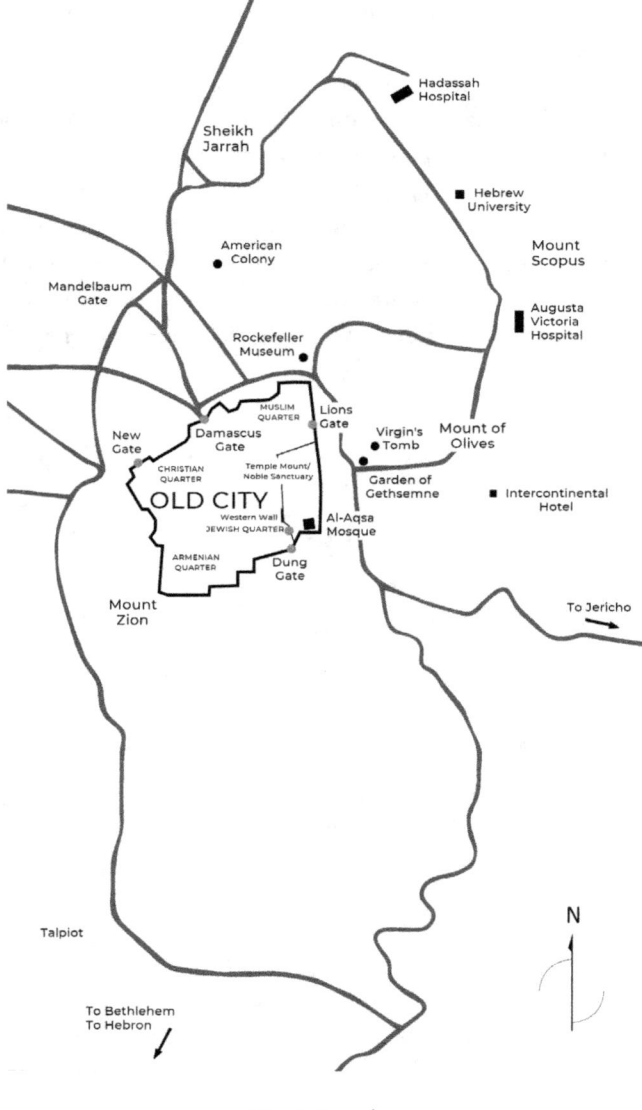

Map 8. Jerusalem

Excavations

I was able to volunteer at two excavations: one in Jerusalem and one in the north. Benjamin Mazar, who had been my teacher at Brandeis, had begun a new excavation at the southwest corner of the Herodian platform just below the alAqsah Mosque. To get to this dig I took the Arab bus from the Mount of Olives down to the bus station at its foot, which is adjacent to a small hill with cavities which make it resemble a skull. This is the site which had been identified by General Charles Gordon as Calvary ("skull" in Latin, Aramaic Golgotha). Adjacent to it is the so-called Garden Tomb, which has been venerated by Protestants. But neither site is authentic.

I would enter the walled city through the Damascus Gate in the north and walk fifteen minutes through narrow cobbled stones to get to the dig site, which was at the other end of the city near the Dung Gate. I would work at the site from 7 a.m. to 3 p.m. Sylvie Nisbet, an enthusiastic volunteer from England, gave me instructions.

One day as I was sifting dirt with a partner we recovered about a hundred copper coins. Every time we found one, we would shout *Echad, Shtayim, Shelosh* "One, two, three!" in Hebrew. Many extraordinary objects were found in this excavation, including a stone object inscribed as "Qorban," and a stone from the parapet, "*LBYT HTQY*" (that is, *lbeyt hateqia*) the place where the priest blew the trumpet to mark the beginning and end of the Sabbath day.[10] Among the other volunteers was Benjamin's granddaughter, Eilat Mazar. She was to become an outstanding archaeologist, uncovering what she believes are buildings of David and Solomon.[11] Other volunteers came from Ambassador College.[12]

---

10. See Benjamin Mazar, *The Mountain of the Lord: Excavating Jerusalem* (Garden City, New York: Doubleday & Co., 1975).

11. Eilat Mazar, *Discovering the Solomonic Wall in Jerusalem* (Jerusalem, Israel: Shoham Academic Research and Publication, 2011).

12. Ambassador College in Pasadena was founded by radio preacher Herbert W. Armstrong in 1947. He started the Worldwide Church of God, which was influenced by the British-Israelite Movement which claimed that the British were descendants of Israelite tribes. He published *The Plain Truth* magazine, which once had a distribution of eight million copies. After Armstrong's death in 1986, the new president Joseph T. Tkatch attempted to reform the denomination to reflect more mainstream evangelical views, which resulted in the splintering of the movement. The Ambassador International Cultural Foundation has provided volunteers for Eilat Mazar's recent excavations.

AN ASIAN AMERICAN ANCIENT HISTORIAN AND BIBLICAL SCHOLAR

Figure 31. Benjamin Mazar at the Temple Mount

The al-Aqsah Mosque

On June 2, I obtained the rare privilege of gaining access to the Herodian passageway still preserved under the al-Aqsah Mosque. This passageway, which was used by Jesus and his disciples, is not open for viewing. On August 21, 1969, Denis Rohan, an Australian follower of the Worldwide Church of God, set fire to the wooden pulpit in an attempt to burn down the al-Aqsah Mosque.[13] He was inspired by reading Zechariah 3:8 to think that he was the appointed "Branch," who would clear the way for the Jews to build the Third Temple. Needless to say, the entire Muslim world was outraged.[14] I may have been the last non–Muslim to see the passageway under the mosque.

---

13. Thomas Idinopoulos, *Jerusalem Blessed, Jerusalem Cursed* (Chicago, Illinois: Ivan R, Dee, 1991), 321322. Tom, a professor of Comparative Religions, once said to me a bit ruefully, "Ed, you really believe in this stuff (i.e. religion)."

14. Michal Artzy wrote to me as follows: "Believe it or not, on that day I was excavating there in charge of an area just across the Western Wall where it was assumed there was the end of the Robinson bridge. It was an experience to remember. I had 16 Arab workers and you can imagine how they felt looking at the fire." Anson Rainey wrote to me on October 31, 1969, as Rohan was being tried in Jerusalem: "Rohan's testimony is making it pretty clear that he is mentally ill. At least his admission that he

Tel Anafa

I also participated as a volunteer from June 3 to 13 at Tel Anafa, a non-biblical site north of the Sea of Galilee. This important Hellenistic town was excavated under the supervision of Saul and Gladys Weinberg of the University of Missouri. There were 25 volunteers from many countries (England, France, Denmark, Australia, Brazil, as well as the US). We stayed at Hagoshrim, a kibbutz. There was a pool there that was quite cold as it was fed by water coming from the snowcapped Mount Hermon to the north.

We woke at 4:30 a.m. and worked until 8:30, when we halted for breakfast. We then worked until lunch at 12:30 p.m., after which we washed pottery sherds until 2:30 p.m. I helped to excavate a *tannur* or oven and pushed a wheelbarrow to move dirt from the pits to a dump. Many coins, glass wares, stucco fragments covered with gold and stamped Rhodian jar handles were evidence of the town's wealth and the far-flung trade connections of this site.[15]

Brian's Fall

While I was away at Tel Anafa, a bomb exploded in Jerusalem only three blocks away from the apartment where Kimi and Brian were staying. No one, however, was hurt.[16] Far more worrisome was an accident which befell Brian. It is described by Kimi as follows:

We had a front porch that was enclosed with windows which rose to seven feet. Brian loved to put a chair against the porch and look at the city of Jerusalem. One afternoon as I was preparing dinner for us, I heard a crash! The chair had slipped under Brian, and he lay motionless on the marble floor. I quickly carried him to our bed and thought, "If only Ed were here to help." Then I prayed silently, "God, please help

---

really did set the fire has gotten us (i.e. Israelis) off the hook."

15. Sharon C. Herbert, *Tel Anafa*, I (Ann Arbor, Michigan: Kelsey Museum, 1994).

16. From time to time, incidents of attacks and counter attacks occurred as recorded in my diary:
Feb. 9, six Israelis killed in a bazooka attack in northwest Jerusalem.
Feb. 16, 21 Fatah terrorists killed.
March 21, 19 Israelis and about 150 Fatah killed.
April 6, explosion in Jerusalem
June 3, when I flew north to work at Tel Anafa, rockets had been fired at Kiryat Shmona, the largest Israeli town in the north.

me." There was no telephone. I couldn't communicate with our neighbors. No one owned a car.

Then I saw droplets of blood on the pillowcase. My heart started beating fast. I couldn't find the source of the blood. Frantically I asked God, "What shall I do now?" He made me recall that Ed had said in passing that the UN supported a hospital on top of the Mount of Olives. Quickly I put on Brian's sweater, put on my shoes, and grabbed my passport and wallet. I started walking up the Mount of Olives on the rocky road. Behind some huge trees I saw the hospital. I pointed to Brian and tried to explain what had happened. The first person shook his head, and then the next and the next. Someone brought a nurse, and she pointed to the old walled city of Jerusalem and said, "Go Government Hospital. This only for mothers." She finally convinced me that this was a maternity hospital.[17] They did not take care of children. I used hand signs and asked, "Where is Government Hospital? I have no car." After what seemed like an hour, an attendant returned. The nurse then said, "We call Government Hospital. Doctor waiting, taxi come."

We rode down the Mount of Olives toward the Old City as the sun was setting. I could see the lights in the homes going on one at a time. After ten long minutes we entered the East Gate (that is, St. Stephen's Gate) and drove down the lonely semi-dark cobbled stone road.

We approached a six-foot high wall. The driver told me to climb the steps and I would find the hospital. I paid the driver and tipped him generously. After I climbed the steps I could see the huge Government Hospital, which used to be a lovely hotel before the war. Looking further up to the second-floor patio, I saw a figure in a white uniform sitting on the ledge. It was a young Arab doctor waiting for my arrival. He spoke fluent English. As he continued to talk and to examine Brian, I could sense that he was becoming friendlier and was pleased that an American was willing to come to an Arab hospital. The doctor suggested that Brian stay overnight. He couldn't locate where the blood droplets came from. He wanted Brian to stay overnight to make sure he had not suffered a concussion.

He said he could put Brian in the women's section on an adult bed. Then I could sleep with him. I was most grateful for this offer. The

---

17. This was not always a maternity hospital. It was the Lutheran Augusta Victoria Hospital built by Kaiser Wilhelm II in 1914 and named in honor of his wife. Just a year before, an Israeli plane had dropped napalm on its grounds to force a key Jordanian force from its grounds.

nurse placed me in a room with four beds. Two of them had elderly Arab women. The third had a young Arab mother with a son about Brian's age. It was such a relief to see someone in a similar situation like me. I was so happy to see her, and so was she to see me. She pointed at Brian speaking to her son in Arabic. My interpretation was, "Look, another boy like you! The doctor is going to help him, too."

After many hand signs and a mixture of Arabic and English, I learned that her husband was a taxi driver. He had learned some English from tourists from Ohio, America! Again, I thanked God for giving me a new friend. Soon a stream of Arab women entered our room. One by one they smiled at me and folded their hands, prayer like. My new friend explained haltingly, "She say she pray for son." As this continued my heart was filled with thanksgiving to God. It showed me that mothers were all alike. They cared for their children.

Then suddenly I heard a loud voice in Arabic on the P.A. system. The women all turned east and started to pray. My new friend quietly told me that it was the evening prayer. As I looked intently through the window, I could see the huge Golden Dome of the Rock. It was beautiful in the evening light. However, as the prayer caller continued, I prayed in my heart that these caring mothers might come to know the only true God and Jesus Christ who walked on the very street outside this hospital.

All through the night the nurses came to check on Brian, shining a light into his sleepy eyes. When morning came the head nurse informed me that Brian seemed to be all right, and that we could go home. As we left the Government Hospital, I saw two ambulance drivers. The drivers told me to "Come, come." They hurriedly invited me to an ambulance, which was painted brown with a red crescent I figured that this was the Arab army ambulance. They kept saying "Americans, Americans," and kept smiling at us. And I kept thanking them for the ride. They took us to the Damascus Gate and hailed a taxi for us and waved a friendly goodbye. All the way back to the apartment, I kept thanking God for the peace He put into my heart and for His watchful care over me.

Greece and Crete

Leaving Israel on June 18, we spent three weeks touring Greece and Crete. In Athens we visited the Agora, the Acropolis, and the national museum. We joined a bus tour for a trip south across the narrow isthmus to get to Corinth. I was excited to visit Mycenae, the legendary home of Homer's Agamemnon. I went all over taking photos of the Lion Gate, the Grave Circle, and the palace until I ran out of film. I hurried back to the bus to get more film but found that everyone else was waiting patiently on the bus for me to show up!

We visited Epidaurus which is famed for its Asklepion or healing shrine and also for its perfectly preserved theater with fifty rows of benches for 14,000 spectators. As I was planning to return that night to view a performance of an ancient Greek drama, I spent all of my time inspecting the ruins of the Asclepion. Alas, my son became ill, so I had to cancel the trip and never got to see this famed theater!

We were able to see Olympia, the site of the ancient Olympic Games begun in 776 BC and continued for a thousand years, as well as the spectacular site of Delphi, the home of the most famous oracle of the Greeks. We rented a Volkswagen beetle for a trip north. As the speedometer reached 100, my wife became alarmed. She did not realize that it was registering kilometers and not miles, so I was going about 60 miles per hour. We were able to view the pass at Thermopylae, where a statue of the Spartan commander commemorates the sacrifice of three hundred Spartans who died trying to stop the massiv army of Xerxes in 480 BC. We also viewed Marathon, where the Athenians had in 490 BC defeated the invading forces of Darius. After the victory a runner ran for twenty-five miles to Athens to announce the victory.[18]

We proceeded north and visited Spiros Zodhiates's orphanage in Katerini near Mt. Olympus, the traditional abode of the Greek gods. On our way to Salonika (Thessalonica) we stopped at Berea. Because I was interested in classical sites, we spent quite a bit of time touring the three-pronged peninsula, the Chalcidice, where we saw Stagira, the birthplace of Aristotle. But in doing so we ran out of time and had to hurry back to Salonika to catch a plane to Athens. We thus missed Philippi, the destination of my favorite New Testament book, Paul's letter to the Philippians!

We sailed from the harbor at Piraeus and stopped at the island of Delos, home to the Athenian Delian League. We then spent a few days on the island of Crete. We visited three Minoan palaces including Knossos

---

18. The marathon race was not a part of the ancient Olympic games. It was included in the revived Olympic games in 1896. The current distance of 26 miles and 385 yards in races like the Boston Marathon was the distance from Windsor Castle to the stadium in London in the1908 Olympics. It became the standard distance after the 1924 Olympics.

excavated by Arthur Evans, Mallia excavated by the French and Phaistos excavated by the Italians. Near the latter was the villa of Hagia Triada, where the largest cache of Linear A tablets had been found. I was able with the help of a guide to descend into the depths of the Dictaean Cave, famed as the birthplace of Zeus. Midway between Knossos and Phaistos is the town of Gortyn, famed for its early law code. Ruins of a cathedral dedicated to Titus, who was sent to the island by Paul, may be seen here. We then returned to Athens and flew home to the US.

Promotion and Tenure

Colleges and universities have an ascending series of ranks: assistant professor, associate professor, and full professor. After a given probationary period, each faculty member is assessed as to whether he or she can be promoted to the next level. In general promotion to the associate professor rank also carries with it the privilege of tenure, that is, a permanent position from which one can only be fired for serious malfeasance. There are generally three factors which are considered: teaching, publications, and service. The weight given to these factors will differ between large research universities and smaller colleges. In the former, publications are most important; in the latter it is teaching and service on committees which is sometimes an onerous burden. Faculty carrying a full load of twelve or more hours of teaching at small colleges have little time for research except in the summer.

Teaching

My time for evaluation at Rutgers came during my fifth year in the fall of 1968. I had not served on any committees, but this was not a problem. As we did not have student evaluations, I had no objective evidence to provide to evaluate my teaching, but this was not a problem.

Three of my Rutgers students developed stellar academic careers. The first of these was Michal Artzy, the daughter of an Israeli who was a professor at Rutgers. Upon my recommendation Michal was accepted to the graduate program at Brandeis, where she earned her PhD in 1972, writing her dissertation "On the Origin of Palestinian Bichrome Ware" under Ian Todd. Michal, who taught at the University of Haifa, directed excavations, particularly at maritime sites such as Tel Akko and Tel Nami.[19]

The second accomplished alumnus was Robert S. Bianchi. Bob, who was a student in my Ancient Egypt class, earned his PhD in Egyptology at New York University. He was the associate curator of the Brooklyn Museum when I saw him again as I was doing research on my book *Africa and the Bible*. He worked with many other museums such as the Getty Museum in Malibu, California. He has also written many books on Hellenistic and Roman Egypt, and on the Nubians.

The third distinguished student is John H. Oakley, who obtained his PhD at Rutgers in 1970. John became an authority on Greek pottery, especially Athenian painted vases, which shed important light on the lives of Greek children. John wrote a gracious letter about my teaching Greek History as follows:

> William & Mary
> Department of Classical Studies
> August 17, 2004
>
> Dear Professor Yamauchi,
>
> It was a great pleasure to see you again several years ago and to have had the chance finally to tell you what an important influence you had on my life. You were the one who first created my interest in the Greek and Roman world when I was a sophomore at Rutgers University. I even remembered that I wrote a paper on the Battle of Marathon for you during the second semester of Greek history. Marathon, by the way, has remained one of my favorite places in Greece, and I remember that enjoyable experience and you whenever I have the chance to teach the battle there on site. And I remember how distraught I was the next year when I learned that you had left Rutgers ... I was greatly looking forward to taking your course on the Persian Empire that year.
>
> Thank you for being the inspiring teacher that you were and for lighting the flame of Classics in me. It is a debt I can never repay.

---

19. Michal wrote in an email (July 22, 2022): "Thank you Prof. Yamauchi! You are still a teacher in my life. I learned so much in your classes. I hope I made as strong an impression as you did to me on some of the many students I introduced the Ancient Near East to."

With the best of wishes.

John H. Oakley
Chancellor Professor and Forrest D. Murden Jr. Professor

P.S. I have recently been named the Mellon Professor of Classical Studies at the American School of Classical Studies at Athens. Please stop by to see us if you come to Athens.

Publications

There was, however, a problem with my publications, not so much their quantity but their nature. Between 1964 and 1968 I had presented eight papers at scholarly conferences. Most of these were published in journals.

In August 1957, I had presented a paper on "The Comparison of Elements in the Mandaic and Coptic Gnostic Sources," at the XXVth International Congress of Orientalists meeting in Ann Arbor, Michigan. There I met with Donald J. Wiseman and W. J. Martin from England and other scholars such as Stanley Walters from Canada to discuss the need for scholarly commentaries by evangelicals on the Old Testament.[20]

During this same time span, I had articles published in the following journals and periodicals: *Berytus, Bibliotheca Sacra, Bulletin of the Evangelical Theological Society, Christianity Today, Journal of Biblical Literature, Journal of Semitic Studies, Journal of the American Oriental Society, Journal of Near Eastern Studies*, and *Westminster Theological Journal*.

In 1966, I had published a small booklet (38 pages), *Composition and Corroboration in Classical and Biblical Studies* and in 1967 a short, illustrated book, *Greece and Babylon: Early Contacts between the Aegean and the Near East*, in which I demonstrated that the Greek words in Daniel did not require a late date after Alexander's conquests inasmuch as Greek influence could be traced at a much earlier date. I was advised that such a publication would not win me any points with some members of the department. My most significant book, *Mandaic Incantation Texts* was judged "philological" and not historical.

---

20. Up to that point, evangelicals had, for the most part, relied on the popular commentaries of Harry A. Ironside of Moody Church and the reprints of the English translations of the German scholars, Carl F. Keil and Franz Delitzsch, first published in 1861! Donald later became the editor of the Tyndale Old Testament Commentary Series, published by InterVarsity Press. See ch. 42.

The department was aware that on the day after I arrived in Israel, I had received a letter from Frank Moore Cross that my monograph *Gnostic Ethics and Mandaean Origins* had been accepted for publication in the Harvard Theological Studies series. But this manuscript was not completed until April 1969 and not published by Harvard University Press until 1970.

Denial of Tenure

The vote was against my promotion and tenure. The chair Dick McCormick informed me that though all the senior professors had voted in my favor, all of the associate and assistant professors had voted against me. He also mentioned an issue of "collegiality," although I did not know what to make of that. Though I did not drink alcoholic beverages, I had attended all of the departmental parties and even hosted one in our home, though we did not serve any liquor. One of my supporters suggested that I should appeal this decision. But though this recourse is sometimes used, even if successful, the result would be highly toxic.[21] Though I had the possibility of teaching a sixth year at Rutgers, I did not care to remain as a kind of "lame duck" member of the department.[22]

A Family Crisis

On December 26, 1968, as I was at the Evangelical Theology Society conference at Westminster Theological Seminary in Philadelphia, I received word that my stepfather Renyu Higa had unexpectedly died. I hurried back to New Jersey and caught a plane to Los Angeles.

---

21. In 1986 when Henry Winkler was the president of the University of Cincinnati, Kathryn Gutzwiller was denied tenure by a unanimous vote of the promotion and tenure committee of the Classics Department. At first, she sued on the ground of sexual discrimination, but lost because another woman had been approved at that same time. She then sued in another court and won reinstatement and promotion. It helped that her husband was a lawyer. But the resulting tensions in the department were such that one of my students Amy Deeds and her husband who were graduate students in classics left the program.

22. Before I left for Israel, I had discussions with Robert Gundry about the possibility of my teaching at Westmont College in Santa Barbara, which would have placed us closer to my family in LA Bob arranged to have his school make me an attractive offer to teach New Testament and Greek, but after due consideration, I decided to remain at Rutgers.

In the meantime, my mother had slit her wrists in an attempt to commit suicide. She blamed herself for Renyu's death and did not wish to live as a widow a second time. Fortunately, my cousins, Gary and Bobby Owan, were staying at the apartment building my parents had been able to buy after they sold their boarding house. Also, two of my uncles were in town, Tom Owan, her brother and Albert Nakama, her brother-in-law. They took my mother to the hospital and to see a psychiatrist. She recovered enough to attend Renyu's funeral service on December 30, led by Rev. Akira Kuroda at the LA Holiness Church. Later she was comforted by friends from the West LA Holiness Church, which she attended. She was baptized in April 1969.

As my parents had bought not only the apartment but also a coffee shop in North Hollywood, they had no cash reserves and no insurance. She had to borrow $2,500 for the funeral. But this was a loan which had to be quickly repaid. My mother therefore asked us for the $2,000 she had given us when we bought a house. We also had no cash reserves. The one way to raise money would be for me to find another position and sell our house in Somerset, which we did for $27,400.

Job Options

In the spring of 1969, there were three openings in ancient history, all in Ohio. One was at Cleveland State University, a second was at Youngstown State University, and a third was at Miami University. I knew nothing about these schools. I had occasionally heard football scores for a school with an odd name, "Miami of Ohio." Henry Winkler, who was quite familiar with the school, wrote me an encouraging letter, praising Miami University as an outstanding school, an evaluation which I was to confirm for myself.

Chapter 15

Miami University

(1809 to 1969)

The Miami Indians

THE WORD "MIAMI" is an anglicized spelling of Myaamia "The Downstream People,"[1] the name of a tribe that once roamed over a large area later settled as the states of Wisconsin, Michigan, Illinois, Indiana, and Ohio.[2] In 1787, the US Congress passed the Northwest Ordinance which claimed the lands northwest of the Ohio River. The Miamis along with other tribes refused to sign treaties ceding these lands to the Americans. After a Miami chief, "Little Turtle," defeated a small American force near Fort Wayne, Indiana, a much larger army led by General Arthur St. Clair marched out of Cincinnati in 1791. But at Fort Recovery near the Wabash River in Indiana the Miamis and their allies inflicted a crushing defeat upon the Americans, killing 634 of them. Then a third expedition set

---

1. As for that better known Miami in Florida it is named after *Myaimi*, the name of Lake Okeechobee and the Indians who lived in that region. In 1899, its population numbered only 1,600. Its later prosperity was due to the decision of Heny Flagler, the wealthy cofounder with John D. Rockefeller of Standard Oil, to extend his East Coast Florida railroad to Miami. In contrast to Miami University, which is a state sponsored institution, the University of Miami founded in 1925 in Coral Gables south of the city of Miami, is a private institution. Its football team is known as the Hurricanes. The president of the University of Miami (2001 to 2015) was Donna Shalala, a 1962 graduate of Western College for Women, which was adjacent to Miami University.

2. For a popular introduction, see Nancy Niblack Baxter, *The Miamis* (Indianapolis, Indiana: Guild Press of Indiana, 1987).

out under General Anthony Wayne, which decisively defeated the Indian coalition at the Battle of Fallen Timbers in northwest Ohio in 1794. The Indians were led by the Shawnee chief "Blue Jacket."[3]

In 1795 at Greenville, Ohio, the defeated Indians were forced to sign a treaty ceding much of their land to the Americans. Eventually by 1846 the remaining 300 or so Miami Indians from Peru (Indiana) were transported in canal boats down to the Ohio River and removed to Kansas. Later the tribe was removed to the Indian Territory which was to become the state of Oklahoma. The vast majority of about 5,000 Miami descendants live in the town of Miami in northeast Oklahoma.[4] The federally recognized tribe elects its chief.[5]

For many years Miami University's athletic teams were nicknamed the "Redskins." But in 1996 at the request of Chief Floyd Leonard of the Miami tribe, the university, not without loud protests from some alumni, changed its nickname to the "RedHawks."

Since 1991 80 members of the tribe have been given free tuition at the university. In 2021 there were 30 Myaamia students at the university. Since 2001 Miami University has had a program called the Myaamia Center which fosters relations with the tribe and seeks to preserve its customs and its language. Indian children had been discouraged from using their native languages and were sent to boarding schools such as the Carlisle Indian School in Pennsylvania and the Sherman Indian Institute in California. In 2016 Professor Daryl Baldwin won a $500,000 MacArthur "Genius Grant" for his work with the Myaamia language. In 2021 Professor Baldwin was named to the National Humanities Council by President Biden.

The Beginnings

Ohio was the first state carved out of the Northwest Territory in 1803. The state then chartered two universities, Ohio University in 1804 at Athens in the southeast corner of the state and Miami University in 1809 in the southwest corner of the state. Miami University was the third

---

3. Near the early Ohio capitol of Chillicothe in south central Ohio, a dramatic outdoor festival commemorates the saga of "Blue Jacket."

4. A much smaller group, which is not officially recognized, still lives in Peru, Indiana.

5. Joe Leonard, Floyd's son and a recent chief, and his wife Etsuko from Japan sang with my wife and myself in a senior Songbirds group.

oldest college west of the Appalachians following Transylvania College which had been established in Lexington, Kentucky in 1780 and Ohio University.[6] It preceded the establishment of the University of Michigan (1817) and the University of Indiana (1820). It is older than the University of Virginia begun in 1819 by Thomas Jefferson.

In 1810 the mile-square village of O ford was established to support the college according to provisions of the Northwest Ordnance. After funds had been raised, a classroom building erected, and a president chosen, classes began in 1824 with three professors and twenty students. Two residence halls that are still used today were constructed in 1828 and 1836.

Miami University's first president was Robert H. Bishop, a graduate of the University of Edinburgh, who had taught at Transylvania University for 20 years prior to 1824. He was a Presbyterian minister, who objected to the selection of a new president at Transylvania who was a Unitarian. Bishop was a critic of slavery and had established one of the earliest "Sabbath schools" for African Americans. President Bishop aspired to make Miami University "The Yale of the West."

In order to matriculate, prospective students had to pass a competency exam in Latin. To matriculate your age did not matter. Students had to take classes in Latin, Greek, and Hebrew along with other subjects. Students were aroused at 5 a.m. with a bugle. Another bugle at 9 p.m. signaled that all the candles had to be extinguished. Silence was required during study hours.

Within thirty years after its founding (1839), Miami's enrollment (250) was surpassed by only five schools: Yale (411), Oberlin (404), Dartmouth (301), Union (286) and Transylvania (269). Miami University had more students at this time than Princeton (237) and Harvard (216).[7]

> From its origins Miami University was "the principal training ground of Presbyterian ministers in Ohio," graduating more than a hundred between 1825 and 1860. "Most of the faculty and all of the presidents between 1824 and 1873 were ordained Presbyterian ministers, as were many of the trustees."[8] This

---

6. *The Miami Student*, begun in 1826, is the second oldest college paper west of the Alleghenies.

7. Curtis W. Ellison, ed., *Miami University 1809-2009, Bicentennial Perspectives* (Athens, Ohio: Ohio University Press, 2009), 29.

8. Phillip R. Shriver and Edith Foth Puff, *A History of Presbyterianism in Oxford, Ohio* (Oxford, Ohio: The Oxford Presbyterian Church, 2000), 11.

was not an anomaly but the rule in higher education in the nineteenth century. "In 1839, of the presidents of the fifty-four oldest colleges in the nation, fifty-one were clergymen; and of these fifty-one, forty were Presbyterians or Congregationalists."[9]

Old School vs. New School

In the first half of the nineteenth century a sharp split occurred among Presbyterians which affected Miami University. The Old School favored a strict adherence to the Calvinism of the Westminster Confession, as championed by Charles Hodge of Princeton Theological Seminary. The New School was championed by Lyman Beecher of Lane Seminary in Cincinnati. The New School accepted Jonathan Edwards's acknowledgement of the role of emotions in conversion and the commonsense recognition of man's abilities and responsibilities. The New School emphasized "revivalism, moral reform, interdenominational cooperation and evangelical piety."[10] President Bishop belonged to the New School, whereas some of his faculty belonged to the Old School.

William Holmes McGuffey

An adherent to the Old School was the new librarian, William Holmes McGuffey, a Presbyterian minister, who also taught ancient languages. He is best known as the author of the *Eclectic Readers*, which taught children how to read.[11] The first Reader was published in 1836. The Readers encouraged the reading of the Bible and upheld high moral standards such as honesty. Eventually over 150 million Readers were sold. Apart from the initial payment which he received, McGuffey earned no royalties. He did receive the bonus of a ham at Christmas each year! His house at the corner of Oak and Spring Streets is a museum today. In it is his custom-made rotating octagonal desk upon which he composed his Readers.

---

9. George M. Marsden, *The Evangelical Mind and the New School Presbyterian Experience* (New Haven, Connecticut: Yale University Press, 1970), 30.

10. Marsden, x.

11. In some circles, they are still being used today. Henry Ford considered McGuffey the third greatest American after Washington and Lincoln.

After serving as the president of Cincinnati College and Ohio University, McGuffey moved in 1845 to the University of Virginia, where he became the first clergyman on the faculty there. He conducted Bible classes in the Rotunda. Jefferson would have been appalled as he wanted no clergy on the faculty. McGuffey is buried in the university's cemetery in Charlottesville.

Women's Colleges

In the middle of the nineteenth century three Presbyterian churches sponsored three women's colleges in Oxford. At one time there were more women attending these schools than men at Miami University. One of Miami's first professors, John Witherspoon Scott, became the president of two of these colleges. In 1849 he established the Oxford Female Institute located on the western edge of Oxford.[12] It enrolled 139 women in its first year. Later after a dispute with the institute's board, Scott became president in 1856 of the Oxford Female College in the northeastern corner of Oxford.[13]

The third women's school which opened in 1855 on a large campus east of Miami University was the Western Female Seminary (later called the Western College for Women). It was planned as the western extension of Mt. Holyoke College. Its first president, Helen Peabody, and all of its first faculty came from Mt. Holyoke. To survive, Western College became co-educational in 1971. When Western College closed in 1974, Miami University acquired its campus and its buildings.[14]

Miami University first admitted women in 1891. Its first women's residence hall, built in 1905, was ironically named after President Andrew Hepburn (1871 to1873), who had been a fierce opponent of co-education!

---

12. Its three-story building with a large ballroom was used as a women's dormitory by Miami University. It has been refurbished as a community center for the arts.

13. After this school ceased, its large building was used as a sanatorium. It was then razed. A replica of the Wren building at William and Mary, the oldest surviving academic building in the US, now serves at the site as the Marcum Conference Center.

14. In 1964 the Congress on Racial Equality and the Student Non-Violent Coordinating Committee aiming to increase Black voter registration in Mississippi, trained about eight hundred mainly white volunteers from June 14 to June 27 on the campus of Western College. Tragically three of the volunteers, James Chaney, Andrew Goodman, and Michael Schwerner were murdered by the Ku Klux Klan in Mississippi on June 21. Chaney was Black, Goodman and Schwermer were Jewish.

Slavery and the Civil War

Walter Havighurst notes:

> For thirty years the question of slavery was a ferment on campus. In 1832 Miami students formed an Anti-Slavery Society and paraded by torchlights through the village streets. In the Literary Halls they debated abolition and colonization,[15] and in the columns of their magazine they argued about nullification and states' rights. President Bishop was a leader in the abolition movement and in liberal (i.e. New School) theology, but his faculty was divided.[16]

An advocate of an anti-Abolitionist stance was George Junkin, who was the second president of Miami University and an Old School Presbyterian. Over a period of two days from September 19 to September 20, 1843, he spoke in Cincinnati in a public debate over abolition. His main thesis was that "believing masters ought to be honored and obeyed by their own servants, and tolerated, not excommunicated from the church of God." He was able to cite many Scriptures, parsing the Hebrew and the Greek words to demonstrate that slavery existed during both the Old Testament and the New Testament eras, and that there was no explicit text which advocated the abolition of slavery either from Moses, Jesus, or Paul. This was in accordance with the view of Charles Hodge of Princeton that Christians should not go beyond the Scriptures. After leaving Miami University in 1844, Junkin taught at Washington College in Lexington, Virginia. One of his daughters married "Stonewall" Jackson, the famous Confederate general.

Abolitionists wanted an immediate end to slavery and urged churches to expel slave owners. An ardent abolitionist was Jonathan Blanchard, who became the pastor of the Sixth Presbyterian Church in Cincinnati. In 1845, he engaged in a four-day long debate in Cincinnati over the issue of abolition. Blanchard became the first president of Wheaton College in Illinois in 1860.

Though most students at Miami were from the North, a fourth were from the slave owning states of the South. When the war broke

---

15. Colonization proposed to send Blacks back to their original home. This eventually led to the founding of Liberia in 1847 as an independent nation. But colonization, though supported by many, could do little to resolve the problem of slavery.

16. Walter Havighurst, *The Miami Years 1809–1969* (New York, New York: G. P. Putnam's Sons, 1969), 140.

out in 1861, students left campus to join opposing armies. G. Wallace Chessman recounts:

> Most saddening was the parting at Old Miami, where the sons of Dixie marched away the same morning as the "University Rifles." The two groups rode together the twelve miles from Oxford to Hamilton, there to separate, the one turning north to Camp Jackson in Columbus, the other south to Cincinnati. The war that set brother against brother would not except classmates.[17]

At this time, five Miami alumni were serving as governors of states: four in the North (Ohio, Indiana, Illinois, Michigan) and one in the south (Mississippi). Ten Miamians served as generals in the Union Army; two of the three Union admirals were Miami grads. Two alumni would serve in Lincoln's cabinet.

Three Miamians were Confederate generals, including Joseph Davis, the nephew of Jefferson Davis, the president of the Confederacy. He would lead troops at the Battle of Gettysburg. Professor Albert T. Bledsoe, who joined McGuffey at Virginia, would serve as the assistant secretary of War for the South. Lottie Moon, an Oxford resident, whose house still stands, served as a noted spy for the South.

As the war deprived colleges of faculty, students, and resources, 408 of the 512 pre-Civil War colleges closed including Miami University. It would not be until 1885 that the college would reopen.

Benjamin Harrison

One of Miami's Union generals was Benjamin Harrison, the grandson of William Henry Harrison, the ninth president of the United States. Benjamin was born at a bend of the Ohio River, west of Cincinnati. He graduated from Miami University in 1833. He married Caroline Scott, the daughter of Professor John W. Scott. Caroline was a charter member and the first president of the Daughters of the American Republic.

After the Civil War, Benjamin established a law practice in Indianapolis. A devout Presbyterian, he had a reputation for honesty and was an excellent public speaker. After serving in the Senate, he became the Republican nominee who defeated Grover Cleveland, to become the

---

17. Wallace Chessman, *Ohio Colleges and the Civil War* (Columbus, Ohio: Ohio State University Press, n.d.), 6.

nation's twenty-third president (1889 to1893). During his administration the Sherman Anti-Trust Act was passed, and six western states entered the Union. He created the national forest system. While tariffs he imposed brought in revenue, they were unpopular. In his unsuccessful bid to be elected again his vice-presidential candidate was a fellow Miami alumnus, Whitelaw Reid (class of 1856), who had become the owner and editor of the *New York Tribune*.

The Twentieth Century

In 1885, "New" Miami was able to reopen its doors to students. The first president of the New Miami was not a Presbyterian minister, but a Mathematics professor, Robert McFarland (1885 to 1888), who abolished compulsory chapel, much to the chagrin of previous president Andrew Hepburn.

Though the village of Oxford remained small (it would reach 5,000 only in 1970), Miami's student body gradually increased from 2,000 in 1923, to 5,000 by 1950.

During World War II, Miami University served as a radio training base for men and women of the Navy. Seventy WAVES arrived at the Oxford railroad depot on April 19, 1943. "Under the cocked Navy hats, all the WAVES had red hair! Later came an explanation: the Navy command had meant to pull the cards of women who could type and instead got the roster of red heads!"[18]

At the height of the program, about 2,000 service men and women were stationed at one time at Miami. Nearly 30,000 were trained in the radio program by war's end. The small town of Oxford had sixteen of its men killed during the war. The airfield hanger west of Oxford is named in honor of Lawrence A. Williams, a sailor who died in the sinking of the battleship Arizona at Pearl Harbor on December 7, 1941. All told about 5,000 alumni served during World War II, with about 150 giving their lives for their country.

---

18. Robert E. White, Jr., *Oxford and Miami U. during World War II* (Oxford, Ohio: The Smith Library of Regional History, 1994), 22.

Walter I. Farmer

A Miamian (class of 1935), William I. Farmer (1911 to 1997), played a key role at the end of World War II. Farmer, who was an architect by training and an interior designer by trade, became one of the so-called "Monuments Men," celebrated in Robert Edsel's 2009 book, *The Monuments Men: Allied Heroes, Nazi Thieves, and the Greatest Treasure Hunt in History*, which was then made into a 2014 movie directed by George Clooney, who also starred in the film.

Though he was at first rejected because of his poor eyesight, Farmer was drafted into the medical corps in 1942. He then became an officer in the Army Corps of Engineers, serving as the adjutant of Colonel Frank Bell, who commanded 10,000 engineers at the invasion of Normandy. He later joined the Army's Monuments Fine Arts and Archives (MFA & A) unit tasked with collecting and inventorying all the art acquired by the Nazis.

Farmer was put in charge of the Wiesbaden collection point, a former museum which had been used as the Luftwaffe headquarters. Though the structure of the building had survived the Allied bombings, all the building's 2,000 windows had been blown out. Farmer was able to locate several tons of glass at an airfield to use in restoring these windows.

Farmer, who spoke no German, was fortunate in locating skilled bilingual workers to assist him in his task of restoring the building. He was hampered by the rule that he could not hire anyone who had belonged to the Nazi party.

Truckload after truckload of German art began arriving, most already crated and labeled. Among the 163 crates of Egyptian antiquities was the famous bust of Nefertiti, which the Germans called *Bunte Königin*. The collection included 700 Torah scrolls and the crown jewels of Hungary. By the end of his assignment, he and his team had inventoried 28,000 crates of artwork.

Figure 32. Walter Farmer and the bust of Nefertiti (courtesy of The Miamian)

In November 1945, he received a most unwelcome order to send master paintings to the National Gallery of Art, supposedly for their safekeeping. The paintings were then sent on a travelling exhibition to raise funds before being returned to Germany.

The 202 paintings, which were from the Kaiser Friedrich Museum, included works by Fra Angelico, Bellini, Bosch, Botticelli, Brueghel, Caravaggio, Cranach, Dürer, Eyck, Hals, Holbein, Lippi, Masaccio, Poussin, Raphael, Rembrandt, Rubens, Tiepolo, Tintoretto, Titian, Velazquez, Vermeer, and Watteau.

Farmer organized most members of the MFA & A officers to sign a protest, which became known as the "Wiesbaden Manifesto." They reluctantly complied with the order, but because of their protest, no further art from Germany was sent back to the US. For this courageous expression of conscience, the German government honored him in 1996 with the Commander's Cross of the Federal Order of Merit. Farmer donated his own art collection to Miami University, where it formed a core collection of the art museum which he helped to establish.[19]

John E. Dolibois

Another Miamian who played a key role at the end of World War II was John E. Dolibois, a native of Luxembourg. Though one of the smallest nations of Europe, Luxembourg is strategically situated, as it is surrounded by Belgium, Germany, and France. John E. Dolibois was born there in 1918. Hansi ("Little Hans") grew up speaking Luxembourgish, French, and German. His mother, who had borne six other children, passed away soon after his birth. In 1931, John and his father emigrated to the US to join his sister and her husband who lived in Akron, Ohio. John learned English, joined the Boy Scouts, and flourished in high school.

John was befriended by a Miami alumnus who encouraged him to apply to the school for a scholarship and if accepted to join a fraternity there. John joined the Beta Theta Pi, founded in 1839. It was one of three national fraternities begun at Miami University.[20] Soon after his graduation in 1942, John was drafted into the army. Though the official credit was given to General Patton, it was John who first discovered and then rescued the famed Lipizzaner stallions of the Spanish Riding School in Vienna. They had been shipped by train out of Austria for their safety to a pasture in Germany.

Because of his fluency in German, Dolibois was then posted as an interpreter to Mondorf (code name "Ashcan"), a spa in Luxembourg, where all the important military and civilian German prisoners were being held prior to their trial at Nuremberg. Dolibois was one of only five Americans with free access to the prisoners. His role as an interpreter allowed him to establish relations with all these notable prisoners, including:

---

19. See Walter I. Farmer, *The Safekeepers: A Memoir of the Arts at the End of World War II* (Berlin, Germany: Walter de Gruyter, 2000).

20. The other two fraternities were Phi Delta Theta, begun in 1848, and Sigma Chi, begun in 1855. About 30 percent of Miami's students are involved in fraternities or sororities.

- Martin Bormann, Nazi party secretary
- Karl Dönitz, admiral of the navy
- Hermann Göhring, chief of the Luftwaffe
- Rudolf Hess, deputy Führer
- Alfred Jodl, commander of the Wehrmacht
- Ernst Kaltenbrunner, head of the Gestapo
- Wilhelm Keitel, defense minister
- Gustav Krupp, industrialist
- Joachim von Ribbentrop, ambassador
- Alfred Rosenthal, racial theorist
- Albert Speer, minister of armaments
- Julius Streicher, editor of the anti-Semitic *Der Stürmer*.

At General Eisenhower's request, Dolibois collected photos and autographs of all the major German prisoners; he kept a duplicate copy of the album for himself.

A short time after his discharge and return to the US, Miami University recruited him to become its first full-time alumni secretary in 1947.[21] Miami's alumni association is the fourth oldest in the country. It was begun back in 1832 when there were only 69 alumni. Dolibois was able to boast that according to the American Alumni Council, "Our program (is) ranked in the top 1 percent of all public and private institutions of higher education."[22]

Later Dolibois, as vice-president for university relations, was able to raise the funds which led to the building of the Art Museum,[23] the Marcum Conference Center, the Murstein Alumni Center, the Sesquicentennial Chapel, and the Yager Football Stadium. In 1968 he was instrumental in establishing Miami's branch campus in Luxemburg, which has been named in his honor.

---

21. Of the 4,100 students at Miami University at this time, about half were veterans taking advantage of the G.I. Bill of Rights.

22. John E. Dolibois, *Pattern of Circles: An Ambassador's Story* (Kent, Ohio: Kent State University Press, 1989), 226.

23. The museum is a striking modernistic building designed by famed architect Walter Netsch, who also designed the Air Force Academy's chapel.

Dolibois was appointed by President Nixon to the board that oversees Fulbright Scholarships. President Reagan then appointed him to serve as the US Ambassador to Luxembourg, a post he held for four years from 1981. He would become the ninth Miamian to serve as an American ambassador.[24]

Phillip R. Shriver

In 1965, Phillip R. Shriver became president of Miami University.[25] After graduating from Yale University, he had served as a naval officer on a destroyer in the Iwo Jima[26] and Okinawa campaigns. After discharge, he had earned a PhD in history from Columbia University and taught at Kent State University. He served as the Dean of the College of Arts and Sciences there.

Like his nineteenth-century predecessors, Phil was a devoted Presbyterian, who with Edith Fath Poff wrote a history of the intertwined relations between Oxford's Presbyterian churches and Miami University. He informed me that at Yale he had sung in the chapel choir.

Students called the extremely affable president "Uncle Phil." After retiring from the presidency in 1981, Phil continued to teach his popular courses on the History of Ohio and the History of Miami University.[27] A unique and admirable trait was that he read and acknowledged the articles I shared with him not with an email or a dictated response, but always with a handwritten note!

A New Home

In the summer of 1969, we left the Boston area, stopped in Ohio, and visited some of Kimi's friends in Illinois. Travelling in a 1961 Valiant nicknamed "Nimrod," we took the northern route through North Dakota,

---

24. Walter Havighurst, *The Dolibois Years 1938–1981* (Oxford, Ohio: Miami University Alumni Association, 1982), 5657.

25. In 1965, tuition and board for a year cost students $1,800.

26. Clarence "Bud" Williamson, who served as the Dean of the College of Arts and Sciences from 1971 to 1982, had served as a marine in the attack on Iwo Jima.

27. See Phillip R. Shriver, *Miami University: A Personal History*, ed. by William Pratt (Oxford, Ohio: Miami University Press, 1998). See also Randall W. Listerman, *Sixteen Years of Miami Memories: The Presidency of Phillip R. Shriver* (Oxford, Ohio: King Printing Co., 2002).

where we encountered numerous problems due to a faulty fuel pump. After visiting my mother in LA, we then returned by the famed Route 66, until we arrived in our new location, where we would spend the next five decades. Our first home was an old university rental, a two-story frame house with dark interiors. I had to hang heavy storm windows on the outside during the winter. It had but one bathroom with a tub and no shower. But the rent was but $80 per month, and its location was most convenient, at the south end of Oak Street. At the north end was McGuffey's home and across from it Irvin Hall, where the History Department was located. I would teach for nearly four decades at a school which later became known as "A Public Ivy"[28] and "The Cradle of Coaches."[29]

The History Department

My first chair was Harris G. Warren. He had served as an intelligence officer in North Africa and was an authority on Paraguay. He was succeeded by Richard M. Jellison, who served as chair from 1971 to 1986. Dick had served as a sailor on board the Light Cruiser USS Honolulu in the Pacific. He had written on the early history of the American Revolution. In his long tenure Dick did come into conflict with some professors such as Michael Hogan,[30] but he was always supportive in my case. Even after his retirement, he would call me by phone to congratulate me on a publication I had sent him. I was honored to deliver his eulogy at the Oxford Presbyterian Church on November 8, 2013.

The history department with about 25 members, including those at the branch campus, was a relatively large department. In fact, when I served as the director of graduate studies, and traveled with Jellison in 1980 to a conference of the chairs of the history departments of the state universities, our department which had grown to 30 members was second only to that of Ohio State University.

Among the many notable colleagues in the department were Jay Baird, an authority on the Nazis and their propaganda; Sam Chandler, who taught Latin American history; David Fahey, a leading authority

---

28. See Excursus I.
29. See Excursus J.
30. Mike Hogan taught diplomatic history in our department for nine years before moving to Ohio State University, where he became the chair of the history department, then the dean of the Colleges of Arts and Sciences, president of the University of Connecticut, and then president of the University of Illinois.

on the British temperance movement; Sherman Jackson, who wrote on Lyndon Johnson and taught African American History;[31] Jeffrey Kimball, who wrote award-winning books critical of Nixon's Viet Nam policies; Jack Kirby who after retirement wrote *Mocking Bird Song; Ecological Landscapes of the South*, which won him the 2006 Bancroft Prize; James Rodabaugh, an authority on Ohio history; Ronald Shaw, who wrote on the Erie Canal; Dwight Smith, an authority on the western US and Canada; and Bill Swanson, an authority on South Africa. Other members of the department in 1977 included Gilbert Chan (Asian History), Tom Coakley (British History), John Dickinson (US History), Bruce Menning (Russian History), Brenton Smith (European History), and Max Welborn (European History).

Herbert Oerter, who had served as a Darby Ranger, a unique US Army unit, and as a member of the staff of General Patton in North Africa and Italy, was a specialist in Medieval and Renaissance Italy. Herb had been teaching ancient history, but the department started looking for a specialist in that area. A candidate from Wisconsin was offered this position but he declined. I was hired for a salary of $13,000 as an associate professor to teach the ancient history classes.

There were no women in the department in 1969. Then in 1974, Marianka Foucek, originally from Czechoslovakia, with a PhD from Harvard was hired as a joint appointment with the Department of Religion.[32] She did not receive tenure, so she left academia to serve in the Lutheran urban ministry. I inherited the class on the History of Early Christianity. I would get about twenty students enrolled in history 232 and twenty students in religion 232 in this class. Marianka had required as a text the Bible. I followed her example not only for this class but also for the large History 121 (Western Civilization class) with about three hundred students. I required the paperback edition of the New International Version as one of the texts. I did not require any of my own books as texts but placed some of them on the library reserve along with other articles I had written.

---

31. The hiring of Sherman Jackson in 1969 was a response to the demands of Black students who asked for a Black professor who would teach African American history. There were only about 100 Black students at Miami at this time.

32. This department now known as the Department of Comparative Religions, was established in 1927 as the oldest or second oldest (with Iowa) religion department at a state university.

In 1969, Miami University had eleven thousand students. Miami was noted primarily as a strong undergraduate college with less than a thousand graduate students. At first only five departments, including History, offered the PhD. This was later expanded to ten departments. In 1974 our department was offering the PhD in American, British, European, Latin American, and Russian history but not in Ancient History, but that was to change with the influx of graduate students seeking to work in this field.

Chapter 16

An Eventful Year

(1970)

"The Gentle Revolution"

STUDENT ACTIVISM AGAINST THE war in southeast Asia and the draft[1] simmered in the 1960's and climaxed at Miami University in the spring of 1970. Students were supported by a relatively small group of faculty who belonged to the Oxford chapter of the New University Conference, which was allied with the Students for a Democratic Society. In the spring of 1969 sixteen faculty had circulated a 26-page pamphlet entitled "The Gentle Revolution."[2]

The pamphlet declared: "In these revolutionary times Miami will make disorderly, even violent revolution in her own internal life inevitable tomorrow if she fails to carry out an orderly, gentle revolution today ..." (p. 2). The pamphlet continued: "Without rehearsing once again and in detail the long and painful history of horrors, we wish to register our profound outrage over the moral condition of our society as expressed in the values which it honors and serves concretely through its allocation of resources and the management of its public affairs; through its inhuman barbarism, colonialism, and militarism in Vietnam and elsewhere at home and abroad ..." (p. 4). The authors laid great stress on freshmen

---

1. In December 1969, the first draft lottery was held, eliminating draft deferments for many college students.
2. See Excursus K.

orientation: "This will mean, in practice, not simply orientation, but re-orientation, since most freshmen come to Miami systematically corrupted by their culture and their society..." (p. 13).

Among specific proposals was the substitution of freshman seminars in place of freshman English; the practice of having other faculty visit classes; a greater number of interdisciplinary courses; the promotion of work studies; the establishing' of a university bookstore; a new governance structure which would provide for an equal role of a Faculty Senate and a Student Senate with the University Council; lessening support for fraternities and sororities: supporting the demands of the Black Students Action Association for more Black students and faculty; eliminating the R.O.T.C. program; and encouraging faculty not to cooperate with the draft board. Some of these proposals, such as a university bookstore and more interdisciplinary courses were eventually adopted by the university.

"The Gentle Revolution" was publicly opposed by a much larger group of 322 faculty and administrators who called themselves "Voices of Reason." Some suspected that the SDS and the NUC were inspired by Marxist or even Communist ideology.

Student Protests

On April 15, 1970, up to five hundred students had gathered in peaceful protest in front of Roudebush Hall, the administration building. In addition to protesters against the Vietnam War. Larry Clark, the president of the Black Student Action Association, called for the enrollment of more Black students and the recruitment of more Black faculty.

Toward evening a small group of about twenty students decided to stage a sit in at Rowan Hall,[3] a brick building used by the N.R.O.T.C., across the street from the Sesquicentennial Chapel on Spring Street. Finding the doors locked, the students broke in. They ordered pizza, and had a jazz band play, as about 300 crowded into the building. At 9 p.m. Robert Etheridge, the Vice-President of Student Affairs, warned the students that they were trespassing and would be arrested and suspended from the university if they did not leave. About half did leave. An hour later campus police assisted by the small Oxford police force

---

3. The building had been named in honor of Stephen Rowan, who had been a Union admiral who commanded the USS New Ironsides.

started arresting the remaining 173 students who went limp. When the church bus that was called to transport them to jail broke down, the Butler County Sheriff Harold Carpenter and his deputies began to help. They used dogs and hurled tear gas canisters to disperse the large crowd that had gathered. A battalion of 700 National Guard troops stationed at the Nike missile base on Todd Road north of the campus were never called onto the campus.

The arrested students were fined $50 and released. Dusty Steytler, the main ringleader, spent some jail time. Much of the student anger was difused by President Shriver's personal willingness to listen to them. On April 16 he addressed a packed Withrow Court audience of about 4,500, agreeing in principle to the demands of the BSAA for more Black students and faculty.[4] He closed the meeting with the prayer that such a disturbance would not occur again.

On April 21, as a demonstration of student power, someone had the bright idea of having students simultaneously flush toilets and open shower heads at 6 and 8 p.m., draining the 300,000-gallon water tower which stood in the Oxford city square and two million gallons of water from the main reservoir. This was no laughing matter for the townspeople as sewers overflowed and a possible fire danger resulted.

Kent State University

After president Nixon ordered the bombing of Cambodia on April 30, a far more serious confrontation between protesting students and the authorities occurred at Kent State University near Cleveland in May. On Saturday, May 2 students protesting the Vietnam War burned down the university's ROTC building. The mayor of Kent had requested National Guard troops from Governor James Rhodes because of earlier disturbances in the city of Kent near the campus.

On Monday, May 4, students sought to assemble at the Commons Area but were prevented from doing so by the National Guard. When students persisted, the soldiers hurled tear gas canisters which some students hurled back at them. At 12:24 p.m. the soldiers shot sixty-seven rounds, killing four students and wounding nine others.

---

4. Despite many efforts at recruiting more Black students, in 2022, only 2 percent of Miami students were Black.

Outraged students at many schools protested in sympathy with these victims. Fires were set around the campus, forcing Miami to close from May 7 to 17. All of the other state universities in Ohio closed. Miami was the only school to reopen and finish this tumultuous semester.[5]

A Daughter Is Born

It was right in the middle of the student protests at Miami on April 16 that our daughter Gail Haruko was born at Fort Hamilton Hospital. As I had driven out of town, I had no notion of anything amiss until people at the hospital asked me what was happening back at the university. Our daughter's middle name, which was also my mother's name, means "Child of Spring." My wife remained for five days at the hospital. We soon learned that Gail was allergic to milk, so we had to nourish her on powdered milk made from soybeans.

A Summer in Europe

I had received a grant from the American Philosophical Society to examine some of the unpublished Mandaic manuscripts that Lady E. S. Drower had donated to the Bodleian Library at the University of Oxford. Our newly enlarged family flew on June 17 to spend three weeks in England.

In Oxford we rented a flat behind the Ashmolean Museum and used a chest drawer as a makeshift bassinet for Gail. We were just up the street from the Sheldonian Theater where I witnessed a graduation ceremony. The manuscripts at the Bodleian were listed in a handwritten catalogue. I was able to meet Lady Drower and obtained her autograph on the Mandaic Dictionary that she and Rudolf Macuch had produced. I also went into London to meet J. B. Segal, a scholar who was to publish the Aramaic magic bowls at the British Museum.

My monograph, *Gnostic Ethics and Mandaean Origins*, was published in 1970 by Harvard University Press (and by Oxford University Press in the U.K.).[6] I had been invited to deliver the annual New

---

5. A detailed and informative account of the events at Miami University in April and May, 1970, is presented by Justin Bruce Keiser, "Where Did the Band Come from? Student Protest at Miami University in April, 1970," MA History Thesis, directed by Jeffrey P. Kimball.

6. Most of the reviews were favorable, but a long, critical review was written by Rudolf Macuch of the Free University of Berlin, the foremost scholar of the Mandaic

Testament lecture at Tyndale House in Cambridge in July. This was a residential library sponsored by the British IV, which had been organized by F. F. Bruce, W. J. Martin, and Donald J. Wiseman. It developed a library superior to that of the University of Cambridge in terms of biblical and cognate subjects. This has been used by scores of American scholars doing research in the UK (see chapter 42.) The warden at the time was Alan R. Millard, who showed me around the university's pointing out the room where the great humanist Erasmus stayed when he came to England in 1511 to teach Greek.

Figure 33. With Alan Millard

My lecture was on "Pre-Christian Gnosticism," which was a critical examination of the variety of evidences, including Mandaic, which had been used by German scholars such as Rudolf Bultmann to assert a pre-Christian origin for Gnosticism, which they assumed had influenced Paul and John. I later expanded this as a book, which was published in

language: "Gnostische Ethik und die Anfänge der Mandäer," F. Altheim and R. Stiehl, ed., *Christentum am Roten Meer* 11 (1973), 733–38. I had met Professor Macuch in Tehran and was indebted to him for his publications of very early Mandaic lead amulets. As to his arguments for an early date for Mandaean Gnosticism, they were quite subjective, based on the resemblance of some Mandaic texts with the Gospel of John. This kind of subjective argument was quite typical of other German scholars including Rudolf Bultmann and Kurt Rudolph.

1973 by Tyndale Press in the UK. Unknown to me, the publishers had asked F. F. Bruce to provide a foreward to the book.

On one trip, I witnessed the Henley Regatta boat races. On another trip, driving between Cambridge and Oxford, I stopped at Bedford, where John Bunyan had been imprisoned. Nearby I saw the tombstone of John Newton who had written the lyrics of the beloved hymn, "Amazing Grace." Our family took trips to London and to Windsor Castle, where we stood but four feet away from Prince Charles. We also visited Stratford-on-Avon, where we saw Shakespeare's play "Measure for Measure."

On July 9, we flew to Vienna, Austria. I rode on the Prater, the famous Ferris wheel beside the Danube. We viewed the beautiful Schönbrunn Palace. While someone babysat our children Kimi and I went out to Baden to view a performance of Strauss's comic opera, *Die Fledermaus* "The Bat."

Renting a Volkswagen I drove to Schloss Mittersill, a castle owned by the I.F.E.S. (International Fellowship of Evangelical Students), where I gave lectures to a conference of internationals including doctors from Egypt and students from Hawaii. The castle had a primitive bowling alley in the basement. My wife made the mistake of trying to flush down disposable diapers in the toilet, which disrupted the ancient plumbing system!

On July 13, we joined a tour group traveling to Venice. At the Italian border I was ordered off the bus and feared that I would be left behind as I had forgotten to bring my passport! The guards relented and let me get back on the bus. In Venice, we rode a gondola, and I climbed the tower of St. Mark's Cathedral, where the relics of St. Mark, which had been stolen from Alexandria, are housed. [7]

Driving westward we visited Salzburg, Mozart's city which had provided the background to "The Sound of Music" movie. We visited the church in Oberndorf, where on Christmas eve 1818 "Stille Nacht, Heilige Nach" (Silent Night, Holy Night) was first played on a guitar because the organ was not functioning. The lyrics were by a priest Joseph Mohr; the tune was composed by Franz Grüber, the organist. Crossing the German border, we visited the town of Berchtesgaden and took the bus up the steep road to get to the elevator to Hitler's "Eagle's Nest." On July 23, we flew from Munich, Germany, back to the US.

---

7. The tradition that Mark started Christianity in Egypt is quite late, dating only to Eusebius (4th c. AD).

December Conference

After Christmas, I flew to California to deliver two papers at the joint meeting of the Evangelical Theological Society and the Near East Archaeological Society at Westmont College in Santa Barbara. I was happy to meet Westmont's provost, John W. Snyder, an ancient historian specializing in Sumerian, who had taught at Ohio State University. Being in southern California gave me an opportunity to visit with my mother in LA. My former Brandeis classmate, Fred Bush, who was teaching at Fuller Theological Seminary in Pasadena, reserved a space for me on the sidewalk so I could witness the 1971 New Year's Rose Parade.

Chapter 17

The Next Three Years

(1971 to 1973)

The Year 1971

The Family

BRIAN, WHO LEARNED THE alphabet at two, started reading at three and a half. He began borrowing books from the library. He composed stories about his one-second car, which travels faster than light. I taught him chess at the age of four. In the fall Brian was accepted into the McGuffey Lab School. He was given preference as the only minority child applying. This school was staffed by professors from Miami's School of Education. Their students could observe the classes from balconies above. Both of our children profited immensely from individualized instruction in small classes taught by master teachers.

In September Kimi's father passed away. She flew with Gail to attend his funeral, the first time she had been back to the Islands since 1964. On the way back they stopped at LA to visit my mother who was delighted to see her granddaughter for the first time.

In October we were able to move into a large new house on Erin Drive on the western edge of Oxford in the midst of cornfields. It was a two-story house, painted sea foam green with a large basement study. We were to occupy this house until April 2019.

Academics

In March I delivered lectures on archaeology at Lincoln Theological Seminary.[1] Then in April I read a paper on the Mandeans at the American Oriental Society conference at Harvard University. An outstanding student who graduated from Miami University with honors in 1971 was Susan Doll, the daughter of a Latin teacher. I encouraged Susan to pursue graduate studies at Brandeis University.[2] In August I saw my first MA student, James Gibbs, graduated. He wrote his thesis on: "Mycenaean Connections with Palestine and Transjordan in the Late Bronze Age."

Ministries[3]

In March I lectured for the IV chapter at the University of Pittsburgh. Then in April I spoke together with Dr. Myron Augsberger to a conference for 250 international students in Philadelphia. In October I spoke at the University of Dayton. Early in November, I spoke for the IV at the University of Colorado. The meetings had been arranged by Bob Olsen, a grad from Rutgers, and sponsored by Professor Ed Miller of the Philosophy Department. Later that month, I spoke for the IV at Oberlin College. I surmised that not many Oberlin students knew the significance of the name Charles G. Finney, the famous evangelist, inscribed on one of the college's buildings.

The Year 1972

Academics

I began teaching large classes of History 121 (Western Civilization) which ranged from 100 up to 300 students. I would lecture twice a week, and grad assistants would hold a discussion session with a section of about 25 students. I provided students with a booklet with outlines of

---

1. It was then that Gerald Mattingly, who later became a leading archaeologist in Jordan, first met me.

2. Susan received a PhD for a dissertation on late Egyptian pharaohs Anlamani and Aspelta. She worked at the Museum of Fine Arts in Boston, and then in the administration of Boston University.

3. I have written a separate chapter (Ch. 46) on the history of the Oxford Bible Fellowship, a church we helped to begin in 1970.

each lecture, a procedure I learned from Frank Sells at C.B.C. My exams were a mixture of 50 objective questions (map, true and false, matching, completion, and identification) together with brief essay questions.

I taught upper division history classes on Ancient Egypt and Ancient Persia with 30 to 50 students. Exams were essay questions. Graduate students could also take the upper division classes. They would have to produce research papers. Robert Wissel, my second MA student graduated, writing on: "The Role of the Elephant in Ancient Warfare."

Publications

In 1972, my *Stones and the Scriptures* appeared in a series edited by John Warwick Montgomery.[4] It was published in the US by J. B. Lippincott[5] and in the U.K. in 1973 by InterVarsity Press. A Spanish version was published in 1977. Because of the yearly increase of archaeological discoveries, much of the content of the book became outdated. But a lasting contribution was my observation of circles of overlapping evidence (traditional, textual, material) and the fractions of what are surveyed, excavated, and published at any given time, making negative assessments of the biblical tradition always inconclusive.[6]

---

4. *Christianity Today* listed *The Stones and the Scriptures* among the twenty-five most significant books published in 1972.

5. At the same time my manuscript titled *Men, Methods and Materials in Biblical Archaeology* was accepted and even advertised by Baker Book House. However, its publication was blocked by Lippincott, noting that my contract prohibited the publication of a competing book.

6. These observations were incorporated by Alfred Hoerth of Wheaton College in his teaching and in his book on Old Testament archaeology.

Figure 34. With John Warwick Montgomery

Library Resources

In 1972 Miami completed the construction of athe four-story King Library to replace the old library with its dark stacks housed in Alumni Hall. Alumni Hall retained a special Art and Architecture Library. Students assembled in a long human chain to transfer the books from the south quad to the west quad.

For someone as myself who was interested in the backgrounds of both the Old and the New Testament I could not have landed at a more ideal place for libraries. Less than an hour south in the Clifton area in Cincinnati was the Klau Library of Hebrew Union College,[7] the oldest seminary for the liberal Reformed Judaism, begun in Cincinnati in 1875 by Rabbi Isaac Wise from Europe. Up the street was the Blegen Library

---

7. After the departure of Cyrus Gordon from Brandeis University, Hebrew Union College became the graduate school of choice for evangelical students seeking a background in Semitic languages. Limiting the list to scholars whom I know personally, the following received their PhDs from HUC: Martin Abegg, Bill Arnold, Bryan Beyer, Hassell Bullock. John Choi, Hélène Dallaire, Sara Fudge, John Halton, Rick Hess, David Musgrave, Benjamin Noonan, Jennifer Noonan, Christine Palmer, David Palmer, Sun Jin Park, Andrew Riley, Michael Thigpen, David Turner, John Walton, Ken Way, and Wilke Winter.

of the Classics Department of the University of Cincinnati, named after Carl Blegen, the noted excavator of Troy and of Pylos. One of the department's chairs had married into the wealthy Taft family, which resulted in a bequest of several million dollars for the department. The librarians, Jean Wellington and Michael Braunlin, allowed both my grad students and myself access to the closed stacks.

Also in Cincinnati was the library of the Cincinnati Christian University perched on Price Hill, with a magnificent panoramic view of the city.[8] The Athenaeum was a Catholic seminary in Cincinnati which housed the Eugene Maly Library.[9]

Two hours southwest was the Southern Baptist Seminary in Louisville. Two hours northeast was Columbus with the Ohio State University and Catholic, Methodist, and Lutheran seminaries.

Judith Sessions, the Dean of Libraries, and her assistant, Dick Pettitt, personally examined library computer systems from Maine to Hawaii to help develop in 1992 the unique Ohio Link, which connected 16 state university libraries and 50 private college libraries[10] in a union catalogue, with members of the participating schools free to borrow from this catalogue. Books would be delivered by a private trucking firm within five days.

Ministries

I began a weekly meeting for what I called the Faculty Christian Fellowship. We met at noon for lunch, prayer, and a Bible exposition. I also included graduate students and staff members in our invitation. We discussed books of such authors as Augustine, Luther, Calvin, James Packer, C. S. Lewis, Dietrich Bonhoeffer, and Francis Schaeffer. One semester Bill Pratt, who is an authority on T. S. Elliot, led us in a discussion of his poems.

Among those attending over the years were: Greg Barger (architecture), Bob Benz (personnel), Michael Buck (English), Reo Christenson (political science), Tom Coakley (history), Phil Cottell (accountancy), Michelle Deardorff (political science), Bob Demaas

---

8. In 2020, this school had to close for financial reasons.

9. Father Maly once led a session for Christian faculty in our home thanks to the personal invitation of Joan Moynagh.

10. Hebrew Union College with its special collection of books chose not to join this consortium.

(education), Charles Flynn (sociology), Dan Hoffman (history), David Kullman (math), Richard Laatsch (math), John Lowery (journalism), Joan Moynagh (music), Anne Pratt (French), Bill Pratt (English), Jerry Sanders (communications), Mary Dean Sanders (paper technology), Fred Schuurmann (math), Brad Simcock (sociology), Dwight Smith (history), Ruth Waggener (audio-visual), and Kimi Yamauchi (German, Russian, and East Asian languages).

Attendance averaged about eight or ten, once reaching as high as twenty-seven. Once, besides my wife, only one person showed up, Greg Barger, an architecture graduate student who, with his professor Hal Barcus, helped to design our church building on Maple Street.

In the spring of 1972, IV sponsored a conference at Miami University with several staff members including Bill Pannell, Tom Trevethan, and John Alexander, the president of IV. John had been the chair of the top-ranked Geography Department at the University of Wisconsin, when he shocked his colleagues by resigning to become the head of IV.

I spoke in February to the IV graduate fellowship at Cornell University. My stay with Dr. Robert Fay, a chemistry prof, was prolonged by a snowstorm. In March I lectured at Western Kentucky University, where Ronald Nash, the chair of the Religion and Philosophy Department had recruited a number of evangelical scholars, including New Testament scholars Bill Lane and Margaret Howe and an Old Testament scholar Ron Veenker. In April, I spoke at the Philadelphia College of the Bible, where I reconnected with Gordon Ceperly, whom I had met in Israel. I also met my Shelton classmate, Lin Crowe who was on the ministerial staff of the Tenth Presbyterian Church in Philadelphia, noted as the church of Donald Grey Barnhouse, the editor of *Eternity Magazine*.

In May, I presented a lecture on "The Dead Sea Scrolls" at the large Fourth Presbyterian Church in DC, which was attended by senators and cabinet members. Its pastor, Rev. Richard Halverson, later became the Senate's chaplain. While in DC, I visited the offices of *Christianity Today*. I met Harold O. J. Brown, one of the editors. Another editor, Don Tinder took me to lunch at the National Press Club. In October I was chosen as an editor-at-large for *Christianity Today*.[11]

---

11. An article on "Historical Notes on the (In)comparable Christ," which I had published in *Christianity Today* in 1971, was reprinted in 1973 by InterVarsity Press as a booklet titled *Jesus, Zoroaster, Buddha, Socrates, Muhammad*. In less than a year, 15,000 copies were distributed. Canadian InterVarsity later reprinted this booklet.

In August, I spoke at a conference of Japanese American Christians in Chicago. This gave Kimi an opportunity to visit her friends at Scripture Press in Wheaton. In October I spoke at Ball State University in Muncie, Indiana. Ball State is best known for its alumnus the talk show host David Letterman.

The Year 1973

Athletics and Music

In 1973 Miami's football team went undefeated, was ranked no. 1 in defense and no. 15th nationally. The 1970s were also the decade of the Cincinnati Reds, the oldest professional team in the major leagues. The "Big Red Machine" featured a number of future Hall of Fame players such as catcher Johnny Bench and second baseman Joe Morgan. Third baseman and later coach, Pete Rose, a beloved Cincinnatian, would have made the Hall of Fame had he not been banned from baseball for life for gambling.

Because of its strong German heritage, Cincinnati has enjoyed one of the oldest choral societies in America. The choir presents four performances at the May Festival each year at Music Hall. Singers, who are volunteers, practice all year round. Especially rousing was their performance of Beethoven's 9th Symphony this year. After doing research at Hebrew Union College and at the UC Classics Library, I often enjoyed going to the opera at Music Hall.

Academics

In January I invited Emmet Bennett from the University of Wisconsin to lecture on Mycenaean texts. In his University of Cincinnati dissertation Bennett had worked on the Pylos texts which provided the key to the decipherment by Michael Ventris of Linear B as Greek. I learned that when he was in Cincinnati, he enjoyed appearing as a supernumerary in the opera. When I first arrived, the opera was being performed at the zoo with animal cries providing background music!

In l973 William R. Holcomb, wrote his MA thesis, "Cimmerian and Scythian Invasions into Western Asia," under my direction. This was a subject I was to incorporate into my book, *Foes from the Northern Frontier*.

Publications

In 1973 my *Pre-Christian Gnosticism* was published by Tyndale Press in the U.K., and by Eerdmans in the US. Elaine Pagels of Princeton University reviewed it favorably in *Theological Studies*.[12] Her teacher at Harvard Divinity School, George MacRae, SJ informed me that though he did not agree with the conclusion of *Pre-Christian Gnosticism*, he did recommend it to his students.[13] James Charlesworth, then at Duke University, wrote to Eerdmans that it was the best work summarizing the issues of Gnosticism.[14] Craig Keener said that the book encouraged him greatly when he was in graduate studies at Duke University. *Pre-Christian Gnosticism*, which I expanded in a second edition a decade later and which has been reprinted, remains one of my most cited publications.[15]

The History Department

In 1973 I was promoted to full professor, an honor that in time made me the most senior professor in rank in the department, entailing certain responsibilities that made me uncomfortable as I had no interest in departmental politics. In fact, I rarely spoke at departmental meetings.

---

12. Elaine sent me her book, *The Gnostic Gospels* (1979) in which she noted: "The many scholars who have shared in this research . . . include Professors R. M. Grant and E. Yamauchi in the United States" (p. xxxiv). In an interview about Gnosticism Elaine Pagels responded: "I thought that Edwin Yamauchi's book was really clear, that there's no pre-Christian Gnosticism." Miguel Bonner, ed., *Voices of Gnosticism* (Dublin, United Kingdom: Bardicx Press, 2011), 143.

13. In a letter dated December 14, 1973, Professor MacRae wrote: "I have urged my students to read your book. I know that a number of them have bought it at our local bookstore. I find it a very useful work indeed, although I am not in full agreement with the way in which the case for pre-Christian Gnosticism is dealt with."

14. In a letter dated August 8, 1973, Professor Charlesworth wrote to Eerdmans: "The full treatment and convenient organization of data along with the balanced arguments suggest that Yamauchi's book is the best available introduction to pre-Christian Gnosticism."

15. Within two years, reviews of *Pre-Christian Gnosticism* appeared in over 3thirty journals published in eight countries. Bruce Winter, the Warden of Tyndale House, Cambridge, wrote to me in 2003: "I can remember when your radical, but entirely unfashionable thesis re the fallacy of Gnosticism in the first century hit the deck and the early response to it at SBL (the Society of Biblical Literature). Who could have guessed that your book would hole that carrier below water line and sink it. Now they shuffle their feet if you mentioned the assured findings in the 1980s of Gnosticism in the New Testament period."

Scholarly Presentations

In September I took part in an interdisciplinary symposium sponsored by the publisher, Tyndale House, at Westmont, Illinois. Among the other participants and their disciplines were: Roger Blackwell (Business), John Brobeck (Medicine), Richard Bube (Material Science), Kenneth Elzinga (Economics), Walter Hearn (Biochemistry), C. Everett Koop (Pediatrics), John McIntyre (Nuclear Physics), Ronald Michaelson (Political Science), Robert Mounce (Religion), Armand Nicholi (Psychiatry), Joseph V. Noble (Art), Ray Robinson (Music), John and Letha Sanzoni (Sociology), John Snyder (Education), Ted Ward (Education), Nicholas Wolterstorff (Philosophy) and James Young (Drama).

As the president of the Conference of Faith and History, I presided over its convention in October at Columbus. Among notable historians present were Edwin Orr, Stanford Reid and Timothy Smith. In November I presented a paper on "The Use of Mandaean Texts for Pre-Christian Gnosticism" at the Society of Biblical Conference in Chicago. I was asked four questions by James M. Robinson. Also present was David Scholer, the bibliographer of the Nag Hammadi Gnostic texts, who was to provide me with fascicles of his annual compilations.

In December, at the meeting of the Evangelical Theological Society at Wheaton College, I served on a panel presided over by Merrill Tenney, which included New Testament scholars F. F. Bruce of Manchester University, George Ladd of Fuller Theological Seminary, Bill Lane of Western Kentucky University, and I. Howard Marshall of Aberdeen University.

Figure 35. NT panel at Wheaton College chaired by Merrill Tenney. From left to right: Bill Lane, F. F. Bruce, Howard Marshall, EMY, and George Ladd

Ministries

As Barney Ford left Miami for Columbus to assume oversight for IV in Ohio, Kent Stephens, a graduate of Ball State University, came in August as the new IV staff worker. Don Fields, the area supervisor, came to speak at Miami University. That same month, in September, Dr. Terry Morrison, IV staff for faculty spoke. Terry had been a chemistry professor at Butler University. I arranged for the Faculty Christian Fellowship an annual spring banquet featuring guest lecturers. Our speaker in 1973 was the noted Quaker author, Elton Trueblood, from Earlham College in nearby Richmond, Indiana.

I lectured at Mt. Vernon Nazarene College, Case Western Reserve University, and Wright State University. I also spoke at a number of churches including a Presbyterian church in College Corner,[16] the church at Hopewell in Hueston Woods Park,[17] Lutheran churches in

---

16. College Corner, northwest of Oxford, straddles the line between Ohio and Indiana. The state line runs through the middle of the high school basketball court!

17. This was the oldest Presbyterian church in the area of Oxford.

Oxford and Hamilton, and a Brethren Church in Youngstown. I also spoke to the Kinney Corporation at a luncheon at the Vernon Manor Hotel in Cincinnati.

In June, I went on a trip to New England to attend a banquet at Harvard University in honor of Cyrus Gordon's sixty-fifth birthday and his retirement from Brandeis University. He was presented with *Orient and Occident*, a Festschrift containing articles by colleagues and former students, edited by Harry Hoffner. It was good to see many former Brandeis alumni and faculty there.

I spoke at the Presbyterian Church in Waltham, at Park Street Church in Boston, and at a Baptist Church in Beverly. I also spoke at a camp on Cape Cod, run by the daughters of Wyeth Willard.

Chapter 18

Near East Travels

(1974 to 1975)

The Year 1974

FOR THE FALL SEMESTER of 1974 and the spring of 1975, I had a sabbatical with a grant from the Institute of Advanced Christian Studies. Cyrus St. Clair from Ohio State University taught in my stead. My original plan to travel in the Near East was based on an invitation to read a paper at the Second International Mithraic Congress in Tehran, Iran. But the patroness, the empress, at the last minute decided to postpone the conference for a year because of its possible conflict with the Asian Games which were being held in Iran. But having obtained visas and shots I decided to go ahead with my travel plans. I was to visit eight countries[1] in eight weeks (Sept. 14 to Nov. 17), traveling on a budget of $20 to $30 per day. I had a suitcase with wheels and a handy denim bag with a loop which I could throw over my right shoulder. I wore white sneakers and a white cap with a red brim with the words "Waikiki" emblazoned on it. I was eager to see many sites that I had included in my lectures on the ancient history of the Near East, Egypt, Persia, and Greece. It helped that I had a rudimentary grasp of some of the local languages. My travel journal had only sketchy entries. My best source of detailed information comes from the 28 letters that I wrote to my family.

1. I was not able to get a visa to Iraq, though I had an invitation from the Baghdad Museum to examine some of the Mandaic magic bowls in their collection.

1. Greece

On September 14 I flew from Dayton to La Guardia in New York, then took Olympic Airlines to fly to Greece. We flew over the Alps and landed at Athens on Sept. 15. Instead of taking a taxi for 200 drachmas (33 drachmas = $1) or nearly $7, I took a bus for 12 drachmas (40 cents). I stayed at the Hotel Eretria, which was a block away from the hotel where our family had stayed in 1968.

On September 16 I rented a car and drove down past Corinth to Sparta in the southeast Peloponnesus. This city state was second only to Athens during the fifth century BC but attracts no tourists because it has few significant remains. Sparta did not even have a city wall as it relied on its superior army. The remains of the altar of Artemis Orthia, where Spartan youths were beaten as a rite of passage still survives.

On September 17 I drove on long winding roads over the Taygetus Mountain where unwanted Spartan babies were exposed to die. I then drove to Pylos in the southwestern Peloponnesus. There I was able to view the remains of the Mycenaean Palace of Nestor that Carl Blegen of the University of Cincinnati had uncovered. I then drove back north and east to Argos, Sparta's main rival in the Peloponnesus.

On September 18 I was back in Athens. On September 19 I went down to the harbor at the Piraeus and took the ferry to Santorini (ancient Thera). This is a fabled volcanic island in the Aegean which exploded with cataclysmic force (c. 1600 BC). This has led numerous writers to associate it with the legendary Atlantis. Arriving on September 20 along with other tourists I rode a donkey up the steep zigzag road to the hill where the hotels are located.

Later that day I took the local bus to the site of Akrotiri where Spyridon Marinatos had unearthed a buried Minoan city. The walls of its houses were still decorated with colorful images of crocuses, monkeys, open bosomed priestesses, and even a naval battle. Mrs. Marinatos led a group of us on a tour. I signed the guest book after the signature of Jaqueline Kennedy. I did not meet Dr. Marinatos but saw him at work through an open window. Just a few weeks later he fell from a ladder and passed away.

On September 21 there was such a crush of passengers boarding the ferry to return to Athens that I paid an extra $6 to go to the first-class section. Returning to the Piraeus at 6:30 a.m. on September 22 I had time to visit the National Museum in Athens where the fabulous frescoes from Akrotiri were on display.

2. Turkey

Later that day I flew from Athens to Istanbul, where I would be housed in the home of Michael and Sylvia Green. A graduate of Rensselaer Polytechnic University, Dr. Green was teaching at Boghazici University (formerly Roberts College). He had attended the Loudanville church pastored by Dennis Kinlaw. Sylvia had once dated Marlin Kreider with whom I had stayed while at Brandeis.

On September 23 I viewed the Ottoman Topkapi Palace in Istanbul with its fabulous throne room and jewels as well as the Hagia Eirene church and the huge Blue Mosque, which the Turks had built to rival the Hagia Sophia. I saw the obelisk of Tuthmosis III which once stood in Constantine's hippodrome where chariot races took place.

Starting from September 24, I rented a Fiat for six days at $30 per day. I had some trouble finding my way out of Istanbul before driving west along the Gallipoli peninsula to the Dardanelles (Hellespont) strait. I experienced a flat on the right rear tire. A hitchhiker I had picked up helped me fix the tire. It took only ten minutes to cross the Dardanelles by the ferry passing as it were from European Turkey to Asian Turkey.[2]

On September 25 I stayed at a spacious but largely empty hotel at Canakkale. I paid $3.50 for a used inner tube to repair the flat tire. I then visited Hissarlik, which Heinrich Schliemann had identified as Troy in 1870. After a busload of German tourists departed, I was left all alone to wander over the ruins, which Carl Blegen of the University of Cincinnati had uncovered in his excavations in the 1930s. A small wooden replica of "The Trojan Horse" stood at the entrance to greet tourists.

I then drove south to Assos, an important site where Aristotle once stayed and where Paul also visited (Acts 20:13). It has some of the best-preserved Hellenistic fortification walls. Just off the coast is the large island of Lesbos which like other offshore islands belongs to Greece. From its association with the female poet Sappho we derive the name "Lesbian" for a female homosexual. More recently Lesbos has become the goal of refugees from Syria who were desperate to reach asylum in Europe.

2. Asia was originally a Hittite word, Assuwa. In Roman times, it was applied to the region around Ephesus (as in the Book of Acts). Later Asia Minor became a designation of Turkey. Currently it means countries in the far east such as China and Japan.

I reached Bergama (ancient Pergamum), once the capital of a major kingdom which was ceded to the Romans in 133 BC I paid $5.60 for the hotel room. The acropolis of Pergamum features an extremely steep theater. It was the site of the second largest library in the Hellenistic world. This was also the site of a magnificent Altar to Zeus. Also of great interest in the plain below the acropolis are the ruins of Pergamum's famous healing shrine dedicated to Asclepius.

On September 26 I drove inland to Sardis, once the capital of the Lydian Kingdom. Sardis with Pergamon and five other cities are listed among the Seven Churches of John's Apocalypse (Rev 2 to 3). There I started photographing the stadium complex and the large synagogue which George Hanfmann of Harvard had excavated and restored, until a guard stopped me, saying that photography was not permitted. There I also experienced a second flat tire, this time on the left rear!

I stayed at a hotel at Izmir (Smyrna) on the coast. At a restaurant next door I was treated during dinner to entertainment by a belly dancer! On September 27 at Izmir I easily found the excavated site of Archaic Smyrna in an orchard. But I had some difficulty in finding the Roman agora as it was squeezed into a crowded urban neighborhood.

Later that day. I was able to visit the marvelous remains of the great city of Ephesus, which the Austrians have uncovered and restored. I ran all over the site to see as much as possible of the great theater, the site of the Temple of Artemis and the two agoras.

On September 28 I drove south to see the ruins of the Hellenistic city at Priene and then visited the important site of Miletus, which was renowned as the home of the pre-Socratic philosophers and noted also as the mother of numerous Greek colonies around the Black Sea. Paul on his way to Jerusalem addressed elders from Ephesus there (Acts 20:15). I also visited Didyma, where there are well preserved remains of the temple to Apollo, designed by the same architect who worked on the temple to Artemis at Ephesus.

On September 29 I drove into the Lycus Valley where there are three cities mentioned by Paul in his letter to the Colossians (Colosse, Hierapolis and Laodicea). Laodicea is also one of the seven churches of Revelation. The modern name of Hierapolis "Sacred City" is Pamukkale "Cotton Castle" after the glistening white terraces that have been formed by its mineral rich hot springs. I stayed in a hotel where I was able to swim in a pool filled with these warm waters. Italians have excavated the site, where one temple was known to the Romans as the Plutonium because its sulfurous fumes seemed to emanate from the Underworld.

Laodicea had been partially excavated by French Canadian excavators. Colosse, however, remained unexcavated. A farmer helped me find the isolated site where ancient remains protrude from the mound. On the way back to the coast I took a side trip to view the ruins of Aphrodisias where an important synagogue inscription has been uncovered that mentions Gentile "god fearers," a group which is prominent in the book of Acts.

On September 30 after returning the rental car to the agency I took a flight from Izmir to Istanbul which cost only $20. I was met at the airport by Michael Green. I took a boat ride up to the Bosporus, the strait leading to the Black Sea. That evening I attended a reception at Michael's university.

On October 1 I toured the Hagia Sophia "Holy Wisdom," the enormous church built by Justinian in the sixth century. After the fall of Constantinople to the Turks in 1453 it had been reduced to the status of a museum decorated with quotations from the Q Qur'ān.[3] I also visited the great museum of antiquities which houses many notable antiquities from Palestine when it was under Ottoman rule, including Hezekiah's inscription from the Siloam Tunnel.

3. Iran

On October 2 I flew to Tehran over the Zagros Mountains which demarcates the upland plateau of Iran from the riverine plains of Iraq to the west. On October 3 I rode on a bus to Kermanshah in northwestern Iran and then took a taxi to view the famous trilingual (Akkadian, Elamite, Old Persian) inscription of Darius at Behistun (modern Bisitun) up high on a mountainside. The heroic copying of this text by Henry Rawlinson led to the decipherment of cuneiform.

On October 4 I then took a three-hour bus ride to get to Hamadan (the site of Ecbatana, capital of the Medes). On October 5, I toured Hamadan, viewing the tomb of the famous Avicena (Ibn Sina), the greatest medical authority of the Middle Ages. On a bare hilltop I viewed the remains of a lion statue left by Alexander the Great. I made a side trip to

---

3. Despite protests from Christians, the Hagia Sophia was reopened as a mosque in 2020.

the Ganj Nameh where an inscription was set up by Darius and next to it a copy by his son Xerxes.

On October 6 I took the bus to Kermanshah and then to Tehran, where I met Mandaic scholar Rudolf Macuch, who was later to teach at the Free University of Berlin. I also had dinner with Paul Rejai, an Iranian who taught Political Science at Miami University.

On October 7 I flew to the Iranian city of Isfahan in the south. At the famous Shah Abbas Hotel. I splurged and charged $6.60 on my American Express card to enjoy a fabulous dinner of lamb and rice. Isfahan is noted for its beautiful plazas, pools and mosques. A teenage boy beckoned me to follow him into a back alley where I witnessed what it takes to create a Persian carpet. Three teachers watched over twelve girls, some as young as seven, who were tying knots to create a pattern. Such a carpet could take up to three years to complete and would sell for $200. I bartered with a merchant for souvenirs for the family. He wanted to charge 900 rials, I offered him 400. We settled at 550 rials ($8.25; 68 rials = $1).

I traveled to the city of Shiraz where I stayed in a second-class hotel for three nights for $3.75 per night rather than in the more expensive NTO hotel for $9 per night or at Persepolis for $18 night. This meant that there were no towels, soap, or toilet paper. The toilet consisted of two holes in the floor. Instead of paying for an all-day taxi for $24, I took the local bus for 30 cents to view the fabulous site of Persepolis, the palatial capital built by Darius and Xerxes. I was able to spend two and a half hours photographing the many well preserved remains which the University of Chicago excavations had uncovered and restored. The air-conditioned tents used for the Shah's celebration of the 2500th anniversary of the Persian Empire which took place during Nixon's presidency were still in place. David Stronach, the head of the British Institute of Persian Studies in Iran, informed me that during the Iranian revolution of 1979 some of the more zealous rebels wanted to destroy the site because of its association with the hated Shah, but cooler heads had prevailed.

When I got back to Shiraz, I found that all the restaurants were closed for the afternoon "siesta." When they opened again, I was able to purchase a lamb kebab for 90 cents.

I rented a car for $34 to get to Pasargadae which is 50 miles north of Persepolis.[4] Though it is important as the capital of Cyrus few tourists visit it as there are relatively few monuments that remain. David Stronach

---

4. Gasoline was extremely inexpensive at 36 cents a gallon. In 2019 when the government tried to raise the price to 50 cents, nationwide riots ensued.

had excavated the site and had unearthed the remains of several buildings. The most striking monument is the Tomb of Cyrus. On the way back I stopped by Naqsh i-Rustam, north of Persepolis. The cliff there holds the rock cut tombs of Darius, Xerxes, and Artaxerxes I. That evening I was able to return to Persepolis to enjoy a magnificent Sound and Light performance there.

On October 8 I flew south passing over the Shatt al-Arab, the single confluence of the Euphrates and the Tigris, which forms the border between Iran and Iraq. I landed at Ahwaz in southwestern Iran. As a direct taxi from the airport would charge $18, I took a cab into Abadan for $1.50 and then a shared taxi for $3.75 into Ahwaz, a trip which took two hours. The temperature was up to 100 degrees. Many of the hotels were full but I was able to find a cheap room next to the kitchen with a ceiling fan for $4.50. In the bazaar of Ahwaz I saw my first Mandaeans in a silver shop in a bazaar.

On October 9 a taxi driver asked for 1200 rials ($18) to take me to Choga Zanbil over dirt roads to view a well-preserved Elamite ziggurat. But I decided to forego this and took a bus and shared taxi for 60 cents to go to Shush (Susa). This was the city where the book of Esther took place. The French have excavated the site for about a century but there are few monuments for tourists to view. The most impressive building is the chateau the French built by reusing ancient bricks.[5] I was tempted to buy a beautiful kerchief in the bazaar for my wife until I noticed that it was "made in Japan"! On October 11 I took a taxi for $2.25 to get to the airport to fly to Kuwait. But as we had to stay over in Kuwait, I then had to pay $16.50 to get to a hotel.

4. Jordan

On October 12 I flew to Amman, Jordan where I saw a doctor about my bronchitis. I paid three Jordanian dollars ($4.50) for my treatment. I visited the museum in Amman where I was able to see the plaster inscription from Deir Allah which mentions the prophet Balaam (Numbers 22). I then viewed the well-preserved Roman theater on the citadel.

On October 13 I traveled north of Amman riding a shared taxi for less than a dollar to visit the extensive Roman and Byzantine remains of

---

5. In the Hebrew Union College library there is a book that contains copies of the fascinating correspondence of Herbert Paper with his wife, written while he helped Roman Ghirshman excavate Susa.

the city of Jerash (ancient Gerasa, one of the cities of the Decapolis). That evening, I attended a Baptist worship service in Amman.

On October 14 I flew south to Aqaba on the Red Sea directly across from the Israeli town of Elath. My cab driver informed me that he had acted as one of the camel drivers in the movie Lawrence of Arabia which was filmed in the nearby Wadi Rum. I then took a tour of the fabulous remains of Petra, the Nabataean capital, with its magnificent tombs carved out of the red cliffs. I climbed up to the high place, which gave a panoramic view of the site. On October 15, I somehow missed the bus to Amman, so I got a ride on a jeep to Ma'an and then took a service taxi to Amman.

5. Syria

On October 16 I flew to Damascus, Syria. A thirteen-year old boy carried my luggage three blocks to the hotel. People were in a very festive mood as it was the Eid al-Fitr, the feast day ending the fast of Ramadan. I was able to view "The Street Called Straight" (Acts 9:11) mentioned in the story of Paul's conversion. I also visited the grand Umayyad mosque. In the evening, I went to see an Arabic movie. Once the doors opened, the waiting crowd rushed pell-mell to grab seats!

On October 17 I had to get to the bus depot by 6:30 am to catch a bus to get to the Roman ruins at the oasis town of Palmyra (biblical Tadmor) in the desert.[6] It took two hours to get to Homs and then another two hours to get to Palmyra. Once there I wandered around the ruins under the blazing heat of the sun with the temperature close to 100 degrees Fahrenheit. I was back at Damascus at 9:30 p.m.

On October 18 I was able to visit the museum in Damascus where the famous wall paintings from the Dura Europos synagogue are displayed. Dura Europos was a city on the western Euphrates in Iraq where three houses of worship were uncovered: a synagogue, a Mithraeum and the earliest Christian church uncovered. The latter's baptistery is now displayed in Yale University's Gallery of Art.

---

6. In 2015 the fanatical ISIS Muslims destroyed much of the "pagan" Roman monuments of Palmyra as they also destroyed the "pagan" Assyrian monuments in Mosul in northeastern Iraq.

6. Lebanon

I then flew to Beirut, Lebanon where I met David Penman from Australia, a staff worker for IFES (International Fellowship of Evangelical Students) allied with IV in the US. He took me to the infirmary of the American University of Beirut where I received a penicillin shot for my lingering bronchitis. I also met Samuel Shahid, a Jordanian citizen born in Palestine, who was the first Arab IFES staff member, as well as Bruce Demarest, the theological secretary for IFES. I was invited to join them and to speak to a conference for college students.

On October 19 I was able to visit the ruins of Roman temples at Baalbek in the Beka'a Valley between the Lebanon and Anti-Lebanon Mountains. A short time later when civil war broke out in Lebanon this area became the territory occupied by the Hezbollah rebels and thus inaccessible to tourists.

On October 20 I went up the coast to view the cliffs on the side of the Nahr al-Kalb "Dog River," where Egyptian and Babylonian kings had placed their inscriptions. Both the pharaohs and Mesopotamian monarchs had coveted the "cedars of Lebanon," which were also praised in the Old Testament. Of especial interest were the ruins of ancient Byblos, the port from which the Greeks obtained papyrus from Egypt.[7]

On October 21 I hired a taxi, which took me to the famous Phoenician harbor cities of Tyre and Sidon. Tyre, once an island, was transformed into a peninsula when Alexander the Great built a causeway to capture it. At this time, very little of the Iron Age Phoenicians had been recovered by archaeologists. I also visited the small coastal site of Sarepta (Zarephath), which is mentioned in both the Old and the New Testaments. In Beirut, I spoke at Haigazian College, an Armenian school, where my former classmate from Brandeis, Andy Bowling, was teaching.

7. Egypt

On October 22, I was met at the Cairo airport by Bruce Demarest, David Penman, and Samuel Shahid, ho had flown to Egypt before me. I stayed with them at Emmanuel House, an Anglican guest house in Cairo for the bargain cost of only 100 piasters ($1.72)!

---

7. This is why the Greek word for scroll was *biblos*, which has given us many English words including the "Bible."

On October 23 I was able to visit the Cairo Museum on Tahrir (Freedom) Square⁸ and view the treasures of king Tutankhamon's unlooted tomb. The lighting on the ground floor, however, was so dim that I had to use a flashlight to see the labels. I had a much better view of these fabulous treasures when they were later exhibited on a tour of museums in the US. I was able to visit Giza on the west bank and climbed into the pyramid of Chephren (Khafre). Nearby was the great pyramid of Cheops (Khufu), the only one of the Seven Wonders of the ancient World to survive. I rode on a donkey to the Sphinx. In nearby Saqqara I was able to descend to the underground burial site of the Apis bulls.

Figure 36. By the Sphinx

On October 25 Bruce Demarest and I bought second-class tickets on a train traveling north to Alexandria on the Mediterranean coast. We had time for just a hurried look at the museum galleries as it closed at 11:30 a.m. as it was Friday, the Muslim holy day. We visited the site of what had been the island of Pharos where the famous lighthouse which was one of the Seven Wonders of the Ancient World once stood.[9] We viewed "Pompey's Pillar," where an annex of the great library assembled by Ptolemy II was located, and the ruins of a small Roman theater. As we

---

8. This square was later to be the center of countless demonstrations against the government.

9. A French underwater expedition has recovered many statues from nearby waters.

had failed to make second-class reservations for our return trip, we had to ride in the crowded third-class coach where we were fortunate to find seats. Four people squeezed into a seat designed for two and the aisles were packed with people. I was astonished to observe people climbing in through the windows and even some riding on the top of the coaches![10] Bruce commented that in India trains were even more crowded with not only people but also with animals!

On October 26 which was a Saturday, I joined in a worship service with about thirty Coptic Christians, singing hymns in Arabic in a crowded flat. Copts comprise about 10 percent of Egypt's population. Presbyterian missionaries have won some of the Coptic Orthodox to an evangelical faith. The Coptic Pope has promoted Bible studies. On October 27 Mary Massoud guided us to the oldest Coptic church in Cairo and led us to the Coptic Museum which houses the Nag Hammadi codices discovered in 1945. These include important Coptic translations of Greek originals such as the Gospel of Thomas.

I took an overnight sleeper train for the fifteen-hour ride south to Aswan, that is, up the Nile River to the site where a huge dam was built to form Lake Nasser. On October 28, I arrived at Aswan at 10 a.m. I took a horse-drawn carriage for 5 piasters (10 cents) rather than a taxi for 25 piasters. I hired a boat for $2.50 to take me to Elephantine Island where a garrison of Jewish mercenaries were posted under Persian rule of Egypt in the fifthcentury BC Aramaic papyri from the site provide important background data for the book of Nehemiah. I hired a guide and a taxi driver for $17 to take me to the High Dam and to the quarry to view an unfinished obelisk. The famous island of Philae was being protected by a coffer dam, as workers were in the process of dismantling the many temples on the island to reassemble them above the waters of Lake Nasser. One of the temples from the time of Augustus rescued from the rising waters of the dam was dismantled and donated to the Metropolitan Museum in New York City where it is housed in a special wing funded by the Sackler family.[11]

On October 29 with other tourists, I boarded a hydrofoil boat which took us to Abu Simbel near the border with Sudan. We left at 5:30 a.m., and traveling at 40 miles per hour, we covered 180 miles and arrived at Abu Simbel at 10 a.m. There we were able to view the

---

10. In Tahrir Square I observed people clinging to the outside of buses.

11. This is the wealthy family that made billions from the drugs marketed during the recent opioid crisis.

four colossal sandstone statues (70 feet high) of Ramesses II, which had been cut apart by Italian stone cutters and reassembled above the waters of Lake Nasser. Advocates of the Late Date of the Exodus believe that Ramesses the Great was the pharaoh of the Exodus. We stayed until 1:30 p.m. and were able to explore the temple of Queen Nefertari. From Aswan I traveled north to Luxor.

On October 30 I wanted to cross the Nile River to the west bank to view the Valley of the Kings. A tour there would have cost $13.60, but as I was running short of Egyptian currency, I rented a bicycle for 68 cents, took the ferry to cross the Nile, rode the bicycle and hopped on a local bus for another 68 cents to the Valley of the Kings. The highlight was a visit to the intact tomb of Tutankhamun, which Howard Carter had discovered in 1929. I accepted the invitation of a boy to ride his donkey for 43 cents, which took me up along the edge of a cliff, giving me a vertiginous view of the mortuary temple of Hatshepsut at Deir elBahri below at the base of the cliff. I had to assure myself that donkeys were surefooted animals!

On the plain, I was able to view the two colossal statues of "Memnon," that is, of Amenhotep III and the temple at Medinet Habu of Ramesses III which depicts on its walls the attacks of the Sea Peoples, including the *Peleset* (i.e. Philistines) in the twelfth century BC. On October 31 I viewed at Karnak the colossal hypostyle temple built by Ramesses II. For transportation I took a horse carriage for 25 piasters (about 38 cents) rather than a taxi which would have cost 50 piasters.

I caught the overnight train leaving at 10 p.m. and arrived at Cairo on November 1 at 9 30 a.m. I stayed overnight again at Emmanuel House where the Anglican bishops of Sudan, Egypt, Iran, Lebanon, Jordan, and Israel had gathered.

8. Israel

As there were no direct flights from Egypt to Israel, I had to go there by way of Greece. I took a plane leaving at 8 a.m. and arrived at Athens at 10 a.m. Rather than taking a taxi I walked about 200 yards dragging my suitcase behind me to get to the TWA terminal. My plane to Israel departed at 12:45 p.m. After arriving at the Lod airport at 2:45 p.m. I took a cab for $18.40 to get to the Institute of Holy Land Studies in Jerusalem.

On November 2 along with Fred Bush and his family I joined a *tiyyul* or field trip led by Anson Rainey. We viewed the Valley of Elah, where David fought the Philistine warrior Goliath. We saw the great mound of Lachish which had been besieged by the Assyrian king Sennacherib in 701 BC and the key site of Tell Beit Mirsim excavated by W. F. Albright. Later I listened to a lecture by William Dever at the American School of Oriental Research in Jerusalem. On November 3 I heard the message of James Monson of the Institute of Holy Land Studies at St. Andrew's Presbyterian Church.[12]

On November 3 I paid $15 to share at taxi with four others to view the excavations of Herod's palaces at the Wadi Kelt in (New Testament) Jericho. On November 4 I went to a lecture by Benjamin Mazar on the Early, Middle and Late Bronze Ages. That evening, I viewed a "Sound and Light" spectacle at the Citadel near the Jaffa Gate of Jerusalem. On November 5 I had lunch with Ethel Wallis, the sister of Wilbur Wallis. I had met her before at the Summer Institute of Linguistics. She was working for Wycliffe Bible Translators on the Circassian translation of the Bible.

On November 6 I visited the office of the Israel Exploration Society and the Hebrew University campus on Mount Scopus, just above our old apartment on the Mount of Olives. I listened to a lecture on the differing factions among the Arabs. On November 7 I went to the Jewish section of the walled city of Jerusalem and spoke with the Israeli scholar Nahman Avigad. I was able to visit the temple area, saw the Rockefeller Museum just outside the walls and peered into "Solomon's" quarry.

On November 8 I rented a car for three days. I first drove to the coast to view Aphek and Caesarea. I then drove inland to see Ein Harod and Mt. Tabor. On the east side of the Sea of Galilee I saw the excavated site of Kursi in the midst of banana fields. I went north to see Banias at the foot of Mt. Hermon and then drove to the northwest shore of the Sea of Galilee to revisit Capernaum. The site of the Byzantine octagonal church I had seen earlier had been excavated to reveal an early house church, which may have originally been Peter's home. I also saw Tabgha, Chorazin, Tiberias and Nazareth. I drove south to Samaria where I saw a new structure over Jacob's well at Sychar (John 4). On Nov 11 I drove south to Beersheba and then viewed Herodium, the site of Herod's burial near Bethlehem.

---

12. It was in a burial nearby this church at Ketef Hinnom that Gabriel Barkay found two silver amulets in 1979 which contain the priestly blessing of Numbers 6:24–26. Dated to the sixth century BC, these are our oldest extant Scriptures.

On November 12 I drove to Tel Aviv to view the museums there. I saw the site of Tel Qasile on the coast which Benjamin Mazar had excavated. On Nov 13 I viewed the Citadel area of the walled city of Jerusalem which once held Herod's palace and which may have been the site of the trial of Jesus rather than the Antonia fortress. I renewed acquaintances with Howard and Bonnie Carlson who were still serving in Bethlehem.

Greece and Home Again

On November 14 I flew back to Athens. On the next day I took a bus out of Athens and then walked to see the remains of the famous silver mines of Laurion which had made Athens prosperous. Some of the entrances were so small that only slaves who were children could have worked in them.

I then flew home on November 17 after an exhausting but exhilarating two months adventure which provided me with photos for two books I later wrote: *New Testament Cities in Western Asia Minor* and *Persia and the Bible*.

The Year 1975

Mithras

Mithras was an ancient Persian god who became the center of an important mystery religion, Mithraism in the early Roman Empire. This exclusively male secret cult became a rival to Christianity.[13] There are no connected texts that reveal its doctrines, but we have thousands of dedicatory inscriptions and sculptures. The sect worshipped in *mithraea,* underground cave like structures. Its central iconographic image is a tauroctony which depicts Mithras slaying a bull, surrounded by astrological symbols.[14]

---

13. Unfounded claims have circulated on the internet that Mithraism influenced Christianity. This is impossible as the earliest date for Roman Mithraism is c. AD 80. It is for this reason that the former legal editor of the *Chicago Tribune,* Lee Strobel, who had interviewed me earlier for his best-selling *Case for Christ,* came to Oxford again to interview me for his sequel, *The Case for the Real Jesus* (2007).

14. All of the papers of the IInd Mithraic Congress were published in the *Acta Iranica* and translated into Farsi. My paper, "The *Apocalypse of Adam*, Mithraism and Pre-Christian Gnosticism," was one of the thirty-four papers to be published in the official report of the congress, *Études Mithriaques* (1978).

The earliest evidence of Mithraism is a quotation from a Roman poet Statius, AD 80. It is highly significant that no mithraea have been discovered at either Pompeii or Herculaneum which were destroyed by the eruption of Vesuvius in AD 79, whereas numerous mithraea have been found at the nearby but later site of Ostia.

The Mithraic Congresses

The interest of the Shah's regime in celebrating its pre-Islamic past led to its sponsorship of the first Mithraic Congress in Manchester, England in 1971 and the second Mithraic Congress in Tehran in 1975. The Shah also subsidized the *Journal of Mithraic Studies.*

I had a special interest in *The Apocalypse of Adam*, a Coptic Gnostic text from Nag Hammadi which had been touted by some scholars as evidence for a pre-Christian Gnosticism. In this text I recognized a Mithraic motif, Mithra's birth out of a rock which demonstrated that this treatise must be post-Christian.

The acceptance of my paper was conveyed to me in a letter dated Jan. 31, 1975, by John R. Hinnells on behalf of the organizing committee (Harold Bailey, R. N. Frye, D. Francis, J. DuchesneGuillemin). Then in a letter dated August 9, 1975, from Shojaeddin Shafa, the Deputy Minister of the Imperial Court of Iran for Cultural Affairs I was assured: "The Pahlavi Library will bear all the expenses of your travel and stay in Iran."

I flew by way of London and Paris to Tehran. While in London I spotted my history colleague from Miami University David Fahey near the British Museum. At the airport in Paris I was able to walk through the narrow supersonic Concorde which had been put on display.

In Tehran, we were housed in a hotel with a pool on the top floor. A bus took us to the sessions at the Melli National University in Tehran. George Cameron of the University of Michigan, who was an old friend of the royal family, was transported in a chauffeur driven car. He once invited me to ride with him.

An opening reception offered us champagne and caviar. I did not drink the former and did not care for the taste of the latter. One lasting image I recall was that of the French scholar Roman Ghirshman waltzing away.[15]

---

15. Ghirshman, who is Jewish, bequeathed his library to the Hebrew University in Jerusalem.

The conference lasted from September 1 to September 8 and featured about a hundred participants from twenty-three countries, including scholars from Australia: William Culican; from Austria: M. Mayrhofer; from Belgium: J. and M. Duchesne-Guillemin; from France: R. Ghirshman, J. Kellens, M. Simon, E. Will; from East and West Germany: H. Humbach. H. P. Schmidt, R Schmitt, W. Sundermann, P. Thieme, H. Von Gall; from India: F. Kotwal; from Italy: U. Bianchi. G. Bonfante; from the Netherlands: H. J. W. Drijvers; from Russia: V. Lukonin; from the Sudan: S. Hashem; from Sweden: P. Beskow; from the United Kingdom: H. Bailey, J. A. Boyle, I. Gershevitch, R. L. Gordon, J. Hansman, J. R. Hinnells, D. Stronach;[16] and from Iran, twenty scholars including E. Negahban.[17]

The scholars from the US included F. A. Bode (Institute of Asia Studies), R. J. Bull (Drew University),[18] G. Cameron (University of Michigan),[19] S. B. Downey (UCLA), D. Francis (University of Texas), R. N. Frye (Harvard University),[20] S. Insler (Yale University), J. Puhvel (UCLA), M. P. Speidel (University of Hawaii),[21] and myself.

We Americans received an official invitation from "The Ambassador of the United States of America and Mrs. Helms for a luncheon on Sept. 3" at his home within the embassy compound. The ambassador Richard Helms was the former director of the CIA.[22]

16. In the summer of 1983, when I was directing an NEH sponsored seminar on archaeology for faculty from a number of Christian colleges at Biola University, I invited Professor Stronach, who was then teaching at UC Berkeley, to give our group a special lecture on ancient Iran.

17. Ezat Negahban, the excavator of Marlik in northern Iran, lectured at Miami University. After the 1979 Revolution, he fled to the US.

18. Robert Bull had just discovered a late mithraeum in a coastal warehouse at the port of Caesarea in Israel.

19. George Cameron, a specialist in the Elamite language, had managed to make latex squeezes of the Behistun Inscription by being lowered in a boatswain's chair from the top of the cliff. This was a far safer procedure than that employed by Henry Rawlinson in the nineteenth century. The intrepid Englishman even stood on the top rung of a ladder that was placed precariously on the eighteen-inch ledge below the inscription!

20. Richard N. Frye, the leading authority on medieval and modern Iran, was later to write a commendation for my book, *Persia and the Bible*.

21. Professor Speidel was a specialist on Roman soldiers among whom Mithraism was popular. They spread Mithraism as far west as Hadrian's Wall in northern England where I photographed a noted mithraeum.

22. In an essay on the Shah's regime published in *Time*, Helms admitted that the CIA had not foreseen the overthrow of the Shah by the followers of Ayatollah Khomeini in 1979. Inasmuch as the CIA had interfered in Iran's internal affairs in the past, the youthful followers of the Ayatollah who stormed the embassy on November 4, 1979, and seized sixty-six American hostages, holding the majority of them for 444

AN ASIAN AMERICAN ANCIENT HISTORIAN AND BIBLICAL SCHOLAR

The participants got to meet and shake hands with the lovely Shahbanu, the Empress Farah, at a reception at the Sa'ad Abad palace. In the group photo which was taken afterwards I found myself in the front row (fourth from the right end) on the right not because of my importance but because I was one of the first to exit the reception hall. On the left of the photo is the empress, flanked on her right by Sir Harold Bailey and on her left by Roman Ghirshman and George Cameron.

Figure 37. Mithraic Congress at Tehran: the empress is flanked on her right by Harold Bailey and on her left by Roman Ghirshman; I am in the front row, the fourth from the right.

After the end of the conference some of us joined David Stronach to inspect Tepe Nush i-Jan, located southwest of Tehran which he had excavated. This was one of the very few Median sites to be uncovered in Iran. We also saw the so-called "Tomb of Esther and Mordecai" in Hamadan. I roomed with William Culican who had authored a book on *The Medes and the Persians*, which I used for my History of Ancient Persia classes.

I befriended an East German scholar, Werner Sundermann, who was the foremost expert on Manichaean texts from Central Asia. He invited me to visit him in East Berlin, where he showed me the Akademie

days, thought that the embassy was full of CIA agents. In actuality, at the time of the seizure, there were only two CIA agents at the embassy, neither of whom knew Farsi (modern Persian), so reliant had the US become on intelligence from the Shah. See Mark Bowden, *Guests of the Ayatollah* (New York, New York: Grove Press, 2006).

der Wissenschaften der D.D.R. I strolled along the famous Unter den Linden, a tree-lined avenue that stretches from the Brandenburg Gate to the former palace of the Kaiser. I was able to view the famous Pergamum Museum that displays the Altar of Zeus from Pergamum and the glazed bricks from the Ishtar Gate of Babylon that Robert Koldewey had uncovered. A side trip to Charlottenburg to a small museum enabled me to view the celebrated bust of Nefertiti.

Family

(1974 to 1975)

In the summer of 1974, after driving to LA, our family flew to Hawaii. In August, we stayed at Kimi's parents' home in Hilo, while I taught at the Hilo branch of the University of Hawaii. On a fishing trip off the coast of Kona I caught two fish. One was a barracuda which was inedible, but the other was the dolphin fish (mahi mahi) which was delicious.

Brian, who turned nine in 1975, loved to read science fiction books. His favorite author was Isaac Asimov. An essay on the electric eel won him an award from the Humane Society. Gail turned five and followed in Brian's footsteps, enjoying the solving of arithmetic problems. When she played tic-tac-toe or Qubic with him, she even won a game or two, to the annoyance of her brother. Her teacher, Dr. Arleen Steen, reported that Gail at five and a half was already reading at a fifth-grade level.

Lectures and Papers

In January 1974, I delivered the annual lectures for the Division of Biblical Studies at Wheaton College. I spoke on Archaeology, Biblical composition, and Gnosticism. In March I delivered the Museum Lectures on the Dead Sea Scrolls and New Testament Archaeology at Anderson College. I spoke in April at McCormick Theological Seminary on Pre-Christian Gnosticism. Also in April, I delivered a paper on "Mandaic Magical Texts" before the American Oriental Society In December I spoke on "The Achaemenid Capitals" to the Near East Archaeological Society.

Easter, History or Myth?

In two March issues of *Christianity Today* in 1974, I published a two-part article titled, "Easter, Myth, Hallucination or History?" In the first article I refuted the widespread conjecture that the resurrection of Jesus was an adaptation of a general myth of rising and dying fertility gods such as Tammuz in Mesopotamia, Osiris in Egypt, Attis in Anatolia and Adonis in Syria.[23] In the second part I discussed the key passages in the Gospels and especially 1 Corinthians 15 that form the basis of the Christian belief in the resurrection of Jesus at Easter. I was to present lectures based on these articles at many universities in the following years.

Other Publications

In 1974 and 1975, I also had articles published in *Bibliotheca Sacra*, the *Journal of the American Academy of Religion*, and the *Journal of the American Scientific Affiliation*. "The Archaeological Confirmation of Suspect Elements in the Classical and the Biblical Traditions" was published in 1975 in a Festschrift in honor of Oswald T. Allis. I also contributed fifteen articles to *The Wycliffe Bible Encyclopedia*, edited by C. Pfeiffer, H. Vos and J. Rea.

A Special Conference

From December 8 to 10, 1975, I took part in a conference held in New York City that featured a dialogue between evangelical and Jewish scholars. This was arranged by Marvin R. Wilson together with A. James Rudin and Marc H. Tannenbaum.

The Jewish scholars were Asher Finkel, Bernard Martin, Emanuel Rackman, Ellis Rivkin, A. James Rudin, Seymour Siegel, Marc H, Tannenbaum, Albert Vorspan, and Michael Wyschogrod. The evangelical scholars were Carl E. Armerding, Leighton Ford, Vernon C. Grounds,

---

23. Over the years, I delivered a talk based on these articles with the same title "Easter—Myth, Hallucination or History" at a number of universities, including the University of North Carolina, l975; the University of Florida, l976; Cornell University, l977; Miami University, 1986; Yale University, 1989; Princeton University, 1989; Gordon College, 1991; the Ohio State University, 1992; the University of Florida, 1994; Azusa Pacific University, 1994; the University of Dayton, 1998; Dennison University, 2001; Kentucky Christian College, 2001; Palm Beach Atlantic College, 2001; Stanford University, 2001; and Washington Bible College, 2002.

Roger Nicole, William S. LaSor, Paul E. Toms, Marvin R. Wilson, G. Douglas Young, and myself.[24]

An interesting exchange took place was when Ellis Rivkin, an authority on the Pharisees from Hebrew Union College, used the phrase "Jesus Christ." One of the orthodox Jews protested audibly more than once, "No, Ellis, not Christ but Jesus!" But Rivkin persisted in using "Christ," that is, the Greek title for the Messiah.[25]

---

24. My paper was published as "Concord, Conflict, and Community," in *Evangelicals and Jews in Conversation on Scripture, Theology, and History*, ed. M. H. Tanenbaum, M. R. Wilson, & A. J. Rudin.

25. Some Jews, such as Hershel Shanks, the editor of the *Biblical Archaeology Review*, prefer the use of the abbreviations BCE and CE (for Common Era), rather than BC (Before Christ) and AD (anno Domini, i.e. Year of the Lord). When I asked two of my Jewish friends, Getzel Cohen of the University of Cincinnati and David Weisberg of Hebrew Union College, they both said they had no objection to the traditional abbreviations as they had become conventional.

Chapter 19

The Rest of the 1970s

The Year 1976

The Family

BRIAN, WHO WAS TEN, was reading at the tenth-grade level. As a fifth grader he participated in a seventh-grade science project by writing a paper on "Black Holes." He was elected the vice-president of the Astronomical Association of Oxford, a small group of high school students and adults interested in star gazing. Gail, who was now six, enjoyed swimming and even went bowling for the first time. She started taking piano lessons from a neighbor who lived behind us. Gail was reading at the sixth-grade level.

We rented a small garden plot from the university near its stables. I had to bring up water in a pail from the nearby creek. We grew an abundance of tomatoes, beans, and broccoli. Kimi enjoyed the experience, but the kids did not care for the weeds and the bugs and did not relish eating the vegetables!

While attending a conference in October in LA, I was able to see my mother. She was working as a maid and cook for the children of a wealthy family in Taiwan, who remained on the island to look after their business of mining gems. My sister Alice (who now prefers the name Alicia) had just graduated from UCLA with a major in Japanese Language and Literature.

Lectures

In January I spoke on "Near Eastern Religions" at the University of Florida, in February on "The Achaemenid Capitals" at Covenant Theological Seminary, and in March on "The Stones and the Scriptures" at Taylor University. In October I gave the Staley Distinguished Christian Scholar Lectures at the University of Virginia on "Near Eastern Religions and the Biblical Faith." It was a privilege to stay in one of the rooms of the Colonnade designed by Thomas Jefferson. My host was the outstanding economics professor Kenneth Elzinga. Ken is a member of the national board of trustees of the InterVarsity Christian Fellowship.

Publications

I had articles published in the *Journal of the Evangelical Theological Society* and the *Near East Archaeological Bulletin*. I published a review essay on Morton Smith's controversial books about a so-called Secret Gospel of Mark, and about Jesus as a magician in the *Christian Scholars Review*. My articles on "Hermetic Literature" and "Mandaeism" appeared in the Supplementary Volume to the *Anchor Bible Dictionary*.

The Year 1977

The Family

Brian became involved in Cub Scouts and was elected president of his class. He enjoyed playing computer games at Miami's computer lab, at times competing with professors who were also playing these games there. Gail joined the Brownies and enjoyed playing checkers and chess. When the family tried ice-skating, she proved to be the most agile pupil.

I took Brian with me as I attended a conference of the American Scientific Affiliation at Nyack, New York. He was the youngest attendant there. We then took a tour of many of the sites not only in New York City but also in Washington, DC. His favorite place was the National Air and Space Museum.

Kimi started to work full time at Miami University as a typist for the food services. I was able to schedule my classes for the mornings so I would be at home when the children returned from school.

A Celebration

In October I was the principal speaker at a celebration of the first Japanese church in the US founded a century before in San Francisco. This was an ecumenical service held at St. Mark's Episcopal Cathedral in Seattle. The occasion was marked by considerable pomp and pageantry. My host Rev. Richard Nishioka treated me to a dinner featuring the city's renowned salmon and mushrooms.

Academics

In December, I presented a paper on "New Light on Gnosticism" at a conference of the American Society of Church History held at the Southern Methodist University in Dallas. There, I was able to view the tiny but sensational "Mani Codex" and to meet the two German scholars Albert Henrichs of Harvard University and Ludwig Koenen of the University of Michigan who had published the codex. They had sent me their publication of the codex in the *Zeitschrift für Papyrologie und Epigraphik*. I had first learned about this important publication from Richard Frye at a conference of the American Oriental Society at Harvard University. Some scholars had believed that Mani had come out of a Mandaean background. But this codex proves that Mani, the founder of the important Gnostic movement known as Manichaeism, arose out of a Jewish Christian sect known as the Elchasaites.

I wrote a critical article on the search for Noah's Ark published in the *Near East Archaeological Society Bulletin* and a bibliographical essay on the Greco-Roman World published in the *Journal of the Evangelical Theological Society*. Brief articles on "The Religion of the Romans," "Manichaeism," and "The Gnostics" appeared in the Lion *Handbook of Christian History*, edited by Tim Dowley.

The Year 1978

The Family

Kimi in addition to caring for the family, working at the university, and being active at church, started taking shorthand and bookkeeping courses at night. Gail at eight was spelling at the sixth-grade level and reading at the eighth-grade level. Brian attended a Deep Sky Conference in July.

Conferences

I took Brian with me as I presented a paper at the American Scientific Affiliation conference in Holland, Michigan in August. Eating at all those restaurants along the way added four pounds to Brian's weight!

In February, I took part in the Panathenaea Conference at Ohio State University. Papers were presented by OSU professors Jack Balcer,[1] Timothy Gregory,[2] and Mark Morford.[3] I presented a paper on "Biblical Documents." I chaired the session on Roman Literature session at the conference of Greek, Roman and Byzantine Studies in April. I also read a paper at the Evangelical Theological Society conference in Chicago in December.

The Conference on Gnosticism

The most important conference in which I took part this year was the International Conference on Gnosticism at Yale University, in March. There were some scholars I had known through previous contacts or correspondence such as: Ugo Bianchi, Andrew Helmbold,[4] Albert Henrichs, Ludwig Koenen, Helmut Koester,[5] Robert Kraft,[6] Elaine Pagels, Birger Pearson, Malcolm Peel,[7] Michael Stone,[8] James M. Robinson,[9] and R. McL. Wilson.[10] Others were scholars whose writings I had read but

---

1. Balcer was an authority on Ancient Persia.
2. Gregory was a specialist in "Byzantine archaeology and history."
3. Morford taught courses on Greek and Roman mythology.
4. I first learned about the Nag Hammadi texts from a paper that Andy had presented at a meeting of the Evangelical Theological Society.
5. Professor Koester, an influential New Testament scholar, was a student of Rudolf Bultmann. When he came to speak at Miami University, as one of the few scholars who supported Morton Smith's claim to have found evidence of a secret proto-Mark, he told me that he thought I was too harsh in my critical review of Morton Smith's claims.
6. Kraft, graduate of Wheaton College, was the chair of the Department of Religious Studies at the University of Pennsylvania. He introduced me when I spoke to the IV graduate fellowship there.
7. Peel, who was part of the team of translators of the Coptic Nag Hammadi Library assembled by James M. Robinson, kindly sent me offprints of his articles.
8. I had attended lectures by Professor Stone, a specialist on pseudepigraphical texts, in Jerusalem.
9. Professor Robinson, a student of Rudolf Bultmann, assembled the team of scholars who successfully translated all the Coptic treatises of the Nag Hammadi Library.
10. Professor Wilson was the leading British scholar on Gnosticism. Though he did

whom I was encountering for the first time such as: Henry Chadwick, Carsten Colpe, Ithamar Gruenwald, Hans Jonas,[11] Bentley Layton,[12] Gilles Quispel,[13] Kurt Rudolph,[14] Alan Segal,[15] William Schoedel,[16] and Frederik Wisse.

I had unwisely packed my paper in a small suitcase which I had checked. When I disembarked from the plane, I learned to my dismay that this suitcase had somehow been left behind! So I had to purchase socks, a shirt, pajamas and sundries from the Yale Co-op. Worse yet, since I do not have the photographic memory of a Michael Astour, I had to make a long phone call to my wife to ask her to read the copy of the paper I had left behind while I jotted as many notes as I could to present my paper as best as I could.

Publications

My paper given at the Yale conference, "The Descent of Ishtar, the Fall of Sophia, and the Jewish Roots of Gnosticism" was published in the *Tyndale Bulletin*. I also had articles published in *Bibliotheca Sacra, Christianity Today, Eternity*, and the *Westminster Theological Journal*.

---

not agree with my conclusions, he was very helpful in supplying me with offprints of his articles. I enjoyed having lunch with him at St. Andrews University in 1985. I learned from a letter from F. F. Bruce that "Robin" was one of his students.

11. Jonas was the leading disciple of Rudolf Bultmann, who published a classic synthesis of Gnosticism by relying in part on Mandaean sources.

12. Layton, who was the organizer of the conference, produced his own translation of the Coptic Nag Hammadi Library.

13. Quispel was the leading European scholar on Gnosticism. One of his students from Norway, Jorunn Buckley came to see me. I was asked to review her dissertation on Mandaic whcih she completed at the University of Chicago. She became the leading scholar of Mandaic and the Mandaeans. I was later invited to contribute to a Festschrift in honor of Professor Quispel.

14. Rudolph was the foremost German scholar on the Mandaeans. He told me that he fled Leipzig in East Germany for the west, leaving all of his books behind him. He wrote the major synthesis on Gnosticism titled *Gnosis*.

15. Though there is evidence of Docetism (the denial of Christ's incarnation) at the end of the first century (Johannine letters) and early in the second century (Ignatius), Segal's seminal work on Two Powers based on his research in Jewish sources supported my own contention that a Gnosticism with dualistic cosmic dimensions did not arise until later in the second century CE.

16. Schoedel wrote the major commentary on the Letters of Ignatius.

The Year 1979

The Family

Brian, who was now thirteen, bought a Kihm I microprocessor. By using it, he earned a "superior" rating for his science fair project. He entered the international "Prisoner's Dilemma" contest and was ranked seventeenth among sixty-two entrants. Gail, who was nine, used her vivid imagination to write stories. She enjoyed swimming and ice-skating. For the Girl Scouts, she sold calendars. She and Kimi joined the boys to view their first Reds baseball game.

The highlight of the year was my mother's visit from May 29 to June 19. This was the first time that she had visited us in Ohio, and the first time in five years that the children had seen their grandmother. In Oxford she joined the children in swimming in the nearby Tri Community Center pool and played tennis for the first time in her sixty-six years! She viewed family movies to catch up on the activities of the children.

In Ohio we took her to the Cincinnati Zoo, the Krohn Conservatory of flowers, Procter, and Gamble's Ivorydale plant. President Grant's home, an Indian mound the Air Force Museum, and the Football Hall of Fame.

In Indiana we saw Metamora, an old canal town, and the racetrack of the Indianapolis 500. In Michigan we visited Holland but were too late to see its famous tulip festival. We visited my cousin Nobu Yamauchi and his family in Ypsilanti. Nobu was a professor of chemistry at Eastern Michigan University.

On a second trip, we went south through Kentucky where we saw a Shaker Village and Daniel Boone's fort at Harrodsburg. We visited the Mammoth Cave. There I took a four-hour tour and then a three-hour tour without taking a break. In Tennessee, we were given a tour of the Oak Ridge facilities by Mark Iskra, a Miami University alumnus.

Academics

John Gregory McMahon, a graduate of the University of Kansas, wrote his MA thesis on "Cults at Corinth: Paul's Interaction with the Mystery Religions."[17] My first doctoral student, John M. Lawrence wrote his dis-

---

17. McMahon went on to study Hittite under Harry Hoffner at the Oriental Institute of the University of Chicago. He served as a professor of history at the University

sertation on "Hepatoscopy and Extispicy in Graeco-Roman and Early Christian Texts."[18] This concerned the practice of divining the future by examining the livers and the entrails of sacrificed animals.

Lectures

In February, I lectured on "Was Nehemiah the Cupbearer a Eunuch?" at the University of Wisconsin. In March, I delivered the Staley Lectures at Grand Rapids Baptist College and Seminary. In April, I spoke at the chapel at Asbury College. In October, I delivered lectures on "Archaeology and the Scriptures" at the Cincinnati Bible College and Seminary. In November, I gave the Griffith Thomas Lectures at Dallas Theological seminary on "The Archaeological Background of the Exilic Era."

Publications

I contributed the essay on "Archaeology and the New Testament" to the introductory volume of *The Expositor's Bible Commentary*, edited by F. L. Gaebelein. Donald J. Wiseman contributed the essay on "Archaeology and the Old Testament." Zondervan later combined both articles as a paperback, *Archaeology and the Bible*. I contributed articles on the "Agrapha," "Apocryphal Gospels" and the "Archaeology of Palestine and Syria" to the *International Standard Bible Encyclopedia*, edited by W. S. LaSor. I also published articles in *Church History* and the *Near East Archaeology Bulletin*.

Miami University's Excellence

The university continued to excel in academic and athletic rankings. The school was ranked the seventeenth most selective public university, just below the University of California at Berkeley. The university was ranked second among small to medium colleges in students who went on to the

---

of New Hampshire and excavated in central Turkey for twenty-five years. He co-edited the *Oxford Handbook of Ancient Anatolia*. His wife Mindy, who is the daughter of a noted professor of mathematics, Charles Hatfield, plays the harp and directs the choir at their church.

18. Lawrence, who came from the Church of Christ background, taught at a number of his denomination's colleges such as Harding College in Arkansas.

PhD behind Oberlin College. Wheaton College was ranked sixth. Miami is the most selective of the twelve state universities in Ohio and has the highest rate of graduation and return of income after graduation.

Miami University won its seventh consecutive Reese Trophy for all around excellence in sports in the Mid-American Conference.[19] The football team won its fourth MAC title in five years.[20] Even when the football team does not do well, Miami excels in the "minor" sports, such as golf, tennis, track and field, swimming, and diving and volleyball. Athletes who participated in these sports in have better grade point averages than the students in general.

19. In 1980, Miami would win its eighth consecutive Reese Trophy.
20. Miami's football team had won three consecutive Tangerine Bowls: in 1973 over Florida under coach Bill Mallory, in 1974 over Georgia, and in 1975 over South Carolina under coach Dick Crum.

Chapter 20

The First Half of the 1980s

The Year 1980

The Family

BRIAN, AT 5 FEET 4 inches, was now taller than his mom. Having finished McGuffey Lab School with all A's, he became a freshman at Talawanda High School. He earned a superior rating for his computer program for playing checkers at a regional science fair. By using his computer skills to compile the indices of one of my books, he earned enough money to buy a Radio Shack TRS 80 minicomputer. He upgraded its memory from 4K to 6K by himself.

Gail, now in the fifth grade, excelled in English and math. She was busy with her pottery making and the Girl Scouts. She also enjoyed playing Brian's computer games. I took her to the circus and her first college football game.

Kimi worked with the dining halls, programming the schedules of the workers. During the noon hours she sat in on courses on computers, small appliance repairs and auto mechanics.

After a lecture tour to Oregon in October, I was able to fly down to LA. My sister Alicia was in charge of a branch bank in West LA where a robber armed with a submachine gun was shot to death by undercover officers from the nearby police station. I took my mother to a theater on Wilshire Boulevard to see the acclaimed new samurai movie, *Kagemusha* "Shadow Warrior" directed by Akira Kurosawa. We arrived late and the theater was completely filled so that the only seats left were in the front row, not a very ideal viewing position!

Ohio's State Universities

The state of Ohio has twelve state universities located as follows:

1. In the center in Columbus is the Ohio State University, the largest.[1]
2. In SE Ohio are Ohio University, the oldest
3. and Shawnee State University, the newest.
4. In the SW is Miami University, the second oldest,
5. and also the University of Cincinnati, once a municipal university.
6. In the NW are Bowling Green State University
7. and the University of Toledo.
8. In the N and NE are Cleveland State University,
9. Kent State University,
10. Youngstown State University.
11. and the University of Akron.[2]
12. Central State University, a school traditionally for Blacks is located near Xenia in SW Ohio.

Miami University with fifteen thousand students at Oxford and two thousand each at branch campuses in Middletown and Hamilton[3] is the smallest of the universities, with the exception of Shawnee State and Central State. By requiring first and second year students to reside in its dormitories, Miami has been able to limit enrollment and to be the most selective of all the state universities. It has more advanced

---

1. Ohio State University plays in the Big Ten, which has been expanded beyond its original ten members. Its main rival is the University of Michigan. Former Miami players and coaches have coached both teams (see Excursus J).

2. Miami University, Ohio University, Bowling Green University, the University of Toledo, Youngstown State University, and the University of Akron play in the Mid-American Conference along with Northern Illinois, Western Michigan, Central Michigan, and the University of Buffalo.

3. The branch campuses are commuter schools with an open enrollment and lower fees. After completing two years, students can transfer to the main Oxford campus. In recent years, the branch campuses have been given greater autonomy and have developed a few four-year programs such as nursing.

placement freshmen than any public or private schools in the state. Of the entering freshmen 40 percent came from the top 10 percent of their high schools. Many are from other states such as Illinois, New York, and New Jersey. It is also one of the most expensive public universities in the US so that most of its students come from middle-class and upper-class families with very few students from minority backgrounds or students needing remedial training.

About a third of the students come from Catholic high schools, of which there are many in the Cincinnati area. Of the entering class in 1980 of 3400, 2500 answered a questionnaire on religious preferences. About six hundred indicated an interest in such evangelical groups as Cru, IV, Navigators, and the Fellowship of Christian Athletes. Only eleven declared that they were agnostics or atheists.

The History Department

In 1980, I became the department's director of graduate studies, a position I was to hold until 1984. I traveled through the state visiting small colleges to recruit students for our graduate program. Periodically all the chairs and directors of graduate programs would meet in what was called the "Hueston Woods Conference" as the first such meeting was held at the Hueston Woods State Park near Oxford. When I flew on the university's plane to Youngstown with Dick Jellison to such a conference, I learned that our history department with 30 professors (including those on the branch campuses) was second only to the history department at OSU with its faculty of over 50 professors.

THE FIRST HALF OF THE 1980S

Figure 38. History faculty: I am fourth from the left; Dr. Shriver is at the far right.

In 1980, I saw my second and third PhDs graduate. Roger R. Chambers wrote a dissertation on "Greek Athletics and the Jews 165 BC to AD 70."[4] Dean Kallander, a Methodist minister, wrote his dissertation on: "The Defense of Jerusalem in the Roman Siege of 70 CE."[5]

Lectures

In January I gave the Earle Cairns History Lecture at Wheaton College. I spoke on "Josephus and the Scriptures." In February I spoke on "Psalms and Near Eastern Poetry" at Malone College. In March I gave a lecture on "The Crucifixion and Docetic Christology" to the Concordia Lutheran Seminary in Ft. Wayne. Also, in March I gave five lectures on "The Bible and Its World" at Grace College. In May I gave the Staley lecture at Asbury College. In October I delivered the Bueerman-Champion Lectures on "Scriptures and Archaeology: From Abraham to Daniel" at the

---

4. Roger taught at the Florida Bible College, a Church of Christ school. His son Adam was to be my seventeenth and last doctoral candidate in 2009.

5. Dean became an Air Force historian at Wright Patterson Base near Dayton.

Western Conservative Theological Seminary in Portland. Mt. St. Helen's erupted on the day I departed!

Scholarly Societies

In February, I read a paper on "Achaemenid Texts and the Post-Exilic Books" at the Midwest Conference of the AOS. In April I gave an invited paper on Gnosticism at the Midwest SBL conference. In August, I presented a paper on "Jewish Gnosticism, the Prologue of John, the Trimorphic Protennoia, and Mandaean Parallel,"[6] in the Judaica section, chaired by Alan Segal at the XIVth Congress of the International History of Religions at the University of Manitoba in Winnipeg. Among other participants on this session were Jorunn Buckley who gave a paper on Mandaic texts, and Kurt Rudolph who showed slides of the Mandaeans. I had a cordial lunch with Morton Smith, who had refuted his many critics in an article in the *Journal of Biblical Studies* but who was unaware of my critical review. It was at this meeting that I met Emperor Hirohito's brother, His Imperial Highness Prince Mikasa, who was a biblical scholar (see Excursus C).

I was elected to the council of the ASA (American Scientific affiliation), an organization of Christians in the natural and social sciences.[7] I had earlier served on the editorial board of the *Journal of the American Scientific Affiliation* and been elected a fellow of the ASA. In March I gave an ASA lecture at Ball State University and in April one at Taylor University. I served as the program chair for the ASA's annual convention in August at Taylor University.

Publications

In 1980 *The Archaeology of New Testament Cities in Western Asia Minor* was published by Baker.[8] My Bueermann Champion lectures were

---

6. I criticized the proposal of Gesine Schenke, who had suggested that the Nag Hammadi tractate was the Vorlage of John's Prologue. When James M. Robinson came to Miami University to receive an honorary degree, I got to meet Gesine, who had divorced Hans-Martin Schenke, a prominent German scholar on Gnosticism and was now Robinson's wife.

7. On the council, I joined Chi–Hang Lee, an old friend. Chi–Hang was born in Viet Nam. He earned his PhD at Rutgers in 1966 and worked for Del Monte Foods.

8. Later reprint editions eliminated the initial words "The Archaeology of." In 2010,

published as *The Scriptures and Archaeology*. I published a comparison of Solon of Athens and Nehemiah in a Festschrift in honor of Cyrus H. Gordon. I also had articles published in *Bibliotheca Sacra, Fides et Historia, Journal of the American Scientific Affiliation, Journal of the Evangelical Theological Society, Themelios,* and *Zeitschrift für die alttestamemtliche Wissenschaft.*

The Year 1981

The Family

Brian, a sophomore in high school, did well in his classes, even in Latin which he took under his father's compulsion. He received his Ham operator's license and organized a computer club with some of his friends. Gail, who was now in the sixth grade, did well in all her classes. In addition to piano lessons, she tried her hand at the violin. She was not happy about having to wear braces.

Kimi and I went to see Agatha Christie's famous play *The Mousetrap* on the showboat Majestic docked on the Ohio riverfront. Years before at a lecture by Sir Max Mallowan on his excavations at the Institute of Advanced Studies at Princeton, I saw his famous wife, Agatha Christie. We also went to see The Music Man. One of the performers was Susan Lowery, who had been a student in one of my classes. She had experienced a remarkable conversion to Christ when she had sung an impromptu solo of Amazing Grace in a Black church.

Lectures

In the spring I gave lectures at the Minnesota Bible College and also an Aslan Lecture at Rochester, the home of the famed Mayo Clinic. In May I spoke on "Herodian Archaeology" at the annual convention of Delta Theta Chi, a sorority. In October, I spoke on "Jesus and Other Religious Leaders" for the IV at Case Western Reserve University.

---

a Japanese tour guide who came to Oxford to visit me produced a Japanese translation of the book.

Papers and Societies

In February, I read a paper on "Ararat, Mini, and Ashkenaz" at the joint Midwest SBL & AOS conference at Ann Arbor. In March I presented an invited paper on "The Present Status of Research on Gnosticism" at the Southeast ETS conference in Knoxville. In August I read a paper on "Divination in the Ancient World" at the ASA convention in Philadelphia. In December I gave the annual IBR (Institute for Biblical Research) lecture on "Magic and Divination in the Ancient World" in San Francisco.

As I was driving to the Cincinnati airport to catch the plane to San Francisco the road was very icy. Though I was driving with other cars slowly at about 30 mph, I came across a patch of black ice and could not control my car, which slid to the left and hit a parked tow truck and barely missed the driver who was standing beside it. After about a half hour waiting, though my left front fender was damaged, I drove to the airport and reported the accident to some police who were at the parking lot. I missed my flight but was able to catch a later flight to San Francisco. I did have to get another used car, a station wagon which had just been turned into the auto dealer with a bumper sticker which proclaimed, "Thank God I am Polish"!

Publications

In 1981, my most widely translated book appeared. I had provided a rather basic text based on my history lectures for *The World of the First Christians*, which the publisher Lion enhanced with numerous colored illustrations and maps. Lion simultaneously released the book in Norwegian, Swedish, German and Dutch editions. Then Lion released in 1983 Finnish and Italian editions and in 1985 Croatian and Spanish editions. The British edition was also issued as four separate booklets: for their use in secondary schools in the United Kingdom. The American edition was called *Harper's World of the New Testament*.

My essay based on the paper presented at Winnipeg was published in *Studies in Gnosticism and Hellenistic Religions*, a Festschrift in honor of Gilles Quispel. I contributed forty entries discussing seventy-five Hebrew words to the *Theological Wordbook of the Old Testament*, edited by R. Laird Harris, Gleason L. Archer, and Bruce K. Waltke. I also published articles in *Christianity Today* and the *Evangelical Quarterly*.

The Year 1982

The Family

Brian won awards in physics, trigonometry, and social studies for his sophomore year at Talawanda High School. During the summer he learned to drive, which proved to be a great help on many of our long trips. Gail who was in the seventh grade did well in classes and enjoyed basketball, volleyball, and cheerleading. She was saddened by Miami University's decision to close its lab school, but one consolation was that her best friends from McGuffey would be with her in the eighth grade at Stewart Middle School.

Kimi's work with the dining halls was now accomplished through computers. She took up a new position as a secretary in the Economics Department. She also attended a graduate class in Gerontology, a field in which Miami's Sociology Department has played a leading role.

In March we drove to Winona Lake, Indiana, where Kimi first worked as a waitress when she came to the mainland from Hawaii. In July we visited the World's Fair in Knoxville. We stayed in the home of Jerry Mattingly at Johnson Bible College.[9] I was able to view the performance of a Japanese *Kabuki* play from the interior of the translator's booth. Kabuki is a popular Japanese dramatic performance in which males, who have heavily made-up faces perform with highly stylized gestures, the roles of females. This tradition is now in danger of ending as few young men want to take up the rigorous training required.

In August Kimi and I attended a reunion of Shelton College at the former campus in Ringwood which was now New Jersey's Botanical Garden. While in the Metropolitan area I visited the Brooklyn Museum, which has some of the best artifacts from ancient Egypt and the Sudan. I was delighted to meet the associate curator of Egyptology, Robert Bianchi who had been my student at Rutgers.

Lectures and Papers

In February I gave the Staley lectures on "Divination and Magic in the Ancient World," and "Russians and Iranians in Prophecy" at Drew University. I delivered a paper on "Pompey and the Mithraic Pirates,"

---

9. Jerry Mattingly's school, now Johnson University, purchased most of my library's books and journals as I downsized in 2019.

at the Ohio Classical Conference at OSU in October. In December I presented a paper on "Sociology, Scriptures and the Supernatural" at the ETS conference.

The C.F.H.

I took some of my graduate students to a meeting of the Conference on Faith and History at Indiana State University in Terre Haute where two of the founders of the CFH, Robert Clouse and Richard Pierard taught. The theme was "Marxism and Christianity." Just the week before, my former Rutgers colleague and noted Marxist historian, Eugene Genovese, had spoken at Miami University. We were able to view the home of the noted socialist Eugene Debs at Terre Haute. I was happy to see a former friend from Shelton, C. T. McIntire,[10] and two former students from Rutgers, Steve Hoffmann[11] and Jim Patterson[12] at the conference.

The A.S.A.

In August Brian and I attended the annual meeting of the American Scientific Affiliation in Grand Rapids. The ASA, a fellowship of evangelicals in the natural and social sciences, was begun in 1941, with annual conferences beginning in 1946. It began the publication of the *Journal of the American Scientific Affiliation* in 1949 (later renamed *Perspectives on Science and Christianity*). There are different categories of members: friends, students, regular members and fellows.[13] The main speaker was Elving Anderson, an outstanding scholar on genetics at the University of Minnesota, who had been president of Sigma Xi.

In 1982 I became the president of the ASA. Its executive director was Robert Herrmann, who had taught at the medical schools of Boston University and Oral Roberts University. Also on the council was

---

10. Carl Thomas McIntire taught history first at the Institute for Christian Studies and then at the University of Toronto.

11. After serving in diplomatic service in Iraq, Steve Hoffmann taught political science at Taylor University.

12. After studying Church History at Princeton University, Jim Patterson served as the dean of Christian Studies at Union University.

13. At its seventy-fifth anniversary in 2017, the ASA listed 163 fellows and 1,035 members. Our fellows have included Richard Bube, Dorothy Chappell, Francis Collins, Owen Gingerich, Robert Kaita, and Charles Townes, a Nobel prize winner.

biochemist Walter Hearn, the editor of the newsletter. Richard Bube, the editor of the *Journal of the American Scientific Affiliation*, was the chair of the Department of Material Sciences at Stanford University. Others who served with me over the years on the council were Chi-Hang Lee a scientist with Del Monte Foods, Kurt Weiss a physiologist from Oklahoma State University, Don Munro a biologist at Houghton University, and Ann Hunt a research scientist at Eli Lilly. Later, Russ Heddendorf, a sociologist from Covenant College who had taught at Shelton College, also joined the council. Later, so did Edwin Olson, a geologist from Whitworth College who worked at the volcanoes in Hawaii.

Figure 39. ASA council: Ann Hunt, Russ Heddendorf, and Don Munro, Tom Olson, and EMY

Publications

I published an article on "Docetic Christology" in the *Concordia Theological Quarterly* and brief articles on "Gnostics," "Mandaeans" and "Manichaeans" in *The World's Religions*, edited by R. P. Beaver. In November, I traveled to Wilmore, Kentucky to attend a dinner in honor of my former Brandeis classmate, Dennis Kinlaw, who had served as a professor of Old Testament at Asbury Theological Seminary and then as president of Asbury College. Among other former Brandeis alumni attending was Father John F. X. Sheehan, SJ, the chair of the Department of Religion at Marquette University. I was honored to contribute an essay on "Nehemiah as a Model Leader" to the Festschrift presented to Denis Kinlaw at this time.

My *Foes from the Northern Frontier* was published, which in its first chapter criticized the widespread interpretation of Ezekiel 38:2 that the words *rosh* ("head"), Meshech, and Tubal were prophetic references to Russia, Moscow and Tobolsk. This interpretation which had gained currency through the Scofield Reference Bible and authors such as Hal Lindsey, I argued was unjustified. A decade later, Roy Rivenburg's article "A Question of Attribution," in the *Los Angeles Times* (July 30, 1992) called attention to the plagiarism of portions of my book, footnotes and all, by Hal Lindsey and Chuck Missler in their book, *The Magog Factor*. Even after my publisher Baker notified these authors of this offense, Missler in a later book continued the plagiarism!

The Year 1983

The Family

In July, we drove across the country visiting many sites such as the George Washington Carver center, the Grand Canyon, and the Roy Rogers Museum in Victoryville. Roy, whose name was originally Leonard Slye, was born in a tenement at a site in Cincinnati occupied by the Reds baseball stadium. We visited the Campus Crusade headquarters in San Bernadino, where we met several Miami alumni, including Chris and Karen Akers. I also visited the missionary center in Pasadena, where I reconnected with anthropologist James Buswell, whom I had met on my first visit to Wheaton College.

We visited Knotts Berry Farm near Disneyland in Anaheim. We also saw the Getty Museum at Malibu, which is a marvelous reproduction of the Villa of the Papyri uncovered at Herculaneum, and the Huntington Library in Pasadena, where Gainsborough's famous painting of a boy in blue is displayed.

In the fall, as Brian was considering applying to college, I took him on trips to visit several campuses including Carnegie Mellon in

Pittsburgh, Rensselaer Polytechnic Institute at Troy, the University of Syracuse, and MIT in Cambridge.

The N.E.H. Workshop

The Coalition of Christian Colleges received a $125,000 grant from the National Endowment of the Humanities to fund five workshops on Christianity and the Humanities for professors from Christian Colleges in the summer of 1983. My workshop on "Christianity & Archaeology" at Biola University during July 23 to 29 was one of the five workshops that were supported. The eight professors who participated were: Leroy Brightup (Friends University), Stephen Brown (Los Angeles Baptist College), Walter Brunn (Messiah College), Charles Davis (Mississippi College), Edwin Olson (Whitworth College), Carl Rasmussen (Bethel College), Arthur Rupprecht (Wheaton College), and Leland Wilshire (Biola University). Ed Olson was a geologist from Whitworth College, who had worked in Hawaii. I lectured every day and each participant worked on a research paper, which was presented at the end of the session. Art Rupprecht made the interesting observation that Paul's famous speech (Acts 17) was not given at the Areopagus (Mars Hill) as a plaque informs tourists, but was given to the Areopagus, a council. I was able to invite David Stronach, who was now teaching at the University of California at Berkeley, to come to LA to give us a special lecture.

Figure 40. With David Stronach

The A.S.A. Convention

While Kimi flew to Hawaii to be with her family, Brian, Gail, and I drove to Oregon, stopping to see the marvelous Crater Lake with its cobalt blue waters. We were headed to George Fox College for the annual convention of the American Scientific Affiliation in early August. I presented a plaque to Dick Bube for his service as our journal's editor, and gave the presidential address on "Proofs, Problems and Prospects of Biblical Archaeology." At the banquet salmon was being cooked, the fumes made Brian so ill that I had to take him back to the motel. Members were taken on an excursion to the site of Mt. St. Helens where many fallen trees could still be seen with some new vegetation slowly reappearing.

Figure 41. As president of the ASA, I congratulated Dick Bube, the editor of the Journal of the ASA.

After the convention we drove east to Idaho, then south to Utah, where we stopped at Salt Lake. At the Latter-Day Saints' Church History Museum, Cyrus H. Gordon's *Before Columbus* was highlighted as it seemed to buttress Mormon claims of an early migration to the New World. We were able to attend the rehearsal of the famed Mormon Tabernacle Choir. We then drove through Colorado, Kansas, Illinois, and Indiana to come home to Ohio.

Presentations

In September at a conference on "Luther" at Wheaton College, I presented a paper on "Erasmus and the New Testament." Erasmus had produced the first printed Greek New Testament in 1516 which greatly influenced Luther. On our western trip I had the opportunity to view a copy of one of the editions of his Greek New Testament at the University of California at Berkeley.

In December, I presented a paper on "The Episode of the Magi" at a special nativity conference in honor of Jack Finegan organized by Jerry Vardaman at Mississippi State University. I coedited with Vardaman *Chronos, Kairos, Christos*, a Festschrift which was presented to Professor Finegan at a later date. Among those participating were Bastiaan Van Elderen of Calvin Theological Seminary, Paul Maier of Western Michigan University and Harold Hoehner of Dallas Theological Seminary. Bas was a student of Finegan at the Pacific School of Religion. Both Maier and Hoehner agreed that the birth of Jesus must be placed before the eclipse of 4 BC associated with Herod by Josephus. An alternative view which favored a later eclipse of 1 BC was resented by Ernest Martin, a professor at Ambassador College. At the other extreme, Vardaman identified the Christmas star with Halley's comet which had appeared in 12 BC.

By participating in this conference, I missed the session of the Evangelical Theological Society at Dallas at which, prompted by Norman Geisler's objections to Robert Gundry's controversial commentary on Matthew, Gundry was pressured to resign from the ETS. Bob and I were selected to serve on the council of the IBR (Institute for Biblical Research) the same year (see ch. 42). While I disagreed with his view that the Magi episode was unhistorical, as the new president of the IBR I wrote a letter to the president of Westmont College affirming Bob's standing as an esteemed scholar in the IBR. At the IBR, I presented a paper on "Pre-Christian Gnosticism a Decade Letter," summarizing the developments I included in the second edition of my book which was published in 1983.

Publications

I had an article on the Scythians published in the *Biblical Archaeologist* and also an article on "Magic in the Biblical World" published in the *Tyndale Bulletin*. Also published in 1983 was *The New International Dictionary of Biblical Archaeology*, edited by E, M. Blaiklock and R. K. Harrison, which contained 41 of my articles. Blaiklock was a Classics scholar in New Zealand whom I never met; R. K. Harrison was an Old Testament scholar teaching in Canada with whom I had collaborated on several projects.

THE FIRST HALF OF THE 1980S

The Year 1984

The Family

Gail was a freshman at Talawanda High School and enjoyed her classes, even Latin though with some grumbling about memorizing all those conjugations! She enjoyed writing but was sometimes carried away as when she wrote a fifty-page short story! She was honored at Northwestern University as one of the few freshmen in the U. S. scoring over 1200 on the SAT exam usually taken by juniors and seniors.

In his final year in high school Brian served as the captain of "It's Academic Team." In May he graduated with a raft of honors in every subject, top ranking as a senior and selection as one of the graduation speakers. He also ranked first in regional competitions in chemistry and math and was a National Merit finalist. He was given a cash award by the Japanese American Citizens League and was offered scholarships by Miami University, Rensselaer Polytechnic Institute, and Carnegie Mellon University. He accepted the offer from CMU, which is in Pittsburgh and is one of the foremost schools in the field of computer science.

My mother came from LA for two weeks to attend Brian's graduation from high school. She spoiled us by cooking us delicious meals of sukyaki, teriyaki, and curried chicken. We took her to hear the May Choral Festival in Cincinnati, and to visit an international festival in Dayton.

Kimi moved to a new position in the spring to become the secretary of the GREAL (German, Russian and Eastern Asian Languages) Department. The Asian languages were Chinese, Japanese, and later Korean. One memorable outing we had was to view the ageless Yul Brynner in a performance of "The King and I" in Cincinnati. In addition to her involvement at church she became a member of TWIGS, a hospital auxiliary. In May she began to feel sharp pains in her side. After doctors misdiagnosed her problem, she had an appendectomy on June 2nd.

Visiting Speakers

In January, I invited Richard Pierard, a historian from Indiana State University to speak at Miami. In March we had the privilege of having Dr. Kenneth Kantzer, the president of Trinity College, come to speak in Oxford. Dr. Kantzer, Kimi's teacher at Wheaton, had married us in the College Church in 1962. In August as I arranged for the annual convention of the ASA to meet at Miami University, Bob Herrmann, its executive director, spoke at our church.

Presentations and Publications

In February I presented a paper on "Archaeology and Persian Religion" at the Midwest AOS conference at Indiana University. In March I gave a series of lectures on "Daniel, Esther, Ezra and Nehemiah" at the Capital Bible Seminary in Lanham, Maryland. In October I presented a paper on "Persians, Egyptians and Jews" at an archaeological conference at Wheaton College. There I finally got to meet Kenneth A. Kitchen, the distinguished Egyptologist from the University of Liverpool, after corresponding with him for twenty years! At the IBR meeting in December in Chicago, I presented a paper on "Demons and Diseases."

I published an article on "Jerusalem" in *Young's Bible Dictionary*, edited by G. Douglas Young. My presidential address was published in the *Journal of the American Scientific Affiliation*.

Figure 42. With Kenneth Kitchen

Chapter 21

The United Kingdom

The Year 1985

The Family

BRIAN IN HIS SECOND year at CMU found the classes informative and challenging. Almost all his introductory classes were large with 150 to 300 students. He worked at the computer lab during the school year and the summer. Gail as a sophomore in high school enjoyed writing and art. She took art classes on Saturday and joined the Artist's League. One of her one-act plays was chosen to be performed by the students. In the fall she went on a science expedition to Lake Erie.

A depression in our driveway damaged Kimi's 1972 Dart. This led to the purchase of our first ever new car, a Horizon. Kimi and I enjoyed hearing "Samson and Delilah" at the May Festival and viewed "My Fair Lady" at the La Commedia dinner-theater. The entire family went to a Reds game and followed with excitement Pete Rose's pursuit of Ty Cobb's hits record, which he surpassed on September 11.

Lectures and Presentations

In February I spoke on "The Trial of Jesus in Jewish Historiography" to the Jewish faculty at Miami's Hillel Foundation. In March I gave a paper on "Cultural Factors in Biblical Interpretation" to the Midwest ETS conference. In October I spoke on "The Retroversion of Vulgate Texts as a Means of Learning Latin" at the Ohio Conference of Classical Studies. In November I spoke on "Cyrus, Politician or Religious Reformer" at the archaeological conference at Wheaton College. Later that month I presented a paper on "Persian Religion, Judaism, and Christianity" at the NEAS conference at the Talbot School of Theology.

Publications

I contributed the notes on Ezra and Nehemiah to the *NIV Study Bible*.[1] I wrote the chapter on "Babylon" for *Major Cities of the Biblical World*, edited by R. K. Harrison. I also contributed articles to the *Journal of the Evangelical Theological Society* and the *Near East Archaeological Society Bulletin*.

A Month in the United Kingdom

I was eager to view many sites in England, Wales, and Scotland that I had lectured on in courses on Roman History and Western Civilization. I arrived on Monday, July 1 at Gatwick Airport south of London. I was met by Mr. Pallister from whom I was renting a brown Ford Granada. Driving in England is a bit of a challenge. The driver's seat is on the right and one drives in the left lane. I soon got used to it. At an intersection when there are no other cars visible, one can turn into the wrong lane. England has many roundabouts which are considered safer than intersections by traffic engineers. Things become more complicated when as many as six routes converge. Then one must circle about to make sure one takes the right exit.

After finding my host's home in Putney, I drove to Wimbledon. After standing in line for about an hour I was able to get a ticket to court no. 1, where I saw an exciting doubles match.

On July 2 I drove to Greenwich, a historic city on the Thames south of London. It is noted as the site of the Greenwich meridian, which marks the point from which longitude is measured. It has the royal palace where Henry VIII and his daughter Elizabeth were born.

---

1. I had been invited to serve on the Old Testament committee of translators of the New International Version but declined as I knew that this would take a tremendous commitment of time and keep me from writing other publications.

It is also the site of the Royal Naval College. Its chapel has a beautiful painted ceiling. The Maritime Museum has a display charting the voyages of Captain Cook and another displaying Admiral Nelson's uniform. Moored at the dock is the Cutty Sark, a famous clipper ship used in the tea trade with China in the late nineteenth century. I took a boat ride up the Thames to go under the Tower Bridge to view Westminster.

I then drove to Cambridge north of London to Tyndale House, a residential library where I had given a lecture back in 1970. Over the next few days scholars from the U.K., US, Germany, and Australia read papers on the subject of the miracles of Jesus. Those whose papers were eventually published in *Gospel Perspectives VI*, edited by David Wenham and Craig Blomberg, included P. W. Barrett, Barry L. Blackburn, Craig L. Blomberg, Bruce Chilton,[2] William Lane Craig, Stephen T. Davis, Murray J. Harris, Gerhard Maier, Graham H. Twelftree, David F. Wright, and myself. My paper was an extensive survey of ancient magic titled "Magic of Miracle," which sought to refute claims by Morton Smith and John M. Hull that Jesus's miracles were no more than magical acts.

On July 4, I walked around the various colleges at Cambridge. On July 5 I had breakfast with Colin Hemer at Newnham College. Colin had been a Classics teacher. He wrote a marvelous dissertation under F. F. Bruce, providing a thorough Greco-Roman background for the Book of Acts. I also met Sir Norman Anderson, the Islamic Law scholar whom I had invited to speak at the chapel of Rutgers University. I visited the Fitzwilliam Museum and King's College chapel. I bought a number of books at Heffer's Bookstore.

On July 6 I drove from Cambridge to Huntingdon, the birthplace of Oliver Cromwell. There was a small museum celebrating the Puritan leader who had defeated the Royalists and had Charles I executed. Though Cromwell died a natural death, Charles II had his body dug up and decapitated.

I saw the magnificent medieval cathedrals of Peterborough and Ely. I was informed that the cost of their upkeep was about a thousand pounds per day! I was especially interested in viewing Colchester,[3] the ancient Roman Camulodunum, where a temple to the emperor Claudius stood. Though Julius Caesar had invaded England twice in 55 and 54 BC, it was not until the reign of the emperor Claudius that Britannia

---

2. Bruce Chilton informed us that he was moving from Sheffield to Yale University.
3. Many of the British sites which end in either "-chester" or "-cester" reflect the Latin *castrum* or military camp.

became a Roman province. Claudius himself accompanied the invasion in AD 43.

On July 7 I visited the important port city of Rochester on the Medway River. As it was Sunday I attended the service at the cathedral. Beautiful music was provided by a boys' choir, but there were only twelve parishioners in attendance, and an additional twelve tourists wandering about the cathedral. As Rochester was a favorite site of Charles Dickens, there was an interesting museum to the famed author here.

I drove to Maidstone to see the nearby Leeds Castle, which has been rightly called "the most beautiful castle in England." Set quite picturesquely in the middle of a lake, it was a favorite domicile of Henry VIII. Today there is a golf course on its grounds where there are colorful peacocks. I then drove to the coastal city of Ramsgate, where a replica of a Viking ship was displayed. I drove south to view the white chalk cliffs of Dover. On a clear day one can see France just 30 miles across the narrow English Channel.[4] I reached my host's home above the town of Hastings at dusk.[5] I asked my host family about the German bombing raids. They reported that about 150 citizens of the town were killed by them.

On July 8 I went down to the shore to examine the remains of the Norman castle at Hastings. Hastings is the name noted for the a 1066 invasion of William and his knights from Normandy[6] in northern France which resulted in their conquest over the Saxons. I drove inland to the site of Battle, where the ruins of the chapel on a hillside commemorate the actual scene of the battle between the besieged Saxon king and the invading Normans. I listened to a guide recount the details of the battle which had been recorded on a marvelous tapestry in Bayeux, Belgium. Most interesting is the depiction of Halley's Comet which appeared at the time.

I continued along the south shore of England until I reached the resort town of Brighton. Its famous pier has appeared in many movie

---

4. In 1994 an underground tunnel called the "Chunnel" was built which allowed both freight and passenger trains to make a speedy journey between England and France.

5. Because I wanted to use as much of the daylight hours sightseeing, I often arrived at my lodging destinations at dusk or even at night! Though I had a good atlas, I did not have the advantage of a cell phone or a GPS, so finding these homes, especially in the countryside, proved quite challenging!

6. The Normans were originally Vikings. To stop their destructive raids, they were granted land in northern France with the condition that they were to convert to Christianity.

scenes. Unlike the beaches in Hawaii, the beaches in England consist not of sand but of small pebbles!

On July 9 I visited Chichester Cathedral. The remains of an ancient Roman amphitheater are marked by an oval depression in the ground. I enjoyed visiting the enormous Roman palace that had been uncovered at Fishbourne with its marvelous mosaics. Elevated walkways allow visitors to view these remains which are protected by an overhead roof. The palace, which was built around AD 75, is estimated to have been as large as Nero's Golden Palace. On this day many school children were visiting.

I went on to the great harbor of Portsmouth and was able to view the remains of Henry VIII's ship, the Mary Rose, which had just been recovered from the sea. I ate dinner at Salisbury after which I was able to visit the nearby site of Stonehenge as light was fading. I arrived at my host's home at Yeovil at 9 p.m. For a long time, I could not find her farmhouse as it was dark, and its address was hidden by trees. I phoned my host who came out to the roadside to guide me.

On July 10 as I was driving west, I noticed that my car was leaking oil. I therefore stopped at the Trinity Car Works in Exeter. I rented a room without a shower at the Hotel Chuffers for 13 pounds. On July 11 as my car was being repaired. I took a train to the coastal resort of Torquay. I knew that the town was the site of a murder mystery by Agatha Christie as it was presented on PBS. It was not until later that I learned that the town was Agatha's birthplace.

On July 12 I drove to Tintagel on the Cornish coast, a picturesque cliff with ancient remains, that are associated in legend with King Arthur. I stumbled in the parking lot and scraped a knee but was glad that I did not break my glasses. I then doubled back to Exeter and north to view the remains of Glastonbury Abbey, where according to legend King Arthur was buried. According to another legend it was here that Joseph of Arimathea brought Christ's crown of thorns. After viewing the cathedral at Wells, I visited the Cheddar Gorge, noted for its caves and also for the origin of "cheddar cheese." I was able to visit the site of Avebury, which has a circle of small standing stones in the midst of a cow pasture!

On July 13 on my way to Wales I drove to the city of Bristol, which was the home of William Penn and of the Wesleys. After crossing into Wales, I viewed the national museum at its capital, Cardiff. I visited Pembroke Castle, one of a series of castles built by the English kings to control the rebellious Welsh. I drove along the coast to Cardigan then to Aberystwyth in the midst of dense fog.

On July 14, which was a Sunday, I attended a Presbyterian church at Tywyn on the coast. The small congregation of about fifty, had women outnumbering the men four to one. I then drove up the coast to Barmouth. Nearby was the well-preserved Harlech Castle perched on a steep hill. It originally had access to the sea, which helped in the many times it was besieged. The castle was built by Edward I between 1282 and 1289.

I drove inland to visit Ffestiniog, the largest slate mine in the world, where I was able to view a demonstration of how miners split the slate from the rock to create slabs for roofing material. In the northwest corner of Wales, I walked along the outer perimeter of the huge Caernarfon Castle, where Charles was officially designated the "Prince of Wales."

I arrived in Liverpool at 10 p.m. I had tried to call Ken Kitchen to inform him that I was running late but found that he had no phone. Neither did he have an automobile. He worked on Egyptian texts while taking public transportation. I stayed overnight with Ken and his father. Liverpool is a major port city but is best known in the US for its quartet of four lads who became known as "The Beatles."

On July 15 I went to the University of Manchester, where I had lunch with John Hinnells. We discussed the contributions of Mary Boyce to the study of Zoroastrianism. He gave me two of her books. He introduced me to Philip Alexander, a young scholar involved in the study of Jewish texts. On July 16 I toured the Lake District and took a ferry across Lake Windemere. I visited William Wordsworth's Dove Cottage and saw some daffodils about which he had written near the spot where I had parked my car. I toured the town of Keswick which was famous for its Bible conferences.

I then viewed the substantial remains of the Roman wall, which the emperor Hadrian had built across the seventy-mile breadth of northern England. I was able to view and photograph the remains of the mithraeum[7] at Carrawburgh.

On July 17 I crossed over into Scotland. At Glasgow I tried to find the remains of the Roman Antonine wall. A man walking his dog led me to a slight depression which was all that remained of this northern wall. After viewing the Museum of Glasgow, I drove east to Edinburgh. I visited the cathedral where John Knox preached against the Catholic Queen Mary and the house where the great Calvinist reformer lived. His burial place is simply marked by a plaque in a parking lot! On a hillside I viewed

---

7. Mithraea were the temples of the devotees of Mithraism, a mystery religion that was popular with Roman soldiers.

the tomb of the famous skeptic of miracles, David Hume. I arrived at my host's home at 9:45 p.m.

On July 18 I drove north to St. Andrews University, where I had lunch with R. McL. Wilson, the foremost British authority on Gnosticism, with whom I had corresponded.[8] He gave me a tour of the university. We discussed various scholars of Gnosticism, including Kurt Rudolph, whose work on Gnosticism he had translated, and Simone Pétrement, a French scholar who had argued as I had for the post-Christian origin of Gnosticism. He commented that my *Pre-Christian Gnosticism* had covered an enormous amount of material, but said, "You are too conservative for me."

On July 19 I toured the city of Edinburgh. At the end of the Royal Mile I visited the Holy Rood, the palace of Mary, cousin of Elizabeth I and her rival. A guide showed us the bedroom where Scottish nobles killed her Italian servant. At the upper end of the Royal Mile, I toured the great fortress castle of Edinburgh. Displays celebrated the military history of the Scottish soldiers. I drove south along the coast but missed the low tide, which was when one could drive out to the Holy Island of Lindisfarne.

On July 20 I drove south and visited the museum at Newcastle-on-Tyne which exhibited remains of various mithraea, including the one at Housesteads. I drove south to Durham where I visited the Museum of Antiquities and toured the cathedral and the university, where my academic hero, J. B. Lightfoot had ministered and taught.

On July 21 I visited York which had been the great Roman capital in the north. The archbishop of York was second only to the primate at Canterbury. On July 9, 1984, a lightning bolt had set fire to the roof of the cathedral. As this occurred shortly after the elevation of David Jenkins who denied the physical resurrection of Jesus, as the new bishop of Durham, this seemed like a celestial rebuke to many. Evidence of the fire was still visible. Remains of the Roman fort of Eburacum are preserved in the undercroft of the cathedral. It was at Eburacum where Constantine was proclaimed emperor by his troops in AD 306. I visited Sherwood Forest near Nottingham, famed for its association with the story of Robin Hood. I was rather disappointed that very few oak trees had survived from antiquity.

---

8. It was only later that I learned from a letter of F. F. Bruce, that Robin had been one of his students.

On July 22 I visited the British InterVarsity Press at Leicester, which had published editions of my *Pre-Christian Gnosticism* and *The Stones and the Scriptures*. It was here that as I stepped off the curb, I was nearly run over as I had looked in the wrong direction. In London there are warning signs on the curb alerting tourists to look to the right first! I also visited Lion Publishers at Tring Herts, which had published my *World of the First Christians* in multiple languages. I was given a tour of the building by David Alexander, who informed me that the American edition, *Harper's World of the New Testament*, had sold over twenty thousand copies, from which I had not received any royalties!

I returned the car to Mr. Pallister and presented him receipts for the repair of the oil leak and new tires I had paid for, totaling 209 pounds! Over the next few days I found lodging at London House, an inexpensive dormitory for students and scholars that my colleague David Fahey, a British historian, had mentioned to me.

On July 23 in London, I bought books at Foyles, which has six stories of new and used books. I secured half-price tickets at Leicester Square to see Mozart's Marriage of Figaro. On July 24 I took the Tube (subway) to visit Aldersgate Chapel, the site of John Wesley's conversion from a nominal Anglican to a fervent evangelical convert. I viewed the graveyard of John Bunyan and Daniel Defoe. I saw the site of the Walbrook Mithraeum and toured the Museum of London. I paid a brief visit to the Tate Gallery, where paintings of John Turner, my favorite artist, are displayed.

On July 25 I visited the Science Museum and the Victoria and Albert Museum. I had lunch with Terence Mitchell, a keeper at the British Museum, who then guided me through the Western Asiatic section, opening for me the closed gallery which housed the reliefs of Sennacherib depicting his siege of Lachish in 701 BC I visited Charles Wesley's tomb at the Mary LeBon Church and made a quick tour of Madame Tussaud's Wax Museum.

I took a long ride on a cab to High Gate to have dinner in her apartment with Mary Boyce, the foremost scholar on Zoroastrianism. It was most gracious of her to invite me, as she was suffering back pains. During three and a half hours of conversation, she revealed that she had been raised as a Presbyterian but was now an agnostic. Her many years of study of Zoroastrian texts and living with Zoroastrians in Iran had given her great empathy for this Persian religion. She had high words of praise for Donald Wiseman, her chair at the School of Oriental and African

Studies at the University of London. Later she generously sent me her major book on Zoroastrian in the Hellenistic period and provided me with photos for my book *Persia and the Bible*.

On July 26 I took the train to the University of Oxford for the joint conference of the American Scientific Affiliation and the British Research Scientists' Christian Fellowship. The theme of the conference was "Christian Faith and Science in Society." There were 160 American scientists and 130 from the United Kingdom attending. We met at St. Catherine's College, one of the newest schools at the University. Among the British scientists were Colin Humphreys, Malcolm Jeeves, David Livingstone, Donald MacKay, and Colin Russell. Among the American scientists were: Elving Anderson, Richard Bube, Edward Davis, Owen Gingerich, David Griffiths, Jack Haas, Russell Heddendorf, Charles Hummel, David Moberg, Walter Thorson, Howard Van Till, David Wilcox, and Davis Young. I met with Roger Beckwith, who had contributed a chapter to the Festschrift for Jack Finegan I had coedited.

On July 27 I visited Latimer House, the counterpart of Tyndale House, at Oxford and also visited Blackwell's bookstore. On July 28, which was a Sunday, we attended a service at Queens College Chapel. Owen Gingerich, astronomer at Harvard, informed me of the recent conversion of the famed cosmologist Allan Sandage to Christianity late in life. I later learned that Allan's father taught at Miami University, I was able to converse with him over the phone to confirm this detail of his life.[9] At a social gathering I got to meet Scottish theologian, Thomas Torrance, and Sir John Templeton, the financier who offers the annual Templeton Prize in Religion, which is worth more than a million dollars. Bob Herrmann, the executive secretary of the ASA, formed a friendship with Templeton, who was interested in the relationship between science and religion.

On July 29, I presented a version of my paper on "Magic or Miracles" before a room filled with nearly a hundred. Questions were raised by Ed Olson, Robert Griffith, and Malcolm Jeeves. Americans were taken on a trip to Stratford-on-Avon, Shakespeare's home. Returning to London, I was able to attend a performance of Beethoven's Leonora Overture.

---

9. Allan's father was Charles Sandage, who came to Miami University in 1929. He was the chair of the Marketing Department from 1937 to 1946. Allan informed me that he had been a physics major at Miami, studying under Ray Edwards. But he was then drafted. After serving in the Navy from 1945 to 1946, he then finished his baccalaureate studies at the University of Illinois.

AN ASIAN AMERICAN ANCIENT HISTORIAN AND BIBLICAL SCHOLAR

On July 30 I took a train from London south to Epsom, to visit with Donald Wiseman and his wife Mary. Donald showed me the inscribed brick of Nebuchadnezzar used as a door stop, which his father brought back from Iraq. It was one of the items which aroused his childhood interest in someday learning to decipher that strange script. Donald mentioned that during World War II he had been a fighter pilot in the Royal Air Force.[10] He showed me the sketches of what he proposed as the site of the Hanging Garden of Babylon as he was about to deliver a lecture to the British Academy on Nebuchadnezzar and Babylon. He was contemplating whether to accept or reject Francis Andersen's commentary on Isaiah for the Tyndale Old Testament series, as the Australian author was advocating multiple "Isaiahs." We spoke about the remarkable phenomenon that so many of the leading evangelical scholars such as F. F. Bruce, Alan R. Millard and Donald all came from the Brethren background. (See ch. 42.)

I departed on July 31 for the United States after a very busy and rewarding month in the United Kingdom.

Figure 43. With Donald Wiseman

10. Donald sent me his privately printed memoir, *Life Above and Life Below*, which has many photos of his service with the R.A.F.

Chapter 22

The Rest of the 1980s

The Year 1986

The Family

BRIAN AS A JUNIOR at CMU made the dean's list every semester. The demands of his computer science major left him no time for extracurricular activities. During the summer he took part in a mapping project in Pittsburgh. In the fall we helped him move out of the dorm into an apartment to get him away from some obnoxious roommates. He learned for the first time how to cook hamburger and pork chops!

As a sophomore in high school Gail took part in the Ohio Tests for Scholastic Achievement. She ranked sixth out of 1800 who took the exam. In her junior year she served as an officer of the Art and the Latin Clubs and was an actress in some of the school's plays. During the summer Gail and I went to Hawaii to attend the wedding of my cousin Iris Nakama, daughter of Albert and Beryl, who offered the free use of a condominium in Waikiki. We shared this with my mother and sister who came from LA to attend the wedding. My mother and I revisited the dozen places in Honolulu where she had worked as a maid.

Gail and I spent several days on the Big Island visiting Kimi's mother and sister in Hilo. We also saw the Kilauea volcano and the black sand beaches. We rode a whale watching boat off the coast of Kona but failed to see any whales. On Oahu, Gail and I went snorkeling in Hanauma Bay. We climbed to the top of Diamond Head which is an extinct volcano that served as a military installation. There is a superb view of Waikiki from the top of this iconic site. We enjoyed a Chinese dinner with Kimi's relatives in Honolulu. Gail learned how to eat with chopsticks but abstained from trying raw fish, octopus, and poi, a purplish paste made from taro root which was a Hawaiian staple.

The History Department

In 1985, Allan M. Winkler had become chair of the department. He was to hold that position for a decade. Allan was the son of Henry Winkler, my chair at Rutgers. He was a graduate of Harvard with a PhD from Yale University. Allan was a distinguished American historian and a popular teacher who wrote both college textbooks and children's books.

I was now supervising five doctoral[1] and four master's students, who were all from evangelical backgrounds. For a seminar in early Church History, I taught a course on Coptic, the language of the early Egyptian church. Important Gnostic tractates including the Gospel of Thomas had been discovered in 1945 at Nag Hammadi in Egypt. I also supervised the teaching fellows and chaired three departmental committees.

Lectures and Societies

In April at the Midwest SBL meeting in Columbus I read a paper on "Böcher's Etiology of Diseases Examined." In May, I lectured on "The Historical Background of Daniel" at Olivet Nazarene College. In September I presented a talk on "Nehemiah, A Model Leader" at the Trinity Episcopal Seminary. Later that month I spoke on "Ancient Near Eastern History" at a faculty seminar on Western Civilization at Wright State University.

Publications

I contributed an essay on "Post-biblical Traditions about Ezra and Nehemiah" to a Festschrift honoring Gleason Archer, edited by Walter Kaiser

---

1. In contrast to the fields of American history, which required competency in only one foreign language, and European history, which required competency in two languages, doctoral candidates for ancient history were required to be competent in French and German and at least two ancient languages (usually Hebrew and Greek).

and Ronald Youngblood. I also contributed eight articles to the *International Standard Bible Encyclopedia*, edited by G. W. Bromiley. The *NIV Study Bible* to which I had contributed was chosen as the "Book of the Year" by *Eternity Magazine*. Nearly a million copies were sold.

Academics and Athletics

The *US News and World Report* took a poll of about two hundred university presidents who were asked to list the top undergraduate schools in the US. Miami University along with the University of Illinois and Cornell University ranked seventeenth.

Ron Harper was a consensus All American basketball player. He ranked among the top five players in the country in scoring, rebounding and steals. Ron had not been recruited by other universities because a speech impediment had hampered his academics. Miami's Speech and Hearing Clinic greatly helped him to overcome this handicap. Chosen by the Cleveland Cavaliers, Ron was later to play for the Chicago Bulls.[2]

The Year 1987

The Family

Brian took advanced courses in computer science. This was such a demanding major at CMU that out of three hundred freshmen who began this major, only seventy-five survived by their senior year. Involvement in his studies caused him to eat one meal a day, which led him to shed not a few pounds. One fun project was making movies with his friends in science fiction plots.

Gail was active in drama and the Honor Society. She took some college courses at Miami University during the summer. She made some friends from Cincinnati and along with them was recruited as an extra in a Molly Ringwald movie! As Gail was named a National Merit finalist, I took her to visit several prospective campuses, including Oberlin

---

2. Ron Harper was chosen in the first round of the NBA draft in 1986 (eighth overall) by the Cleveland Cavaliers. He later earned three NBA titles playing with Michael Jordan and the Chicago Bulls (1995–1998) and one title with Kobe Bryant and the Los Angeles Lakers (1999–2000).

College, Bard College, [3] Vassar University, Yale University, and Brown University. It helped that she had learned to drive by this time.

Athletic Competitions

During the summer Kimi and I went to attend the Pan-American Games in Indianapolis. We enjoyed viewing the pomp and pageantry of the opening ceremonies, swimming events, and track and field events. We were seated in the "cheap seats" up high watching a basketball game when I experienced severe back pains, so much that I could not drive. Kimi drove me to the emergency room of the Methodist Hospital, where I lay under a blanket for two hours before a doctor came to examine me. X-rays revealed the cause of the problem, kidney stones. These were dissolved by sound waves so that by 11 p.m. I gained some relief. We reached our motel by 1 a.m. A week later Kimi herself felt similar pains, and then shortly thereafter our pastor was hospitalized by the same ailment!

The Russian skaters were in town for an international competition in Cincinnati. They used Miami's hockey arena for their practices, so we got to watch them from a ringside view. One of the annual events which I have enjoyed viewing is the ATP tennis matches at Mason near the King's Island Amusement Park north of Cincinnati. Held just a week before the US Open in Flushing Meadows, the tickets, especially early in the week are relatively inexpensive. The very top men's players and eventually women's players as well participated in this event. This year I got to see Boris Becker, the redhaired young German who had created such a sensation in the 1985 Wimbledon matches. I also saw Ivan Lendl, whom I had seen at Wimbledon, as well as Jimmy Connors. In later years I also got to see Rafael Nadal and my favorite player Roger Federer.

Academics

The teaching of Greek and Latin was foremost in importance in the earliest years of Miami University's history. It housed the American Classical League which fosters the teaching of Latin in high school. Miami's Classics Department was a small one without a graduate program but with outstanding teachers such as Judith de Luce, who was

---

3. We were shown around its campus by Bruce Chilton, a New Testament scholar of my acquaintance.

recognized as the national teacher of the year for her popular courses on mythology. I was appointed to be the chair of the promotion committee for Elizabeth Thornton, whose Latin course I had audited. Liz was an excellent teacher and also a renowned scholar, who had contributed essays to the prestigious German reference work, *Aufstieg und Niedergang der römischen Welt*.

Lectures

In January I lectured at the Concordia Theological Seminary in St. Louis on "Pre-Christian Gnosticism Reviewed" and "Docetic Christolgy and Gnosticism." In March I gave lectures on "The New Testament World" at the Catherine Booth Salvation Army College in Winnipeg, Manitoba. In April I spoke at Covenant Theological Seminary in St. Louis on "Gnosticism and the New Testament" and on "Babylon." During the summer I taught a course on Gnosticism at Grace Theological Seminary in Winona Lake, Indiana. In November I gave a message on "Nehemiah as a Model Leader" at the chapel of Wheaton College.[4]

Special Conferences on Ancient Egypt

The year 1987 marked the centennial of the discovery of the Amarna tablets in Egypt from the reign of Amenhotep III and his son Akhnaton. A conference to celebrate this centennial was organized by the Midwest AOS branch. I gave a paper on "Akhnaton, Moses and Monotheism" in the crowded Breasted auditorium at the Oriental Institute of the University of Chicago. Many notable Egyptologists, including James K. Hoffmeier, Donald B. Redford, and Otto Schaden, read papers.[5]

Also on April 4 to 5 I had the honor of chairing a symposium on "The Date of the Exodus" sponsored by the NEAS at the Memphis Convention Center in conjunction with a traveling exhibit on Ramesses II.[6]

---

4. It was on this occasion that I learned that Stephen Kellough, Wheaton's chaplain, had graduated from Miami University. In an email (March 14, 2019) Steve wrote: "Although we have not been in touch recently, I think of you from time to time and recall the significant influence you had on my life during my time at Miami University."

5. The papers from the conference were to be published by Eisenbrauns. Though it was advertised, for unexplained reasons the volume never appeared.

6. The exhibit, which ran from April to August, drew nearly 700,000 visitors. It was curated by Rita Freed, whom I met many years later after she had moved to the

Among the 18 scholars from Israel, Jordan, the United Kingdom, and US reading papers were: Gleason Archer, John Bimson, Itzhaq BeitArieh, Gordon Franz, Hans Goedicke, Rivka Gonen, Cyrus Gordon, Adnan Hadidi, James Hoffmeier, Kenneth Kitchen, David Livingstone, Gerald Mattingly, Maxwell Miller, William Shea, David Ussishkin, Bruce Waltke, Bryant Wood, and Ronald Youngblood.

The subject of "The Date of the Exodus," concerns the choice between an Early Date (c. 1440 BC) and a Late Date (c. 1270 BC). On the one hand, the majority of evangelical Old Testament scholars adhere to the Early Date (based on 1 Kings 6:1), which relates that Solomon built his temple 480 years after the Exodus (c. 960 BC), whereas most other scholars including Egyptologists favor the Late Date based on the reference to the city of Ramesses (Exodus 1:11). Hans Goedicke proposed an idiosyncratic date about 1500 BC by citing a text of Hatshepsut and correlating certain features of the Exodus with the cataclysmic explosion of the volcanic island Thera (Santorini).[7]

Publications

I contributed "History and Hermeneutics" to the *Evangelical Journal*, "The Nag Hammadi Library" to *The Journal of Library History*, and "Erasmus' Contributions to New Testament Scholarship" to *Fides et Historia*.

The Year 1988

The Family

Brian began the year by having four wisdom teeth extracted! On May 15 Brian graduated with honors from Carnegie Mellon University with a BSc degree in Computer Sciences. In the summer he worked with McDonnell Douglas Aircraft in St. Louis. He was offered fellowships by universities in California, Massachusetts, and New York. He chose to pursue graduate work at the University of Rochester.

During her senior year in high school Gail served as the president of the Artists League and appeared as an actress in several plays. She and her best friend Elizabeth Scott produced a play. Both served as

---

Museum of Fine Arts in Boston

7. The papers from the conference were never published.

valedictorians at graduation in June. She was accepted at all the schools we visited. She chose to enroll at Brown University in Rhode Island.

My seventy-five-year-old mother Haruko Higa moved to Ohio in May and was able to witness the graduation of both of her grandchildren. In October she was able to move to the Talaford Manor, a federally subsidized set of apartments but three blocks away from us. As the rent was adjusted to her income, she initially paid sixty dollars a month and then as little as twenty-five dollars a month! I was able to enroll her into Medicaid. Though she missed her Japanese friends, she enjoyed a number of first-time experiences including the fall foliage, flower shows, an ice-skating exhibition, and even a college football game! She spoiled us by cooking delicious Japanese *gochisō*.

The History Department

I served on a search committee as the department added four new members. Three of my students completed their MA theses: 1) Thomas Nowak wrote on "Darius's Invasion of Scythia," using Russian sources. 2) Robert Smith wrote on "The Antipatrids and Their Eastern Neighbors," and 3) John Wineland on "The Region of the Decapolis." Both Bob and John were students of Reuben Bullard, an archaeologist and geologist at Cincinnati Bible Seminary. They both worked at the excavation at Abila in Jordan directed by Harold Mare of Covenant Theological Seminary. In November I took Jim Murdoch, a grad student, to the archaeological conference at Wheaton College, where the main speaker was Alan Millard of the University of Liverpool.

Lectures

In April I gave a series of lectures on "Persia and the Bible" at Bethel Theological Seminary in St. Paul and a talk on "Pre-Christian Gnosticism and the New Testament" to the Minnesota Consortium of Theological Schools. I visited Roger Palms, our former pastor, who gave me a tour of the building where *Decision Magazine*, which he was editing, was being published. In November I gave the Staley Lectures at Northeast Bible College in Essex Fells, New Jersey at the invitation of Melvin Dahl, my former teacher at Shelton College.

Publications

Eight years after the completion of the manuscript, my commentary on Ezra and Nehemiah finally appeared in *The Expositor's Bible Commentary*, edited by Frank Gaebelein. I contributed "Religions of the World, Persia," to the *International Standard Bible Encyclopedia*, edited by G. W. Bromiley. I also contributed "Gnosticism," "History of Religions School," and "Zoroastrianism and Christianity" to *The New Dictionary of Theology*, edited by S. B. Ferguson and D. F. Wright as well as "Justin Martyr" and "Ignatius of Antioch" to *The Great Leaders of the Christian Church*, edited by John D. Woodbridge. Two publications that were translated were my *World of the First Christians* into Spanish and my chapter on "Magic or Miracle" into Italian.

The Year 1989

The Family

Brian in his second year at the University of Rochester developed a program which enabled a robot to perceive in three dimensions. His project of having a robot bounce a ball on a racquet was featured in *The Chronicle of Higher Education*. He spent the summer in research.

In her second year at Brown Gail enjoyed classes in Art and in English. She made friends from many different states and countries. During the summer she worked at Arby's in Oxford. In the fall she worked as a supervisor in the university cafeteria and served as a counselor to students from the Third World.

When the brakes on our station wagon failed twice even after repairs, we gave up on our 1977 Dodge Aspen and bought a 1986 Dodge Aries with 40,000 miles on its odometer for our extensive travels east. We toured the Civil War battlefield at Antietam and then stayed with my uncle Tom Owan and his wife Frances in Silver Springs, Maryland. This allowed us to view various sites in Washington, DC, including the Vietnam Memorial, where we found Kimi's brother's name, Kaoru Honda. We drove to New York City where we attended the Ebla Conference at New York University, held in honor of Cyrus Gordon who had been teaching there and who was now eighty.

The History Department

In the spring my upper division class on Ancient Persian History had thirty-two undergraduates and seven graduate students. In the fall the department adopted a new policy of having very large survey courses, with teachers lecturing twice a week and teaching assistants conducting small discussion sessions. I volunteered to teach a Western Civilization survey with four hundred students and five TAs. During the summer, I had prepared slides and overhead transparencies for this course.

James Murdoch completed his MA thesis on "The Concept of Perfection in the Thought of Clement and Origen of Alexandria." Jim was a graduate of Cedarville University where his father Murray Murdoch taught history.[8] Scott Carroll completed his PhD, writing on "The Melitian Schism: Coptic Christianity and the Egyptian Church." Melitius was an opponent of Athanasius, the bishop of Alexandria. Scott, who is a charismatic teacher and accomplished scholar, obtained a teaching position at Gordon College. Though he had not yet completed his PhD Jerry Pattengale gained a position at Azusa Pacific University in California. There had been about two hundred applicants for each of these two positions.

Conferences

In February I took a carload of graduate students to attend the Ancient History Symposium at Ohio State University. Ice had coated the roads making driving exceedingly treacherous. After going north to Eaton, I yielded the wheel to Tom Nowak to drive east to Columbus. I counted about forty cars abandoned on the sides of the highway. We arrived just in time for me to read a paper on "The Early Church." In August I read a paper on "Aphrodisiacs, Abortion, Contraception and Infanticide" at the ASA conference in Marion, Indiana. In early November I spoke on "The Jews and the Persians" before the Biblical Archaeology Society of Madison, Wisconsin.

Also, that month I presented a paper on "The Persians" at the archaeological conference at Wheaton College. The conference, which was organized by Alfred Hoerth, also featured lectures by David Howard on "The Philistines," by Ralph Younker on "The Ammonites," by

---

8. Jim went on to earn his PhD in philosophy at Fordham University, writing on the German philosopher Hegel. He then taught at Villanova University.

Daniel Block on "The Babylonians," by Harry Hoffner on "The Hittites," by Keith Schoville on "The Canaanites," by James Hoffmeier on "The Egyptians," and by Jerry Mattingly on "The Moabites," It was Jerry who proposed that we take these papers to produce a book to supplement *Peoples of Old Testament Times*, edited by Donald J. Wiseman (1973), Later in November I presented a paper on "Zoroastrianism, Judaism, and Christianity" at the ETS conference in San Diego.

Yale and Princeton Universities

Tom Woodward, a graduate of Princeton University, while serving as a missionary in the Dominican Republic, read my article on Easter published in *Christianity Today*. He then arranged for me to speak on "Easter: Myth, Hallucination or History?" at both Yale University and Princeton University in October. I flew into New York City and was then driven to New Haven. The director of Campus Crusade at Yale was David Mahan, an alumnus of Miami University.

I was then driven south to Princeton where I was hosted by Robert Kaita, who had received his PhD from Rutgers and who had attended the same Highland Park Baptist Church that we had when I had taught at Rutgers. When I first received a letter from Bob, indicating that he was a Group Head of the Plasma Physics Lab at Princeton, I mistakenly assumed that this had something to do with blood! Rather, he was in charge of researchers attempting to produce energy by nuclear fusion. He led Tom Woodward and me on a tour of his lab, showing us his unique tokamak machine. The head of Cru's mission to faculty and grad students was Dr. Scott Luley, who had formerly taught at Miami University. My lecture at Princeton was posted by Tom Woodward on YouTube under the rubric "Princeton Chronicles." I was also invited by Thomas Gillespie, the president of Princeton Theological Seminary to speak to the Theological Students Fellowship on "Gnosticism and Christianity." I spoke on "Biblical Archaeology" to the Princeton Evangelical Fellowship.[9]

I accompanied Bob and his family to view the Takarazuka dancers, a Japanese version of the Rockettes, at the Radio City Music Hall in Rockefeller Center. Bob's mother who was with us had once been a member of this famed troupe. I was able to speak on "Nehemiah" at the First

---

9. The PEF was founded by Dr. Donald Fullerton at Princeton before the advent of either IV or Cru. Among notable alumni are Harry Hoffner, James Menninger, and John C. Whitcomb.

Baptist Church in Highland Park and to meet the new pastor, George Whittemore, and his wife Carol.

Publications

Chronos, Kairos, Christos, a Festschrift in honor of Jack Finegan, which I edited with Jerry Vardaman was published by Eisenbrauns. Most of the chapters were papers presented at a Nativity Conference arranged by Vardaman at Southern Mississippi State University. I contributed an essay on "The Magi Episode." Other articles included: Bastiaan Van Elderen, "The Significance of the Structure of Matthew 1"; Konradin Ferrari-D'Occhieppo, "The Star of the Magi and Babylonian Astronomy"; Jerry Vardaman, "Jesus' Life: A New Chronology"; Ernest L. Martin, "The Nativity and Herod's Death"; Douglas Johnson, "'And They Went Eight Stades toward Herodeion'"; Harold W. Hoehner, "The Date of the Death of Herod the Great"; Paul L. Maier, "The Date of the Nativity and the Chronology of Jesus' Life"; Nikos Kokkinos, "Crucifixion in AD 36: The Keystone for Dating the Birth of Jesus"; Colin J. Humphreys and W, G, Waddington, "Astronomy and the Date of the Crucifixion"; Roger T. Beckwith, "Cautionary Notes on the Use of Calendars and Astronomy to Determine the Chronology of the Passion"; S. Dockx, "The First Missionary Journey of Paul: Reality or Literary Creation of Luke?"; and Dale Moody, "A New Chronology for the Life and Letters of Paul."

Chapter 23

The First Half of the 1990s

The Year 1990

The Family

BRIAN PRESENTED PAPERS ON robotics at conferences in Massachusetts and in New Mexico. His project with a robotic arm and balloons was featured in *Optic News*. He received the MSci in Computer science from the University of Rochester. During the summer he worked at the Hughes Laboratory in Malibu.

Gail, in addition to her studies at Brown, served as a counselor to minority students. During the summer she took art classes at Miami University. She then took a year off to work for the poor with the Fourth World, an organization that had been started in France by a Catholic priest. After orientation in Washington, DC, she worked in lower Manhattan.

In July Kimi was able to fly back to Hawaii to spend two weeks there. She was able to see her mother and sisters in Hilo and sisters in Honolulu after an absence of many years.

The History Department

I taught a large Western Civilization class of 370 students with the assistance of six graduate TAs who led weekly discussion sessions. At the invitation of Karl Mattox, the chair of the Botany Department, I gave a lecture on "Creation and Evolution" to an honors seminar. I gave a response to a speaker on "The Asian American Myth" and responded to a film on "The New Yellow Peril." Lester Ness completed his PhD dissertation on "Judaism and Astrology in Late Antiquity."[1]

Lectures and Conferences

In April I lectured on "Persia and the Bible" at Andrews Theological Seminary.[2] In August I read a paper on "Gnostic Views of Creation" at the ASA conference. In November I then presented papers in three successive weeks: on "Christians and the Jewish Revolts" at the CFH conference, "The Current State of Old Testament Historiography" at the Wheaton Archaeological Conference, and "Africa and the Bible: Cush and Meroe" at the NEAS conference.

Publications

Baker published my *Persia and the Bible*, which included a foreward by Donald J. Wiseman. This was endorsed by a number of scholars including Richard Frye of Harvard University and Robert North, SJ of the Pontificio Istituto Biblico whose *Guide to Biblical Iran* had been the only previous publication on this subject. My essay on "Archaeology and the Gospels" was published in *The Gospels Today*, edited by John Skilton. An article on Gnosticism and the New Testament appeared in *The Evangel: The British Evangelical Review*.

Little Man Tate

One of the highlights of 1990 was the filming of "Little Man Tate" on Miami's campus. It was the touching story of a seven-year old genius who enrolled at a university. Because of his outstanding intellect he could not relate to others of his own age. Nor could he relate to his

---

1. Lester had served in the navy and was a graduate of Wheaton College. He served as an English instructor in several schools in China.

2. Andrews is a Seventh Day Adventist school. Staying at a dorm, I found the cafeteria food rather bland. There were no fast food restaurants in Berrien Springs at this time, so I went out of town and found a pizza place. But when I got back I found the gate to the main entrance locked. Luckily I found an unlocked side entrance!

older college classmates. The film starred famed actress Jodie Foster as the boy's mother in her directorial debut. One setting was the Tau Kappa Epsilon fraternity house on Campus Avenue. Another was Upham Hall, a large U-shaped building which housed the History Department. The large classroom at Upham which was used was one where I have given lectures. I witnessed from the second floor the filming of the scene in which a college student tosses a large globe which hits the little boy. Many Miami students got involved as extras. The movie was both a critical and a commercial success.

The Year 1991

The Family

Brian worked at the Jet Propulsion Lab in Pasadena on the prototype of the rover which would be sent to Mars. He was shown around LA by my sister Alicia and introduced to her friends.

Gail worked in Washington state with the Third World to unionize hotel workers. For these efforts she was awarded a Starr Fellowship by Brown University. She was among ten chosen out of four hundred nominees for this award. When she began her junior year, she declared Art as her major. She also took some courses at the adjacent Rhode Island School of Design.

In August my mother became seriously depressed. After hospitalization and a short stay with us, she recovered enough to return to her own apartment. She was encouraged by Noriko, a student from Japan, and a neighbor Elsa Swenson, a woman from Sweden.

The History Department

In addition to the six graduate students in Ancient History, the fall saw the addition of three new students including: 1) Laura Dunn, a graduate of Xavier University and Trinity Evangelical Divinity School. 2) John DeFelice, a graduate of Gordon College. John and his wife Gwen, who is the granddaughter of the noted Yale historian Roland Bainton, were both professional optometrists. 3) Kenneth Calvert, a graduate of Wheaton College and Gordon-Conwell Divinity School, where he was student body president. Ken also studied under Helmut Koester, a student of Rudolf Bultmann, at Harvard Divinity School. Students in Ancient History garnered about a third of all the grants and fellowships awarded by the department.

MA applicants for assistantships and PhD applicants for fellowships are screened by the Graduate Studies Committee on which I served with six other professors. After assessing their GPAs (grade point averages), GRE (graduate record examination scores), and letters of recommendation, we would each assign a candidate scores, usually ranging from 6 to 9, with 10 being the highest score. Someone with a calculator would total the scores. The candidates with the highest scores would be granted these awards.

At one meeting Jennifer Hevelone, a student of Scott Carroll's from Gordon College applied. She had excellent GPA and GRE scores, great letters of recommendation, and had studied Coptic with Scott. But when the members responded with their assessments, Jack Kirby, a US historian, gave her a zero! Other members of the committee and I were in a bit of a shock. When I asked why, Jack said with some justification, "Ed, there are already too many ancient history majors."[3] It has been said that sometimes God closes doors only to open other doors. Jennifer earned an MA at the University of Chicago and then a PhD at Princeton University under Peter Brown, the foremost scholar of Christianity in Late Antiquity. She became the chair of the History Department at Gordon College!

Lectures and Conferences

In February, I gave my talk on "Easter" to a faculty conference in Fort Wayne, Indiana and at a convocation at Gordon College in April. I spoke on "The Bible and Archaeology" to the college's Phi Alpha Chi (a history honorary group). In June I gave one of the keynote addresses at a conference on Christianity and the Classics in Toronto. I spoke on "Gnosticism and Christianity in the Second Century." In August I read a paper on "Gnostic Views of Creation" at the ASA conference. I then read a paper on "The Archaeology of Biblical Africa: Cyrene" at the NEAS conference.

---

3. Jack and I remained good friends. After his retirement to St. Augustine, Florida, he wrote *Mockingbird Song: Ecological Landscapes of the Souti,* which won the 2007 Bancroft Prize. He kindly sent me an inscribed copy.

Africa and Africans in Antiquity

In March, with the aid of the McClellan Lecture Fund, I organized a major conference featuring leading scholars on ancient Africa. These included: William Y. Adams (University of Kentucky), Reuben G. Bullard (Cincinnati Bible College and Seminary), Stanley M. Burstein (California State University at Los Angeles), Carleton T. Hodge (Indiana University), Edna R. Russmann (Brooklyn Museum), Frank M. Snowden Jr. (Howard University), Maynard W. Swanson (Miami University), Donald White (University of Pennsylvania), and Frank Yurco (Chicago Field Museum of Natural History). These papers were later published in *Africa and Africans in Antiquity*, which I edited for Michigan state University Press.

Publications

I contributed "Jews in the New Testament," "Libraries," and "Nineveh" to *The Holman Bible Dictionary*, edited by Trent Butler. An article on "Christians and the Jewish Revolt against Rome" appeared in *Fides et Historia*.

The Year 1992

The Family

Brian worked for Boeing Aerospace at the Kennedy Space Center in Cape Canaveral. He developed the software for the robotic inspection of the panels on the space rafts. In the fall he entered the doctoral program in Computer Science at Case Western Reserve University in Cleveland. He joined a science fiction writing club and also a lobbying group which promoted the Delta Clipper, a reusable space craft. He read a paper in Hawaii at an interdisciplinary conference which sought to apply insights from animal behavior to robots.

Gail served as a peer counselor at Brown and earned money by washing vessels for the Biochemistry Lab. She did research for a community organization in Providence called D.A.R.E. (Direct Action for Rights and Equality).

In June Kimi and I visited Brian at Cape Canaveral and viewed a rocket launch with him. In Orlando we visited the Epcot Center, Disney World and Universal Studios. We met Chris and Karen Akers, Miami alumni, who were working with Campus Crusade for Christ at its headquarters in Orlando. We also visited the adjacent headquarters of the Wycliffe Bible Translators.

The History Department

I taught a Western Civilization survey class of 350 students with the help of seven TA's, including one from China and one from Kenya. I was supervising the research of seven doctoral and three master's students.[4] Carl Smith completed his MA thesis on "Mark the Evangelist and his Relationship to Alexandrian Christianity in Biblical, Historical and Traditional Literature."[5] Daniel Hoffman completed his PhD dissertation on "The Status of Women in Gnosticism, Irenaeus, and Tertullian."[6]

Lectures

In April I gave my lecture on "Easter" to the students at Ohio State University, and a talk on "The Bible and Archaeology" to the Christian faculty fellowship. That same month I gave a series of lectures on "The Bible and the Ancient World" at Beeson Theological Seminary, an interdenominational school which is housed at the Baptist Samford University in Birmingham. I lectured on Gnosticism for Frank Thielman's class. I also spoke in the chapel and observed uninterested football players in the balcony who were there by compulsion! I witnessed the arrival of Margaret Thatcher, who had come to Samford University for a fundraising event.

---

4. Since ours was a PhD granting department, we had relatively light teaching loads (6 hours), including even those who did not have grad students to supervise.

5. The tradition that Mark founded the church at Alexandria does not date earlier than the fourth-century historian Eusebius.

6. This was later published. Daniel criticized Elaine Pagels assertion that the Gnostics treated women more favorably than the Orthodox such as Tertullian. Daniel showed that some Gnostics exploited women and that Tertullian admired women martyrs. In 1995 at the SBL session on the Nag Hammadi Library, Elaine, who had read his book, conceded to me that Daniel did have a point.

Conferences

In August, I presented a paper on "Metal Resources and Metallurgy in the Biblical World" at the ASA conference held at the Youth With a Mission College in Kona, Hawaii.[7] I roomed with Bob Kaita from Princeton. A featured speaker was Philip Johnson, a law professor from Berkeley, who had written a number of books published by InterVarsity Press critical of naturalism in general and of evolution in particular. There was a spirited discussion between Johnson and Harvard astronomer Owen Gingerich over these issues. A field trip took us up the 14,000-foot Mauna Kea to view the many observatories located at the summit. The thin air made my feet quite wobbly!

In November, I presented a paper on "Sensational Claims for the Dead Sea Scrolls Reexamined" at the NEAS conference in San Francisco. This enabled me to visit nearby Walnut Creek to reconnect with Chi-Hang Lee, a Chinese scientist from Viet Nam,[8] who had served as the first Asian president of the ASA. I was the second and Bob Kaita was the third. We all had Rutgers connections: I taught there, and Chi-Hang and Bob earned their doctorates there.

Publications

I contributed articles on "Ahasuerus," "Assos," "Astyages," "Herodotus," "Myra," "Troas," and "Tyrannos" to *The Anchor Bible Dictionary*, edited by David N. Freedman. Several of my graduate students also wrote articles for this major reference work. An article "Mordecai, the Persepolis Tablets, and the Susa Excavations" appeared in *Vetus Testamentum*.

---

7. I had dinner with Merry Puff and Bob Hoffman from Oxford and Jerry and Angel Jackson who were working at the college. Merry and Bob married upon returning to Oxford. I had baptized Jerry and Angel, who later moved to Switzerland.

8. Chi-Hang wrote: "I was born in a small village in Vinh-Long province, in southern Vietnam. One of the childhood memories I have was the small 'house' with straw/grass roof, with mud floor. It's right next to a small river (or creek). Almost daily before dark, my grandmother would carefully examine the floor and corners or crevices, to make sure no snakes were around when we went to bed! Another vivid memory were the majestic clouds at sunset, and the total dark sky with stars. I often saw meteorites. Perhaps my interest in astronomy began at that time. At age 8 we moved to Saigon, where electricity was available. After high school I came to the US for college. My first two years were at Houghton College; then I finished a BA in Southern Illinois University. Then at Rutgers (1960 to 1966) I was grateful you befriended me, and we became good friends since then."

THE FIRST HALF OF THE 1990S

Christianity Today

In June, I was appointed to a two-year term to serve on the board of senior editors of *Christianity Today*, an influential periodical begun by Billy Graham. The editor-in-chief was Kenneth Kantzer.[9] This afforded me the opportunity to write occasional editorials.[10] Other members of the board included: George Brushaber, Robert Cooley, Mark Noll, Thomas Oden, James Packer, and Haddon Robinson. The book review editor was Michael (Mickey) Maudlin, a Miami University graduate.[11] Other members of the CT staff included Harold Myra, Tim Morgan, and David Neff.

Figure 44. With Mickey Maudlin

9. Kantzer, who was one of Kimi's teachers at Wheaton, had married us in the College Church in 1962. He had moved from Wheaton College to become the academic dean of Trinity Evangelical Divinity School in Deerfield, a suburb north of Chicago. He had transformed a small seminary of the Evangelical Free Church into a major seminary by being given the freedom to hire leading scholars without restriction as to their denominational backgrounds.

10. My first editorial highlighted the exemplary Christian witness of Bill Wilson, a Botany professor at Miami University (see chapter 46).

11. When Mickey's wife Karen went to Wheaton College for graduate work in psychology, Mickey worked at a Christian bookstore and then at IV Press, before joining CT.

The Year 1993

The Family

Brian continued his program in Computer Science at Case Western. An interesting commentary on the status of this demanding field is that out of fifty doctoral students, there was only one other American. He spent the summer programming robots at the Naval Intelligence Laboratory in Washington, DC. He connected with a cousin Clyde Owan, the son of my uncle Tom, who worked in naval intelligence.

Together with Brian, Kimi and I were able to witness Gail's graduation from Brown University in May. One of Brown's traditions is a parade of the graduates down a hill with the oldest alumni marching first. What was quite striking was that all of the early alumni were white. It was only after World War II that a noticeable increase of alumni "of color" could be observed. With her own hard earned money Gail bought a 1977 yellow Volvo. She managed to drive it back to Ohio even though it had a hole in the floor! In the summer she went to study French in Paris as an intern with the Fourth World.

On the way to Gail's graduation Kimi and I got to visit Cooperstown, where the Baseball Hall of Fame and the home of James Fennimore Cooper are located. On the return trip, as we were hauling Gail's things in a U-Haul trailer, a tire on it blew out on the Pennsylvania Turnpike. Fortunately, this happened close to an exit, so I was able to walk to a service station to get help.

In June we witnessed the Brown crew win the national collegiate rowing race at Harsha Lake near Cincinnati. In July we visited Greenville directly north of Oxford, where the sharpshooter Annie Oakley was born. Her museum also features the journalist Lowell Thomas, who publicized the exploits of "Lawrence of Arabia."[12]

The History Department

Due to retirements, I was now the most senior full professor in rank in the department. During the spring I taught an overload course on Western

---

12. T. E. Lawrence began his career as an archaeologist working with Leonard Woolley. Because of his knowledge of Arabic, he became an invaluable agent of the British in aiding the Arab revolt against the Turks. He later returned to Oxford under a pseudonym.

Civilization at the Middletown campus.[13] In the fall I taught a course on Ancient Egyptian History and a graduate colloquium on Eastern Christianity. I also taught a course on Syriac to students in this course. Jerry Pattengale completed his PhD dissertation on "Benevolent Physicians in Late Antiquity: The Cult of the *Anargyroi*," The latter were doctors who offered their services "without silver," that is without fees.

The Religion Department

Miami's Department of Comparative Religions is one of the oldest if not the oldest such department at a state university. While the department offers only the MA degree, some of its faculty have served on the doctoral committees of my students.[14] This department arranged for the granting of an honorary degree to James M. Robinson of Claremont University, the scholar who had organized a team of Coptic specialists to translate the Nag Hammadi Library into English. Robinson was a student of Rudolph Bultmann. I had met him before, but this was the first time that I was to meet his new wife Gesine, whose writings I had also criticized for maintaining that a pre-Christian Gnosticism had influenced the New Testament.

Lectures

In March through the university's program board, I spoke on Easter at Miami University. Among those in attendance was my history colleague and the university president, Dr. Philip Shriver. In April I presented lectures on "Sensational Claims for the Dead Sea Scrolls" and "The Effect of Gnosticism on the Early Church" at Covenant Theological Seminary. I lectured on Daniel for Robert Vasholz's class.[15] In October I spoke on

---

13. I also taught nearly every summer in order to support our children, who chose to go to private universities. If they had been content to go to Miami University, which after all is a pretty good school, tuition would have been free!

14. Notably Roy Bowen Ward, a graduate of Harvard, who served on two such committees. The later chair, James Hanges, who earned his PhD at Chicago, was a student in my Church History class while pursuing the MA at Miami.

15. As this was Easter weekend and as I was teaching a course on Eastern Christianity, I decided to attend a Coptic Orthodox and a Greek Orthodox service. I was welcomed by the priest of the first to join in a service meeting in a home, but I came late and made the mistake of sitting in the women's section! I had great difficulty finding the Greek Orthodox church as it met in a garage like structure. As is typical in such

"Ancient Persian Capitals" at Millikan University in Decatur, Illinois. I was happy to meet Professor Michelle Deardorff, who had attended the Bible study I had led at Miami University. In November I presented a paper on "God and the Shah" at the ETS conference.

Publications

Two Kingdoms, a church history textbook I coauthored with Robert Clouse and Richard Pierard, was published by Moody Press. Bob and Dick, who were both at Indiana State University, were friends from the Conference on Faith and History which they had helped to begin[16] and which I had served as president. I covered the early history, Bob the Middle Ages and Dick the recent developments.[17] I also contributed articles on "Gnosticism" and "Hellenism" to *The Dictionary of Paul and His Letters*, edited by Gerald Hawthorne, Ralph Martin and Daniel Reid, and an article on "Archaeology and the Bible" to the *The Oxford Companion to the Bible*, edited by Bruce Metzger. I was interviewed by Timothy Jones for the article "Dead Sea Scrolls Hype" published in *Christianity Today*.

The Year 1994

The Family

In July, Brian gave a paper at the International Conference on the Simulation of Adaptive Behavior in Brighton, England. In August he gave another paper at the International Symposium on Robotics and Manufacturing at Maui, Hawaii. He contributed a paper for a journal published by MIT Press. In March Kimi and I went to see Brian. We joined him in listening to a concert by the Cleveland Symphony Orchestra.

Gail was assigned by the Fourth World to work with impoverished children in the slums of Bangkok, Thailand. There she learned the Thai language but normally spoke with her colleagues in French. In October

---

traditions all except a few elderly were standing. I lasted for about two hours before I left!

16. The Conference on Faith and History was started by Clouse and Pierard with Robert Lindner who taught at Kansas State University. All three were graduate students at the University of Iowa.

17. This was translated into Portuguese in Brazil. Moody also published an abridged illustrated version called *The Story of the Church*.

she returned to the States to join 300 other delegates from 40 countries for a conference on poverty in Peekskill, New York. As she did not have time to return to Chio, Kimi and I traveled to Peekskill to spend some time with her there While in upstate New York we visited F.D.R.'s home at Hyde Park, Eleanor Roosevelt's cottage, West Point, and Bear Mountain. The foliage was at its most colorful peak.

The History Department

A new master's student was Steven Stannish, a graduate of the University of Nebraska at Omaha. He had read my *Persia and the Bible*. Another new MA student was Daniel Master,[18] a graduate of the Philadelphia College of the Bible, where his father taught the Old Testament. He had read my *Pre-Christian* Gnosticism. Dan served as a site supervisor at the excavation of Ashkelon, an important Philistine city on the Mediterranean coast. John DeFelice completed his MA thesis on "Tin and Trade: An Archaeometallurgical Approach to Dating the Exodus." Robert Smith completed his PhD dissertation on "*Arabia Haeresium Ferax*? A History of Christianity in the Transjordan to CE 395." Bob obtained a teaching post at Florida Bible College in Kissimmee.

Lectures

In April, I spoke on "Easter-Hoax or History?" in an auditorium seating five hundred at the University of Florida in Gainesville and gave a talk to the Christian faculty on "Nehemiah, a Model Leader." Tom Woodward of Trinity College, who had earlier arranged for me to speak at Yale and Princeton, set up a luncheon for me in Tampa. I also gave a message at an Easter service held at the University of Florida's baseball field.

Early in October, I gave the Lyman Stewart Lectures on "Africa and the Bible" at Talbot School of Theology in La Mirada, California. I also spoke to Clinton Arnold's seminar. I then gave my talk on "Easter" at Azusa Pacific University, where Jerry Pattengale was teaching. While in the LA area, I was able to meet with George Giacumakis, who was at Fullerton

---

18. Daniel Master asked for permission to enter our program not in the fall, but in the following semester. When I asked him why, he wrote that he was involved in a soccer tournament for his college!

State University. I also visited the Nixon Library at Yorba Linda, the Getty Museum at Malibu, and the Huntington Museum at Pasadena.

Later in October, I spoke on the Reliability of the New Testament at a Veritas Forum at the Oho State University. There were about a thousand in attendance. Other speakers at the forum included Philip Johnson on Darwinism, Peter Kreeft on Relativism, and Paul Vitz on Freudianism. The Veritas Forums were begun by Kelly Monroe, an InterVarsity staff member at Harvard. Her daughter attended Miami University.

Figure 45. With Kelly Monroe

Societies and Conferences

In May, I gave a paper on "Adaptation and Assimilation in Asia" before the Association of Ancient Historians at Wright State University. In November I presented a paper on "Afrocentric Biblical Interpretation" at the ETS conference in Chicago. The IBR banquet speaker was the noted British New Testament scholar, James Dunn. I was able to attend a special dinner honoring Cyrus H. Gordon, who was now 85.

Publications

Peoples of the Old Testament World, which I coedited with Alfred Hoerth and Gerald Mattingly was published by Baker. This was selected for a prize by the Biblical Archaeology Society as one of the best popular books on biblical archaeology. A foreward was written by Alan R. Millard. I contributed the essay on "Persians." Other chapters included: "Sumerians" by Walter Bodine, "Babylonians" by Bill Arnold, "Assyrians" by William Gwaltney, "Hittites" by Harry Hoffner, "Canaanites and Amorites" by Keith Schoville, "Phoenicians" by William Ward, "Arameans" by Wayne Pitard, "Philistines" by David Howard, "Egyptians" by James Hoffmeier, "Ammonites" by Randall Younker, "Moabites" by Gerald Mattingly, and "Edomites" by Kenneth Hoglund.

I contributed the essay "The Current Status of Old Testament Historiography" to *Faith, Tradition and History*, edited by David Baker, James Hoffmeier and Alan Millard. I also wrote "The Political Background of the Old Testament" for *The Foundations for Biblical Interpretation*, edited by David S. Dockery, Kenneth A. Mathews and Robert B. Sloan. My essay on "Gnosticism and Early Christianity" appeared in *Hellenization Revisited*, edited by Wendy Helleman. An abridged version of my commentary on Ezra and Nehemiah appeared in the *NIV Bible Commentary*, edited by K. L. Barker and J. Kohlenberger III. I contributed the article on the "Pergamum Library" to *The Encyclopedia of Library History*, edited by W. A. Wiegand and D. G. Davis and essays on "Nebuchadnezzar," "Cyrus," "Darius," and "Xerxes" to *Historic World Leaders*, edited by A. Commire.

Chapter 24

The Rest of the 1990s

The Year 1995

The Family

IN MAY, KIMI AND I attended Brian's graduation from Case Western Reserve University, where he earned a PhD in Computer Science. Brian's research enabled robots to maneuver in changing environments. After a summer at a science fiction workshop at Michigan State University, he began a post-doctoral assignment at the Institute for Learning and Expertise at Stanford University.

Gail used her skills in art to work with the children in the slums of Bangkok. She also took a course in art from a university in the city. She surprised us by returning from Thailand unannounced at Christmas.

In July Kimi and I went to Bethesda, Maryland to attend the wedding of my cousin Douglas Owan. In October we observed the spectacle of "Tall Stacks," the gathering of paddle wheelers on the Ohio River at Cincinnati. We enjoyed the movie "Picture Bride," which related the story of immigrants from Japan who worked in the sugar plantations of Hawaii, just as both of our families did.

The History Department

I had seven students who were completing their dissertations. A new doctoral student was Darlene Brooks Hedstrom, who had both a BA and an MA from Wheaton College. Dar worked at the excavation of an early monastery at Wadi Natrun, Egypt, under Bastiaan Van Elderen. Daniel Master completed his MA thesis on "The Origins of Jewish Elements in Early Ethiopian Christianity," and was accepted into the doctoral program of Near Eastern Archaeology at Harvard to study under Lawrence Stager, the director of the excavation at Ahkelon. Robert Winn, a graduate of Cedarville University, finished his MA thesis on "An Evaluation of the Theory of a Semitic Influence on Stoicism."[1]

Lectures

In April, I gave the Dwight Lecture on "Implications of the Dead Sea Scrolls" at the University of Pennsylvania. I was introduced by Robert Kraft, the chair of the Department of Religious Studies. Donald J. Wiseman was in the audience. After the lecture Donald and I retired to the home of Francis Rue Steele, the head of the North Africa Mission. Steele, who had once been an assistant to Samuel Noah Kramer at the University Museum, had translated one of the earliest Sumerian law codes.

In May, I gave the Horn Museum Lecture on "Babylon and the Bible" at Andrews University Seminary. In September I spoke on "Adaptation and Assimilation in Asia" and "Traditions, Archaeology and Inscriptions in Reconstructing Ancient History" at Indiana State University. I stayed at a motel in Terre Haute owned by ISU basketball player Larry Bird, my favorite NBA player.

Special Session on Nag Hammadi

I was invited to read a paper on "Pre-Christian Gnosticism in the Light of the Nag Hammadi Texts" at the special session of the SBL celebrating the 50th anniversary of the discovery of the Nag Hammadi Library. This was held in Philadelphia, where there was also a banquet honoring Cyrus Gordon at Penn's University Museum.

---

1. Bob Winn went on to study the ancient Armenian language and earned his PhD at Catholic University of America. He then served as the chair of the history department at Northwestern College in Iowa.

Publications

I wrote the chapter "Jesus Outside the New Testament" in *Jesus Under Fire*, edited by M. J. Wilkins and J. P. Moreland. This was an attempt by evangelical scholars to rebut the negative conclusions of a group of liberal New Testament scholars known as the Jesus Seminar organized by Robert Funk. Members of the group used colored tokens to vote on the authenticity of sayings of Jesus found in the four Gospels and the Gospel of Thomas. Their overwhelmingly negative conclusions were published in *The Five Gospels* in 1993, which garnered widespread media attention. *Jesus Under Fire* caught the eye of the former skeptical journalist for the *Chicago Tribune*, Lee Strobel, who sought to popularize our responses by interviewing various evangelical scholars. He came to Oxford to interview me for the chapter "The Corroborating Evidence" in his book, *The Case for Christ* (Zondervan, 1998) which became a best seller.[2] I also contributed the article "Hellenistic Bactria and Buddhism" to *Humanitas*, and "On the Road with Paul: Ease and Dangers of Travel in the Ancient World" to *Christian History*.

---

2. Among other scholars who were interviewed were: Craig Blomberg for "The Eyewitness Evidence," Bruce Metzger for The Documentary Evidence," John McRay for "The Scientific Evidence," Ben Witherington III for "The Identity Evidence," Donald A. Carson for "The Profile Evidence," William Lane Craig "The Evidence of the Missing Body," Gary Habermas "The Evidence of the Appearances," and J. P. Moreland "The Circumstantial Evidence."

Figure 46. With Lee Strobel

Various Media

I was one of the scholars interviewed for the twentieth anniversary edition of *Biblical Archaeology Review*. In March I appeared on the Arts and Entertainment television show on Esther. I was cited in an article on "The Mysteries of the Bible" in the April issue of *US News and World Report*. I was also interviewed on a Jubilee radio program from St. Louis and on a talk show from Cincinnati.

The Year 1996

The Family

Brian accepted a two-year postdoctoral research fellowship at the Naval Research Lab in Washington, DC, where he had worked before. During the summer he took part in the Clarion science fiction conference at Michigan State University.

During the summer, I got to visit Thailand and see Gail's work firsthand. She provided art materials and books for children in the slums of the city. I met her French co-worker Jaqueline and a Thai engineer friend named Golf. Bangkok was hot and smoggy, but travel on a narrow swift boat on the river was pleasant. In addition to observing the gilded palace in Bangkok, we took a rail trip to the former capital to view some ancient Buddhist remains. Gail had become fluent in Thai and had become accustomed to Thailand's spicy foods.

In July, Kimi and I explored southern Ohio. We visited Athens in southeast Ohio, the home of Ohio University, Miami's sports rival and the oldest school in the state. We visited Marietta on the Ohio River, the earliest settlement in the state, and Chillicothe, the state's earliest capital. We visited a nearby Indian mound and viewed the outdoor spectacle celebrating the famous Indian chief Tecumseh.

The History Department

Brett Griffith finished his MA thesis "On the Effectiveness of Julian the Apostate's Military Leadership." John Wineland, a graduate of Valparaiso University and of Cincinnati Christian Seminary, completed his dissertation on "Abila of the Decapolis: A Historical and Archaeological Examination from the Hellenistic Period to the Arab Conquest."[3]

Eric H. Cline

In the fall of 1995 and the spring of 1996, I enjoyed a sabbatical, while Eric H. Cline taught in my stead. His wife Diane was a member of the Classics Department at the University of Cincinnati. With a PhD from the University of Pennsylvania, Eric was an authority on the relations of the Mycenaeans, the Hittites, and the Egyptians. He had a profound influence of three of my graduate students, John DeFelice, Jason Larson, and Steve Stannish. Eric moved on to George Washington University and excavated at Megiddo and Tel Kabri in Israel. He published many influential and well received books on archaeology and ancient history.

3. This was published by the British Archaeological Reports in Oxford, England. John continued to excavate in Jordan, working with Jerry Mattingly in Moab.

Lectures in Asia

In conjunction with my trip to see Gail in Thailand, I visited a number of Asian countries from May 13 to June 14. Philip Lam, a missionary from Hawaii, arranged speaking engagements in Taiwan for me. On May 15 I spoke on "The Travels of Paul" at Chong Yuan University in Chung Li. On May 16 I lectured on "Old Testament Archaeology" and on "Gnosticism" at the Taiwan Theological Seminary in Taipei. On May 17 I discussed "Magic and Divination" at Sheng-Te Christian College in Chung Li. On May 20 I spoke on "Buddhism and Christianity in Hawaii" at the Tung Hai University in Taichung. On May 21 I lectured on "Nehemiah" at Chung Tai Theological Seminary in Taichung.

I then spent a week in Singapore with my former Shelton student, Dr. Swee Hwa Quek, and taught a course on The Biblical World and a course on Gnosticism in his Biblical School of Theology. I shared my testimony and gave a public lecture on Archaeology at the National University of Singapore. I spoke at the Serangon Church on "The Spread of Christianity" and at the Zion Bishan Church on "Nehemiah" and "The Cross and the Empty Tomb." In Singapore I renewed acquaintances with Philip Heng from Shelton College and David Chan from Brandeis.

I flew into Hong Kong with the airplane flying just over the tops of buildings to land. I spoke on "Biblical Archaeology" and "Gnosticism and Early Christianity" at the China Graduate School of Theology where one of Cyrus Gordon's students, Wilson Chow (Brandeis PhD 1974) taught. Among other faculty was Walter Louie, who had been a student when I taught one summer at Grace Theological Seminary.

I flew into Japan where I spoke on "Archaeology and the Bible," "The Chronology of Jesus' Life," "Pre-Gnosticism and the Dead Sea Scrolls" at the Tokyo Christian University located near the airport. David Tsumura, who earned his PhD from Brandeis in 1973, was my host as I spoke at his Museum of Biblical Archaeology in Tokyo, at a laymen's institute in Yokohama, and lectured at his Japan Bible Seminary on "Old Testament Archaeology," "New Testament Archaeology," and "The Dead Sea Scrolls." I also spoke on "Biblical Archaeology" to the Hamadayama Biblical Archaeology Society.

The Japan Bible Seminary (*Seisho Senkyokai*), which was begun in 1958, moved to its location in Hamura northwest of Tokyo in 1989. At the time of my lecturing there in 1996, there were but thirty-two full time students and twelve faculty members. My wife knew Shin Funaki who had gone to Wheaton College and Henry Ayabe from Hawaii who had gone to Moody Bible Institute. Henry was the brother of Nobu Ayabe whom I knew at Columbia Bible College.

There was very little time for sightseeing, but I did get to meet Steve Lambacher, a former MA student from Miami, who was teaching at Aizu University. I met Kimi's friends, Akiko Minato,[4] Shin Funaki, and David Shimada. I also got to visit with my mother's brother, Dr. Choko Owan, and his family. I stayed in Tokyo in the small apartment of Yokichi and Nancy (Ohama) Suzuki, missionaries to Japan. Nancy was a member of Kalihi Union Church.

Other Lectures

In February, I spoke at the Rocky Mountain section of the ASA in Colorado Springs, where Dr. John Vayhinger was my host. In March, I taught a course on Biblical Archaeology to grad students at Toccoa Falls Bible College in Georgia. I also gave lectures at Lee College, in Cleveland, Tennessee, where my student Dan Hoffman was teaching. In April I spoke at the on "Nehemiah as a Model Leader" in the chapel of Trinity Evangelical Divinity School.

On October 22 I took part in a Veritas Forum at the University of Virginia. Ken Elzinga, distinguished professor of Economics, who had been my host during my lecture at the school twenty years earlier was my host again. I had lunch at Michie Tavern and was given a tour of nearby Monticello. I stayed at the Colonnade Club, an inn located on the historic lawn of the university. Drew Trotter, the executive director of the Center for Christian Study, was the one who had invited me to take part in the Veritas Forum, mainly on the basis of my contribution to *Jesus under Fire*, edited by Michael Wilkins and J. P. Moreland. I spoke on "What Can We Know about Jesus" in a dialogue with Harry Gamble, the chair of the Religious Studies Department. I also spoke in one of Professor Gamble's classes.

Also speaking earlier that day was the physicist John Polkinghorne, President of Queens College, Cambridge University,[5] who spoke

---

4. Akiko was Kimi's classmate at Wheaton College, who was honored in 2008 as the Wheaton alumna of the year. She served as the president of the Japan's Women Christian College, where Prince Mikasa taught the Old Testament.

5. Polkinghorne was awarded a Templeton Prize for his work on science and religion as they related to the cosmos.

on "Should a Scientist Pray?" The next day after I left George Marsden, historian, and Alvin Plantinga, philosopher, both from the University of Notre Dame spoke. Marsden spoke on "Has Truth Been Silenced in Our Passion for Pluralism?" and Plantinga on "An Evolutionary Challenge to Atheism." In November I lectured at Covenant Theological Seminary on "Ancient Persian Capitals" and "Zoroastrianism and Judaism."

Figure 47. With John Polkinghorne

Publications

I contributed an essay "Cambyses in Egypt" to *"Go to the Land and I Will Show You,"* a Festschrift in honor of my teacher Dwight Young, edited by J. E. Colson and V. E. Matthews. I published an article "Cyrus H. Gordon and the Ubiquity of Magic in the Pre-Modern World," in a special issue of the *Biblical Archaeologist* dedicated to Professor Gordon. My articles appeared in *The Journal of the Evangelical Theological Society*, and in *Stylos*, a theological journal published in Indonesia.

The Year 1997

The Family

Brian presented papers on his research at the Naval Research Lab at several conferences. He headed a team which developed "Coyote," a robot which was entered in a hors d'oeuvres serving contest. It won first place in the Technical Competition and placed second in overall scoring. In April Kimi and I visited Washington, DC, to join Brian in touring such sites as the Kennedy Center, the Library of Congress, the Supreme Court, the Jefferson Memorial, and the White House.

Gail continued to work in Bangkok. In April a fire devastated the slum where she worked, killing two of her pupils. In the fall she traveled to Paris for a debriefing of her work with the Fourth World organization.

In October Kimi's mother who was ninety-six and in a nursing home in Hilo passed away. Kimi flew to Hawaii and spent time with her sisters, two in Hilo and three in Honolulu. At the end of 1997 Kimi retired from her position as the secretary of the German, Russian and East Asian Languages Department. She began restudying New Testament Greek through a correspondence course from Moody Bible Institute.

Visiting Lecturers

In January James Sire, the editor of InterVarsity Press came to speak at our Faculty Christian Fellowship banquet. In February I arranged through the McClellan Lecture funds of the History Department to invite noted US historian George Marsden of Notre Dame to our campus. He spoke on "Is There a Place for Religious Perspectives in the Classroom." Notre Dame, the premier Catholic university in America, has been remarkably receptive to having evangelical scholars join their faculty. George had taught at Calvin Theological Seminary. After he retired, he was succeeded by Mark Noll of Wheaton College.[6]

Lectures

In March I lectured on "The Reliability of the Gospels" to the Graduate Christian Fellowship at the University of Michigan. Its president was Dennis Keeler, a graduate of Miami University.[7] I also spoke at Hillsdale College in Michigan, where my student Ken Calvert served as a history professor and headmaster of Hillsdale Academy. I presented lectures on

---

6. Other evangelicals who taught there include Nathan Hatch, a US historian who served as provost, Alvin Plantinga, noted philosopher, and James VanderKam, a Dead Sea Scrolls scholar.

7. Dennis Keeler was named the outstanding graduate student in the university. After earning his PhD in mathematics, Dennis did a postdoc at MIT, before joining the faculty at Miami.

"Acts and Archaeology," "Afrocentrism," and "Radiometric Dating." Also in March I spoke on "What Can We Know about Jesus" in a Veritas Forum at Ball State University in Muncie, Indiana.

At the end of May and at the beginning of June I taught a doctoral seminar on Gnosticism at Trinity Evangelical Divinity School. Among my seven students were two from Africa (Nigeria and Sierra Leone), two from Korea, and one from Hong Kong. I enjoyed meeting such faculty as Harold O. J. Brown, Donald Carson, Wayne Grudem, Murray Harris, and Grant Osborne.

In June I presented a paper on "Death and the Afterlife in the Ancient Near East" at a conference at McMaster Divinity School in Hamilton, Ontario, Canada, which had been organized by Richard Longenecker.[8] Kim and I stayed with Dick and his wife Fran in the charming village of Niagara-on-the-Lake. Prior to the conference we were able to visit Toronto, Montreal, and Ottawa. In November I presented a paper on "Pre-Christian Gnosticism" at the ETS conference in Santa Clara, California. While I was in the San Francisco Bay Area I took a boat ride to the island of Alcatraz, which had housed infamous prisoners and had been the scene of many movies.

Publications

I published "The Issue of Pre-Christian Gnosticism in the Light of the Nag Hammadi Texts," in *The Nag Hammadi Library after Fifty Years*, edited by John Turner and Anne McGuire. I contributed "Greece and Babylon Revisited" to a Festschrift in Honor of William H. Shea, *To Understand the Scriptures*, edited by David Merling, and "Herodotus Historian or Liar?" to a Festschrift in honor of Michael C. Astour, *Boundaries and Linking Horizons*, edited by G. D. Young, M. W. Chavalas, and R. E. Averbeck. I also contributed three articles to the *New International Dictionary of Old Testament Theology and Exegesis*, edited by Willem A. Van Gemeren.

---

8. Dick Longenecker had been teaching at Trinity Evangelical Divinity School when he voiced some complaints about their graduate program. He was then told by the dean, that he should go elsewhere. He obtained a position at the evangelical Wycliffe College of the University of Toronto, where Roland K. Harrison taught, before joining McMaster Divinity School.

The Year 1998

The Family

Brian presented papers on his research on robots at an International Conference on Autonomous Agents at Minneapolis, a conference on integrating robotics at Stanford, a conference on Automatic Learning at Pittsburgh, and a conference on graphics in Orlando. He continued his involvement in science fiction and acting groups.

In January Gail served as a bridesmaid in the wedding of her best friend, Elizabeth Scott. She took up a position as an editorial assistant for the Human Rights Watch located on the thirty-fourth floor of the Empire State Building.[9] In October Kimi and I were able to visit with Gail and her Thai friend Golf. We took a boat ride around Manhattan, observed the Statue of Liberty, visited Ellis Island, and viewed the Tenement Museum

Kimi and I also traveled south to New Brunswick to visit Rutgers University and Princeton University. At Princeton we had lunch with Bruce and Isobel Metzger, Samuel Moffett, and Scott Luley. Moffett, a former missionary to Korea, had written an important history of Christianity in Asia which I had reviewed. Scott was a former Miami professor who served with Cru ministering to grad students and faculty at Princeton.

Kimi enjoyed her first year of retirement as she took up watercolor painting lessons from Jean Vance, joined the Songbirds, a senior singing group, and volunteered to deliver Meals on Wheels.

---

9. The renewed King's College was located in the basement of the Empire State Building. The evangelist Percy Crawford had founded The King's College. In the 1960s, when I was at Shelton, the college was located in Tarrytown, NY, but then went bankrupt. Its state license was purchased by Campus Crusade.

Figure 48. With Samuel Moffett, Scott Luley, and Bruce Metzger

The History Department

In the fall I taught a graduate colloquium on Eastern Christianity. One of the students in this course was James Cattapana from Argentina who was teaching modern Hebrew at Miami. An outstanding student who graduated in 1998 was Jonathan David. Jonathan, who came from Appalachia, excelled as a triple major (Classics, History, Religion) and was given the honor of addressing the graduating class. He took my course on Herodotus.[10] Jason Larson, a graduate of Gordon College, completed his MA.thesis on "The Northeast Mediterranean at the End of the Bronze Age."[11] Laura Dunn completed a dissertation which I codirected with Roy Ward on "The Evolution of Imperial Roman Attitudes toward Same Sex Relationships."[12] John DeFelice was named an outstanding teaching assistant by the College of Arts and Sciences. John was greatly

10. Jonathan David received his PhD in History from Penn State University in 2006. He taught at California State University Stanislaus, before moving to Gettysburg College. Jonathan has excavated in Israel at Megiddo and at the site of the VIIth Ferrata Legion's camp.

11. Jason Larson went on to earn the MLS from the University of Kentucky and the PhD in religious studies from Syracuse University. He has taught at the prestigious Hotchkiss School in western Connecticut.

12. Laura Dunn has served as the director of distance learning at Eastern Florida University.

aided by photos of Pompeii given to him by Roy Ward, as he completed his dissertation on "The Women of the Roman Inns: A Study of Law, Occupations and Status."[13] Darlene Brooks Hedstrom was also named one of the outstanding teaching assistants of the College of Arts and Sciences. She was granted a fellowship to do research in Egypt. Carl Smith, a doctoral student, assumed the post of the Dean of Ministries at Palm Beach Atlantic University.

Lectures

In April I spoke on "Easter" at the University of Dayton. Later that month I gave a lecture on "The Crucifixion of Christ in Historical and Archaeological Context" at Indiana Wesleyan University. I returned in October to speak on "The Historicity of Easter." Jerry Pattengale was serving as an assistant to the vice-president at his alma mater. Also, in October I spoke on "The Dead Sea Scrolls" to the graduate IV group at the University of Illinois and on "Archaeology and the Old Testament" to the Christian faculty group there.

Conferences

In September I presented a paper on "Ancient History in Global Perspective: Two Case Studies" at the CFH conference at David Lipscomb University in Nashville. This shared insights I had gained in teaching a graduate course on Eastern Christianity about the spread of Christianity into Central Asia and China. The theme of the conference was "Globalization and the Historian's Craft." The keynote speaker was Paul Spickard of the University of California at Santa Barbara. Richard Pierard and Robert Clouse both spoke on false hopes of millennial movements. We were led on a tour of nearby Civil War battlefields. Kimi and I also visited the Country Music Hall of Fame and attended a concert at the Grand Ole Opry.

In October, I read a paper on "Rome and Meroe" at an international conference on Italy and Africa convened at Miami University. In November I presented a paper on "Divination and the Ancient World" at the

---

13. After teaching at Charleston College in South Carolina, John DeFelice became a professor of history at the University of Maine at Presque Isle, near the Canadian border. He also was ordained as a Methodist minister.

NEAS conference in Orlando. I got to meet two notable German New Testament scholars. At the ETS conference I met Etta Linneman, a one-time student of Rudolf Bultmann, who had rejected his critical views and had served as a missionary in Indonesia. Martin Hengel, the outstanding evangelical scholar from Bengel Haus, Tübingen, was the speaker at the IBR conference. Martin Hengel's lecture at the IBR became the substance of his book, *Four Gospels — One Gospel*.

Publications

My essay "Life, Death and the Afterlife in the Ancient Near East," was published in *Life in the Face of Death*, edited by Richard Longenecker. I contributed a chapter on "An Ancient Historian's View of Christianity" to *Professors Who Believe*, edited by Paul M. Anderson.

The Year 1999

The Family

Brian began working as a senior software engineer for iRobot. As his work was classified, he was not at liberty to discuss the details of his research. Several of his superiors and former professors appeared in a PBS special on robots. He moved from Nashua, New Hampshire to an apartment in Boston.

Gail moved into an apartment in Jersey City in northern New Jersey. She had a long hour and a half commute by train and subway to her work in Manhattan. She became the union representative of the staff at the Human Rights Watch. On weekends she enjoyed working with children in a poor neighborhood of Brooklyn.

In June, as Kimi and I traveled east to see Gail and Brian, we also met with former Miami students including Jim Murdoch, who was pursuing the PhD in philosophy at Fordham University and David Mahan, who was the head of Cru at Yale University. Later during the summer, on our trip to attend the ASA conference in Arkansas, we saw the Merrimac Caverns, a passion play, George Washington Carver's Museum, Mark Twain's home in Hannibal, and a musical at Branson, Missouri.

The History Department

I taught a course on the History of Early Christianity, which was cross listed as a course in the Department of Comparative Religions, with half of the thirty-four students enrolled as students in History 232 and the other half in Religion 232. I gave a pre-test on the knowledge of the New Testament. This revealed that half of the students knew a great deal and the other half virtually nothing about the Bible. A graduate colloquium on Early Christianity included seven students, including a Muslim woman.

An outstanding student in my senior seminar on Judaism and early Christianity was Kirk MacGregor, who graduated *summa cum laude* as a Mathematics and Statistics major. The class helped to direct him into the study of theology and philosophy.

I gained three new MA students, including Deirdre Fulton and Abigail Rush, graduates of Wheaton College, and Adam Chambers, the son of Roger Chambers, one of my earliest PhD students. Adam suffered from a tumor in his brain, which forced him to learn to walk and to speak again. Kenneth Calvert, a graduate of Wheaton College, Gordon-Conwell Theological Seminary, and Harvard Divinity School, completed his dissertation on "Conflicts of Providence: The Roman Web of Power and the Rise of Christianity."

The Mandaean Conference

In June, the first ever conference on "The Mandaeans" was held at Harvard University. Three high priests, one from Detroit and two from Iran attended. They conducted their *masbuta* "baptismal" ceremony in the Charles River along with other rituals and prayers.

Figure 49. With Mandeans at the Charles River

Cyrus Gordon was present along with Margaret (Drower) Hackworth-Jones, the daughter of his friend Lady Drower. I presented a paper on "Mandaic Magic," including the translation of a new magic bowl which Miami University purchased for its art museum. I got to meet Karen King of Harvard Divinity School, who had cited my publications on the Mandaeans in her book on Gnosticism. as well as John Huehnegard of Harvard's Department of Near Eastern Languages, who had used my *Mandaic Incantation Texts* as a textbook. I also met Erica Hunter, the scholar from Cambridge University, who had become a leading authority on the magic bowls. Other scholars who presented papers were Roberta Borghero (Italy), Jorunn Buckley, Nathaniel Deutsch, Sinasi Gündüz (Turkey), Edmondo Lupieri (Italy), Brian Mubaraki (Australia), Fabrizio Pennachetti (Italy), Francesca Rochberg, James Tabor, and Roberto Valencia (Mexico).

Figure 50. Mandean Conference at Harvard

In August, I presented a paper on "Ancient Astrology" at the ASA conference in Siloam Springs, Arkansas, and in November a paper on "The Curse of Ham among Jews, Muslims and Mormons" at the ETS conference in Nashville.

Various Media

In September I was interviewed for the Hugh Ross apologetics radio program in California. Later that month I flew to Charlotte, North Carolina, to be interviewed for the John Ankerberg television program along with Darrell Bock, William Lane Craig, Gary Habermas, and Ben Witherington III. This program was a response to a Peter Jennings special on ABC. I was then interviewed on campus for the Coral Ridge Ministries in Florida for a program which was aired on NBC to an estimated 12 million viewers.

Publications

My article "God and Shah: Church and State in Sasanid Persia" appeared in *Fides et Historia*. A Danish translation of "Zoroaster's Teaching and the Old Testament" was published in the journal *Tel* in Denmark. Kenneth Calvert wrote the chapter reviewing my publications in *Bible Interpreters of the Twentieth Century*, edited by Walter A. Elwell and J. D. Weaver (see Excursus L).

InterVarsity Christian Fellowship

After having served as the faculty advisor to the IV at Rutgers University for five years, and at Miami University for twenty-five years, I retired from this position in 1995. Dennis Dudley, the IV staff member, arranged a surprise reception in my honor. I was presented with a scrapbook of letters from many appreciative alumni.

Chapter 25

The First Two Years of the 2000s

The Year 2000

The Family

BRIAN BEGAN WORKING WITH the iRobot Company in Boston, chaired by Rodney Brooks, a professor at MIT. He helped to develop a robot that was described by *Wired Magazine* as "the smartest webcam on wheels." It was on display at the electronics convention in Las Vegas attended by 250,000 visitors.

Haruko[1] joined Arts Excellence, an organization which placed various artists (musicians, dancers, painters) in public schools in New York City. Its office was located near Macy's at Herald Square. She also began taking courses in creative writing at the New University, formerly the New School for Social Research.

My Sister's Wedding

My sister Alicia had met Heinz Saurer from Switzerland in California. Their wedding was to take place in Hawaii in March. Heinz's mother and sister flew all the way from Switzerland to attend. Kimi and I with my mother flew from Ohio joining Brian and Haruko in Hawaii. I presided

---

1. Gail, from this time forth preferred to go by her middle Japanese name, which means "Child of Spring." It was also my mother's name.

over the wedding in a guest house near the University of Hawaii. The wedding reception was held at the Hale Kulani, a hotel in Waikiki. The occasion proved to be a grand reunion of my mother with many Owan and Yamauchi relatives.

Figure 51. Wedding in Hawaii: Brian, Gail, Kimi, Alicia, Heinz, EMY, my mother, Tama from Taiwan, and Tom Owan

I met with a number of friends from C.Y.C. in Wahiawa including Kathleen Curtis, Alice Araki, Nora Handa, and Chieko Komata. We were also able to share meals with Kimi's sisters and their families in Honolulu and in Hilo. On our way back to Ohio we stopped at Los Angeles, where my mother had a tearful reunion with her friends at the West LA Holiness Church.

The History Department

Brannan Becknell, a graduate of Georgia State University and Gordon-Conwell Theological Seminary, completed his dissertation on "Almsgiving,

The Jewish Legacy of Justice and Mercy."[2] His study followed the important development of alms as a work of merit before God from Tobit to the church fathers such as John Chrysostom.

Charlotte Newman Goldy became the first woman to receive tenure in the department. Her research involved post-Norman England, i.e. after 1066, and the history of medieval women. She served as the chair of the department from 1996 until 2005 except for her sabbatical year of 2000 to 2001 when Andrew Cayton served as the chair. An observant Jew, Charlotte was involved in the Jewish Studies program and served on the committees of many of my master's and doctoral students.

In 2000 when the department discussed the reduction of doctoral fields to US History and European History, Charlotte proposed Ancient History as a third field in view of the many outstanding graduate students in that field, with the proviso that this would hold true only until my retirement. Among those who raised concerns about this proposal was Michael O'Brien.[3] In order to meet his objections, I asked Jeri Schaner, our secretary, to compile the numbers of PhDs and of ABDs (that is "all but dissertation") in the various fields from 1970 to 2000. These were the results:

1. United States: 64 PhDs; 9 ABDs
2. Modern Europe: 18 PhDs; 3 ABDs
3. Early Modern Europe: 6 PhDs
4. Africa: 2 PhDs
5. Near East: 1 PhD.
6. Ancient: 12 PhDs; 4 ABDs

One of my colleagues, David Fahey, once remarked to me that he thought I had more doctoral students than all of the non-US faculty combined. Although this was not true of the years 1970 to 2000, it was true of the last decade, 1990 to 2000.

1. United States: 29 PhDs; 9 ABDs
2. Modern Europe: 2 PhDs; 3 ABDs

2. Brannan Becknall served as a pastor of different churches in Maine.

3. Michael O'Brien was a historian of the US South from England. He taught both at Miami University and at Jesus College, the University of Cambridge. His two volume work, *Conjectures of Order: Intellectual Life and The American South 1810–60* won the Bancroft Prize for 2006.

3. Early Modern Europe: 1 PhD
4. Africa: 2 PhDs
5. Ancient: 8 PhDs; 4 ABDs

This tally shows that there were more PhDs and ABDs (eight and four) than in all of the non US fields combined (five and three). As a result of these numbers, the department voted to support Ancient History as a third doctoral field.[4]

Lectures and Papers

In April, I spoke on "The Jesus Seminar" and "The Reliability of the Gospels" at an IV Faculty Conference held at Ohio State University. In May, I gave a series of lectures on Philippians to about two hundred Chinese Christian youths held at Crestville, a camp 5,000 ft. above the San Bernardino Valley in California. The conference was organized by Shi Pei Chu, a pastor who had moved from Cincinnati to Claremont. As I was leaving, I marveled that as early as six a.m. there was a long stream of workers commuting into Los Angeles. Housing was so expensive in the city that many had to live at a distance, a situation that has grown only worse over the years.

I read a paper on "A Tale of Three Cities: Mecca, Medina and Jerusalem" at the ETS conference in Nashville. Mecca was where Muhammad was born and Medina where he was buried. Jerusalem (al-Quds) is the third holiest city in Islam based on an interpretation of a passage in the Qur'ān (17:1) that Muhammad made a miraculous flight on a winged horse to Jerusalem, ascended to consult with Allah, and returned the

---

4. By 2009 I had directed 17 PhDs and 28 MAs. Other professors who also had relatively large numbers of graduate students included

David Fahey 17 MAs and 10 PhDs
Mary Frederickson 14 MAs and 9.5 PhDs
Richard Jellison 11 MAs and 10 PhDs
Jeffrey Kimball 12 MAs and 9 PhDs
Jack Kirby 13 MAs and 6 PhDs
James Rodabaugh 11 MAs and 4 PhDs
Ronald Shaw 12 MAs and 7 PhDs
Allan Winkler 20 MAs and 5.5 PhDs

Fahey taught World and British History.
All the others taught US History.

same night to Mecca. The name *Masjid al-Aqsah*, "the farthest mosque" has been given to the building with the silver dome on the Ḥaram al-Sharif "the noble sanctuary," a name given to the Herodian platform. Muslims deny that there ever was a Jewish temple there.

Publications

My articles on "Synagogues" and on "Gnosticism" were published in the *Dictionary of New Testament Backgrounds*, edited by Craig A. Evans and Stanley E. Porter. An article on "Attitudes toward the Aged in Antiquity" appeared in the *Near East Archaeological Society Bulletin*, and one on "Mandaic Incantations: Lead Rolls and Magic Bowls" in *Aram*, a journal published in Oxford, England.

The Year 2001

The Family

In April, Brian, who continued working for iRobot, gave a well-received lecture on robots for the Computer Science Department of Miami University. In the audience were a number of his teachers from elementary school, who were no doubt proud of their pupil's accomplishments.

On September 11 we received a brief message from Haruko, "I am okay," without any details. Only in October when we went to see her in New York City did we learn how close she was to the fall of the Twin Towers. That morning about 9 a.m. she was in a meeting for Arts Excellence in the basement of the Deutsche Bank building[5] immediately south of the Twin Towers. When they heard the sound of the first plane crashing, they continued their meeting until they heard a second crash and realized what was happening. Haruko and her associates somehow managed to board a subway to escape to midtown Manhattan. Many others were not so fortunate.[6]

Kimi and I got to see her place of work on West Forty-Sixth Street, a building which housed the Jaqueline Kennedy School of Performing Arts featured in the movie Fame. We enjoyed going with Haruko to

---

5. This building was so badly damaged that it had to be torn down.

6. Two officers from Oxford were at the Pentagon where a third terrorist plane crashed: Captain David Foley of the navy and Colonel David Bliesner of the air force. Neither was hurt.

performances of the Music Man and the Mikado in modern dress. We also visited the Museum of Natural History, the Metropolitan Museum, and the Guggenheim Museum.

Back in Ohio, Kimi and I attended the May Choral Festival in Cincinnati, and an outdoor performance of the Blue Jacket near Xenia. At a supper sponsored by the Japanese American Citizens League in Dayton, we got to meet the actor George Takei of Star Trek fame.

A Week in Israel

During the spring break in March I joined a tour group to Israel led by Bob Hostetler. Kimi backed out of the trip as she was disturbed by the violence between the Palestinians and Israelis shown on television. On March 10, we flew from Cincinnati to Chicago, then to Zurich and arrived at Tel Aviv on March 11. We stayed in a hotel at Tiberias by the Sea of Galilee. On March 12 while the rest of the group went to a baptismal service in the Jordan River, I rented a car as I wanted to see the newly excavated site of Sepphoris, but I arrived at 4 p.m. just as the gate closed. I then drove to the northern end of the Sea of Galilee to see the excavated site of Bethsaida, Peter's home, but that excavation was also closed!

On March 13 we boarded a tour bus which took us to the Herodian harbor at Caesarea. I had seen this site before but saw the nearby aqueducts for the first time. We then went north to Mt. Carmel, Megiddo, Nazareth, Cana and returned to Tiberias.

On March 14 we went to Beit She'an (Scythopolis), which I had not seen. I ran up to the top of the steep ancient tell and raced to see as much of the ruins of the Roman city as I could. This was the only city of the Decapolis in Cis-Jordan, all the others were in Transjordan. We then went to Qumran and ascended to Bethphage and Bethany, before descending to Jerusalem to view the Garden of Gethsemane.

On March 15 our bus traveled through a check point to get to Bethlehem in the West Bank, where we visited the Church of the Nativity and spent two hours at gift shops. We returned to Jerusalem and viewed the Church of St. Peter in Gallicantu. We visited the Dormition Abbey and various parts of the walled city of Jerusalem including the Damascus Gate and the Citadel by the Jaffa Gate.

On March 16 we went to the Herodian fortress of Masada by the Dead Sea. We ascended to the top by means of a cable car; some of us walked down the snake path. We went down to the Dead Sea and some floated on the buoyant water, and even plastered themselves with black mud! In the evening, we heard a lecturer from the Bethlehem Bible College.

On March 17 we went through St. Stephen's Gate and saw the ruins of the pool of Bethesda at St. Anne's Church, the Ecce Homo Arch, the ruins of the Fortress Antonia, and the Church of the Holy Sepulcher. I climbed up the 158 steps of the nearby Lutheran Church's tower to gain a spectacular view of the Church of the Holy Sepulcher. We then walked to the site of the Wailing Wall, and the area of Benjamin Mazar's excavation where I had worked as a volunteer in 1968. Returning north of the walled city we visited Gordon's Calvary near the Arab bus station and the Garden Tomb. Dan Parkinson, a retired professor from Miami, had a pickpocket steal $1800 from his money belt! Fortunately, this amount was in American Express traveler's checks, so Dan was able to recover his money.

On March 18, which was a Sunday, we attended a service at the Garden Tomb with a British pastor presenting the sermon. We visited Michael Avi-Yonah's model of Herodian Jerusalem at the Holyland Hotel, and the Holocaust memorial museum at Yad va-Shem. I led a guided tour of nine from our group through the walled city, including a visit to the excavations of the Burnt House in the Upper City and the Armenian Quarter. We then departed for the States on March 19.

The History Department

An outstanding student who was a member of my senior seminar on Judaism and Early Christianity was Jeffrey Morrow. Jeff, who came from a Jewish background, was converted to Christ by Cru, and then became a Catholic. He majored in Comparative Religions and in Classical Greek. Jeff was a prodigious researcher, who became a prolific author. He eventually expanded his research paper from the seminar on the resurrection of Christ into a book.[7]

Three of my doctoral students completed their dissertations. Steven Stannish was a graduate of the University of Nebraska at Lincoln, who had read my *Persia and the Bible*. He was competent in Russian

---

7. Jeff Morrow wrote his PhD dissertation at the University of Dayton on Scott Hahn, a prominent evangelical convert to Catholicism. My wife and I attended his wedding to Maria at the chapel of Notre Dame. He has served as the chair of Undergraduate Theology at Seton Hall University in New Jersey.

and in ancient Egyptian hieroglyphs. He had written an MA thesis in 1995 on "An Investigation of the Amarna Revolution." His dissertation was on "Evidence for the 'Amarna Period from the Memphite Tombs of 'Aper-El, Horemheb, and Ma'ya."[8]

Carl B. Smith II was a graduate of Tennessee Temple University, where he was a classmate of Scott Carroll. He also earned the MDiv from Temple Baptist Theological Seminary and served as the academic dean of the Baptist Bible College East in Boston. While pursuing graduate studies at Miami, Carl served as the pastor of the Fairhaven Community Church. His dissertation "'No Longer Jews': Gnostic Origins and the Jewish Revolt under Trajan 115–117 CE" was published by Hendrickson in 2004 upon the recommendation of David Scholer, the bibliographer of the Nag Hammadi texts.[9] It won many favorable reviews and has been used as a text on courses on Gnosticism.[10]

Darlene Brooks Hedstrom received her BA in Near Eastern Archaeology at Wheaton College under Alfred Hoerth and wrote her MA there under James Hoffmeier. She participated in numerous excavations including those at Abila in Jordan under Harold Mare and at Wadi Natrun in Egypt under Bas Van Elderen. Her dissertation was on "'Your Cell Will Teach You All Things': The Relationship between Monastic Practice and the Architectural Design of the Cell in Coptic Monasticism, 400–1000."[11]

Lectures

In March I spoke on "Easter" at Denison University in Ohio. At the end of March, I delivered the Gresham Lectures on "The Achaemenid Capitals," "Sites Related to the Life of Christ," and "The Gospel of Thomas, the Jesus Seminar and Pre-Christian Gnosticism" at Kentucky

---

8. Steve Stannish obtained a position in the History Department of the State University of New York at Potsdam, where he won an award for teaching excellence.

9. David Scholer, who was at Fuller Theological Seminary, was dealing with cancer at the time he agreed to review Carl Smith's manuscript.

10. Carl Smith taught at several schools, including Palm Beach Atlantic University, Cedarville University, Payne Theological Seminary, and South University. He served as the rector of an Anglican Church in Yucaipa, California. He then moved to Phoenix, Arizona, to serve as the associate rector of an Anglican church alongside his son Peter.

11. Dar began teaching at Wittenberg University, where she became the chair of the History Department. She was honored with an endowed chair in the humanities. Her 2017 book, *The Monastic Landscape of Late Antique Egypt* won a prize from the Biblical Archaeology Society. See ch. 41 for her later promotion.

Christian University, where my student John Wineland was teaching. I gave a talk on "Nehemiah as a Model Leader" in chapel. Then early in April I delivered lectures on "The Jerusalem Temple," and on "Easter" at Palm Beach Atlantic University, where Carl Smith was teaching. Renting a car, I drove south to Miami and saw the campus of the University of Miami at Coral Gables.

On April 12, I gave my lecture on "Easter" at Stanford University at a very full Cubberly Auditorium. What struck me was the high proportion of Asian students in the audience. I was introduced by Richard Bube, who before his retirement in 1992 had been the chair of the Material Science and Electrical Engineering Department. Dick had served as the editor of the *Journal of the American Scientific Affiliation* when I was the president of the ASA. I had been invited to Stanford by Campus Crusade. Ron Sanders of Cru wrote: "There is a possibility of at least three discussion groups of investigative Bible studies as a result of your lecture. We have also given out approximately 75 'The Case for Christ' books to interested persons." After the lecture I ate breakfast with a number of Christian faculty including L Art Boyer (Medicine), Marga Jann (Art), Charles McLure (Hoover Institute), Fred Mihm (Medicine) and Jeff Strand (Law). A junior history major Josh Hawley also joined us.[12]

Papers

In February I presented a paper on "Mandaic Incantation Texts" at the AOS conference at Notre Dame. I was elected the vice-president of the Midwest AOS section. In August I was asked to present the concluding talk at "The Future of Biblical Archaeology" at a conference of evangelical and Jewish scholars organized by James Hoffmeier at Trinity Evangelical Divinity School. In November I presented a paper on "Moses' Cushite Wife" at the ETS conference in Colorado Springs.[13]

---

12. After graduating from Stanford and Yale Law School, Hawley served as a clerk to Chief Justice John Roberts. He became Missouri's attorney general and then was elected as a senator from Missouri in 2019. A conservative Republican Hawley has supported Donald Trump's claim that the 2020 election was stolen from him.

13. On my way to get to the airport a car struck a deer, the car behind it stopped suddenly, and I hit that car. My air bag deployed, and my right fender was damaged. I was delayed for an hour but managed to catch my Delta flight at the Cincinnati airport, which is in northern Kentucky. The cost to repair the damage was $4,200, which the insurance covered except for the deductible.

Publications

After a long delay *Africa and Africans in Antiquity*, which I edited was published by Michigan State University.[14] This contained the papers presented at the conference I had organized at Miami University in 1991. An additional chapter was contributed by Kathryn Bard and Rodolfo Fattaovich, who were not at the conference. The book was dedicated to my colleague Maynard W. Swanson, who had passed away in the interim. The essays that were included: Carleton T. Hodge, "Afroasiatic"; Frank J. Yurco, "Egypt and Nubia: Old, Middle, and New Kingdom Eras"; Edna R. Russmann, "Egypt and the Kushites: Dynasty XXV"; Stanley M. Burstein, "The Kingdom of Meroe"; William Y. Adams, "Ballana Kingdom and Culture: Twilight of Classical Nubia"; Reuben G. Bullard, "The Berbers of the Maghreb and Ancient Carthage"; Donald White, "An Archaeological Survey of the Cyrenaican and Marmarican Regions of Northeast Africa"; Frank M. Snowden Jr., "Attitudes towards Blacks in the Greek and Roman World: Misinterpretations of the Evidence"; Kathryn A. Bard and Rodolfo Fattovich, "Some Remarks on the Processes of State Formation in Egypt and Ethiopia"; and Maynard W. Swanson, "Colonizing the Past: Origin Myths of the Great Zimbabwe Ruins."

I contributed a chapter on "Meroe and Rome" to the book *ItaliAfrica*, and Martin Bernal's *Black Athena*" to the Journal *of Ancient Civilization* published in China.

Beauty, Brains, and Brawn

A Christian student from Miami was chosen Miss Ohio. Another Miami student won a Rhodes scholarship to study at Oxford University. Ben Roethlisberger was the outstanding freshman quarterback in the nation. Miami lost a thrilling 52 to 51 game to the University of Hawaii in Honolulu.

---

14. One of the reasons for the delay was that the publisher had sent out a single contract to be signed seriatim by each contributor, who was supposed to send it on to the next person on the list. Edna Russman had not only refused to sign the contract but had placed it in her file cabinet in Brooklyn. She was in California when I reached her. The publisher then sent individual contracts to each author, which Edna did sign.

Chapter 26

The E. T. S.

The Years 2002 to 2004

The Year 2002

The Family

IN MAY, KIMI AND I flew to New York to attend Haruko's MA in Creative Writing graduation ceremonies at the New School University. As Kimi had forgotten to take her driver's license, we had to return to Oxford to retrieve it. We took a later flight and just barely made it in time for the ceremonies! We went with Haruko to view the musical Oklahoma.

In August, Kimi and I flew to Boston where Brian showed us the building of iRobot located to the northwest of the city on the 128 outer corridor. Many of the robots Brian and his colleagues have designed appeared in the news including the Roomba, a disk-shaped vacuum cleaner and a robot which pierced a blocking stone in the Great Pyramid. Brian obtained a patent for the pack-bot, a mobile robot a soldier could carry which would help detect mines and probe dangerous situations. About six thousand of these were used by the army in Iraq and Afghanistan. We walked the "Freedom Trail" with Brian and viewed a participation mystery play called "Shear Madness."

Kimi kept busy in retirement, helping at the church, taking watercolor lessons from Jean Vance, singing with the Songbirds, and tutoring international students in English. For our fortieth anniversary she got her first new car, a silver Saturn which she loved!

This year's highlight for my mother was the surprise April visit of my sister Alicia with her daughter Sabine, who had just learned to walk. My mother had some strained relations with Alicia because of her resentment over Alicia's using up my mother's hard-earned money to travel to different countries. But my mother's heart melted at the sight of her very cute granddaughter!

The History Department

A brilliant student with a most unusual background was Foy Scalf. By his own admission, in high school, he was more interested in drugs and rock-and-roll music than studies. He enrolled in a vocational program at Cincinnati State University. At night he worked for a trucking firm. But he developed an interest in Egyptian history. A fellow driver from Cincinnati Bible College, when asked where he could study Egyptian history, suggested "Try Edwin Yamauchi at Miami University." When Foy enrolled in my Ancient Egyptian History course, he proved to have a near photographic memory and produced research papers that were superior to my graduate students. He graduated *summa cum laude* from Miami. Though offered an assistantship at Miami, Foy chose to enroll without aid at the Oriental Institute of the University of Chicago.[1]

Four new Ancient History students began their MA studies: Beth Troy, a graduate of Miami, Abigail Rush, a graduate of Wheaton College, John Fortner, a graduate of Beeson Divinity School, and Eva Mwanika from Kenya.[2] Three MA students completed their theses. Mark Fletcher wrote on "The Earthen Rampart's Origins and First Appearance in Palestine." Adam Chambers wrote on "Judaism, Hellenism, and the Greco-Roman Theater." Adam was accepted into our doctoral program. Deirdre Fulton completed her thesis on "Classical Perceptions of the Galatians:

---

1. Foy Scalf proved to be such a brilliant student there that he was offered a full scholarship. He wrote his dissertation on Demotic, the most cursive and difficult form of Egyptian writing. He became the Head of the Research Archives at the Oriental Institute.

2. Allan Winkler made annual visits to Kenya and helped to bring Kenyans to Miami to pursue graduate studies in history.

Attalos' Statues at Pergamon." She was accepted into the doctoral program at Pennsylvania State University.[3]

In addition to classes, I offered individual tutoring to some graduate and undergraduate students during my office hours, for example to Eva Mwanika in Hebrew and to Deirdre Fulton in Greek. I took some students to a special exhibit of objects from Old Kingdom Egypt at the Cincinnati Art Museum. I often took students with me to the annual archaeological conferences at Wheaton College. This year's featured speaker was Lawrence Stager of Harvard University, two of whose students, John Monson[4] and Daniel Master were teaching at the college.

Figure 52. With Daniel Master and Larry Stager

Lectures

In January, I gave seven lectures on Ancient Mesopotamia at an International Symposium on Biblical Archaeology organized by Steve Collins

---

3. Deirdre Fulton became the star pupil of Gary Knoppers, the chair of the Department of Ancient History. She became a professor of Old Testament at Baylor University.

4. John Monson grew up in Israel as his father taught at the Institute of Holy Land Studies.

at Albuquerque. Charles Aling of Northwestern College in St. Paul offered lectures on Ancient Egypt. In February I gave lectures on "Moses' Cushite Wife" and "Why the Ethiopian Eunuch Was Not from Ethiopia" at Covenant Theological Seminary. Also, in February I was invited by Getzel Cohen, the chair of the Classics Department at the University of Cincinnati, to speak on "Greece and Palestine" to his seminar.

In March, I was invited by historian Paul L. Maier to speak on "Jerusalem, Sacred City of Judaism, Christianity and Islam," and "The Saga of the Dead Sea Scrolls." Paul, the son of famed Lutheran Hour speaker Walter Maier, wrote his dissertation on a Reformation figure, but then taught Ancient History and served as the Lutheran chaplain at Western Michigan University. He has published illustrated translations of Josephus and Eusebius, which I used in my classes.[5]

Also, in March I spoke on "Easter" at Washington Bible College. In October I lectured on "Jerusalem" at Indiana Wesleyan University. In October at the Conference on Faith and History at Huntington College I served on a panel which honored Richard Pierard, one of the original founders of the CFH.[6] The other members of the panel were Thomas Askew of Gordon College, Robert Linder of Kansas State University, Chuck Weber of Wheaton College, and Ronald Wells of Calvin College. The keynote speaker was George Marsden, who spoke on "Christians and the History Profession."

---

5. Paul Maier has also written popular historical novels including *The Constantinian Codex* (2011), which is a Christian response to Dan Brown's *DaVinci Code*. He inserts some contemporary figures in the narrative including Daniel Wallace of the Center for the Study of New Testament Manuscripts and Edwin Yamauchi "of Oxford" (pp. 258, 261).

6. Richard Pierard, Robert Clouse, and Robert Linder, who had met in graduate school at the University of Iowa, began the Conference on Faith and History in November 1967 at a conference at Greenville College in Illinois. Pierard was a critic of the close alliance of evangelicals with "The Religious Right." He authored *The Unequal Yoke* (1970), and co-authored *Protest and Politics* (1968), *The Cross and the Flag* (1972), and *Politics: A Case for Christian Action* (1973).

Figure 53. Officers of the CFH congratulate Dick and Charlene Pierard. From left to right: Tom Askew, Bob Linder, Ron Wells, Chuck Webber, and EMY

In May, I gave a lecture on "Akhnaton, Moses and Monotheism" at Cornerstone University at Grand Rapids, where Scott Carroll was teaching. This was an updated version of the paper which I gave at the Oriental Institute at the centennial of the discovery of the Amarna tablets in Egypt in 1987.

Papers

In February, I presented a paper on "Banquets in the Biblical World" at the Midwest SBL and AOS conference at Mundelein, Illinois. I was accompanied by two of my grad students, Deirdre Fulton and Abigail Rush. Abigail also read a paper at the conference. Deirdre arranged for a stretch limousine to transport us from the airport to the Catholic retreat center at Mundelein. In March at the Midwest ETS conference, I presented two papers: "Moses and Akhnaton, 100 Years after the Amarna Discovery," and "Pre-Christian Gnosticism, 50 Years after the Nag Hammadi Discovery."

My former Rutgers colleague, Eugene Genovese, invited me to chair a session at the conference of his Historical Society in Atlanta which featured the theme of "Reconstruction." I invited David Weisberg of Hebrew Union College to offer a paper at the session I chaired. I presented a paper on "The Reconstruction of Jewish Communities in the Persian Era."[7]

In November in Toronto I presented a paper on "Jesus in the Qur'ān" at the ETS conference, and on "Zoroastrianism" at the NEAS conference. I roomed as I often did with Harold Mare of Covenant Theological Seminary. He asked me to walk with him to the American Schools of Oriental Research conference at another hotel. Against a wintry headwind he walked slowly but with steely determination one step at a time. At the age of eighty-four, he was still directing the excavation at Abila of the Decapolis in Jordan, where several of my students (Robert Smith, John Wineland, Darlene Brooks Hedstrom, and Adam Chambers) had worked.[8]

---

7. This paper was published in the *Journal of the Historical Society*, edited by Elizabeth Fox Genovese.

8. Harold Mare died on June 21, one month before his eighty-sixth birthday, in Jordan as he was taking David Chapman of Covenant Theological Seminary, his successor as director to the site of Abila. After a long journey both were tired, but he insisted on seeing the excavation site as soon as possible. David was drowsy driving a jeep when he suddenly saw a car coming toward them, he turned to avoid a head on collision but in so doing their jeep overturned and Harold was killed.

Figure 54. With Harold Mare

Publications

My essay "The Eastern Jewish Diaspora under the Babylonians" appeared in *Mesopotamia and the Bible*, edited by Mark W. Chavalas and K. Lawson Younger Jr. Articles on "Achaemenian Dynasty," "Astyages," "Cyaxares," "Kassites," "Manichaeanism," "Zurvanism," appeared in the *Encyclopedia of the Ancient World*, edited by J. Sienkewicz. My essay "Banquets in the Biblical World" was published in the *Proceedings of the Eastern Great Lakes and Midwest Biblical Society*.

The Year 2003

The Family

Brian's company iRobot was praised by *Scientific American* for its highly mobile robot with a web camera. Brian described the creation of rescue robots at a conference at Tampa. He was the lead roboticist in a $1.3 million Department of Defense project called the Wayfarer, a robot which would be equipped with vision, laser and global positioning sensors.

Haruko was happy with her work in Manhattan where she obtained a bicycle for transportation. One of her highlights was meeting her favorite author, Lynda Barry, the creator of Ernie Pook's Comeek. She met another author, Steve Adams, through classes at the New School University.

In March Kimi and I heard the performance of the Vienna Boys Choir, which included two singers from Cincinnati. We also enjoyed the performance of Madame Butterfly in a new opera house in Dayton. In June we attended a Shelton College alumni gathering at the old campus in Ringwood, which had become New Jersey's Botanical Garden. I enjoyed seeing many former students and teachers for the first time in forty years!

Later in June we toured the Wright Patterson Airforce Museum, where President George Bush had just spoken to commemorate the centennial of the Wright Brothers' invention. We visited the replica of their bicycle shop and the nearby home of the poet Paul Dunbar in Dayton.

We also saw the Cirque du Soleil in Columbus. While in Columbus we enjoyed seeing James Thurber's museum. We visited the family of Ramadan Hassan, refugees from the Sudan whose children Kimi had tutored. In October we celebrated Kimi's birthday by attending the performance of Showboat at the La Comedia dinner theater.

The History Department

Two new Ancient History students were Jenny Rempel, a graduate of Wheaton College, and Brandon Walker, a graduate of Longwood College. Brandon had worked for a Bible software company in Virginia so he had exceptional computer skills. Abigail Rush obtained her MA in History without a thesis.[9]

Lecturers

In October, I invited James Hoffmeier, an archaeologist from Trinity Evangelical Divinity School, to lecture on "New Evidence for the Exodus." Jim had grown up in Egypt where his parents had served as missionaries. He

---

9. A history colleague tried to dissuade Abigail Rush from further graduate studies when she revealed that she had already accumulated about $50,000 in student debt. But Abigail persisted and obtained the MLS from the University of South Carolina and gained positions as a librarian at Newberry College and later at the Presbyterian College in South Carolina.

had obtained his PhD at the University of Toronto, studying under the noted Egyptologist Donald Redford and worked with him at the site of Amarna. Jim had begun his own excavations in the northern Sinai and had discovered new evidence for the route of the Israelites out of Egypt.

In November, through a Templeton grant I secured through the ASA, I was able to invite Owen Gingerich, a noted astronomer who had served as the chair of the History of Science Department at Harvard University, to speak at Miami on the topic "Dare a Scientist Speak on Design?" The dinner before the lecture was attended by Miami's president, James Garland, a physicist, and Muriel Blaisdell, one of his former students who was on Miami's faculty. Owen spoke to an auditorium with 230 seated and another 50 standing along the walls and in the back. He spoke of the "anthropic principle" detailing the extraordinary features which make life possible on earth. Owen fielded numerous questions from students and faculty. J. K. Bhattacharjee, a microbiology professor pointed out that humans and chimpanzees share 94 percent of the same genes. Owen agreed but pointed out that the 4 percent distinction makes all the difference in the world.

Lectures

In August I presented lectures on "Africa and the Bible" and "Gnosticism" at Northwest Theological Seminary, a small new seminary in Seattle. While in the area I had lunch with Ward Gasque, a New Testament scholar who had written the foreword to my book on the *Archaeology of New Testament Cities in Western Asia Minor*.

Figure 55. With Ward Gasque

I also did some sightseeing, including riding an amphibious "duck" around Seattle's harbor and touring the enormous Boeing plant. I made a quick trip to ascend Mount Rainier. Margaret Cottle, a friend in Vancouver, told me of a little-known entry into Canada which would bypass the crowded Peace Bridge. Sure enough, there was no customs delay as I zipped on through. The only problem as I headed west to Vancouver was that there had been two accidents which caused a long delay and left me only a half hour to tour Vancouver and its famous park before I had to head south to Seattle.

In October, I gave a lecture on "The Historical Evidence for Jesus" at Middlebury College in Vermont. I visited a church started by Wes Pastor, a former Miami faculty member, who had persuaded three Navigator couples (Mike and Heather Battig, Joel and Lisa Dyke, and Stuart and Kim Pratt) from Miami to join him in establishing a church to minister to the University of Vermont. This ministry evolved into NETS, which trains seminary graduates to plant churches in New England.[10]

---

10. The first church plant was in Hanover, New Hampshire, to minister to the students at the Dartmouth College, founded in 1769 as the ninth oldest university in the US. Its original mission was to educate native American tribes.

Conferences

In February, I read a paper on "Solomon and the Queen of Sheba" at the Midwest AOS and SBL conference. In April I attended the annual meeting of the AOS (American Oriental Society) in Nashville. Founded in 1842 the AOS is the second oldest scholarly society in America. It is devoted to the study of Near Eastern and Far Eastern languages.[11] As president of the Midwest AOS branch, I served on its national board of directors.[12]

The E.T.S.

The ETS (Evangelical Theological Society) was begun in 1949. It is a society that meets annually and publishes a journal at first called the *Bulletin of the Evangelical Theological Society,* and later the *Journal of the Evangelical Theological Society*. Evangelical biblical scholars and theologians, most of whom are professors at Christian colleges and seminaries, agree to a doctrinal statement, which reads: "The Bible alone, and the Bible in its entirety, is the Word of God written and is therefore inerrant in the autographs." Later a clause concerning the Trinity was added: "God is a Trinity, Father, Son, and Holy Spirit, each an uncreated person, one in essence, equal in power and glory."

According to a letter sent to me by Roger Nicole (October 15, 2005) it was Burton L. Goddard who initiated the formation of the ETS. Other members of the founding fathers were: R. Laird Harris, Carl F. H. Henry, Kenneth Kantzer, Roger Nicole and Samuel J. Schultz. Charter members who joined in 1950 included: Gleason L. Archer, Robert D. Culver, Lloyd A. Kalland, W. Harold Mare, Charles C. Ryrie, and John F. Walvoord. In 1949, the first president was Clarence Bouma, and the first conference was held at Calvin Theological Seminary.

In addition to signing the doctrinal statement, full members must have the equivalent of a ThM beyond the basic seminary degrees of the BD or the MDiv, that is, usually a total of five to six years of seminary

---

11. My *Mandaic Incantation Texts* had been published in the AOS Monograph series; I had also published an article and reviews in the *Journal of the AOS.*

12. I was one of our successive evangelical scholars who held this position. I followed Harry Hoffner of the University of Chicago, and was then followed by Richard Averbeck and Lawson Younger, both of Trinity International University. Harry, a Brandeis classmate, was the editor of the *Chicago Hittite Dictionary*. Dick was a specialist in Sumerian texts and Lawson in Akkadian texts.

studies. An exception can be made for those with the PhD in biblical languages or related subjects. I came in under this exception clause, as I had not taken any seminary classes, though I have presented lectures and papers at a number of seminaries (see Excursus Q).[13]

At its annual convention three affiliated societies meet with the ETS: the Evangelical Philosophical Society, the Adventist Theological Society, and the Near East Archaeological Society. I first attended an ETS conference when I was a student at Shelton College. I presented my first paper, "The Slaves of God," when I was graduate student in 1962. My first article "Cultic Clues in Canticles" had been published in the *Bulletin of the Evangelical Theological Society* in 1961. In the following years I presented papers almost annually at either the ETS or the NEAS. I served as the chair of the eastern section of the ETS from 1965 to 1966 and served on the editorial committee of the *Journal of the Evangelical Theological Society* from 1983 to 2000.

At the ETS conference in November in Atlanta, two friends, Linda Belleville and Dick Pierard, who had been a president of the ETS, asked me if I would be willing to accept the nomination as the new vice-president if they were chosen to serve on the nominating committee by the business meeting. I thought that when neither was chosen that would be the end of the matter. But then much to my surprise I was elected the vice-president of the Evangelical Theological Society.

The officers of the ETS include a president, president elect, vice-president, secretary, and the editor of the journal. Retiring presidents serve an additional four years on the council. When I joined the council, James Borland of Liberty University had been its longtime secretary, Andreas Köstenberger of Southeastern Baptist Theological Seminary was the journal editor. Previous presidents on the council included John Sailhamer of Southeastern Baptist Theological Seminary, Darrell Block of Dallas Theological Seminary, Millard Erickson of George Truett Theological Seminary, David Howard of Bethel Theological Seminary, and Gregory Beale of Wheaton College. Craig Blaising of Southwestern Theological Seminary was the president.[14] The only responsibility of the vice-president was to present a short devotional at the annual meeting.

---

13. According to Ken Magnuson, the executive director, in 2021 the ETS had 2,565 full members, 471 associate members and 1,074 student members.

14. Richard Pierard and I were the only presidents of the ETS from state universities rather than from seminaries or Christian colleges. I have been the only Asian American elected president.

Open Theism

As Scriptures in some passages stress God's sovereignty, while other passages even in the same book, e.g. the Gospel of John, set forth man's freedom to choose, there has been a tension between these two poles throughout the history of Christianity. Many of the early Church Fathers stressed man's freedom to choose. It was Augustine who set the emphasis on God's sovereignty, which was to be reinforced by the Reformer John Calvin. His views were opposed by Jacob Arminius, whose emphasis on free will was embraced by John and Charles Wesley. On the other hand, their contemporary, the evangelist George Whitfield was a staunch Calvinist.

Encouraged by some trends in philosophy, a number of evangelicals embraced what has been called "Open Theism." These proponents emphasized not only God's freedom but man's as well, so that God's knowledge of man's choices is not fixed but will be determined by man's choices. Though the term had first emerged in in 1980 with Richard Rice's book *The Openness of God*, the concept did not become an issue until the publication of *The Openness of God: A Biblical Challenge to the Traditional Understanding of God* published by InterVarsity Press in 1994. This volume contained essays by David Bassinger, William Hasker, Clark Pinnock, Richard Rice, and John E. Sanders. Pinnock and Sanders were members of the ETS.

While both Calvinists and Arminians have been welcomed in the ETS,[15] this form of what some have characterized as extreme Arminianism was not welcomed by some influential members. Roger Nicole, a Swiss born Reformed theologian and one of the founders of the ETS, who had served as the president of ETS in 1956, circulated a statement signed by eleven of the founding fathers and charter members of the ETS, declaring "the denial of God's foreknowledge of the decisions of free agents is incompatible with the inerrancy of Scriptures." In 2001 the ETS endorsed the proposition "We believe the Bible clearly teaches that God has complete, accurate and infallible knowledge of all events, past, present and

---

15. One attempt to bridge the chasm between Calvinism and Arminianism has been the adoption of God's Middle Knowledge by some evangelical philosophers, most notably by William Lane Craig. Middle Knowledge is God's "prevolitional knowledge of all true counterfactuals of creaturely freedom." It is a concept first put forward by the Spanish Jesuit theologian Luis de Molina in the sixteenth century. Kirk R. MacGregor, one of my students, has written *Luis de Molina: The Life and Theology of the Founder of Middle Knowledge* (Zondervan, 2015).

future, including all future decisions and actions of free moral agents" by a vote of 253 Yes to 66 No votes, with 44 abstentions.

Roger Nicole brought forward a motion in 2002 to expel Pinnock and Sanders from the society on the grounds that their views were incompatible with the understanding of Scripture as inerrant. The executive committee of the ETS held formal hearings with both scholars in October 2003. As Pinnock was willing to make changes in his *Most Moved Mover* and *The Scripture Principle,* the executive committee unanimously recommended that Pinnock should not be removed from the ETS. This resolution was approved by a 432 to 212 vote. On the other hand, Sanders, while acknowledging that he had used some inappropriate language in asserting that God makes mistakes (*The God Who Risks,* pp. 132, 205), still insisted that some prophecies relate to probabilities and not to certainties regarding the future. The executive committee voted 5 to 2 for his dismissal. The majority of members voted 388 to 231 to dismiss Sanders. This was 63% which was just short of the 67% needed to expel him. When David Neff of *Christianity Today* quoted me as suggesting that the expulsion of Pinnock and Sanders would have been "an impoverishment of the ETS," Roger Nicole wrote me a personal letter to chide me for that remark. One prominent evangelical who publicly resigned from the ETS for its failure to expel Sanders was Norman Geisler, who had been the ETS president in 1998 as well as the founder of the Evangelical Philosophical Society.[16]

Publications

I contributed an essay "Athletics in the Ancient Near East" to *Life and Culture in the Ancient Near East,* edited by R. Averbeck, M. Chavalas, and David Weisberg. I also wrote the chapter, "The Exilic and Post-Exilic Period," for *Giving the Sense: Understanding and Using Old Testament Texts,* a Festschrift in honor of Old Testament scholar Eugene Merrill, edited by David M. Howard, Jr. and Michael A. Grisanti. *Dois Reinas,* a Portuguese translation of *Two Kingdoms,* which I had co-authored with Robert Clouse and Richard Pierard was published in Brazil.

---

16. Norman Geisler, who was a classmate of my wife Kimie Honda at Wheaton College (class of '58) was a prolific author, popular apologetics speaker and fervent champion of inerrancy.

Figure 56. With Eugene Merrill

The Year 2004

The Family

Brian helped to develop urban navigation abilities for mobile robots. Some of iRobot's robots were used to disarm roadside bombs in Iraq. Brian returned to his alma mater, Carnegie Mellon, to recruit employees for his firm. While in Pittsburgh as a Honda Prelude owner he had an opportunity to drive his car several laps on the BeaveRun racetrack at over 100 miles per hour! He was chosen for inclusion in Marquis's *Who's Who in Science and Engineering*.

Haruko placed various artists, dancers, and musicians in twelve schools and two homeless shelters in New York City for Arts Connection.

She biked through busy traffic to her work and also for pleasure on weekends to New Jersey. She enjoyed writing nonfiction narratives and short stories. During the Republican National Convention, she served as a street monitor of police activities for the American Civil Liberties Union.

Because my mother had left the water running at night when the manager of Talaford Manor paid an unannounced visit, she was asked to vacate her apartment. We showed her an assisted living apartment at the Knolls, a new retirement community on the edge of Oxford, but my mother refused to move. Then one day Kimi found her collapsed on the floor, so she was taken to the hospital. She was then transferred to the dementia wing of the Knolls at the end of 2003. She found the staff helpful and the other residents friendly. She gained weight (from 79 to 96 pounds). She spoke in Japanese, not realizing that others could not understand her! We were delighted to have Alicia and her charming three-year old Sabine visit us in September. At first Sabine was wary about being embraced by her grandmother, but she did warm up later in the week.

Kimi continued many activities in her retirement, including the tutoring of children and of internationals in English. Among the latter were women from China, Japan, Korea, Peru, Turkey, Jordan, and the Sudan.

Early in June I traveled to Hawaii for the fiftieth class reunion of Iolani's Class of 1954. I had gone to Iolani for four years, but through circumstances I have related (chapters 7–9) I did not actually graduate with my class. But my former classmates graciously extended an invitation for me to join them. I was especially delighted to see Virginia Haas, the teacher who had first introduced me to Latin.

Later in June Brian and Haruko joined us for an Owan family reunion at Camas near Portland organized by my cousin Diana Gibson. There we met many relatives, some for the first time. We also had the opportunity to see such sights as Portland's famous rose garden, Multnomah Falls, and Mount Hood.

A Visiting Lecturer

In April, through Templeton funds received from the American Scientific Affiliation I was able to invite Dorothy Chappell, the Dean of Natural and Social Sciences at Wheaton College, back to Miami to give a lecture. Dot had earned her PhD in Botany from Miami University, which had one of the premier Botany Departments in the nation. While at Miami in the early 1970s she was influenced by professor of Botany Bill Wilson and his wife Enid, both graduates of Wheaton College. It was Kimi, also an alumna of Wheaton, who urged Dot to apply for a position at Wheaton College.[17]

The History Department

Three MA students completed their theses. Beth Troy wrote on "Legally Bound: A Study of Women's Legal Status in the Ancient Near East."[18] John Fortner wrote on "'Much More Ours Than Yours': The Figure of Joseph the Patriarch in the New Testament and the Early Church."[19] Eva Nthoki Mwanika wrote on "Ancient Egyptian Identity."[20]

Conferences

In January I took part in a special conference organized by Daniel Block at the Southern Baptist Theological Seminary in Louisville. Its theme was "Israel: Ancient Kingdom or Modern Invention," with papers aimed at countering the claims of the so-called Minimalists, scholars from England and Denmark who dismissed the Old Testament as an unhistorical collection of documents from very late dates. The featured speaker was Alan Millard of the University of Liverpool. My contribution was titled "Did Persian Zoroastrianism Influence Judaism?" Other scholars who presented papers included: Joel Drinkard, Daniel Fleming, Richard Hess,

---

17. After forty years of service at Wheaton College, just before her retirement, Dot wrote my wife and myself a gracious letter (December 12, 2019) in part as follows:
"Thank you for being a significant Christian Influence in my life when I was a student at Miami University of Ohio. . . . The fellowship you led in Oxford Bible Fellowship, in student and other groups were wonderful! Of course, you pointing me toward serving at Wheaton College was a pivotal event in my life. You are among the most important people in helping shape my Christian faith for service in academic institution. Your mentoring of, and commitment to, seeking the Lord's guidance to shape the integration of faith and learning was excellent and helped cast a vision for much of my life's work. . . . Your example, in word and deed, for our Lord Jesus Christ has had an enormous influence on many lives, not the least of which is mine, and I thank the Lord for His provision of your influence in my life. Thank you!"

18. Beth Barovian was hired as an instructor in Miami's Farmer School of Business.

19. John Fortner became the director of adult education at Tony Evans megachurch in Dallas.

20. Eva Mwanaika earned an MA in Biblical Languages from Gordon-Conwell Theological Seminary.

James Hoffmeier, Harry Hoffner, Gerald Mattingly, Simon Sherwin, John Walton, and Lawson Younger.[21]

Figure 57. Louisville Conference: from left to right: Harry Hoffner, Simon Sherwin, John Walton, Lawson Younger, Rick Hess, Alan Millard, Jerry Mattingly, Daniel Fleming, Daniel Block, Jim Hoffmeier, Joel Drinkard, and EMY

In February at the Midwest AOS conference, I read a paper on "Kerma, Capital of Kush. In March I attended the annual meeting of the AOS in San Diego. I did not read a paper but met with the AOS board of directors. I visited the "Old Town" of San Diego and viewed many interesting exhibits, including an original Wells Fargo carriage. I took a trolley to visit Tijuana, Mexico. Wandering off from the main street with its tourist shops and cafes, I entered a Catholic church and wondered why it was not larger.

Publications

My book *Africa and the Bible* was published by Baker Academic. Noted Egyptologist Kenneth A. Kitchen of the University of Liverpool provided a foreward. I was indebted to Kitchen's scholarly book on *The Third Intermediate Period* for much of my material. I had written this book because I noted that on the one hand, the books on the subject at the Harvard Divinity bookstore were written by African American preachers, and on the other hand the scholars who contributed essays to *Africa and Africans in Antiquity* which I had edited, made no reference

---

21. Our papers were edited by Daniel Block and published as *Israel—Ancient Kingdom or Late Invention?* (Nashville: B & H Academic, 2008).

to the Bible with the exception of Frank Snowden. I also contributed an essay "Homer and Archaeology: Minimalists and Maximalists in Classical Context" to *The Future of Biblical Archaeology*, edited by James K. Hoffmeier and Alan R. Millard.[22]

---

22. This essay caught the eye of Hershel Shanks, who invited me to contribute a condensed version of the essay to the *Biblical Archaeology Review*, which he was editing.

Chapter 27

Retirement

The Years 2005 and 2006

The Family

BRIAN CONTINUED HIS MILITARY research for iRobot, working on projects with a total value of nearly four million dollars from DARPA (Defense Advanced Research Project Agency) of the Defense Department. He developed navigation and obstacle avoidance software for autonomous vehicles in urban environments.

While working with Arts Connection, Haruko found time to write about the impoverished communities in Bangkok where she had worked with children and women. She received a 2005 Artist's Fellowship in Non-Fiction from the New York Foundation for the Arts. This sizable sum of money enabled her to reduce her student debt, purchase a laptop computer, and pay for dues to a Manhattan group which provided her a quiet space to write.

My mother Haruko Higa, who was in the dementia wing of the Knolls needed hospice care and passed away on June 14, just ten days before her ninety-second birthday. Her memorial service was held on June 25. Our pastor Win Clark gave the message. Brian, Haruko, and Alicia flew into Ohio and her brother Tom Owan and his son Douglas drove from Maryland for the service. I later took her ashes to be placed in the vault with the ashes of her husband Renyu Higa at the Inglewood Cemetery in Los Angeles.

Retirement

My official retirement after teaching for thirty-five years in the History Department[1] was celebrated by two banquets on Saturday and Sunday (April 29 and 30). The first was hosted by the History Department and was attended by many former students who came from many states (see Excursus M). Several of them offered tributes. Carl Smith mentioned that when I had given him some bibliography cards, he noticed that one was in Italian. He recalled with a chuckle that I had responded, "Is that a problem?" Some of my history colleagues such as Charlotte Goldy and David Fahey also voiced their appreciation.

The event on Sunday evening was held at the Shriver Student Center for a wider group of about 140 friends from our church. My history colleague, President Philip Shriver offered some kind words. My cousin Roy Yamauchi and his wife Charlene came all the way from Hawaii, bringing floral leis for our family.

Figure 58. With Dr. Philip Shriver at my retirement

---

1. I took the opportunity to teach for one semester for three years to obtain a supplementary bonus added to the pension from the State Teachers Retirement System. This enabled me to build an additional room annexed to my basement office, so I could move my books from my university office into this annex.

Lectures

In February, I spoke on "Akhnaton, Moses and Monotheism" at Cornerstone University in Grand Rapids where Scott Carroll was teaching. I gave the same lecture in May to the Cincinnati Christian Seminary. In August I spoke on "The Message of Ezra" at the Bethel Grove Baptist Church in Ithaca. My host was Bob Fay, the chemistry professor at Cornell who had hosted my previous visits to speak at the university.

Trips and Travel

Kimi and I took several long trips which combined business with pleasure, including sightseeing and reconnecting with friends. In March we flew to Philadelphia and took the Amtrak train to Penn Station in New York City. We stayed at the Red Roof Inn on thirty-second Street near the Empire State Building. The street was filled with Korean restaurants as one could tell from the pungent odor that wafted out of their kitchens. This enabled me to indulge in my favorite dish, *bulgogi*, Korean barbecue!

We took the tour of Rockefeller Center and the NBC studios and joined the audience of the Jane Pauley Show. We viewed Der Rosenkavalier at the Metropolitan Opera and with Haruko obtained front row seats for Fiddler on the Roof. We viewed the memorial to the victims of the 9/11 attack at the site of the former Twin Towers.

We then boarded the Amtrak for Philadelphia where I attended a board meeting of the AOS. At the conference I presented a paper on "New Texts Shedding Light on the Exilic Era." We viewed a special exhibit of Salvador Dali at the Philadelphia Art Museum, the front steps of which were featured in the movie Rocky. We also went to Independence Hall and the Norman Rockwell Museum. We then flew back to Ohio from Philadelphia.

In May we drove to Holland, Michigan, to attend the Conference on Faith and History at Hope College. I had a good visit with Robert Swieringa of Kent State University. Bob was conducting research on the Dutch church in America. We visited Holland, the charming Dutch Village, and saw numerous fields of colorful tulips. We met with Dave and Kim Netzley, Miami alumni. Dave, who had been teaching at Hope college, had left his position there to become a minister.

In July, we flew into Orlando and rented a car. We visited the Believe It or Not Museum and ate dinner at a Medieval Times banquet. We visited Disney's Animal Kingdom and the Holy Land Experience, where some of the Scriptorium's treasured Bibles were on display. Attendance was very sparse, however, which did not bode well for the survival of this Christian theme park (see chapter 44).

Later in July we drove to Charlotte to attend the wedding of Jesse and Lindsey Rhodenbaugh. While there we had lunch with Robert Cooley and his wife. Bob was an archaeologist who had helped start the Near East Archaeological Society with Joseph Free and Samuel Schultz when he taught at Wheaton College in 1958. He had served as the president of Gordon-Conwell Theological Seminary and then as chancellor of the school's branch at Charlotte.

We drove to Savannah, Georgia, and took a boat ride to Fort Sumter in the harbor. It was the rebel bombardment of this federal fort that started the Civil War. We had dinner with Garvin and Kathleen McClain from Oxford. Garvin was a beloved gynecologist and obstetrician, and Kathleen was a nurse. They were both converted to Christ and were baptized at our church before they retired to Savannah.

On our way to Atlanta we took a detour to the small town of Plains and viewed the school and the church of the peanut farmer who became the president of the United States. Jimmy Carter still taught Sunday School in that church. Sarah Pechan from Oxford, who served a stint at The Carter Center in Atlanta, gave the president a copy of my book *Africa and the Bible*. In Atlanta we viewed the home of Margaret Mitchell, the author of *Gone with the Wind*. We went to the Coca Cola visitors center and the Martin Luther King tomb and museum. We also visited the Olympic Park and took a tour of the CNN building. We went to view the famous carving on the Stone Mountain, but rain obscured our view.

We then drove to Chattanooga, where we climbed up Signal Mountain to visit Covenant College at its summit. I saw an old friend who had been active in the ASA, sociologist Russell Heddendorf. He told us that the college's main building had been a hotel where Elizabeth Taylor had once honeymooned. Also, in Chattanooga I had a reunion with Sally Sharp from Shelton, who with her husband Ed Koehn completed translation work with the Apalai Indians of northern Brazil. We then made the trip back to Oxford.

Later we drove to Boston to visit with Brian. We stopped by Gordon-Conwell Theological School and saw my former student, Eva Mwanika. We also visited Brandeis and then moved west on the Massachusetts Turnpike. We stopped at Springfield to visit the National

Basketball Hall of Fame. Basketball was invented by James Naismith at a YMCA in Springfield in 1891.

We drove to Albany and then to Buffalo. Along the way we saw the Erie Canal Museum, and the Susan B. Anthony home. At Buffalo we visited with Mark and Angie Fulk, Miami Phds in English, who were teaching at Buffalo State University. At Erie in the far northwest corner of Pennsylvania, we visited George and Katie Hill, originally from Oxford. George Hill was an industrial consultant and an early member of the Oxford Bible Fellowship. His office was in a farm building which now sits at the northern entrance to the Knolls. He had given his property to his alma mater, Allegheny College, which in turn sold it to the Knolls.

The ETS Conference

I did not know when I was chosen to be vice-president of the Evangelical Theological Society, that in 2005, as the president elect, I would have the responsibility of working out the details of the November convention at Valley Forge. I made a scouting trip with Jim Borland to learn the layout of the hotel, the rooms, and their capacities. I could not have arranged the conference without the aid of Brandon Walker, my graduate student who had computer skills. I did not even know what a spreadsheet was! As I received about 400 proposals for papers, I had to group them in sessions with chairs chosen over the sessions. I worked in a crude fashion spreading proposals into groups around tables at the church. As some members wanted to present two papers, it was important to arrange these so they would not be scheduled at the same time.

The theme of the conference was "Christianity in the Early Centuries." This was suggested by Darrell Bock in the light of the confusion which was being spread about the Dead Sea Scrolls, the New Testament canon, and the Nag Hammadi library by Dan Brown's enormously popular *The DaVinci Code* published in 2003.[2] Craig Blaising, a patristics scholar from Southwestern Baptist Theological Seminary, gave the presidential address. One of the plenary speakers was Nicholas Perrin, one of the few scholars who knew both Coptic and Syriac and who had pointed out parallels between the Gospel of Thomas and the Syriac Diatesseron, a harmony of the Gospels. This demonstrated the late date of Thomas. He

---

2. Translated into many languages, 80 million copies were sold. In 2006, a movie featuring Tom Hanks was released.

had served as an assistant to Bishop N.T. Wright. I contacted Tom, who vouched for him. He spoke on "Thomas, the Fifth Gospel?"[3]

Figure 59. With Nicholas Perrin

The three other plenary addresses were: 1) "What Evangelicals and Liberals Can Learn from the Church Fathers" by Christopher Hall of Eastern University. 2) "Development and Diversity in Early Christianity" by D. Jeffrey Bingham of Dallas Theological Seminary. 3) "Gnostics on Asia Minor in the Early Second Century CE?" by Paul Trebilco of the University of Otago in New Zealand.

The NEH

In December I had been invited to sit on a committee which reviewed applications for fellowships from the National of Endowment for the Humanities in Washington, DC. The chair of our committee was Michael Poliakoff. We met in the old Post Office building, which had rooms around a huge open atrium. This was the building which Donald Trump later transformed into a luxury hotel.

3. After teaching at Wheaton College, Nicholas Perrin in 2019 became the president of Trinity Evangelical Divinity School.

I was able to visit the new Museum of the American Indian, the Sackler Museum of Near and Far Eastern Art, and the World War II monument. I was given a tour of the capitol by Bill Fairback, a Cru staff member who had served at Miami University. He and his wife Critty knew many of the congressmen and women and their spouses. The House was in session voting on a bill proposed by Democrats to offer more subsidies to the poor, which was opposed by the Republicans. It was fascinating to observe the progress of the voting as this was indicated in a lighted panel over the door. The bill was defeated as the Republicans held a majority in the House of Representatives at this time.

At a café in the Union Terminal, I had lunch with Bill and two others from Oxford, including Jim Coltharp, who worked with Comcast and Wood Parker, who was a vice-president of Northrup Gruman. Jim was active with the Navigators at Miami University; his father Jerry was one of the earliest elders of the Oxford Bible Fellowship.[4] Wood had served as the NROTC director at Miami University.[5]

Publications

Christianity Today in its annual survey of books in 2005, cited *Africa and the Bible* as "the outstanding book on the Bible" published in 2004. I contributed the essay, "Elchasaites, Manichaeans, and Mandaeans in the Light of the Cologne Mani Codex," to *Beyond the Jordan: Studies in Honor of W. Harold Mare*, edited by Glenn A. Carnagey. I wrote the article on "Ezra and Nehemiah, Books of," to the *Dictionary of the Old Testament: Historical Books*, edited by Bill Arnold and H. G. M. Williamson.[6] I also

---

4. Jim Coltharp and the Fairbacks both attended The Falls Church Anglican in Virginia which had originally been George Washington's church. The evangelical pastor John Yates had led most of the congregation out of the liberal Episcopal denomination over the ordination of an openly gay bishop in 2003. After a long seven-year legal dispute the new Anglican congregation lost all rights to the church properties. After meeting in multiple locations Falls Church in 2019 erected a large new building. Jim discipled the new rector Sam Ferguson, who succeeded Rev. Yates in 2019.

5. Wood Parker later commanded a destroyer, which went aground during a storm in the Gulf of Mexico. He lost his naval commission as a result, but he eventually ascended into a position which oversaw billions of dollars of military orders.

6. Hugh Williamson is the Regius Professor of Hebrew at Oxford University who wrote the definitive Word Commentary on Ezra and Nehemiah. So, it was a considerable honor for me to be invited to write this entry by Hugh. One of my MA students, Deirdre Fulton, is now teaching the Old Testament at Baylor University. She has been asked by Zondervan to write a replacement for the Williamson Word Commentary on

wrote an article on "Josephus" for the *New Dictionary of Christian Apologetics*, edited by C. Campbell-Jack and Gavin J. McGrath.

The Rivendell Institute

David Mahan, the son of Dr. Hal Mahan, the director of the Cleveland Museum of Natural History, was a student at Miami University, who took my History of Christianity course. He wrote, "You were the first Christian professor I ever met, for which I am profoundly grateful."[7] David was active in Cru at Miami and graduated as a history major in 1982.[8]

After serving on the Cru staff at Virginia Tech University (1982 to 1985) and Springfield College (1985 to 1987), David became the director of Yale Students for Christ (1987 to 1999). In 1995 he helped to establish the Rivendell[9] Institute to minister to the graduate students and faculty at Yale. David recruited several highly educated associates to promote three goals: a research program, a mentoring program, and round tables involving both Christian and non-Christian faculty. In 1995 Rivendell sponsored lectures by distinguished evangelical scholars to counter the Jesus Seminar's radical assault on the historicity of the Gospels.

In addition to David, the initial staff included Gregory Ganssle with a PhD in Philosophy from Syracuse University[10] and Jon Hinkson, a graduate of Princeton and Cambridge.[11] In 2000 Donald Smedley with a BA in Molecular Biology, and a ThM from Dallas Theological seminary was added to the staff. In 2002 Frederick Schneider, a graduate of Harvard in Russian Area Studies joined Rivendell's staff.[12] It cannot be overlooked that their wives Karen Mahan, Jeanie Ganssle, Anita Hinkson, Sue Smedley, and Soozie Schneider have played key roles, particularly in activities for women faculty members and graduate students.

Ezra and Nehemiah.

7. In an email September 15, 2020.

8. David Mahan later earned the MAR from Yale Divinity School in 1995, and the PhD in Literature from the University of Cambridge in 2005. He has served as an adjunct lecturer at the Yale Divinity School.

9. According to J. R. R. Tolkien, Rivendell is the place where wisdom and learning flourish.

10. Greg Ganssle became a professor of philosophy at Talbot School of Theology.

11. While continuing on the staff at Rivendell, Jon Hinckson also gained a position in the Office of Chaplains at Yale.

12. Frederick Schneider later earned a PhD from the Moscow Institute of International Relations.

In September 2005 I was invited to serve on Rivendell's first Board of Advisors. Among others who were invited to serve on this board were:

- Swede and Judy Anderson, directors of Cru's Mission to Eastern Europe and Russia
- Chris Green, assistant professor, School of Law, University of Mississippi
- Mary Habeck, associate professor of Strategic Studies, Johns Hopkins University
- John Hare, Noah Porter Professor of Philosophical Theology at Yale.[13]
- Kent Hucheson, founder and president of Colorado Uplift
- Roy Rosedale, coordinator of the International Consortium of Seminaries
- Drew Trotter, president of the Center for Christian Study at the University of Virginia.

I had dinner at Mory's, a famed restaurant in New Haven, with David and Karen Mahan. Also joining us were Maurice and Beth Lee, and Tolivar and Samantha Wills. Maurice, the son of my friend Chi-Hang Lee, was at Yale Divinity School. Tolivar had served on the staff of Athletes in Action at Miami University and had graduated from Gordon-Conwell Theological Seminary. He was an assistant pastor at the First Presbyterian Church in New Haven.

The Year 2006

The Family

Brian worked as the lead roboticist in iRobot's entry into DARPA's Urban Challenge. He was the principal investigator for the Army Tank-Automotive and Armaments Research Development's Daredevil Project to develop radar sensors to see through foliage, rain and snow. He also worked on the navigation system of the R-Gator, an autonomous vehicle that iRobot was developing with the John Deere Company. He enjoyed driving his new silver 2006 BMW.

---

13. John Hare succeeded Nicholas Wolterstorff. They both taught at Calvin Theological Seminary before coming to Yale.

After working for six years in New York City, Haruko decided to return to Thailand where she had lived from 1994 to 1998. In Bangkok she worked with the Foundation for Women, writing and editing publications to advance the status and rights of women. She also volunteered briefly with Big Brother Mouse in Laos, an organization that published children's books.

In July Brian and Haruko joined us for a family reunion in Hawaii. On Oahu we were able to have meals with the Owan and Yamauchi families, and with Kimi's sisters Jane, Helen, and Ellen and their families. We also worshiped at Makiki Christian Church, Kimi's home church which Ellen also attended. On the Big Island we had meals with Kimi's two other sisters, Miyoko and Janet and her family. On Kauai we visited the Waimea Canyon and sailed up the Wailuku River. On Maui Brian rented a car and drove the winding road east to Hana, while Haruko went swimming. Kimi and I visited a sugar cane plantation museum and the Iao Valley. All of us then drove went west to Lahaina, which had been the whaling harbor of Maui before returning to the mainland.

In September Kimi and I took a trip to Chicago and to Cleveland. In Chicago we visited Moody Church, which I saw in 1958 when I first met Kimi. We went to see the special exhibit of objects from Tutankhamun's tomb at the Field Museum of Science and Industry. The objects were well displayed in contrast to when I first viewed some of them in the Cairo Museum in 1974. Then I needed a flashlight to read the labels. In Cleveland we visited the Maltz Museum of Jewish Culture, where some extraordinary objects from Israel were being displayed. The exhibition, which was not publicized widely outside of the Jewish community, displayed two unique objects, the stone inscription from Caesarea which contained the name of Pontius Pilate and the only physical evidence of crucifixion that up to this date had ever found, the heel bones of a young Jewish man with the iron nail still transfixed.[14] This had been discovered in an ossuary, a limestone box, in 1968 when we had been in Jerusalem.

In October Kimi and I went to Circleville, south of Columbus, to enjoy the hundredth annual Pumpkin Festival. Huge pumpkins were on display, one weighing over a thousand pounds! Little girls competed to earn the title "Miss Pumpkin," and there were all sorts of pumpkin edibles including pumpkin ice cream.

---

14. In 2019 a heel bone (right calcaneus) with a hole was found at Gavetto in northern Italy, from the first c. AD. It had a hole apparently caused by a nail and is the second archaeological evidence of crucifixion.

RETIREMENT

Professional Travels

On April 28, I represented Miami University at the inauguration of Dr. Eugene B. Habecker as the thirtieth president of Taylor University in Upland, Indiana.[15] I spoke at the dedication of the Venture for Victory display and met all the original team members who had visited Hawaii in 1958 on their initial mission to the western Pacific. I was photographed with the team members, from one of whom I had first heard the Gospel at Kalihi Union Church.

Figure 60. Venture for Victory Team

In May I traveled to Boston to attend the banquet celebrating the retirement of Walter Kaiser from the presidency of Gordon-Conwell Theological seminary. Walt and I had been fellow graduate students at Brandeis University in the 1960s. Walt had also taught at Wheaton College and had served as the academic dean of Trinity Evangelical Divinity School.

In June I directed "The History Track" for Campus Crusade's conference at Washington, DC, which was attended by eighty of their staff, 320 faculty members, and forty internationals. I presented a paper on

---

15. On April 26 a great tragedy had occurred. A semitrailer northbound crossed the barrier and hit a Taylor van traveling south from Taylor's Fort Wayne campus. Four Taylor students and one employee were killed; five others were hurt.

"The DaVinci Code, Apocryphal Gospels, and Gnosticism." Featured speakers included Peter Kreeft, philosopher from Boston College, Marla Fredericks of the African Studies Department at Harvard, and Francis Collins, who in 2000 had directed the successful project to map the human genome.[16] Robert Kaita of Princeton was honored for his outstanding witness as a Christian professor by Scott Luley, who had organized the conference.

In October, I went to New Haven for a meeting of the council advising the Rivendell Institute. During my second (and final) year in 2006 additional board members were added, most of them Yale alumni.

- Pam Cochran, lecturer in Religious History at the University of Virginia
- Steward Davenport, assistant professor of History at Pepperdine University
- Will Imboden, Policy Planning staff, US State Department
- Bo Karen Lee, professor of Theology, Loyola College (MD)
- David Legg, managing director, Gerson Lehrman Group, Hong Kong
- J. P. Moreland, professor of Philosophy, Talbot Theological Seminary
- Robert Murchison, partner, Murchison Capital Partners

I spoke to a number of the Christian faculty at Yale. I had time to visit the New Haven cemetery and view the tombs of so many notables including Eli Whitney and Lyman Beecher. I also saw the baptistery and frescoes from the earliest Christian church, which had been recovered from Dura Europos and were on display at the Yale Gallery of Art.

Annual History Lectures

At my retirement in 2005 Dennis Dudley, the IV staff worker, and Win Clark, the pastor of the Oxford Bible Fellowship, established a fund with the Oxford Community Foundation to support an annual lecture in my name, which would be sponsored by the History Department and

---

16. In 2009 Francis Collins was named the director of the National Institute of Health.

co-sponsored by various churches and campus ministries. The first of these lectures was presented in May by Darrell Bock of Dallas Theological seminary, who spoke on "Breaking the DaVinci Code, and on the so-called Gospel of Judas." (For a list of the subsequent lecturers and lectures, see Excursus N.)

The Evangelical Theological Society

In November Kim and I attended the ETS conference in Washington, DC. I spoke on "An Anomalous Asian Ancient Historian" to a session on "Asians and Asian Americans." At the banquet I gave the presidential address on "Talisman, Specimen or Dragoman," about three different attitudes toward the Bible, one regarding Scriptures as magic, the opposite as an academic object of study. Evangelicals regard the Bible as a "dragoman" or guide. Prior to my address John D. Wineland presented to me *The Light of Discovery*, a Festschrift in my honor, which he had edited.[17] This included essays by my students: Kenneth R. Calvert, Scott Carroll, John F. DeFelice, Darlene L. Brooks Hedstrom, Daniel Hoffman, Lester Ness, Jerry Pattengale, Steven M. Stannish, Carl B. Smith II, and Robert W. Smith. The volume included a bibliography of my publications and a foreward by Paul L. Maier, the Russell H. Seibert Professor of Ancient History at Western Michigan University.

Figure 61. With doctoral students at the ETS conference: From left to right: Bob Smith, John DeFelice, John Wineland, Jerry Pattengale, Steve Stannish, Adam Chambers, and Carl Smith

17. This is volume six in the ETS Studies series.

Ben Roethlisberger

"Big Ben," who stands 6' 5", had broken all kinds of Mid-American Conference records during the three years he played as the quarterback of the Miami Red Hawks. He was drafted in 2004 in the first round by the Pittsburgh Steelers. In his first season he was named Offensive Rookie of the Year. In just his second season he led the Steelers to a victory over the Seattle Seahawks in Super Bowl XL on February 5 to become, at the age of 23, the youngest quarterback to win such a victory.[18]

---

18. Ben Roethlisberger would go on to win a second Superbowl XLIII in 2009 over the Arizona Cardinals and lose in a third Superbowl XLV in 2011 to the Green Bay Packers. After he retires, he is regarded as a future Hall of Famer.

Chapter 28

Switzerland and Scotland

The Year 2007

The Family

BRIAN SERVED WITH IROBOT as the principal investigator for three projects: 1) Daredevil, a project funded by the Army to use radar sensors to enable robots to see through rain, snow, fog, and dust. 2) Stingray, another Army project to develop remotely operated vehicles which could be driven at high speeds through urban environments. 3) Sagittarius, funded by the Air Force, to develop air and ground vehicles for reconnaissance. For this project he worked with professors and researchers from Carnegie Mellon University.

He moved into a corner apartment of a new building near Fenway Park. The only other previous occupant had been a Boston Red Sox second baseman, Dustin Pedroia. Brian is not a sports fan so that name did not mean anything to him. Dustin in 2006 had won American League Rookie of the Year honors.[1]

Haruko was the sole foreigner working with a Thai group that promoted women's rights and their participation in civil society. She served as a contact with international donors, writing grant proposals, translating Thai documents into English, and editing reports.

---

1. Later in 2008, Pedroia was named Most Valuable Player of the American League. When I was growing up in Hawaii, my favorite team was the Boston Red Sox, and my favorite player was Ted Williams.

The History Department

After two failed searches, the department finally hired a young ancient historian to replace me, Kevin Osterloh. Kevin had studied under Samuel Meier at Ohio State University and then under Daniel Fleming at New York University. He received his PhD from Princeton University, specializing in Hellenistic and Roman Judaism. He spent time on a kibbutz in Israel, married an Israeli woman, and became an adult convert to Judaism.[2]

Lectures and A Lecturer

In February, I gave a series of lectures on "Africa and the Bible" at the Peninsular Bible Church in Palo Alto, California. This had been the influential church pastored by Ray Stedman with an outreach to students and faculty at nearby Stanford University.

In March, Rick Hess, the chair of the Old Testament Department at Denver Seminary gave the second of my Annual History lectures on "Israelite Religions." Rick received his PhD from Hebrew Union College and taught at the Glasgow Bible College before securing his position at Denver Seminary. His special research on ancient Semitic names was aided by Anson Rainey.[3]

Papers and Conferences

In March, Kimi and I went to San Antonio to attend the annual AOS conference. We enjoyed the famed River Walk, riding a boat along the canal which came up to our hotel. We visited the Alamo and the Museum of Texas, featuring various nationalities. It was there where I saw a video of my aunt, Carmen Higa Mochizuki, relating her experiences at Crystal City in Texas (see Excursus E).

---

2. Kevin taught at Miami until 2014, when he left for Oregon State University where his wife had secured a position. Thereafter no ancient historian was hired as his replacement. In 2019 Miami dissolved the Classics Department, and the History Department was assigned its former chair, a most distinguished Roman historian and outstanding teacher, Stephen Tuck. In 2023 when the Department of Comparative Religion was dissolved, Scott Kenworthy, a historian of the Russian Orthodox Church, was added to the History Department.

3. Rick Hess served as the editor of the *Bulletin for Biblical Research* (2005–2015) and became the editor of the IBR Monograph series.

In November, we traveled to San Diego to attend the ETS and NEAS conferences. We had time to see the famous Coronado Hotel, the lighthouse at Point Loma, the numerous museums in Balboa Park, including one with a special exhibit of the Dead Sea Scrolls, and San Diego's famed zoo. We also went on a bus tour of religious sites that included the early Franciscan mission, a Serbian Orthodox Church, and the former Spaulding Theosophical Center, now Point Loma Nazarene College.

Interviews

In January Lee Strobel came to Oxford to interview me for his new book, *The Case for the Real Jesus*. He was concerned to refute allegations now spread on the internet that Christianity was based on Mithraism, a Roman mystery religion centered on a Persian god. I had taken part in an international congress on Mithraism in Tehran in 1975 and had devoted a chapter to Mithraism in my book *Persia and the Bible*.

In June Joseph Hovsepian, a film producer from California, came to interview me about ancient Persia for a film he was making about the martyrdom of his father Haik, who was killed in 1994 in Iran. The documentary which is available as a DVD is called "A Cry from Iran."

Switzerland

In July, Kimi and I flew into Zurich. We then took a train to Bern, the capital city, where we were met by my sister Alicia and my six-year old niece Sabine. Alicia and her husband Heinz Saurer lived in a charming chalet overlooking Lake Thun. She drove us to Chillon, where its lakefront castle was immortalized by Lord Byron's poem "The Prisoner of Chillon." She then drove us west to Geneva to view the cathedral where the French Reformer Jean Calvin preached. We also toured the former League of Nations building, now used by the United Nations. We did not have time to tour the headquarters of the Red Cross. On our way east we stopped at Lausanne about 4:30 p.m. I raced up the hill and walked rapidly through the International Olympic Museum before it closed at 5:00 p.m. Heinz later drove us back to Zurich, where we caught a plane for the United Kingdom.

Scotland

We flew into London's Heathrow Airport, where there was a mass of people struggling to get through customs. We then traveled north to Edinburgh, where I would participate in a joint conference of the American Scientific Affiliation and the British Christians in Science at the University of Edinburgh from August 2 to 5. There were 154 American scientists and 121 British scientists in attendance. I read a paper on "Africa, India and Russia: Biblical Misinterpretations" in a session on the History of Science chaired by Edward Davis of Messiah College. I also chaired a session on "Creation, Fall and Sabbath." Among other American scientists were Walter Bradley, Calvin deWitt, Mark Kalthoff, George Murphy, Nancey Murphy, Joseph Spradley, and Kenell Touryan. There were also speakers from Canada, Australia, and Europe.

The theme of the conference was "New Frontiers in Science and Faith." The keynote speaker was Alister McGrath, professor of historical theology at the University of Oxford. Before his ordination to the Anglican ministry, McGrath had been a researcher in molecular biology. Other plenary speakers included John Polkinghorne, Sir John Houghton, chair of the Panel on Climate Change, and Sir Ghillean Prance, Director of the Royal Botanic Gardens at Kew. Houghton and Prance warned about the dangerous consequences of global warming for humanity.

We had lunch with David Wright, a New Testament scholar from New College (the divinity school) at Edinburgh, with whom I had participated on "The Miracles of Jesus" seminar at Tyndale House in 1985. We also had lunch with the renowned missiologist Andrew Walls, who made a special trip from Aberdeen to Edinburgh to meet me. Walls had endorsed my book *Africa and the Bible*.

An exciting excursion was a boat ride to the Scottish National Bird Preserve on Bass Island, where millions of birds nested. After the conference there were about 40 of us who boarded a bus to tour Scotland from east to north and then west. We first toured Edinburgh's historic sites from the castle down to the Holy Rood palace, John Knox's house, and St. Giles Cathedral where he preached. We also visited a small museum dedicated to Robert Burns and Robert Louis Stevenson. On the evening of August 6, I joined others to view the "Tattoo," a celebration of bands with bagpipes at the castle. Kimi was too tired to venture out.

After leaving Edinburgh we visited St. Andrews where golf was invented. We viewed the battlefield of Culloden, where the British in 1746 decisively defeated the Scottish "Jacobite" forces supporting the claim of James Stuart to the throne.[4] The Jacobites were led by his son Charles, who had arrived in Scotland from France. We toured Dunrobin Castle, which has been occupied since 1300. Its picturesque gardens have been the setting of many weddings. We enjoyed a demonstration of falconry here. We sailed to the Orkney Islands off the northern coast of Scotland, where Neolithic (c. 3000 BC) structures were visible. We stayed at a hotel on Loch Ness and viewed the ruins of Urquhart Castle on its shore. We visited the great fortress of Stirling Castle. After the ASA tour ended, Kimi and I took our own tour of Glasgow before departing for the US.

Francis J. Beckwith

Francis J. Beckwith was elected the vice-president of the ETS the year after I was. I was not familiar with his important publications on such issues as abortion nor had I ever met him before the ETS executive council meeting at the Southwestern Baptist Theological Seminary in Fort Worth. Frank was a professor of Church State Relations at Baylor University in nearby Waco.

Frank was responsible for the planning of the ETS meeting in Washington, DC., in 2006 on "Christians in the Public Square." Because of the topic and the location of the conference, the ETS hired a Christian public relations firm to prepare the executive council to answer questions from reporters. Though I was the president of the ETS for this conference, I was averse to any public pronouncements, so I was happy that Frank, who was legally trained, was quite adept at expressing his opinions on blogs.

At first unbeknown to the executive council Frank had decided in April 2007 to return to the Catholicism of his youth. This posed a dilemma for the ETS as his conversion became the subject of evangelical bloggers. Frank affirmed that he could still sign the ETS doctrinal statement. Thomas Howard, who had been forced to resign from Gordon College in 1985 after his conversion to Catholicism, when queried by Andreas Köstenberger also affirmed that he could also sign the ETS statement of faith.[5]

---

4. The term "Jacobite" is derived from Jacob, which is the English rendering of Hebrew *Yaʿaqōb*, Greek *Iakōb*. The latter assumed two Latin variants *Iacobus/Iacomus*. The former developed into *Iago* as in *Sant Iago*, the patron saint of Spain. The latter form developed into the Spanish *Jaime*, which gave us the English *James*.

5. Thomas Howard is the brother of Elizabeth Elliott and the uncle of David

I was the only one on the executive council who at first agreed that Frank could remain in the ETS. But then Jim Borland, our secretary, in response to my query stated that ETS had no Catholic members as the framers of the original statement "the Bible alone" had intended to exclude Catholics. When it was revealed that Scott Hahn, a former evangelical had converted to Catholicism, he was removed from the ETS membership.[6]

The problem is that Catholics do not rely on *Sola Scriptura* as their authority but also rely on the Old Testament Apocrypha accepted as deuterocanonical Scriptures at the post-Reformation Council of Trent. Catholics also regard the *magisterium* or teaching of the Fathers and the encyclicals of popes as authoritative.[7]

Faced with the opposition of the rest of the executive council, Frank graciously tendered his resignation. Craig Blaising, in a public statement crafted for the council, thanked Frank for his contributions. David Howard Jr. (president of the ETS in 2003) wrote an article "Rome-ward Bound" for the *Wall Street Journal* (May 18, 2007) explaining the situation for the public at large. Frank wrote his own *apologia pro vita sua, Return to Rome: Confessions of an Evangelical Catholic* (Brazos Press, 2009). Frank asked me for an endorsement for the book, which I was happy to provide. Frank has continued to read papers at subsequent ETS conferences as a non-member, whose name is marked by an asterisk in the program. In the program for 2023, his name appears without an asterisk. This may have been an oversight or as Frank responded, it may be because he is still a member in good standing of the Evangelical Philosophical Society.

Howard, Jr.

6. Scott Hahn has joined the IBR, so has a student of mine Jeffrey Morrow, who wrote a dissertation on Scott Hahn at the University of Dayton. Jeff, who came from a Jewish background, was converted to Christ at Miami University by Cru, but then converted to Catholicism.

7. A somewhat similar situation in 2006 had involved the firing by Wheaton College of Joshua Hochschild, a professor of philosophy who after his conversion to Catholicism had affirmed that he could still sign Wheaton College's statement of faith.

Chapter 29

Japan and Okinawa

The Year 2008

The Family

BRIAN SERVED AS THE principal investigator for the Army's Stingray Project to develop fast, mobile robots for reconnaissance. Operators wore headsets that controlled motions of the robots as though they were riding the robots. Brian presented papers on his research at the Autonomous Vehicles Conference at Carnegie Mellon University and at the biennial Army Research Conference at Orlando.

From January to August Haruko served at the Foundation for Women in Bangkok. She worked on a project researching the experiences of young women who were trafficked abroad and who had returned to their villages. She also completed a report on the organization's history of working for women's rights in Thailand. In September Haruko returned to work again with Arts Connection in New York City. She also volunteered for Barack Obama's presidential campaign in the city and in Pennsylvania.

In May I went with Kimi to Wheaton College for the fiftieth reunion of her class of 1958. Her former housemate Akiko Minato, who was the president of Tokyo Women's Christian College, was honored as the Alumna of the Year. We also met with Dot Chappell, the Dean of Natural and Social Sciences and my former student, Daniel Master, who had just become the field director of the excavation at Ashkelon, succeeding his mentor, Larry Stager of Harvard University.

A Lecturer and Lectures

In March, noted New Testament scholar Craig Evans spoke in my Annual History lecture series on "Jesus and the Ossuaries," the subject of his recent book. Ossuaries are limestone boxes in which Jews deposited the bones of the dead. Many of them bear names relating to the New Testament, such as "James, the brother of Jesus."

In June, I presented a lecture on "Gnosticism" to Campus Crusade's conference for Christian faculty in Washington, DC.[1] Among the keynote speakers were Ken Elzinga, professor of economics at the University of Virginia and J. P. Moreland, philosopher from Talbot Theological Seminary. Kimi and I were able to visit two Civil War sites, Harper's Ferry in West Virginia and the Manassas battlefield in Virginia. Also in Virginia, we visited the Luray Caves, Williamsburg, Yorktown, and Jamestown. In DC, we viewed the Museum of Natural History and the Spy Museum. We saw the newly installed Japanese American Citizens League monument.

In September, at the CFH conference at Bluffton College, I presented my first power point lecture on "Hellenism." An American History professor at the college was Perry Bush, the son of Frederic Bush, who had been my classmate at Brandeis University.

As the president of the Near East Archaeological Society, I arranged for a special session on the Dead Sea Scrolls at our conference in Providence in November. Speaking at the session were James VanderKam of Notre Dame, and Martin Abegg and Peter Flint of Trinity Western University.

In 1969, Nelson Glueck, the president of Hebrew Union College had acquired a set of the negatives of all of the Dead Sea Scrolls, which were secretly kept in a vault at the Klau Library for safekeeping. This was not available to the professors or students of the college. Abegg, however, discovered in the reference cage of the library a set of the hand-copied concordance of all the words in the scrolls, published and unpublished, that had been made by scholars such as Joseph Fitzmyer.

---

1. Cru's faculty outreach known as CLM (Christian Leadership Ministries later known as the Faculty Commons), had been co-founded by Stan Oakes and Scott Luley, who had taught at Miami University and then ministered to the faculty at Princeton University.

This had been acquired by Professor Ben Zion Wacholder. By devising a software program that would link the references of each word with its context, Abegg was able to reconstruct the original texts. In March 1991, I had lunch with Wacholder and his friend Stanley Burstein, who had been a graduate student together with Wacholder at UCLA. In September, 1991 Abegg and Wacholder released the first volume of their reconstructed texts with the help of Hershel Shanks, the editor of the *Biblical Archaeology Review*, to the consternation of the official Scrolls Committee, which had limited access to the unpublished materials. Stephen Kaufmann from HUC, who had been on Abegg's committee, also disapproved and refused to sign his dissertation. Wacholder then got Lawrence Schiffman to serve as the second reader.

Shortly thereafter, a second set of negatives, which James Sanders had acquired, was made public by William Moffett, the new director of the Huntington Library in Pasadena. Then Robert Eisenman, a professor at California State University at Long Beach acquired a set of photographs, which he published with James M. Robinson. He did not reveal the source of these photos even to Robinson.[2]

Publications

I wrote a chapter on "Did Persian Zoroastrianism Influence Judaism" for *Israel—Ancient Kingdom or Late Invention?* edited by Daniel Block. I contributed the article on "Magic, Sorcery" to *The Encyclopedia of the Historical Jesus*, edited by Craig Evans, and articles on "Susa" and "Vashti" to the *Dictionary of the Old Testament: Wisdom, Poetry & Writings*, edited by Tremper Longman III and Peter Enns.

Japan and Okinawa

In September, Kimi developed pains in her upper shoulder and had to be taken to the hospital. The diagnosis was not serious. She had some arthritis in her spine, which could be relieved by massage. But we agreed that she should not join me in a three-week tour we had planned to visit Japan and Okinawa.

---

2. See Jason Kalman, *Hebrew Union College and the Dead Sea Scrolls* (Cincinnati, Ohio: Hebrew Union College—Jewish Institute of Religion, 2012).

On October 13, I left Cincinnati and arrived in LA at 6 p.m. Renting a car, I stayed in a Days Inn at Inglewood. On October 14, I went to the Inglewood Cemetery, where I bought some flowers to place by the crypt that holds the ashes of my mother and stepfather.

The Yamato Travel Agency in LA had sent me a packet with information, including a Japanese Air Lines (JAL) envelope. I had pulled out the itinerary cards and thrown the envelope away. When I arrived two hours before flight time, the agent who examined the cards asked where was the paper ticket? I said that I had not seen a paper ticket. She said that there must have been one in the envelope. Most US airlines had converted to electronic tickets, but this was not the case with JAL. The staff worked with my travel agent to reconstruct the necessary documentation, but this took an hour and a half. Finally at 12:50 p.m. they gave me a ticket and a boarding pass. A JAL agent went with me to whisk me through security, while a crowd of passengers stood in the regular security lines. I made it to the gate with the very last passengers at about 1:05 p.m. The plane was scheduled to leave at 1:20 p.m., but actually left at 1:14!

On October 15, I arrived at the Narita Airport, which is an hour and a half east of Tokyo. I easily made it through immigration and found the airport bus. Though it was only 6 p.m. it was already dark as there is no daylight savings time in Japan. The sun had set about 5:15 p.m. My agent had booked me into the luxurious Grand Prince Akasaka Hotel in the center of Tokyo. The $160 a night rate was not unreasonable for the most expensive city in the world.

I had arranged to have Scott and Jen (Bystrom) Thomson, Campus Crusade staff, to come to my hotel at 9 p.m. Jen was a grad of Miami. I was going to treat them in one of the hotel restaurants, but we walked out when we looked at the menu which priced a meal at 15,000 yen (about $150)! We went down the hill and found a small local restaurant, which served *yakitori* (grilled chicken on a stick) for just $6.

On October 16, I woke up early to catch the bus at 6 a.m. to visit the famous Tsukiji fish market by the wharfs. My uncle Tom Owan had urged me not to miss this experience. This was a very busy site that did not welcome tourists. I saw numerous large tuna fish being prepared for auction to provide *sashimi*, the raw fish slices Japanese love to place on their sushi.

I had signed up for a bus tour that picked up tourists from different hotels. We first went up to the Tokyo Tower, where at a height of about

450 feet we had a superb panoramic view of the city. We stopped briefly at the outskirts of the Imperial palace. We then went to see the famous temple of Kannon, the goddess of Mercy, whose statue was found by fishermen in the Sumida River nearby.[3] The approach was lined with shops and the atmosphere was festive with many pilgrims as this day was a special anniversary for the temple. I asked to be let off at the Ginza shopping district as I wanted to purchase a back up camera. I also bought a pricy pair of pajamas as the one Kimi had packed for me did not fit.

Later that evening, Professor David Tsumura and his wife (who is from Indiana) came to my hotel. David, who studied at Brandeis after me, is a preeminent Old Testament scholar. I had lectured for him at the Tokyo Bible Seminary when I was last in Japan in 1996. We went by subway to the busy Shinjuku area in west Tokyo.[4] After supper we hurried to get back to the Christian Student Center in Ochanomizu, which houses the offices of both Cru and IV, as well as David's small biblical archaeology museum where I was to lecture. There were about seventy-five present, mainly older men and women. I gave a power point presentation (only my second one) on Ancient Persian Capitals. I had sent David the text of my presentation. It seemed that when I spoke for a minute, he elaborated in his Japanese translation for two minutes!

On October 17, Steve Lambacher, a professor of linguistics at Aoyama Gakuin University, came to my hotel to guide me around Tokyo. Steve graduated from Ohio University and did an MA in History at Miami. He served with the Navigators in Korea. He married a Japanese woman, Kimiko, and moved to Japan. We went by subway to the northeast district of Ueno, which is noted for its parks and museums. We saw a small museum which depicted life in *Shita Machi* (the lower city of Tokyo) during the Emperor Hirohito's era early in the twentieth century. We then went to the large and modern *Edo* Museum. Edo was the earlier name of Tokyo under the Shogun, that is in the age of the samurai, before the Meiji era of the nineteenth century. We had only 45 minutes to spend, though we could have spent all day with the many informative models and exhibits there, but Steve had to go back to his campus for a class. He later came to the hotel, and we went for supper

---

3. I later learned that the Japanese camera company, Canon, is named after Kannon.

4. At this time my passport listed my height as 5'11". Most striking to me was the fact that in the crowded subways I seemed to stand head and shoulders above the mass of riders.

back to the busy Shinjuku area, which resembles Times Square with its flashing neon lights and crowds of young people.

On October 18, I took a taxi to the smaller Haneda airport, where I boarded a JAL flight that left at 3:30 p.m. and arrived in Naha, Okinawa, at 5:00 p.m. I took a taxi to the Naha Terrace Hotel and went on a stroll along the mile long main street which was crowded with Okinawans visiting the many shops and restaurants. The weather here was warm and humid. I found a restaurant that featured two women performing traditional Okinawan dances.

On October 19, which was a Sunday, Mildred Kiyuna, a missionary from Makiki Christian Church, came to take me to her church. Millie and I had been at Columbia Bible College in 1955 to 1956. She had helped to convert Paulo, a Brazilian Japanese, who came with her.[5] They took me to a small church with about twenty members. I gave a short testimony in Japanese. I could understand about 80 percent of the singing and sermon in Japanese, both of which were lively and forceful. The song-leader was originally from Korea. The pastor was the son of an Okinawan mother and a Mexican-American soldier.

After the service, they drove me to the southern fishing village of Itoman, from which my father had emigrated to Hawaii and where my mother, who was born in Hawaii, lived for several years as a child. Through the help of a recently discovered relative in Dayton who had phoned ahead, I was able to contact two distant relatives on my mother's Owan side of my family in Naha.

We then visited the very interesting reconstructed red castle at nearby Shuri, which displayed marked Chinese influence. Though it was late, we pressed on to Nago in the north, where we met my stepfather Renyu Higa's brother and other family members. He was a member of the Okinawan legislature.

On October 20, I flew from Okinawa to Fukuoka, a city on the southern island of Kyushu. After depositing my luggage at the Miyako Hotel, I went across the street to the Hakata train station and boarded the "bullet train," which travels about 180 mph, for Iwakuni, just south of Hiroshima. Iwakuni in Yamaguchi prefecture was where Kimi's mother came from as a "picture bride" to Hawaii. I arrived in the late afternoon and strolled about the city, which was rather deserted with a few people

---

5. I learned that there were now about 300,000 Japanese from Brazil who had emigrated to Japan for work.

riding their bicycles. I went into an arcade where I ate supper.[6] I then went to see an American movie, where I could see but one other customer.

On October 21, I toured Iwakuni, which is famed for the *Kintai-kyo*, its unique Kintai Bridge over a river in a picturesque valley below a mountain. The Kintai bridge is a five-arched wooden bridge which is about 200 m. long and 5 m. wide. It was first built in 1673 and destroyed and rebuilt many times thereafter. Its use was originally restricted to official travelers. A cable car takes visitors up to the mountain top, where there is a reconstructed *shiro* or castle.[7] Japanese castles usually have five floors. From the top floor one could get quite a panoramic view of the scenery below. There was a fine museum of antiquities, including numerous samurai swords and sets of armor. At the base of the mountain was a museum of the unique white snakes living in this area which are believed to bring good luck. There was also a beautiful pond with colorful carp. I tried to feed these fish, but ducks would inevitably gobble up the pieces of bread I threw to the fish.

On October 22, I took the bullet train back to Fukuoka, arriving about noon. As it was too early to check into the Miyako Hotel, where I was to meet the group from the Japan Evangelical Missionary Society (JEMS) for a tour of southern Japan, I decided to do some sightseeing in the area. I took a train to Kokura a port town to the north, which was the original site of the atomic bomb which was dropped on Nagasaki instead because of cloudy conditions. Kokura has a splendid castle in the middle of the town. I then took two local trains to get to a peninsula, where there is a large aquarium with a dolphin show.

Late that night at the hotel, I met Rev. Sam Tonomura, the leader of the tour, and our Japanese guide, Yumi-san. Besides Sam and myself, there were thirteen others, all Japanese-Americans from California, except for one Caucasian woman, who had been married to a Japanese man from Kauai. Besides Kimi three others had canceled at the last minute. These were one couple whose husband had developed shingles and a single woman who tripped over her ironing cord and had broken her wrist. Six of us were over seventy years old.

On October 23, we first visited the 360-foot high Fukuoka observation tower, which gave us a splendid view of the port city of Hakata. We then visited the Kyushu National Museum, which is housed in a

---

6. While in Japan I enjoyed my favorite Japanese dishes, shrimp tempura and *unagi* (broiled eel).

7. All but three of the many castles in Japan are reconstructions built about 1960.

large domed building with exhibits on various eras of Japanese culture and history. These illustrated the importance of early Korean influence upon Japan.

On October 24 we toured the important port city of Nagasaki. which was the site of the second atomic bomb, which killed 74,000 on August 9, 1945, and injured another 75,000. At the Peace Park stood the colossal figure of a man with one arm pointing upward toward danger from the sky and the other arm pointed horizontally pleading for peace. Other statues in the park have been donated by various nations. The Atomic Bomb Museum gives graphic details of the devastation wrought with relics from the debris. The most poignant details of that fateful day are those recorded by children, who survived and recorded their memories in 1949.

Christianity was introduced into Japan through Nagasaki in 1549 by Francis Xavier, an early Jesuit. He and his colleagues had considerable success in this area in the late sixteenth century. But then the Shogun, the military leader, disliked the Christian teaching of equality which threatened the strict hierarchical order of Japanese society, and feared a foreign invasion. He banned Christianity and threatened death any Christian who did not recant.

We visited a hill where twenty-six Christians, including six foreign priests, were crucified in 1597. These martyrs were canonized by the pope in 1962. We then walked up a steep hill to visit the Oura Catholic church built by French priests in 1864. This is the oldest wooden church of Gothic style in Japan. In its school buildings Japanese converts were taught Latin.

On the other side of the hill overlooking Nagasaki harbor is a cluster of western type buildings known as the Glover Garden which housed a number of important Europeans. These Europeans introduced many western technologies to Japan through Nagasaki, including the railroad and paved roads. Their houses reminded me of the house of Madame Butterfly in Puccini's opera, as she watched for the return of the father of her son, Captain Pinkerton, as he sailed into Nagasaki harbor. On the path below is a statue of Puccini.

After the tour group returned to the hotel, I set out on my own by streetcar to see some other sites in Nagasaki. On a hillside I located the oldest Chinese Zen Buddhist temple, called *Kofukuji*, built in 1620. I walked along the river and saw the *Megane* (eyeglass) bridge, built in 1634, the oldest stone arch bridge in Japan. But by the time I reached *Dejima*, the island where Europeans were allowed to stay, it had become dark.

On October 25 our bus drove south to the Shimabara peninsula, which lies in the shadow of Mount Unzen which erupted for five years in the 1990s with devastating effect on the areas below. Shimabara castle was the center of the Christian revolt in 1637 and 1638 against oppressive taxation. The 120-day revolt was led by a charismatic sixteen-year-old named Amakusa Shiro. His 35,000 soldiers were crushed by the 125,000-man army sent by the Shogun. We viewed the Gion stone bridge, which marks the site of a famous battle during this revolt. The drive along the coast was breathtaking with small islands set in the sea. We took a ferry to the island of Amakusa, which was rather isolated until the 1960s, and stayed in Hondo City. Our hotel Alegria was sited on a beautiful palm lined bay. Like many hotels in volcanic Japan, it featured a hot spring spa.

On October 26, which was a Sunday, we worshiped at a small Baptist church with 20 mainly younger members. The sermon was in Japanese, which was translated into English. Nearby was a site where Christians were beheaded and their skulls buried. We were joined by Susan Maeda, a JEMS missionary in the area. Originally from Kauai, Sue attended Wheaton College, graduating in 1956. She then taught for 40 some years in Azusa, California, before coming to Amakusa in 2005.

After lunch we went around the coast of the island to visit two Catholic churches built in the 1930s, one atop a steep hill and the other by a bay. We visited the Amakusa Christian Museum which displayed the original banner used by Shiro in his revolt. He and all of his followers were killed. We viewed the Amakusa Shiro Hall, which was opened in 1993 to commemorate this figure. While we were in the area there was a special anniversary celebration in his honor.

We also saw evidence of the so-called *Kakure* ("Hidden") Christians. During the persecution images of Christ or Mary were placed on the ground and everyone was required to step on these images or the *fumiei* (tablet of the crucifix). Those who refused were executed. [8] Some did step on the image, but they and their descendants hid their Christianity hence their name. They made such items as *kakushi jujibotoke*, that is a hidden cross in a Buddha image.

---

8. This is the background of Shusaku Endo's acclaimed novel *Silence*, which was made into a film directed by Martin Scorsese in 1966. The book was recommended summer reading for incoming freshmen at Miami University.

On October 27 we drove over five bridges connecting islands in the Amakusa region to get to the city of Kumamoto. There we visited the huge castle, one of the three most famous in Japan along with those of Osaka and Nagoya. This had originally been built in 1588. We viewed the magnificent Suizenji gardens arranged about a small lake filled with colorful carp. We then visited Tabaruzaka park, the scene of the "Last Samurai" battle that inspired the Tom Cruise movie. The movie anachronistically depicted samurai wearing clothing from the seventeenth and eighteenth centuries, whereas the battle took place in 1873. Lord Saigo of the southern city of Kagoshima and his samurai were no match for the larger and better equipped imperial forces. The great grandfather of one of our tour members, Ryoko Narusawa, who with her husband Ray, had served as missionaries to the Japanese in Brazil, fought in this war. Ray and I both graduated from Leilehua High School in Wahiawa.

On October 28 we left Kumamoto by express train back to Fukuoka, where we transferred to the bullet train for Hiroshima. We were fortunate that we had our energetic guide Yumi-san holding her yellow flag aloft, to make the quick connection. We arrived at Hakata at 10:50 a.m. and then had only ten minutes to transfer to the bullet train, which left precisely as scheduled. Upon arriving at Hiroshima at noon, we ate near the train station and then took a trolley to the Hiroshima Peace Park. The first atomic bomb fell without warning on this port city at 8:15 a.m. on August 6, 1945. The bomb killed 140,000 citizens of the city in an unimaginable inferno. The shock and radiation waves destroyed almost everything within a mile or so and set off fires through the rest of the city. Those who survived suffered terribly from the radiation. The skeletal remains of the domed Genbaku building were left standing as a grim reminder of this holocaust. The peaceful river flowing by it was once filled with corpses. Shortly after the second bomb on Nagasaki Japan surrendered unconditionally on August 15.

On October 29 we drove to a ferry, where a short ride took us to the lovely island of Miyajima. Its famous red *torii* (a Shinto ceremonial gate), rising from the sea at high tide is considered one of the three most memorable sites in Japan. Visitors are greeted by a herd of very tame deer, who sometimes nibble at objects such as packages. The Shinto shrine of Itsukushima, which is built on stilts, is held as a national treasure. While we were there, we witnessed a ceremony asking for good luck.

Shintoism, an animistic religion, was the indigenous religion of Japan. During the World War II it was used to exalt the emperor as a god and to arouse patriotic fervor. In the past Japanese used to call upon the Shinto priest at weddings. Today most young couples prefer a western style of wedding, with the bride wearing a white gown rather than the traditional kimono. In the past Japanese called upon the Buddhist priest for funerals (all Japanese are cremated). Today there are funeral parlors with a Buddhist priest at hand, which threatens the independent existence of the temples.

While others went shopping, I climbed up to get a closer look at the five-storied red pagoda built in 1407. I was able to visit the large *Senjokaku* (one thousand mat) Shinto hall, built by the shogun Toyotomi Hideyoshi. This heroic but tragic figure who rose from low origins to become the supreme head of Japan, built this hall in 1587.

I ate the region's special eel. I did not try the oysters; Hiroshima Bay provides half of Japan's oysters. Nor did I venture to try another of the region's specialty which was raw horse meat, reputed to be very tender!

We went to view the lovely Shukkeien Gardens, built in 1620, around a small lake. The garden where some had sought refuge was destroyed by the bomb. After it was rebuilt, the garden has drawn nearly a million visitors a year. A stone bridge bisects the garden. We were fortunate to view a traditional wedding couple there, with the bride in her kimono. On display were gigantic chrysanthemums.

On October 30 we took the bullet train from Hiroshima to Osaka, the port town that grew up close to the early imperial capital of Kyoto. On the train, I gave a brief devotional talk on the apostle Paul's hope to visit Rome expressed in his letter to the Romans, which God fulfilled later in an unexpected way when Paul was taken to Rome as a prisoner.

We first went to view a very large aquarium. We ate at a nearby department store. I had *sukiyaki*, which I cooked myself on a small *hibachi* stove. I had not had this dish of thin sliced beef and vegetables since my mother last cooked this for us. We then went to view the magnificent Osaka castle, which shone brilliantly with its gilded ornamentation. There was a special exhibit on the capture of this key castle from Toyotomi's family by the Tokugawa clan in 1615 which established the two-century era centered in Edo. An ancient silk screen depicted the bloody conflict with its individual scenes highlighted with a narrative text.

I hailed a taxi to get back to check in at our hotel since Atsuko Hirose, who lives in Osaka, was coming to see me at 5 p.m. I discovered that after being born in Taiwan, she moved to the island of Amakusa. There she met Melvin Ishikawa, a missionary from Wahiawa, who had told her about me. The photo she had sent to me of myself and Melvin, was one he had given to her. She was converted to Christ at the age of fifteen. She traveled widely in Asia and Europe for her research on Amakusa Shiro, the Christian leader of the revolt. She came along with the group for our final dinner together at a Chinese restaurant on the thirty-third floor of a building in Osaka. There we ate *nabe* ("pot"), where a large pot of broth is set boiling at each table. One can throw into it any of about two dozen ingredients. At this dinner we met two of the JEMS missionaries who are working in Osaka: a businessman and pastor who has a unique ministry to his peers, and a Caucasian married to a Yonsei (4th generation Japanese) from California.

On October 31 we flew out of Osaka to arrive at the Haneda airport. We then took a bus to the larger Narita airport. We flew from Japan at 5:20 p.m., arriving on the same day in Los Angeles at 10:50 a.m., where I parted company with the JEMS tour group. I took a Delta flight at 10:45 p.m., to arrive in Atlanta at 6 a.m. to fly back to Cincinnati.

Chapter 30

The Year 2009

The Family

BRIAN WAS AWARDED A patent for his invention of the Wayfarer, a portable robot that can explore and map urban environments by using laser and vision sensors. He served as a member of the program committee for the Defense, Security and Sensing Symposium, one of the largest gatherings of scientists and engineers in the Defense Industry. He presented a paper on the Stingray robot he had developed. He also contributed to *Book: The Sequel*, a collection of imaginary sequels to famous books, in his case to George Orwell's *1984*.

In January, Haruko attended the inauguration of President Barack Obama in Washington, DC. She moved from Queens to Brooklyn and continued to work with Arts Connection in all the New York City boroughs. She started studying Spanish and began working toward a graduate degree in Library Science. She also volunteered at two public libraries.

Kimi ended her ten years of helping to deliver Meals on Wheels on Monday mornings[1] in order to take her watercolor painting classes in the mornings rather than in the evenings. On Tuesdays, she tutored internationals in English; on Wednesdays, she was involved in a women's Bible class; and on Thursdays, she sang with the Songbirds. In September she joined other members of Jean Vance's art class to visit the new

---

1. I took her place driving for Meals on Wheels. I drove with Richard Laatsch, a retired mathematics professor.

women's cancer wing of the Bethesda North Hospital where two of her paintings were hung.

My Health

A urology test in January reported an elevated PSA (prostate specific antigen) and a biopsy revealed a small cancer. Radioactive seeds were implanted in July. PSA tests in November revealed that the cancer had been successfully treated. While jogging around the track at the Health and Recreation Center, I was praying and not paying attention to my feet. I stumbled and knocked myself unconscious! I stayed overnight at the hospital to make certain I had not had a damaging concussion. This incident led me to buy a treadmill I can use at home.

I was healthy enough to participate in the annual Senior Games sponsored by the senior center near our home. I was terrible in all the games including shuffleboard, horseshoes, darts, and corn toss. To my surprise I won a second prize ribbon for bowling because there were so few others bowling in my age category!

New England Travels

In May, I traveled to New England to attend the wedding of Dennis Keeler and Elan Hanson in Carlisle. Dennis grew up in Oxford, attended Miami University, and earned his PhD in mathematics at the University of Michigan. He then did a postdoc at MIT and attended Park Street Church, where he met Elan. Dennis joined the Miami faculty, and Elan's parents, Don and Phoebe, moved to Oxford.

After the wedding, I went to Rockland, Maine, where one of my doctoral students, Brannan Becknall, was pastoring a church. I had lunch with Art and Peggy Hill, who were living nearby. I had first met Art when he was a serviceman at Scofield Barracks some 52 years before. We had corresponded annually, but this was the first time since then we had met in person! Art had served as the principal of a Christian school in Delaware and as the chair of the trustees of Eastern University.

Washington, DC

In July, Kimi and I went to Washington to do some sightseeing and to meet with relatives. We toured Baltimore, visiting the Museum of Dentistry, the Baltimore & Ohio Railroad Center, and Babe Ruth's home. We viewed the harbor on a "duck." We had lunch with Joe and Angela Geyer. Joe, a graduate of Miami, was working for the NSA. On another day we went to Richmond, Virginia, to view Jefferson Davis's home and the Museum of the Confederacy. In Virginia City we met my student Brandon Walker, who showed us around the campus of Regent University.

In DC, we visited the newly reopened Museum of American History, where the flag that flew over Fort McHenry was displayed. We were also able to take a tour of the Capitol. On July Fourth, I went into the city to view the parade and saw characters in costume portraying Jefferson, Adams and Franklin reading the Declaration of Independence from the steps of the National Archives.

We had a family reunion in Germantown, Maryland, with my uncle Tom Owan, and his sons Clyde Owan and Douglas Owan and his family. My sister Alicia, her husband Heinz, and their daughter Sabine had also come over from Switzerland. We all watched a tremendous fireworks display at night.

New York City

At the end of August Kimi and I traveled to New York City. We met with Stan Oakes, the president of King's College, which was located in the basement of the Empire State Building. We viewed the memorial site of the Twin Towers and toured Theodore Roosevelt's Home. We also visited the Jewish Museum and the Metropolitan Art Museum. With Haruko we saw the delightful Japanese cartoon movie *Ponyo*. We traveled to Coney Island, where I rode the famous Ferris wheel with Haruko. Kimi and I also saw the Broadway play, Mamma Mia.

A Visiting Speaker

In March, Walter Kaiser, president of Gordon-Conwell Theological Seminary, who had been a fellow graduate student with me at Brandeis University, came to speak at Miami University in my Annual History

Lecture series. He spoke on "The Bible and Archaeology" to a standing room audience.

The Last PhD

In August, I was able to hood my seventeenth and last PhD candidate, Adam Chambers, who is the son of one of my first PhD student, Roger Chambers. Adam graduated from Florida Bible College, where his father taught. He then earned the MA from Cincinnati Christian University under Reuben Bullard, a noted archaeologist and geologist. Adam wrote his dissertation on "Churches of the Decapolis: Origin and Expansion 4th to 7th c. CE." Adam along with my other doctoral students Robert Smith and John Wineland worked at the Decapolis city of Abila in Jordan.

A Lecture and a Paper

In June, I spoke on "Gnosticism" to a group led by Doug Franck of Search Ministries in Columbus. Kimi and I visited the COSI Museum, which had a special exhibit on Ancient Egypt. In November I presented a paper on "Moses, Akhnaton and Monotheism" before the Near East Archaeological Society in Atlanta.

Publications

I wrote "The Curse of Ham" for the *Criswell Theological Review* and contributed "Did Persian Zoroastrianism Influence Judaism?" in *Ancient Israel: Ancient Kingdom or Late Invention?* edited by Daniel Block. I wrote the commentary on Ezra and Nehemiah for the *Zondervan Illustrated Bible Backgrounds Commentary*, edited by John H. Walton. I also contributed a short essay on the introduction of football in 1888 by President Dudley Warfield (the brother of B. B. Warfield) for the volume celebrating the bicentennial of Miami University.

Miami Athletics

Miami's hockey team lost the championship game against Boston University, but teams in seven other sports won MidAmerican Conference championships. As a rule. apart from the football and basketball teams, athletes in the minor sports (swimming, diving, volleyball, golf, tennis, track) have higher grade point averages than the student body in general.

Chapter 31

Glaciers and the Canadian Rockies

The Year 2010

The Family

WORKING FOR IROBOT IN the Boston area Brian was the principal investigator for a number of military projects: for Daredevil to enable robots to see through smoke and fog, for Stingray to develop small high-speed robots, for Dynamo to develop vehicles with skills like race cars, and for Labrador to develop robots with doglike intelligence to recognize and fetch objects. In May, Brian traveled to Anchorage, Alaska, to present a paper at the International Conference on Robotics and Automation.

Haruko, while living in Brooklyn, continued to work with Arts Excellence in various boroughs. She pursued her graduate courses in Library and Information Technology at Queens College and volunteered at a public library in the lower east side of Manhattan.

In January, we took advantage of Saturn's demise as a company to purchase for Kimi a dark blue Aura for $18,000 at a savings of $8,000 off the list price. I joined her in singing with the Songbirds, which had about a dozen women and two other men. We had a talented pianist, John Bercaw, who taught jazz music at Miami University.

Mark A. Noll

In March, Mark A. Noll, the Francis A. McAnaney Professor of History at Notre Dame, spoke on "The Bible and Slavery" in my Annual History Lecture series. Mark, a graduate of Wheaton College, had taught for many years at that college before succeeding George Marsden at Notre Dame. I had known Mark through the Conference on Faith and History and served with him from 1992 to 1994 on the board of senior editors of *Christianity Today*. We were joined in a supper before the lecture by my history colleague, Mary Cayton, who was an authority on New England Transcendentalists and Evangelicals, and Peter Williams, the chair of the Comparative Religions Department. Peter knew Mark from the Society of Church History.

Figure 62. Mark Noll

Marvin R. Wilson

In May Kimi and I attended the commencement of Gordon College during which Marvin R. Wilson was honored with the presentation of a Festschrift, to which I had contributed an essay on "Abraham and Archaeology." Marvin and I had been fellow students in graduate school at Brandeis. I had used his classic text *Our Father Abraham*, which highlights the Jewish background of Christianity, in my seminar on Judaism and Early Christianity.

Shelton College Reunion

Later in May I attended a reunion of more than one hundred former students and faculty of Shelton College at Bird-in-the-Hand in Pennsylvania Amish country. It was good to see so many friends such as George and Joan Giacumakis, Bonnie Carlson, Bill and Carole Broadwick, Johnny and Carolyn Hibbard, Al and Bev Monroe, John and Jane Schimmer among others.

Glacier National Park and the Canadian Rockies

Glacier National Park in northern Montana is remote and open only during the summer. Therefore, relatively few tourists visit this park. In 1960, there were one hundred and fifty glaciers there, but in 2010 there were only twenty-seven left, surely incontrovertible evidence of global warming. Glacier National Park is continued on the Canadian side by the Waterton Lakes Park. Our tour from July 16 to 24 was with Tauck World Discovery, which uses the very best hotels. My one reservation was the food was too abundant and too rich for me. I purposely ate only two meals per day and as a result of walking about an hour a day, I lost four pounds in eight days!

On July 16, I flew from Cincinnati to Toronto, where I had only an hour to go through customs and make connections. I had to hurry from one end of the corridor to the end of another corridor, arriving only five minutes before the departure of the 1 p.m. flight!

The province of Alberta is quite wealthy with its resources of oil and natural gas. The southern city of Calgary is a boomtown. I had time to ascend the Calgary Tower with an overview of the city, as this was located next to our hotel, the historic Fairmont Palliser. Though we did not get to see the parade and festivities, the annual Stampede, a rodeo and horse wagon event, was taking place.

That evening we had an introduction to the twenty-eight members of the tour, which included mainly retired couples, with the exception of one extended family. There were two single women and two single men including myself, since Kimi, who had sprained her knee, decided not to come along. Our guide, Jennifer Ovens, a forty-four-year-old redhead, was vivacious, well informed, and had a delightful sense of humor.

On July 17, we drove south from Calgary to stop at the Head-Smashed-In Buffalo Jump, which was used for 5,500 years. An Indian guide described how braves would herd about five hundred bison at a time to jump over the cliff, which was only about thirty feet high, to be killed and then butchered for meat.

We then drove to the Waterton Lakes National Park, where the group had lunch at the scenic Prince of Wales Hotel on a bluff overlooking a lake. We arrived in the afternoon at the Many Glaciers Hotel, located in the eastern part of Glacier National Park.

On Sunday, July 18 following a suggestion made by Jennifer, I woke up at 5:30 a.m. to hike around the lake in front of our hotel to catch the sun as it rose at 6 a.m. This was probably the highlight of my trip as I was able to photograph the mountains burnished red by the rising sun as they were reflected in the mirror like surface of the lake. I also encountered deer during the walk and saw some fresh (bear?) poop.

Our party boarded three replicas of the red "Jammer" open roofed touring cars, which are today found only here and in Yellowstone National Park. They took us on the spectacular "Going to the Sun Road" which wound about the side of the mountains beneath glaciers and above lakes and rivers. We encountered heavy traffic, including many motorcycles at the continental divide at Logan Pass. This is where rainwater divides into three directions, not only west to the Pacific and east to the Atlantic, but also north to the Hudson Bay. We arrived in the afternoon at Lake McDonald on the western side of Glacier National Park and stayed in a lodge there.

On July 19 we traveled north and east through Radium Hot Springs, where despite a drizzle, Canadians and foreigners were enjoying the therapeutic waters of warm springs that filled two pools. We then traveled to Lake Louise (elevation 5,700 ft.), where our hotel Chateau

Lake Louise was located on a lovely turquoise blue lake bounded by mountains and glaciers.

In the morning on July 20 I took a shuttle to the skiing area, where I went up on a lift to the top of the mountain, first in an enclosed car and then descended (somewhat nervously) on an open ski lift type of chair. The view from the top was quite magnificent with a view of the hotel and its lake in the far distance We then traveled north to Jasper (elevation 3,500 ft.), where we were lodged in cabins around a lake.

As we had the entire day free on July 21, I spent the morning in a paddle boat on the lake and then decided to go horseback riding. I was given a large brown horse named "Rocket," but I was assured that he was the slowest in the pack. As the tour ended, I waited on my horse, so I could get a photo taken. And then near disaster! As I dismounted, my left foot got stuck in the stirrup, with my knee twisted in the process. It took two guides to free my foot. My knee remained sore as I had strained the medial collateral ligament.

In the afternoon I took a forty-five-minute shuttle to ride a boat on Maligne Lake, which at first did not look especially impressive. But once we were on the boat we were treated to a spectacular vista of surrounding mountains and glaciers. We stopped at the small Spirit Island, which is one of the most photographed sites in the Canadian Rockies.

On July 22 we drove south on the Icefields Parkway and stopped to actually go on to the Athabasca Glacier by riding on a specially built Ice Explorer with huge wheels. As it was very cold, we did not spend much time outside on the glacier. En route we also stopped at the Athabasca Falls. We then arrived at the famous tourist town of Banff (elevation 4,500 ft.) where we would stay in the historic Banff Falls hotel. The original hotel was first built in 1888, to take advantage of hot springs discovered on the mountain side. I walked down a steep hill behind the hotel to view the Bow River Falls, and then walked along the river to the town of Banff. I was then able to catch a bus back to the hotel.

On July 23 I took an early shuttle to ride the Banff gondola, which gave me a marvelous view from about a thousand feet higher. I then took the bus into the town of Banff to visit in turn the Cascade Gardens, an Indian Trading Post, a most informative Buffalo Indians Museum, and the Whyte Art Museum, where I viewed a video on what to do if you confront a grizzly or a black bear.

In the afternoon a large group of guests were led around the hotel by the hotel's historian, who regaled us with stories of the famous royalty, musicians, actors, and politicians who had stayed at the hotel. He told the story of an elevator girl who was asked by Prince Philip of England what she did. She answered that she was a college student. She then asked what he did. He replied, "I am a prince." Not knowing the identity of the guest she responded, "If you are a prince, then I am the Queen of Sheba!" The prince was more amused than offended.

Prior to our farewell dinner, we were entertained by an informative talk by a retired Royal Canadian Mounted Policeman, a title which is a bit anachronistic as the officers no longer use horses. After breakfast on July 24, we traveled ninety minutes back to the Calgary airport, where I boarded a plane for Denver to get back to Cincinnati.

Summer Trips

In July, Kimi and I attended the Butler County Fair in Hamilton and witnessed the judging of animals raised by youths for prizes. One young boy could barely handle the huge cow he had raised! The sight of hens, rabbits, goats, sheep, and cows reminded me of the missionary "ranch" in Wahiawa. In August, we headed north to Greenville, the home of the famed sharpshooter Annie Oakley to attend the festival commemorating her life. Annie as an impoverished young girl managed to shoot game for her family. In Cincinnati she out-dueled professional sharpshooter Frank Butler and later married him. She was the main attraction in Buffalo Bill's Wild West Show and astounded monarchs in Europe with her extraordinary skills.

The World Equestrian Games

In October Kimi and I spent two days viewing the World Equestrian Games. This was the first time that these prestigious events were ever in the United States. They were held at the Kentucky Horse Park just north of Lexington. At the park's museum there was an informative history of thoroughbreds from the first Arabian horses imported into England. We witnessed jumping, vaulting, and dressage among other events. Miami University has its own stable of horses which are used by students to compete in equestrian games.

Lectures and Conferences

In September I presented three Staley Lectures at Cedarville University where my student Carl Smith was teaching. In November, Kimi and I spent a week in Atlanta attending conferences of the ETS, the NEAS, and the IBR. I was honored with a plaque at the ETS, as I rotated off the executive council after seven years on it. At the Zondervan breakfast Kimi found under her chair a gift certificate for three New Testament commentaries.

Publications

This year saw the publication of my revised commentary on Ezra and Nehemiah for *The Expositor's Bible Commentary*, edited by Tremper Longman III. My *Persia and the Bible* was translated into Korean and my *New Testament Cities in Western Asia Minor* into Japanese.

Athletics and Academics

In August at Mason, I saw a match featuring the number one women's tennis player in the world, Kim Clijsters of Belgium. Miami's football team became the most improved in the nation. After a one win and eleven losses record last year, it improved to eight wins and three losses this year. The *US News & World Report* (August 19) ranked Miami University just behind Dartmouth College as the school with the best undergraduate teaching, ahead of Princeton, Notre Dame, William and Mary, Brown, and UC Berkeley.

Chapter 32

Hawaii

The Year 2011

The Family

BRIAN CONTINUED AS THE lead roboticist for two projects, Dynamo and Labrador, funded by DARPA (Defense Advanced Research Projects Agency). He also led a group that coordinated artificial intelligence research between the military and domestic divisions of iRobot.

Haruko continued her work with Arts Connection and her graduate studies in Library Science. The big news of the year was her engagement to Denis Cretinon from Paris. Haruko had spent six years in Thailand working for the Fourth World; Denis had spent five years with the same organization in the Central African Republic. He taught mathematics at a middle school in Newark. He had two teenage sons, William and Eddie, from a previous marriage.

California

On March 3, Kimi and I flew to Los Angeles en route to a return visit to the Islands after an absence of five years. In LA, I did some research at the library of Fuller Theological Seminary and met former Miami students Joe Webb and his wife Diane. Joe was serving as the vice-president of the seminary in charge of fund raising. After his graduation from Miami University, he became the director of Cru in New England and then the director of Here's Life in Europe. The latter movement began fifty thousand new Bible study groups. Upon his return to the US he began Global Village, an organization that advised missionaries.

We stayed at the Kyoto Hotel in Little Tokyo. While walking through Little Tokyo we saw the new monument to the famed 442 Battalion of Japanese American soldiers from Hawaii who fought so valiantly in Europe during World War II. We also visited the the Japanese American National Museum. My cousin Shoan Yamauchi, who had a tofu factory where I worked in 1952 and 1953, had donated a large sum of money to the museum. I had been invited to give lectures on Jerusalem and on Nehemiah by Rev. Sam Tonomura, the head of JEMS (Japanese Evangelistic Missionary Society) to a group of Nisei and Sansei pastors. The JEMS headquarters is located in Little Tokyo.

On March 5. we drove to the new Irvine campus of California State University at Fullerton, where my good friend George Giacumakis had arranged for me to give a series of lectures. George was a fellow student both at Shelton College and at Brandeis University. George eventually became the chair of the History Department at Fullerton's main campus, then the president of the Institute of Holy Land Studies in Israel. George also served as the chair of the History Department at Biola University. We went in the afternoon to Yorba Linda to see the Richard Nixon presidential library, which includes the modest home where he was born and also his presidential helicopter.

On March 6 we drove west to see the new Ronald Reagan Library in Simi Valley. We arrived 15 minutes before closing time. Instead of being turned away, we were admitted free of charge and dashed through the galleys and even boarded the presidential plane! That evening at Van Nuys in the San Fernando Valley, we had dinner with Roy and Mary Hayden. Roy, a fellow student at Brandeis, taught for over 40 years at Oral Roberts University. He translated Ezra and Nehemiah for the New International Version. He was now teaching at the small King's College affiliated with Jack Hayford's church.

Hawaii

On March 7, we flew from Los Angeles to Honolulu and arrived at about 1 p.m. We went to Waipahu near the airport to view a small but interesting museum on the city's sugar plantation. One of the haole managers of the plantation was a great sports enthusiast who fostered a unique pride in athletics in this rural town, which has produced Little League champions for Hawaii. The photos and equipment of cutting the sugar cane reminded Kimi of the days when as a teenager garbed in protective clothing, she helped cut the canes and placed them on the water flumes.

We went to the Arizona Memorial at Pearl Harbor where two new museums had been built, one devoted to the prelude to the December 7 attack and the other devoted to the attack itself. What was most interesting were the testimonies of some of the Japanese pilots and of children who witnessed the attack. One interesting fact I learned was that all the thirty civilian casualties died as the result of friendly fire as artillery shells fell to earth.

We had arranged to have supper at a restaurant in Pearl City. Those who came included Nora Handa, Judy Galley, Kay Curtis, Joe and Barbara Grimes. I had worked with Nora at the Christian Youth Center in Wahiawa. She later served as a missionary in Japan with Judy. Kay, who was in her eighties, was the widow of Claude Curtis. With her son she ran a Christian bookstore in Millilani and still pursued her husband's goal of bringing Bibles into China. The Grimes were Wycliffe missionaries whom I first met at the Summer Institute of Linguistics in Norman, Oklahoma. After teaching at Cornell University, Joe and Barbara were translating the Bible into Hawaiian Pidgin.

We got to our hotel in Waikiki late at night, only to be sent across the street to another hotel. We later learned that a ten-inch water main next to the hotel had burst that morning. Most of the tourists seemed to be from Japan.

On March 8 we went up to Nuuanu Valley to meet with Ada and Richard Lum, who lived on Old Pali Road. My mother had worked as a maid for the Hites, a family who lived on the right side of the road; Kimi had worked as a maid for the Marks family, who lived almost across the street. Ada Lum, who was in her eighties, was a noted Bible teacher for the International Fellowship of Evangelical Students in Asia. It was her younger brother, Dick, a classmate at Iolani who had invited me to Kalihi Union Church where I first heard the Gospel in 1952.

After my father died in 1940 my mother worked as a maid in a dozen locations in Honolulu in a dozen years. We tried to retrace some of these locations. She had worked at two homes on Pacific Heights, which we ascended on a constantly curving road. I located Pauoa School, which I had attended in the third grade in the area below these heights. Kimi had also worked on the heights as a maid during her first summer on Oahu.

We then proceeded around the base of Punchbowl, a crater with the military cemetery, to Manoa Valley, where my mom had worked in several places. I located Manoa Elementary School, which I had attended in the first grade. It was in Manoa that my mom was working on December 7, 1941.

We visited the campus of the University of Hawaii, which I attended in 1957 to1958, ostensibly as an anthropology major while spending most of my time studying languages and working as a columnist and feature editor for the university's newspaper *Ka Leo*.

On March 9 we visited Queen Emma's summer home in Nuuanu. Unfortunately because of heavy rain, we could not view the spectacular Pali lookout. At Kaneohe we had lunch at a Chop Suey restaurant with my aunt Beryl and her husband Albert Nakama and my uncle Bob Owan and his wife Grace. That evening we had been invited to an apartment on Emerson Street below Punchbowl, near where my mom and I had once stayed in a boarding house. Our hosts were Yokichi and Nancy Suzuki, missionaries to Japan, who had housed me on my visit to Tokyo in 1996. They had invited Bong and Alma Ro, as well as a couple, Dennis Kawamura and his wife from Kalihi Union Church. Bong, who had been born in North Korea, recalled that he had met me briefly when I was at Columbia Bible College, which led to his enrolling there. He later attended Wheaton College where he knew Kimi, Covenant Theological Seminary, and Concordia Theological Seminary, where he earned a PhD in Church History. He served in Singapore, Korea, and Taiwan.

On March 10, Dennis Kawamura invited me to address the Joy Fellowship, a group of senior citizens who meet weekly at Kalihi Union Church. I spoke on the significance of Jerusalem in the current political and religious contexts. In Kalihi we visited the Bishop Museum, which has the finest exhibit on ancient Hawaiians and especially their royalty. We ate Hawaiian *laulau*, *poi*, and *kalua* pig at a small local restaurant called Helena's which was to be featured in April on the Travel Channel. We then went to Makiki Christian Church, Kimi's home church, which has the unusual architecture of a Japanese castle. We also visited the new Ala Wai campus of Iolani, a private Episcopal school that I had attended when it was up at Nuuanu Valley.

That evening, word of the earthquake in Japan created fear of a possible tidal wave in Hawaii. Many guests were either sent above the third floor or were evacuated inland from hotels both on Oahu and the Big Island. We were fortunate in that we were on the fifth floor and did not have to move. Damage was minimal on the eastern side of the islands but was considerable on the western side, especially at Kona on the Big Island and near the bay where Captain Cook was killed.

On March 11 we had breakfast with June Fujimoto, Kimi's good friend from Hawaii who had been her maid of honor at our wedding in 1962 at Wheaton. We caught up on all of her activities since then as a missionary to Japan and then as a staff member at Makiki Christian Church.

After flying to Hilo on the Big Island we had dinner at a Japanese restaurant on the bayside with Kimi's younger sister, Janet. We stayed at Uncle Billy's Hotel on Banyan Drive. Had we come a day earlier, we would have been evacuated with all the other guests of the hotels to higher ground.

On March 12 with Janet as our chauffeur, we viewed the burial site of Kimi's parents and her brother. We then visited with her oldest sister, Miyoko, who was in a nursing home. We were surprised at her good spirits and her talkativeness, though it was difficult to fully understand her.

We then visited the Volcano National Park on our way to Kona. There had been sizable eruptions recently which led to the closure of some roads, and to a phenomenon called *Vog*, fog with sulphur dioxide. Fortunately, the trade winds were blowing the fumes away from Hilo. The only way to see the red molten streams of lava was by an expensive helicopter tour. We did get to see a sizable plume of smoke from the Halemaumau crater.

Along the way to Kailua, we stopped by in Kau, the southern part of the Big Island, where Kimi grew up. She was born in Hilea, a village that no longer exists and attended school in Naalehu, the southernmost city in the US. We visited the black sands of Punaluu where she swam and saw the monkey pod tree Mark Twain planted when he visited the Islands in 1866. As the sun was setting, we reached Uncle Billy's Hotel in Kailua.

On Sunday, March 13 we attended the 9 a.m. service at the historic Mouaikaua Church in Kailua, the first church built in the Islands in 1820 by the missionaries who came from New England. After the service a guide gave a brief but fascinating talk on the arrival of the missionaries and the history of the church. The speaker was from Youth With a Mission from their University of the Nations. I had been on the campus during a convention of the American Scientific Affiliation in 1992. As Kimi wanted to get to the small Kailua Kona airport as early as possible, we arrived at 3 p.m. only to learn that the Delta agent would not be on hand until 7 p.m. for our 9 p.m. flight to California!

On Monday, March 14 we arrived in Los Aangeles at 5 a.m., with a two hour interval before our 7 a.m. flight to Cincinnati on Delta. I asked the agent where we needed to catch the plane to Cincinnati. We were told it would be Gate 69A in another terminal, and that we could avoid a second security checkpoint, by going downstairs by the McDonald's. But Kimi was so anxious that we should not be late, that she went ahead of me as I paused to check our flight status. In doing so she went past the point where she could return, so we had to proceed. At first, I was upset with her but her action proved to be providential, as we discovered that our suitcases were on the luggage carousel and had not been forwarded to our final destination. I had not realized the implication of the fact that our round trip between Cincinnati and LA (which included a free companion ticket) and the round-trip between LA and Hawaii were two separate flights, which needed separate check ins and sets of boarding passes. I asked an agent for the use of a wheelchair for Kimi to hasten our passage to the next terminal. An important result was that we were able to bypass the long security line to arrive at the gate with about twenty minutes to spare!

Donald A. Carson

On March 26, the noted New Testament scholar Donald A. Carson spoke on "Christ and Culture Revisited" in my Annual History Lecture series. Don, who was originally from Quebec, received his PhD from the University of Cambridge. He had taught at Trinity Evangelical Divinity School from 1978. He is known for his commentaries on the Gospels of Matthew and of John. He is also a popular international speaker.

Lectures and Conferences

On March 30, I traveled to Wilmore, Kentucky, and had supper with Dennis Kinlaw, the president emeritus of Asbury College. Dennis had been a fellow graduate student at Brandeis. He later served as a professor of Old Testament at Asbury Theological Seminary and became the president of

Asbury College. A popular speaker, Dennis had also founded the Francis Asbury Society to promote Wesleyan teachings. I spoke in the chapel of the seminary on "Moses, Akhenaton and Monotheism," and gave a lecture on "Abraham and Archaeology" to a class of doctoral students.

Figure 63. With Dennis Kinlaw

At the end of July Kimi and I drove to Naperville, Illinois, where I presented a paper on "Physicians in the Biblical World" at the ASA conference. We visited Wheaton College where Dot Chappell, the Dean of Natural and Social Sciences, who had received her PhD in Botany from Miami University, gave us a tour of the new science building that she had personally designed. In Chicago, we stopped at the Oriental Institute of the University of Chicago where my former student Foy Scalf was now the director of the Research Archives.

Figure 64. With Dot Chappell

On August 15 I flew to Oklahoma City, where two of my doctoral students, Jerry Pattengale and Scott Carroll, were working with Steve Green, the president of Hobby Lobby, to develop a national Bible museum. I viewed Passages, an exhibit of 300 select objects from the Green collection, which Scott with the aid of his daughter Joy had curated. I had dinner with them and with David Green, the patriarch of the family who had begun Hobby Lobby. I gave a lecture to a sold-out auditorium on "The Old Testament and Archaeology." The scholar who responded was from Oral Roberts University, a school that the Greens had recently rescued from financial collapse with an infusion of several million dollars (see chapter 45).

Jerry Pattengale and I visited Thomas Oden, noted Methodist theologian, who lived in Oklahoma City. Tom and I had served together on the board of senior editors of *Christianity Today*. At one time a flaming liberal theologian at Drew Theological Seminary in New Jersey, Tom had become an evangelical through reading Augustine. He was editing a new patristics commentary of the Bible for InterVarsity Press with the financial support of the Green family.

In November in San Francisco, as the president of the Near East Archaeological Society, I arranged a special session featuring the important contribution of Seventh Day Adventist archaeologists, inspired by the leadership of Siegfried Horn, to conduct excavations in Jordan. The speakers included: Constance Clark Gane, Michael G. Hasel, Larry Herr, Efrain Velazquez, and Randall Younker.

Chapter 33

A Wedding

The Year 2012

The Family

BRIAN WAS PROMOTED TO Principal Roboticist at iRobot. He was awarded a second US patent as the coinventor of a system which allows land robots and unmanned air vehicles to work cooperatively to track targets.

On September 29 in Jersey City Haruko was married to Denis Crétinon by Rev. Elizabeth Scott, a friend from childhood. Many of her other longtime friends from Oxford were in attendance as well as members from Denis's family from France. Later a celebratory picnic was held at Battery Park on the southern tip of Manhattan.[1]

The family members spent some time in cabins in the Catskills near the farm where the famous Woodstock music festival was held in 1969. Kimi and I then visited Bear Mountain and spent some time in New York City. We viewed the 9/11 monument, a square sunken pool with the names of the dead inscribed. We were also able to view the musical The Phantom of the Opera. I also took a cab to see a docked carrier with the space shuttle Enterprise displayed on its deck.

---

1. Just a month later in October, Hurricane Sandy would devastate much of the coastline of New Jersey and New York, flooding the subways and train tunnels, prolonging Haruko's daily commute, which normally took an hour and a half!

Our Fiftieth Wedding Anniversary

To celebrate our fiftieth wedding anniversary, we stayed overnight at the Netherlands Hilton Hotel in Cincinnati and dined at their famous Orchid Room. On May 4 we boarded the American Queen, a paddle-wheel boat, for a cruise down the Ohio River and the Mississippi River to Louisville to view the running of the Kentucky Derby. A bus dropped us off near the gate. I had bought expensive bleacher seats near the final turn. But when the horses came racing by everyone stood, so that Kimi, who is short, could not see a thing. The horse that was leading did not win the race.

Among the most interesting sights were the elaborate hats worn by many women. I had a hard time finding non-alcoholic drinks. As I was leaving the men's bathroom a well-dressed woman appeared. I told her "This is the men's room." She replied, "I know but I have to pee!" She had evidently had a lot of mint juleps and the women's line to their bathroom was evidently too long as is usually the case. On our way back we stopped at Madison, Indiana, famed as the site of speed boat races.

We were pleasantly surprised to receive a certificate from the Ohio House of Representatives celebrating our golden wedding anniversary! This had been arranged by Tim Derickson, a representative of the House, who is a member of our church.

Paul L. Maier

In March Paul L. Maier spoke on "Josephus and the New Testament" in my Annual History Lecture series. Josephus was an important first-century Jewish historian, who wrote about John the Baptist and Jesus and who chronicled the Jewish Revolt that resulted in the Roman destruction of the Temple in AD 70. Paul is the son of Walter Maier, famed preacher of the radio program, the Lutheran Hour. He studied Reformation History under Karl Barth and the New Testament under Oscar Cullmann at the University of Basel. He taught Ancient History at Western Michigan University. He has produced illustrated translations of Josephus and of Eusebius, which I used as texts for my classes. He is also an author of bestselling historical fiction. In *The Constantinian Codex*, which is a Christian response to Dan Brown's *DaVinci Code*, Maier inserts in this text contemporary figures such as New Testament textual authority Daniel Wallace and Edwin Yamauchi (of Oxford).

Figure 65. With Paul Maier

A Week in Switzerland

My sister Alicia, her husband Heinz, and their daughter Sabine had moved to Switzerland in 2006. They lived in Sigriswill, a village on the northern shore of Lake Thun. Kimi and I had spent three days visiting them in2007. I planned to spend a week with them in August.

On July 31 I flew from Cincinnati to Charlotte on US Airways, and then from Charlotte to Munich on Lufthansa. I then flew from Munich to Zurich on Swiss Air. On August 1, Alicia and I were able to stay overnight in her friend's apartment in the suburbs of Zurich. As I had only three to four hours of fitful sleep on the Trans-Atlantic flight, I needed a two-hour nap. Alicia and I then took a bus and then a tram to the Bahnhof (train station).

Zurich is Switzerland's largest city and a transportation center, which is renowned for its banks. We walked along the Limmat River and viewed St. Peter's Church, and the Gross Münster, where Ulrich Zwingli preached and began the Swiss Reformation in 1519. After supper we attended an organ concert at the Frauen Münster, where the organist played Rossini's *William Tell Overture*, as well as music by Richard Strauss on a magnificent organ with nearly 6,000 pipes. This church has colorful stained-glass windows created by the famed French Jewish artist, Marc Chagall.

On August 2 we returned to the Gross Münster, where I viewed a most informative historical exhibit (in German) in the cloister, which narrated the key role played by Zwingli and his influential successor, Heinrich Bullinger. I then climbed the 190 steps of one of the twin steeples for a magnificent view of the city and Lake Zurich. We then visited the Swiss National Museum, which is near the Bahnhof. We took the train to Bern, then another train to Thun, and then the bus to Sigriswil.

I had bought a Swiss Flexi-Pass for 54 Swiss francs. As Switzerland is not part of the European Union it does not use the euro. The Swiss franc was equivalent to the American dollar. This pass not only gave me free rail for five days, but also free bus and boat rides, and also free access to all museums!

On August 3 Alicia and I spent the day in Bern, where she works in a consulting firm. The city is the capital of Switzerland and is famed for its arcaded shops and colorful fountains. By the river we saw an enclosure with four bears, which are the iconic animal of the city. I climbed the 230 steps of the cathedral's steeple for a panoramic view of the city. It was at Bern, where he worked in the Patent Office, that Albert Einstein formulated his theory of Special Relativity in 1905 and his famous formula $E = mc^2$ in 1907. I spent two hours following an audio tour of Einstein's life in the Historical Museum. Back at Sigriswil, I was introduced to the Swiss dish of raclette cheese, which is heated in a special device.

On August 4 the weather was especially sunny, which is why Heinz carefully planned my trip on this day to Interlaken. As he anticipated freezing weather at Kleine Scheidegg (elevation 6762 feet), he provided me with a heavy jacket in a bulky backpack. I wore a flannel shirt and a suit, all of which proved unnecessary as the temperature was about 60 degrees at the site!

I boarded a ship at Gunten, below Sigriswil, and took a very pleasant two-hour boat ride to Interlaken West. As I walked to Interlaken East, I was treated to the sight of parasail gliders who were landing on a park after leaping from a high cliff. I took the blue train up to Lauterbrunnen (2612 ft.), and then transferred to the green train which made the steep winding ascent to Kleine Scheidegg, where I had a breathtaking view of the three famous mountains: the Jungfrau (Virgin), the Mönch (Monk), and the Eiger (Ogre), towering respectively 13,642 ft., 13,475 ft., and 13,026 ft. The latter was made famous by the movie, *The Eiger Sanction*, which was filmed on location with Clint Eastwood performing all the mountain climbing scenes himself.

That evening, Heinz and Alicia met me at Interlaken East, and Sabine and I attended the rousing patriotic pageant of Friedrich Schiller's (1802) play, relating the tale of William Tell (in German), complete with a large cast of actors, some mounted on horses. It reprised the legendary tale of the (thirteenth-century) crossbowman who was compelled to shoot an apple off the head of his son by an Austrian official. This led to the sealing of a compact by three men near Lucerne in 1291 that eventually produced the united Swiss confederation of separate cantons, an event celebrated on August 1.

On August 5 Alicia and I traveled north from Thun to Bern, then to Basel by train. Basel has over thirty museums. I saw the special exhibit on Renoir at the main art museum. We also saw a small Jewish museum. In the plaza before the colorful Rathaus (Town Hall), young children frolicked as oscillating jets of water shot in the air. We crossed and recrossed the Rhine River in a small wooden boat, which was propelled by a wire connected to an electrical wire overhead festooned with the banners of the twenty-six cantons of the nation.

As I had written an article on Erasmus's contributions to New Testament scholarship, I was very interested in seeing the cathedral where Erasmus is buried. Erasmus was the Dutch humanist who published the first printed Greek New Testament in 1516, which greatly influenced Martin Luther to begin the Reformation in 1517.

On August 6 we traveled by train toward Lucerne, but then had to take a bus because of construction through the Emmental region, famed for its cheese. This was the ancestral home of Ben Roethlisberger, Miami's former quarterback who has won two Super Bowls with the Pittsburgh Steelers. The Swiss of the region are aware of Ben's exploits, as he has visited this area.

Lucerne is one of the most popular tourist sites in the country. Large groups of Chinese tourists were in evidence. I walked across the famed wooden Kapelbrücke (Chapel Bridge), and then took an hour and a half boat ride. What impressed me most were the abundant swans on the river. Unfortunately rain soon obscured any view. I went inside into the boat's café and ordered the cheapest item on the menu, carrot soup for

10.5 Swiss francs. What was the shocker was the bill for the water which was 6.5 francs! I went to view the famous carved lion that commemorates the fate of the hundreds of Swiss mercenary guards who died protecting the French king in 1792. Nearby was a large circular auditorium that presented a multimedia story, including contemporary paintings, of the debacle of the French army led by General Bourbaki, crushed by the Prussians in 1871. About 70,000 French soldiers fled into northern Switzerland, where they were disarmed and interned briefly before being repatriated. This was the first major operation of the Red Cross, which was founded in Geneva by Henry Durant in 1863.

On August 7 I ascended the tower of the well-preserved castle at Thun, which has an informative historical display, listing many famous visitors to the city, including Brahms, Mendelsohn, Matthew Arnold, and Napoleon III. The museum also highlighted the role of soldiers from Thun, who helped to defeat the invading Burgundians from France at the nearby site of Murten in 1476. Jakob Amman, the founder of the Amish movement, was born near Thun. His followers were imprisoned in this castle, but they were not noted in the display.

Later that day Alicia drove me to Zurich, where we stayed in her friend's apartment. We ate at a Japanese restaurant in the city. Prices were quite high. She had six sushi with *sashimi* (raw fish) for thirty-seven francs; I had two slices of *unagi* (eel) with rice for twenty-six francs.

On August 8 we woke up at 4 a.m., as we had to leave at 4:30 a.m. for the 7 a.m. flight from Zurich. I flew on Swiss Air to Munich, arriving at 8 a.m. and then left on a Lufthansa for the nine-hour flight to Toronto. I was originally scheduled to have a three-hour layover in Toronto, but this was reduced to two hours by a delay in Munich. Unlike my outbound trip where my suitcase was checked all the way to Zurich, for some reason my suitcase was checked only to Toronto and not to Cincinnati. Therein lay a huge problem. I was directed with all the other travelers to go up to section F upstairs to pick up my suitcase, and to check it through US customs. After waiting in vain for a half hour for my suitcase to appear on the carousel, I approached an agent who told me to go downstairs and go through Canadian customs. I went downstairs with another traveler, who seemed to have a similar problem. She was turned back and went upstairs, so I followed her. She did finally find her suitcase on the carousel. I, however, was told again to go downstairs and find my suitcase on Carousel 7. When I did so, I could not find it. It had come on Carousel 10. My Cincinnati flight had been delayed from 4 p.m. to 5:30 p.m., but it was 5:45 by the time I found my suitcase. I was then told to go up to the Air Canada desk with my suitcase to see if there was another later flight. But there was none. With the exception of four to five hours of fitful sleep on the Transatlantic flight, I had now been up for nearly twenty-four hours. I was grateful that Air Canada gave me a voucher for an overnight hotel stay and a meal. On August 9 I was able to catch an 8 a.m. Air Canada flight to Cincinnati,

In conclusion, I felt that I had lived one of Rick Steves's travel adventures. The coordination and precise timing of all modes of transportation in Switzerland enabled Alicia to plan our trips with a minimum of waiting. This also meant that I was forever two steps behind as she hurried to catch buses, trams, and trains. In the process of walking and climbing four to six hours per day, I lost three pounds, which I quickly regained once back in the US.

The NEAS

The annual meeting of the NEAS (Near East Archaeological Society) takes place with the ETS (Evangelical Theological Society) conference in November. When I arrived at the hotel in Milwaukee, I had somehow failed to make a reservation and was directed to another hotel across the river. Just at this time quite providentially my friend Dick Pierard appeared and offered to share his room with me.

The NEAS is an evangelical society of scholars involved in biblical archaeology, which was formed in 1958 by three Wheaton College professors, Joseph P. Free, Samuel Schultz, and Robert Cooley. Sam Schultz was an Old Testament scholar, and Bob Cooley was an archaeologist. Joe Free, whose PhD was in French Literature, purchased the tell of Dothan in Israel and dug there. The site is associated with the story of Joseph (Genesis 37:17).

As the president of the NEAS, I organized a special session to highlight the contributions of Wheaton College. Alfred Hoerth, the longtime professor at the college who had inspired many students to pursue archaeology and who had hosted annual conferences on archaeology at Wheaton, spoke on "Wheaton College's Contribution to Biblical Archaeology: From Joseph P. Free to the Present." Daniel M. Master, my MA student who had earned his PhD at Harvard, spoke on "Recent Excavations at the Leon Levy Expedition to Ashkelon." John Monson, who likewise earned his PhD. at Harvard, spoke on "A Legacy of Integration in an Age of Specialization." Tom Davis, who earned his PhD at the University of Arizona, spoke on "Biblical Archaeology from Albright to Dever: The Collapse of the Paradigm." Darlene Brooks Hedstrom, my doctoral student, spoke on "Transgressing Early Monastic Narratives: The Revision of Monastic Archaeology in Egypt."

Chapter 34

The Year 2013

The Family

BRIAN DEVELOPED ADVANCED TECHNOLOGY for iRobot's home robots. He contributed a chapter, "Beyond Rosey: Consumer Robots in the Twenty-First Century," to *Autonomous Technologies: Applications that Matter*, published by the Society of Automotive Engineers. He also sold a short story "Fall Forever" to the online magazine *Daily Science Fiction*.

Haruko and Denis both earned master's degrees; hers in library and information science, his in education. They both began working in new positions in the fall: Haruko as a reference and instruction librarian at the Hostos Community College in the South Bronx; Denis as a math teacher at Community Roots Middle School in Brooklyn.

Ten Days in Paradise

Mark Twain, who visited Hawaii in 1866, described the islands as "the loveliest fleet anchored in the Seven Seas." With azure skies, lush tropical vegetation, sandy beaches, and balmy trade winds, they do seem like a "paradise." Temperatures are generally in the 70s. Those in Ohio would not be sympathetic with Islanders who complained of the cold when the temperature there dipped into the 60s! On the other hand, gasoline costs $4 a gallon, but you cannot travel very far. It takes about 3 hours to go around Oahu and about 6 hours to go around the Big Island. The median price for houses and condominiums was $300,000.

Kimi and I had been going back to the Islands about every five years, most recently in 2011. But then my uncle Tom Owan offered us a week free at his time share apartment between the Ala Wai Canal and Kalakaua Avenue in Waikiki. I also had a free Delta Companion ticket for Kimi's travel to and from Los Angeles.

So on Saturday, January 5 we flew to LA and spent a couple of days there. We stayed in a motel in Fullerton, and I did some research at the library of Talbot School of Theology in nearby La Mirada. We had supper at a Mexican restaurant with our good friends George and Joan Giacumakis.

On Sunday, January 6 we went to the 9:30 a.m. service at the Evangelical Free Church in Fullerton, where we heard Mike Erre preach a powerful sermon. Mike was the first youth leader at the Oxford Bible Fellowship. He succeeded Dale Burke, OBF's first pastor, who in turn had succeeded Chuck Swindoll. We were impressed with the full church, and its vast campus with many buildings and activities. We were greeted warmly by Mike afterward. That afternoon we walked on the star-studded Hollywood Boulevard and saw familiar names including Billy Graham's. We went to the Hollywood Wax Museum, where we encountered such figures as Tom Hanks and Lucille Ball.

On Monday, January 7 we left LA at 3 p.m. and arrived at Honolulu at 7 p.m., with a two-hour time change. On Tuesday Tom took us out to the local McDonalds, which served a breakfast menu with rice and spam. He explained that the affection for spam in the Islands was created when after World War II the army, which had tons of leftover spam in their warehouses, distributed cans of them free to the Islanders.

On Wednesday, January 9 we picked up Kimi's sisters Helen Oh and Ellen Eshima and had lunch with them at a Japanese restaurant. Ellen was a world traveler, who had visited more than a hundred countries! Intrigued by the Hawaii Five O series on television that depicts the building behind the iconic King Kamehameha statue as the squad's headquarters, we ventured into the building, only to discover that it was an old courthouse. It contained a fascinating display of the evolution of law in Hawaii, from its days as a kingdom to the period after the United States, at the instigation of white sugar planters, overthrew the monarchy in 1898 and established Hawaii as a Republic.

On Thursday, January 10 we went toward Koko Head and located the Spitting Cave. I descended a steep path at the dead end of a residential street to gain access to this little-known site at the edge of eroded cliffs. Most tourists stop at the nearby site of Blow Hole, where the incoming waves shoot a spray of water upward. We enjoyed the dolphin show at the Sea Life Park in nearby Waimanalo. I then hiked part way up the Botanical Garden on the slopes of Koko Head, which like Diamond Head, is an extinct volcanic crater, to view some colorful Bougainvillea flowers.

On Friday, January 11 Tom drove us to Kaneohe, where we were pleasantly surprised that my aunt Beryl, who had been afflicted with cancer, was well enough to come with her husband Albert to join us for lunch at a Chop Suey House. Tom then drove us to his old home in Kahuku in the northern end of Oahu to show us where the family store had been. There was a brand-new Buddhist temple that was for sale, as there were no more Japanese in Kahuku!

Tom then took us to Sunset Beach, the scene of the international surfboarding contests, though the surf this day seemed pretty calm. At Haleiwa he treated us to the famous "shave ice" that President Barack Obama has helped to popularize. It is crushed particles of ice with added flavors.

On Saturday, January 12, we drove out to Waipahu to the Sugar Plantation Museum, which has preserved restored houses for each of the ethnic plantation groups, the Chinese, Japanese, Okinawans, Koreans, and Filipinos. Our guide stressed that Hawaii was not a melting pot, but a multiethnic society, with each group retaining its own traditions and contributing some to the whole. For example, as the Japanese took off their shoes before entering a home, most people in Hawaii do the same. The Korean practice of lavish parties for their babies' first birthday has also caught on.

We then went to Kapolei to have lunch with Joe and Barbara Grimes, Wycliffe Bible Translators, whom I had first met at the Summer Institute of Linguistics at Norman, Oklahoma in 1960. They were translating the New Testament into Hawaiian Pidgin English.

I went to see the bird sanctuary at the remote Kapena Point, the westernmost part of Oahu. While Kimi waited in the parking lot, I had to walk over a rocky rutted road for an hour to reach the sanctuary. It was a bit of a disappointment as I saw only one albatross nesting and three others walking. I had also taken my binoculars as whales have been known to emerge at the point, but I saw none during the ten minutes I spent there. A service couple in a four-wheel drive vehicle gave me a lift halfway back. They had stayed longer and seen a dozen birds and a dozen whales!

We then had supper with Nobu and Myrneth Ayabe and Kay Curtis at the Mililani Shopping Center. Kimi had known Nobu at Fort Wayne Bible College and I had known him at Columbia Bible College. Kay was the ninety-year-old widow of Claude Curtis, who had gone the year before with her son Philip to bring Bibles to China.

On Sunday, January 13 Tom went with us to attend the service at Makiki Christian Church, which is the home church for both Kimi and her sister Ellen. Kimi was happy to see many of her friends, including June Fujimoto, who was in our wedding, and Milly Kiyuna, a missionary who hosted me when I visited Okinawa in 2008.

I was able to purchase a seat on a small submarine leaving the Hilton Dock at 3 p.m. The voyage on a boat for a mile to the sub yielded a grand view of Diamond Head and the row of hotels lining Waikiki Beach. The sub had about fifty passengers, including many Asian tourists. It descended to a depth of about one hundred feet to hover just above the beach floor and some deliberately sunken wrecks of planes and ships designed to serve as a base for new coral growth. During the 45-minute trip we saw only about five species of fish and that only for about ten minutes.

On Monday, January 14 we took a Hawaiian Air Lines flight for the hour flight to Hilo on the eastern side of the Big Island where I was born in 1937. As it is a wet area, tourists prefer the western or leeward side of the island in Kona. We stayed at a motel on Banyan Drive where gigantic banyan trees are identified with bronze plaques listing those who planted them, including Cecil B. Demille, Franklin D. Roosevelt, and Harry Truman, during the period from 1934 to 1938. We then had supper with Kimi's youngest sister, Janet at a nearby Japanese Restaurant.

On Tuesday, January 15 Janet drove us to the Meishin Buddhist columbarium, where the ashes of Kimi's parents had been placed. Janet then took us to the nursing home, where Kimi's oldest sister, Miyoko, now 90, resided. When she saw Kimi, she spoke in a loud, excited voice but it was difficult to understand what she was saying.

We left at 10 a.m. on Highway 11 south to Naalehu, Kimi's home in the Kau or southern section of the Big Island. She looked for the plantation store where her dad had worked but it had long disappeared. We then drove to South Point, the most southern site in the US. Fish abound in the seas at the base of the cliff. We saw firemen's trucks here. We only learned later that they were there to search for the body of a fisherman who had drowned the day before.

On Wednesday, January 16 while Kimi stayed at the motel, I headed up the Saddle Road between Mauna Loa and Mauna Kea (13,796 ft.), which appeared surprisingly easy on the ascent, with two lanes of cars speeding at 55 mph westbound, and one lane east bound. Before the road was improved, rental cars were not allowed to drive on the unpaved road. The road crests at 6,578 ft. The summit of Mauna Kea with its famed observatories was clearly visible above the level of the clouds. The western descent followed a winding, roller coaster road through many one-lane bridges down to Kamuela, the center of the famous Parker Ranch. At 225,000 acres it was at one time the largest privately held cattle ranch in the US.[1] After a drive through a forest of tall trees, I reached the Hamakua coast road and just before Hilo turned up toward Honomu, the site of the awesome 420-foot Akaka Falls.

We flew at 5 p.m. to Honolulu and then boarded a Delta overnight flight to LA. After a seven-hour layover, we flew to Cincinnati to arrive on Thursday evening, January 17.

Back in Oxford

I replaced Kimi as a driver for Meals on Wheels on Mondays. I had also joined her in singing with the senior Songbirds. In February our group sang the national anthem at the Miami women's basketball game. Also in February, we attended Miami's Hall of Fame banquet, where Ben Roethlisberger was honored as the Pittsburgh Steelers quarterback who had led the team to three Super Bowls, winning two of them. Last year's winner, the Baltimore Ravens, was coached by another former Miami player, John Harbaugh.

---

1. Long-horned cattle were first brought to Hawaii as a gift to King Kamehameha I by the British captain George Vancouver in 1793. John P. Parker, who was born in 1790 in Newton, Massachusetts, came to the Islands in 1815. He was befriended by the king and married his granddaughter. Through royal favor Parker was able to acquire a massive amount of land near the town of Waimea on the slopes of Mauna Kea. By the late 1800s the Parker Ranch had an estimated herd of 25,000 head of cattle. See David Wolman and Julian Smith, *Aloha Rodeo* (New York, New York: Harper Collins, 2019), 121.

William Lane Craig

In March William Lane Craig spoke on "Theism, Atheism and the Big Bang" in my Annual History Lecture series. Craig, a graduate of Wheaton College and Trinity Evangelical Divinity School, earned a PhD at the University of Birmingham and a D'Theol at the University of Munich. He has written a scholarly defense of the historicity of Christ's resurrection and has served as president of the Evangelical Philosophical Society. He is also a popular speaker at universities and has debated notable atheists such as Antony Flew and Christopher Hitchens.

Figure 66. With William Lane Craig

Lectures

In April, I gave lectures on "Archaeology and the Old Testament" at Northwest Oklahoma State University at Alva. This was in the remote area of the Oklahoma panhandle that had been Cherokee territory. At Oklahoma City I was able to have lunch with my former graduate student Jenny Rempel, who was working at the city's library. A few weeks later a devastating tornado hit Moore, a southern suburb of Oklahoma City.

In October, I gave a lecture on "Archaeology and the Old Testament" at Colorado Springs in connection with the "Passages Exhibition" of select objects from the Green Collection. One of the organizations that cosponsored my lecture, which was devoted to a ministry to unwed mothers, was headed by Dr. Diane Foley. I was pleasantly surprised that her parents Dr. and Mrs. James Blackburn were present. Jim had been a neighbor and a history doctoral student, who had later served for many years as an administrator of Marion College, which became Indiana Wesleyan University. While in Colorado Springs I was given a tour of the Navigators headquarters.

In November, I was asked to speak on behalf of the History Department at the memorial service at the Oxford Presbyterian Church for Dr. Richard Jellison, the longtime chair of the department. Jim Blackburn, as one of Dick's doctoral students. also shared memories of his mentor.

Conferences

From November 18 to 25, I attended multiple conferences in Baltimore (ETS, NEAS, IBR, SBL). As the outgoing president of the NEAS, I had arranged for the speakers at two sessions. One session honored the late Reuben Bullard of Cincinnati Christian University, who had been the first geologist to work at an excavation. Reuben had contributed a chapter on "The Berbers of the Maghreb and Ancient Carthage" to a book I had edited, *Africa and Africans in Antiquity*. A number of his students came to pursue doctoral studies with me. Those who spoke at this session included Adam Chambers, Daniel Hoffman, and Robert Smith. John Wineland became ill, and his place was taken by David Avila of John Brown University, the director of the Abila excavations in Jordan.

For the other session, I had invited Ed Cook, chair of the Semitics Department at the Catholic University of America,[2] Theodore Lewis, who had served as the chair of the Department of Near Eastern Studies at Johns Hopkins University, and Rami Arav from the University of Nebraska at Omaha, who had been excavating at the site he believed to be Bethsaida, the home of Peter, on the northern shore of the Sea of Galilee.

I was invited to present a lecture on "Unexpected Insights into the Biblical Texts" gained from my research on a dictionary of daily life at a breakfast sponsored by Tyndale House in Cambridge for about 150 scholars.

---

2. Ed Cook, a graduate of Fuller Theological Seminary, received his PhD from UCLA. He labored from 1988 to 1997 in a basement office of the Klau Library at Hebrew Union College on the Comprehensive Aramaic Lexicon Project edited by Professor Stephen Kaufman. When the funding ran out, Cook was out of academia for about a decade, but he kept publishing and became a leading authority on the Aramaic texts from Qumran. I was happy to review his manuscript on *Solving the Mystery of the Dead Sea Scrolls* and to recommend its publication by Zondervan. I also served as an outside evaluator for his tenure review at the Catholic University of America in 2012.

Chapter 35

The Year 2014

The Family

BRIAN MOVED INTO A new apartment in a high-rise building in Boston's Back Bay area. When we visited Boston, he took us around iRobot's headquarters in Bedford on the western outskirts of Boston's 128 loop. He showed us the company's museum which displayed various robots including some he had helped to develop. He had been working on future domestic projects such as an autonomous lawnmower.

Haruko served as a teaching librarian at the Eugenio Maria de Hostos Community College in a largely Puerto Rican neighborhood of the South Bronx. She helped students develop critical thinking habits and research skills. Denis taught math at a community charter school in Brooklyn. Attempting to integrate students with special needs among mainstream students proved to be challenging.

During the July Fourth weekend on a visit to Ohio, Haruko and Denis joined us in going to the centennial celebration of Darrtown, a small village south of Oxford. It is such a small community that the town has no stop lights or even a stop sign. It does have a very famous native son, Walter Alston. "Smokey," as he was known, was a graduate of Miami University who became the celebrated manager of the LA Dodgers from 1954 to 1976. He won seven National League titles and four World Series. He was named Manager of the Year six times. During the off season he returned from LA to his home in Darrtown.

Marvin R. Wilson

In March, Marvin R. Wilson, professor of Old Testament at Gordon College, spoke on "Our Father Abraham" in my Annual History Lecture series. This was the subject of his award-winning book emphasizing the Jewish background of Christianity. I had used this as a textbook for my senior seminar on Judaism and Early Christianity. Marv, a graduate of Wheaton College and Gordon-Conwell Theological Seminary, was a fellow grad student with me in the Mediterranean Studies Department of Brandeis University. Marv had invited me to speak both at Barrington College and Gordon College.

Marv became the foremost evangelical scholar in promoting dialogue with Jewish scholars. With Jewish funding Marv produced the television documentary "Jews and Christians: A Journey of Faith." Marv with his Jewish friends promoted the visit of Christians to synagogue services and of Jews to church services. His lecture was cosponsored not only by churches and Christian ministries but also by the Jewish Hillel Foundation

InterVarsity Christian Fellowship

In October, I was invited to address the national board of trustees of I.V.C.F. which was meeting at the University of Cincinnati. Dr. Santa Ono, the new president of UC, is a member of this board. Also among the trustees present was noted economics professor, Kenneth Elzinga, who had been my host when I spoke at the University of Virginia. Barney Ford, the first IV staff at Miami University eventually became one of IV's vice-presidents. His successor at Miami, Kent Stephens, became a trustee. Barney also served as the president of the International Fellowship of Evangelical Students. Kent later became the vice-president of IFES. Another Miami alumnus who served on IV's national board was Bill Gates, no not the billionaire, but the president of an auto dealership in South Bend.

Conferences

In November, I went to a series of conferences in San Diego. I was picked up by Ben Connaroe, an alumnus of Miami, who was working in a ministry to imprisoned servicemen. We ate dinner at a Mexican restaurant in the Old Town of the city. I also saw Brandon Walker, my MA student, who had earned a PhD in New Testament from the University of Nottingham, after serving as a missionary in Mozambique.

For the NEAS, I arranged a session that featured Ian Jones (University of California at San Diego) reporting on the tenth c. BC copper mines that Thomas Levy had discovered in the Aravah Valley of Jordan. Jeffrey Morrow, my former student who was a professor at Seton Hall University, read a paper on the background in Semitic studies of Alfred Loisy, noted Catholic modernist. Scott Bartchy (UCLA) spoke on Roman slavery. Rami Arav (University of Nebraska at Omaha) discussed the controversial Talpioth ossuaries that Jewish TV director Simcha Jacobovici had claimed were from the tomb of Jesus and his wife Mary.

After the conference, I flew to Fresno in an attempt to see my cousin Wayne Owan, who was in prison in nearby Corcoran for life without parole for a double murder. We had been corresponding, and he had accepted Christ as his savior. When I showed up, I was denied entry because I had missed a deadline in my application. I was able to spend a few days in a cabin at the nearby Yosemite National Park that our family had visited many years before.

Publications

In July, I received an unexpected visit from Yutaka Nomachi, who had translated into Japanese my book *The New Testament Cities in Western Asia Minor*. Nomachi-san worked for a travel agent and used my book as he guided tours of western Turkey. I also received the Korean translation of *Peoples of the Old Testament World*, which I had coedited with Alfred Hoerth and Gerald Mattingly. I learned that in Korea in 2013 this translation had gained the Best Book of the Year Award.

Academics and Athletics

Miami University earned the dubious distinction of being rated the most expensive public university in the United States. On the other hand, as our students arrived with many advanced credits, most graduated in less than four years. Of the incoming freshmen 40 percent ranked in the top 10 percent of their senior classes. The *US News & World Report* ranked Miami University only behind Princeton and Dartmouth in its dedication to teaching undergraduates. With 38 percent of its students participating, Miami University was ranked second in its study abroad programs. The town of Oxford was ranked the third best college town in the United States by Livability.com.

Alumnus John Harbaugh, the coach of the Baltimore Ravens, last year's Super Bowl champions, had his statue installed in Yager stadium's "Cradle of Coaches" courtyard. His statue joined those of Earl Blaik, Paul Brown, Carmen Cozza, Paul Dietzel, Ara Parseghian, Weeb Ewbank, and Bo Schembechler.[1] Ben Roethlisberger of the Steelers became the first NFL quarterback to throw for six touchdowns in two successive games!

---

1. See Excursus J "The Cradle of Coaches."

Chapter 36

New England

The Year 2015

The Family

FOR THE LAST THREE years, Brian worked with a team to develop iRobot's first autonomous lawnmower. On my visit to Boston in October I had dinner with Brian and his friend from high school Kyle Killian and his wife Anna Aganthangelou and their two sons. Kyle is a psychology professor for Capella University. Anna, who came from Cyprus, had been one of my students. She was a political science professor with a research grant from Harvard University.

Haruko continued to commute an hour and a half each way to get to the Hosios Community College in the South Bronx, where she served as a teaching librarian. Denis took up a new position as a teacher and part-time administrator at the Discovery Charter School in Newark. Denis and Haruko were delighted to be able to purchase their own home in Jersey City which even had a garden. In their visits to Oxford, they both enjoyed sitting under a tree in our backyard. In visiting Jersey City I discovered why. There were no trees that I could see in that urban environment!

As early as 2009, I had noticed that Kimi was having problems with her short-term memory. At the insistence of our children, I had her undergo a battery of tests from both a memory specialist and a psychiatrist. They both concluded that she had a moderate dementia of an Alzheimer type. Happily, the loss of short-term memory is her only symptom so far. I bought her a new dishwasher, a new television set, and a new recliner.

For myself, I bought a new Ford Fusion, which Brian recommended for its safety features. There was a single Fusion available on sale at Northgate Ford. Its most important feature is a rear-view television monitor. My last three accidents were backing into other cars that I did not see. It also has warning sensors on either side when I back out of our garage. When I swerve out of line on the highway, it chimes and displays a coffee cup, suggesting that I need to take break!

Alan Ullman

Charlotte Goldy, the chair of the History Department, informed me that a former student, Alan Ullman (class of 1980), had designated an estate gift to the department for a scholarship in my name with a special preference for those majoring in ancient history. According to the university's press release:

> "Professor Yamauchi was amazing in his ability to bring to life events and people from thousands of years ago," Ullman remembered. "He taught me to do more, read more, research more, and I still love history to this day. I've never had a professor who inspired me as much as he did."
>
> A Cincinnati native who felt drawn to history as a boy browsing the family's encyclopedia set, Ullman first met Yamauchi in a freshman-year western civilization course. The two clicked immediately, and Ullman took every undergraduate course Yamauchi offered over the next four years. In the end, though, Yamauchi's candor steered Ullman away from a career in history.
>
> Alan first became a successful lawyer, and then after a life-threatening illness became a nurse practitioner. He formed a consulting service that combined his legal and medical backgrounds.

I arranged for my wife and I to have lunch with Alan and his wife Marjorie at the Montgomery Inn, which was famous for its ribs that Bob Hope loved to eat when he came to Cincinnati. During the course of our conversation, Alan remembered that I had attended a church in Oxford. When I asked him what church he had attended, Alan revealed that he and his wife were Jewish. Later Alan wrote me a gracious letter in which he wrote: "I have met many notable and successful people over the years who were foremost in their respective fields. Your humility and quiet confidence has always resonated with me as a role model for how a successful individual should carry himself. Thank you for lunch and more so for the books which I will always treasure."

Daniel Wallace

In March, Daniel Wallace of Dallas Theological Seminary spoke on "The Greek New Testament Text" in my Annual History Lecture series. Wallace is the founder of the Center for the Study of the New Testament Manuscripts. His aim is to photograph all the available manuscripts of the Greek New Testament. Just before he came to Oxford, he had been busy photographing ten thousand pages in the libraries and monasteries of Greece, at times in trying circumstances without air condition. Like Bruce Metzger of Princeton Theological Seminary, Wallace believes in the essential trustworthiness of the Greek manuscript traditions. He has debated Bart Ehrman of the University of North Carolina, a student of Metzger's, who has emphasized the corruption of the copying of New Testament manuscripts.

Figure 67. With Daniel Wallace

A Week in New England

I planned to spend a week (October 4 to 10) in New England to see the editor at Hendrickson Publishers in Peabody, Massachusetts, to visit various friends, and to view the fall foliage. Kimi, who developed back pains, decided not to go on the trip.

When I arrived in Boston on Sunday at 6:30 p.m. it was already dark. My hotel in Peabody where I had stayed before was just an hour away, north on Route 1. After renting a car I made the mistake of trusting my Garmin GPS, which must have been led astray by my entering a tunnel. I found myself on Storrow Drive headed west instead of north! I stopped at a coffee shop where a policeman gave me simple directions to get on Route 1 north. But as I traveled north on the right lane, I was forced to turn off the route into a dimly lit neighborhood. After some trouble I found my way back on Route 1 and arrived at the hotel at 10:30 p.m.!

On Monday Marvin Wilson and I met with Jonathan Kline of Hendrickson (for details see chapter 43) about our dictionary project. I then stopped by at Newburyport, Massachusetts, where I photographed the Old South Church, where George Whitefield, the famous British evangelist is buried. I once had the privilege of speaking there. I then viewed the seaport of Portsmouth, New Hampshire.

At Durham I had dinner with Greg and Mindy McMahon. Greg, a graduate of Kansas University, earned his MA in history from Miami in 1979, and his PhD.in Hittite from Chicago in 1988 under Harry Hoffner, a former Brandeis classmate. Greg had just returned from his excavation in Turkey. He was a history professor at the University of New Hampshire and the faculty advisor to IV. Mindy, who plays the harp, directed a choir at their church in Rye.

On Tuesday after leaving my motel in Concord, I drove north to Hanover in northern New Hampshire. Because of my poor eyesight I missed the name Hanover on a sign and drove past exit 13. Moreover, my Garmin indicated that I was on IS 89, when I was really on IS 91. I backtracked and was thirty minutes late for a lunch with Ryan and Jenny Bouton (and their 6 children) and Don Willeman, who had wanted to meet me. The Boutons were on the staff of Cru at Dartmouth College, an Ivy League school. Jenny is the daughter of Duane and Martha (a Miami University grad) Conrad, who have served as the head of Cru in Germany.

Don, a graduate of Bowling Green and Dallas Theological Seminary, is the pastor of a church in Hanover, which was the first and one of the most successful of the church plants sponsored by Wes Pastor's NETS organization. Meeting in a high school they had about 300 attending, half of them students from Dartmouth. Ryan and Don gave me a tour of Dartmouth, which was founded by Eleazar Wheelock, to evangelize and educate Indians.

On the way to Burlington, Vermont, I took a side trip to Stowe, where the Von Trapp family (featured in *The Sound of Music*) settled after coming to America. They chose Stowe because the setting reminded them of the Austrian mountainscape and developed a popular lodge there. Along the way I passed by the headquarters of Ben & Jerry's Ice Cream factory, but I did not have time to take a tour of their plant.

On Wednesday morning Heather Battig took me to the top of Mount Philo, where there was a panoramic view. The color of the foliage was not yet fully developed because of the warmer than usual weather. She also showed me the former school for autistic children that NETS hoped to purchase, if they could raise a million and a half dollars by June. In the afternoon, Mike Battig took me on a boat ride on Lake Champlain.

In the evening, I treated the Pastors, the Battigs, the Dykes, and Stuart Pratt[1] to a dinner in a restaurant near my motel. Wes Pastor, a grad of Ohio State University, came to Miami to teach accountancy. He served as an elder at our church. Wes spent four years at Dallas Theological Seminary but was not granted a degree there because he had come to reject dispensationalism. He then went on to Westminster Theological Seminary. His wife Sue is a nurse.

Wes had established a church to minister to the University of Vermont in Burlington and had invited to join him three Navigator couples he had mentored at Miami University: Mike and Heather Battig, Joel and Lisa Dyke, and Stuart and Kim Pratt. Mike taught computer science at St. Michael's, a Catholic college; and Heather had babysat our children. Lisa was a student in my history classes. Stuart is the son of Professors Bill and Anne Pratt, who faithfully attended the Bible studies I led for faculty.

On Thursday I drove south to Springfield, Massachusetts, stopping on the way to view Amherst College. In Springfield, I visited an interesting exhibit of Theodore Geisel (Dr. Seuss), who grew up there, and

---

1. Kim Pratt was away at a conference.

bought a copy of his posthumous book, *What Pet Shall I Get*. Next to my hotel was the NBA Hall of Fame.

On Friday my Garmin directed me via the scenic route to Lakeville in western Connecticut, where the Hotchkiss School is located. Jason Larson was teaching philosophy and religion there. Jason, a Gordon College graduate, earned his MA in History at Miami University in 1998. He then gained a PhD in Religion from Syracuse University. Jason, who is hearing impaired, is able to read lips.

Founded in 1891, the Hotchkiss School is an exclusive and expensive ($55,000 annual tuition) high school of six hundred students. Among its many distinguished alumni are: Pulitzer Prize winners (John Hershey, Archibald MacLeish, Tom Reiss), statesmen (Strobe Talbott, Paul Nitze), a commissioner of baseball (Fay Vincent), publishers (William Loeb, Henry Luce), industrialists (Edsel Ford, Henry Ford II), a director of the Metropolitan Museum of Art (Thomas Hoving), judges (Robert Bork, Potter Stuart), and governors (Lawrence Judd,[2] Ernest Gruening, William Scranton). MacKenzie Scott, a graduate, as the former wife of Jeff Bezos, is one of the wealthiest women in the world and a generous philanthropist.

Jason invited me to speak to his class of fifteen freshmen on the subject of the Crucifixion and Resurrection of Christ. Afterwards he emailed me as follows: "It was wonderful to see you again and to be in your classroom. The students really appreciated it as well, and several have spoken to me since then to ask if we might continue the discussion next week."

Taylor University

Later in October, Kimi and I were invited to attend the Hall of Fame weekend at Taylor University in Upland, Indiana. I had first heard the Gospel from a member of Taylor's Venture for Victory basketball squad in 1952. I was made an honorary member of that squad. Among the later members of the basketball team was Gary Friesen, the son of missionaries, who had earned his MA.in mathematics at Miami University. Gary and his wife Janet served at Faith Academy, a school for missionary children in Manila. We also met Steve Hoffmann, a professor of political sciences, who had been in the InterVarsity chapter at Rutgers

---

2. Lawrence Judd served as the governor of the Territory of Hawaii from 1929 to 1934.

University when I taught there and served as the IV advisor. Steve had served in the State Department in Iraq.

Conferences

In November I spent a week in Atlanta attending various conferences. I read a paper on "Education and the Age of Spouses in Antiquity" at a session of the Near Eastern Archaeology Society. I met former students Kirk MacGregor, Jeffrey Morrow, and Brandon Walker, all of whom had authored recent books. Other Miami alumni at the conference were Carl Smith, Dean of Ministry at the Southern University in Savannah, and Paul Gould, who was teaching Apologetics at Southwestern Theological Seminary in Fort Worth. Charley Warner, a Miami alumnus, who was ministering to Eastern European countries, introduced me to Gegham Bdoyan, who taught Old Testament at a seminary in Armenia. I donated books to his seminary library. I also had breakfast with Andy Rhodenbaugh from our church, who with his wife Reisha, was ministering to athletes in Atlanta. I attended a church at which Tolivar Wills, who had been with Athletes in Action at Miami University, served as pastor.

Figure 68. With Paul Gould

Chapter 37

The Year 2016

The Family

BRIAN CONTINUED WORK ON the robotic lawnmower. This project involved frequent trips to California to work with engineers there. He purchased a 2016 Corvette Stingray and enjoyed cruising around Boston with this new sports car. Brian also moved into a new apartment complex overlooking the Science Museum in Cambridge which had been designed by a Japanese architect.

At the Hostos Community College in the Bronx, Haruko became the library faculty's coordinator of teaching. As the vice-president of an association for New York City's college librarians, she led the planning of the group's annual symposium which addressed the issues of power and money among the city's libraries and archives. In the summer Haruko and Denis were able to take a trip to Montreal, where they met some of Denis's cousins. They went hiking and kayaking in a beautiful national park.

Kimi enjoyed going to church, attending our community group, and singing with the Songbirds at the Senior Center. She went to the gym with me once a week to walk around the indoor track but then developed pain in her right knee because of arthritis. The physical therapist prescribed exercises at home to resolve this problem.

I experienced myopic degeneration in the retina of my right eye. This means that I need a magnifying glass to read. I also experienced double vision when driving, at twilight, which meant that I should not drive when it is dark. Since 2014, I have also had a problem with my neck bent forward at a 25-degree angle. I believe that this was caused by my spending endless hours hunched forward reading to meet deadlines for a dictionary project. This has not been painful but is awkward, making it difficult to read signs at stores, at streets, and even at hotels. I consulted numerous specialists who ruled out an operation. The best solution offered was to do daily physical therapy exercises.

Santa J. Ono

In March Santa J. Ono, the president of the University of Cincinnati, spoke on "To Whom Much Has Been Given, Much Is Required" in my Annual History Lecture series. Miami University's president, David Hodge, attended the banquet before the lecture. When asked about his first name, Dr. Ono explained that it had nothing to do with "Santa Claus" but was taken from a Japanese popular figure "Santoro." Santa was born in Vancouver. His father Takashi Ono was a prominent mathematician from Japan who had been invited to the Institute for Advanced Studies at Princeton. According to a talk given to the Cincinnati chapter of the Japanese American Citizens League that my wife and I attended, growing up in Maryland, Santa and his family faced anti-Asian prejudice. Once someone fired a bullet through their kitchen window!

Santa felt inferior to his two talented brothers and became depressed as a freshman at the University of Chicago. Befriended by members of InterVarsity, he became a Christian.[1] He went on to do graduate work at McGill University, where he met his wife Wendy Yipp, a fellow cellist. He then had a distinguished career as a research scientist specializing in eye diseases at Harvard University and the University College in London.

Unlike older Japanese Americans like me, Santa is an extrovert and gregarious. He served as a popular provost at Emory University and then as the provost at the University of Cincinnati. When the president of UC, Gregory Williams suddenly resigned, without going through a national search Santa was named as his successor in 2012 so popular was he with students, faculty, and trustees alike. During his tenure at UC, he increased the university's student body, its faculty and research funding as well as its national standing. Later in 2016 he became the

---

1. I first met Santa Ono through Dennis Dudley, InterVarsity staff at Miami University, who knew Dr. Ono as he was on InterVarsity's national board of trustees.

president of the University of British Columbia in Vancouver, Canada's second largest university. In 2022 Santa Ono became the president of the University of Michigan.

Figure 69. With Santa Ono

Interviews

I was interviewed by Patrick Zukeran on "The Bible and Archaeology" for his apologetics program which was broadcast in Hawaii and in the Philippines. Patrick, a 1984 graduate of Iolani High School, is on the staff of Probe Ministries. I was also interviewed by Jeff Baxter of the Day of Discovery television series for a documentary on "Iran and the Bible," which was later translated into Farsi and broadcast into Iran.[2] Some years ago a graduate student in Tehran had informed me that my "famous book" *Persia and the Bible* was available in Iran in an (unauthorized) Farsi translation.

---

2. According to an email from Jeff Baxter (June 17, 2021): "The Iran in the Bible documentary has now been viewed on YouTube 2.6 million times since January 2020. It also has been broadcast via satellite in Turkish and in Arabic."

THE YEAR 2016

Blacks in the Bible

On Thursday, October 27 Denis Dudley took me to the Cincinnati airport. I flew into Boston for a conference on "Blacks in the Bible" at Boston University. I took a cab to the university campus and was lodged in the Hotel Commonwealth, a famous and very expensive hotel ($300 per day), which lacked amenities of cheaper hotels such as a fridge in the room, a gift store, or a restaurant. There was a nearby 7-Eleven store which was convenient. Access through a corridor and stairway did lead to a restaurant, which was very crowded. So, I ordered a most delicious and most expensive ($30) hamburger in my room!

On Friday the workshop "Blacks in the Bible" was convened by John Thornton, chair of the African American Studies at Boston University. John is the son of Elizabeth Thornton, who taught Latin at Miami University. I had sat in on one of her classes and chaired the committee which led to her promotion as full professor.

The first speaker was Jeremy Pope from the College of William and Mary. He spoke on the alleged "Rescue of Jerusalem" by Taharqo (biblical Tirhakah) from Sennacherib's invasion in 701 BC, an event that I discuss in my *Africa and the Bible*. Jeremy, who earned his PhD writing a dissertation on Taharqo at Johns Hopkins University, said that he assigned this book to his students. He was quite familiar with John Oakley, the chair of the Classics Department, who had been my student at Rutgers University. Jeremy was a dynamic speaker, which encouraged me to speak forcefully also.

My own Power Point presentation "Why the Ethiopian Eunuch Was Not from Ethiopia" was based on chapter 6 from *Africa and the Bible*. Through contacts made at this conference, I later learned that I was featured in over one hundred YouTube videos in Amharic, which denounced me because I denied the two great traditions of the Orthodox Ethiopian Church, that the Queen of Sheba (1 Kings 10) and the Ethiopian Eunuch (Acts 8) came from their country. The queen came from Yemen in southwest Arabia and the eunuch came from the Sudan.

In the afternoon, Wendy Belcher of Princeton University spoke on the *Kebra Nagast*, the legendary tale of the encounter between Solomon and the Queen of Sheba, which produced a son, Menelik from whom Ethiopian kings such as Haile Selassie have traced their ancestry. She expressed appreciation for my *Africa and the Bible* and was pleased to learn that I had read her *Honey from the Lion*, which is a fascinating account of the translation work of Mary Steele in Ghana, who was awarded the MBE by England for her fifty-plus years of labor. I loaned her book to Palma Daawin, a grad student in statistics from Ghana who attended our church. He and I later had breakfast with John and Rachel Schaeffer. The Schaeffers are graduates of John Brown University, where they studied English under Mark Fulk, a Miami PhD. John's parents and his brother have worked with Wycliffe in Ghana.

John Thornton spoke about the remarkable Beatriz Kimpa Vita, a Joan of Arc figure, who claimed that she was possessed by the spirit of St. Anthony. At the urging of Capuchin monks, she was burned at the stake in 1706 in the kingdom of the Kongo (Angola).

Steve Vinson of Indiana University related how the ancient Egyptian tale of Setneh with hidden magical powers in a box guarded by a serpent and by a voluptuous ghost inspired countless successors in novels, including African American literature.

The audience for the morning session was sparse, perhaps twenty, in a room that could have held one hundred; the afternoon audience was even smaller. But what it lacked in quantity, it made up in quality. Among those whom I had invited were: 1) Ben Thomas, director of the Archaeological Institute of America, which is housed at Boston University. His wife, Kim Berry, is one of my daughter's best friends from Oxford. 2) Susan Doll, who was one of my students at Miami. She received her PhD in Egyptology at Brandeis University specializing in Kushite history (700 to 400 BC). Susan worked at Boston's Museum of Fine Arts. 3) She invited her former Brandeis classmate, Janice Yellin, who teaches at Babson College, and is the authority on Meroitic pyramids. Janice was able to confirm that my proposed candidates for the Candace of Acts 8 are possible. 4) Rita Freed, the curator of Egyptian Art at the Museum of Fine Arts. Back in 1987, she had been the curator at the Memphis Museum, when a conference on the date of the Exodus was held at Memphis, which I had the privilege of chairing. 5) Rodolfo Fattovich of the University of Naples, who had coauthored a chapter with Kathryn Bard of Boston University for *Africa and Africans in Antiquity*, which I had edited for Michigan State University Press.

We were joined at a dinner I had arranged in the nearby Indian Quality Restaurant by Kathryn Bard who had been teaching classes at the time of the conference sessions. Kathryn and Rodolfo had recently excavated a fabulous Red Sea port, which had preserved wooden planks, coils of rope, and inscribed cargo boxes from c. 2000 BC.

On Saturday, I took a cab driven by a Moroccan driver to Somerville, where I had brunch with Andrew Pottorf, a student of Marv Wilson at Gordon College, and a graduate of Gordon-Conwell Theological Seminary. Andrew helped us check the bibliographies of the articles in the dictionary Marv and I edited. Andrew was pursuing graduate studies at Harvard University. He had just returned from a summer of excavations at Ashkelon, directed by Daniel Master. Andrew and I walked a half mile to the Harvard Divinity School, where I did some research. I then walked several blocks to Harvard Square with some difficulty in reading street signs. A note on the third floor of the large Harvard Coop bookstore announced that at 5 p.m. Kareem Abdul Jabar would appear for a book signing. I took the subway back to the hotel with some difficulty reading the subway map. The Kenmore stop was conveniently located right by the hotel.

On Sunday I took a cab to Park Street Church at the bottom of the hill below the golden dome of the capital building. I met John Carlson, the architect from Boston who supervised the building of the new dormitories at Miami University. When he came to Oxford, John was advised to look me up by Gordon Hugenberger, the pastor of Park Street, who had taught Old Testament at Gordon-Conwell Theological Seminary and who was familiar with some of my books. Pastor Hugenberger, who had just returned from Australia, announced his intention to retire. John Carlson took me to a Legal Seafood restaurant by the port of Boston, which I had never seen. We were driven to the airport by a driver, who had been born in Ethiopia. When I arrived at the Cincinnati airport, Tim and Sue Cameron were waiting to give me a ride back to Oxford.

Conferences

In November at San Antonio, I presented a paper on "Worship in Islam, the Dome of the Rock, and the al-Aqsah Mosque" before the Near East Archaeological Society. At Brandeis University I had studied the Qurʾān and the Hadith ("Traditions") in Arabic. In 1968 I had taken part in the first excavations at the southwest corner of the Herodian platform led by my former teacher Benjamin Mazar. I had been given the rare opportunity to go under the al-Aqsah mosque to view the original Herodian passageway which Jesus and others would have used for entry and egress from the temple platform.

Instead of preparing a Power Point presentation, I had planned to use overhead transparencies. I had even donated funds to the NEAS to get the hotel to provide an overhead projector. When the time came, however, the projector would not work because it had a burnt-out bulb! This may have worked out for the best as I was able to finish my paper in the allotted time. I had expected an audience of perhaps thirty, but there were about sixty present, with some standing. At the end of my presentation, which was to be my last at such conferences, I received a standing ovation. Also, an unprecedented honor was given, naming me the honorary president emeritus of the NEAS (see Excursus O).

Publications

Notes from my commentary on Ezra and on Nehemiah published in the Zondervan *Illustrated Bible Backgrounds Commentary* (2009) were included in the *Bible Backgrounds Study Bible*, edited by John H. Walton and Craig S. Keener.

Academics and Athletics

For financial reasons, Miami University like many other schools sought to recruit international students who pay the full tuition. As a result, out of 15,000 students, 2,000 are from abroad, mainly from China. These students are primarily interested in the majors in the Farmer School of Business. The school is named after Richard Farmer, alumnus and CEO of the Cintas Corporation, which provides service uniforms. He donated $40 million dollars to Miami University for the school. In its annual review of Best Colleges *US News & World Report* ranked Miami University second only to Princeton University for "Best Undergraduate Teaching."

Miami's football team lost its first six games, but then with the return of an injured quarterback won its next six games, the first time this has happened in NCAA history. The Miami RedHawks earned the right to play Mississippi State University on December 26 in the Gasparilla Bowl. Alas, Miami lost 16 to 17!

Chapter 38

A Family Reunion

The Year 2017

The Family

Brian continued his work for the navigation software for iRobot's autonomous lawnmower. Haruko served as the president of the New York City's Association of College and Research Libraries. At the Discovery Charter School Denis with his colleagues worked on an interdisciplinary project on the history of the city of Newark. Students from grade four to eight studied the Newark Rebellion of 1967 from multiple perspectives. Denis also coordinated a schoolwide presentation of Disney's *The Lion King*. Haruko helped to make a papier mâché elephant.

A Family Reunion

In late July Kimi and I took a trip back to the Islands for the first time in four years to see relatives, and in my case to attend a family reunion of the Owans, my mother's family. The reunion was held on July 22 in Laie. It was organized by my cousin Diana Gibson, who lives in Washington State. She had learned of the Owan *mon*, the kanji symbol of the Owan family and had tee shirts made displaying it for the reunion.

On Wednesday, July 19, Dennis Dudley drove us down to lodge at the hotel at the Cincinnati airport the day before our departure so we could catch an early flight on Delta to Honolulu by way of Salt Lake

City. I had requested wheelchair assistance for Kimi, which proved most helpful. At Salt Lake City we had to move a long distance to another terminal. The young man who pushed Kimi did so at such a fast rate that I had difficulty following them.

Haruko and Denis had flown in from New Jersey to spend two weeks in the Islands. They found homes to stay in through Airbnb and enjoyed hiking trips. We arrived at the Honolulu airport about 4 p.m. and were picked up by Brian, who had flown in from Boston. I had arranged for an early dinner in Mililani with some women who were associated with the Christian Youth Center in Wahiawa, where I had worked on a "missionary ranch" from 1953 to 1957. We drove past Scofield Barracks and Wahiawa to the northern end of Oahu and just past Kahuku on the northern tip of Oahu where my mother's parents, the Owans, lived on a sugar plantation. We went a short distance to Laie, where the Owan reunion was to take place. We stayed at the Marriott Hotel near the Polynesian Cultural Center, a key tourist attraction which is run by the Mormons. My cousin, Bobby Owan, who is in charge of purchases for the Brigham Young University in Laie, had helped make arrangements for the reunion.

On Friday afternoon, Brian, Kimi, and I visited the Polynesian Cultural Center, viewing dances and talks of different Polynesian island populations (Fiji, Samoa, Tahiti, the Cook Islands, etc.). We were planning to eat a luau and view the evening show. Brian and I took turns pushing Kimi through the park in a wheelchair. In retrospect, I came to realize that during three hours of a hot and humid afternoon Kimi and I had not taken the opportunity to drink anything though Brian had done so.

About 5:45 p.m. while sitting in the gift shop, Kimi experienced a short but severe pain in her chest as she was sitting before an air conditioning unit. Alarmed that she might be suffering a heart attack, I asked for medical assistance. The EMT workers had her swallow four baby aspirins and took her to the emergency room at Kahuku Hospital ten minutes away. After three hours of EKG tests and blood analysis, Dr. Scott Sanderson concluded that she had not had a heart attack but had experienced angina, which could be a precursor to a heart attack. He prescribed a daily dose of baby aspirins and a nitroglycerin spray to be applied under her tongue in case of future episodes. He also recommended that she see a cardiologist in Honolulu. Upon hearing the news Haruko and Dennis drove all the way up from Kailua an hour away to see Kimi. That night they then drove all the way back to Kailua to the only 24-hour pharmacy on Oahu to obtain baby aspirins and a nitroglycerin spray and drove back to Laie to give these to me.

On Saturday Kimi felt well enough to attend the Owan reunion at Bobby's house in Laie, where I was glad to see a surviving uncle Albert Nakama and a surviving aunt Grace Owan, both in their 90s, and numerous cousins, who had come to Hawaii from Washington State and Maryland, as well as second cousins.

On Sunday my cousin Roy Yamauchi picked us up to attend his church in Kailua. Roy and his wife Charlene had come to Oxford on the occasion of my retirement from Miami University in 2005. Roy's father, Shoyei, had been the best friend of my father Shokyo, so during our trips with Roy I learned many details of my father's life that I had not known before.

Roy was the head of the search committee for a pastor for his church. They had twenty-two candidates, all from the mainland except for one local candidate. The problem in attracting candidates is the high cost of living in Hawaii. Gasoline is above $3 per gallon. A recent article in the *New York Times* announced that the median cost of homes in California had risen to $500,000; the median cost of homes in Hawaii was $800,000! After the service we had lunch in Kailua with Haruko, Denis, and Brian. Kailua, where President Barack Obama and his family vacation, is crowded with tourists.

Brian drove us to our Ala Moana Hotel, which was right next to the Ala Moana shopping center, a huge complex. That evening we had a seven-course Chinese dinner at a restaurant at the hotel, which was arranged by Roy. I was happy to see his mother Kameyo, who was a healthy 100 years old, as well as many other Yamauchi relatives.

On Monday, as Kimi slept in, I took a walk to the Ala Moana Park to view the boat basin and the beach. I then crossed back to the parking area under the Ala Moana shopping center. But as there was construction going on and no clear signs as to how to get up to the store level, I wandered around for about a half hour. When I finally managed to emerge, I found that I was at the end closest to the hotel, when I had wanted to get to a drugstore at the opposite end. I was rushed as I came back to a Macy's Store, so I grabbed four Aloha shirts off the rack without looking at their prices. I was shocked later when I saw their prices. Each cost close to $100!

Brian picked us up so that Kimi could see a cardiologist, Dr. Robert Wong, a cousin of Patrick Chang, a dentist who is married to one of my cousins. Dr. Wong recommended that during the long plane rides Kimi get up and walk to prevent blood clots. Like the doctor in Kahuku he also suggested that when we returned to Ohio, that Kimi undergo stress tests.

We then went to see Kimi's sister Helen, who was in a skilled nursing home recovering from a stroke. She was in a deep sleep when we saw here. This was very close to the site in Kuakini where my father leapt from a bridge and committed suicide in July 1940, when I was but three years old.

We planned to have dinner with Brian before his departure the following day. Brian said he had found a restaurant that had the best steaks in the Island for $50 a plate. When I asked if he was going to treat us, he said "No." So we opted for a Macaroni Grill which was at the shopping center, where we enjoyed a delicious but less expensive meal!

On Tuesday Roy came by early to take us to visit my cousin, Mitchan, who lives in an assisted living apartment in Aiea near Pearl Harbor. Though lacking a few front teeth, she was alert and lively. I had worked with her for four years on weekends, when I was eleven to fifteen years old at the Yamauchi tofu factory. In the afternoons we worked at the saimin (noodle soup) stand attached to the tofuya. Mitchan and I enjoyed playing canasta. I almost resented customers who came and interrupted our card game!

Afterward, Roy took us to the plantation museum at nearby Waipahu. We had seen this before but had never been able to take the guided tour. After only a few minutes of walking, it became clear that Kimi could not keep up with the tour, so she and Roy rested while I took the tour.

That afternoon I was picked up for a helicopter tour of Oahu. In addition to myself there was a young Korean couple and three women from Tennessee. I was given the best seat on the left, as the copter went around the island in a counterclockwise direction. One surprise was that there are still some verdant valleys without any houses. One of these pristine valleys was used as the setting for the movie, Jurassic Park. The final leg of the tour took us over Pearl Harbor and the monument of the sunken battleship Arizona.

On Wednesday Roy picked us up to see several places I wished to see. For the first time, I got to visit Kamehameha High School, perched on a hill overlooking the city. It is run by the wealthy Bishop Estate for the benefit of those with any Hawaiian blood. We were also able to visit the Buddhist temple, where my father had served and to view his tombstone in Kaimuki.

At the Japanese Cultural Center bookstore I was able to buy a number of books dealing with the fate of Japanese in Hawaii who were arrested, detained at Sand Island in Pearl Harbor and later transported to the mainland. My mother worked as a maid for a Seiichi Tsuchiya, a Japanese journalist, who was seized by the FBI and then kept in a prison near Ewa.

At noon we had arranged a luncheon at the Chinese restaurant at our hotel with Ellen, Kimi's younger sister, and with Bong and Alma Ro. Bong is a Korean professor of theology who had met Alma, a Japanese American from Hawaii, at Wheaton College. Also joining us was Tom Weiner, who had worked with the Navigators at Miami University and who headed the Navigators ministry at the University of Hawaii. We waited in vain for the arrival of Patrick Zukeran, who had once interviewed me for his radio ministry. It turned out that he had been waiting in the lobby according to the directions of my email letter but had not listened to my phone message directing him to the restaurant on the third floor.

Roy picked us up to get to the Inter-Island terminal to fly to Hilo, on the Big Island. He had helpfully engaged the services of a private company to hold our two large suitcases while we were gone for just one day before returning to the airport. I had originally planned to rent a car but Haruko and Denis, who were already on the Big Island, offered to pick us up and drive us around. After we arrived, they took us north of Hilo to a private home where they were staying before delivering us to our Seaside Hotel on Banyan Drive. That evening we were able to meet with Kimi's youngest sister, Janet, at a restaurant overlooking Hilo Bay as the sun set.

On Friday Haruko, Denis and I had planned to take a helicopter ride but rain canceled those plans. We were able to visit Kimi's oldest sister, Miyoko, now 95 in a nursing home. She was alert, cheerful, and spoke in a loud voice, though we could not understand what she was saying.

We caught the Hawaiian Air Lines flight back to Honolulu, arriving about 6 p.m., for our Delta flight leaving at 8:41 p.m., plenty of time to make the transfer or so we thought. But then the shuttle, which was supposed to arrive every 20 minutes, did not arrive for 40 minutes. When I called for the delivery of our two large pieces of luggage, the agent said that he would be there in five minutes. But I waited and waited, and called and called, and said "I cannot see you." I said I was on the street in front of the Delta gate, but he replied, "I cannot see you there." It turned out that there were two street levels, and I was on the lower level and he was on the upper level. When we finally got the bags to the Delta agents, they said they could not assure us that the bags would arrive in LA with us (they did!). Taking two wheelchairs they rushed us through security (we fortunately have the TSA pre-check numbers) and pushed us through the waiting crowd of passengers to board first. It is a great advantage in such cases to be passengers in wheelchairs!

On Saturday we arrived at 5 a.m. at Los Angeles. I had changed our itinerary to make a stopover here when I learned that my sister, Alicia and her 16-year-old daughter, Sabine, would be visiting LA from Switzerland. Having grown up in LA, Alicia was adept at negotiating the freeway traffic in LA. She was staying in Montebello to the east of LA with her aunt, Carmen (Yoshie) Mochizuki, who is the sister of my stepfather Renyu Higa. Carmen was the lead plaintiff in the suit against the US government for the illegal and unjust treatment of the Japanese from Latin America (see Excursus E). That night we ate at a Korean barbecue restaurant where I enjoyed a favorite dish *bul goghi*.

On Sunday Alicia took us to a church in Yorba Linda, where my good friend George Giacumakis was teaching an adult class on Daniel. After gaining his PhD at Brandeis University, George taught in the History Department at Fullerton State University when it first began. It now had forty-thousand students. That afternoon I spent two hours at our hotel lobby with Matthew Bustamante, a friend of Alicia's, who had read some of my books. In the evening Alicia took us to a Ramen restaurant.

On Monday Alicia took us to the airport and helped us with our luggage. The return nonstop flight seemed short by comparison with the long two-stage flight to Hawaii. Don Hanson picked us up. But then I could not find the house key in my suitcase. Fortunately, I had left a spare key with the Pettitts, and Dick brought it over just as we arrived at Erin Drive. I later found the key in Kimi's suitcase.

James K. Hoffmeier

In March James K. Hoffmeier spoke in my Annual History Lecture series on "New Light on Egypt and the Bible." Hoffmeier was born in Egypt to parents who were missionaries there. Later when he met the British Egyptologist Kenneth Kitchen of the University of Liverpool, he learned that Ken had prayed for his family. After graduating from Wheaton College, Hoffmeier received his PhD from the University of Toronto, where

A FAMILY REUNION

one of his teachers was the noted Egyptologist Donald Redford. He worked with Redford on the Akhnaton Temple Project in Egypt from 1975 to 1977 at Luxor. Hoffmeier served as the chair of the Bible and Archaeology Department at Wheaton College. He then transferred to Trinity Evangelical Divinity School when the college would not give him time off to conduct excavations in Egypt during the winter semester. He directed excavations at Tell el-Borg, north Sinai, from 1998 to 2008. The project was funded in part by a wealthy Jewish donor.

Figure 70. With Jim Hoffmeier

Hoffmeier has appeared in and served as a consultant for television programs on the Discovery, History, Learning, and National Geographic Channels. He has authored two important books published by the Oxford University Press: *Israel in Egypt: Evidence for the Authenticity of the Exodus Tradition* (1997) and *Ancient Israel in Sinai: The Evidence for the Authenticity of the Wilderness Tradition* (2005). He has coedited two volumes to which I have contributed chapters: *Faith, Tradition and History: Old Testament Historiography in Its Near Eastern* Context (1992) and *The Future of Biblical Archaeology* (2004). He contributed the chapter on "The Egyptians" for *Peoples of the Old Testament World*, which I coedited.[1]

---

1. Hoffmeier's wife, whom he met as a student at Wheaton College, is of Chinese descent. No doubt this motivated him to write *The Immigration Crisis: Immigrants, Aliens and the Bible* (Wheaton, Illinois: Crossway, 2009).

Ambience and Athletics

The village of Oxford, which has about ten thousand permanent residents, was named the number one college town in America by WalletHub as announced by Forbes Magazine. The website surveyed 415 cities and analyzed twenty-six academic, economic, and social factors. Oxford had earned this distinction once before in 2014.

Miami alumnus Sean McVay (class of 2007) became the youngest NFL coach at the age of 30. He transformed the Los Angeles Rams from the lowest scoring team to the top scoring team in leading them to Super Bowl LIII. He was recognized as NFL's "Coach of the Year." His grandfather John McVay, who coached the New York Giants and served as the general manager of the San Francisco 49ers, also played at Miami University (class of 1952).

Chapter 39

The Year 2018

The Family

AFTER NINETEEN YEARS IN Boston working for iRobot, Brian moved to San Francisco for a new position as a technical director at Anki, a company started by three PhDs from Carnegie Mellon University. Boris Sofman, the company's CEO, had been one of Brian's interns at iRobot back in 2005. Anki focused on developing robots with compelling personalities. Brian worked with animators from Pixar and the video game industry. Anki's robotic toy Cosmo was the best seller on Amazon in 2016 and 2017. Brian moved into a new apartment building in San Francisco with a great view of the bay and the city.

Haruko published a chapter about progressive library training programs in the inner cities in *Reference Librarianship & Justice*. In the summer Haruko and Denis were able to visit France to meet members of Denis's family and coworkers from the Fourth World Movement. They also went to Switzerland to meet my sister Alicia, her husband Heinz, and their daughter Sabine.

Kimi's sister Helen passed away. Her sister Ellen lived on Oahu, and her sisters Miyoko and Janet lived in Hilo on the Big Island. We watched in fascination for months as slowly moving lava streams from Kilauea destroyed 700 homes south of Hilo. Those who build in this area are aware of the risks, as lava has destroyed many homes in this area before. But they build there as this is the cheapest land available. Even a modest house in Hawaii costs $900,000!

Kimi and I watch Hawaii Five O as it reminds of Hawaii. It is about the only television program that features Asian and Pacific Island characters. We also like watching Jeopardy, which was my mother's favorite program, which she called "Jalopy"!

We enjoyed going to our church's small community group, which meets bi-weekly in homes. We have a time of food, the sharing of prayer requests, and a study based on the week's sermon, which is led on a rotating basis by members of the group. As I no longer drive at night, we are dependent upon the kindness of Dick and Ruth Pettitt for rides.

I attended a weekly luncheon of Christian faculty arranged by Dennis Dudley, the IV staff member, who is also responsible for helping with my annual History Lecture series. A key faculty member in both activities is Tim Cameron, the chair of the Mechanical and Manufacturing Engineering Department. Tim and his wife Sue have been faithful participants in the monthly service I have conducted at the nursing home at the Knolls.

Ben Witherington III

Ben Witherington III spoke in March on "A Singular Jesus in a Pluralistic World" in my Annual History Lecture series. Witherington received his BA from the University of North Carolina, his MA from Gordon-Conwell Theological Seminary, and his PhD from the University of Durham. He is the Amos Professor of New Testament for Doctoral Studies at Asbury Theological Seminary.

Witherington is a renowned author of numerous books on the New Testament and on Jesus, including: *Invitation to the New Testament*, *New Testament History*, *Jesus of Nazareth*, and *What Have They Done with Jesus?* Two of his books were recognized as the outstanding books in their category by *Christianity Today*: *The Jesus Quest* (1995) and the *Paul Quest* (1999).

Figure 71. With Ben Witherington III

Publication and Books

For *Biblical Leadership: Theology for the Everyday Leader*, edited by Benjamin R. Forrest and Chet Roden, I revised an essay I had earlier contributed to a Festschrift in honor of Dennis Kinlaw, "A Model Leader: Leadership in Nehemiah."

In preparing to downsize in order to move to a retirement community, I had two Christian booksellers go through my library.[1] But since I was too busy to pay careful attention to what they were removing, I lost a few books that I did not want to part with. I gave away ten boxes of church history books to Jonathan Armstrong, a professor at Moody Bible Institute who was asked by InterVarsity Press to revise the church history textbook *Two Kingdoms* that I had coauthored with Robert Clouse and Richard Pierard.

---

1. One of the book dealers was James Stock of Wipf & Stock Publishers in Salem, Oregon, which has reprinted several of my books. James related how he began and continues as a used book dealer. He joined with Wipf, who was also a used book dealer in southern California. They then began reprinting books, keeping a very low inventory, and printing them on demand. Later Wipf & Stock under various labels published original and eventually scholarly books.

Former Students

A number of my former graduate students recorded notable achievements. Darlene Brooks Hedstrom, the chair of the History Department at Wittenberg University, was given an endowed chair in the Humanities. I was able to travel to Springfield, Ohio, with Judith de Luce, former chair of Miami's Classic Department, on the occasion of this honor for Dar. Robert Winn, the chair of the History Department at Northwestern College in Iowa, published *Christianity in the Roman Empire*. Daniel Master of Wheaton College began excavations at Tel Shimron, the largest unexcavated mound in Israel. He was joined by Deirdre Fulton of Baylor University in the dig, which is sponsored by the Museum of the Bible. Jerry Pattengale coedited *The State of the Evangelical Mind*.

Chapter 40

Downsizing and a Move

The Year 2019

The Family

BRIAN AND HIS COLLEAGUES from Anki, a robotic toy company in San Francisco, traveled to Hong Kong to interest wealthy capitalists in investing in their company. When those investments failed to materialize, Anki shut down in May. After considering offers from a number of robotic companies, Brian moved to Mountain View in the heart of Silicon Valley. As a senior software engineer, he began working with others on the development of a self-driving car for Argo. Argo, which is funded by the Ford Motor Company, has a fleet of autonomous Fusion sedans that were being tested in Palo Alto, Pittsburgh, Detroit, Miami, and Washington, DC.

This year, Haruko earned tenure as an assistant professor and library teaching coordinator at the Eugenio Maria de Hostos Community College in the Bronx. Hostos (d. 1903) was an outstanding Puerto Rican educator, writer, and politician, who worked for the independence of his island from Spain. He was disappointed that after the Spanish American War, Puerto Rico became an American territory rather than an independent nation. The name of the school is a tribute to the dominant Puerto Rican population of its neighborhood in the South Bronx. Denis was named the school leader of the Discovery Charter School in

Newark, after he had already been doing much of the supervisory work without this title.

Downsizing

Like many other older couples, we decided we should try to sell our two-story three-bedroom home with a full basement study and an annex that I had added as I retired in 2005 to house books from my office at the university. But first we needed to dispose of so much stuff! Kimi, who grew up in the Depression, is a bit of a hoarder. She had stored away untold boxes in a lower room that we had built for my mother but that had turned into a storeroom. Additional boxes were piled high in the garage. Then in the backyard there were two storage sheds full of boxes!

Brian got rid of his stuff, which included boxes of comic books that I gave away. Haruko had some of her art materials in one shed. She and Denis helped to fill scores of plastic bags for the trashmen to take away. We gave away clothes to the Goodwill Store and loads of books to the Lane Library.

I had given my extensive collection of the Loeb Classical Library of Greek and Latin authors to Scott Carroll. As I did not have an accurate catalogue, I found myself at times ordering duplicate copies of the Loeb, which I would then send to John DeFelice. But that still left the major part of the library intact, including books, journals, and slides. I was happy that Jerry Mattingly of Johnson University in Knoxville, Tennessee, had his school buy almost all of these items.

An inspector detected hail damage on our roof, but our home insurance denied this claim, so we had to pay for a new roof and also for the painting of the exterior. Volunteers from our church cleaned and painted the interior. Two auctioneers did not think that what we would leave behind (an upright piano, a ping-pong table, bookshelves, some furniture, filing cabinets, etc.) were worth auctioning. A third auctioneer said he would take all the items which were moved into the garage. But instead of making a modest profit, we wound up having to pay the auctioneer for getting rid of all these items!

Marty Creech, our realtor, is a member of our church. Even before our house was listed, he had buyers in hand, a young couple who were graduates of Miami University. They had been involved in the Navigators and were middle-school teachers. We were able to sell our house for $165,000, which enabled us to buy a cottage at the Knolls for $190,000.

The Knolls of Oxford

The retirement community, the Knolls of Oxford, is located on the western edge of the city. It is part of the Maple Knolls Community, which has quite a venerable history. In 1848 Lydia Beecher founded the Society for the Relief of Indigent Aged Women. In 1879 this was merged with the Old Men's Home. In 1834 the Protestant Home for the Friendless and Foundlings became the Hospital and Home for the Friendless. In 1950 this became the Maple Knolls Hospital and Home. Then in 1973 this merged with the Widows and Old Men's Home. In 1975 a retirement village was built on the former grounds of the hospital in Springdale, just south of the Tri-County Mall in Cincinnati. In 2000 a branch of the Maple Knolls Community was opened in Oxford, spurred by a committee of members from the Oxford Presbyterian Church including President Philip Shriver.

The Knolls of Oxford has 107 "villas" or "cottages" which are either two- or three-bedroom dwellings. These are arranged in duplexes or triplexes, which are grouped into five neighborhoods with a central location for mailboxes in each. There is also a Clubhouse for activities, and a large main building, the Commons, which is connected to an assisted living section with twenty-eight apartments and a nursing unit with sixty-two beds. In the center of the Knolls is a large pond with two resident swans. There were thirty-six couples, fifty-six single women, and only ten single men occupying 102 of the 107 available cottages at the time of our move. Most are retired faculty and staff of Miami University and their relatives and friends.

I hired a professional to help coordinate the boxing of items and their transfer to the Knolls. She and her crew proved extremely helpful. The move in date was postponed until April 13, providentially as it happened that Haruko and Denis had planned to stay with us for several days beginning on April 14! They were thus able to help us unpack, build shelves, and hang paintings on the walls.

We moved into the oldest part of the Knolls in a triplex. Our next-door neighbor Agnes McDonough is a member of the Songbirds. Just beyond her was my history colleague Jay Baird. The previous occupant of our cottage, John Blocher, lived to be a hundred. Other centenarians have celebrated their birthdays, including June Goggin, the widow of Lloyd Goggin, who was a vice-president of the university. On the other hand, given the average age of the residents, there is hardly a month that goes by without a notification of the passing of one of the residents.

Living in a smaller single floor dwelling simplified many tasks, such as doing the laundry, bringing in the groceries, and taking out the trash and recyclables. The newspapers were delivered by the garage door. I no longer had to mow the lawn. Meals can be eaten at a café in the Commons or delivered to the door. A monthly fee of $2,400 covers all the utilities, taxes, phone, internet, and cable tv fees. This includes once a week maid service. Maintenance issues are promptly addressed.

I donated some of my books on the Bible and archaeology to the library in the Commons. I also had the opportunity to give two lectures in the clubhouse, which is the center of many activities. In warm weather, Kimi and I were able to walk down to the swan pond. While she sat on a bench I would take a quick brisk walk around the pond.

DOWNSIZING AND A MOVE

Figure 73. Ed and Kimi at the Knolls

The Knolls of Oxford was built on the grounds of the Kettler farm between Contreras Road and Fairfield Road. It had been bought by George M. Hill in 1962 and then bequeathed to his alma mater, Allegheny College, which then sold it to the Knolls. George had served as the director of hiring at Armco Steel Company in Middletown and taught Industrial Psychology at Miami University. He then established a consulting firm George M. Hill Associates with its offices in the building which now sits at the northern entrance of the Knolls. George and his employees and that building played a key role in the early years of the Oxford Bible Fellowship (see ch. 46).

Jennifer Wiseman

In March Jennifer Wiseman, the astrophysicist at NASA's Goddard Space Center in charge of the Hubble Space Telescope, spoke on "Planets, Stars, Galaxies, and Life" in my Annual History Lecture series. Wiseman received her BS in physics from MIT, and her PhD in astronomy from Harvard University. She is a leader in the dialogue between science and religion for the Association for the Advancement of Science. I had heard Jennifer at a conference of the American Scientific Affiliation. She showed stunning images of colorful distant galaxies taken by the Hubble Telescope.

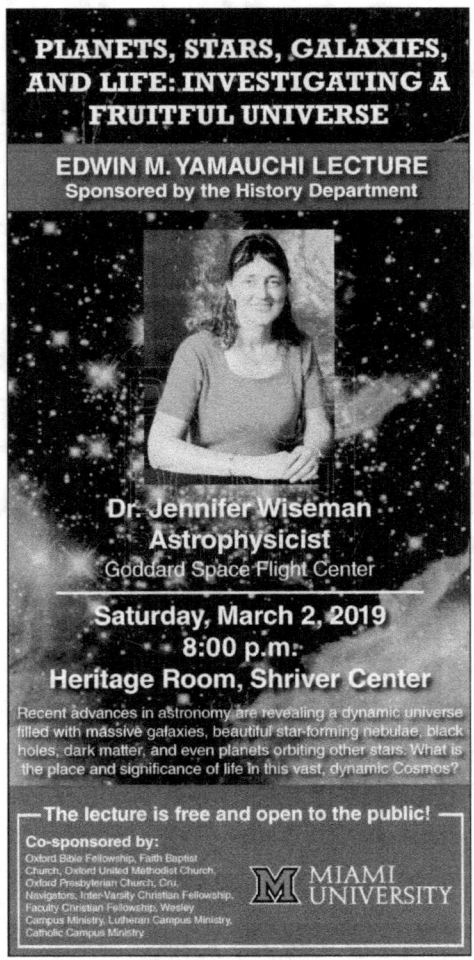

Figure 74. Poster for Jennifer Wiseman's lecture

The Myaamia Center

One of the couples who joined us in the Songbirds was Joe and Etsuko Leonard. Etsuko, who is from Japan, taught Japanese. Joe, a professor of management, has served as chief of the Miami (Myaamia) Tribe. It was his father Floyd Leonard, a longtime chief of the tribe, who established relations between Miami University and the tribe. One of the results of that relationship was the dropping of the athletic teams' nickname "The Redskins" for "The Redhawks," a move which upset not a few alumni!

A most positive development of that relationship was the granting of free tuition to members of the tribe and the development of the Myaamia Center to help preserve the culture of the tribe. Daryl Baldwin, a professor of linguistics, won a MacArthur "Genius" grant of $500,000 for his efforts at preserving and teaching the Myaamia language. George Ironstrack, who was a graduate student in history, is on the staff of the center which holds an annual conference on campus. Miami University also encourages students to visit the main location of the Myaamia tribe in the town of Miami in northeastern Oklahoma.

Publication

I revised and expanded the first part of my *Christianity Today* article on "Easter—Myth, Hallucination or History" as "Did Christianity Copy Earlier Resurrection Stories?" for *The Harvest Handbook of Apologetics*, edited by Joseph M. Holden. I added a section on Mithras, the Persian god of a Roman mystery religion since so many websites were falsely claiming that Mithraism influenced Christianity.

Chapter 41

The Year of the Pandemic

Year 2020

The Family

BRIAN MOVED BACK TO Boston in February to join Boston Dynamics to work on their four-legged yellow doglike robot Spot. Spot weighs about seventy-six pounds. Boston Dynamics has sold hundreds of Spot robots to commercial, industrial and entertainment customers throughout the world. Customers use Spot for a wide range of tasks, from inspecting nuclear power plants and patrolling offshore oil platforms to performing at theme parks. SpaceX uses their Spot robot to inspect their launch pad for their next generation Starship spacecraft. The Brigham and Women's Hospital in Boston used Spot to perform initial intake on patients over a video screen. The New York Police Department leased a Spot robot for $94,000 in 2020 but then canceled this contract in the face of fierce public opposition.

Brian is a senior roboticist with the Autonomy Group for the Spot Project. During the pandemic he worked from his apartment in the Brighton area of Boston. In December Boston Dynamics released a YouTube video of their robots dancing including Spot, which attracted millions of viewers worldwide. The Korean automaker Hyundai has acquired an 80 percent stake in Boston Dynamics for $1.1 billion dollars.

Haruko worked remotely as her college shut down. She learned how to offer research instruction through Zoom. She got involved with her college's union to press the administration to do all it could to preserve the health and safety of the college community. After the pandemic started Denis had to figure out how to support all his teachers and to quickly make his school (grades 4 to 8) remote for the spring. He spent the summer grappling with the complicated logistical, pedagogical and communication challenges of opening the school as "hybrid" in the fall with some children at home and some at school. With his team of teachers, he did so with some success. But then the Covid infection rates in Newark spiked, so he had to move the school to all remote.

Both Haruko's college in the South Bronx and Denis's school in Newark are in very low-income neighborhoods. So, the Covid toll was very high for their students and families in terms of sickness, death, the necessity of underpaid "essential" services, and sudden unemployment. At the same time Haruko and Denis have enjoyed the respite of being able to spend much time outdoors, hiking and bicycling.

On October 13, Kimi reached her ninetieth birthday! Partly to celebrate this occasion and also because of an all-day cleaning of our cottage, we spent two days at the nearby Hueston Woods State Park. We had a lakeside room and enjoyed the beautiful foliage on display. One of Kimi's paintings was hung in the living room of the guest house at the northern entrance to the Knolls.

In early March, I was notified by Deborah Anderson, the chair of the Prayer for Oxford Committee, that I would be honored with a crab apple tree planted in the Community Park opposite the southern entrance to the Knolls and that my name would be added to the bronze plaque below the flagpole. I was the third recipient of this honor after the late police chief, Bob Holzworth, and the late Bob George, a middles-school teacher. Both had been members of our church.

Daniel Master

On March 7, Daniel Master, professor of archaeology at Wheaton College, spoke on "Ashkelon Uncovered, a Philistine City in Israel" in my Annual History Lecture series. Daniel was a graduate of Philadelphia College of the Bible, where his father taught the Old Testament. He had been serving as a volunteer at the excavation at Ashkelon directed by Lawrence (Larry) Stager of Harvard University, who accepted him into Harvard's Near Eastern Languages and Civilization program. Daniel earned his PhD there in 2001. At a SBL book display Larry Stager told me that Daniel was the "best student I had ever had." When I repeated this to someone, he replied "Ah, Larry says that about all of his students!" But in truth Daniel was Larry's best student and succeeded him as the field director of the large Ashkelon dig in 2007 and became the series editor of the Final Reports of the Leon Levy Expedition to Ashkelon in 2015. He is also the editor of the *Oxford Encyclopedia of the Bible and Archaeology*.

There were five Philistine cities: three on the coast (Ashdod, Ashkelon, Gaza) and two inland (Ekron, Gath). All except Gaza, which is occupied by Palestinians, have now been excavated. Daniel's team uncovered the first Philistine cemetery ever discovered. One of the members of his team was Deirdre Fulton, who also gained her MA at Miami University before earning her PhD at Penn State University. Deirdre, who is teaching Old Testament at Baylor University, has become a specialist in the archaeology of animal bones.

Figure 72. With Deirdre Fulton

Miami University

On March 11, the Republican governor of Ohio, Mike DeWine, a Miami University alumnus, ordered the closing of schools in the state because of the spread of the Coronavirus. In the fall Miami offered students three options: 1) they could put off studies for a year, 2) they could opt for distance learning, or 3) they could plan to come to live on campus. In September before the freshmen returned, some students living off campus made national news as they partied and disregarded the governor's orders for masks and social distancing. About 4,000 fewer students returned to campus. About 2,500 tested positive for the virus, though none had to be hospitalized. They were subject to various degrees of quarantine. They finished classes by Thanksgiving. At first fall sports for the Mid-American Conference were suspended and then commenced late. Miami's football team which won the championship could only play three games because of cancellations.

Darlene Brooks Hedstrom

During the summer one of my doctoral students Darlene Brooks Hedstrom, who had received her BA and MA from Wheaton College, received a signal honor. She was named the Myra and Robert Kraft and Jacob Hiatt Associate Professor in Christian Studies at Brandeis University with a joint appointment in Classical Studies and Near Eastern Studies. Jacob Hiatt, the father of Myra Kraft, had served as the chair of the board of trustees at Brandeis University. Robert Kraft is well known as the owner of the New England Patriots. Hedstrom's book *The Monastic Landscape in Late Antique Egypt* (Cambridge University Press) had won an award from the Biblical Archaeology Society.

Figure 75. With Darlene Brooks Hedstrom

The ETS Conference

The last annual conference of the Evangelical Theological Society and the Near East Archaeological Society I had attended was in 2016. This year's conference with its theme of "Christianity and Islam" was held virtually because of the pandemic. Though missing personal contacts and the opportunity to examine the books in publishers' booths, this format was much cheaper and more convenient as it saved the expense of travel, hotels, and meals. It also allowed me to view pre-recorded papers in different sessions at my convenience. I thus got to listen to papers by some of my former students such as Kirk McGregor and Bob Smith, as well as papers by Paul Gould, Bill Spencer, and Aida Spencer, which I would not have been able to do had I attended the conference in person, as I would have remained in place in the Near East Archaeological Society sessions. The presidential address by Craig Keener of Asbury Theological Seminary was especially moving and challenging.

Publication

My essay, "In Praise of a Venerable Scribe," an annotated bibliography was published in a Festschrift for Alan R. Millard, *Write That They May Read: Studies in Literacy and Textualization*, edited by Daniel Block and others. Alan is a distinguished Assyriologist and Old Testament scholar, now retired from the University of Liverpool. I first met Alan in 1970 when he was the warden of Tyndale House in Cambridge, where I presented a New Testament lecture. Alan guided me around the colleges of Cambridge and pointed out where the distinguished humanist Erasmus had come to teach Greek. I have contributed essays to volumes coedited by Alan, and Alan has written forewords to two of my books, *Foes from the Northern Frontier* and *Peoples of the Old Testament World*.

Forthcoming

Though an unmitigated disaster for almost everyone, the pandemic was for me somewhat of a blessing in disguise, as it freed me from meetings, allowing me more time to concentrate on writing my memoir. I did participate in a men's Zoom Bible study led by Timothy Cameron. For the most part, with a few exceptions, Kimi and I viewed our church services remotely rather than in person.

One essay I was able to complete for a Festschrift in honor of David T. Tsumura[1] was "The Philistine Giant Goliath." This was stimulated by Daniel Master's discovery of the Philistine cemetery at Ashkelon, which revealed that the average height of Philistine men was only 5 ft. 1 in., with the tallest only 5 ft. 4 in. Almost all scholars, translators and commentators including David T. Tsumura have favored the Hebrew Masoretic Text describing Goliath as "six cubits and a span" or 9 feet 6 inches tall. This was also reflected in a recent CNN documentary on Jerusalem. But Daniel Hays has made a persuasive case that the true height was "four cubits and a span" or 6ft. 9 in. tall as attested in a fragment of 1 Samuel from Qumran, the Septuagint and Josephus.[2]

---

1. *The Legacy and Current State of Japanese Hebrew Bible and Ancient Near Eastern Studies: Essays in Honor of David Toshio Tsumura*, ed. By Kaz Hayashi and Masashi Tamura (Louvain: Peeters, forthcoming). All the editors and contributing scholars except for myself are scholars from Japan.

2. J. Daniel Hays, "Reconsidering the Height of Goliath," *Journal of the Evangelical Theological Society* 18 (2005), 701 to 714.

I have gathered additional evidence on the height of ancient individuals to support the shorter height. Like Hays I have refuted the argument that the shorter height could not have carried the weight of the body armor of Goliath. In addition, I have pointed out the weakness of the feet of a giant like Robert Wardlow (d. 1940), the tallest man in recent history, who was 7 ft. 11 in. tall.

Chapter 42

The I.B.R.[1]

THE INSTITUTE FOR BIBLICAL Research (IBR) is a society of evangelical scholars involved in biblical research. It was inspired by the British Tyndale Fellowship, which met annually at the Tyndale House in Cambridge, England. IBR fellows have PhDs in the Old Testament, New Testament or related studies such as Near Eastern Languages. Prospective fellows are nominated by two other fellows. Associates are PhD candidates who have been nominated by a fellow to the Executive Committee.[2]

Tyndale Fellowship and Tyndale House

Concern with the growing liberal orientation of the Student Christian Movement led evangelical students at the University of Cambridge to form InterVarsity Fellowship in 1919, which in 1928 became known as the Universities and Colleges Christian Fellowship. Tyndale House, a residential research library, was established in Selwyn Gardens, Cambridge in 1944. It was to host many doctoral students and professors doing research in the United Kingdom. Annual conferences featured

---

1. As a charter member and as the oldest surviving president, I was asked by Beth Stovell, the secretary of the IBR, to provide an account of the earliest years of the organization.

2. Master's level students may be nominated as student members without voting privileges, as is the case with friends such as publishers.

papers on the Old Testament and the New Testament. From 1953 an annual *Tyndale Bulletin* was published.

The three founding scholars of the Tyndale House were all from the (Plymouth) Brethren background: W. J. Martin, Donald J. Wiseman, and F. F. Bruce. William James Martin (1904 to 1980) received his BA from Trinity College, Dublin. He then graduated with a BTh from Princeton Theological Seminary, where Robert Dick Wilson advised him to study Semitic languages in Germany. Martin studied in Berlin and Leipzig from 1929 to 1935, earning his PhD in Assyriology. He was appointed Rankin Lecturer in Hebrew and Ancient Semitic Languages at the University of Liverpool, where he taught from 1937 to 1970. He then moved to Vancouver to serve as the vice-principal of Regent College. Apart from an important but brief critique of the Documentary Hypothesis, Martin did not publish many scholarly works after his initial cuneiform studies. But it was Martin who began promoting a biblical research center as early as 1937.

Donald John Wiseman (1918 to 2010) was the son of P. J. Wiseman who had served in Iraq (1923 to 1925, 1931 to 1933) and who had brought home inscribed cuneiform bricks which first aroused his son's curiosity. Donald studied history at King's College but was then persuaded by W. J. Martin to study Hebrew and Akkadian. During World War II Donald served as a decorated RAF pilot.[3] After graduating from the University of Oxford in 1948, Wiseman was appointed an assistant keeper at the British Museum. He transcribed and published the tablets from Alalakh discovered by Leonard Woolley and the Chaldean Chronicles of Nebuchadnezzar. He worked with Max Mallowan at Nimrud and published the Esarhaddon Vassal Treaties discovered there. In 1961, he was appointed the chair of Assyriology at the School of Oriental and African Studies of the University of London, a position he held until his retirement in 1982. He was chosen a Fellow of the British Academy in 1969.[4] Wiseman headed the Old Testament Study Group at Tyndale House.

Frederick Fyvie Bruce (1910 to 1990) earned his BA and MA. in Greek and Latin at the University of Aberdeen, and a BA in Classics at Cambridge. In 1934, he went to the University of Vienna to study

---

3. As recounted in his self-published memoir, *Life Above and Below* (2003), a copy of which Donald kindly sent to me.

4. I stayed at Donald's home in 1985 as he was preparing to deliver the Schweich Lecture on Nebuchadrezzar and Babylon to the British Academy. I learned that this was a highly select group which numbered only about 200 at this time.

Indo-European languages including cuneiform Hittite but did not complete a PhD. Then in 1938, he obtained a position teaching Greek and Latin at the University of Leeds. Despite his lack of any formal theological training, Bruce became the head of the new Department of Biblical History and Literature at the University of Sheffield in 1947. In 1959, he became the Rylands Professor of Biblical Criticism and Exegesis at the University of Manchester,[5] from which he retired in 1978. Bruce became a Fellow of the British Academy in 1973. He headed the New Testament Study Group at Tyndale House.[6]

In August 1967 at the XXVIIth International Congress of Orientalists at Ann Arbor, where I read a paper on "The Comparison of Elements in Coptic and Mandaic Gnostic Sources," I met with W. J. Martin and Donald Wiseman to discuss the great need for informed evangelical commentaries on the Old Testament. At this time evangelicals were relying on the popular commentaries of Harry Ironside (the Brethren) pastor of Moody Church, and the reprints of the conservative Keil and Delitzsch series.[7] Donald asked me about qualified American evangelical Old Testament scholars, and I provided him a short list, mainly students of the Jewish scholar Cyrus H. Gordon, who had mentored doctoral students at Dropsie College and Brandeis University, including myself.

In 1970 I published *Gnostic Ethics and Mandaean Origins* in the Harvard Theological Studies series. In that year I was invited to present the New Testament Lecture on "Pre-Christian Gnosticism" at Tyndale House, a paper which I expanded into a book, *Pre-Christian Gnosticism* published by Tyndale Press in 1973. Without my prior knowledge the

---

5. The other candidate for this position was J. A. T. Robinson, who when asked about the Dead Sea Scrolls, declared that he did not read Hebrew texts. Bruce, on the other hand, besides becoming the president of Studiorum Novi Testamenti Societas also became president of the Society for Old Testament Study.

6. See Alan Millard, "Brethren and Biblical Scholarship in Britain in the Twentieth Century," in Neil Dickson and T. J. Martinello, eds, *Bible and Theology in the Brethren: Studies in Brethren History* (Glasgow, United Kingdom: Brethren Archivists and Historians Network (2018), 95–105. I owe this reference to Alan R. Millard, who succeeded W. J. Martin at the University of Liverpool. Alan was the warden of Tyndale House when I first went there in 1970. Alan, who also came from a Brethren background, was the protégé of Donald J. Wiseman and the mentor of Daniel I. Block, who served as president of the IBR (2001 to 2005). Daniel has recently co-edited with David C. Deuel, C. John Collins and Paul J. N. Lawrence a Festschrift in Alan's honor: *Write That They May Read: Studies in Literacy and Textualization in the Ancient Near East and in the Hebrew Scriptures: Essays in Honor of Professor Alan R. Millard* (Eugene, Oregon: Pickwick Publications, 2020).

7. E. J. Young had begun his scholarly commentaries on Isaiah in 1965.

publishers who were affiliated with IVF, had asked F. F. Bruce to contribute a foreward. In December 1973 at the meeting of the Evangelical Theological Society at Wheaton College, I served on a panel presided over by Merrill Tenney, which included F. F. Bruce, George Ladd of Fuller Theological Seminary, Bill Lane of Western Kentucky University, and I. Howard Marshall of the University of Aberdeen.

I continued to correspond with and exchange publications with Fred Bruce and Donald Wiseman. Donald kindly contributed a foreward to my *Persia and the Bible* (1990). I coedited with Alfred Hoerth and Gerald Mattingly, *Peoples of the Old Testament World* (1994), which was designed as a sequel to *Peoples of Old Testament Times*, edited by Donald J. Wiseman (1973).

E. Earle Ellis

Edward Earle Ellis (1926 to 2010) was born in Fort Lauderdale, Florida. After graduating from high school Earle served in the US Army and became a Second Lieutenant in the military police (1944 to 1946). He studied law at the University of Virginia, graduating in 1950. But then the Lord called him to a career in the study of the New Testament. He began his theological studies at Faith Theological Seminary in Delaware, but then transferred to the graduate program at Wheaton College, where he earned the BD and the MA in 1953. At Wheaton he and Gerald Hawthorne were housemates and became lifelong friends. Earle then received the PhD at the University of Edinburgh in 1955. He pursued post-graduate studies at Tübingen, Göttingen, Marburg and Basel (1954 to 1962).

Earle taught courses in the New Testament at Aurora College (1955 to 1958), at the Southern Baptist Theological Seminary at Louisville (1958 to 1960), at Bethel Theological Seminary (1960 to 1961), at the New Brunswick Theological Seminary (1962 to 1985), and finally at the Southwestern Baptist Theological Seminary in Fort Worth from 1985 until his death in 2010.

I met Earle when I started teaching at Rutgers in New Brunswick in 1964. The Dutch Reformed seminary had moved from New York City to New Brunswick in 1810. This is the oldest Protestant seminary in America. Earle lived in a basement apartment of a seminary building.

Earle came to a weekly Bible study I led for a small group of faculty from Rutgers and from Douglass College, a women's school that had been acquired by Rutgers. He commuted to New York City to attend the Marble Collegiate Church pastored by Norman Vincent Peale. When Bruce Metzger[8] retired in 1984 Earle told me that Bruce had hoped Earle could succeed him as the George L. Collard Professor of New Testament at Princeton Theological Seminary. But Earle said his views on women and the New Testament proved to be too conservative for the seminary faculty. Instead, Metzger was succeeded by James Charlesworth from Duke University.[9]

Earle was honored with the presentation of two Festschriften, the first at his sixtieth birthday[10] and the second at his eightieth birthday.[11] These list his many publications, lectures, and honors. Jerry Hawthorne contributed an insightful account of Earle's life in the second Festschrift, which has also been published separately.[12] It is a testimony to Earle's stature as an admired New Testament scholar, that distinguished scholars not only from the US but also scholars from Australia, Belgium, Canada, Germany, Korea, the Netherlands, Norway, Sweden, Switzerland, and the United Kingdom contributed essays to these Festschriften.

---

8. While I was at Rutgers, I regularly did research at the Speer Library of Princeton Theological Seminary but had no direct contact with Bruce Metzger. Some 30 years later we both served with Walter Kaiser and Bastiaan Van Elderen on the advisory board of the Scriptorium.

9. Upon the publication of *Pre-Christian Gnosticism*, I received a letter from Professor Charlesworth commenting that he thought this was the best introduction to the problem of Gnosticism. Craig Keener informed me that while he was pursuing doctoral studies at Duke University, this book was a source of encouragement to him. Bruce Winter, the warden of Tyndale House wrote me in 2003: "I can remember when your radical, but entirely unfashionable thesis re the fallacy of Gnosticism in the first century hit the deck and the early response to it at SBL (the Society of Biblical Literature). Who could have guessed that your book would hole that carrier below water line and sink it. Now they shuffle their feet if you mentioned the assured findings in the 1980s of Gnosticism in the New Testament period."

10. Gerald F. Hawthorne, ed., *Tradition and Interpretation in the New Testament: Essays in Honor of E. Earle Ellis* (Grand Rapids, Michigan: Eerdmans, 1987).

11. Sang-Won (Aaron) Son, ed., *History and Exegesis: New Testament Essays in Honor of Dr. E. Earle Ellis for His 80th Birthday* (New York, New York: T & T Clark, 2006). I am indebted to Aaron Son for retrieving invaluable information about the IBR from Earle's archives housed at the library of Southwestern Baptist Theological Seminary.

12. Gerald F. Hawthorne, "A Biographical Sketch." This essay has been reprinted in *Index Theologicus*. Jerry reports that despite the pleas of the IBR executive committee not to do this, Earle "walked out on an invited guest-lecturer at its annual banquet" (p. 13), as he felt that this scholar should not have been invited. Jerry does not mention the scholar's name. He was James D. G. Dunn of the University of Durham, speaking in 1994. Earle objected to what he perceived as Jimmy Dunn's "Adoptionist Christology."

Figure 76. With Earle Ellis

The Institute for Biblical Research

Earle had regularly spent summers doing research at Tyndale House. Earle recounts that his first visit was in 1953 when Andrew Walls was the librarian. On October 1, 1970, he sent out an invitation to other American scholars who had been at Tyndale House to implement his vision of an American version of such a residential library. At the SBL meeting later in 1970 in New York City he met with nine others in a café. He mentions specifically Robert Meye, the father of Marianne Meye Thompson, and Robert Gundry, the father of Judith Gundry Voth, as members of this original group.[13] No doubt his good friend Jerry Hawthorne was also there. This group met as a Tyndale Committee at Atlanta in 1971 and at Los Angeles in 1972. I was not a member of this committee. I was

---

13. E. Earle Ellis, "Institute for Biblical Research 1973–1993 Prologue and Prospects," *BBR* 4 (1994), 35–40.

present at the first organizational meeting of the IBR when Earle gave his inaugural "Tyndale Lecture" in Chicago on November 8, 1973.

Earle kept meticulous records of those who participated and served as officers of the IBR. He reported that by the second year (1974), there were about 50 charter members of the new organization. But he did not provide a list of those who were. I do know that Lee McDonald was one of those who joined in 1974.[14] As one of the charter members my best estimate is that the following were those who were active in the IBR in the 1970s. (I include the schools from which they received their PhDs.) David Aune (Chicago), Gerald Borchert (Princeton), Donald Carson (Cambridge), Peter Craigie (Edinburgh), Raymond Dillard (Dropsie), Earle Ellis (Edinburgh), Gordon Fee (Southern California), Ward Gasque (Manchester), Robert Gay (Manchester), Robert Guelich (Hamburg), Robert Gundry (Manchester), Donald Hagner (Manchester), Murray Harris (Manchester), Gerald Hawthorne (Chicago), George Ladd (Harvard), William Lane (Harvard), William LaSor (Dropsie), Richard Longenecker (Edinburgh), Ralph Martin (King's College), Lee M. McDonald (Edinburgh), Bruce Metzger (Princeton), Robert Meye (Basel), Ramsey Michaels (Harvard), Charles Pfeiffer (Dropsie), Peter Richardson (Cambridge), David Scholer (Harvard), Julius Scott (Manchester), Moisés Silva (Manchester), Klyne Snodgrass (St. Andrews), and Bastiaan Van Elderen (Pacific School of Religion).

It will be seen at a glance that the overwhelming number of fellows were New Testament scholars; the only Old Testament scholars in my list are Dillard, LaSor, and Pfeiffer. Of the New Testament scholars, seven were students of F. F. Bruce at Manchester.[15] When Bruce retired, American NT students after 1980 flocked to study under I. Howard Marshall at Aberdeen, Scotland. These included Darrell Bock, Gary Burge, Roy Ciampa, Joel Green, Grant Osborne, Philip Towner, and Ralph Yarbrough.[16]

---

14. Lee later served as president of IBR from 2006 to 2012.

15. See F. F. Bruce, *In Retrospect: Remembrance of Things Past* Grand Rapid, Michigan: Eerdmans 1980).

16. See Jon C. Laansma, Grant Osborne, and Ray Van Neste, ed., *New Testament Theology in Light of the Church's Mission: Essays in Honor of I. Howard Marshall* (Eugene, Oregon: Cascade Books, 2011).

AN ASIAN AMERICAN ANCIENT HISTORIAN AND BIBLICAL SCHOLAR

Gerald F. Hawthorne

Gerald Foster Hawthorne (1925 to 2010) was born in Los Angeles. When his father lost his accounting job during the Depression, he bought a small farm of nut trees in the San Joaquin Valley. The family attended the Brethren Church. Jerry took courses at Visalia Junior College and then received a BTh from the Bible Institute of Los Angeles. He then earned his BA and his MA in Greek at Wheaton College. In 1969 Jerry earned his PhD from the University of Chicago, writing a dissertation on Melito of Sardis. He continued teaching Greek at his alma mater for forty-two years to 3600 students, many of whom went on to distinguished academic careers. Jerry was an enormously popular and effective teacher and received numerous accolades. He was also involved in numerous aspects of the college life and as an elder at the Brethren Chapel. In his honor Wheaton College established an endowed chair, which has been held by Scott Hafemann, Karen Jobes, and Jon Laansma. Friends also raised funds for a Hawthorne House near the Tyndale Library which can be used by visiting Wheaton faculty.

Jerry's major scholarly contribution was his commentary on Philippians in the Word Commentary Series. He was honored with a Festschrift[17] with an appreciative foreword by Ralph P. Martin with whom he coedited *A Dictionary of Paul and His Letters* (1993).

Jerry was an admiring and loyal supporter of his friend Earle Ellis in the work of the IBR. He served as IBR's treasurer from 1973 to 1989, and then as its president from 1989 to 1993.

I first met Jerry when I started dating Kimie Honda (class of '58), who had been one of the few women in his graduate Greek course. I also met his wife Jane Elliot, the sister of Jim Elliot, one of the five missionaries killed by the Auca Indians in Ecuador in January 1956. The Hawthornes were serving as dorm parents in a men's dormitory in 1958.

---

17. Amy M. Donaldson and Timothy B. Sailors, ed., *New Testament Greek and Exegesis: Essays in Honor of Gerald F. Hawthorne* (Grand Rapids, Michigan: Eerdmans, 2003). The contributors who are all former students include: David E. Aune, Peter H. Davids, Bart D. Ehrman, Stephen E. Fowl, G. Walter Hansen, William W. Klein, William J. Larkin, Jr., John R. Levison, Bruce W. Longenecker, Douglas L. Penney, Jeffrey L. Staley, and Frank S. Thielman.

Figure 77. With Jerry Hawthorne

Bastiaan Van Elderen

Bastiaan Van Elderen (1924 to 2004) was born into a Dutch American community in Ripon, California. Bas graduated from Calvin College and earned an MA at the University of California at Berkeley in 1955. After obtaining the BD from Calvin Theological Seminary, he was hired to teach the New Testament at the school. In 1961 he earned the PhD from the Pacific School of Religion in Berkeley under Jack Finegan. He credited Professor Finegan with inspiring him to work as an archaeologist on early sites of Christianity.[18]

In 1972 Bas became the director of the American Schools of Oriental Research in Amman, Jordan. He conducted excavations at Abila,

18. See Bastiaan Van Elderen, "Jack Finegan: A Tribute," in *Chronos, Kairos, Christos: Nativity and Christological Studies Presented to Jack Finegan*, edited by Jerry Vardaman and Edwin M. Yamauchi (Winona Lake, Indiana, Eisenbrauns, 1989), ix–xi.

Hesban and Madaba in Jordan. In Egypt he excavated Pachomius's basilica at Chenoboskion and the early monastery of St. John in Wadi Natrun in northern Egypt.[19]

From 1974 Bas taught for another decade at Calvin Theological Seminary. He received the Distinguished Alumnus Award from Calvin in 2004. Among his outstanding students was James VanderKam, who after teaching at Calvin moved to the University of Notre Dame, where he became a leading scholar of the Dead Sea Scrolls and the editor of the *Journal of Biblical Literature*.

In 1984 Bas accepted a position at the Free University of Amsterdam. After Earle had retired from the position as the chair of the IBR,[20] Bas had become the second chair from 1981. But in view of his move overseas, he relinquished this position. That was when I became chair from 1983 to 1986. Then the title was changed, and I continued as the president of the IBR from 1986 to 1989. When Klyne Snodgrass retired prematurely from his term as president,[21] I suggested to Earle that we approach Bas to serve again as he was now back in the States. So, Bas served a second term as president from 1995 to 2001. Bas was tall and spoke deliberately. He exuded *gravitas* as our president.

In 1997 Bas became the second executive director of the Scriptorium in Grand Haven, Michigan, succeeding Scott Carroll in this position. This was an organization funded by the Christian financier Robert Van Kampen, who had a small museum of ancient Bibles and other texts related to the Bible at his gated mansion. The Scriptorium sponsored six annual conferences on the Bible which hosted international scholars at a manor house in Hereford, England (see ch. 44). Bas was in charge of planning the 2000 conference on the Dead Sea Scrolls together with Emanuel Tov of Israel. Bas was unfortunately unable to attend this conference because of the unexpected death of his son Marlin, who had been working with the World Council of Churches in Geneva. Bas was able to arrange a major exhibit of the Dead Sea Scrolls at the Grand Rapids Public Museum in 2003.

---

19. Two of my doctoral students, Scott Carroll and Darlene Brooks Hedstrom, worked with Bas at this site.

20. Earle continued as an annually re-elected member of the executive committee until 1993.

21. Klyne became vexed at Earle's micromanaging the affairs of the IBR.

Figure 78. With Bas Van Elderen

The Bulletin for Biblical Research

Members of the IBR subscribed to the *Tyndale Bulletin,* and also contributed articles to this excellent journal. During my six-year tenure as the chair and then president (1983 to 1989) the number of fellows had more than doubled from 140 to about 300.[22] As the number of our fellows grew, I developed the idea that it was time for us to produce our own journal, not to supplant the *Tyndale Bulletin* but to supplement it.

At a meeting of the executive council in my hotel room at Chicago in 1988, I proposed such a journal. The other men in the room responded favorably, even enthusiastically. Ward Gasque offered to donate money to such a cause as did others including Andrew Bandstra,

---

22. By 1976 the membership had more than doubled to 83 Fellows. In 1994 the number had grown to 311 Fellows and 90 Associates. In 2006 the IBR had 412 Fellows, 41 Associates, 32 Friends and 36 Retired for a total of 521 members.

Earle Ellis, Daniel Fredericks, Jerry Hawthorne, Tremper Longman III, Klyne Snodgrass, and Richard Stegner.

As I set about getting a publisher, I approached the Eisenbrauns. Jim Eisenbraun as a grad student at the University of Michigan had begun ordering Near Eastern language books for his fellow students. Then he and his wife Merna established their publishing house in Winona Lake, Indiana. They published the *Journal of the American Oriental Society*, which required specialized skill in dealing with the diacritics of Near Eastern and Far Eastern languages. Jim agreed to publish a journal for the IBR.

As for an editor, I had met Bruce Chilton, a specialist in Aramaic targums, at Tyndale House in 1970 just as he was about to leave for Yale University.[23] I knew that he had edited the *Journal for the Study of the New Testament* when he was at the University of Sheffield. He had moved on to Bard College at Annandale-on-Hudson north of New York City, where he also served as the Episcopal Chaplain. I asked Bruce if he would be willing to edit a journal for the IBR and he accepted that responsibility.

The first issue of the *Bulletin for Biblical Research* is dated 1991 but actually appeared in 1992. In that issue, Bruce included an article by his good friend Jacob (Jack) Neusner, a renowned Jewish scholar. I thought that this was a coup for the journal and the society.

I had first been contacted by Jack Neusner shortly after the publication of my *Mandaic Incantation Texts*. He had written that his doctoral advisor Morton Smith at Columbia University, who was interested in magic, wanted to have a copy.[24] Jack used my monograph for his history of the Jews in the Sassanid period of Mesopotamia. He was one of the most prolific authors in history, having written and edited almost a thousand volumes! I have used his books in my seminar on Judaism and Christianity.

But my positive reaction was not shared by other members of the IBR, including Earle Ellis. The continuing critiques of the journal by

---

23. I did not learn until later that Bruce Chilton was one of the few evangelical scholars with Ramsey Michaels who had participated in the Jesus Seminar. For a sharply critical assessment of the Jesus Seminar, see Bruce Chilton and Craig A. Evans, "The Jesus Seminar," in Craig A. Evans, ed., *Encyclopedia of the Historical Jesus* (New York, New York: Routledge, 2009), 333 to 336.

24. Morton Smith did review my book, and I critically reviewed his books on Jesus, magic and the so-called Secret Gospel of Mark mentioned in a letter of Clement of Alexandria he said he had found in the Mar Saba Monastery in Israel, but which many suspect he had forged. See Craig A. Evans, *Jesus and the Manuscripts* (Peabody, Massachusetts: Hendrickson, 2020), ch. 8.

Earle led Bruce to resign before the fifth year of his term as editor. When he did so Earle asked me to chair a committee to find a successor. Earle favored Donald Carson, but our committee chose Craig Evans.

I had recruited Craig to join the IBR because I admired his many publications. I later learned that Craig had been a protégé of Lee McDonald, who was to serve as the IBR president from 2006 to 2012. Craig had served as the associate editor of the *BBR* from 1993. Craig continued as editor for the next decade (1995 to 2005), increasing the publication from one to two issues per year.

I usually supported Earle but not always. In 1998, at our meeting in Orlando Earle proposed a by-law that Craig and I opposed. Craig recalls the proposal better than I do as he recounts in an email letter (August 28, 2020):

> In 1998, at the annual meeting of IBR and SBL in Orlando, Florida, Earle Ellis put forward a motion requiring the IBR and *BBR* to adopt a very conservative statement that was to be printed in the issues of the *BBR*. I and many others vigorously opposed adoption of this motion. At the Saturday morning business meeting, when this motion would be put to the vote, several IBR members remarked that Earle's motion didn't have a chance of passing and saw no reason to stay for the meeting or the vote. I urged some of these members to remain. Earle stood up, speaking in support of the motion, and claimed that he had the support of several senior members, including Richard Longenecker (who had left the room). I later learned that most of the IBR members named by Earle denied that they had told Earle they supported the motion. Earle had also aggressively recruited a number of very conservative IBR members to attend the business meeting.
>
> The question was called. 125 votes were cast, with 63 in favour of the motion and 62 against. The ballots were recounted, and the tally was the same. Earle was very pleased. At the Executive meeting that afternoon, he stated that I should resign as editor of the *BBR* because I had not supported the motion. I might mention that at earlier SNTS meetings Earle urged me to add an inerrancy statement to the *Bulletin* and to refuse to publish papers or reviews by scholars who did not embrace inerrancy. I reminded him that he himself had founded IBR as a scholarly evangelical society that would not have inerrancy at its centre, as ETS historically has had. Earle was at Southwestern Baptist Theological Seminary in Fort Worth, Texas, and was under

pressure to conform to the new fundamentalism that had swept the Southern Baptist Convention and its seminaries.

Bas Van Elderen was President of IBR in 1998. He chaired the Executive meeting and he responded to Earle by saying that his motion may have passed but it would be up to the IBR Executive to interpret it and enforce it as it saw fit. He turned to me and said for all to hear: "You're doing a good job, Craig. Keep doing what you're doing." That was the end of the matter. I greatly appreciated Bas's support. Earle never spoke of the matter again. Earle's statement appeared on the front page of the *Bulletin* but the editorial policies and practices were not altered.[25]

---

25. Craig Evans adds: "The first issue of *BBR* 2005 was my last issue as editor. With the second issue of *BBR* 2005 Rick Hess began his tenure as editor. Under his editorship the *Bulletin* expanded to four issues per year. In his second or third year of his first term Earle's motion was rescinded at the annual IBR meeting and Earle's inerrancy statement no longer appeared in the *Bulletin*. Rick's last year as editor was 2015. In my view, Rick did an excellent job. I thought the book review section was greatly improved."

The next editor was Nijay Gupta, a graduate of Miami University. Nijay, who came from a Hindu background was converted through his brother, who had earlier been converted to Christ through Cru. After graduating from Gordon-Conwell Theological Seminary Nijay earned his PhD from the University of Durham. Teaching at Portland Theological Seminary and Northern Theological Seminary, Nijay has become a prolific and influential New Testament scholar.

THE I.B.R.

Figure 79. With Craig Evans

An IBR Library

Earle Ellis steadfastly, some would say stubbornly, pursued his original dream of establishing a residential library in the US, which like its model in Britain would house scholars doing biblical research and would host conferences. To that end he established a separate committee of Library Trustees that he chaired from its inception in 1993. Jerry Hawthorne served as its treasurer, and I served as its secretary from 1993 to 1998. Others who served on this committee included: Darrell Bock, Donald Carson, Donald Engelhard, Buist Fanning, Gordon Fee, Scott Hafeman, Harold Hoehner, Sam Kistemaker, William Lane, Robert Mounce, Bas Van Elderen, and Paul Wolfe.

Martin Hengel, the outstanding New Testament scholar from Tübingen, was the featured speaker at the IBR conference in 1998. In an article "Raising the Bar" published in *Christianity Today* (October 22, 2001), he assessed North American evangelical New Testament scholarship as follows: "In the field of New Testament text research in America, Princeton Theological Seminary's Bruce Metzger has distinguished himself with his books about the text, the early versions, and the canon of the New Testament." "A hopeful development in America is the supra-denominational evangelical Institute of Biblical Research with its fine scholarly journal." He continued, "Allow me to make a daring proposal. Why not found an IBR-run institute of advanced studies at a traditional renowned university center in the United States?" Speaking of a number of "first class" New Testament scholars in the US and Canada, he wrote: "It is impossible to list all of their names, but they include Craig A. Evans, E. Earle Ellis, Darrell L. Block, Ben Witherington III, Seyoon Kim, Donald A. Hagner, Ed Yamauchi, Gordon D. Fee, Donald A. Carson, James Scott, Judith Gundry-Volf, Craig L. Blomberg, Scot McKnight, and Klyne Snodrass. I think they and other scholars can cooperate in creating a Tyndale House like institution in America."

Earle had named the IBR after the Institute of Advanced Studies at nearby Princeton, when he was at New Brunswick. Princeton would have been an ideal center for such a residential library, but though it was considered, the costs were too high for our limited resources. I did write to Bruce Metzger to see if he might consider bequeathing his house and library to the IBR, but I was not surprised that I did not receive a reply.

Once Earle moved to Fort Worth he favored that location. He hired a professional fund raiser for about $50,000. Though there are many wealthy Christians in Texas few were inspired to contribute to a research library. Then in 1992, Bill Lane, who was on the board of Rutledge Hill Press, which had made a fortune in selling small booklets of pithy sentiments, offered a million dollars to fund the research library. In 1993, the president of Southwestern Baptist Theological Seminary, Russell Dilday, offered Earle a sizable property at some distance from the seminary for the nominal rent of $1 per year. I traveled in January 1994 to Fort Worth to examine the site with Earle and to witness the signing the contract. Earle had architects draw up plans for the library. But unexpectedly the Southern Baptist Convention later in 1994 fired President Dilday for being "too moderate."

In a letter written on April 26, 2007, to IBR secretary Lynn Cohick, Earle explains somewhat ruefully, "But the rising IBR generation was not interested in an IBRL (IBR Library), and some were opposed to the Fort Worth location which the IBR-LT (i.e. Trustees) for a number of reasons, had in 1994 unanimously chosen. Consequently, in 2004 IBR and IBRL separated into two non-profit corporations in friendly relationship."

Before his death in 2010, the new president of Southwestern Baptist Theological Seminary, Paige Patterson, gave Earle a two-story house just a short distance from the seminary library for the IBR Library. It has its own small library, a small room for meetings, and an upstairs apartment for a visiting scholar. This is a far cry from replicating the Tyndale Library in Cambridge which Earle and Martin Hengel had envisioned.

Conclusions

The example of our British colleagues "from across the Pond" have had an incalculable impact on North American evangelical scholars. Though Earle Ellis's original vision of a residential library like Tyndale House was not fulfilled, the Institute of Biblical Research which he began has flourished with a growing society of over 500 fellows, who are influential biblical scholars and authors. The IBR has produced bibliographies and monographs and has encouraged women and minority scholars as well. In these ways the IBR has far exceeded Earle's original vision.

Chapter 43

The D.D.L.

The *Dictionary of Daily Life in Biblical and Post-Biblical Antiquity* (DDL) is a unique reference work which I coedited with Marvin R. Wilson and which was dedicated to Roland K. Harrison. The completion of this project took about thirty years. It represents the culmination of my scholarly research and writing, but it had a long and complicated history and came close to never seeing the light of day.

Human Relations Area Files

As an anthropology major at the University of Hawaii in 1957 to 1958, I had learned of the Human Relations Area Files begun at Yale University in 1949. The HRAF categorized all of human behavior including abortion. I had been struck by the fact that though abortion had become such an issue for Christians it was not an entry in any of the Bible dictionaries and encyclopedias except in one, the massive six-volume *Anchor Bible Dictionary*. This was because standard reference works had been keyed to the words that appear in the Bible, such as "abomination," but the word "abortion" does not appear. From my forty years of teaching ancient history, I was well aware that abortion was practiced in antiquity. I therefore proposed to Stanley Gundry, senior editor at Zondervan, a new approach based on a grid of cultural categories provided by the HRAF data. Stan accepted my proposal and Zondervan gave me an advance of $2500 in October 1983 to purchase an Apple MacIntosh computer for the project, one of the earliest uses of such a device for the publisher. We were initially going to divide 150 articles, ranging from long, medium, and short essays among Roland K. Harrison, Marvin R. Wilson, and myself.

Roland K. Harrison

Roland K. Harrison (1920 to 1993) was an evangelical scholar of the Old Testament, who earned his PhD at the University of London in 1952 with a dissertation on "The Problem of Evil with Special Reference to Disease." He came to Canada to teach at Huron College in western Ontario in 1950. In 1960 he became the professor of Old Testament at Wycliffe College, an evangelical Anglican school of the University of Toronto, where he taught until his retirement in 1986. Roland was best known for his massive *Introduction to the Old Testament* (1969). This 1,325-page book was reprinted by Hendrickson in 2016. He was a prolific author and a tireless editor. I had contributed articles to *The New International Dictionary of Biblical Archaeology* (1983)o, which he coedited with E. M. Blaiklock of New Zealand, as well as the chapter on "Babylon" to *Major Cities of the Biblical World* (1985), which he edited.

In an appreciative foreword to a Festschrift presented to Roland, Peter C. Craigie wrote:

> Above all else, however, has been the steady stream of publications from Roland Harrison's pen that has made him known to a wider audience. I have, I must confess, long since lost count of the numerous books that Harrison published. To call him *indefatigable* is an understatement, and his productivity in scholarship is all the more remarkable in the light of an early life scarred by ill health.[1]

Roland's character is summarized by his longtime colleague at Wycliffe College Richard Longenecker as follows:

> He seemed never to be in a hurry, yet he worked very hard and for long hours—almost always being at his office before breakfast and often continuing late at night.... He had an obvious interest in everything philological, historical and archaeological,

---

1. Peter C. Craigie, *Israel's Apostasy and Restoration: Essays in Honor of Roland K. Harrison*, ed. Avraham Gileadi (Grand Rapids, Michigan: Baker Book House, 1988), viii.

yet he also prided himself on his understanding of the medical sciences and psychology.[2]

Roland's dedication to the project may be seen in letters which he wrote to me.[3] Especially poignant is his letter of October 6, 1986, just after he had retired.

> Dear Ed:
>
> By now you must think me the most ungracious person that you have ever met for not answering your letters. I apologize most profusely for my physical inability to do so, the fact being that I have had two sessions in hospital this spring and summer.
>
> When I saw you in Anaheim (in November) I had already been feeling increasingly unwell for eighteen months, and really should not have journeyed to California, tired and ill as I was. I contracted a virus in February of this year, which along with the basic infection which was making me ill brought on a stomach disorder and anemia. I spent two weeks in hospital over Easter and was released "on probation" for six weeks.
>
> I did not improve significantly, although I did not need any more blood transfusions, so was readmitted to hospital for a month. I had tests of various kinds, since a stomach ulcer was suspected, and when surgery was finally decided upon I was found to have an occluded pyloric opening to the duodenum. The surgeon didn't even need to make any cuts and, having realigned the stomach (a condition which is an occupational hazard of authors I discover!), I began to feel better within two hours of coming out of anesthetic.
>
> I have been home for six weeks or so recuperating and trying to replace the 35 lb. of weight that I lost while I was ill. I have regained 20 lbs. so far and am feeling very much better. My appetite, which was virtually nil at the time of operation, has now returned marvelously, and my only problem is that I tire quickly when I do things. This weakness will last till next spring, the doctor thinks, and then I should be as good as new.
>
> Until now I simply haven't had the strength to write to you and explain my appallingly bad manners. I have no secretarial help, having now retired from Wycliffe, so have to wait until I muster some strength. I am delighted with the bibliographies

---

2. Cited by J. Glen Taylor, "R. K. Harrison," *Bible Interpreters of the Twentieth Century*, ed. Walter A. Elwell and J. D. Weaver (Grand Rapids, Michiigan: Baker Books, 1999), 315.

3. I am indebted to Graham Harrison for permission to cite his father's letters.

> which you sent me and am using some of the material as I read up on the entries. My doctor doesn't want me to do much writing until Christmas, but if I feel energetic enough, I may decide to disobey him!
>
> Again, please accept my profound apologies for delinquency. I pray that the Lord will bless you richly and that we may produce a piece of work that will be to His glory.
>
> Cordially and sincerely,
> Roland

From a letter dated December 6, 1988, Roland wrote:

> Finally and at last I am able to begin sending you material for the DICTIONARY OF BIBLE MANNERS AND CUSTOMS, or whatever it will be called eventually!
>
> I would like to hear from you if the enclosed is unsuitable in any way, and then I can modify subsequent material. I am working continuously on the entries, which I am enjoying very much.

In a letter dated February 16, 1989, Roland wrote:

> Please feel free to add whatever material will enhance the articles which I send in. I am most willing to countenance improvements, because, like yourself, I want this Dictionary to be absolutely the best on the market for years to come!

In a letter dated June 2, 1989, Roland wrote:

> Please feel free to make whatever additions are necessary for emphasis in special areas. I am most anxious for this work to be outstanding!

Roland completed all of his assigned articles, which were typed with hand-written annotations and corrections, before he passed away in 1993.

Marvin R. Wilson

Marvin is a graduate of Wheaton College and of Gordon-Conwell Theological Seminary. He completed his PhD at Brandeis under Dwight Young in 1963, writing on "Syntactical Studies of Future Tenses in Sahidic." Marvin taught courses in the Old Testament and Jewish Studies at

Barrington College in Rhode Island for eight years and then at Gordon College from 1971 until his retirement in 2018.

By forging friendships with leading Jewish spokesmen such as Marc Tanenbaum and James Rudin, Marvin helped to convene conferences of Jewish and evangelical scholars, and also encouraged Jews to attend church services and Christians to attend synagogues in New England. His classic work, which I used as a text, *Our Father Abraham, Jewish Roots of the Christian Faith* has been translated into French, Italian, Czech, Chinese, Japanese, and Korean. Marvin served as the primary scholar for an award-winning documentary based on this book supported by Jewish funding that was presented on PBS. In 2010, he was surprised at the commencement of Gordon College by the presentation of a Festschrift, *Perspectives on Our Father Abraham*, edited by Steven A. Hunt. I had the privilege of contributing an essay, "Abraham and Archaeology," and attended the ceremony with my wife.

Marvin recalls writing the earliest articles for the DDL while he was on sabbatical leave at the Tyndale House in Cambridge in the summer of 1987. He had one of his students John F. Kutsko[4] compile bibliographies for him.[5] Marvin also finished his assigned articles.

Reasons for the Delay

But even after enlisting a number of my students to help on the dictionary, the completion lagged as I took on too many other writing assignments including some from Zondervan. But all along I was gathering bibliographic data and photocopying articles on all the topics. It was not until my retirement in 2005 that I was able to give undivided attention to this dictionary project. Part of the problem was my penchant to want to track down and read every book and article on any given topic.[6] Another reason for the delay was my dissatisfaction with the ar-

---

4. After graduating from Gordon College in 1986, John Kutsko received the MA from the University of Michigan in 1991 and the PhD from Harvard University in 1997. He worked at Hendrickson Publishers (1996 to 2003) and Abingdon Press (2003 to 2010), before becoming the executive director of the Society of Biblical Literature in 2010.

5. I hired another of Marvin's students, Andrew Pottorf, who was just beginning his doctoral studies in Near Eastern Languages and Civilizations at Harvard University to doublecheck all the bibliographies.

6. It was a fortunate development that I was somehow dropped from Jack Sasson's Agade list serve, which presents daily the titles of a score of publications on the ancient

ticles which had been completed, as they seemed to be similar to those already available in numerous Bible reference works. I wanted to see more extrabiblical refences. Then I made perhaps a foolhardy decision to extend the coverage beyond the biblical period to what I designated as "Post-Biblical Antiquity," covering the "trajectories" of this subject into the later "Jewish World" and the later "Christian World."[7]

In a letter dated August 17, 2010, Stan Gundry informed me that Zondervan was cancelling our contract. Zondervan did not, however, ask for the initial $2500 back! Over the next years I tried in vain to interest other publishers such as InterVarsity Press for whom I had written many reference articles, and Baker Book House which had published many of my books. But after due consideration, the answers were negative. At this time I doubted that the dictionary would ever be published, so I paid a modest sum to Graham Harrison, for all the work his father had done.

Hendrickson Publishers

Then Craig Keener, who had gone to Central Bible College with Steve Hendrickson, suggested I try Hendrickson, a publisher in Peabody, Massachusetts. Two teenage sons of an Assembly of God pastor in Lynn, Massachusetts, Steve and Ray Hendrickson, in 1978 had begun a small book distributing business out of their parents' home. The business thrived. Eventually the family-owned business became Christian Book Distributors, the largest Christian mail order business.[8] The name of the company was later changed to ChristianBook. Ray is the owner of the firm with Paul, Ray's brother, running Hendrickson Publishers beginning in 1980, which is housed in the same building as ChristianBook.

At the SBL conference in Chicago in 2012 I met Allan Emery, the senior editor of Hendrickson. He was a tall man with a full beard. I recognized the Emery name as one connected with Park Street Church in Boston. Allan and his family did have a long association with the

---

world, or I would never have been satisfied!

7. As originally planned, the articles completed by R. K. Harrison and Marvin R. Wilson covered the Old Testament and the New Testament. In the articles I coauthored with R.K.H, I updated the bibliographies and added sections on The Near Eastern World, the Greco-Roman World, The Jewish World, and The Christian World. Due to teaching and other writing commitments Marvin was unable to update or expand his articles. I therefore enlisted other contributors as coauthors to do this with his articles.

8. The advertising of the firm as CBD had to be changed because of its confusion with the abbreviations for Cannabidiol, an ingredient of marijuana!

church. He had served on the staff of the church and knew both Marvin Kreider, with whom I had roomed as a grad student at Brandeis, and also Douglas Calhoun, a Miami grad who had served as a young adult minister at the church. Allan served in the armed services in Germany, where he befriended Dennis Dudley, who became the InterVarsity staff worker at Miami University. Allan went to Gordon-Conwell Theological Seminary and had earned his PhD in Near Eastern Languages and Civilizations from Harvard University.

Though he was scheduled to retire in two years Allan discussed the project with his colleagues at Hendrickson, and they agreed to accept it for publication. I had updated and expanded 60 of the 120 articles by this time. Allan told me, "Ed, you are not going to live long enough to finish this dictionary by yourself." He informed me that I could hire contributors and pay them myself. The usual practice is for publishers to pay contributors 5 cents per word for dictionary articles. In order to finish the project, I contacted scholars and offered to pay them 10 cents per word up to 2500 words, and 5 cents up to 5,000 words, but no more beyond that though they could write more. I tried to limit the bibliographic entries to about 50 references. I provided the contributors with my bibliographies and files of photocopied articles.

Upon Allan's retirement the editorial duties were taken on by Jonathan Kline, a newly minted PhD from Harvard's Department of Near Eastern Languages and Civilizations. Jonathan is the grandson of the noted Old Testament scholar, Meredith G. Kline, a student of Cyrus Gordon who taught at Westminster Theological Seminary and at Gordon-Conwell Theological Seminary. Jonathan's father Meredith M. Kline taught at Westminster Seminary in California and also at Gordon-Conwell. His family lived on the same street as Marvin Wilson.

But first there was a major obstacle. In citing ancient and modern authors I had not bothered to indicate the source as some major references such as the four-volume *Civilizations of the Ancient Near East*, edited by Jack Sasson and reprinted as a two-volume set by Hendrickson had not done so. But Hendrickson insisted that this requirement was absolutely essential. Now it was my custom that after I had completed updating an article and noting the bibliographic titles I disposed of the photocopied sources. I did not know how to scan the relevant pages, so I had no record of the sources of all these citations. To go back and look up all the books and journal articles of these citations would have been an impossible task!

Fortunately, I had a former student, Foy Scalf, come to the rescue! Foy, who had earned a PhD in Egyptology at the University of Chicago, was the head of the Research Archives at the Oriental Institute. Foy has a remarkable memory and has unparalleled search resources at the OI, which enabled him to trace every ancient and modern citation I had included! Foy also arranged for the provision of numerous photos from the OI for the dictionary without charge.

The initial plan was to issue the DDL in three volumes, but as Hendrickson to my delight did not limit the length of the articles, the project eventually resulted in four paperback volumes. Volume I (A to Da) appeared in 2014, volume II (De to H) in 2015; volume III (I to N) and volume IV (O to Z) in 2016. Hendrickson offered these volumes at affordable prices.

Hendrickson was able to obtain endorsements from prominent scholars for each of the four volumes. For volume I, endorsements were provided by Craig A. Evans of Acadia Divinity College, Tremper Longman III of Westmont College, Jacob Neusner of Bard College, and Mark W. Hamilton of Abilene Christian University. For volume II, endorsements came from Clinton E. Arnold of Talbot School of Theology, Victor H. Matthews of Missouri State University, and James K. Hoffmeier of Trinity Evangelical Divinity School. For volume III, endorsements came from Walter C. Kaiser Jr. of Gordon-Conwell Theological Seminary, Eugene H. Merrill of the Southern Baptist Theological Seminary, and Peter J. Williams of Tyndale House. For volume IV, endorsements were provided by Scot McKnight of Northern Seminary, Alan Millard of the University of Liverpool, Nijay K. Gupta of George Fox Evangelical Seminary, and Peter Machinist of Harvard University.

Figure 80. With Peter Machinist

A comprehensive case bound volume (A to Z)[9] appeared in 2017. Electronic versions of separate articles have also been offered digitally on Amazon, as well as the entire set by Logos Bible Software.

The reviews in journals and the response from purchasers were quite favorable. Gordon Hugenberger, the former pastor of Park Street Church and senior Old Testament Professor at Gordon-Conwell Theological Seminary posted this review on the Amazon website:

> Serious readers of the Bible, whether laypersons or scholars, are greatly indebted to Edwin Yamauchi and Marvin Wilson, and the team of respected scholars they assembled, for this much needed resource. Packed into this single 1818-page volume are 120 exceptionally readable and well researched articles on almost every major aspect of the culture of the biblical and post-biblical world of antiquity. These articles, arranged alphabetically, go from Abortion, Adoption, Adultery, Age & the Aged, and Agriculture, to Wealth and Poverty, Weapons, Widows & Orphans, Wild Animals & Hunting—with everything else in between. Each fascinating article is followed by an extensive bibliography which reflects respectful and judicious attention to the competing views and contributions of a wide range of responsible scholars. As a result, readers, whether or not they share the mainstream conservative Christian faith of the

---

9. The (to Z) designation is somewhat misleading as the last entry is on "Wild Animals & Hunting."

editors, are bound to find the articles highly informative and reliable—and truly just fun to read!

Gordon then listed the DDL as his top recommendation for the alumni of Gordon-Conwell Theological Seminary in the GCTS newsletter.

As of July 2021, the World Catalogue listed 320 libraries that had acquired the DDL, including libraries in the following foreign countries: Australia (13), Brazil (1), Canada (17), China (3), Denmark (3), Ecuador (1), England (4), France (3), Germany (8), Ireland (1), Israel (2), Jamaica (1), Netherlands (4), New Zealand (5), Nigeria (1), Peru (1), Poland (1), Scotland (1), South Africa (2), Spain (1), Sweden (2), Switzerland (2), and Turkey (2).

Allan Emery expressed his opinion that the DDL was the most important work published by Hendrickson under his editorial supervision. In November 2016, Marvin Wilson and I were able to celebrate the completion of the DDL project at the Hendrickson booth during the SBL convention in San Antonio. Graham Harrison was gratified that the contributions of his father were updated, enhanced, and finally published. In 2018, the DDL was one of the five finalists for the Christian Book Awards in the category of Bible reference works at a ceremony held at the Museum of the Bible in Washington, DC.

Figure 81. With Marvin Wilson

Chapter 44

The Scriptorium

TWO OF MY DOCTORAL students played key roles in the development of two institutions the Scriptorium and the Museum of the Bible (see chapter 45).

Jerry A. Pattengale

Jerry Pattengale grew up in a dirt-poor family with an abusive alcoholic father in Buck Creek.[1] Jerry graduated from high school when he was but sixteen, but he was homeless at that time. Jerry was rescued by a church pastor who arranged for him to gain a full scholarship at Marion College. He spent a semester in 1977 in Israel, studying archeology and biblical history. Jerry was on the tennis and track teams. He started a teen program (J.C. Body Shop), which is today centered in a multimillion dollar complex adjacent to the campus. He graduated as the outstanding senior in 1979.[2] Jerry doubled in History and Religion and served as the student body president. He then earned an MA in Interpersonal Development from Wheaton College in 1981. At Miami University after earning

---

1. Jerry Pattengale has described his life in this impoverished unincorporated area in over 250 "Buck Creek Chronicles" for the Marion newspaper, *The Chronicle Tribune*. This newsprint series was recognized with awards from the Indiana Associated Press (2015) and the Hoosier State Press Association (2016). He has also published four books with selections from this series.

2. Marion College, founded in 1920, changed its name in 1988 to Indiana Wesleyan University, in part to distinguish it from Marian College, a nearby Catholic school.

an MA in Tudor-Stuart England in 1986, he completed his PhD in 1993 by writing a dissertation on "Benevolent Physicians in Late Antiquity: The Cult of the *Anargyroi*." The *anagyroi* were Christian physicians who did not charge fees for their services. While in graduate school Jerry contributed 13 entries to *The Anchor Bible Dictionary*, wrote two sections for *The Great Events in American History*, and a chapter for the *Historical Dictionary of the Modern Olympic Movement*. Even before finishing his doctorate Jerry joined the faculty of Azusa Pacific University in southern California, where he was twice named "Professor of the Year" and once "Honors Faculty of the Year." He received a Fulbright Award to study in Greece, while assisting at the excavations at Isthmia. He helped to direct as a volunteer The Night of Champions in the greater Los Angeles area. This involved scores of Olympic and professional athletes. He helped build the event from an involvement of 100 to 6,000 teens participating in an event that is still held annually decades later.

Scott T. Carroll

Scott Carroll was quite an athlete at West Virginia University. He was a free style and Greco-Roman wrestling champion who competed in Iran on a Junior Olympic team. His conversion to evangelical Christianity caused a rift with his parents who had hoped he would continue to pursue his athletic career. Scott dropped his scholarship to attend Tennessee Temple University, where he received his BA. He studied ancient history under Charles Aling, an Egyptologist, who later taught at the University of Northwestern in Minnesota.[3] He then earned his MA in Church History at Trinity Evangelical Divinity School studying under John Woodbridge. At Miami University, in association with a graduate course on Eastern Christianity, I taught Scott and other students Coptic and Syriac. Scott also took courses at Hebrew Union College. He was a superb teaching fellow and won the Stein Award as the outstanding graduate student in the university. He completed his dissertation in 1989, writing on "The Melitian Schism: Coptic Christianity and the Egyptian Church." Melitius, the bishop of Lycopolis, led a schism which opposed the authority of Athanasius, the bishop of Alexandria.

In 1988, Scott obtained a position teaching ancient history and ancient languages at Gordon College. He was a demanding but also

---

3. Charles Aling and I were both involved in the Near East Archaeological Society.

an inspirational teacher.[4] He also taught courses on Patristics at Gordon-Conwell Theological Seminary.[5] Scott led the college's European Seminar in touring sites in Greece and Italy. He had a number of articles published in journals such as *The International Journal of African Historical Studies*, *The Journal of Sport History*, *Markers*, *The Journal for the Study of the Pseudepigrapha*, *The Second Century*, and *Vigiliae Christianae*. He also contributed twenty-seven articles to *The Anchor Bible Dictionary*. Scott was also on NPR's two-hour Talk of the Nation program with Donald Redford discussing the historicity of the biblical account of Joseph and the Exodus. He was given the Junior Faculty Excellence in Teaching Award for 1992 to 1993. After all these activities and achievements, Scott was disappointed in the delay of his tenure and decided to leave Gordon College.

The Van Kampen Collection

Robert (Bob) Van Kampen, a graduate of Wheaton College (class of 1960), had developed a fortune through the Van Kampen funds. Bob and his wife Judith built a mansion on the eastern shore of Lake Michigan in a gated compound at Grand Haven, Michigan.

In 1986, Van Kampen acquired his first ancient Bible, the so-called "Martyr's Bible," pages of which were purportedly stained with the blood of a martyr (it was a Matthew's Bible 1537). The stain was later verified to be mold. He then began acquiring ancient Bibles and other objects, which became one of the more prominent collections of Bibles and related items in the world. The Van Kampen Collection eventually included: several Greek New Testaments, one dating to the ninth century, an Ethiopic Lectionary (eighteenth century), the Eliot Indian Bible (1663), the illuminated Ruskin Septuagint (seventeenth century), the Gospels in Old Slavonic (seventeenth century), the Gospels in Armenian (seventeenth century), map of the Bible, Antwerp (1541), a Coverdale Bible (1535), a first edition of Tyndale's Pentateuch (1530), a second edition of Tyndale's New Testament (1534), the Complutensian Polyglot (1522), German manuscripts of Scripture dating before Luther, the first printed Hebrew edition

---

4. Scott Carroll inspired twenty-one of his students from Gordon College and from GordonConwell Theological Seminary to pursue PhDs.

5. Scott encouraged his students and friends to pursue graduate studies with me at Miami University, including Brannen Becknell, John DeFelice, Jason Larson, and Carl Smith.

of Daniel, Ezra and Nehemiah (1487), early Prophets in Hebrew printed by the famous Soncino Publishing House (1485), the Ulm Latin Bible (1480), the Mollenbecke Tabula (1480), the largest holdings of first edition German Bibles before Luther outside of Germany, the Bible in Latin (Venice 1479), the Seville Bible in Hebrew (1468), the complete book of Daniel from the Gutenberg Bible (1455), the largest collection of Wycliffe New Testaments and manuscripts outside of England (c. early fifteenth century), several Latin Vulgates (eleventh to thirteenth centuries), Latin Glossed Epistolary (twelfth century), a Latin New Testament with interlinear translations in Bohemian (1409), Gospels in Greek (ninth century), a Gospel leaf in Armenian, Psalms in Syriac (seventh century) originating from the Monastery of St. Catherine's in the Sinai, the fabled Syrian Yonan Codex, a portion of a Kaifeng Torah (Genesis 1–27, sixteenth century), unpublished cuneiform tablets,[6] including a fragment of an ancient copy of the Taylor Prism, preserving Sennacherib's failed attempt to conquer Jerusalem, Greek papyri, the Mississippi Coptic Codex II, and untranslated Coptic parchment leaves and papyri.

This collection was all amassed between 1986 and 1998. The objects were initially stored in the basement of Bob Van Kampen's home in Chicago. Some books were damaged when it flooded. The collection was moved to the top floor of his mansion in Grand Haven, Michigan. Turkey buzzards often perched on the window ledges, pecking at the glass windows while scholars attempted to do research.

In 1987 a chance meeting one summer at a rural church in Virginia brought Scott in contact with David Smith, who was assisting Robert Van Kampen at the time in collecting antiquarian Bibles and related materials. David Smith had his own sizable collection. Scott stayed in contact with David and began identifying manuscripts in his collection. Bob Van Kampen acquired from David a collection of over 120 early Coptic leaves in 1992. David allowed Scott to work on the leaves at Gordon College prior to Van Kampen's acquisition of them. Scott incorporated students in his research, teaching them Coptic manuscript studies and history. The project was commended by the *Journal of Higher Education*. One student, Jennifer Hevelone, received a NEH grant to continue her work on Coptic; several other students also went on to pursue doctoral work.

Eventually Scott was put in touch with Van Kampen, who hoped to have his manuscripts researched. In 1994 Scott accepted Van Kampen's

---

6. Among the scholars who looked at these tablets were Alan Millard, Brian Webster ,and Gordon Young.

offer to work with his collection. Scott proposed to Van Kampen a broader vision that would necessitate the establishment of a research center. Van Kampen agreed and The Scriptorium, Center for Christian Antiquities, was established. Scott was tasked with identifying items in the Van Kampen Collection and making them available to researchers and the public.

Figure 52. With Scott Carroll at the Van Kampen home

Bob Van Kampen had originally committed to build a public access museum, but he decided to repurpose a building that was under his tennis courts on the grounds of the mansion. The space was built out into a gallery with library space, offices, a small conference room and a vault. Van Kampen's daughter Kimberly Molinari, who was a PhD candidate at the time in Medieval and Renaissance English Literature at Northern Illinois University was employed as the curator of the collection. Beverly Van Kampen, Bob Van Kampen's sister-in-law, served as the administrative director of the Scriptorium. In 1995, Scott persuaded Jerry Pattengale to come as the Scriptorium's director of education. Jerry left the Scriptorium to accept a position at Indiana Wesleyan University, his alma mater, in 1997.[7]

7. Candida R. Moss and Joel S. Baden have written a fascinating critique, *Bible Nation: The United States of Hobby Lobby* (Princeton, New Jersey: Princeton University

The Scriptorium reached out to the community and to schools. The Scriptorium hosted lectures by scholars such as John Sailhamer, Bruce Waltke, Bruce Metzger, and Bastiaan Van Elderen. Bruce Metzger, Bastiaan Van Elderen, Walter Kaiser, and I were appointed to the advisory board of the Scriptorium.[8]

Figure 83. Walt and Marge Kaiser

Press, 2017). Their book was based on extensive research and on two interviews with Scott Carroll and Jerry Pattengale as well as interviews with others. They write in the endnote to page 22, "Carroll received his doctorate from the University of Miami, where he studied with the prominent ancient historian Edwin Yamauchi." And again on p. 64: "At the University of Miami in the late 1980s Pattengale, like Carroll, had studied under Edwin Yamauchi, a conservative evangelical Christian apologist/historian. Yamauchi and Pattengale would go on, in 1996, to cofound the Scriptorium, a private Bible oriented foundation that would eventually become part of The Holy Land Experience, a Christian theme park in Orlando." The authors like many others in the public at large do not know the difference between Miami University, a state school founded in Oxford, Ohio in 1809 and the private University of Miami founded in Coral Gables, Florida in 1925. They are completely in error about the formation of The Scriptorium.

8. In 1999 Richard Marsden of the University of Leeds was added to the board.

The Eberhard Nestle Library

Eberhard Nestle (1851 to 1913) was the German scholar who produced the standard Greek New Testament text with a critical apparatus of readings from various manuscripts in his monumental *Novum Testamentum Graece* in 1898, which he and later his son Erwin revised. The latest revision by Kurt Aland is the twenty-eighth edition published in 2012. Nestle was a scholar of many languages including Hebrew and Syriac. He also had a special interest in the Septuagint.

The house where Nestle's library was housed was formerly the home of twin sisters Agnes Lewis and Margaret Gibson, who learned Syriac and who were close friends with Nestle. He bequeathed his library to them. Scott traveled to Westminster College to apprise Van Kampen of the value of the collection. Scott was astounded by what he saw. In 1995, Van Kampen purchased the entire library for $100,000, much to the chagrin of some at Cambridge. The library was crated and shipped to the United States. The crates arrived at the Scriptorium a day before Bruce Metzger's seminar on textual criticism conducted at the Scriptorium.

Among the treasures were: the edition of the Septuagint commissioned by Pope Sixtus V (1588), Quadriplex Psalterium (1516), the first four editions of Erasmus's Greek-Latin New Testament, Blomberg's first edition of the Pentateuch (the First Rabbinical Bible; 1517 to 1519), and innumerable Bibles illustrating the development of critical texts, along with grammars and lexical works dating from the fifteenth to the nineteenth century. A number of volumes contain Nestle's copious notes. Some letters were also found interleafed in the books.

Wadi Natrun and the Odyssey Program

The Scriptorium sponsored Bastiaan Van Elderen's excavations of the early monastery of John the Little in Wadi Natrun northwest of Cairo. Among those participating were my doctoral student Darlene Brooks Hedstrom and her husband Mark. In 1996, Scott created and wrote an inter-curricular program for Middle School students in southwestern Michigan, integrating live access to the excavation. This was quite a feat with the internet only in its infancy. The program was called Odyssey in Egypt. Jerry coordinated the program with participating schools, and Mark provided photos and support in Egypt. The computer programming was done by Steve Boggus in the US. This innovative interactive program generated great interest with the teachers and students and demonstrated the potential of online education. It was featured in *Newsweek Magazine* and was a finalist for the prestigious Webby Award for innovations in technology and education. The program is archived in the Smithsonian Museum. It cost less than $30,000 to create. Van Kampen believed that the internet would never catch on, so he cancelled the program.

Hampton Court[9]

In 1994, the Van Kampes purchased Hampton Court, the largest manor house in England. It is located in Herefordshire in southwestern England near the Welsh border. The cathedral in the nearby town of Hereford houses the largest chain library in England and the huge *Mappa Mundi*, one of the most famous medieval maps of the world with Jerusalem in the center. It is five feet in diameter. This map was stored at Hampton Court during the English Civil War.

Hampton Court was built in 1435 by Henry IV, who gave it to Sir Rowland Lenthal, who was knighted for his bravery at the famous battle of Agincourt (1415) against the French. It is purported that the Hereford breed of cows was developed on the farm of Hampton Court. The only books left in the impressive library were volumes of the farm's top bovine specimens.

The castle has 160 rooms, including twenty-eight bedrooms. The master bedroom contains one of England's first indoor bathtubs. Van Kampen spared no expense to refurbish the ancient building as a modern conference center. The interior was decorated with ancient suits of armor and a stuffed lion's head. He added numerous bathrooms and a commercial kitchen and installed new wiring and a new central heating system. The restoration of the ancient roof required fifty-four tons of lead and thirty-thousand Welsh slate tiles.

---

9. There was a later Hampton Court Palace built by Henry VIII in London.

Figure 84. Portrait of Bob and Judith Van Kampen

The Bible as Book

Hampton Court would serve as the venue for six annual conferences on "The Bible as Book." The Scriptorium paid for the expenses of numerous distinguished scholars to travel to the conferences. Their papers would be published by the British Library. The appearance of Hampton Court resembled that of Downton abbey in the PBS series.

Figure 85. Kimi at Hampton Court, Hereford

The first conference, from May 31 to June 3, 1995, was on "The Manuscript Tradition." This conference was planned by Scott and Jerry with the aid of Scot McKendrick of The British Library. I gave the inaugural address on "Scripture as Talisman, Specimen, and Dragoman."[10] While the other scholars were lodged in a hotel in Hereford, Scott gave my wife and me the privilege of staying in the master bedroom in the manor house. Among the speakers at the conference were: Géza Vermes (Wolfson College, Oxford), Vivian Mann (The Jewish Museum), Dan Rettberg (Emory University), Stephen Emmel (Brown University), T. S. Pattie (The British Library), John Sharpe (Duke University), Allison Salveson (The Oriental Institute, Oxford), Sylvie Merian (The Pierpont Morgan Library), Andrew Lowth (Goldsmith's College), John Skillen (Gordon College), Bernard Meehan (Trinity College, Dublin), David Ganz (University of North Carolina), Christopher de Hamel (Sotheby's), Lillian Randall (Walters Art Gallery), Nancy Netzer (Boston College), Christina von Nolcken (University of Chicago), Richard Marsden (Girton College, Cambridge), Adelaide Bennett (Princeton University), Martin McNamara (Milltown Institute of Theology, Dublin), Jennifer

---

10. Eleven years later after expanding this paper, I gave it as the presidential address to the Evangelical Theological Society in 2006.

O'Reilly (University College, Cork), Lucy-Anne Hunt (University of Birmingham), and P. Leonard Boyle (Biblioteca Apostolica Vaticana).[11] Scott presented a paper describing the goals and objectives of the Scriptorium at the concluding banquet in the long hall of the castle.

Figure 86. Hereford Conference 1995. In the center, I am flanked by Scott Carroll on my right and Jerry Pattengale on my left.

Because I was traveling in Asia, I missed the second conference in 1996 on "The First Printed Editions." That conference opened in London at The British Library with an address by Sir Anthony Kenny, the chairman of The British Library, followed by a demonstration of the library's Incunable Short Title Catalogue. An exhibition of Wycliffe and Tyndale Bibles from the Van Kampen Collection was displayed with related treasures from The British Library that evening at a special event arranged by Scott and Jerry with the help of staff from The British Museum at a London hotel that had been rented by Van Kampen. Because of other commitments, I also missed the conference on "The Reformation" in 1997.

11. Father Boyle's arrival coincided with an unfortunate development. The theft of illuminated leaves from the Vatican Library by an Ohio State professor had just come to light. As he arrived at the castle Father Boyle handed Jerry a *Time Magazine*, which he had been reading on the plane and said, "Jerry, all these years I have been doing good for people, and a friend of 20 years steals from me and damn it, now I'm famous!"

The Septuagint Project

It was well known that Robert Van Kampen had a consuming interest in biblical prophecy. He wrote several books on this topic promoting his premillennial beliefs. He wanted to sponsor a new English translation of the Septuagint into English, hoping that this would support his theological positions. When John Sailhamer withdrew from this project, it devolved to Scott Carroll. Before beginning his translation, Scott expended a great deal of time and effort in developing a critical apparatus of the early chapters of Genesis with the help of Brian Webster. It was hoped that such an apparatus might provide academic credibility to this undertaking. This was an overly ambitious project as such a task as this would require a large committee of scholars.[12] I received a letter of concern from Robert Kraft of the University of Pennsylvania who had been working on such a committee. Walter Kaiser also received a similar message of concern from Moisés Silva. Because of his dissatisfaction with Scott's work on the Septuagint and interpersonal conflicts, Van Kampen replaced Scott with Bastiaan Van Elderen as the executive director of the Scriptorium in 1998. The Septuagint project was terminated. Scott found a teaching position at Grand Valley State University in Allendale, Michigan, where he taught courses in history.

Later Conferences

The fourth conference, on "The Transmission of the Greek Text," was held on May 27–30, 1998, commemorating the centennial of the publication of the *Novum Testamentum Graecae* by Eberhard Nestle. The speakers included: Warren Kay (Merrimack College), Robert A. Kraft (University of Pennsylvania), Stanley E. Porter (Roehampton Institute, London), L. Neville Birdsall (University of Birmingham), John Brogan (Northwestern College, Iowa), Scott McKendrick (The British Library), David C. Parker (University of Birmingham), Michael W. Holmes (Bethel College), Tjitze Baarda (Vriej Universiteit, Amsterdam), Bart D. Ehrman (University of North Carolina), Paul McReynolds (Hope International University), Karen Jobes (Westmont College), Emanuel Tov (Hebrew University), Michael Welte (Institut für Neutestamentliche Textforschung, Münster), Keith Elliot (University of Leeds), Jacob van Bruggen

---

12. In 2007 Oxford University Press published *A New English Translation of the Septuagint*, edited by Robert Piertsma and Benjamin C. Wright.

(Theologische Universiteit, Kampen). The conference concluded with addresses on "The Future of Septuagint Textual Studies" by John Weavers (University of Toronto) and "The Future of New Testament Textual Studies" by Bruce M. Metzger (Princeton Theological Seminary)

The fifth conference on "The Latin Bible" was held on May 26 to 29, 1999. This was a relatively small conference with scholars mainly from Ireland[13] including: Aidan Breen (Trinity College, Dublin), Helen Conrad O'Brain (Trinity College, Dublin), Martin McNamara (Milltown Institute of Theology, Dublin), Thomas O'Loughlin (University of Wales),

---

13. After this Hereford conference I spent a week touring Ireland. Flying into Dublin I rented a small car. As in England one drives on the left and the driver's seat is on the right. I had a bit of a scare after viewing the spectacular Cliffs of Moher on the west coast. As the sunlight was fading, I came down a hill and while rounding a curve my left wheels went off the road into a ditch. I would have been in grave difficulty had not soon after two cars stopped. Eight men lifted my car back on to the road!

I visited a number of sites associated with St. Patrick (fifth century AD), an English lad who was captured by the Irish. After his release, he trained as a priest in France. In a dream which he recorded in his diary which has been preserved, he heard the Irish calling to him to return and evangelize them, and so he did. The Celtic Christianity which he began was both monastic and missionary. It spread to Scotland and northern England and then to Europe.

In Dublin I visited Trinity College (founded in 1592) and viewed a page of the Book of Kells, the most celebrated illuminated manuscript from the Middle Ages.

In the north of Dublin, I viewed the River Boyne, where the Protestant King of England, William III, inflicted a massive defeat on the Catholic Irish, a victory which is still celebrated by Protestants on July 12 to this day in Northern Ireland.

In Dublin I also visited the Post Office building, where Irish rebels on Easter 1916 were barricaded and assaulted. Bullet marks from that raid can still be seen. I viewed the courtyard of the British government, where the rebels were hanged.

At the port city of Cork, I stayed in a hotel where a plaque marked the room where Michael Collins, the famed Irish Republican Army. leader stayed. He was assassinated in 1922 by more radical IRA members who were opposed to his willingness to sign a treaty with the British

I took a tour of the Guinness distillery but did not accept the sample drink they offered to the tourists. Guinness is known worldwide for all kinds of achievements that they record.

The one site in Dublin I wished to see most of all was the Chester Beatty Museum, which I had some difficulty finding as it was located in a suburb. (In 2000, the museum was moved to the Dublin Castle.) Chester Beatty was an American who had gained a fortune through copper mining enterprises in Africa. He became an avid collector of manuscripts and artifacts. He moved his vast collection from London to Dublin. At his death in 1968 he was honored by the Irish government. There are three early papyri codices which he obtained which contain some of the earliest Greek manuscripts of the Gospels, Acts, Pauline epistles, and Revelation dated to AD 200 to 300. I bought a poster from the museum, which depicts a scribe copying a manuscript. I placed this on the door of my office in the History Department. The title of the poster was THE WORD OF GOD.

Anne Marie D'Arcy (Trinity College, Dublin), Orlaith O'Sullivan (The Scriptorium), Laura Light (Harvard University), J. D. Pheifer (Trinity College, Dublin), Malgorzata Krasnodebska-D'Aughton (University College, Cork), and Tjitze Baarda (Vrije Universiteit, Amsterdam). An excursion went to Hay on Wye in Wales, a town noted for its many used bookstores.

The sixth and final conference of The Bible as Book series was on "The Text of the Bible in Light of the Discoveries in the Judean Desert" held on June 18 to 21, 2000.[14] The opening lecture on "The Emergence of a Canon of Scriptures in Light of the Fragments of Biblical Books from Qumran" was presented by Shemaryahu Talmon (Hebrew University).[15] Papers were then given by: Arie van der Kooij (University of Leiden), Armin Lange (University of Tübingen), Eugene Ulrich (University of Notre Dame), Donald Parry (Brigham Young University), Ted Herbert (International Christian College), Peter Flint (Trinity Western University), Martin Abegg (Trinity Western University), Philip Alexander (University of Manchester), Eibert Tigchelaar (University of Groningen), Timothy Lim (University of Edinburgh), Jesper Hogenhaven (University of Copenhagen), Sarianna Metso (Umiversity of Helsinki), George J. Brooke (University of Manchester), James VanderKam (University of Notre Dame), Steven Daley (Jerusalem), Harold Scanlin (United Bible Societies), and Sidnie White Crawford (University of Nebraska). The closing address "The Biblical Texts from the Judean Desert: An Overview in Light of the Full Publication of the Texts" was given by Emanuel Tov (Hebrew University).[16]

---

14. Bastiaan Van Elderen who had planned the conference was unable to attend because of the death of his son who had been working with the World Council of Churches in Geneva.

15. At Brandeis University I had the privilege of studying under Shemaryahu Talmon, who was the leading Israeli scholar on the Dead Sea Scrolls.

16. Emanuel Tov, a student of Talmon, had been placed in charge of the official Oxford University series, *Discoveries in the Judean Desert*.

THE SCRIPTORIUM

Figure 87. Hereford Conference 2000. I am kneeling in the front row on the left.

After dinner, Géza Vermes, the foremost British scholar on the Dead Sea Scrolls spoke on "Living with the Dead Sea Scrolls—Personal Reminiscences over 50 Years." We were able to celebrate Géza's eightieth birthday at this occasion.[17] We also had the public presentation of *The Dead Sea Scrolls Bible* by Martin Abegg, Jr., Peter Flint, and Eugene Ulrich, which translated all the Qumran biblical fragments together with commentaries on these texts.[18]

---

17. I have used Géza Vermes's *Jesus the Jew* for my senior seminar on Judaism and Christianity.

18. Published by Harper San Francisco in 1999. All the non-biblical Qumran fragments were translated by Michael Wise, Martin Abegg, Jr. and Edward Cook in *The Dead Sea Scrolls* (San Francisco, California: HarperOne, 1996; second edition 2005).

Figure 88. With Géza Vermes

Robert Van Kampen's Death

After waiting in vain for a heart transplant for three years, Robert Van Kampen died on October 3, 1999, at a hospital in suburban Chicago at the age of 59. At the time of his death, his wealth was estimated to be about 400 million dollars. Prior to his death, the Van Kampens had authorized the building of the elaborate Van Kampen Garden at Hampton Court. Complete with a 150-year-old Wisteria walk and a new maze, the garden was opened for the first time to the public by Judith Van Kampen together with her daughter Karla and son-in-law Scott Pierre on June 24, 2000. After its sale by the Van Kampens, Hampton Court was renovated and its gardens enlarged. Today, it is a popular site for visitors and for the hosting of weddings.

The Van Kampen family moved from western Michigan into a gated community in Orlando, Florida. In 2002, the family loaned the Van Kampen Collection to the custody of Marvin Rosenthal, the founder of Zion's Hope, an organization that Bob Van Kampen had supported.

Bastiaan Van Elderen and Bruce Metzger publicly lamented the loss to scholars of this vast collection, which included not only a large collection of ancient Bibles but also about 1,500 cuneiform tablets and 2,500 Greek and Coptic papyri.

The Holy Land Experience

In 2001, Marvin Rosenthal, a messianic Jew, had opened The Holy Land Experience, a Christian theme park in Orlando, Florida, on Interstate 4 just a half hour from Disney's Magic Kingdom. For an estimated 16 million dollars, he replicated a Qumran cave, Herod's temple, and the Garden Tomb. A Jerusalem street market was created, and actors in ancient costume were employed. The Oasis Palm Cafe served "Goliath burgers." In one corner of the park, a Coptic-styled building housed a selection of the Van Kampen Bibles in thirteen galleries.

Despite its prime location, The Holy Land Experience failed to attract enough visitors. In 2007, the park was eight million dollars in debt and was sold to the Trinity Broadcasting Network for 37 million dollars. In February 2020, the park closed even before the onset of the corona virus pandemic in March.

Chapter 45

T.M.O.B.

The Museum of the Bible (TMOB) was opened in Washington, DC in 2017 to considerable acclaim, but the museum has also experienced a number of controversies. It was largely funded by Steve Green, the president of Hobby Lobby. Scott Carroll and Jerry Pattengale played key roles in its development.

Hobby Lobby

Hobby Lobby is a large chain of arts and crafts stores that was begun by David Green, the son of a Pentecostal preacher. David considered himself "the black sheep" of the family since unlike his five brothers he did not become a preacher but became a retailer. In his own words David "squeaked through high school" and entered the Air Force Reserves. He worked for a five and dime store TG&Y. He began his own business in 1970 selling pets. He then borrowed $600 from the bank to start making picture frames with the help of his wife Barbara and his sons Steve and Mart, whom he paid seven cents per frame.

In 1972, David opened his first Hobby Lobby store in Oklahoma City in a tiny 300 square foot space. He adopted four key principles: 1) Run your business in harmony with God's laws. 2) Focus on people more than money. Make sure you never stop focusing on the customer's perspective. 3) Be a *merchant* . . . Your core activity is *buying and selling merchandise.* 4) Install the proper systems to support the first three keys.[1] Though there were times when the business almost went bankrupt, the Hobby Lobby chain prospered over the years despite closing on Sundays.

According to Candida R. Moss and Joel S. Baden:

> What began as a living-room family photo-frame assembly line grew into a retail giant. By 2012 Hobby Lobby had 520 superstores[2] in 42 states, and the Green family which owns 100% of the company was ranked at number 79 on the Forbes list of the four hundred richest Americans, with an estimated net worth of $4.5 billion. Every step along the way Green stayed true to his religious beliefs, often at the expense of company profits.[3]

In 2004 Steve Green succeeded his father as the C.E.O. of Hobby Lobby. He and his wife Jackie have a son and five daughters, including a daughter adopted from China in 2008. He and his family attend a Baptist church in Oklahoma City.

Johnny Shipman

D. Jonathan "Johnny" Shipman was a Christian businessman from Dallas. He was the son of a pastor of a Baptist church in Cleburne, a small town south of Fort Worth. He collected Bibles and had a dream of starting a national Bible museum in Dallas. For this he needed both funding and some expert advice. Johnny was a friend of David Smith and through him he learned about Scott Carroll and his work for the Van Kampen Collection. The two met in 2000 as Scott was teaching at Cornerstone University in Grand Rapids.[4] Shipman had worked with Mart Green to raise money for Mart's film company which produced the movie *The End of the Spear* (2005) chronicling the martyrdom of five missionaries in Ecuador.

---

1. David Green with Dean Merrill, *More than a Hobby* (Nashville, Tennessee: Nelson Business, 2005), 11–12.

2. Such stores average 60,000 square feet.

3. Candida R. Moss and Joel S. Baden, *Bible Nation: The United States of Hobby Lobby* (Princeton, New Jersey: Princeton University Press, 2007), 3.

4. Cornerstone University until 1999 had been known as Grand Rapids Bible College. It and the adjacent Grand Rapids Theological Seminary were affiliated with the General Association of Regular Baptists.

The Green family was the wealthiest and most generous patron of Christian causes.[5] They receive annually thousands of requests for money for projects, ministries, and property. In weekly family meetings they decide which of these projects to fund. They have, for example, provided $60 million dollars to aid Oral Roberts University in Tulsa in 1997 and have also aided the Assembly of God Evangel College in Springfield, Missouri. The family is also a generous supporter of Wycliffe Bible Translators.

Shipman and Carroll made presentations once a year beginning in 2006 to Steve Green about their vision of a national Bible museum but the project failed to interest him. Mart Green told Shipman and Carroll that his family did not collect anything. Steve had been buying properties, improving them, and after a year and a day, donating them to gain a tax write off. Shipman believed that Steve Green might be interested in buying a distressed property in Dallas and in donating it for a national Bible museum. Considerable effort was expended in looking for a suitable property. Carroll mentioned this plan in *The Herald*, Cornerstone University's school paper, in 2008. In 2010 an article in *The Dallas Observer* quoted Carroll as describing plans to acquire a 900,000 square foot building in downtown Dallas to be financed by $300 million dollars from an unnamed family. But these plans fell through.

Steve Green then became interested when he learned that by buying antiquities and then donating them, he could earn a similar tax write off as his real estate ventures.[6] In this case, Hobby Lobby would purchase the items and donate them to a museum of the Bible on the assumption that the estimated appraised value of these items would become worth at least three times their purchase cost.

Johnny Shipman played a key role in the earliest acquisitions by Steve Green. In 2009 Steve acquired a few items from US dealers including a sizable collection of American Bibles and a Dead Sea Scrolls fragment, which later turned out to be a forgery. In late 2009 Steve gained at auctions from Sotheby's and Christie's very important works including a German Bible printed by Anton Koberger (1483), a Bodmer Papyrus Psalms codex (c. 4th c. AD), and most significantly Richard Rolle's Middle English translation of the Psalter and Canticles (c. AD 1450). Shipman also helped to negotiate the acquisition of the Codex

---

5. In 2011, the sales of the Hobby Lobby chain and affiliated companies totaled $2.2 billion dollars.

6. Under a stipulation known as 501(c)(3) charities. See Moss and Baden, 23–24.

Climaci Rescriptus from Westminster College, Cambridge, to the chagrin of scholars in Cambridge.

Early in 2010, Shipman arranged a trip for Steve and Scott to meet antiquities dealers in Turkey and Israel. In Istanbul, Steve acquired papyri and Egyptian funerary masks made of papyrus cartonnage. In Israel Steve met the well-known dealer Kando, who showed him a list of biblical fragments that were kept in a bank vault in Zurich. Shipman also introduced David and Scott to Alan Baidun. In one of his shops by the Via Dolorosa, Baidun uncovered a trap door to disclose an opening to a large storeroom filled with antiquities. Shipman also introduced David and Scott to a Jewish dealer who showed them a Genizah, or storeroom for discarded Hebrew scrolls. Shipman purchased numerous antiquities and had them shipped to the Hobby Lobby office in Oklahoma City.

In the late spring of 2010 a reporter from the *New York Times*, who had been contacted by Shipman, came to Oklahoma City to view some of these acquisitions which were put on display in the Hobby Lobby office. But at the time Shipman himself was not present for the interview. Because Steve could no longer stand Shipman's idiosyncrasies, he had fired Johnny! Johnny Shipman's role in starting a Bible museum was erased from the official record. But to his dying days Shipman continued to hold on to that dream. At his funeral, following his death on March 16, 2013, mourners were encouraged to donate to his National Bible Museum Fund.

Passages

Once the Green family became convinced of the value of a national Bible museum to educate Christians and as a witness to non-Christians, they went all out for this project. After Johnny Shipman was dismissed, Scott was given the responsibility of building the Green Collection. While he made suggestions as to what the Greens might wish to buy, the decision to buy always fell to the Greens. Payments and sales agreements were handled directly between the Greens and the dealers.

Scott traveled throughout the world to meet private owners and antiquities dealers. He attended the auction houses Sotheby's and Christie's in London. Because of the financial crisis of 2008, this period was a buyer's market. Individuals and institutions were selling remarkable items. During Scott's tenure, it has been estimated that the Greens expended about

$60 million dollars, securing about 40,000 items. While the final appraised value of these items is not fully known, they may now approach one billion dollars in value. The market adjusted and prices went up, which made the acquisitions by the Greens much more valuable.

The Greens hoped that the collection they were acquiring would have an impact on people worldwide. In the summer of 2010 Scott took selected items for exhibits in Liberia, Nigeria, and Sierra Leone. Large numbers of people came to see the exhibits and to hear Scott's lectures.

In view of the impending five hundredth anniversary of the publication of the King James Bible in 2011, Scott suggested that an exhibit should tell the story of the translation of the Bible into English, culminating in the publication of the King James version. Scott created a children's route through the exhibit, led by a friendly lion! The traveling exhibition, which included four hundred select items from the Green Collection, would be called "Passages."

Scott curated Passages and wrote an illustrated catalogue for the exhibitions.[7] Passages was arranged in rooms with life-like figures such as a figure of William Tyndale bound to a stake, urging people to read the Bible. A virtual tour guide met the visitor at each gallery. 1) The recreation of the Dura Europos synagogue illustrated the Jewish scribal tradition with a Qumran fragment of Genesis, Torah scrolls, Megillah scrolls, and synagogue lamps including a marble lamp from the Herodian period. 2) A recreation of the cave in Bethlehem with a figure of Jerome translating the Bible into Latin, later known as the Vulgate. 3) An artist's room showing the adornment of illustrated medieval manuscripts such as a gilded Spanish Psalter. 4) A monastic cloister with Carolingian manuscripts (c. AD 800), and the *Codex Climaci Rescriptus*, one of the earliest complete Bibles in the world.[8] 5) A medieval peasant's hut with the *Roseberry Rolle*, the earliest translation of the Psalms into Middle English. 6) Early English Bibles: first editions of the Coverdale Bible, Matthew's Bible, the Geneva Bible, and the King James Bible.

---

7. When Scott asked for royalties for this publication, he was rebuffed.

8. The Codex Climaci Rescriptus was discovered at the library of Saint Catherine's Monastery in Sinai. This is a palimpsest, that is a manuscript which has a later text written over a previous text. The Christian Palestinian Aramaic version of the Old and the New Testament (sixth century AD), lay under the later Greek uncial New Testament (c. eighth century AD). Westminster College, Cambridge, the owners of the codex put it up for sale in 2010 at Sotheby's for a million dollars. When it was not sold, the Green Collection bought it for an undisclosed price. In February 2012, the 137-page codex was entrusted for study to the scholars associated with Tyndale House, Cambridge.

7) Gutenberg's Print Shop with Gutenberg's Bible (fifteenth century), and a first edition of Thomas à Kempis's *The Imitation of Christ*. 8) A Reformation Theater featuring figures of Erasmus, Luther, and Johann Eck. This room displayed Luther's letter written the night before he was excommunicated. Also on display was William Tyndale's *Obedience of a Christian Man* and the 1535 translation from Latin of the New Testament he was working on as he was imprisoned in the Tower of London just before his execution. 9) The final room has a printer preparing to make corrections to the notorious "Wicked Bible," an edition of the King James Bible that had an egregious omission so that Exodus 20:14 commanded "Thou shalt commit adultery"!

The logistics of mounting such a traveling exhibition were enormous. There was, first of all, the securing of a large space for several months. Then packing, shipping, and insuring the items to be exhibited. Along with the exhibits there were lectures by noted scholars who would complement the exhibitions. Jerry Pattengale, the director of the Green Scholars Initiative, made the arrangements for these speakers.[9]

Passages was first mounted in Oklahoma City, then moved over the years to Atlanta, Charlotte, Colorado Springs, Springfield (MO), Los Angeles, the Vatican twice, Jerusalem, Havana, and Buenos Aires.

The world premiere was held at the Oklahoma City Museum from May 16 to October 16, 2011, commemorating the four hundredth anniversary of the publication of the King James Bible.[10] The exhibits were held in a 15,000 sq. foot hall space. Among the speakers invited to give lectures were Gordon Campbell (University of Leicester), Ralph Hanna (Keble College, Oxford), David Lyle Jeffrey (Baylor University), Alistair McGrath (Kings College, London), and Dirk Obbink (Christ Church, Oxford).

In 2011, I had the privilege of being one of the speakers at Oklahoma City in the sold-out lecture series. It was good to see Jerry as well as Scott, his wife Denise, and their daughter Joy who was the Curator of the Green Collection from 2010 to 2012. She worked with Lauren Green McAfee, one of the Green daughters. I had dinner with Steve and Jackie Green and Mart Green. When I gave a PowerPoint presentation on "The Greatest

---

9. Jerry continued as the assistant provost for public engagement at Indian Wesleyan University with reduced responsibilities so he could work for Steve Green.

10. Through contacts made with Mario Parades, the Catholic liaison with the American Bible Society, Scott was able to exhibit a selection of 20 items from the Green Collection at the Vatican Embassy in Washington, DC, in March 2011.

Archaeological Discoveries and the Old Testament," David and Barbara Green were sitting in the front row.[11] Bradford Young of Oral Roberts University served as the respondent to my talk.

On the next day Jerry and I went to visit Thomas Oden, who lived in Oklahoma City. Tom, a once liberal Methodist theologian who was converted to evangelical Christianity upon reading Augustine, and I had served as senior editors of *Christianity Today*. The Green family was subsidizing the scholarly patristic commentaries published by InterVarsity Press that he was editing.

I was also one of the lecturers when Passages was exhibited from June to December 2013 in a 40,000 sq. foot venue in Colorado Springs. The other speakers were Gordon Campbell (University of Leicester), Donald Fairbairn (Gordon-Conwell Theological Seminary), Bill Yarchin (Azusa Pacific University), Ben Witherington III (Asbury Theological Seminary), Christopher B. Hays (Fuller Theological Seminary), Ken Schenk (Wesley Theological Seminary). Jennifer HeveloneHarper (Gordon College), Brett Foster (Wheaton College), Peter Williams (Tyndale House, Cambridge), Andrew Atherstone (Wycliffe Hall, Oxford), David Lyle Jeffrey (Baylor University), Tim Laniak (Gordon-Conwell Theological Seminary, Charlotte), Daniel B. Wallace (Dallas Theological Seminary), Filip Yukosavovic (Bible Lands Museum, Jerusalem), Robert Duke (Azusa Pacific University), Stan Rosenberg (Wycliffe Hall, Oxford), Craig A. Evans (Acadia Divinity College), Simon Gathercol (Fitzwilliam College, Cambridge), Curt Niccum (Abilene Christian University), and Walter Kaiser (Gordon-Conwell Theological Seminary). All the speakers were given very generous honoraria.

The Green Scholars Initiative

It was Scott Carroll's idea to loan unpublished texts from the Green Collection to selected scholars with the proviso that they include students in the project of examining and studying such texts. He believed that such an experience would not only excite scholars, engage them in the work of the collection and provide credibility, but would also motivate the students to pursue further study of the Bible and related rare books.

---

11. David Green gave me an autographed copy of his book, *More Than a Hobby*. Steve Green gave me an autographed copy of his book, *Faith in America: The Impact of One Company Speaking out Boldly*.

Jerry Pattengale, as the director of the Green Scholars Initiative, invited senior scholars to serve as an advisory board in fields of their specialty, Marian Ayad (Coptic texts), Robert Duke (Hebrew Texts), Jeffrey Fish (Greek Texts), Curt Niccum (Ethiopic Texts), David Riggs (Latin Texts), Peter Williams (Aramaic Texts), and Dirk Obbink (Papyri). Jerry then identified the scholars, mainly from the evangelical consortium of Christian Colleges and Universities, who would be designated as Green Scholars. Their schools would have to insure the manuscripts. The participants were pledged to nondisclosure agreements until after the texts were published.

For example, a three-inch wide and six-inch long Greek papyrus was entrusted to Septuagint specialist Karen Jobes of Wheaton College. Authors Moss and Baden seem to view these projects as a cynical exploitation of unpaid labor.[12] But the eight Wheaton students who participated were quite excited and enthusiastic about this hands-on experience as were other students the authors interviewed.

Funerary Masks

Especially during the Ptolemaic era Egyptians created decorated funerary masks made from discarded papyri moistened with gesso to form a papier mâché mold. The Egyptians sometimes also used linen strips along with the papyri and gesso. Cartonnage usually survives as corroded chunks of gesso and twisted layers of papyri. Researchers have been dismantling masks since the late nineteenth century and have recovered many important papyri in this manner.

Dirk Obbink of Oxford University sold twenty Egyptian funerary masks to the Museum of the Bible. Dirk held that when papyri are collected randomly about 80% are documentary and about 20 percent are literary. He surmised that the same ratios would hold true of papyri extracted from cartonnage. As the use of such funerary masks ceased with the end of the Ptolemaic period, it is not possible that New Testament papyri were used in this manner.

Scott found that by dissolving cartonnage with a mild detergent he could extract the papyri infrastructure which at times contained literary papyri. In 2010, a student videotaped a day long demonstration and posted a two-minute excerpt without Scott's permission on YouTube. In

---

12. See Moss and Baden, ch. 2.

2010 Scott identified fragments of Homer and a fourth century AD fragment of the LXX version of 1 Samuel extracted from such masks. Scott demonstrated this procedure at a seminar sponsored by the Christian apologist Josh McDowell. In early January 2012, Scott and Dirk dismantled some of the masks bought by the Museum of the Bible in Dirk's office. Later, on January 16, Scott led a demonstration of this process for students and faculty from Baylor University. He dismantled two leg coverings that produced documentary papyri. Scott also brought with him the papyri he and Dirk had earlier extracted. The use of the two sources of papyri led to the unintended conclusion that all of the papyri came from the same source according to Scott. He showed a literary papyrus to a Baylor professor who correctly identified it as from the poems of Sappho.[13] Some scholars were appalled by the destruction of the Egyptian mummy masks, but others applauded the identification of literary works such as the rare fragment from Sappho.

Scott Carroll's Dismissal

Because of unstated personality and policy differences,[14] Scott Carroll was suddenly dismissed from his employment with the Greens in 2012, just two weeks after the closing of the Vatican exhibition. When Scott asked why he was being dismissed, Steve replied "for no reason in particular" and added that as Scott was an "at will" employee, he did not have to provide a reason. Scott was offered a severance package, but he chose not to accept it.

Moss and Baden suggest:

> What is clear, however, is that once Carroll left, the Greens began to rewrite the story of his contributions. They both scrubbed the internet of reference to Carroll's involvement and subtly created a public narrative in which Carroll was responsible for any mishandling of acquisitions and artifacts. After years of

---

13. Sappho lived on the large Greek island of Lesbos, just off the coast of Turkey. Because of her erotic poems about her female companions, the term "Lesbian" came to designate a female homosexual.

14. In its first 2010 filing for tax purposes, the museum indicated that its primary purpose was "to bring to life the living word of God, to tell its compelling story of preservation, and to inspire confidence in the absolute authority and reliability of the Bible." A revised 2013 mission statement declared: "We exist to involve all people to engage with the Bible. We invite Biblical exploration through museum exhibits and scholarly pursuits." This latter view was more in accord with Scott's own vision for the collection.

representing the Green Collection in the press and around the world, Carroll had effectively become a scapegoat.[15]

Hobby Lobby and the Supreme Court

One provision of President Barack Obama's 2010 Affordable Care Act (ACA), popularly known as Obamacare, required employers to provide their female employees with health insurance coverage for contraceptives such as Plan B and Ella, which some Christians considered abortifacients since they prevented a fertilized egg from being implanted in the womb.

In September 2012, Hobby Lobby filed a lawsuit in a state district court of Oklahoma against the enforcement of this ACA provision on the basis of the Free Exercise of Religion of the First Amendment and on the Religious Freedom Restoration Act (RFRA) passed by Congress in 1993. In March 2013, the US Court of Appeals for the Tenth District ruled that Hobby Lobby was "a person who has religious freedom." Hobby Lobby's case passed through several more appeals courts before reaching the Supreme Court on March 25, 2014.

The case was called Burwell[16] vs. Hobby Lobby. Hobby Lobby had about 21,000 employees. Its case was joined with a similar appeal from Conestoga Wood Specialties, a company with about a thousand employees owned by the Mennonite Hahn family. If Hobby Lobby lost the case, it would have been subject to fines of over $1 million dollars per day. But Hobby Lobby won the case by a vote of 5 to 4, with Justice Alito writing on the basis of the RFRA: "The companies in the case before us are closely held corporations, each owned and controlled by a single family, and no one has disputed the sincerity of their religious beliefs."[17]

A High School Curriculum

Steve Green had a vision of creating a high school curriculum that would highlight the Bible's contributions to the world and to the nation's history. Jerry Pattengale, with the input of scholars who wrote brief essays, wrote the textbook for such a curriculum. In 2016, this

---

15. Moss and Baden, 46.
16. Sylvia Burwell was the Secretary of Health and Human Services.
17. Cited by Moss and Baden, 9.

was offered to the Mustang School District near Oklahoma City. But criticism and opposition from such groups as the ACLU stopped the distribution of this material in the United States.

But it had some success in the United Kingdom. Most surprising was its enthusiastic reception by Orthodox Jews in Israel in 2015 after the curriculum had been revised to eliminate references to Christianity. An interactive program called TAMAR created with the help of an Israeli technological company Compedia together with the donation of iPads, allowed Jewish students to access the internet for resources such as maps and visuals to illuminate the text of the Tanakh, i.e. the Old Testament.

The Museum of the Bible Building

After a study of possible locations, Steve Green concluded that the best possible location was in Washington, DC. One possible site was the old Post Office Building, which was later made into a luxury hotel by Donald Trump.[18] In July 2012, Steve was able to purchase the Washington Design Center located just a few blocks from the Sackler Museum on the National Mall for about $50 million dollars.[19] This had originally been built in 1929 as a refrigerated warehouse. The exterior was completely refurbished. The interior was rebuilt to provide 430,000 square feet of space for exhibits. The cost of the renovation is estimated to have been about $400 million dollars. The latest high-tech features were installed. Visitors would be given a tablet on which they could program what they wanted to see. If they spent too much time at one exhibit, the tablet would tell them to move on!

The Topping Out

I was among those who were invited by Cary Summers, the president of the Museum of the Bible, to attend "The Topping Out" of the building on September 13, 2016. "The Topping Out" designates the stage at which the concrete and steel structures are completed. I and others were provided with free airfare and lodging at the Washington Hilton for the occasion.

---

18. I had served on a committee reviewing NEH Humanities grants in this building in December 2005.
19. The museum is located at 400 4th Street SW.

At breakfast, we were given TMOB tee shirts. On the bus, we were issued yellow green vests, gloves, and hard hats. I sat next to Mart Green on the bus. At the construction site some of us who had difficulty walking were taken up to the sixth floor on a construction elevator. There, box lunches were provided for the guests and for the workers. Jerry Pattengale came by with Steve Green, who is the chair of the museum's board. The three of us were photographed together, hard hats and all.

The former mayor of Washington, DC, greeted us. He announced that with the opening of the new Museum of African American History and Culture[20] on the National Mall there were now fifty museums in the city. There was a long speech by the president of the construction company and applause for the 500+ workers.

Figure 89. With Jerry Pattengale on my right and Steve Green on my left

As I had difficulty walking and seeing, Jerry accompanied me on the tour of the building which required walking up and down several

---

20. I had hoped to visit this new museum but discovered that reservations had to be made months in advance. One of my history colleagues, Jack White, had worked at the Smithsonian in the Transportation Section and knew the director of the new museum, Lonnie Bunch III. I sent Dr. Bunch a copy of my *Africa and the Bible* and received a gracious response. In 2019 Dr. Bunch was made the head of all the Smithsonian museums.

flights of stairs, some of them more than once. The heat in the high 80s fogged up my glasses so I could see very little detail. There were busy construction crews everywhere.

In the evening, there was a banquet with several speeches. At my table sat Ken Blackwell, former Republican secretary of Ohio and his wife who had been the head of the Cincinnati Public Schools. Also at our table was Terence Chapman from Atlanta, who headed an association of CEOs of Christian companies like Hobby Lobby and Chick-fil-A. It was revealed that his association had just sent in a check of $500,000 for the museum! I then realized that most of those in attendance were wealthy potential donors.

It was announced that the museum would open on November 17, 2017, so I made travel plans and hotel reservations to attend the opening. And quite remarkably, given the magnitude and complexity of the task and the numerous possibilities for delays, the deadline was indeed met![21]

The Opening of the Museum

Visitors enter through forty-feet-high bronze doors.[22] The floors have a trapezoidal shape. As one enters there is a museum gift store with a limited selection of books on the right. There are many items with the museum's logo for sale. In a room on the ground floor is a small but very interesting set of books and objects on loan from the Vatican. These objects will be replaced on a six-month rotation. Among the objects loaned for the Vatican room was the prayer book of the Emperor Charles V who condemned Luther. Manuscripts illustrating the Nativity were on loan from the Bavarian State Museum. Some fascinating items connected with the Jewish Messianic pretender Sabbatai Zvi (seventeenth c) were on display. An interesting documentary on the Vatican Library was shown.

The second floor focuses on the Bible's impact upon the world in general and on America in particular.[23] There are displays illustrating the

21. I had donated $1,000 to the museum but this did not meet the threshold for an invitation to the opening. Jerry Pattengale secured a complimentary invitation for me.

22. During the first year, admission was free with a donation of $15 suggested, though one needed to obtain dated and timed tickets. Even before opening all the tickets for the first three months had been allocated. About one million visitors came to the museum during the first year. When admission fees of $2025 were charged during the second year, attendance numbered about a half million visitors.

23. This is the subject of Steve Green, *Faith in America: The Powerful Impact of One Company Speaking Out Boldly* (Decatur, Georgia: Looking Glass Books, 2011).

use of the Bible both for and against slavery. The many organizations inspired by the Bible such as Habitat for Humanity are highlighted. There is one section where the numerous Bibles translated by Wycliffe Bible Translators and other organizations are displayed.

The third floor is the Narrative Floor, recounting the story of the patriarchs (Abraham, Isaac, Jacob), Moses, the Conquest, the kings, the Exile, etc. A separate ticket was required to view the Torah scrolls.[24] The Passover seder is explained. A recorded testimonial from Lawrence Schiffman, a Jewish scholar, describes how he got interested in the Dead Sea Scrolls. In a separate section there is a recreation of a village like Nazareth from Jesus's day, with actors and actresses in costume explaining food items, the olive press, and a synagogue service.

The fourth floor is the History Floor, where there are exhibits on the history and archaeology of the Bible. There were only a few actual monuments but many photos of objects and some replicas, e.g. of the Hammurabi Stele in the Louvre Museum. There are many Bibles on display, such as the Tyndale New Testament (1535), the Geneva Bible (1560), the Bishop's Bible (1568), and Jefferson's Bible (1819), which deleted all the miracles of Jesus.

The fifth floor contains a restaurant and a performing arts theater seating an audience of about five hundred. A dedicated space exhibits artifacts on loan from the Israel Antiquities Authority.

The sixth floor has a rooftop viewing area overlooking the National Mall and the Capitol. It also contains a ballroom that can accommodate a thousand guests.

The dedication ceremony held in the evening of November 17 was impressive for the number of dignitaries who took part. After a welcome by Tony Zeiss, executive director of the museum, popular singer CeCe Winans sang. This was followed by "Blessings" by Cardinal Donald Wuerl, archbishop of Washington, who brought greetings from the Pope. Prayers were offered by Rear Admiral Margaret Kibben, Chief of Chaplains, US Navy, and by Rabbi Stuart Weinblatt, representing the Jewish Federations of North America. Then remarks were made by Cary Sommers, president of the museum and Muriel Bowser, mayor of the District of Columbia. Yariv Levin, Israeli Minister of Tourism spoke, and Ron Deimer, Israeli Ambassador brought greetings from Prime Minister Netanyahu of Israel. Finally, Steve Green offered a brief speech.

---

24. The museum has a collection of over 3,000 Torah scrolls.

I did not go down with others to the street level to witness the ribbon cutting ceremony, as I wanted to spend as much time in the galleries, knowing that this would be my only visit to the museum.

At the banquet Jerry seated me between himself and David Trobisch, the director of collections. I recognized the name Trobisch as I had read articles in *Practical Anthropology* by his parents, Walter and Ingrid, who were missionaries to Cameroon. David is a distinguished New Testament textual scholar. I took the opportunity to ask him about the museum's Dead Sea Scrolls that had just been published (see below), but whose authenticity had been doubted by scholars such as Eibert Tigchelaar.[25] Trobisch responded that the museum was now subjecting these fragments to chemical tests. I also asked if the museum had considered buying the so-called first-century fragment of Mark. He indicated that he and Jerry had seen it, but gave me the impression that no, the museum had not considered buying it. After the banquet Jerry introduced me to Rick Warren, pastor of Saddleback Church and author, who is on the board of the museum. Rick, who said he was familiar with some of my writings, mentioned that the first church he had founded was one he had started as a teenager in Japan.

---

25. Other scroll fragments purchased by Azusa Pacific University and Southwestern Baptist Theological Seminary have also had their authenticity questioned.

Figure 90. With David Trobisch, Rick Warren, and Jerry Pattengal

The Museum's Dead Sea Scrolls

In 2016, the museum's prized collection of thirteen Dead Sea Scrolls fragments had been published by the prestigious firm of Brill in Leiden, The Netherlands, as *Dead Sea Scrolls Fragments in the Museum Collection*, edited by Emanuel Tov, Kipp Davis, and Robert Duke. This was volume I of Publications of the Museum of the Bible: Semitic Texts, edited by Emanuel Tov with Jerry Pattengale as the managing editor. The thirteen texts included: Genesis 31:23–25, 32; Exodus 17:4–7; Leviticus 23:24–28; a fragment of Leviticus; Numbers 8:3–5; Jeremiah 23:6–9; Ezekiel 28:22; Jonah 4:2–5; Micah 1:4–6; Psalm 11:1–4; Daniel 10:18–20; Nehemiah 2:13–16; and a Fragment of Instruction.

I was particularly interested in the fragment of Nehemiah as I had written commentaries and studies on Nehemiah. No Qumran fragment of Nehemiah had been reported before but as in the Hebrew canon Ezra and Nehemiah were considered one book, Nehemiah unlike Esther was not counted one of the missing books of the Old Testament from the Qumran collection. I contacted its translator Martin Abegg, whom I had known since his days as a doctoral student at Hebrew Union College. Marty has usually responded promptly, but when I did not get a reply, I sensed that something may have been amiss.

These scrolls had been purchased by the museum between 2009 and 2014 in three lots. In April 2017, the museum asked for the testing of five fragments by the Bundesanstatt für Material Forschung und Prüfung. Its report in October 2018 raised suspicions about the authenticity of these five fragments. In February 2019, the museum contracted Art Fraud Insights to do a thorough examination of the thirteen published fragments. Their conclusion released in October 2019 branded all these fragments as modern forgeries! The museum sponsored an academic symposium on March 13, 2020, to discuss these results.

Questions of Provenance

Especially since wars broke out in the Middle East after 1970, questions of provenance had become important, since the instability in countries like Iraq and Syria had led to widespread looting. Provenance relates to the attested origin of an object being sold and imported. In 2010 Patty Gerstenblith, a law professor at DePaul University, gave a lengthy presentation to several Hobby Lobby executives and to the staff of the Green Collection about the legal ramifications of purchasing poorly provenanced artifacts. Steve Green came into the conference room intermittently during Gerstenblith's presentation. These warnings were ignored by the Greens.

In 2011, Federal authorities seized at the Memphis airport a shipment of about three hundred cuneiform tablets imported from Israel that were destined for the Hobby Lobby warehouses in Oklahoma City with the misleading label "handcrafted clay tiles." By 2017, The Museum of the Bible had acquired at least 5,500 artifacts from a dealer in the United Arab Emirates, which included 1,500 cuneiform tablets, 500 cuneiform bricks, thirteen extra-large cuneiform tablets, and 3,000 clay bullae or seal impressions. These were judged looted objects, and the museum was fined three million dollars for this breach of the antiquities laws.

For a cuneiform tablet that contained a text about "Gilgamesh's Dream," the museum in 2014 paid $1.67 million dollars to Christie's, a London auction house. The museum's staff became suspicious about the tablet's provenance and reported this to the Department of Homeland

Security. In May 2020, Federal authorities secured the tablet to repatriate it to Iraq. The museum is suing Christie's for its false provenance of the tablet. Jeffrey Kloha, the new curator since 2017, concluded that several thousand items in the museum lacked sufficient evidence of their provenance. The museum agreed to return about 12,000 clay tablets to Iraq.[26] The museum also paid the Iraqi government a $15 million dollar settlement. The museum also agreed to return 5,000 papyrus fragments to Egypt.

The Oxyrhynchus Papyri

The Egypt Exploration Society (EES) sponsored two Oxford scholars, Bernard P. Grenfell and Arthur B. Hunt, on an expedition to Egypt at the end of the nineteenth century. They came across a huge dump of about 500,000 discarded papyri scraps at Oxyrhynchus. So far only about 1 percent of these have been published. On just the second day of the expedition, Grenfell and Hunt found a sensational papyrus which contained the "Logia" of Jesus. This was published in 1898 as Oxy. P. 1. This and Oxy. P 654 contained the "The Sayings" of Jesus, which were later identified as the Greek text underlying the Coptic Gospel of Thomas which was found at Nag Hammadi in 1945.

Dirk Obbink

Dirk Obbink of Christ Church, Oxford University, is an American who was recognized as the world's foremost authority on Greek papyri. In 2001 he was awarded a $500,000 MacArthur "genius" grant. He was engaged by Jerry Pattengale to serve as one of the senior scholars for the Green Scholars Initiative program. Obbink was the general editor of the Oxyrhynchus Papyri stored in the Sackler Classics Library at Oxford.

In November 2011 as Scott Carroll and Jerry Pattengale[27] were about to leave his office, Dirk laid on the pool table in his office four

---

26. These tablets were returned to Iraq in August 2021 along with about 5,000 cuneiform tablets from Cornell University. David Owen, the chair of the Near Eastern Department at Cornell, had informed me about the donation of these Sumerian tablets by a wealthy donor.

27. For Jerry's first-hand account, see Jerry Pattengale, "The 'First-Century Mark' Saga from Inside the Room," *Christianity Today* (June 28, 2019). Scott's recollection of Obbink's offer is somewhat different: "In preparation for the exhibit at the Vatican,

papyri fragments of Matthew 3:7–12; Mark 1:8–9, 16–18; Luke 13:25–27; John 8:26–28,33–35. He indicated that these were from a private collector and wondered if the Greens might be interested in buying them. Obbink thought that the Matthew, Luke, and John fragments were from the second century but that the Mark fragment might possibly come from the first century. This was indeed sensational![28]

Scott revealed the existence of this Mark fragment to Daniel Wallace, who cited this evidence in a debate with Bart Ehrman at the University of North Carolina on February 1, 2012.[29] Wallace, a professor at Dallas Theological Seminary is the founder of the Center for the Study of New Testament Manuscripts. He is attempting to photograph all the Greek New Testament manuscripts in the world.

As news of a "first-century Mark" spread, the EES realized that this was one of its Oxyrhynchus papyri. Obbink admitted showing the New Testament papyri to Carroll and Pattengale but denied offering them for sale. The EES commanded him to cut all ties with the Museum of the Bible and ordered him to publish the Mark fragment forthwith, which he did, dating it now to the late second or early third century, still the earliest fragment of Mark's Gospel. [30]

Michael Holmes, a New Testament textual scholar from Bethel Theological Seminary, who had replaced Jerry Pattengale in 2014, published a purchase agreement dated February 4, 2012, with Dirk Obbink's signature for the sale of the four Gospel papyri to the museum in January 2013. The four papyri remained in Oxford for further study. The museum paid Obbink $760,000 for the four Gospel fragments.[31] In 2016, the EES

Scott mentioned to Dirk Obbink that it would be fascinating to have papyri from each of the four Gospels to display. In October (2011), Dirk showed Scott a papyrus from Mark 1 which he said emphatically dated to the late 1st century. Scott pressed him on the source, but Dirk had no reply. But he clearly indicated that the papyrus was for sale, but he gave no price. Scott mentioned it to Steve Green but there was no further mention of it to him. Scott has consistently maintained (this) recollection of events since 2013."

28. The earliest known New Testament papyrus is a fragment of the Gospel of John dated to the early 2nd century held at the John Rylands Library in Manchester, England.

29. See Ariel Sabar, "A Biblical Mystery at Oxford," *The Atlantic* (June 2020).

30. The papyrus P. Oxy. 5345, which is now listed in the Nestle Aland catalogue of New Testament manuscripts as P1137, was published in 2018 by Dirk Obbink and Daniela Colomo in *Oxyrhynchus Papyri* vol. LXXXIII, pp. 4–7.

31. According to a *New York Times Article* "Ancient Texts Embroiled in a Covetous Tale" published on September 27, 2021, the museum sued Obbink for the return of this money. He had returned at this date only $10,000.

did not renew Obbink's contract as the general editor of the Oxyrhynchus Papyri. On April 16, 2020, *The Oxford Blue*, a student newspaper, reported that Obbink had been arrested as the EES had discovered thirteen missing papyri, which had been sold without authorization to the Museum of the Bible, which returned the purloined papyri. Then, as the EES began studying its files, they found, by examining a duplicate catalogue, that about a hundred other papyri were missing. Obbink, who was dismissed from his teaching post at the University of Oxford, has protested his innocence. He was freed on bond, as the case was continued in the courts.[32] In 2021, Hobby Lobby sued Obbink for seven million dollars.

Karen King

Karen King studied under John Turner of the University of Montana, a leading scholar of the Coptic Nag Hammadi texts.[33] Karen, who secured a position at Harvard Divinity School, became an authority on the Nag Hammadi treatise on Mary Magdalene. I met her when I read my paper at the conference on the Mandaeans at Harvard in 1999. She cites two of my books on the Mandaeans in her book *What Is Gnosticism?*[34]

In September 2012, at the International Congress of Coptic Studies in Rome,[35] Karen King announced that she had acquired a small Coptic papyrus that has Jesus calling Mary Magdalene "my wife." Her preliminary analysis dated the papyrus to the fourth century AD and the composition of the text to the second century AD. She gained the support of Roger Bagnall of Columbia University, a leading scholar of Greek and Latin papyri. She planned to have her essay published in the *Harvard Theological Review*. But scholars such as Egyptologist Leo Depuydt raised doubts about the authenticity of the papyrus, which caused a delay. The editors of the *HTR* finally published Karen King's article along with Depuydt's critique in 2014.

---

32. See Charlotte Higgins, "A Scandal in Oxford: The Curious Case of the Stolen Gospel," *The Guardian* (January 9, 2020); Ariel Sabar, "The Case of the Phantom Papyrus," *The Atlantic Monthly* (June 2020), 62–73.

33. Professor Turner invited me to read a paper at the SBL session celebrating the 50th anniversary of the discovery of the Nag Hammadi Library in 1995.

34. (Cambridge, Massachusetts: Harvard University Press, 2003).

35. Darlene Brooks Hedstrom, one of my students, also read a paper at this conference.

There had been hints of a special relation between Jesus and Mary Magdalene in Coptic Gnostic texts, and a popular tradition that she was Jesus's wife, a theme exploited in Dan Brown's sensational novel, *The DaVinci Code*. So, the publication of this so-called "Gospel of Jesus's Wife" gained Karen King enormous public attention. That this was a patent forgery was conclusively proved by Christian Askeland,[36] a Green scholar who completed his PhD dissertation at Cambridge on Coptic translations of John's Gospel. He recognized that the handwriting of The Gospel of Jesus's Wife was identical to a known forgery of a fragment of John's Gospel. In a fascinating tale of persistent detective work, Ariel Sabar identified the forger as a German student of Egyptology, Walter Fritz.[37] Much to her chagrin and embarrassment, Karen King did acknowledge that indeed the Coptic text that had gained her so much fame was, alas, a forgery![38]

Postscript: Scott Carroll

Scott Carroll taught from 2000 to 2010 at Cornerstone University where he was honored twice with "The Teacher of the Year Award." He inspired nine Cornerstone students to pursue the PhD. He directed two NEH Junior Scholar's grants overseeing students working on unpublished manuscripts. He has continued to teach regularly at the Asia Biblical Theological Seminary, headquartered in Chiang Mai, Thailand. The school has multiple extensions throughout Southeast Asia and is affiliated with Cornerstone University.

Scott has also worked with faculty and graduate students several times a year since 2013 at the University of Jos in Nigeria. He directs seminars where participants have hands on opportunity to work with manuscripts. Two participants in the seminars were awarded post-doctoral grants by the African Humanities Program in conjunction with the American Council of Learned Societies to continue their work on manuscripts with Scott. He has begun a similar program at St. Paul's University

---

36. Christian Askeland, who was hired by Jerry Pattengale to work with the Green Scholars Initiative, taught at Indiana Wesleyan University.

37. See Ariel Sabar, *Veritas: A Harvard Professor, A Con Man and the Gospel of Jesus's Wife* (New York, New York: Doubleday, 2020).

38. See Craig A. Evans, *Jesus and the Manuscripts: What We Can Learn from the Oldest Texts* (Peabody, Massachusetts: Hendrickson, 2020), 316 to 323.

in Lumuru, Kenya, attracting professors and students from the greater Nairobi area.

Scott's Manuscript Research Group supports private collectors of manuscripts and rare books. He has worked with several patrons who have donated Torahs to over 100 leading seminaries, universities, and museums, where Scott has given lectures and led seminars. Scott and his research team have developed an extensive database of the codicological and textual features of Torahs and other Hebrew manuscripts, working in consultation with scholars at the National Library of Israel.

Scott and his staff organize exhibitions of Bibles and other biblically related texts, which are called "Inspired." These contain about a hundred objects. The first exhibit was in Hong Kong (2017), followed by Minsk, Belarus (2018) in partnership with the National Library of Belarus. An exhibit was then mounted in St. Petersburg, Russia (2018) at the International Cultural Forum. Scott wrote catalogues for the exhibitions which have been translated into Chinese, Belarusian and Russian. These exhibitions have attracted over one million visitors.[39]

Postscript: Jerry Pattengale

Jerry Pattengale has worn many hats and won many awards. As an assistant provost at Indiana Wesleyan University, Jerry was nationally recognized for his work in student motivation and retention, winning the National Student Advocate Award in 2000. In 2012 IWU presented him with the World Changing Faculty Award. Then in 2014 IWU named him the school's first University Professor.

In addition to writing about Buck Creek in the local Marion paper, Jerry has contributed articles to the *Chicago Tribune*, *Wall Street Journal*, *Washington Post*, and *Inside Higher Education* and has written reviews for *Books & Culture*. Jerry was on the membership committee of the National Press Club. He is on the board of Yale University's Jonathan Edwards Center and on the board of *Christianity Today*. He serves as an associate producer of *Christian Scholars Review*. He is a senior fellow of the Sagamore Institute.

He served as the interim codirector of the Religion News Foundation. In this capacity he spoke on a panel discussing the protection of world

---

39. Scott has also spoken in Australia, India, Liberia, Mexico, Nigeria, Philippines, Romania, Sierra Leone, Singapore, and South Korea.

religious sites at the United Nations in February 2020. He wrote the script for Inexplicable, the six-part TBN series on the spread of Christianity broadcast in 2020 and wrote a book developed from the series.

Among the many books that Jerry has authored or edited, I will just mention one which is destined to become a bestseller. *The World's Greatest Book*,[40] co-authored with Jewish scholar, Lawrence H. Schiffman, is an informative introduction to the history of the Bible including the writing of various books, the copying of manuscripts, the printing of Bibles and the translations of Bibles. It is written in a most engaging manner that should appeal to visitors to The Museum of the Bible. Jerry retired from his position at The Museum of the Bible in 2018, but then was rehired in 2020 as a special advisor to President Steve Green.

Edwin M. Yamauchi Awards

In July 2013, Jerry Pattengale shared with me a press release from Oklahoma City that was headlined: "Green Scholars Initiative Honors Young Biblical Scholars: First Edwin M. Yamauchi Awards for Textual Studies Given to UCLA and Cambridge Students." The two students were Peter Malik from Slovakia, sponsored by Peter Williams, warden of Tyndale House, for doctoral studies at the University of Cambridge, and Josiah Chappell sponsored by the St. Shenoude Archimandrite Coptic Society for doctoral studies at UCLA.

The Edwin M. Yamauchi Award for Excellence in Textual Studies are for $30,000 each year for up to three years.[41] "The award is given to scholars who have demonstrated rare aptitude in biblical language studies, shown exceptional academic performance and are pursuing terminal degrees." The recipients are invited to present papers on their research at the Green Scholars Initiative summer workshops in Oxford, England, and will also be given "priority access to artifacts in The Green Collection." The awarding of the grants is administered by a committee of the Scholarship and Christianity in Oxford.[42]

---

40. (Franklin, Tennessee: Worthy Books 2017).

41. Students who already have a full scholarship are given supplemental awards.

42. As of 2020, nine awards have been given for doctoral studies on ancient texts and manuscripts at Baylor, Cambridge(two), Durham, Edinburgh, Fuller Theological Seminary, Notre Dame, Oxford, and UCLA.

Chapter 46

O.B.F.

THE OXFORD BIBLE FELLOWSHIP (OBF) is a church that was begun in 1970 to minister to the students and faculty of Miami University as well as to the community of Oxford. OBF's influence over the decades has impacted thousands throughout the world (see Excursus T). OBF has cooperated closely with parachurch organizations such as InterVarsity Christian Fellowship (IV), Campus Crusade for Christ (Cru), and the Navigators (Navs).

Our Prior Church Experiences

Kimi after her conversion became a member of the evangelical Congregational Makiki Christian Church in Honolulu. As a student at Moody Bible Institute and Wheaton College she was involved in two Japanese churches in Chicago: Lakeside Christian Church near Wrigley Field and the Chicago Avenue Japanese Church. During the year that she was in graduate school at Columbia University she assisted at the Riverside Church in Manhattan.

After my conversion, during my year in Los Angeles, I attended the Westwood Bible Presbyterian Church near UCLA. While I was at the Christian Youth Center in Wahiawa, I was involved in the very small Oriental Bible Church pastored by Rev. Claude Curtis. During the year I attended the University of Hawaii, I lived with Dr. Robert Hambrook and visited different churches with him including the Kaimuki

Community Church, a member of the American Council of Christian Churches. During my first year of graduate school at Brandeis University, I roomed with Marlin Kreider and Wally Sims and attended Park Street Church in Boston with them.

After my wife and I were married, we became active in the Waltham Presbyterian Church pastored by Dr. Wyeth Willard, who had been an assistant to the president of Wheaton College. Upon moving to Rutgers University, we at first attended the First Baptist Church in Highland Park, pastored by Roger Palms, and then the New Brunswick Bible Church.

When we first came to Miami University in 1969, we visited a number of Oxford churches. We were invited to attend the Greenhills Baptist Church by Jerry and Evelyn Coltharp[1] and the Brethren church in North College Hill by Bill and Enid Wilson.

William and Enid Wilson

William E. Wilson, after graduating from Wheaton College, earned the MA and PhD from the University of Illinois, specializing in plant diseases (phytopathology). Bill served as a first lieutenant in Italy during World War II. After teaching at Muskingum College for a year, Bill came to Miami University in 1947 and taught in the Botany Department until his retirement in 1979. "Prof" as he was affectionately known was a master teacher who was honored as one of Miami University's Outstanding Faculty. He was tall, with a sonorous voice, and emphatic teaching style. His hair which had once been red had become white. When a student went to sleep in the back of the room, he would be struck by a piece of chalk unerringly thrown by Bill, who used to be the catcher on Wheaton College's baseball team!

It was Bill who introduced InterVarsity Christian Fellowship to Miami University in 1958. He served as its faculty advisor. As I had served in that role at Rutgers, I soon joined him as another advisor. On Sundays Bill taught a Bible class to about 50 IV students at the student center.

Enid (Dresser) Wilson was not only a graduate of Wheaton College, she was the direct descendant of Jonathan Blanchard, the college's first president. According to the information provided to me by her son Mark:

1. Jonathan Blanchard Jr. married Mary Avery Bent. They had twelve children, one of whom was Nora Emily.

---

1. Jerry Coltharp was on the staff of Miami's Audiovisual Department.

2. Nora Emily Blanchard married Henry Lyman Kellogg. One of their eleven children was Geraldine Cynthia.

3. Geraldine Cynthia Kellogg married Amos Dresser IV. My mother, Enid Dresser Wilson, is one of their five children.

Enid was a gifted musician who sang in a trio on a radio station in New England. She was an organist and pianist,[2] who also taught piano lessons. Enid was a most gracious hostess. The Wilsons had planned their Maxine Drive home so that it could accommodate large student gatherings both upstairs and downstairs. Enid and a group of women in her Bible study had been praying for years that God would someday establish a church in Oxford that would minister to the university's students.

Figure 91. Bill and Enid Wilson

2. Enid Wilson knew 600 hymns by memory.

Beginnings

Late in 1969 a small group gathered in our living room at 716 Oak Street, where the school's Recreational Center is now located. The group included Bill and Enid Wilson, Dan and Barb Fulton, Alice Peo, Mary Stout, Joe and Diane Webb,[3] and my wife and I. Dan was a businessman who led a home Bible study. Alice was a secretary, and Mary was the wife of a mailman (see Excursus S). Joe and Diane Webb were seniors who had been active in IV.

After prayerful consideration we agreed to start a new church to minister especially to the students of Miami University. We could use the upstairs room of the Municipal Building, normally used as a courtroom, without cost. It was Bill who proposed the name The Oxford Bible Fellowship. I preached the inaugural message "The Slaves of God" on January 11, 1970. There were about fifty present, mainly IV students. For the first eight months we followed the Brethren pattern of having lay speakers in a three-man rotation including Dan Fulton,[4] Bill Wilson, and myself. By February, there were sixty-five present and by April, eighty-four present. In November, Don Fields, an IV staff member, spoke.

In the fall of 1970 Barney Ford, a graduate of the University of Evansville, came as IV's first staff member at Miami University. In January 1971, Barney joined us in a four-speaker rotation. On March 14, 1971, eleven were baptized in the baptistery of the Victory Church of Christ. Bill baptized the men, and I baptized the women.

Barney Ford, who was an effective "soul winner," reported that he had led 65 students to Christ in 1970 and 1971. As a result, attendance at OBF rose to 150 in 1971. By 1972 attendance had risen to 250 with students literally sitting on the window ledges (cf. Acts 20:9). In 1971 Dave and Debbie Iverson became the first staff members of Cru at Miami University. Dave, a communications major at North Dakota State University, joined OBF's speaker rotation.

Once a month on Sunday evenings we would celebrate communion at the university's Sesquicentennial chapel with about a hundred present. In a number of ways, the facilities of the municipal building were not adequate to minister to families of Oxford. The only space for children's

---

3. Joe and Diane Webb graduated from Miami University in 1970. They were active in IV but joined Cru as staff at Boston University.

4. Dan Fulton was a devoted follower of Rev. Bob Thieme, the pastor of Berachah Church in Houston.

Sunday school was on the back stairs behind the courtroom. As a result, only two families with children attended in the first two years. Besides the Yamauchis with our two small children, there were Richard and Stephanie Moore and their two young daughters.

An important early member of OBF was George Hill, a part-time instructor in Industrial Psychology who had a consulting firm that employed Dan Fulton and Jack Hendry. George had been a Presbyterian elder when he and his wife were converted to Christ in 1970. In August, Sophie Goldfliess, a seventy-year-old Jewish grandmother who had been befriended by Katie in their karate class, accepted Christ. In November, Bill baptized eight including Mrs. Goldfliess.

George had bought the Kettler farm on the western edge of Oxford. He allowed the leaders of OBF to meet in his office on that property on Saturday mornings to pray and plan for the Sunday services. When we needed a larger venue for our growing congregation, it was George who suggested that we consider Presser Hall on the Western College campus.[5]

Presser Hall

Western College, one of four women's colleges in early Oxford and the only one to survive, was situated across Patterson Avenue to the east of Miami University. Presser Hall housed the Music Department and had an auditorium with a stage. This could seat about 400 with a balcony which could seat an additional 120. Jerry Coltharp approached Will Keebler, the business manager of Western College, and he agreed to rent us not only the auditorium but also the classrooms for the weekly fee of just $25! OBF began meeting at Presser Hall on Easter April 2, 1972. I gave the message to a capacity crowd. Even when Western College, a private school, was absorbed by Miami University, a state university, in 1974 we were allowed to continue our meetings at Presser Hall.[5]

Late in 1972, attendance averaged about four hundred. At the end of 1972, Bill baptized fifteen students. Among those who gave their

---

5. In later years George Hill offered several acres of his farm at no cost to the church, but OBF declined this generous offer as it would have removed us too far from the university campus.

6. I later learned that it was due to the support of President Philip Shriver, a devoted Presbyterian who appreciated OBF, that we were granted this privilege.

testimonies in 1972 were David Gill, Larry Hoop, Bill Gates, Sophie Goldfliess, Alice Peo, Bill Cressey, Doug Rumford, and Beth Moore.

In February 1973, Don Shrader[7] and eight women were baptized. In September, my history colleague Dwight Smith and his wife came to a service. OBF was attended by about 200 IV students and 100 Cru students. In 1973, from a group of thirty seniors, three joined IV and one joined Cru as staff members. In 1974, out of forty graduating seniors, ten joined the staff of IV and Cru.

In March 1975 four women and four men were baptized. In May, history professor Cyrus St. Clair, who was taking my place while I was on leave, gave his testimony. In June 1975 we honored two high school students, fifty-nine receiving baccalaureate degrees and six with graduate degrees. Eight of these grads joined the staff of IV or Cru. On July 20, Dan Fulton gave his last message at OBF. In November Al and Carole Jamieson, Wycliffe Bible Translators working in Mexico, spoke. I had met them at the Summer Institute of Linguistics in 1961. Al's grandfather had been the pastor of the Presbyterian church in Oxford. In December a children's cantata directed by Karen DeRight sang.

A survey taken of the congregation in 1975 included representatives of thirty-five different denominations, including: Methodists 23 percent, Presbyterians 20 percent, Baptists 15 percent, Lutherans 8 percent, Catholics 6 percent, Episcopalians 3 percent, and Church of Christ 3 percent, as well as a variety of other backgrounds, including no affiliation, 22 percent. The budget for 1975 was $11,000, of which 35 percent went to IV, 27 percent to Cru, and 8 percent to overseas missions.

I served as the worship coordinator, choosing hymns and the order of the service. Enid Wilson and Karen DeRight played the piano. Mindy McMahon, the wife of one of my grad students played her harp. Soloists included Mary Frieg, Kay Raplenovich, and Dennis DeRight. Dennis and Karen also sang duets. On occasion a men's quartet or a women's trio would sing. Bill Wilson and I served as greeters and passed out hymn books which were stored in a movable "ark" built by Don Fairburn, a physics professor. No collections were taken but baskets for contributions were placed in the rear.

Barney Ford recalls:

---

7. Don and his parents Bob Shrader, a professor at Miami, and his mother Berniece, a teacher at Talawanda High School, began Faith Baptist Church affiliated with the General Association of Regular Baptists. Dick and Ruth Pettitt were at first part of this small church but joined OBF for the sake of their son Christian.

My favorite memory occurred on a Sunday morning during our days of worshipping in Presser Hall. On that Sunday I was speaking and Dr. Wilson was standing at the top of the aisle in the back. There were several hundred in attendance. During my talk I asked all those who had come to Christ during their time at Miami to raise their hands. Over half of the audience raised their hands. As I looked out over that sea of raised hands, I saw Dr. Wilson with tears streaming down his face in joy and thanksgiving.

In 1975, new staff members, Kent and Linda Stephens for IV and Bill and Critty Fairback for Cru came to Miami University. Kent and Linda were graduates of Ball State University. Bill was a graduate of the University of Pennsylvania, who had been a member of the school's rowing team. Also Wally Cirafesi, a graduate of Penn State University, began the Navigators ministry[8] in this year.

In 1976, Bill Wilson presided over the marriage of Cyprian Ejiasa, a graduate student from Nigeria, to Grace who had arrived from Nigeria. I stood in for Grace's father during their wedding. In June OBF honored two high school graduates, 62 BA and eight MA candidates. Five of the graduates enrolled in seminaries. Nearly 100 Miami students attended the Urbana Missionary Conference sponsored by IV in December. During 1976 I had the privilege of baptizing 30 students in three services.

In 1977 two new staff members, Bruce Tucker with Cru and Kent Schellhause with the Navs, joined the speakers rotation. In May, Samuel Shahid, founder of Good News for the Crescent World, whom I had

---

8. The Navigators is a parachurch organization was begun by Dawson Trotman (b. 1906). The son of an atheist father and a Pentecostal mother. As a teenager Daws attended the Lomita Presbyterian church's youth group where his team was challenged to memorize Bible verses for a contest. He was good at this challenge, so his team won the contest. But in the third week he became convicted and made a profession of faith, but he backslid. After two years Daws returned to the church and made a recommitment and became a zealous follower of Jesus. He attended the Bible Institute of Los Angeles for two years. Daws began converting and discipling hundreds of seamen at the port of Long Beach, hence the name of his new organization, the Navigators, begun in 1933. Over a hundred sailors were won to Christ on the USS West Virginia, which was one of the battleships sunk at Pearl Harbor on December 7, 1941. Trotman's methods of Bible memorization and discipleship were shared with Billy Graham, Wycliffe Bible Translators, and other evangelical organizations. In 1951 the Navs began their first campus ministry at the Univedrsity of Nebraska at Lincoln. In 1953 Billy Graham alerted Trotman of the possibility of purchasing Glen Eyrie, an estate in Colorado Springs, if sufficient funds could be raised in a very short period of time. Trotman died in 1956 in a boating accident at Jack Wyrtzen's Schroon Lake conference grounds.

invited to speak at the Faculty Christian banquet, spoke at OBF.[9] That spring OBF honored seventy BA students, eight MA students, and one PhD, Dorothy Chappell, who earned her doctorate in botany. By this year, the OBF Alumni newsletter that I edited went out three times a year to five hundred OBF alumni. Among those who attended that summer were Mr. and Mrs. John Dolibois. In October, Roger Palms, the editor of *Decision Magazine* and our former pastor from Highland Park, spoke.

In 1978 Larry Hoop, an alumnus, who was now on the staff of IV, joined the rotation of speakers. In March seven men and seven women were baptized. In April George Giacumakis, whom I had invited to speak at the Faculty Christian Fellowship banquet, spoke at OBF. George, a fellow grad student at Brandeis, was a history professor at Cal State Fullerton. Among those giving their testimonies were: Jane Armstrong, a graduate of Southern Mississippi University and a new Cru staff member, Jane Becker, Dot Chappell, Scott Luley, and Dale Nichols. We recognized twenty-five graduating seniors, as well as an additional fifteen in absentia.

H. Dale Burke

As we had reached a kind of plateau by the end of 1978, twenty-six members of OBF met at our home on 807 Erin Drive to discuss the possibility of calling a full-time pastor. We were not a full-service church without one. Twenty-four OBF members voted to call a full-time pastor. The Wilsons because of their Brethren background were at first not in favor of such a move. One of those at the meeting, Cru staff member Bruce Tucker, said that he had a friend from West Virginia, Dale Burke, who might be interested in ministering at a campus church because of the impact of Cru at Marshall University.

Dale and his wife Becky were from Hurricane, West Virginia. He had graduated *summa cum laude*, receiving his BA with a major in Speech Communications with minors in Classics and Sociology from Marshall University in 1975. At Dallas Theological Seminary, he received the ThM for a thesis on "A Post-Marital Preventative Counseling Program."[10] The Burkes came to Oxford in November. Becky gave her testimony and Dale preached at Presser Hall. He was so well received that without going

---

9. I had first met Samuel Shahid in Lebanon in 1974.

10. Among his classmates at Dallas Theological seminary were Jeff Baxter, Darrell Bock, J. P. Moreland, and Daniel Wallace.

through the usual search process the OBF council voted to call Dale as our first pastor. He was offered a salary of $13,000 a year.

Dale began as our first full-time pastor on January 1, 1979. One of the first things he did after a year was to have an election of elders. The first elders were Dale Burke, Dennis DeRight, Bill Wilson, and I. Soon thereafter, Jerry Coltharp was also chosen an elder. Dale began a youth program and started premarital counseling classes. There were four classes for about 120 students held before the worship service, which were taught by Dale, Dennis DeRight, George Hill, and I. In August, OBF honored Bill and Enid Wilson with a plaque reading "You were there when we needed you."

J. Herbert Kane

When J. Herbert Kane, a professor of Missions at Trinity Evangelical Divinity School, was diagnosed with cancer at the age of seventy in 1980, he and his wife Winnifried (Winnie) moved to Oxford to be with their son Stanley, who was the chair of the Philosophy Department (see Excursus K). Born in Montreal, Quebec, Herb graduated from Moody Bible Institute in 1935. Herb and Winnie served until 1950 under the China Inland Mission in China until the Communists expelled all missionaries.

After returning to the States, Herb earned a BA from Providence Bible Institute (later called Barrington College) and an MA from Brown University. He taught missions at Barrington College (1951 to 1963), Lancaster Bible College (1963 to 1967), and Trinity Evangelical Divinity School (1967 to 1980). He was the author of influential books on missions such as *A Global View of Christian Missions*, *Understanding Christian Missions*, *Christian Missions in Global Perspective*, *A Concise History of the Christian World Mission*, and *Life and Work on the Mission Field*. He served as the president of the Association of Evangelical Professors of Missions and of the American Society of Missiology.

After Herb came to Oxford, he was chosen an elder of OBF and preached and taught Sunday School. After successful treatment for his cancer, Herb was able to commute back to TEDS to teach courses there.[11] He and his wife Winnie had a great impact on many students whom they entertained in their home. As a result of his classes at OBF

---

11. The portrait of Herbert and Winnifred Kane which hangs on a wall in the Carl F. Henry Library at Trinity Evangelical Divinity School was paid for by Ralph and Florence Jones. Ralph was the chair of the Marketing Department at Miami University.

on missions, about fifty students committed to become missionaries. Herb invited many noted missiologists to speak at OBF, including his successor David Hesselgrave from TEDS.[12]

Figure 92. Portrait of Herb and Winnie Kane

The Early 1980s

In 1980, about three hundred students were attending OBF; twenty-six of them were baptized. OBF was financially supporting ten alumni in seminaries. There were a dozen alumni studying at Trinity Evangelical Divinity School (TEDS). OBF was also supporting eighteen individuals or couples in campus ministries and twelve as missionaries. Many OBF alumni were now in positions of leadership: Barney Ford as an associate

12. Herb Kane passed away in 1988.

director of IV supervised seventy staff members. Kent Stephens was IV's regional director of Ohio, West Virginia, and western Pennsylvania. Mark McCloskey directed Cru's work in North Dakota, South Dakota, and Minnesota. Jim Toy did the same for Washington, Oregon, and Idaho. Joe and Diane Webb headed Cru's Here's Life program in Europe. Jane Becker was a leader of Cru's Stop Out program in West Africa. Bill Fairback was in charge of Cru's Middle East training program.

In 1982 during a service in January, a deranged woman cried out "You can have this spell. I am the Devil!" We called Miami University's security, who removed her. There were three Sunday School classes attended mainly by students: Dale had a class of about seventy-five, Herb Kane a class of about thirty-five, and I had a class of about forty-five. In February, Herb spoke on the history of the China Inland Missions (later called Overseas Missionary Fellowship), under which he and his wife had served in China. In April, six men and seventeen women were baptized. In May, we honored forty-seven graduating seniors, ten of whom joined the staff of Cru. Also, in May Jim Read, a Salvation Army officer from Canada and a visiting professor of philosophy, spoke "On Knowing God." In June Dennis Stokes, a graduate of Penn State University and a new Navs staff, spoke. Also that month, Mick Pechan, a new physics professor, spoke at the monthly service at the Oxford View Nursing Home, which I had begun.[13] In November eight women and six men were baptized.

In 1983 Dale organized mini-churches that met in homes. In February noted apologetics speaker, Norman Geisler, whom I had invited for the Faculty Christian banquet, spoke at OBF. In April eleven were baptized. In October Richard Friedman, a graduate of Denver Seminary, became the IV staff person at Miami; his wife Sherry became active in the Pro-Life movement in town. In November, Joe Waggener, a professor of Education accepted Christ; his wife, Ruth, an audiovisual staff member, had attended my weekly Bible studies at the university.

800 S. Maple Street

In 1980, Miami University had asked OBF to move to other quarters. The reason was not as we had suspected, the issue of church and state

---

13. In later years Dorothy Benz, who worked at this facility, and her husband Bob led monthly services at this nursing home.

separation but the fact that other churches were asking for the same privilege of meeting at the university, which put the school in an awkward situation. A preliminary search indicated that there were no suitable rental facilities to accommodate a congregation of about four hundred.

OBF was therefore faced with the formidable challenge of finding a place, then of raising the funds necessary to build a church. In 1981, Miami University gave OBF another year's extension to use Presser Hall, provided that we made substantial progress toward finding our own facilities by the spring of 1982.

In 1981 as he was driving south on Maple Street, Dale observed a woman in her house coat putting up a "For Sale Sign" at 800 S. Maple Street, next to the freshmen dormitories. She did not want to sell to the university. As the vast majority of our congregation consisted of students, we had a small base of community members who contributed the $47,000 needed for a down payment on the property. Hal Barcus, a professor of architecture, and Greg Barger, his grad student and a member of OBF, drew up plans for the building. Now we faced the daunting challenge of raising funds necessary for the church building.

Many different means were used to raise money: some $2500 was raised through garage sales; Rich and Chuck Bostwick designed some stationery; a cookbook was edited by Linda Hill. By the fall of 1982, $53,000 had been raised. Plans were made to break ground in May 1983. A week before that date the Stewards Foundation agreed to loan OBF $295,000 at 6% interest for its building. The foundation normally restricts its loans to Brethren churches but favored us because of the Brethren background of the Wilsons.

Figure 93. Bill Wilson at the groundbreaking at 800 S. Maple Street

Dwain and June Freels helped to lay down the new lawn. Jay Bennett and his crew erected the new sign. Among key individuals who contributed to the completion of the building were: Dale Burke, who was the site supervisor; Howard Krauss, chair of the Building Committee; Jonathan Brant and Barbara Samuelson, chairs of the Building Finance Committee; Judy Bennett, chair of the Furnishings Committee; and Ron Mahurin, supervisor of painting. New hymnals were donated by Dennis and Karen DeRight.

The first service in the new building was held on March 18, 1984. Richard Friedmann spoke on that day. Its formal dedication took place on May 1. The church's red brick structure blends in well with the red brick freshmen dormitories which are just adjacent. We went to two services on Sundays to accommodate the 250–300 students who attended.

The Later 1980s

In 1984 Wes Pastor, a graduate of Ohio State University, and an accountancy instructor who was active with the Navs, became an elder. Roger

Hershey, a Penn State University grad, who had been an elder since 1982, resigned in 1984 as he became the new director of Cru.[14] In 1984 I arranged for special speakers to come to Miami University who also spoke at OBF: in January, Richard Pierard, a historian from Indiana State University; in February Bob Herrmann, the executive director of the American Scientific Affiliation in connection with the ASA conference I had arranged to meet at Miami University; and in March Kenneth Kantzer, the president of Trinity College, who had been Kimi's teacher at Wheaton College and who had married us in 1962.

In 1985 OBF added a ministry intern, Gary Taylor, a graduate of Dallas Theological Seminary (DTS). We also had two professors from DTS speak: John Hannah, professor of church history and Ron Blue, professor of missions. I edited a newsletter that went out to seven-hundred alumni. Of these 165 were pursuing full-time Christian ministries, sixty-five with Cru. We bade farewell to Bill and Enid Wilson, who were moving to a retirement home near their son Craig in West Liberty.

In March 1986 Swee Hwa Quek spoke to the Faculty Christian Fellowship and then to OBF. Swee Hwa had been my student at Shelton College. After graduating from Faith Theological seminary, Swee Hwa earned his PhD under F. F. Bruce of the University of Manchester. He is the pastor of a Bible Presbyterian Church and the president of the Graduate Biblical School in Singapore. In May OBF honored forty graduating seniors, including three who graduated *summa cum laude*. In the last fifteen years, seventy-five alumni have enrolled in seminaries. Many others had become parachurch staff members serving at such universities as: Alabama, Arizona State. Georgia Tech, Illinois, Illinois State, Marquette, Mt. Holyoke, Northwestern, Ohio State, Smith, and West Virginia. Others have served as missionaries in: Canada, Hong Kong, Indonesia, West Germany, Kenya, Moluccas, Philippines, and Togo. In the summer, forty students and staff from Cru shared the Gospel in Japan. In November, Ralph Winter, a friend of Herb Kane, and founder of the US Center for World Missions in Pasadena, spoke at a missions conference at OBF. Kimi served as the chair of OBF's missions committee.

---

14. Three of the campus staff at Miami were contemporaries at Penn State University. Roger Hershey was a cheerleader, Wally Cirafesi (Navs) was a football player, and Dennis Stokes (Navs) was a member of the marching band.

Figure 94. With Ralph Winter and Herb Kane

Miami alumni, Dave and Janine Sylvester, were serving as Cru staff at Northwestern University. In 1986 OBF launched Operation Timothy, sending Gary Taylor and Dale Burke to help start the Evanston Bible Fellowship to minister to students at Northwestern University. A key leader in this new church plant was Tom Mason, a professor of Physics at the university.[15]

In March 1987, Howard Hendricks of Dallas Theological seminary spoke on "Marriage and the Family." In the summer of 1987 Dave Smetana and his new bride Terry came to OBF, initially to succeed Gary Taylor as a seminary intern to be trained by Dale Burke. Dave, a graduate of Michigan State University had been active with the Navs there and had graduated from Dallas Theological Seminary. But Dave, who had superior computer skills, was to stay and serve at OBF in various roles. Terry would be active in the women's ministry and was also an outstanding salesperson for Mary Kay cosmetics.

---

15. By 2010 in rented facilities Evanston Bible Fellowship had a membership of 200, with 350 in attendance, approximately 100 of whom were university students. EBF was established a number of branch churches.

In 1988 Ralph Gutowski, who was an assistant to a Miami's vice-president, joined the elder board. Ralph, who had been a colonel in the Air Force, had served as the vicepresident of a small Bible College in Centerville near Dayton. Ralph led a Perspectives on Missions class at OBF.

Ward Ballard and the Navigators

Ward Ballard, the son of the mayor of Akron, was a *summa cum laude* pre-med graduate of Miami University in 1982. He returned to Miami in 1985 to serve as the director of the Navigators for the next fifteen years. In 1994 he began leading summer missions trips to Vladivostok, Russia. In 1996 he met his wife Kari in Vladivostok and married her in 1997. She was the daughter of Navigator missionaries to Sweden. Ward comments, "I was single and the only staff my first 12 years. OBF provided the family-like support I needed to survive." Ward became an OBF elder in 1987 and served until 1995.[16]

Dale Burke's Resignation

In the summer of 1989 Dale Burke accepted a call to become the pastor of Grace Bible Church in northern California near Cal Polytechnic University at San Luis Obispo.[17] Dave Smetana was approved as the interim pastor. I stepped down temporarily as an elder to chair a search committee. At this time the other elders were Ward Ballard, Tim Rhodenbaugh,[18] and Dave Smetana.

---

16. Ward and Kari Ballard served as Navigator missionaries in Bergen, Norway, from 2000 to 2005, ministering to students at the Medical School and the Business School there. On his return to the States, Ward became the regional director for the Navigators in Ohio, Michigan, and Kentucky for twenty years. In 2018, Ward became the national director for outreach to internationals at the Navigator headquarters in Colorado Springs.

17. Dale Burke was to remain there until he was called in 1995 to become the pastor of the 5,000 member EFCA church in Fullerton, California, founded by Chuck Swindoll. He was to serve here for the next 15 years. He then moved to Seacoast Church in Encinatas, and established Leverage Leadership to train leaders in Africa. He also served as an adjunct faculty member at Dallas Theological Seminary. Dale was succeeded at the Fullerton church by Mike Erre, OBF's first youth director.

18. Tim Rhodenbaugh, who had been active with Cru at Miami, was a dentist who had served with his wife Becky as missionaries in Swaziland.

In 1990, three new elders were added: Bob Evans,[19] Howard Krauss,[20] and Mick Pechan. After Kimi resigned as the deacon of missions, I became the acting deacon. OBF was blessed by the visit of some of our missionaries, including Sue Swieringa from the Philippines, Doug Boone from Zaire, and Bill and Critty Fairback from Singapore. Blair and Jane Cook had presented a Christian education curriculum based on the Jesus Film in Estonia and Russia. Charley and Cheryl Warner moved to Odessa in the Ukraine, where Charley taught at a seminary in Odessa. Two of our high schoolers went on a mission trip to Okinawa.

Winston Clark

The search committee I chaired reviewed the files of about a hundred applicants, many from Dallas Theological Seminary, several from Trinity Evangelical Divinity School, and one candidate from Gordon-Conwell Theological Seminary, Winston Clark. He was the committee's unanimous choice to become OBF's new lead pastor in 1990.

Win, whose father was a doctor originally from Maine, took premed courses at the University of Massachusetts. He became active there in Cru and married vivacious Nancy, a cheerleader from Florida State University, who was also involved in Cru. Win served for sixteen years in Nova Scotia, first in a rural church and then in a large Baptist church in Halifax. Many in that congregation were elderly, but there were also students and internationals from Dalhousie University. The Clarks had three children, Brian who was 16, and his younger siblings, Tim and Amy.

A funny incident occurred when the Clarks first met the Smetanas. Upon opening the door Terry said in a loud voice "Winston go to the other room." It happened that their dog was named "Winston" also![21] The Clarks bought a home on Maxine Drive, only a few houses away from the former residence of the Wilsons.

---

19. Bob and Karen Evans were graduates of Juniata College. Bob, who had earned a master's degree in chemistry from Miami, was in charge of the IT services at Oxford's hospital.

20. Howard Krauss was a chemist with Proctor and Gamble.

21. For the first decade, Dave Smetana served as the associate pastor. Then in 2001, Dave and Win became co-pastors with equal salaries until Dave's resignation in 2006.

The Early 1990s

In January 1992 there was a memorial service for Bill Wilson at OBF. When a university professor passes away, it is usually the members of his or her department who form a committee to write the deceased's official obituary. In the case of Bill Wilson, Karl Mattox, the chair of the Botany Department, knowing my close relation to Bill, appointed me as the chair of this committee which consisted of Botany professors. We recognized not only Bill's outstanding reputation as an inspiring teacher, but also his character as a Christian gentleman.

In July Frank Jenista, who had served in the US Embassy in the Philippines, spoke. He is the brother of Ruth Pettitt. Frank after earning a PhD with a dissertation on a tribe in the Philippines, taught at Cedarville University. In August we had a reception for Steve and Kimiko Lambacher. Steve, a *summa cum laude* grad of Ohio University, received his MA in History from Miami University. He served with the Navs in Korea and returned to earn an MA in teaching English as a second language. Kimiko from Japan was one of his students.[22] In the fall Bob and Robin Hostetler, both former Salvation Army officers who were serving as staff at a boys' home in nearby Riley, started attending OBF. Bob was a gifted speaker and a popular author who had written books for the apologist Josh MacDowell.

Among alumni who reported on their missions were Wes and Sue Pastor, who were beginning a ministry in Burlington for the students of the University of Vermont, as well as Wally and Connie Cirafesi, who were ministering to Hispanics in Florida. They had just moved to Homestead before a hurricane struck, but fortunately their home was spared. Blair Cook and Doug Franck spoke about their mission to Russia. Cru students and staff described their spring blitz to Albania, a previously closed country. An IV student spoke about his visit to Kazakhstan.

The Buryat Jesus Film

It was in 1992 that OBF began raising $25,000 to pay for the translation of the Jesus Film into Buryat, a Mongolian dialect spoken by a group of 600,000 Buryats residing near southern Lake Baikal in Siberia

---

22. Steve and Kimiko Lambacher returned to Japan where Steve earned a PhD in Cognitive Science from Shukyo University. He then taught at Aizu University and at Aoyama Gakuin University in Tokyo.

just north of Mongolia. This was a project spurred by Tim and Becky Rhodenbaugh.

In August 1994 after the film's translation was completed six OBFers traveled for a two-week trip to Ulan Ude for the showing of the film. These included Tim Clark, Bob Evans, Keith Rhodes, Tom Taylor, Tom Troke, and Paul Vermilion. Tim was the high school son of Pastor Clark, Bob and Paul worked at hospitals, Tom Troke was a mailman, Keith was a university student, and Tom Taylor was on the staff of *The Cincinnati Enquirer*. The total travel expense for each team member was $2,500.

They left on July 30 and flew to Moscow, where they were delayed for two days because of customs problems. The team took advantage of this delay to do some sightseeing at the Red Square, the Kremlin, Lenin's tomb, and a Russian Orthodox Church.

According to Tim Clark's report:

> When we got to Ulan Ude the assistant minister of Culture, who is a hardline Communist, provided us with a bus, theaters to show the movie in, and two of his assistants, to guide us around Ulan Ude for two weeks. Stottler Starr, who works with Inspirational Films, a branch of Campus Crusade for Christ, had made these arrangements a month earlier. . . . We got to show the film five times in Ulan Ude and then again in four of the surrounding villages. Everyone said the film was translated very well and the message was very clear, but all the Buddhists have been taught that when Jesus turned twelve, he went to Tibet and studied under the Dalai Lama.

According to the account from Bob Evans:

> The Buddhists were, at least, willing to listen to our presentation and did take a copy of the film. In fact, they were quite hospitable, especially in comparison with the Russian Orthodox representative. The Russian Orthodox Church was far less interested in the film and refused to even allow our team's "ambassadors" past their gates. They did not want a copy of the film and they did not want to hear about it or our goals to reach out.
>
> From my perspective, the entire project was a great success; it unified OBF in an effort to sponsor the film's translation; it allowed a group of OBFers to travel overseas to present the Gospel of Hope.

The Light of the World, a church in Ulan Ude, provided translators who knew the Buryat language. Tom Taylor fell in love with a lovely Russian translator, Vera Goldina, and later married her in America.[23]

New Elders

In 1993 three new men were added to the elder board: Marty Creech, the owner of The Bike Center, Tom Troke, a mailman, and Jim Lillibridge, a research scientist with Procter and Gamble. A new member of the congregation was Jim Collard, the city manager of the town of Oxford. A noted visiting speaker was Haddon Robinson of Gordon-Conwell Theological Seminary.

In March 1994 I went up to Chicago to attend the ordination of Martin McCorkle as the pastor of the Evanston Bible Fellowship, which OBF had helped to develop. OBF hired its first youth director, Mike Erre, a graduate of Miami University who had been working at a bank when Nancy Clark invited him to attend OBF. OBF also acquired some property behind our lot.

OBF's Twenty-Fifth Anniversary

On September 16 and 17, 1995 OBF celebrated our twenty-fifth anniversary. At a banquet on Saturday night, many old timers, including Enid Wilson, Barney and Arlene Ford, Bill and Critty Fairback, Douglas Boone, and others, shared their memories of OBF. On Sunday, a special service was held at Presser Hall. Tom Mason represented the Evanston Bible Fellowship. The featured speaker was Dale Burke, our first pastor, now the pastor of the Evangelical Free Church in Fullerton, California. President Philip Shriver, who attended the service expressed his appreciation for the ministry of OBF to the university and to Oxford.

The Later 1990s

In 1997, Greg Bryan, a graduate of Kent State University and Columbia Bible College and Seminary, arrived in Oxford to serve with the Navs. Greg served as the director of the Navigators until 2002. He married Emily

---

23. He is a copy editor on the staff of *USA Today*, and Vera teaches and translates Russian.

Burke, a Miami grad in 2000. Greg comments, "OBF practically treated Navigator staff as pastoral staff members. Allowing us to use the church for campus work, allowing us to use their office to make copies, and providing encouragement for our work! It was a great partnership!"[24]

In 1998 OBF purchased a property across Maple Street, which Miami University then acquired in exchange for an equivalent property behind OBF. Then in the fall a host of volunteers including children worked under the supervision of Rob Compton, Brian Ruby, and Don English to create an extension of our parking lot by laying down thousands of individual stone pavers.[25] These were laid down with interstices filled with gravel which allowed water to drain when it rained. Later, as OBF allowed Miami University to use our parking lot on special occasions, the university reciprocated by allowing the church to use their adjacent parking lot on Sundays. In contrast to uptown churches members of OBF have experienced no difficulty in finding a parking space!

By 1999 Kimi had organized the Prime Timers, a group of older members of OBF who would meet occasionally for fellowship. The young people's ministry among junior high and senior high students was flourishing. Twenty young people went to help build an orphanage in Monterrey, Mexico in November. Several OBFers went abroad to serve including Ward and Kari Ballard to Norway, Christian and Lisa Pettitt to the Netherlands, Josh Kaufmann to Argentina, Marlene Benz to Macedonia, Jim and Cindy Fath to Uzbekistan.

In 2000 OBF was able to acquire the corner lot at the south end of Maple Street facing Chestnut Street, a major east west corridor. We demolished the dilapidated house and cut down the trees, which had resembled a jungle. The lot had been occupied by a recluse who was hostile to the church, but his heirs sold the property to OBF for $137,000. When Miami University renovated the nearby housing for graduate students, the school donated the playground equipment which was erected on the cleared space.

---

24. Greg and Emily Bryan served with the Navigators at Kent State University from 2002 to 2014, the University of Hawaii, from 2014 to 2016, and back to Kent State, where their focus is on international students.

25. Pat Parkinson donated a generous gift of $10,000 for the project.

LOVE Inc. and Darryl Jackson

Pastor Win Clark was challenged by Joan Baidenmann to mobilize the Oxford churches to unite to minister to the poor and the needy through an organization called LOVE Inc. sponsored by World Vision. As Pastor Clark recalls:

> Our first meeting was held in the fireside room of OBF, and we organized and had 15 churches working together from 1992 to 2004. We received training through World Vision and Joannie Baidenmann and I attended sessions in Naperville, IL and Atlanta, Georgia. I was the president of LOVE Inc for 10 years and spoke at many of our area churches to encourage maximum participation. I spoke to the Rotary, Kiwanis, and Lions Clubs in Oxford to promote the working of the churches for the poor and marginalized in Oxford.

It was through LOVE Inc. that Win in 1992 first met Darryl Jackson, the pastor of the Black First Baptist Church. Win reports:

> Pastor Darryl was very involved from the outset, and I began by speaking at First Baptist to invite all his people to sign up and keep a list of all who were willing to register their abilities to serve in the Name of Jesus. Our two congregations sponsored an oil change together for widows and single women. While OBF hosted the Kids Club at the Oxford trailer park throughout the 1990s and well into the new century, Pastor Darryl and his wife, Cheryl, headed up a similar outreach in Parkview Arms.

> Pastor Darryl and I became lifelong prayer partners after I attended the 10,000 men Promise Keeper event with a dozen men of OBF in Boulder, CO in 1993. I was challenged to go home and find an African American Pastor to befriend and pray with on a regular basis. We began to exchange pulpits and joined together for Easter sunrise services at First Baptist together each year.[26] Pastor Darryl taught me far more about the love of Christ and bridging the racial divide in our community than I ever could have imagined. We went together with 12 area pastors to the Promise Keeprs Clergy Conference in 1996 with 50,000 other pastors around the country. Our friendship has extended beyond Oxford.

---

26. The pulpit exchanges between the two churches lasted from 1996 to 2000.

One of my highlights with Pastor Darryl was when their congregation moved from Beech Street to College Corner Pike near Wal Mart. I dropped by their new church and saw that their women were looking for a pulpit in a church magazine. I contacted Virg Otto and together we built them a pulpit that matched their dreams. Then on Mother's Day 2004, Virg and I rolled in the pulpit in the middle of their church service to the delight of their women and Pastor Darryl. He's been preaching behind that pulpit ever since.

Refugees from the Sudan

In the summer of 2000 OBF welcomed a family from the Sudan. Ramadan Hassan, his wife and two young daughters were refugees. Ramadan, a Christian, had been imprisoned and tortured by Muslims from northern Sudan. They escaped to a refugee camp in Egypt. The Catholic Refugee Services brought them to the US and Ohio. Through Carol Schaber, OBF agreed to serve as a host church. We housed them at an apartment in Candlewood Terrace and provided them with furniture and other necessities. Kimi tutored the young girls in English. I tried to help Ramadan get a driver's license. Though he had driven a truck in the Sudan, he failed the test twice, as he could not parallel park and once when asked to make a left turn at an intersection he froze. We later helped them move to Columbus where there is a large refugee community chiefly from Somalia. Ramadan aspired to become a veterinarian as he had served as a game warden. I knew a Christian professor at OSU's veterinary school and introduced Ramadan to him. But as it is more difficult to get into veterinary school (as there are fewer of them) than to get into medical school, Ramadan could not get in. We visited them several times in Columbus. The last we heard was that he had become a truck driver!

A Major Split

At the end of 2000, there was a major split at OBF. Two of our elders, Bob Hostettler and Jim Lillibridge became dissatisfied with the ministries of the co-pastors Win Clark and David Smetana. Bob was the chair of the elders and set the agenda for our elder meetings.

A problem had arisen over the supervision of the Tennessee Trek, an annual summer event for the young people which Dale Burke had begun on Geiger Island near the Tennessee border where the young people would be isolated for a time of fun, fellowship, Bible study, and bonding. Usually one of the pastors would attend but this year neither could do so and some things occurred that were unsupervised such as baptisms. The elders therefore decided to revise the by-laws to require greater accountability from the youth director. While we were at it, we decided to also look into accountability for the pastors.

Bob who came from a Salvation Army background, and Jim from a position at Procter and Gamble were used to working with detailed rules of conduct. They wanted to require the pastors to announce a year in advance their vacation plans, a position which was opposed by the pastors and the two other elders (Marty Creech and myself). After protracted meetings it became clear that the differences were too great and personal that agreement could not be reached.

At the end of the year at a church meeting Bob and Jim read out a list of complaints and resigned from the elder board. The pastors chose not to respond. About fifteen families left, including the office coordinator, Lynette Holzworth.[27] After a short time, the dissidents were able to purchase a sizable property on Kehr Road and begin Cobblestone Church. Though many feelings were hurt, after a period cooperation between the two churches resumed on such projects as missions to Mexico and the Tennessee Trek.

The Evangelical Free Church of America

In January 2001 Chuck Warner, the regional director of the Evangelical Free Church of America spoke. OBF had been an independent church since 1970. The late Herb Kane had urged OBF to affiliate with the EFCA, a denomination founded by the Norwegian and Swedish free church immigrants, who had left their state church countries. The EFCA had a seminary, Trinity Evangelical Divinity School in Deerfield north of Chicago. The EFCA proved attractive to OBF as it gave great latitude to local churches. One issue was its premillennial stance on the Second Coming of Christ. But once it was clarified that this did not require the

27. Her husband Bob Holzworth, who was a police officer, later became the chief of police. Their son Andrew, who graduated from Moody Bible Institute, became one of the pastors at Cobblestone Church.

dispensational understanding of premillennialism the elders agreed to OBF's joining this denomination, though OBF does not emphasize its denominational affiliation.[28]

Cru at Miami University

Roger Hershey, a graduate of Penn State University, came to Miami University in 1980. Succeeding John Whitehouse as the director of Cru, Roger served at Miami University until 1997. Commenting on Cru's relationship to OBF, Roger observed:

> The relationship OBF had with the campus ministries for all of those years was so unique. I know of so few other places like this anywhere in the country in which the local church worked so cooperatively, with you, Dale and Win, bringing in speakers together, mission conferences, etc. I do believe that is one of the reasons we saw so much fruit and so many laborers raised up because of working together rather than competing and OBF being so supportive and seeing the students being ministered to and sent out by the campus ministries and OBF together.

Mark Brown, a graduate of Northern Illinois University, with his wife Diane joined the staff of Cru in 1991. He worked with fraternities until 1997, when he succeeded Roger Hershey as the director of Cru at Miami. In 2001, Mark took a leave of absence to work on Cru's national campaign to distribute a magazine. He reports:

> During this time, Cru at Miami grew to the largest in its history, over 900 students were in small group Bible Studies during my absence. This affirmed in me that Cru did not need me. Also, during the following years, we had close to 45 staff, interns, and volunteers. Additionally, Grant Scott directed our international partnerships to Albania and Macedonia. We also would see 80- students put their faith in Christ annually. We also would see during this time 15+ students a year going into full-time ministry.[29]

---

28. Though the denominational affiliation was once noted on an outdoor sign, that is no longer the case. Nor does the EFCA affiliation appear on the opening page of OBF's website.

29. Mark Brown developed a father and son retreat and also served as a chaplain with the Oxford Police Force. He served on a search committee in 2015 and became an elder of OBF in 2016.

Jane Armstrong, who has been the codirector of Cru, has organized Bible studies for the women, who outnumber the men by a ratio of three to one in Cru. She also annually accompanied other staff and students on missions trips to Fiji, Italy, Albania, and Montenegro. She bought the Waggener's house on Maple Street across from the Rec Center and has had a number of women living with her. Jane, who arrived in 1978 and is still a member of OBF, has impacted the lives of thousands of Miami women in the forty-plus years of her ministry.

The Early 2000s

In 2001 Marcus Jobe, a professor in the Farmer School of Business who had taught in the Ukraine, brought visiting Ukrainian professors and administrators to OBF. At OBF Marcus was active in supervising the Angel Tree gifts to the children of prisoners. New members included Col. Stuart Wagner and his wife Susan; Col. Wagner was the head of the NROTC program at Miami University.

By 2002, a Bible study for Chinese students was meeting at OBF, taught by a leader from the Chinese church in Mt. Healthy, a northern suburb of Cincinnati. Numerous students from Africa were attending. Bob and Karen Evans, and Sarah Pechan went to Casablanca, Morocco to teach at an elite private school, the George Washington Academy. Susan Swieringa, one of our earliest missionaries who had served as the vice-principal of Faith Academy, a school for missionary children in Manila, returned to the states to become one of the vice-presidents of her mission, Christar.

In 2003, a new men's fellowship meeting on Monday nights drew about fifty men. Newcomers to OBF were Reid Christenberry and his wife. Reid was the new vice-president for Information Technology at Miami University. A welcome addition to Miami and to OBF was Dennis Keeler, who grew up in the church and made a decision for Christ as a child in a Vacation Bible School. His father Art was on the staff of the Audio-Visual department and his mother Debbie was a secretary for the Department of Computer Sciences. After graduating from Miami, where he was involved in IV, Dennis received his PhD from the University of Michigan and did a post-doc at MIT. He chose to teach at Miami, because he was interested in working with the children at OBF.

OBF hired a new youth director, David Friedrich. David, a Canadian, had been working with his wife Anna at L'Abri, the center established by Francis Schaeffer near Lausanne, Switzerland. In August, I was able to visit the Evanston Bible Fellowship. EBF had just hired as its assistant minister, John Kim, a Miami University alumnus who had graduated from Trinity Evangelical Divinity School.

In 2004, OBF added three new elders. Bob Benz and his wife Dorothy, a nurse, were originally from New Mexico. Bob had graduated from Cincinnati Bible College and Seminary and worked at the Church of Christ publishing house in Mt. Healthy, before becoming the head of personnel at Miami University. He had served as the part-time pastor of the small Victory Church of Christ. For the sake of their children, David, Glenn, and Marlene, the Benzes had joined OBF. Bob supervised the counting and recording of offerings.

Another new elder was Alan Oak, the assistant dean of the Farmer School of Business. Alan, who was originally from Maine, and his wife Diane had lived in Jamaica, where Alan had worked for a bank. When they first came to Miami University, they lived in a cottage next to Presser Hall. Attracted by the music and singing, they then attended the services at Presser. Alan's financial acumen and experience were a great asset to the elders. The Oaks have also been active in supporting McCullough Hyde Memorial Hospital.

Ben Voth, a professor of communications, also became an elder. Ben, a graduate of Baylor University, initially thought of training for the ministry. But after receiving a PhD in Communication Studies from the University of Kansas, Ben became a professor. Ben was an outspoken witness for Christ both on campus and in the public square. He coached Miami's award-winning debate teams. A Jewish student who had studied under him later joined the staff of the Holocaust Museum and invited Ben to coach Holocaust survivors to tell their stories in public.

In 2005 Mike VanHook, a campus minister, spoke at OBF. Mike would later establish International Sports Alliance, an organization which ministers in the island of Haiti. In March Darrell Bock, a New Testament scholar from Dallas Theological Seminary spoke at OBF. Bock was the first speaker of the Annual History Lecture series, which had been established in my honor by Win Clark and the IV staff-worker Dennis Dudley, by creating a fund with the Oxford Community Foundation.

Most of the speakers in the series would speak at the university on Saturday evening and at OBF on Sunday morning.[30]

It's All About Jesus

This is the title of a book taken from the motto on the front of a barn on Somerville Road near Oxford, a photo of which is displayed on the front cover.[31] The authors, Dr. Peter Magolda and his graduate assistant Kelsey Ebben Gross were from the Department of Educational Leadership at Miami University. The authors comment, "The academy remains largely ignorant of the intricacies of evangelical organizations . . . ."[32] They at first considered four evangelical organizations including the large Faith Nite (i.e., Cru), with its thousand members and thirty staff, but for a number of reasons restricted their "ethnographic" study to a medium sized (eighty members, two staff) organization they called Students Serving Christ (SSC), which was the Navigators, directed by Matthew (i.e., Justin Gravitt). The authors were given unlimited access to all of the Navs meetings, including not only the large group meeting but smaller Bible studies and training sessions, which they report in detail with sympathy but also with critical analysis. The research began in October 2004 and concluded in September 2006. The authors were both raised at Catholics and so observed the Navs staff and students as "outsiders."

Their book twice mentions OBF, where the Nav meetings took place. Once as "a modest-size interdenominational Christian church on the edge of campus."[33] And as "the Christian Fellowship church on the edge of campus" with a sign "An Evangelical Free Church."[34] One interesting question they raised was how evangelical groups could proselytize in dorms when the university forbids solicitations in residence halls. The answer is that these groups pass out surveys, and if a student indicates an interest in studying the Bible and gives his or her residence room information, then Christians are free to contact them there.[35]

30. Exceptions occurred in 2016 when the speaker was Dr. Santa Ono, the president of the University of Cincinnati, and in 2022 with Philip Jenkins of Baylor University.

31. Peter Magolda and Kelsey Ebben Gross, *It's All about Jesus: Faith as an Oppositional Collegiate Subculture* (Sperling, Virginia: Stylus, 2009).

32. Ibid., 10.

33. Ibid., 93.

34. Ibid., 113.

35. Ibid., 148.

Justin Gravitt and other Nav staff members, such as "Don" (who is Richard Jarvi, the regional trainer for the Navs) and "Nancy" (who is his wife Lois), were able to record their reactions to the observations and conclusions of the authors at the end of the book. Justin, who had majored in comparative religions at Miami, had succeeded Ward Ballard as the director of the Navs in 2002. He and his wife Kristen, a *summa cum laude* graduate of Miami University continued as the Navs staff until 2006.³⁶

Jeremy Carr

By 2006 the elders and congregation had decided to conduct a search for a new lead pastor to supplement the ministry of Win Clark. When such an arrangement proved to be unworkable, Win Clark decided, after seventeen years at OBF, to retire in 2007. He and Nancy moved to Carmel, Indiana, where he joined the staff of Horizon International, an organization that worked with Aids orphans from five countries in Africa who sang in American churches to raise funds.

The search committee was led by Mick Pechan. I had suggested to the committee that it place an ad in the classified section of *Christianity Today*. Only one applicant responded to the ad. He was the successful candidate. In the fall of 2007, OBF welcomed a new lead pastor Jeremy Carr, along with his wife Michelle and their two young daughters. He was a graduate of Faith Bible College in Iowa, which was a school of the General Association of Regular Baptists. Jeremy had also taken seminary courses at Liberty Theological Seminary. He had been serving as the youth pastor in Crown Point in northern Indiana. Jeremy proved to be a skilled expositor of the Scriptures who attracted large crowds of Miami students.

In October 2007 during the celebration of Halloween, Jeremy came into conflict with Kelli Voth, who had been directing the Christian education. She asked him to do certain things, but he was not ready to take "orders" from a subordinate. Since Kelli was the wife of Ben Voth, an elder, this led to serious tensions that were not resolved.

---

36. The Gravitts spent four years in Lampang, a large city in northern Thailand, working with a government school and bearing witness to Christ. Upon returning to the States Justin became a director for Innovation and Advancement for the Navigators Church Ministry.

Ben and his family left Oxford in 2008 as he accepted a position at the Southern Methodist University in Dallas.

In March 2008 Craig Evans, a noted New Testament scholar from Acadia Divinity School spoke at OBF. In May, OBF honored forty-two graduating seniors. In November, Chris McCune spoke. Chris, a West Point grad, married Liz Schaber. He graduated from Reformed Theological Seminary in Mississippi. He and Liz served with North American Missions to plant a church near Edinburgh, Scotland. Upon returning to the States, they attempted to plant a new church in Denver. This attempt was frustrated by a split in the church leadership.

Two New Elders

In 2009 two new elders were chosen: Richard (Dick) Pettitt and Michael (Mick) Pechan. Dick was a grad of Cedarville University, as was his wife Ruth. Dick's father was a GARB pastor in New Jersey. Ruth's parents were missionaries with the Association of Baptists for World Evangelism (ABWE). Her father is buried in New Guinea; her mother, Sophie Jenista, served as a missionary to women prisoners in Manila. Sophie, who turned ninety-nine in December 2021, and her Filipino co-worker Deb Anat managed to involve 1,800 women in prisons in Manila in their "Light Bearers" ministry!

Dick and Ruth served as teachers in a private school in the Philippines. Ruth taught as a beloved English teacher in the Middle School in Oxford. Dick entered Miami's graduate history program but was drafted to serve in Vietnam. After discharge, he completed his PhD in US history under Professor Richard Jellison. When Dick could not find a teaching job, he began as a janitor at Miami University, then eventually became the associate dean of libraries and finally the assistant provost in charge of buildings, including the erection of the Farmer School of Business. His background was very beneficial in OBF's remodeling efforts.

Mick Pechan was originally from Wisconsin. He earned his PhD at Iowa State University. He was the chair of the Physics Department at the time he became an elder. He and his wife Kathy, a trained counselor, have three daughters, Sarah, Jessica and Hannah.[37]

---

37. After retiring as the chair, Mick accepted a position with the Department of Energy in DC and oversaw the granting of about 50 million dollars in grants.

In March Walter Kaiser, noted Old Testament scholar from Trinity Evangelical Divinity School, spoke at OBF, preaching two different sermons at the two services. Walt and I had been at Brandeis University. In November Mark and Shirley Wilson visited OBF. Mark is the older son of the Bill and Enid Wilson. A graduate of Wheaton College, Mark was employed by IBM when Dennis Stokes (a former OBFer) persuaded Mark and Shirley to serve for about a decade as Navigator missionaries in Russia.

Derek Whalen

In 2010 OBF hired Derek Whalen to serve as an associate pastor. Derek grew up in Valley Forge, northwest of Philadelphia. After graduating from Cedarville University, he continued his studies at Grand Rapids Theological Seminary. He then served as a youth pastor at Ann Arbor, Michigan. He and his wife Christy have three children, including Derek, Jr., who is an avid golfer; Deanna who was an outstanding tennis player; and a daughter Charis. Derek himself received a scholarship as a soccer player. Derek was placed in charge of overseeing the various community groups of OBF with occasional opportunities to preach.

OBF's Fortieth Anniversary

In February 2010 OBF celebrated its fortieth anniversary with a series of events. On February 7, Barney Ford spoke at three services; on February 13 and 14, Dale Burke spoke at four services. On February 14 a banquet was held at the Shriver Student Center with 140 in attendance, about half of whom were returning alumni. I created a booklet "Celebrating the 40th Anniversary of the Oxford Bible Fellowship," which contained photos of the three venues of OBF: the Municipal Building (1970 to 1972), Presser Hall (1972 to 1981), and 800 S. Maple Street (1981 to 2010). This also included a portrait of Bill and Enid Wilson. A letter of congratulations from the Ohio House of Representatives secured by Representative Timothy Derickson, who was a member of OBF.[38] Also included was a proclamation from Richard Keebler, the mayor of the city of Oxford, and a letter from President Phillip Shriver of Miami University.

---

38. Tim Derickson received the second most Republican votes in Ohio to succeed retiring speaker of the House of Representatives, John Boehner of West Chester.

AN ASIAN AMERICAN ANCIENT HISTORIAN AND BIBLICAL SCHOLAR

Dr. Shriver wrote:

> As President of Miami University in 1970, I remember so well your founding and your phenomenal and inspirational growth and impact on the students, faculty, and staff and townspeople of Oxford over the past four decades. I recall my conversation with my good friend and colleague, Dr. Edwin Yamauchi, about your use of Presser Hall on the Western Campus until a permanent site in Oxford could be identified. I also recall our rejoicing as we celebrated your 25th Anniversary in 1995.
>
> As I reflect on your wonderful years of the O.B.F., I remember my undergraduate involvement with the Yale Battelle Chapel Fellowship and my participation in its meetings and discussions and as a member of the Chapel Choir.
>
> To the Oxford Bible Fellowship go my heartfelt thanks for your positive and beneficial impact on the lives of thousands who have been, are now, and will be touched by the O.B.F. May the Father Almighty and His Holy Son our Lord and Savior Jesus Christ, bless the Oxford Bible Fellowship for all time to come

In this booklet, I also included a brief history of OBF, a description of the ministries and vocations of some of its alumni, and testimonials from alumni as well as the earlier testimonials collected on the occasion of our twenty-fifth anniversary.

In March Professor Mark Noll, an eminent historian from the University of Notre Dame, spoke at OBF. Mark, a graduate of Wheaton College, had taught for many years at his alma mater. He and I had served together as senior editors of *Christianity Today*. In November the elders prayed for Bob Scholl, a retired education professor whom I had invited to OBF. He had approached me during a basketball game because he had read *The Case for Christ*. It turned out that his son and Marty Creech had been best friends in high school.

In 2011, New Testament professor Donald Carson of Trinity Evangelical Divinity School spoke at OBF. The preaching of Jeremy Carr attracted large numbers of university students to our three services on Sunday morning. In May, we recognized eighty-seven graduating seniors who had attended OBF. Two new elders were added, Ron Knopf, a supervisor at the Ford Motor Company in Cincinnati,[39] and Ayodele Abatan,

---

39. Ron Knopf would later be sent by Ford to supervise the building of three automobile factories in Chongqing China.

who was head of the Engineering Technology Departments at the branch campuses in Middletown and Hamilton. Ayo, who had a PhD in civil engineering from Virginia Tech University, and his wife Adetutu, were from Nigeria. Tutu was a lecturer in English.

In 2012 Professor Paul Maier, ancient historian from Western Michigan University spoke at OBF. Paul also served as the Lutheran chaplain at the university. He has translated highly readable and illustrated editions of Josephus and Eusebius, which I have used in my classes. The Lord continued to bless the ministry of Jeremy Carr with about 400 university students and 300 community members attending, including many young families with children. We had two morning services at OBF and a third service in between at Benton Hall until the end of 2012. Nick Cattin, who was on the staff of the Farmer School of Business, served as the site supervisor for the services at Benton Hall. He became an elder in 2013.

Among those attending were the vice-principal, the athletic director of the high school, and the principal of the elementary school. Faculty from the following university departments attended: Botany, Business, Computer Sciences, Educational Psychology, Engineering Technology, English, History, Kinesiology, Manufacturing and Mechanical Engineering, Marketing, Mathematics, Microbiology, Music, Physics, Psychology, and Statistics.

From the beginning of 2013 until May we were able to use the site of the old Talawanda High School for services and classrooms while also using the Maple Street church for one service directed to the college students. We contemplated buying the site, but Miami University purchased it. In March evangelical philosopher William Lane Craig of the Talbot School of Theology spoke at the Palm Sunday services. About 600 to 700 were attending, half of them students. Also in attendance were the assistant men's basketball coaches, the women's basketball coach, and the interim football coach with some of their players.

In February 2014 led by Charley Warner, an OBF supported missionary with Barnabas International, a team of OBFers (Bob and Dorothy Benz, Derek and Christy Webb, and Brian Woodruff[40]) traveled to Armenia to develop a partnership with an Armenian church and the Evangelical Theological Seminary of Armenia, which is located at Ashtarak, west of Yerevan, the capital. OBF raised funds to help the pastor and to provide scholarships for the seminary students. Charley, a Miami

---

40. Brian Woodruff, who is the director of housing at Miami University, together with his wife Jackie, a nurse, actively support the ministry of the Navigators.

graduate, has taught in this seminary as well as at seminary in Odessa in Ukraine. He has served as a coordinator of seminaries in Eastern Europe and in the former Soviet Republics.

In March Marvin Wilson of Gordon College spoke at OBF. He had been a fellow student with me at Brandeis University. Marvin has been the foremost evangelical leader in reaching out to Jewish leaders. In May OBF honored about seventy graduating seniors. Steve Becker, who had been involved with the Navigators received his PhD.in Psychology.

Mark Smith, a graduate of Miami University, served as the director of the Navs from 2007 to 2014. He comments: "We fluctuated between 75 to 100 students. But we noticed towards the end of the time that it seemed there were less and less believing freshmen at Miami and our ministry began to feel the numerical effects of secularization."[41]

IV and OBF

From its beginnings in 1970 OBF has had a symbiotic relationship with IV (InterVarsity Christian Fellowship). Its earliest members were the IV students in Bill Wilson's Bible class at the student center. One of the earliest speakers was Barney Ford, an IV staff member. Barney became one of the vice-presidents of IV. He directed IV's quadrennial "Urbana" Missionary Conferences and served as the president of IFES (International Fellowship of Evangelical Students), student groups in many international countries affiliated with IV. Kent Stephens has served as the vice president of IFES. Bill Gates serves on IV's national board. Through the years, most IV students have attended OBF. Many OBF alumni have served as IV staff members.

I served as the faculty advisor for IV at Miami University for twenty-five years (1970 to1995). Unlike most faculty advisors of student organizations, I was not content to simply sign a form for IV but followed the example of Bill Wilson in attending IV's weekly meetings. I also went to several conferences and camps with the students. We

---

41. In 2014 Mark and Megan Smith moved to Orlando to start a successful new Navigators chapter at Central Florida University, one of the largest universities in the US. They served there until 2020. They intended to move to Croatia, but then the pandemic struck. They then planned to move to Austria, when Mark had a very bad accident which precluded that move. They were reassigned to the Cincinnati area where they minister to students at the University of Cincinnati, Xavier University, and Northern Kentucky University.

sang the great British hymns of Isaac Watts and Charles Wesley acapella from the blue IV hymn books. The chapter ranged from thirty to sixty and formed a tight-knit community which led to lasting friendships and not a few marriages!

Matt Troy recalls:

> My years in IV as an undergrad student would have been 1998 to 1999, and then I volunteered as staff at a retreat or two over the next couple of years. IV was important for me because it provided a Christian community in college as well as training on Bible study methods.

Beth (Barovian) Troy reports:

> I was in IV during my undergraduate years at Miami, 1999 to 2002, and attended weekly meetings, retreats, and a couple of Bible studies in that time frame. . . . Since I wasn't raised with any religious background, IV was instrumental in introducing me to inductive Bible study, and I learned a lot of the basics of Bible structure as a whole. Matt and I met at my first meeting as a freshman, and we married in December 2001.

Down through the years, all IV staff members, including Barney Ford, Kent Stephens, and Rich Friedmann, were active members of OBF. Rich, a graduate of Denver Seminary, served as the IV director from 1983 to 1988 and as an elder of OBF from 1986.[42]

In 1990, Dennis Dudley, a graduate of Central Michigan University and of Grand Rapids Baptist Seminary was assigned by IV to staff the chapter at Miami University.

Dennis had served in the army in Germany where he was involved with the Navigators and married his wife, Carolyn, a graduate of Cedarville University. When he first visited the chapter from Columbus, it had only five members But due to the recruiting zeal of Meg Schwarzmueller and Tom Kidd the chapter had grown to 70 by 1992, which is when Dennis and his wife moved to Oxford to a home on Maxine Drive next to the home of pastor Win Clark.

---

42. For a brief interval between 1988 and 1989, Ben Connaroe drove down once a month to serve as the IV staff at Miami University. Ben, a graduate of Indiana University earned a master's in English from Miami. He was involved in IV and was a member of the OBF choir. Ben joined the Navs Military Ministry in 1994 and served in Hawaii and San Diego. Since 2004 he has been on the staff of RPJM, ministering to military prisoners in the San Diego area.

Dennis felt that OBF did not need his gifts. He and his wife therefore went to the large First Baptist Church in Hamilton where he had opportunities to teach and to preach on occasion. Dennis was supported as a missionary by OBF and frequently visited the church. Over time, however, the lack of his presence, especially in the fall when many freshmen from the nearby dorms attended OBF meant that in contrast to the Navs and Cru, IV lacked a staff presence to promote its meetings.[43] This led to a gradual decline. From 2010, for the next six years, IV was "dormant." That is, Miami University continued to recognize IV as a student organization but there were no actual students in the chapter.

The national IV advised Dennis to redirect his efforts to the faculty, which he did. He was able to compile an email mailing list of about fifty Christian faculty and organized two weekly meetings, which met at the Mechanical and Manufacturing Department on Thursdays at noon and at Bachelor Hall, which housed the English and Mathematics Departments, on Fridays at noon. Even after my retirement in 2005, I attended the Thursday meetings, which were facilitated by Tim Cameron, the chair of Mechanical and Manufacturing, who was a member of OBF. An average of about six faculty members attended each session. With but a few rare exceptions these faculty were all male.[44]

Dennis also facilitated occasional webinars produced by IV. He assisted in arranging banquets for faculty and spouses held at the student center prior to the lectures in my annual series, which Dennis had originated with Win Clark. He also promoted the books of IV Press. Dennis became a member of Miami's Men's Glee Club and arranged their European tours including a concert at the Vatican. He continued to lead Bible studies for the Glee Club. One of these Glee Club members was Connor McInnes, who attended OBF has become the IV staff worker who revived IV in 2016. He travels from Columbus to encourage the reemerging IV chapter with about 20 to 30 members.

---

43. One of the new directors of the Navs and his wife began attending a Baptist church in Camden to get away from the students on Sundays. But Ward Ballard advised him in no uncertain terms to attend OBF.

44. A separate Bible study for five women faculty at the Farmer School of Business and the College of Education, Health and Society by Allison Farmer in 2017. Allison and all the others were members of OBF.

Jeremy Carr's Resignation

In the summer of 2014 after six and a half years of a highly successful ministry and the birth of three additional daughters, Jeremy Carr resigned and accepted a pastorate in Des Moines to be near Michelle's parents who had developed health problems. The attendance declined from 700 at three services to about 350 at two services, with half of those attending consisting of students. A search committee for a new lead pastor was constituted with Matt Cable as chair. Derek Whalen, who declined to become a candidate for the position of lead pastor, served as a capable and popular interim pastor.

Garrett Nates

In 2015 OBF welcomed as its new lead pastor Garrett Nates, who had served for fourteen years as the associate pastor of the large College Church in Wheaton.[45] As it was just across the street from Wheaton College, many of the school's faculty and students attended it. Garrett, who was originally from Colorado Springs, was a graduate of Biola University and had taken courses at the graduate school of Wheaton College. His wife Naomi was the daughter of noted missiologist Luis Bishop, who gave Garrett's installation charge. Garrett and his children (Ezekiel, Landon, Moriah, Breck) were avid soccer players.

In March Daniel Wallace of Dallas Theological Seminary spoke at OBF. Wallace has sought to photograph all the ancient New Testament manuscripts in the world. Several new professors in Business, Mechanical and Manufacturing Engineering, and NROTC began attending OBF. Some of the over a thousand Chinese students were also in attendance, as well as three Chinese professors (of biology, computer engineering, and physics).

In 2016, OBF hired Emanuel Istrate, who had been ministering in a church in Carol Stream near Wheaton, as our full-time youth director. Among churches in Oxford only OBF had such a full-time youth director. His parents were refugees from Romania who had settled in northern California. Emanuel was a graduate of Moody Bible Institute.

The children's ministry thrived with about a hundred children in attendance under the leadership of Angie and Rich Dunn. Miami

---

45. This was the church where Kimi and I were married in 1962.

University now had about 2,000 students from China enrolled. About forty of these students met at OBF for a weekly fellowship and Bible study, led by a teacher from the Chinese church in Mt. Healthy.

OBF commissioned Ross and Mary Hunter to return as missionaries to the Quechua Indians in Ecuador under a new board, the Pioneers. Retiring missionary Peggy Lowry, who served in Indonesia for thirty years teaching under Overseas Missionary Fellowship, visited OBF. After being active in IV and serving as a staff member with IV, Peggy had been among our earliest missionaries.

In the spring of 2017, Garrett Nates challenged the church to raise $10,000 following messages on "Generosity." The congregation responded by donating $12,500. Half of this was used to support students at a seminary in Armenia. The other half was used to build a picnic shelter for Parkview Arms in Oxford, a subsidized housing complex. Ken Baker donated the concrete foundation. Men of the church supervised by Derek Whalen built the structure working ten hours in a single day. This effort was reported by Bob Ratterman in *The Oxford Press*.

New Elders

Garrett Nates with the approval of the other elders instituted a new policy of having rotating elders so that long-time elders Bob Benz, Dick Pettitt, and myself were rotated off the elder board.[46] Marty Creech was retained as a holdover elder. In 2017, Matt Troy was chosen as a new elder. After Matt graduated from law school at Case Western University, the Troys lived in Louisiana before returning in 2009 to Oxford, where Matt practices law. Beth teaches at the Farmer School of Business.[47]

Two new elders were chosen in 2018. Daryl Nelson, a graduate of Asbury Theological Seminary, was the owner of a franchises of Chick-fil-A, one in Oxford and one in Hamilton. Samuel Perry, a graduate of Murray State University, serves the city of Oxford as the Director of Community Development and oversees issues of planning, building, and

---

46. After the departure of Win Clark in 2007, I succeeded him in leading monthly services at the nursing center of the Knolls. I preached consecutively one chapter a month through Matthew, the Acts and the Epistles and had reached 2 Peter when the covid pandemic brought an end to our services. Among those who regularly assisted me in these services were Mary Vincent, Tim, and Sue Cameron, Byran and Amy Smucker. The Smuckers are Mennonites, whose young children sang with them to the delight of those assembled.

47. Beth had been my graduate student in History.

zoning. Sam was a great help just as OBF sought to expand its facilities as we had to meet various city requirements and ordinances.

In 2019 two additional elders were chosen. Jeff Blakeley who served as a construction manager for Kokosing Industrial. Steve Hricko, a graduate of Miami University who earned a master's degree from Bowling Green State University, has served as a teacher, counselor, and coach at the Middle School in Oxford.

OBF had a pressing need for rooms for children and youth ministries and office spaces. In 2018 OBF with the help of a professional fundraiser launched a two-year building campaign. The elders authorized the borrowing of two million dollars at low interest from a bank in Bath, Indiana. On September 29, 2019, in front of the office building groundbreaking ceremonies were held. The festive occasion was covered by Bob Ratterman and made the front page of *The Oxford Press*. A photo of six elderly members sitting on chairs included surviving founders Alice (Peo) Winterrod, Evelyn Coltharp, and Kimi and Ed Yamauchi.

The Year of the Pandemic

In 2020, two new elders were added. The first was Page Farmer, whose wife Allison holds an endowed chair in the Farmer School of Business. Page works for IBM on IT security. The second was Bob Mack, a graduate of the Air Force Academy, who had worked at Wright Patterson Air Force Base.

On March 18, Daniel Master, my former student and former OBF member who is a professor of Bible and Archaeology at Wheaton College, spoke at OBF. But the next week the state of Ohio instituted a lockdown ordered by the governor, Mike DeWine. Schools were closed and in-person gatherings were banned because of the covid pandemic. Church services were live streamed on YouTube.

A small committee chaired by Derek Whalen met weekly during the summer to plan for a fiftieth anniversary celebration in September. A list of about 1500 alumni was compiled and postcards and emails were sent notifying them of our plans. But alas, the pandemic continued unabated so that these plans had to be cancelled. On September 25, Bill Fairback organized a Zoom reunion of a number former OBFers and Cru members who had attended OBF during our years at Presser Hall.

The lack of a congregation meeting at OBF proved in some way to be a boon for the construction workers who could work on the new educational building without impediment. Also, the pandemic caused banks to lower their lending rates, so that OBF was able to refinance its initial loan at the low rate of 4.125%. With $400,000 raised by the building campaign OBF borrowed the remainder to pay for the $2,550,000 cost. The building was completed with its many facilities and a partially finished full basement in the early fall.

Missions to Mexico

Under the leadership of Ryan Massey, who was the youth director, and his wife Jody, OBF began to send annually short-term youth missions to Monterrey in northern Mexico from 1999 for the next dozen years. They worked with an organization called Back2Back. The first mission included sixteen adults and youth who served at four locations: Casa Hogar Douglas, Casa Hogar del Norte, La Coyetera, and El Retiro Juvenil. Ryan and Jody moved to Monterrey and served there from 2001 to 2005. They worked with kids from the Casa Hogar Douglas and served as captains of El Retiro Juvenil, a children's home. The Masseys also helped start the Hope Program for teens.

Ellen Joyce, the daughter of OBFers Brian and Susan Joyce, was an anthropology major with a minor in Spanish. Ellen became involved in spring and summer trips to Mexico through IV's partnership with Merge Ministries. Upon her graduation from Miami University in 2002 Ellen moved to Saltillo, where she led the children's ministry and taught English at a local church. In 2004 she married a member of that church, Oscar Hernandez. Oscar and Ellen then were invited by the Masseys to join them in the Back2Back ministry, where they worked from 2004–2006. They returned to work with Merge Ministries for northwest Mexico from 2006–2010. They then returned to Back2Back to serve as house parents for teenagers. Ellen also served as the principal of the Sierra Madre Christian Academy and Oscar as one of the captains for the orphanage El Retiro Juvenil. They returned to the States in 2016.

Hope Maglich, the daughter of OBFers Jeff and Becky Maglich, after graduating from Miami University, joined the Back2Back staff in 2008 to teach English to staff children in Monterrey. She met and married Cheque Garcia. Together they served as captains of children's homes, first over Mantiel de Amor, then over Casa Posibilidades. In 2017 Back2Back commissioned them to begin a new ministry in the Dominican Republic, where they work with existing churches and the Jubilee Community Center in Santiago.

OBF's Youth Ministry

Since the hiring of Emanuel Istrate in 2016, OBF has enjoyed a robust youth ministry. When he first arrived, there were twenty high school and middle school youth involved with nine adult leaders. By 2020 there were thirty high school and twenty middle school youth involved along with fourteen adult leaders. There have been annual kick-off events and retreats as well as special mission trips during the summer. The youth went to New Orleans in 2017. Middle schoolers went to Big Creek, Kentucky, and high schoolers to Camp Friedenswald, Michigan, to work with inner city kids from Chicago in 2018. In 2019, Justin Kailer was added as part-time staff responsible for middle school youth. In 2019, middle schoolers went again to Big Creek, Kentucky, and high schoolers to Camp Friedenswald, Michigan.

A Postscript

Early in 2021 Derek Whalen resigned to take up a post as the associate pastor of a church near Allentown, Pennsylvania, which his parents had begun. This would allow him greater opportunities to preach and place him near his parents. OBF did not seek to replace him with a new candidate due to the budget restrictions caused by the decline in giving during the pandemic year and the added expenses of the mortgage for the new educational building.

In July 2021 OBF issued a Mid-Year Impact Report with the following statistics:

- 300 to 350 average in-person attendance and engagement[48]

---

48. Most community members appear to be families with young children. There are few single adults or retired individuals. Some long-time members have moved on to other churches such as Cobblestone, the Methodist Church, and the Vineyard. The congregation is almost entirely white. There are very few people of color (Asians, Hispanics, Blacks), though there have always been a few faculty and graduate students from countries in Africa (Eritrea, Ethiopia, Ghana, Kenya, Mali, Nigeria, Senegal, Tanzania, Zambia, and Zimbabwe). OBF helped the family of a grad student, Moses

- 423 unique church online viewers from thirty different states and five different countries[49]
- 112 women and men in a Bible study or small group
- Ninety kids attending VBS (Vacation Bible School) and sixty-six servant leaders
- Forty-two college students meeting weekly to go deeper in Christ[50]
- Thirty-three students and leaders serving at Big Creek Mission in KY
- Eighteen missionaries serving in eleven countries
- Fifteen lives transformed in Oxford with benevolence assistance[51]
- Ten baptisms

In the spring of 2022 as a result of conflicts with the staff and with some members, as well as other issues, the elders asked for the resignation of Garrett Nates. In his stead, they appointed Emanuel Istrate, the director of youth ministries, to serve as the interim pastor. In 2023 without

---

Romano, move out of Zimbabwe to the US.

49. During the pandemic year we became accustomed to watching the services online and prefer this mode today because of my wife's age and my visual impairment.

50. There was a noticeable decline of college students attending OBF during 2016 to 2019. A branch of Crossroads, a mega church in Cincinnati meeting at Benton Hall attracted 300 students. But this ministry ended in 2018. Cru has 11 staff members with 250 students involved. Many of the students of Cru began attending Cobblestone, along with the new director Ian Mansfield, who arrived at Miami in 2016. Most of the 70 students involved in the Navigators attend OBF. The Navs have been led by Taylor and Christy Scott who arrived from Kansas in 2013. Pastor Nates in the fall of 2021 reported: "I believe we have between 175 to 200 students now coming to OBF. Many of the Cru students are attending OBF this year."

51. Most of the members of OBF are from the affluent middle class. There was but one welfare dependent family in the church, but it was an important one. The benevolence committee provided $400 a month for her medical expenses. Doris Sharp was stricken by polio and lived in rural Somerville with her beloved dogs and cats. Her daughter Virgi was invited to OBF by some of her friends. Doris and Virgi started attending the mini-church that included the Wilsons and the Yamauchis, meeting at the home of Bill and Maggie Bliesner near Woodland Manor. Doris was a "prayer warrior" whose faith impressed all those who knew her. Doris and Virgi were able to move to a home on Vereker Drive in Oxford, where they gained custody of a young girl Kayla, whose father was a dealer in drugs and whose mother was a drug addict living in Park View Manor. They succeeded in raising Kayla to become a bright and successful high school student. After Doris died on December 24, 2012, I had the privilege of giving the eulogy at her memorial service at OBF on February 2, 2013.

a search for an external candidate, OBF confirmed Emanuel as the new pastor. Under his more collaborative style of leadership with the counsel of the elders and a host of volunteers, OBF has continued to flourish.

Excursus A

Barack Obama in Hawaii

PRESIDENT BARACK OBAMA (2009 to 2017) has been rightly hailed as the first "Black" president of the United States. What many people do not realize is that he is biracial, his mother was white. In Hawaiian terms he was a *hapa haole*, that is "half white." The two most important adults in his life were not his absent father or his often-distant mother, but his white maternal grandparents who raised him in Hawaii from the fifth grade until he graduated from high school. Obama himself says relatively little about this background in Hawaii and the Wikipedia pages on him say nothing at all.[1]

His father Barack Hussein Obama was born in 1934 in western Kenya as a member of the Luo tribe. He was an excellent student who assisted in the Laubach program of literacy. When he left Kenya for the University of Hawaii half-way around the world, he left behind a nineteen-year-old wife Grace Kezia Aoko and a young son Roy.

Barack was the first and only African when he enrolled at the University of Hawaii in 1959. He was a smart, confident man, who attracted women and attention from the start. He was featured in stories published in *Ka Leo*, the university's paper and in the *Honolulu Star Bulletin*. He lived in an apartment on Tenth Avenue in Kaimuki. During the summers he worked for Dole Corporation for $1.34 an hour.

---

1. Fascinating details of Obama's life in Hawaii are contained in a mammoth (1460 page) account based on extensive interviews and meticulous research titled *Rising Star: The Making of Barack Obama* by David J. Garrow (New York, New York: Harper Collins, 2017).

EXCURSUS A: BARACK OBAMA IN HAWAII

Obama's mother Ann Dunham was the daughter of Stanley and Madelyn Dunham, who were originally from Kansas. In 1960, Stan had moved to Hawaii from Seattle to take a job with the Isle Wide Furniture distributor and Madelyn secured work at the Bank of Hawaii. Ann moved to Hawaii after graduating from high school and enrolled at the University of Hawaii. Both Ann and Barack took Russian 101, but it is not clear if that is how she met Barack, who got her pregnant. On the insistence of her parents the couple was married in Wailuku, Maui. But Barack never lived with his second wife. Barack[2] Hussein Obama II was born on Friday August 4, 1961, at the Kapiolani Maternity & Gynecological Hospital on Punahou Street.

Barack did well in his studies at the UH. He was elected to the Phi Beta Kappa honorary society. He took part in a Peace rally with the prominent Democratic politician Patsy Mink. He graduated in 1962 and was awarded a graduate fellowship in economics at Harvard University. He would complete all his course work but was then forced to leave the US and never completed his dissertation. The Immigration and Naturalization Service was disturbed about his reputation for liquor and women.

Soon after Barack junior was born, his mother went to Seattle to study at the University of Washington for one year before returning to the UH. She stayed with her parents while taking courses. They called her son Barry; he in turn affectionately called his grandparents "Tutu" and "Gramps."

At the UH, Ann met and fell in love with Lolo Soetoro, a graduate student from Indonesia, who was a student at the UH's newly opened East West Center. In March 1964 Ann was granted a divorce from her Kenyan husband. Ann and Lolo were married in Molokai a year later. By June 1966 Lolo's visa expired and he had to return to Jakarta. Ann completed her BA in Anthropology at the UH in 1967 and flew with her six-year-old son to rejoin her husband in Indonesia.

Barry, whom the Indonesians pronounced "Berry," was enrolled in Indonesian schools, at first in a Catholic school St. Francis Assisi. Teachers recalled that he struggled with the Indonesian language. His classmates remember him fondly as a chubby boy with large ears and a friendly smile. One of Barry's lasting impressions was the sight of abject poverty in Jakarta. Lolo became well off after he was hired by the Union Oil Company of California. This enabled him to enjoy "the good life,"

---

2. The name "Barack" is an Arabic loanword in Swahili which means "Blessed." It is cognate with the Hebrew name "Baruch."

which became at odds with the idealism of his mother.³ In 1970, Ann gave birth to Maya Kassandra.

In1971 just after his tenth birthday, Barry would move back to Hawaii to live with his grandparents and to enroll as a fifth grader at Punahou School just four blocks away from their small apartment in a high rise at 1617 S. Beretania Street. Tuition at this time cost $1,165, which his grandparents could afford, now that Tutu was a vice-president of the Bank of Hawaii and Gramps was selling insurance.⁴ In his new memoir speaking of his mother Obama writes: "Despite the financial strain she and my grandparents would send me to Punahou, Hawaii's top prep school."⁵

At the end of 1971 when Barry was ten and in the fifth grade his father came from Kenya to spend a month with his former wife and son. He had a booming voice and made a positive impression on his son, though a fleeting one as he was never to see him again. He brought with him trinkets from Kenya and that Christmas gave Barry his first basketball, which was to transform his life as basketball became his passion. As he grew older, his grandmother recalled that Barry wanted to become a professional basketball player.⁶

From the fifth to the tenth grade, besides Barry there was just one other African American student at Punahou, Joella Edwards.⁷ But she and Barry were never close friends. During his last two years in high school there was one other black student, Kim Jones, out of a student body of about 1600 students at Punahou.⁸

---

3. Barack Obama recalls vivid memories of Indonesia in ch. 8, "The World beyond Our Borders" in *The Audacity of Hope* (New York, New York: Broadway Paperbacks, 2006).

4. In 1978, his senior year Punahou's tuition had risen to $2,050.

5. Barack Obama, *A Promised Land* (New York, New York: Crown,2020), 7.

6. In 1972 Barry's mother Ann with his two-year-old half-sister Mayar returned to Hawaii so she could pursue graduate work in Anthropology at the UH. Ann and Maya returned to Indonesia in 1973. By 1974 she and Lolo had agreed to an amicable separation. She later divorced him.

7. Obama was aware of his status as one of two Blacks at Punahou. See Barack Obama, *Dreams from My Father* (New York, New York: Broadway Paperbacks, 2004), chs. 4 and 5.

8. The reason that there were so few Blacks at Punahou was not because of discrimination against Blacks. Rather, it was a reflection of the relative absence of Blacks in the population of Hawaii. Neither my wife nor I encountered any Blacks while growing up in the Islands. According to Eleanor C. Nordyke, "Blacks in Hawai'i: A Demographic and Historical Perspective," *The Hawaii Journal of History* 22 (1988), 241, a state survey in 1980 counted 24,215 Blacks in Hawaii, but of these 86.4 percent were military

EXCURSUS A: BARACK OBAMA IN HAWAII

In 1976, when Barry was fifteen and in the tenth grade, he played on Punahou's junior basketball team. Though he was a reserve, he was the third leading scorer as the team won nine of its fourteen games. The yearbook has a photo of Barry sporting an Afro. This was the year that he read *The Autobiography of Malcolm X*, which made a great impression on him.

In his junior year Barry took the mandatory American History class and not the advanced placement class. His teacher Bob Torrey remembers him as a "totally average student." He made the basketball team but as a reserve. The school paper *Ka Punahou* recorded that the team had seven wins and ten losses. During the summer Barry worked at a newly opened Baskin Robbins Ice Cream store on King Street a few blocks from his apartment.[9]

Up to this point, Barry was known mainly as a genial "jock." His mother worried that his concentration on athletics rather than on academics might hurt his chances of getting into a top college. But in his senior year Barry enrolled in the school's most demanding elective course, Law and Society, which was taught by the attorney Ian Mattoch at 7:15 a.m. three mornings a week. It was a college level course in which Barry earned an A-.

Barry made Punahou's twelve-member varsity team coached by Chris McClachlin. While he was talented, Barry's free style did not fit into the coach's structured system, so he remained mainly on the bench as the team won the state championship. Gramps who attended many games was Barry's biggest cheerleader.

Most revealing about Barry's rather carefree attitude to school was his page on the 1979 yearbook. In the upper left was a photo of Barry on a basketball court with the caption "we go play hoop." At the bottom was a photo of a beer bottle and a record player captioned "still life." In the middle was his message: "Thanks Tut, Gramps, Choom Gang, and Ray for all the good times." The Choom Gang were his buddies who drank

---

personnel and their dependents who lived in such places as Scofield Barracks near Wahiawa. This means that even at this date there were only 3,293 Blacks in the general population of Hawaii.

9. On his first date with Michelle Robinson, who was his supervisor at a Chicago law firm, Barack offered to buy her an ice cream cone from a Baskin-Robins store. He writes, "I told her about working at Baskin-Robbins when I was a teenager and how hard it was to look cool in a brown apron and cap. . . . I asked if I could kiss her. It tasted of chocolate." *The Audacity of Hope*, 330

beer and smoked cigarettes and *pakolo* (marijuana), and Ray was the dealer who provided the latter.

Barry applied to but was rejected by Swarthmore College. But he was accepted at Occidental College near Pasadena, no doubt on the strength of the recommendation by his teacher Ian Mattoch, an alumnus of the college. When he left the islands, he was not driven by an ambition to "become president" as he had written as a child in Indonesia, but rather to play basketball at a college.

Excursus B

The MIS in Okinawa

FROM THE BEGINNING OF World War II the army's Military Intelligence Service (MIS) sought Nisei, the second-generation sons of *the* Issei, first generation immigrants, who knew or could learn the Japanese language. They trained at the MIS Language School at Camp Savage, Minnesota. About 3,000 MIS graduates served in the Pacific theater. As theirs was a secret mission, they did not receive the publicity accorded to the Nisei who served with the 442nd in Europe.

A preliminary survey of Nisei by the Army found that only 10 percent of them were fluent in Japanese. Most of the latter were Kibei "Returned to America" who had been born in America but who had spent considerable time in Japan. There were two categories of Kibei: 1) sons from prosperous farm families on the mainland who were sent back to Japan to be educated, and 2) children of poor plantation families in Hawaii who had sent their children, like my mother and her siblings and my Yamauchi cousins sent back to Okinawa to be cared for by relatives as their mothers could not continue to do so as they worked in the sugar fields.

The first class of the MIS Language School graduated in May 1942. This class included 117 Nisei enlisted men and twelve Caucasian officers. They were trained to learn Japanese military terminology to interrogate prisoners and to translate documents.[1] But for a number of reasons there

---

1. One important document translated by the MIS in Australia revealed the Japanese plan for the battle of the Philippine Sea.

EXCURSUS B: THE MIS IN OKINAWA

were relatively few prisoners to interrogate. First, American soldiers often preferred to kill the Japanese soldiers rather than to take them captive. Second, trained in the samurai code of *bushidō*, Japanese were taught from their earliest schooling that there were only two alternatives: to die fighting or to commit suicide. Surrender was not an option.[2]

Takeo Higa emigrated from Okinawa to Hawaii in 1915 to work on the planation at Waipahu on Oahu. In 1925, his wife took two boys and a girl back to Okinawa to live with relatives. While his older brother and sister were later taken back to Hawaii, the youngest, Takejiro, who was born in 1923, was left behind. When his parents passed away, he became an orphan who was cared for by his kind relatives. He was raised in the small village of Shimabuku in the center of the island. In 1939 to avoid being drafted by Japan to serve in Manchuria, Takejiro asked his brother and sister to pay for his voyage back to Hawaii. In 1943 when his older brother Warren volunteered to join the 442nd, Takejiro could not pass the Army's English proficiency test. But as Army officials learned of his fourteen years living in Okinawa, Takejiro was recruited to join two hundred other Nisei from Hawaii in the first MIS Language School class. As the army was preparing to invade Okinawa, Takejiro was shown arial reconnaissance photos. He was asked about concrete structures on hills which could be fortifications and holes in the fields which could be machine gun pits. Suppressing a smile, Takejiro explained that the former were *haka*, funerary tombs, and the holes were manure composting pits! The battle for Okinawa, which lay 350 miles south of Japan, was the costliest battle in the Pacific for both sides. The invasion began on April 1, 1945. As the only MIS interpreter who was fluent in Okinawan, Takejiro was assigned to the commander of the invading forces who landed in the middle of the western coast of the island, aiming to create a wedge between the sparsely occupied north and the heavily defended south. This was very close to his home. Those turning north by April 13 secured the Kadena Airfield, but those turning south faced stiff resistance as the enemy was dug in on high ridges north of the ancient palace of Shuri and the capital city of Naha and its harbor. On June 13, three

---

2. According to Bruce Henderson, *Bridge to the Sun: AThe Secret Role of the Japanese Americans Who Fought in the Pacific in World War II* (Nedw York, New York: Alfred A. Knopf, 2022), 261, "By the war's end, only about 35,000 Japanese soldiers had been taken prisoner Allied forces, a fraction of the 945,000 German and 490,000 Italian POWs captured in the war." Of the total enemy prisoners taken captive, 7,400 were captured in Okinawa, including conscripts who were unwilling to die for a distant emperor.

to four thousand Japanese sailors and their commander Admiral Ota committed suicide in their underground bunker. Many other Japanese soldiers who had taken refuge in underground tunnels or caves killed themselves rather than surrendering.

After the island was secured on June 21, some Japanese soldiers removed their uniforms to mingle with the civilian survivors. Takejiro's task was to determine who among the survivors were actually military men. When he interrogated one individual who claimed to be an Okinawan, he asked him where his home was. A small village named "Yamauchi" he answered. This was but three miles from Takejiro's home at Shimabuku. After asking him rapidly some questions in Okinawan, the man was unable to answer and confessed that he was actually a lieutenant colonel in the Imperial Japanese Army An older man who had been caught at night digging up sweet potatoes was suspected of being a Japanese officer, though he protested that he was but a schoolteacher. When he was brought for interrogation, Takejiro recognized him and cried out, "Sensei." He was Shunsho Nakamura, who had been his middle school teacher.

Two bedraggled Okinawan conscripts who claimed that they had only been given shovels and not weapons by the Japanese were brought before Takejiro. They looked vaguely familiar. He asked them if they had studied under sensei Nakamura. They were astonished at this question. They then recognized Takejiro as their classmate who had returned to Hawaii before the war![3] The Japanese had warned the Okinawans that the Americans would do horrible things such as raping their women if taken prisoner. This led some mothers with their children to leap to their deaths off the cliffs of southern Okinawa. Many other women and children cowered in caves prepared to blow themselves up with explosives. Takejiro hurried to the entrance of as many caves as he could to proclaim loudly at the entrances:

> My name is Takejiro Higa. I am an Okinawan son. I grew up in Shimabuku. My family is still here. They are fine. I am an American soldier now. I can tell you Americans are not savages They are good people. You will not be mistreated. We have food and water. If you are hurt or sick, we will care for you. Don't waste your life. Please save yourselves.[4]

---

3. Henderson, 294300.
4. Ibid, 301

Thanks to the efforts of Takijiro and other MIS interpreters, some eighty-thousand Okinawan civilians emerged from caves instead of committing suicide.

At the Prefectural Peace Museum in Naha are listed the names of 14,009 Americans killed in action. Defending the island had been 80,000 Japanese soldiers and 40,000 forcibly conscripted Okinawans, including schoolboys. Listed among those killed are the names of 77,485 members of the Imperial Japanese Army. From a population of about 300,000 on Okinawa, half were killed. The museum lists the names of 149,611 Okinawans who perished. Of those who survived, 90 percent were left homeless.

The high casualties suffered in the battle of Okinawa factored into President Truman's decision to drop two atomic bombs on Japan on August 6 on Hiroshima and on August 9 on Nagasaki to avoid even higher casualties in an invasion of the main islands of Japan. If Japan had not surrendered, the US had seven more atomic bombs which they could have used.[5] Shortly after bombs were dropped against the urging of his military advisors to keep on fighting to the bitter end, Emperor Hirohito, on August 15, 1945, in a surprise radio address, announced that Japan was surrendering. It was the first time that the Japanese people had heard their revered emperor's voice.

After the war Okinawa was ruled by Americans for twenty-seven years. Only in 1972 was the island returned to Japan. The Americans still retain major bases there occupying much of the scarce land. Okinawa has 75% of the American bases in Japan, a sore point with the Okinawans.

---

5. Japan and Germany were also working on atomic bombs, but they did not have access to the amounts of uranium necessary, an essential ingredient which the US had obtained from the Belgian Congo.

Excursus C

Japan's Imperial Family

IN OCCUPYING POST-WAR JAPAN, General Douglas MacArthur made the shrewd decision not to prosecute Emperor Hirohito for war crimes as was the case with General Hideki Tojo. Instead, Hirohito renounced his exalted position and became a figurehead. He devoted his time to marine biology.

His youngest brother, H.I.H. (His Imperial Highness) Prince Takahito Mikasa, studied Christianity and Judaism, learned Hebrew, and became an Old Testament scholar. He taught at Tokyo Women's Christian University from 1955 to 1978. Dr. Akiko Minato, the school's president, was my wife's classmate at Wheaton College (class of 1958).

Prince Mikasa was present at the first Japanese excavation in Iraq in 1956. He started the Society for Near Eastern Studies in Japan and translated into Japanese books by Jack Finegan.

Donald J. Wiseman and I had contributed essays on Old Testament Archaeology and on New Testament Archaeology to the introductory volume of *The Expositor's Bible Commentary*. Zondervan combined the two articles into a slender book, *The Bible and Archaeology*, which was translated into Japanese. In 1975, Prince Mikasa was a visiting professor at the School of Oriental and African Studies of the University of London, which was chaired by Professor Wiseman, who presented Prince Mikasa with the Japanese version of our book.

I had the privilege of meeting H.I.H. Mikasa at a conference of the International History of Religions at the University of Winnipeg in 1980. In 2016, Prince Mikasa died at the age of one hundred.

Excursus D

The Higa Boarding House

My mother did not know about any government benefits she might have been entitled to as an American citizen. Even if she had known, as an older Japanese she probably would not have applied for them as she believed in *gaman*, the virtue of enduring. She worked long hours to supplement Renyu's income, which was only $275 per month in the 1950s. In the 1960s, it had increased only to $300 per month.

For seven months, she worked until 9 p.m. as a seamstress in a "sweatshop" in downtown Los Angeles. By 1954, my parents were renting a three-story frame building in on W. 35th Street near the University of Southern California. They used the extra rooms to board some Japanese single men who worked as independent gardeners. When I examined her books in 1954, I found that she was working 100 hours a week with a net profit of only $200 per month, in other words she was working for the equivalent of fifty cents an hour!

Before World War II, the Japanese had dominated the nursery industry. Their horticultural skills in raising flowers also served well in caring for the yards of wealthy Angelenos in Hollywood and Bel Air. As of 1934 30 percent of all Japanese laborers in LA were involved in gardening. By 1940 the League of Southern California Japanese Gardeners had grown to some 900 members (mainly in Hollywood, Uptown LA, and West LA).[1]

---

1. A stained-glass panel featuring a push lawnmower in St. Mary's Episcopal Church in Los Angeles honors the labor of Japanese gardeners, according to *Green*

EXCURSUS D: THE HIGA BOARDING HOUSE

During the internment years the Japanese gardeners used their skills to beautify their camps. For example, at Manzanar, Kuichiro Nishi, a former rose grower, built a Japanese garden with more than a hundred species of flowers, pine trees, a waterfall, a bridge, and a tea house.

The Refugee Act of 1953 permitted the immigration of *nammin* "new immigrants," primarily from Kagoshima which had experienced natural disasters. Many of these men turned to gardening. Other Japanese gardeners came from Hawaii and some came illegally from Mexico.

In 1959 by obtaining $45,000 from Okinawan friends and from Shoan Yamauchi as well as a bank, my family was able to buy three adjoining properties at 2215 W. Venice Boulevard, between Crenshaw and Western. On two lots, old houses were used; on the third lot they built the first new boarding house in LA for gardeners. All told she could board about fifty gardeners.

My mother had the assistance of an older Japanese woman in the kitchen and a younger woman for housecleaning. But she did all the daily shopping at Von's supermarket for her family of hungry boys! She provided not only breakfast and dinner but also *bento* (box lunches) for the men before they set out for work in the mornings. This meant working from 5 a.m. to 10:30 p.m. By 1960, she had gotten more help but still worked to 9 p.m. There was no dishwashing machine, so everything had to be washed by hand. When Renyu returned from work my mother wanted him to help with the dishes, whereas he wanted to relax, drink a beer, and watch the Dodgers play. This demanding schedule meant that my mother had little time to enjoy taking care of Akichan, who by default became Daddy's little girl.

During the summer of 1965 I was able to come to LA to work at the boarding house so my parents and sister could at long last after about 40 years revisit Okinawa. While they had sent money and gifts, they had not sent photos. So, when my mother encountered her relatives, they asked, *Anata, dare desuka?* "You, who are you?" My mother said she recognized a tree she had climbed as a child. Later in 1965, my parents were able to sell the boarding house for $50,000 to Mr. Yamajuta, who wanted to raise the room and board charges.

From their profits, my parents invested in an apartment building and a small coffee shop in North Hollywood. Since she no longer had to work evenings, my mother took *ikebana* (Japanese flower arrangement)

Makers: Japanese American Gardeners in Southern California (Los Angeles: Southern California Gardners Federation, 1967), 133.

classes. She enrolled in a school for immigrants where she was the only one of Japanese ancestry in her class. We were all proud of her when in June 1967 she earned the equivalent of a junior high school diploma at the age of fifty-four!

Excursus E

Carmen Higa Mochizuki

My step-father Renyu Higa's younger sister, Carmen Yoshie Higa, had been born on December 9, 1932 in Callao, Peru. While Renyu refused to leave America, she had returned with her parents and eight other siblings to war devastated Okinawa. In 1958, she came to LA to help my mother at the boarding house. But to my mother's chagrin, she fell in love with Mike Mochizuki, a gardener from Hawaii, and married him in 1959. She then worked at the Bank of Tokyo in Little Tokyo.

It was in 2004 while my wife and I were attending a conference in San Antonio that I first became aware of Carmen's key role as the lead plaintiff on behalf of Latin American Japanese against the US government. We visited a museum celebrating various ethnic groups in Texas. Prior to the influx of Peruvian Japanese to Crystal City there had been less than 1,000 Japanese in the state of Texas. In an alcove dedicated to the Japanese of Texas, a videotape of Carmen was on display.[1]

The West Coast Japanese had been illegally moved under specious reasons to remote internment camps and except for those who could entrust their properties to trusted Caucasian friends, had to sell all their properties at short notice at bargain basement prices. A campaign for redress led by the Japanese American Citizens League and others finally succeeded. In 1987 the House of Representatives voted 243 to 141 to express an apology for the internment of the Japanese Americans. In 1988

---

1. Carmen's recollections are reported in Jan Jarboe Russell, *The Train to Crystal City* (New York: Scribner, 2015), xix–xx, 245–46, 253–50.

the Senate voted 69 to 27 in favor of this bill. Then in 1989 President George Bush signed The Civil Liberties Law awarding each survivor of the internment camps $20,000.

The Latin American Japanese, the majority from Peru, had suffered even worse treatment and lost everything. This led to a campaign for similar redress for the Latin American Japanese with Carmen as the lead plaintiff in the case "Carmen Mochizuki vs. the United States of America" in 1996. Congress in 1999 authorized a payment of $5,000 for each of the Latin American Japanese still residing in the US. The disparity in payments led some to reject the settlement and to appeal to the InterAmerican Commission on Human Rights for a judgment against the US.[2] One complainant, Art Shibayama declared, "The letter of apology stinks because it doesn't say anything about Japanese Latin Americans or specify wrongs which were committed, like forced deportation." To add insult to injury, Art was drafted into the army, but was not allowed to become a US citizen until 1970!

In 2000 the National Committee for Redress and Reparations awarded Carmen, along with Alice Nishimoto, their "Fighting Spirit Award."

---

2. Martha Nakagawan, "Japanese Latin American Abductee to Testify before International Commission," *The Pacific Citizen* (March 10–23, 2017), 7–8.

Excursus F

Kimie Honda

KIMIE WAS BORN ON October 13, 1930, at the small plantation town of Hilea in the Kau district in the southern area of the Big Island. Her father Haruichi was born on January 4, 1898, in Pahala on the Big Island. His father was Shinanosuki Honda, who was born in 1862 and came to Hawaii in 1886. Her mother Sen Ishihara (1900–1997) came as a picture bride to Hawaii in 1920 from Iwakuni in Yamaguchi-ken near Hiroshima.

Kimie was the middle of seven children, including five sisters (Miyoko, Jane, Helen, Ellen and Janet) and a brother (Kaoru). Haruichi was the manager of the Hutchinson Sugar Plantation store at Hilea. The family moved to Naalehu, the southernmost city in the US, where the youngest child Janet was born.

As a young teenager Kimi worked in the sugar cane fields. She attended Pahala School up to the 10th grade. She moved to Honolulu and graduated from McKinley High School. She supported herself by working in the pineapple cannery during the summers and by working as a maid. In Honolulu she lived at the Okamura Home next to Makiki Church. Coming from a strong Buddhist home, she first encountered Christianity in a small Bible class with two other friends from McKinley that was taught by Harold DeGroff, a member of the Navigators. She made her decision for Christ in 1948 at a Youth for Christ meeting.

She then attended Makiki Christian Church and also helped out at a number of other churches, including a Missionary Church, which encouraged her to attend Fort Wayne Bible College in Indiana. Prior to enrolling there in the fall of 1952, she worked as a waitress at the Winona Lake Bible Conference.

Finding the Arminian theology of Fort Wayne not to her liking, she transferred to Moody Bible Institute. Upon graduating from Moody after two years, she transferred to Wheaton College. She was a Christian Ed major but was also one of the few women to take theology courses under teachers like Kenneth Kantzer. She studied the Old Testament under Laird Harris and J. Barton Payne who both commuted from Covenant Theological Seminary in St. Louis. She also took Greek from Jerry Hawthorne, who wrote in a letter to me (May 22, 2007): "Kimi Honda was the best Greek student I have ever had the privilege of teaching Greek." Her favorite teacher was Merrill Tenney.

To support herself through Moody and Wheaton, she worked at the Sunday School supply company Scripture Press, which moved from Chicago to Wheaton just as she was transferring there. She walked the mile to the company as it was faster than waiting for the bus. Upon graduating in the class of 1958, she enrolled in the Wheaton grad school to do research on the subject of "slavery" in Paul's letters.

Excursus G

Gordon's PhD Students

IN AN APPENDIX TO his memoir, *A Scholar's Odyssey*, 113–118, Gordon lists 91 students who received the PhD: eighteen at Dropsie College (1946 to 1956),[1] sixty-one at Brandeis (1957 to 1973),[2] and twelve at New York University (1973 to 1989).[3] From my own admittedly incomplete knowledge, I would estimate about half (44) came from evangelical backgrounds, about a quarter (22) from Jewish backgrounds, and the rest from other backgrounds or backgrounds unknown to me. The majority of those at Dropsie were from evangelical backgrounds, all of those at New York University from Jewish backgrounds. The one notable Catholic student John F. X. Sheehan (Brandeis 1968) became the chair of the

---

1. Among outstanding Jewish scholars who received the PhD at Dropsie were David Neiman (1955), who taught at Boston College and Nahum Sarna (1955), who taught at Brandeis and wrote commentaries on Genesis and Exodus.

2. Some of those receiving PhDs at Brandeis had other professors as their chief advisors: Hammond (one), Hoffner (two), Lacheman (three), Morrison (one), Newby (one), DeSomogyi (one), Young (three), and Jabkar (one).

3. Much to Gordon's chagrin one of his closest collaborators Gary A, Rensburg (New York University, 1980) was inadvertently left off this list. See See Cyrus H. Gordon and Gary A. Rendsburg, *The Bible and the Ancient Near East* (New York: W. W. Norton, 1997). Rendsburg has confirmed my guess that most of Gordon's NYU students came from Jewish backgrounds. In an article on Cyrus Herzl Gordon in the *Encyclopedia of the Bible and Its Reception* (Berlin, Germany: De Gruyter, 2015) Gary Rendsburg lists among Gordon's adoctoral students who enjoyed their own academic careers: "Nahum Sarna, Anson Rainey, Michael Astour, Baruch Levine, Harry Hoffner, Edwin Yamauchi, Jack Sasson, David Owen, David Tsumura, Mark Geller, and Gary Rendsburg."

Religion Department at Marquette University. I was not the first Nisei from Hawaii to study under Gordon at Brandeis. I was preceded by Roy Uyechi (Brandeis 1961),[4] There were also a few students from Egypt, England, Hong Kong,[5] Japan,[6] Korea, and Turkey.

I have already mentioned many of Gordon's earlier students. Of course, it is impossible to mention everyone, but let me briefly comment on a dozen fellow students, whose subsequent careers I know best, in the order of their graduation.

1. Michael C. Astour (1962). Michael was born in 1916 into a secular Jewish family. He grew up in Poland speaking Yiddish. From 1934 to 1937 he studied at the Sorbonne in Paris, where he was introduced to the study of Ugaritic. The Nazis murdered his mother. The Russians killed his father, and imprisoned Michael in a series of labor camps. After he was freed, he came to Brandeis to teach Yiddish and Russian. He had long seen connections between Greek myths and Semitic parallels. His erudite dissertation was published as *Hellenosemitica* by Brill in 1965.[7] Astour was content to teach at the Edwardsville branch of Southern Illinois University. He contributed many learned articles on ancient geography.

   I might relate one anecdote about him. While the Astours were at a fast-food restaurant near Times Square, Michael was victimized by a couple, one of whom distracted him from the front, while a partner from behind snatched away the valise which contained the paper which he was to read at a conference at New York University in honor of Professor Gordon. But as Michael had a near photographic memory, he was able to give his talk. There was one

---

4. Roy had attended McKinley High School, Wheaton College, University of Pennsylvania, and Westminster Theological Seminary. He taught at Jarvis Christian College, in Hawkins Texas. Roy attended Kalihi Union Church. His niece Caroline married Dick Lum, my Iolani classmate. (See ch. 7)

5. Wilson Chow (Brandeis 1973) was to teach at the China Graduate School of Theology, where I lectured in 1996.

6. David T. Tsumura (Brandeis 1973) became an outstanding Old Testament and Ugaritic scholar. He taught at the Japan Bible Seminary outside of Tokyo, where I lectured in 1996. He also maintains a small Biblical Archaeology Museum, which sponsored my lecture in Tokyo in 2008. David wrote the commentaries on I and II Samuel for the New International Commentary series

7. The writings of Gordon and Astour inspired Martin Bernal of Cornell University to write a most controversial work, *Black Athena*, which claimed that Egyptians migrating to Greece inspired much of Greek civilization.

problem, however, he did not know when to stop, so his wife Miriam spoke up, "Michael, enough already!" But he responded, "They are still listening to me," and so we were!

2. Andrew C. Bowling (1962). Andy was a graduate of John Brown University in Siloam Springs, Arkansas. His dissertation was on the Late Egyptian language. He taught for a number of years at Haigazian College, an Armenian school in Beirut, Lebanon, where I spoke in 1974. After retiring from teaching at John Brown University, Andy was involved with Robert Longacre in teaching Hebrew at the Summer Institute of Linguistics in Dallas.

3. Roy E. Hayden (1962). Roy was a graduate of Fuller Theological Seminary. Roy wrote his dissertation on Nuzu Court Procedures under Professor Lacheman. Roy taught at Huntington College and then at Oral Roberts University in Tulsa. Because some problems arose when he was teaching at its branch in England, he was unfairly blamed and dismissed. He then taught at a branch of King's University in the San Fernando Valley until that school closed in 2017.

4. George Giacumakis (1963). George was a year ahead of me at Shelton College. George wrote his dissertation on the Akkadian of Alalakh,[8] which my wife typed. This was before the age of computers, so a single error meant retyping the page! George taught at the new California State University at Fullerton, and then served for six years as the president of the Jerusalem University College (earlier known as the Institute of Holy Land Studies). On his return to the US, in addition to teaching at Cal State Fullerton, he also chaired the History Department at Biola University. He developed a Museum of Biblical Archaeology and was involved in Bible translation.

5. Harry A. Hoffner. Jr. (1963). Harry was a German major at Princeton University. He was influenced by the Princeton Evangelical Fellowship to attend Dallas Theological Seminary, where he studied Hebrew under Dwight Young. When Gordon invited Dwight to join the faculty at Brandeis, Harry came as a graduate student into our department. Though Gordon knew Hittite, the Indo-European language written in cuneiform, which was used in Anatolia, i.e.,

---

8. Alalakh (fl. 1600–1200 BC) was a site in northwestern Syria excavated by Leonard Woolley.

ancient Turkey (1600 to 1200 BC), Harry learned it on his own. Since much of the scholarly works were in German his language major gave him an advantage. After teaching at Brandeis and then at Wheaton College, Harry taught at Yale University, and finally at the Oriental Institute of the University of Chicago, where he became the editor of the *Chicago Hittite Dictionary*. Harry contributed the chapter on "The Hittites" both to *Peoples of the Old Testament*, edited by Donald J. Wiseman, and to *Peoples of the Old Testament World*, which I coedited. He did not believe that the biblical "Hittites" were identical with the Anatolian Hittites.

6. Anson F. Rainey (1963). Anson was a graduate of John Brown University and the Baptist Theological Seminary. After writing his dissertation on "The Social Stratification of Ancient Ugarit," Anson lectured on Historical Geography at the Institute of Holy Land Studies established by G. Douglas Young in Jerusalem. He became fluent in modern Hebrew and taught for many years at Tel Aviv University and at Bar Ilan University. Somewhat pugnacious in nature, Anson joined Yohanan Aharoni in his feud with Yigael Yadin of the Hebrew University in Jerusalem. He later became critical of William Dever. He disapproved of the proposed late dating advocated by his former student Israel Finkelstein,[9] He produced a four-volume study, *Canaanite in the Amarna Tablets*. At the time of his death in 2011 he was involved in examining again the 382 Akkadian tablets found at Amarna in Egypt.[10]

7. Marvin R. Wilson (1963). Marv was a graduate of Wheaton College and of Gordon-Conwell Theological Seminary. He wrote a masterly dissertation on Coptic. He taught at Barrington College and then for many years at Gordon College. Marv is the leading evangelical scholar who has reached out to the Jewish community. His important book, *Our Father Abraham*, stresses the Jewish roots of

---

9. In opposition to Yigael Yadin's identification of three identical triple chambered gates at Hazor, Megiddo and Gezer as Solomonic (10th c. B.C.), Finkelstein dated these structures to the 9th c. BC and therefore as not Solomonic. His revisionist dating has been opposed by other archaeologists such as Amihai Mazar and Steve Ortiz.

10. In 1887 a peasant woman found a cache of cuneiform tablets at the Middle Egyptian site of Amarna. These turned out to be the diplomatic correspondence between the pharaohs Amenhotep III and Amenhotep IV (14th c. BC) and the kings of Babylonia, Assyria, the Hittites, Mitanni and Cyprus, and petty chieftains in Lebanon and Palestine.

Christianity. With Jewish funding, he developed a PBS program on this subject. He hosted a number of conferences bringing together Jewish and evangelical scholars. He coedited the *Dictionary of Daily Life in Biblical and Post-Biblical Antiquity* with me.

8. Frederic W. Bush (1965). Fred was a graduate of Fuller Theological Seminary. He wrote his dissertation on the Hurrian language,[11] which he managed to learn on his own. Though Gordon knew Hurrian, he did not offer any courses on this language. Fred taught Hebrew to many generations of students at Fuller Theological Seminary in Pasadena. Together with his mentor, William Sanford LaSor, and David Hubbard,[12] he wrote an introduction to the Old Testament, and also wrote the Word Commentary on Esther and Ruth.

9. Donald H. Madvig (1966). Don, a graduate of Fuller Theological Seminary wrote his dissertation on "A Grammar of the Royal Assyrian Annals of the Sargonid Dynasty" under Dwight Young. He taught at the North American Baptist Seminary, the North Park Theological Seminary, and Bethel Theological Seminary. He took part in the Old Testament translation of the New International Version and contributed the commentary on Joshua in the first edition of the *Expositor's Bible Commentary*.

10. Jack M. Sasson (1966). Jack was born in Aleppo, Syria in 1941. He and his family emigrated to the US in 1955. He related how the first time his mother went to a supermarket and was presented with a bill for let us say $30, she offered to pay $20, so used was she to bartering in the Middle East! And Jack, who was translating, was deeply embarrassed. After graduating from Brooklyn College, Jack entered the program at Brandeis. He was already fluent in French, which stood him in good stead as he wrote on the cuneiform archive found at Mari,[3] a site on the Euphrates in western Syria, which the

---

11. Hurrian was the unique language of the kingdom of Mitanni in northrn Mesopotamia which flourished in the fourteenth century BC.

12. David Hubbard, the president of Fuller Seminary, had written his dissertation at St. Andrews University on the *Kebra Negast*, the ancient Ge'ez epic which tells of the romance between Solomon and the Queen of Sheba. When I visited the University of London, I met his supervisor, Edward Ullendorf, who expressed his regret that Hubbard never had his dissertation published.

13. The important site of Mari was accidentally discovered in 1933. It had been destroyed by Hammurabi (18th c. BC). The French excavators found a vast archive of

French had excavated. Jack taught at the University of North Carolina, where he served as the chair of the Religion Department, and then became an endowed professor at Vanderbilt Divinity School. He was elected president of the International Association for Assyriology and the president of the American Oriental Society, which is devoted to the study of Near Eastern and Far Eastern languages. He wrote commentaries on Judges, Ruth, and Jonah. He produced a very useful compendium of the wealth of information found in the Mari tablets, *From the Archives of Mari* (2015). He maintains a listserv on the ancient Near East, Agade, which has over 5,000 subscribers.

11. Dennis F. Kinlaw (1967). Dennis, a graduate of Asbury Theological Seminary, was already a successful pastor at Loudonville in upstate New York, when he entered the graduate program at Brandeis. Dennis became an Old Testament professor at Asbury Theological Seminary and then the president of Asbury College. He contributed the commentary on the Song of Solomon in the first edition of the *Expositor's Bible Commentary*. He started the Francis Asbury Society to promote Wesleyan values.

12. David Owen (1969). David was a graduate of Boston University. While at Brandeis David participated with George Bass in diving to investigate a shipwreck in the Mediterranean. David became the chair of the Near Eastern and Judaic Studies at Cornell University. David has translated and published numerous Sumerian and Akkadian texts.

13. Walter C. Kaiser Jr. (1973). Walt, who taught at Wheaton College and later at Trinity Evangelical Divinity School, came into the graduate program in 1961 with Fred Bush and me, but it took him longer to finish his doctorate because after he had done years of research, Gordon changed his mind and had him work on an altogether different topic, "The Ugaritic Pantheon." Walt served as the Academic Dean of TEDS, and then as the president of Gordon-Conwell Theological Seminary. Cyrus Gordon attended the special service at Park Street Church, celebrating Walt's inauguration as president of the seminary. A prolific author and a popular speaker, Walt was elected the president of the Evangelical Theological Society. He and I served

---

25,000 cuneiform tablets, including 4,000 letters.

together with Bastiaan Van Elderen of Calvin Theological Society and Bruce Metzger of Princeton Theological Seminary on the advisory board of the Scriptorium.

While we were at Brandeis, Charles F. Pfeiffer (Dropsie 1953), who was then teaching at Gordon-Conwell Theological Seminary came to Brandeis to recruit writers for a reference work, *The Biblical World*, he was editing for Baker Book House. Seven of us (Andrew Bowling, George Giacumakis, Roy Hayden, Harry Hoffner, Anson Rainey, Gerald Swaim, and Edwin Yamauchi) contributed articles to this volume.

Excursus H

Tributes to Cyrus H. Gordon

1. *A Student Tribute Presented to Cyrus H. Gordon.* Waltham, Massachusetts: Privately printed, 1962. I edited this volume which contained: a) an annotated bibliography of Gordon's publications; b) essays by Michael Astour, Andrew Bowling, Frederic Bush, Roy Hayden, Harry Hoffner, David Huttar, Gerald Swaim, and Edwin Yamauchi. c) a list of Gordon's past and present students and their publications.

2. *Orient and Occident: Essays Presented to Cyrus H. Gordon on the Occasion of His Sixtyfifth Birthday,* ed. Harry A. Hoffner, Jr. Kevelaer, Germany: Butzon & Bercker, 1973; Neukirchen-Vluyn, Germany: Neukirchener Verlag, 1973.

3. *The Bible World: Essays in Honor of Cyrus H. Gordon,* ed. Gary Rendsburg, Ruth Adler, Milton Arfa, and Nathan H. Winter. New York, New York: KTAV Publishing House, 1980.

4. *Cyrus H. Gordon: A Synthesis of Cultures.* Special issue of the *Biblical Archaeologist* 59.1 (March 1996). The issue contains articles by Meir Lubetski and Claire Gottlieb, Louis H. Feldman, Howard Marblestone, Martha A. Morrison, Gary A. Rendsburg, David Toshio Tsumura, and Edwin M. Yamauchi.

5. *Boundaries of the Ancient Near Eastern World,* ed. Meir Lubetski, Claire Gottlieb, and Sharon Keller. Sheffield, United Kingdom: Sheffield Academic Press, 1998.

Excursus I

A Public Ivy

IN 1985 RICHARD MOLL in *The Public Ivys* (New York, New York: Viking Penguin, 1985) identified eight schools which he considered "America's Best Public Colleges and Universities." Among them was Miami University together with:

1. University of California
2. University of Michigan
3. University of North Carolina
4. University of Texas
5. University of Vermont
6. University of Virginia
7. William and Mary College of Virginia

Miami University is the smallest, the most selective, and the most expensive of the state universities in Ohio. Its beautiful campus with uniform red Georgian brick buildings is located in a bucolic rural setting surrounded by fields of corn. The poet Robert Frost, who came to visit his fellow poet Percy MacKaye who was an artist in residence at Western College, called Miami's campus "the prettiest campus there ever was." In a survey conducted by WalletHub and cited by Forbes Magazine in 2016 Oxford, a town with only 8,000 residents, was ranked the best college town in the nation. At the main Oxford campus incoming students are required to stay in dormitories. Smaller branch campuses located at Middletown and Hamilton are commuter schools.

1. In various national rankings, Miami University has distinguished itself.
2. *Newsweek* (1993) listed five schools as "Public Ivys": University of California, Miami University, University of North Carolina, University of Texas, University of Virginia.
3. Miami has ranked high in the *US News & World Report* list of schools, public and private, in their commitment to undergraduate teaching. In 1995 Miami ranked eighth; in 2011 Miami ranked second.
4. In 1996 Money Magazine ranked Miami third in producing chief executive officers of Fortune 500 businesses.
5. Miami has ranked high in the number of its students studying abroad. In 1994 it ranked fourth; in 1996 it ranked first.
6. It has been ranked among the nation's ten most efficient schools by *US News & World Report* (1994, 1995, 1996).
7. *Businessweek* (2015) ranked the Farmer School of Business as the eighth best among public universities.
8. Its accountancy program has been ranked sixth in the nation.
9. Its entrepreneurship program has been ranked among the top ten in the nation.
10. *Money Magazine* (1995) listed Miami as the nineteenth best college value.
11. Miami is one of twenty public schools listed as a "best buy" in *the Fiske Guide to Colleges* (1996).
12. Miami's acceptance rate for zoology majors into medical schools is 80 percent.
13. Miami's acceptance rate for law schools is 82 percent.
14. Its graduation rate of 80 percent is among the highest in the nation. Among NCAA Division I schools, Miami is ranked first in Ohio and ninth nationally for the graduation rates of its athletes (2005).
15. Miami was ranked twenty-fifth in producing Peace Corps volunteers (2002).

16. Miami has one of the oldest and strongest alumni associations in the nation.

Among noteworthy alumni are:

- **CEOs:** Michael Armstrong of AT & T; Richard T. Farmer of the Cintas Corporation; Charles Meacham of the Taft Broadcasting Company; Marvin Pierce of the McCall Corporation;[1] John Smale of Procter and Gamble; Richard Smucker of Smucker Foods
- **Writers:** Ira Berkow of *The New York Times*; Rita Dove US poet laureate; Will Haygood of *The Washington Post*; P.J. O'Rourke of *Rolling Stones*
- **Broadcaster:** Bill Hemmer of Fox News
- **Politicians:** Benjamin Harrison, 23rd president (1889 to 1894); Paul Ryan, Republican vice-presidential candidate, speaker of the US House of Representatives; Mike DeWine, governor of Ohio

---

1. Pierce was the father of Barbara Bush, whose brother also attended Miami University.

Excursus J

The Cradle of Coaches

MIAMI UNIVERSITY'S FOOTBALL TEAM plays in the Mid-American Conference, which is regarded as a mid-major conference. It has achieved modest success in some years rising as far as the 10th ranked team in the nation. In 1973, 1974, and 1975 it won three successive Tangerine Bowls in Florida against Florida, Georgia, and South Carolina. But its true fame lies in the fraternity of former players and coaches who have achieved extraordinary success as coaches of the college and National Football League teams, which led sportswriter Bob Kurtz to designate the university as "The Cradle of Coaches." See Bob Kurtz, *Miami of Ohio: The Cradle of Coaches* (Piqua, Ohio: Hammer Graphics, 1983).

The following is a selected list (* played at Miami; ** coached at Miami.)

1. Bill Arnsparger (*) N. Y. Giants 1974–1976; Miami Dolphins 19761983; LSU 1984–1986

2. Earl Blaik (*, **) Army 1941–1948. tthree national championships, 1944, 1945, 1946

3. Paul Brown (*) Ohio State University 1941–1943; national champion 1942; Cleveland Browns 1946–1962; AFC champions 1950, 1954, 1955; Cincinnati Bengals 1968–1975

4. Carmen Cozza (*, **) Yale 1965–1996. ten Ivy League championships, 1967, 1968, 1969, 1974, 1976, 1977, 1979, 1980, 1981, 1989

EXCURSUS J: THE CRADLE OF COACHES

5. Dick Crum (**) Miami 1974–1977, North Carolina 1978–1987. three MAC championships 1974, 1975, 1977; one ACC championship 1980

6. Paul Dietzel (*) Louisiana State University 1955–1961, Army 19621965, South Carolina 1966–1975. Won national championship in 1958 with LSU.

7. Weeb Ewbank (*) Baltimore Colts NFL champions in 1957 and 1958 with Johnny Unitas; New York Jets Super Bowl III champions in 1969 with Joe Namath.

8. Sid Gillman (**) Miami, 1944–1947; University of Cincinnati, 19491954; LA Rams 1955–1959; San Diego Chargers 1960–1969.

9. John Harbaugh (*) Baltimore Ravens. In 2013 John won Superbowl XLVII over his brother Jim, who coached the San Francisco 49ers.

10. Woody Hayes (**) Miami 1949–1950; Ohio State University (19511978). Five national championships 1954, 1957, 1961, 1969, 1970.

11. Terry Hoepner (**) Miami 1999–2004; Indiana 200–2007. In 2003 with Ben Roethlisberger Miami finished 10th in the nation.

12. Bill Mallory (*, **) Miami 1969–1973, Colorado 1974–1978, Northern Illinois 1980–1983, Indiana 1984–1996. Won two MAC championships, in 1973 and 1983, and one Big Eight championship in 1976.

13. Sean McVay (*) L. A. Rams. In 2017 Sean became the youngest NFL coach at 30. He also won Coach of the Year honors and took his team to the Superbowl LIII in his first year of coaching!

14. Joe Novak (*) Northern Illinois 1996–2007.

15. Ara Parseghian (*, **) Miami 1951–1955; Northwestern 1956–1963; Notre Dame 1964–1974. Two national titles with Notre Dame, 1966, 1973

16. Bo Schembechler (*, **) Miami 1963–19168, Michigan 1969–1989. Tied for two MAC championships, 1965, 1966, Tied or won 13 Big Ten championships, 1969, 1971, 1972, 1973, 1974, 1976, 1977, 1978, 1980, 1982, 1986, 1987, 1988.

17. Randy Walker (*, **) Miami 1990–1998; Northwestern 1999–2005. BigTen champion 2000.

18. Ron Zook (*) Florida 2002–2004; Illinois 2005–2011

Miami has produced three notable N.B.A. basketball players.

Wayne Embry (class of 1958) averaged 19.5 points and 15.9 rebounds, leading Miami to the MAC championship. He was an all-star five times in the NBA, playing for the Royals, Celtics, and Bucks. He became the first African American general manager, managing the Bucks, the Cavaliers, and the Raptors. He has been installed in the Naismith Basketball Hall of Fame, and his statue has been erected in front of Millett Hall.

Ron Harper (class of 1986) played for the Bulls and Lakers. Harper had a severe stuttering problem. Miami's Speech and Hearing Clinic was a great help to him.

Wally Szczerbiak (class of 1999) played for the Timberwolves, Celtics, Sonics, and Cavaliers. He is currently a television commentator.

The one famous alumnus in Major League Baseball was Walter "Smoky" Alston (class of 1935). Alston was the manager of the Brooklyn/Los Angeles Dodgers from 1954 to 1976, winning seven National League and four world championships. In the off season he retired to his home in Darrtown, a village so small that it had neither a stop light nor even a stop sign! When he died in 1984, I witnessed the procession of Tommy LaSorda and other Dodgers coming to Alston's memorial service at Miami's Sesquicentennial service.

Excursus K

Signers of the Gentle Revolution

(* = grad instructor)

	Name	Department
1	William Owsley	Architecture
2	Robert Meredith	English
3	Roland Delattre	Religion
4	Martin Benjamin	Philosophy
5	Robert Deming	English
6	Roland Duerksen	English
7	Robert Oldham*	English
8	Stanford Luce	French
9	David Bromberg*	Fine Arts
10	Richard E. Johnson	English
11	Melvin Bloom	Mathematics
12	Ralph Stone	History
13	Brian Holm	Philosophy
14	Roy Bowen Ward	Religion
15	Anthony Paul	Philosophy
16	Robert J. Smith	History

EXCURSUS K: SIGNERS OF THE GENTLE REVOLUTION

Those who signed the Gentle Revolution pamphlet earned the displeasure of President Shriver and Provost Charles Wilson. For their "disservice to the university" they were not awarded their expected salary increments. For example, Anthony Paul was awarded a salary increase of only $200 instead of the $2,000 recommended by the chair of the Philosophy Department. So dispirited by what they regarded as unfair treatment, four of the members of this small department, including its chair, Robert Harris, resigned. The remaining members were afraid that their department would be merged with the Department of Religion.

I was not at all aware of the tension between the administration and the department when, in 1972, I was appointed to head a search committee to find a new chair for the Philosophy Department. I contacted my friend, Ronald Nash, the chair of the Philosophy Department at Western Kentucky University for suggestions. He recommended Stanley Kane, who had completed a PhD on Anselm at Harvard University. Stan had been born in China to missionary parents Herbert and Winnie Kane. It was not until later that I learned that his father was a leading authority on Christian missions.

Stan had just the right temperament to mediate between his department and the administration. Though other members of the department did not share his Christian convictions, they all admired his character and his teaching classes on the History of Philosophy and the Philosophy of Ecology. Stan and his wife Nancy attended the Oxford United Methodist Church.

Excursus L

Bible Interpreters of the Twentieth Century
edited by Walter A. Elwell & J. D. Weaver

(Grand Rapids, Michigan: Baker, 1999)

1. J. C. Ryle
2. William H. Green
3. J. Albert Broadus
4. Theodor Zahn
5. Adolf Schlatter
6. Robert Dick Wilson
7. Geerhardus Vos
8. A. T. Robertson
9. R. C. H. Lenski
10. Oswald T. Allis
11. Arthur W. Pink
12. William Hendricksen
13. Ned B. Stonehouse
14. E. M. Blaiklock
15. Merrill C. Tenney

16. Edward J. Young
17. Merrill F. Unger
18. F. F. Bruce
19. George E. Ladd
20. William S. LaSor
21. J. W. Roger Beckwith
22. Bruce M. Metzger
23. Leon L. Morris
24. Donald Guthrie
25. Donald J. Wiseman
26. R. K. Harrison
27. Joyce Baldwin
28. J. Barton Payne
29. Ralph P. Martin
30. Walter C. Kaiser, Jr.
31. Gordon D. Fee
32. Edwin M. Yamauchi
33. Peter C. Craigie
34. D. A. Carson
35. N. T. Wright

Excursus M

Schools, States, and Countries Where My Students Have Taught

ARKANSAS: Harding College

CALIFORNIA: Azusa Pacific University, California State University at Stanislaus

CONNECTICUT: Hotchkiss School, Yale Divinity School

FLORIDA: Eastern Florida State College, Florida Bible College, Palm Beach Atlantic University, Southeastern University

GEORGIA: South Georgia State College

ILLINOIS: Chicago State University, College of DuPage, University of Chicago, Wheaton College

INDIANA: Indiana Wesleyan University

IOWA: Northwestern College, University of Iowa

KENTUCKY: Kentucky Christian University, Northern Kentucky University

MAINE: Bates College, University of Maine Presque Isle

MASSACHUSETTS: Boston College, Boston University, Brandeis University, Gordon College, University of Massachusetts at Boston

MICHIGAN: Cornerstone University, Hillsdale College

EXCURSUS M: WHERE MY STUDENTS HAVE TAUGHT

MINNESOTA: Metropolitan State University

NEW HAMPSHIRE: University of New Hampshire

NEW JERSEY: Seton Hall University

NEW YORK: State University of New York at Potsdam

NORTH CAROLINA: MidAtlantic Christian University

OHIO: Bowling Green State University, Cedarville University, Cincinnati Christian University, Lakewood Community College, Miami University, Oberlin College, Payne Theological Seminary, Wittenberg University

PENNSYLVANIA: Gettysburg College, Villanova University

SOUTH CAROLINA: College of Charleston, Newberry College, Presbyterian College

TENNESSEE: Lee University

TEXAS: Baylor University

VIRGINIA: College of William and Mary, James Madison University, Regent University

WEST VIRGINIA: Concord College

WISCONSIN: Carthage College

FOREIGN SCHOOLS

CANADA: York University

CHINA: College of Foreign Languages, Yunnan University of Finance and Economics, Kunming Teachers College, Graduate School of Theology (Hong Kong)

ISRAEL: University of Haifa

JAPAN: University of Aizu, Aoyama Gakuin University

MALAYSIA: University of Malaya

SINGAPORE: Singapore Bible College

Excursus N

Annual History Lectures

Year	Speaker, Topic
2006	Darrell Bock, "Breaking Up the DaVinci Code"
	(Dallas Theological Seminary)
2007	Rick Hess, "Israelite Religions"
	(Denver Theological Seminary)
2008	Craig Evans. "Jesus and the Ossuaries"
	(Acadia Divinity School)
2009	Walter Kaiser, "Archaeology and the CT: Top Fifteen Finds"
	(Gordon-Conwell Theological Seminary)
2010	Mark Noll, "The Bible and Slavery"
	(University of Notre Dame)
2011	Don Carson, "Christ and Culture"
	(Trinity Evangelical Divinity School)
2012	Paul Maier, "Josephus and the New Testament"
	(Western Michigan University)

EXCURSUS N: ANNUAL HISTORY LECTURES

Year	Speaker, Topic
2013	William Lane Craig, "Theism, Atheism, and the Big Bang"
	(Talbot Theological Seminary)
2014	Marvin Wilson, "Our Father Abraham"
	(Gordon College)
2015	Daniel Wallace, "The Reliability of the New Testament Text"
	(Dallas Theological Seminary)
2016	Santa Ono, "To Whom Much Is Given, Much Is Required"
	(President, University of Cincinnati)
2017	James K. Hoffmeier, "New Light on Egypt & the Bible"
	(Trinity International University)
2018	Ben Witherington III, "A Singular Jesus in a Pluralistic World"
	(Asbury Theological Seminary)
2019	Jennifer Wiseman. "Planets, Stars, Galaxies, and Life"
	(Goddard Space Flight Center)
2020	Daniel M. Master, "Ashkelon—A Philistine City Uncovered"
	(Wheaton College)
2021	Cancelled because of the pandemic
2022	Philip Jenkins, "Christianity in Asia"
	(Baylor University)
2023	Craig L. Blomberg, "The Historicity of the New Testament"
	(Denver Seminary)

Excursus O

The Near East Archaeology Society Honors

SUBJECT: Appointment of Dr. Edwin Yamauchi as President Emeritus

The title of President Emeritus is being conferred by the Board of Directors upon Dr. Edwin Yamauchi who has been a long-term member of the Near East Archeological Society (NEAS) and has served many years as its president.

WHEREAS, Dr. Yamauchi has rendered distinguished service to the Near East Archaeological Society, and has continually distinguished himself and served NEAS throughout his professional career in a multitude of volunteer positions. Dr. Yamauchi is an expert in ancient Near Eastern languages including Hebrew, Aramaic, Akkadian, Ugaritic, Arabic, Syriac, and Coptic. In all, he has immersed himself in twenty-two different languages. Dr. Yamauchi's nonlinguistic areas of expertise include Ancient History, Old Testament, New Testament, Early Church History, Gnosticism, and Biblical Archaeology. His contributions to the academy are enormous, with specialized chapters in several books, several articles in reference works, and over eighty essays in thirty-seven scholarly journals. In addition, Dr. Yamauchi has also written about the social and cultural history of First Century Christianity, the relevance of the discovery of the Dead Sea Scrolls for New Testament studies, the primary source value of Josephus's writings, and the role of the Magi in both ancient Persia and in the Nativity Narrative of the Gospel of Matthew. Furthermore, Dr. Yamauchi has served his profession by being a board member and president of NEAS, as well as being past a member and officer of the Institute for Biblical Research and a member and past president of the Evangelical Theological Society

THEREFORE, BE IT RESOLVED that in recognition of Dr. Yamauchi's long and committed service to Biblical Archeology and his profession in the areas of teaching, research, and service, the Board of Directors hereby confers upon Dr. Edwin Yamauchi the title and position of President Emeritus, with all the rights, privileges, and responsibilities pertaining thereto.

Submitted by the Executive Committee
Approved by the Board of Directors
November 15, 2016
Clyde E. Billington

Excursus P

Colleges & Universities Where I Have Given Lectures & Papers

Schools	Place	Date
1. Anderson C.	IN	1974
2. Asbury C.	KY	1979, 1980
3. Azusa Pacific U.	CA	1994
4. Ball State U.	IN1	1972, 1974, 1980
5. Barrington C.	RI	1964
6. Biola U.	CA	1983
7. Bluffton C.	OH	2008
8. Boston U.	MA	2013, 2016
9. Brandeis U.	MA	1963
10. California State Fullerton	CA	2011
11. Calvin C.	MI	1967
12. Capital U.	OH	1973
13. Case Western U.	OH	1973
14. Catherine Booth C.	CANADA	1987
15. Cedarville U.	OH	2010

EXCURSUS P: WHERE I HAVE GIVEN LECTURES & PAPERS

Schools	Place	Date
16. Chon Yuang U.	TAIWAN	1996
17. Cincinnati Bible C.	OH	1979
18. Cornell U.	NY	1972, 1977
19. Cornerstone U.	MI	2002, 2005
20. Dennison U.	OH	2001
21. Drew U.	NJ	1982
22. European Bible Inst.	FRANCE	1958
23. Gordon C.	MA	1991
24. Grace C.	IN	1980
25. Grand Rapids Baptist C.	MI	1979
26. Haigazian C.	LEBANON	1974
27. Harvard U.	MA	1971, 1999
28. Hebrew Union C.	OH	1980
29. Hillsdale C.	MI	1997
30. Huntington C.	IN	2002
31. Indiana State U.	IN	1995
32. Indiana U.	IN	1984
33. Indiana Wesleyan U.	IN	1998, 2002
34. Inst. for Christian Studies	CANADA	1991
35. John Brown U.	AR	1999
36. Kentucky Christian U.	KY	2001
37. Lee C.	TN	1996
38. Lipscomb U.	TN	1998
39. Malone C.	OH	1980
40. Melli National U.	IRAN	1974
41. Middlebury C.	VT	2003
42. Millikin U.	IL	1993
43. Minnesota Bible C.	MN	1981

EXCURSUS P: WHERE I HAVE GIVEN LECTURES & PAPERS

Schools	Place	Date
44. MIT	MA	1962
45. Mississippi State U.	MS	1983
46. Mt. Vernon Nazarene C.	OH	1973
47. National U.	SINGAPORE	1996
48. North Central C	IL	2011
49. Northeast Bible C.	NJ	1988
50. Northwest Oklahoma State U.	OK	2013
51. Oberlin C.	OH	1971
52. Ohio State U.	OH	1975, 1978, 1982, 1989, 1992, 1994, 2000
53. Olivet Nazarene U.	IL	1986, 2004
54. Palm Beach Atlantic U.	FL	2001
55. Philadelphia C. of the Bible	PA	1972
56. Princeton U.	NJ	1989
57. ShengTe Christian C.	TAIWAN	1996
58. Southern Methodist U.	TX	1977
59. Stanford U.	CA	2001
60. Taylor U.	IN	1976
61. Temple U.	PA	1968
62. Toccoa Falls Bible C.	GA	1996
63. Tokyo Christian U.	JAPAN	1996
64. Trinity Southwestern U.	NM	2002
65. Tung Hai U.	TAIWAN	1996
66. U. of California at LA	CA	1987
67. U. of Chicago	IL	1968, 1987
68. U. of Colorado	CO	1971
69. U. of Dayton	OH	1971, 1998
70. U. of Edinburgh	U.K.	2007

EXCURSUS P: WHERE I HAVE GIVEN LECTURES & PAPERS

Schools	Place	Date
71. U. of Florida	FL	1976, 1994
72. U. of Hawaii Hilo	HI	1974
73. U. of Illinois	IL	1998
74. U. of Manitoba	CANADA	1980
75. U. of Michigan	MI	1967, 1981, 1997
76. U. of North Carolina	NC	1975
77. U. of Notre Dame	IN	2001
78. U. of Oxford	U.K.	1985
79. U. of Pennsylvania	PA	1995, 2005
80. U. of Pittsburgh	PA	1971
81. U. of the Nations	HI	1992
82. U. of Virginia	VA	1976, 1996
83. U. of Wisconsin	WI	1979, 1989
84. Washington Bible C.	MD	2002
85. Western Kentucky U.	KY	1972
86. Western Michigan U.	MI	2002
87. Westmont C.	CA	1970
88. Wheaton C.	IL	1970, 1973, 1974, 1980, 1984, 1985, 1987, 1989, 1991
89. Wright State U.	OH	1973, 1986
90. Yale U.	CT	1965, 1978, 1989

Excursus Q

Seminaries Where I Have Given Lectures & Papers

	School	Place	Date
1	Andrews U. Sem.	MI	1990, 1995
2	Asbury Theol. Sem.	KY	2011
3	Beeson Divinity School	AL	1992
4	Bethel Theol. Sem.	MN	1988, 1989
5	Bethel Theol. Sem. West	CA	1939
6	Biblical Graduate School	SINGAPORE	1996
7	Calvin Theol. Sem.	MI	1957
8	Capital Bible Sem.	MD	1984
9	Graduate School of Theology	HONG KONG	1996
10	Chung Tai Theol. Sem.	TAIWAN	1996
11	Cincinnati Chr. Sem.	OH	1979, 2005
12	Concordia Theol. Sem.	IN	1980
13	Concordia Theol. Sem.	MO	1987
14	Conservative Baptist Sem.	CO	1983
15	Covenant Theol. Sem.	MO	1976, 1987
16	Dallas Theol. Sem.	TX	1979

	School	Place	Date
17	Evangelical School of Theol.	PA	1966
18	Faculté Evangélique Theol.	FRANCE	1968
19	Grace Theol. Sem.	IN	1987
20	Japan Bible Sem.	JAPAN	1996
21	Lincoln Theol. Sem.	IL	1971
22	McCormick Theol. Sem.	IL	1974
23	McMaster Divinity Sch.	CANADA	1997
24	Minnesota Consortium	MN	1988
25	Mundelein Cath. Sem.	IL	2002
26	New Brunswick Theol.	NJ	1964, 1968
27	New Orleans Bap. Sem.	LA	1990
28	Northwest Theol. Sem.	WA	2003
29	Princeton Theol. Sem.	NJ	1989
30	Southern Bap. Sem.	KY	2004
31	Taiwan Theol. Sem.	TAIWAN	1996
32	Talbot School of Theol.	CA	1985, 1989, 1994
33	Trinity Evangelical Divinity School	IL	1978, 1996, 1997, 2001
34	Trinity Epis. Sem.	PA	1986
35	Union Theol. Sem.	NY	1963
36	Western Con. Sem.	OR	1980
37	Westminster Theol. Sem.	PA	1968

Excursus R

Chapters Contributed to Festschriften

	Scholar Honored	Major Field
1	Oswald T. Allis (1974)	Old Testament
2	Gleason Archer (1986)	Old Testament
3	Michael C. Astour (1997)	Near Eastern Studies
4	Jack Finegan (1989)	New Testament
5	Cyrus H. Gordon (1973)	Near Eastern Studies
6	Cyrus H. Gordon (1980)	Near Eastern Studies
7	Harold W. Hoehner (2005)	New Testament
8	Dennis F. Kinlaw (1932)	Old Testament
9	W. Harold Mare (2005)	New Testament
10	Eugene Merrill (2003)	Old Testament
11	Alan R. Millard (2020)	Near Eastern Studies
12	John W. Montgomery (2008)	Apologetics
13	Gilles Quispel (1981)	Gnosticism
14	William H. Shea (1997)	Old Testament
15	David T. Tsumura (forthcoming)	Old Testament
16	Marvin R. Wilson (2010)	Old Testament
17	Dwight W. Young (1986)	Near Eastern Studies

Excursus S

Mary Stout

JAMES 1:27 (NIV) STATES: "Religion that God our Father accepts as pure and faultless is this: to look after orphans and widows in their distress." In the history of OBF there was one widow who required my special care for many years. Mary A. Stout (1934 to 2008) was a member of Enid Wilson's Bible study group and was one of the original founders of OBF. She was a proud member of the Daughters of the American Revolution. Mary was fair in complexion and rather heavyset in physique. She was married to Ora Stout, a veteran and a mailman, who died in 1978. She was a housewife with little work experience, but Ora had left her a home on College Corner Pike and three Medicare supplemental insurance policies. Mary was a devout Christian but had a difficult personality. She falsely accused a young woman, Cana Copley, who tried to help her of stealing from her.

As she was driving to Hamilton on Route 27, she changed her mind and made a U turn near the Marshall Elementary School, which resulted in a terrible accident. I received a call from the emergency room at Fort Hamilton hospital to come and see her. She was able to recover and bought another car. But she later gave up driving.

I drove her to numerous locations including to a mall for shopping, to dentists and doctors including a cancer specialist in Richmond, to a psychiatrist in Cincinnati, and to a bankruptcy lawyer in Hamilton.

I arranged to fix her leaking toilet. I mowed her small but hilly lawn. Once with some trepidation I used a ladder to climb on the roof to dislodge a branch that had fallen on it. Each week I took out her garbage can to the curb. Roxanne Hershey who lived nearby would then bring the empty can to her garage door. On October 10, 1996, when I went to her home, I found Mary passed out on the floor. I called 911 and she was taken to the hospital.

After Mary was examined by physicians and a psychiatrist, she was declared "incompetent." None of her siblings wanted to have anything to do with Mary, including a brother who lived in Middletown. I therefore accepted the responsibility of becoming her "probate guardian" in January 1997. This would mean that I would have charge of her income, expenditures, and taxes. Each year for the next decade I had to render an annual account to the Butler County Probate Court in Hamilton.

I arranged for the sale of her automobile and the sale of her house. Many members of OBF including Win Clark, Dave Smetana, Marcus Jobe, Ruth Pettitt and Dorothy Benz helped to clean Mary's house. Her house sold for $74,000, which after fees netted her $58,000. A yard sale earned Mary about $700.

I placed some furniture, clothes, and books in a storage shed in Middletown. After a number of years I concluded that the monthly fee for the storage was wasted money, and contacted her relatives to go through her belongings for any mementos. After her funds became depleted, I enrolled Mary in Medicaid.

Mary was such a demanding resident that I had to move her from one nursing home to another: from the Oxford View Nursing Home to Garden Manor in Middletown, to Schroder Manor in Hamilton, to Hawthorn Glen in Middletown, and finally back to the nursing home in Oxford, which was now called the Liberty Matrix Nursing Home, where she passed away in 2008. Sadly, Mary remained bitter at me for selling her home when she could no longer live in it.

Excursus T

Notable OBF Alumni

Abbreviations

ABWE	Association of Baptists for World Evangelism
AIA	Athletes in Action
CIU	Columbia International University
Cru	Campus Crusade for Christ
CT	Christianity Today
DMin	Doctor of Ministry
DTS	Dallas Theological Seminary
EPS	Evangelical Philosophical Society
ETS	Evangelical Theological Society
GCTS	Gordon-Conwell Theological Seminary
IFES	International Fellowship of Evangelical Students
IV	InterVarsity Christian Fellowship
MBI	Moody Bible Institute
MDiv	Master of Divinity
Navs	Navigators
OMF	Overseas Missionary Fellowship
OSU	Ohio State University
TEDS	Trinity Evangelical Divinity School

EXCURSUS T: NOTABLE OBF ALUMNI

TST   Talbot School of Theology
WBT   Wycliffe Bible Translators
WTS   Westminster Theological Seminary

Note: Unless otherwise indicated degrees are from Miami U.

Anna Agathangelou. Anna, who is originally from Cyprus, was a student in my Western Civ survey class. She is married to Kyle Killian (see below). After receiving her PhD from Syracuse U. she taught at Oberlin C. and then at York U. in Canada. She served as a visiting scholar at the John F. Kennedy School of Government at Harvard (2014–2015) and is a professor of Politics at the U. of Massachusetts in Boston. She is a co-director of the Global Change Institute in Cyprus, and the author of several books including a coedited work with Kyle Killian, *Time, Temporality and Violence in International Relations*.

Chris and Karen Akers. After graduating from Miami in the 1970s, Chris, an arts major, joined Cru's headquarters when it was at Arrowhead Springs in San Bernadino County, CA. When Cru moved its headquarters to Orlando, the Akers also moved there. In recent years Chris and Karen have served with Cru's inner-city mission in Orlando.

Katie (Armington) Reid. Katie Armington was led to Christ by Jane Armstrong. She joined the staff of Cru at OSU. There she met and married Tim Reid. They attended CIU. The Reids are ministering with IDEAS to missionaries in North Africa and the Near East.

Ken and Lois Baker. Ken as a high school student attended OBF when we began at the Municipal Building. Later after marriage to Lois, a Wheaton grad and nurse, Ken lived in St. Louis and took classes at Covenant Theological Seminary. Ken's older brother Dan while he was attending Miami, began in Oxford the Baker Concrete Co. This eventually grew and moved to Monroe, becoming one of the largest companies in the area, employing 2,000 and earning 700 million dollars annually! After returning to Ohio Ken began his own concrete repair and reconstruction company in Middletown. He and Lois have worked on many relief efforts in New Orleans, Nicaragua, Peru, Iran, and Mozambique. The Bakers are active with Serve City in Hamilton which ministers to the poor.

Ward Ballard. Ward, the son of the mayor of Akron, was a *summa cum laude* pre-med major. He joined the staff of the Navs and became the director of the Navs at Miami for a dozen years and also served as an elder at OBF. After marrying Kari, the daughter of missionaries to Sweden, the Ballards served as missionaries in Bergen, Norway, from 2000 to 2005, ministering to students at the Medical School and the Business School there. Upon returning to the States, Ward then served the Navs as their Mid-Western director. In 2018 he moved to the Navs headquarters as the national director for outreach to internationals.

Mike Bath. Mike was an outstanding quarterback for Miami, who preceded and welcomed Ben Roethlisberger as his successor. He served as an assistant coach at Miami and then as the interim coach when he and his family attended OBF in 2013. He later served as an assistant coach at the U. of Wyoming and then at Western Michigan U. In 2022 he joined the coaching staff of Indiana State U.

Michael and Heather (Babcock) Battig. The Battigs were active with the Navs and along with two other Miami couples, Joel and Lisa Dyke and Stuart and Kim Pratt, joined Wes Pastor as he began a ministry in Vermont. Mike became the chair of the Computer Sciences Dept. and Heather served as a member of the Applied Linguistics Dept. at St. Michael's College, where they also work with international students.

Jane (Becker) Cook. Jane was led to Christ by Barney Ford. She joined the staff of Cru in 1977. On overseas missions she met Blair Cook, who earned a PhD from Penn State University in Education and married him. They presented the Jesus film to more than 800,000 people in several African countries. They then spent six years with Cru in Canada. For Cru in 1988 Blair began the International School Project featuring a curriculum based on biblical and Christian principles, which was introduced to hundreds of thousands of teachers in 39 countries including: Albania, Armenia, Belarus, Brazil, Bulgaria, Cambodia, China, Cuba, Ecuador, Egypt, Estonia, Ghana, Greece, Grenada, Guam, Guatemala, Honduras, Hong Kong, Iraq, Jordan, Kazakhstan, Kenya, Kyrgyzstan, Latvia, Lebanon, Lithuania, Moldova, Mongolia, Myanmar, Nepal, Poland, Romania, Russia, Slovakia, Slovenia, Taiwan, Thailand, Ukraine, and Zimbabwe.

Marlene Benz. Marlene, the daughter of OBFers Bob and Dorothy, was active with Cru and joined its staff. From 2000 to 2003 Marlene served in Macedonia, training national staff. During 2003 to 2005 she served at Miami U. while raising support. She then served at Cru's Indianapolis office from 2005 to 2015 overseeing new interns and staff. After raising support and a long visa process, Marlene served with Cru in New Zealand during 2018 and 2019. After leaving Cru Marlene found a position with the state of Indiana.

Carol Bibighaus. Carol, a grad of Wheaton C., earned her MA in Zoology, and was one of the earliest members of OBF when we began. She served as a counselor for the Billy Graham film that OBF sponsored. She then served for many years as a missionary under ABWE in Hong Kong. Upon returning to the States, she ministered to single women missionaries.

David Bliesner. David, the son of OBFers Bill and Maggie, was a member of Miami's AFROTC program. He rose in rank to become a colonel. By 2010 he was chief of Plans, Policy, and Integration of the Divisions of the Air Force Global Strike Command at Clarksdale AF Base (LA), in charge of nuclear missiles and bombs. In 2011 David became the commander of the 341 Missile Maintenance group at Malmstrom Air Force Base, Montana. He was in the Pentagon during the attack on 9/11.

Douglas Boone. Doug is from Boone, NC, and is a relative of Daniel Boone. Doug earned both a BA and MA in Mathematics. He was active in IV and sang in OBF's choir. After linguistic training he joined WBT and was assigned to the Democratic Republic of Congo (the former Belgian Congo). He rode his motorcycle over vast areas of the countryside surveying languages. After his marriage to Jennings the Boones have worked in the northeastern section of the DRC at Bunia.

Craig Boreman. Craig was active in IV. After earning his MD, Craig served as a physician for the military at Wright Patterson Air Force Base. A specialist in pediatrics, Craig has taught at the Dayton Children's Hospital.

Jonathan Brant. Jonathan and Mindy Brant were in charge of Christian Education during OBF's early years. Jonathan has served as the foundation director of Beta Theta Pi, one of three national fraternities founded at Miami University. He served for a term at the national headquarters of fraternities in the US, where he advocated for more non-alcoholic functions at fraternities.

Greg and Emily Bryan. Greg graduated from Kent State, and then attended CIU. He succeeded Ward Ballard as the director of the Navs at Miami from 1997 to 2002. Greg married Emily Burke, a grad of Miami. The Bryans returned to serve at Kent State U. from 2002 to 2014. The chapter there grew from 12 students to close to 200. The Bryans then went to Hawaii to start a Navs chapter there from 2014 to 2016. Returning to Kent State the Bryans have concentrated on a ministry to internationals, and have also reached out to the U. of Akron and Youngtown State U.

Michael Buck. Mike organized the softball teams for OBF. After receiving his PhD in English, Mike taught briefly at Taylor University, before spending over 30 years at Indiana Wesleyan U. as the Dodd Elder Endowed Professor in English and Literature. Mike is an authority on Sir Walter Scott.

Tom Bullard. Tom was involved in IV. After receiving a PhD in Physics, Tom became a researcher in super conductivity and microwave properties at the Wright Patterson Air Force Base.

Deidre (Butler) Shelden. Deidre was the daughter of the chairman of the Art Dept. She became involved at OBF when we were at Presser Hall. She did not graduate from Miami, but joined CURE, a mission to the inner-city slums of Cincinnati, where she lived. There she met and married Howard Shelden. After attending MBI, they went out with WBT to the island of Ambon in the Molucca archipelago of Indonesia. They began their translation but had to depart after violent conflicts arose between Muslims and Christians. They continued to work on translation and literacy materials from the States.

Jennifer (Bystrom) Thomson. Jennifer was involved with Cru and joined its staff. She met and married Scott Thomson, a grad of Syracuse U., who was on the staff of Cru at the U. of Massachusetts. The Thomsons then served with Cru at Yale for four years. They then went to Tokyo in 2008. Since 2011 the Thomsons have been on the Cru staff at the U. of Connecticut. They have taken students on mission trips to nine countries in the Caribbean, Central America, Europe, the Middle East and Asia.

EXCURSUS T: NOTABLE OBF ALUMNI

Doug Calhoun. Doug was led to Christ by Barney Ford on the first day he came to OBF in September 1970. He served on the staff of IV from 1974 to 1985: three years on Long Island, four years as the team leader for Maine and New Hampshire, and two years overseeing seminary interns. He and his wife Adele served as missionaries under IFES in Trinidad and Tobago. Doug received the MDiv and DMin degrees from GCTS. From 1986 to 1994 Doug served as the Young Adult pastor at Park Street Church, then from 1996 to 2008 as an Associate Pastor of the Christ Church of Oak Brook, IL. He and Adele then served as the co-pastors of a Presbyterian Church in Needham that ministered to students from Brandeis U., the Babson School of Business, and Wellesley C.

Ken Calvert. Ken was a grad of Wheaton, who attended GCTS, where he was the student body president. After studying at Harvard Divinity School under Helmut Koester, he earned his PhD in Ancient History. He became a professor of History at Hillsdale C. and also the headmaster of Hillsdale Academy.

Mark Carlsson. After earning the MDiv from TEDS, Mark and his wife Christie moved to Sweden. He served as an assistant pastor at a Vineyard church in Norrköping (2003–2006), and then as a campus minister in the same city (2006–2011). He became the lead pastor of the Bethlehem Church in the center of Stockholm (2011–2019). In 2019 he was called to become the lead pastor of the 4,000-member Good Shepherd Lutheran Church in Naperville, IL.

Scott Carroll. Scott was a grad of Tennessee Temple U. and of TEDS. His wife Denise sang in the OBF choir. After he earned his PhD in Ancient History, Scott taught at Gordon C. and at Cornerstone U., and played a major role in the development of the Scriptorium and of the Museum of the Bible (see chapters 44 and 45).

Dorothy Chappell. Dot was one of the first women to graduate from the U. of Virginia. She was a member of OBF when it began. After earning her PhD in Botany, Dot taught for many years at Wheaton C., with a brief interlude at Gordon C. She served as the Dean of Natural and Social Sciences at Wheaton and has served on the board of Gordon C. Dot designed Wheaton's new Science Building. She has served as the president of the American Scientific Affiliation.

EXCURSUS T: NOTABLE OBF ALUMNI

Wally and Connie Cirafesi. Wally was a grad of Penn State U., where he played as an end on Joe Paterno's football team. It was Wally who first brought the Navs to Miami in 1974. Wally and Connie served as Navs missionaries in Venezuela for nine years (1978–1987). He then led the Hispanic ministry in New York and New Jersey (1987–1992), and the Hispanic ministry in south Florida ((1992–2000). He taught English as a Second Language for many years at MBI.

Brian Clark. Brian, the son of pastor Win Clark, accompanied his father when Win was working with Horizons International to aid orphans in African countries. Brian had a very effective ministry among junior and senior high school students in Carmel, a suburb north of Indianapolis. He and his father formed an organization called People Bridge. Win mentors men in Carmel while Brian and Erin moved to Orlando where they encourage people personally and online. Brian's website attracts a thousand viewers. He helped raise over $170,000 in 2020 to send to his partners in Africa.

Jim Coltharp. Jim, the son of Jerry and Evelyn, early members of OBF, was active with the Navs. He became a chief economist with the media giant Comcast, and represented it before the FCC in Washington, DC. After retiring from this position, he started the KeePressingOn project to serve as a coach. Jim has also worked to help disadvantaged children and youth in the DC area. He has been active in The Falls Church Anglican, and worked alongside the current rector, Rev. Sam Ferguson. Jim and his dance partner, Olga from Belarus, have won numerous awards at national competitions.

Ben Conarroe. Ben, a grad of Indiana U., earned the MA. in English. He sang in the OBF choir and was active in IV. He served briefly as an IV staff at the U. of Toledo, visiting Miami's chapter once a month. He then worked with the Navs in Hawaii. He has served for many years with RPJM (Re-Entry Prison and Jail Ministry) with servicemen jailed at the Navy Brig at San Diego.

Janice (Creswell) Doemland. Janice was active in IV. She is petite but with a powerful voice and sang solos at OBF. She then sang with an opera company in Germany. Dr. Peter Kim, a friend from IV, on an overseas mission in Africa met a German, Dr. Marco Doemland from Mainz. Peter put Marco in touch with Janice with the result that they married!

During Miami's 2017 Glee Club tour of Europe, Janice sang with the group in Wiesbaden.

Casey Davis. Casey was active in IV. After graduating from Asbury Theological Seminary, he earned a PhD in New Testament from Union Theological Seminary in Richmond, VA. He has been a professor of Theology at Roberts Wesleyan University.

Dan and Christina Dorsey. The Dorseys were both active with Cru. Christina taught Sunday school at OBF. They served on the staff of Cru at Arrowhead Springs, CA, Sacramento State U. and Georgia Tech, and went on mission trips to Australia, Thailand, the Philippines and Israel. Dan earned the MDiv from CIU and served as a pastoral intern at a Korean church in Columbus. Since 2000 Dan has served as the Executive Pastor of the Calvary Baptist Church in State Park ministering to students of Penn State U.

Philip Dudley. Philip is the son of IV staff Dennis Dudley and his wife Carolyn. Philip joined the army as a Military Intelligence Officer in 2007 and served in Operation Iraqi Freedom. He helped create the first Multi-Function Team that targeted and helped capture high value insurgents. His team assisted in the capture of five high value insurgents in the first four months of their creation. He was awarded numerous medals including the Iraq Campaign Medal with two stars. Following active duty, Philip transitioned to the state of Washington Army National Guard (2013 to 2018) to serve as an Information Operations Officer. During this time, he helped plan dozens of joint interactions with allied nations including Indonesia, the Philippines, Korea, Taiwan, Malaysia, Mongolia and Japan.

Cyprian Ejiasa. Originally from Nigeria, Cyprian earned the MBA at Miami and then a PhD in Economics from OSU. He has served in high positions at several government agencies including serving as a deputy director for finance at NASA's Goddard Space Center (2009–2014). He is the chief financial officer of the Corporation for National and Community service.

Mike Erre. After graduating from Miami, Mike became OBF's first youth director. He then attended TST and became a college pastor for the Mariner's Church in southern California. After Dale Burke retired from the pastorate of the Evangelical Free Church in Fullerton, CA Mike became his successor. Mike then resigned and started a new church in a former movie complex. Mike is now the Teaching Pastor at the Journey Church in Franklin, TN. He is a best-selling author and popular conference speaker.

Bob and Karen Evans. Bob and Karen, graduates of Juniata C., came to Miami as grad students in Chemistry. At OBF Bob served as a choir member, song leader, and elder. Karen taught Sunday School. Bob served as the director of IT services at McCullough-Hyde Memorial Hospital. Bob and Karen taught science courses at George Washington Academy, an elite school in Casablanca, Morocco for a number of years. Bob then taught Missions at Crown C., a Christian and Missionary Alliance school in Minnesota. Bob completed a PhD in Biochemistry and Biophysics at the U. of Minnesota and serves as an assistant professor in that department. Karen serves as a professor of Secondary Science Education at Crown College.

Don and Peg Faimon. Don Faimon was a graduate of Taylor U., where he was an outstanding golfer. Don was elected to the school's Hall of Sports Fame. He came originally to Miami as a grad student in Political Science. But he then studied at Yale's Medical School, becoming a doctor specializing in ophthalmology. When Don was pursuing grad studies at Miami, he worked as the manager of a Long John Silver's restaurant. He hired a high school waitress, Margaret, whom he later married. Peg earned a BFA from Indiana U. and then an MFA from Yale. She taught in Miami's Art Dept., eventually becoming its chair. Peg has written many books on design and has won awards for her designs. In 2015 she became the founding dean of the Eskenazi School of Art, Architecture + Design at Indiana U.

Bill and Critty Fairback. Bill, a grad of the U. of Pennsylvania, served his first assignment as a member of Cru at Miami. Thereafter the Fairbacks served Cru in Singapore, Jordan, and the United Nations. For the last two decades they have served Cru in Washington, DC, ministering to the officials on Capitol Hill. They have recently also been involved in Cru's urban ministry. They attend the Anglican Falls Church.

Jim and Cindy Fath. Jim was a Computer Science grad student at Miami. The Faths went out as "tent" missionaries to Uzbekistan, supported by the Mennonites. When that Muslim country expelled Christian missionaries, they relocated in southeastern Turkey near Adana. They came back to the US for family reasons and have relocated to the Columbus area. Cindy teaches English to immigrants, and Jim supervises the distribution of Covid kits and vaccinations for the Ohio Dept. of Health.

Tyler Flynn. Tyler was active in IV. He served in a ministry to college students in western Pennsylvania, and then earned the PhD in US History from Penn State U., writing on "Calvinism and Public Life: A Case Study of Western Pennsylvania 1900 to 1955.' He teaches in the History Dept. at Eastern U. in St. David's, a suburb of Philadelphia.

David Foley. David grew up in OBF as his parents Charles and Elizabeth were early members. He was in the NROTC at Miami and rose to the rank of Captain in the Navy (the equivalent of a Colonel in the Army). He served on a carrier and taught at the War College in Rhode Island. David was in the Pentagon at the time of the attack on 9/11. Though not a smoker, David died prematurely from lung cancer.

Barney Ford. Barney, a grad of the U. of Evansville, became IV's first staff member at Miami He was one of the original four speakers at OBF beginning in 1971. He kept being promoted with greater responsibilities for IV, first over Ohio and then Michigan. He finally became one of the vice-presidents of IV, directing its triennial "Urbana" missionary conferences. He also served as the chair of IFES.

John Fortner. John graduated from Bryan C. and Beeson Divinity School. He earned a master's in Ancient History. He undertook further graduate studies in the NT at Marquette U. He has served as the Director of Adult Education at the mega church of Tony Evans in Dallas.

Gary Friesen. Gary is the son of missionaries to Japan. He was an outstanding basketball player at Taylor U. and was part of the school's Venture for Victory team that played national teams in Asia. He earned the MA in Mathematics. He then taught Mathematics and Computer Science at Faith Academy, a school for missionary children in Manila (1984–1996). On returning to the States, Gary became the director of Academic Technology (1997–2014) at Taylor U. After his retirement (2015), he became the executive director of Innovative Technology, an organization that aids schools in Liberia.

EXCURSUS T: NOTABLE OBF ALUMNI

Mark and Angie Fulk. Mark and Angie were both grads of Marietta C., where they were active in IV. While grad students in English at Miami, they were active with the interdenominational campus ministry. They both earned PhDs in Medieval English. After teaching at John Brown U., both Mark and Angie have been teaching English at Buffalo State U.

Deirdre and Jamey Fulton. Deirdre is the daughter of professors at Ball State U. Both Deirdre and her husband Jamey were grads of Wheaton C. Jamey taught science courses at Talawanda High School as Deirdre earned the MA in Ancient History. She then earned the PhD in OT studies at Penn State U., while Jamey earned the PhD in Geology. She is now a professor of OT at Baylor U., while he is a professor in Geosciences. They have participated in many archaeological excavations in Israel.

Jerry Gannod. Jerry's parents emigrated from the Philippines to Michigan where he received his BA, MA and PhD in Computer Sciences from Michigan State U. Jerry joined Miami's Computer Sciences Dept. He was active in the Faculty Christian Fellowship and played stringed instruments on OBF's worship team. Jerry is now the chair of the Computer Sciences Dept. at Tennessee Tech.

Bill and Susan Gates. Bill was active in IV and joined the staff of IV, serving for five years at Purdue U. He then became the head of the Gates Automotive Dealership in South Bend. Bill and Susan have a winter home on Kauai, where they have been active in the church in Koloa. Bill serves on the national board of trustees of IV.

Paul Goodwin. Paul, a graduate of Huntington C., became involved in the Navs while pursuing grad studies at Miami. Since 2004 he has served as the Funding Coach for World the Navs ministry at the U. of Wyoming in Laramie.

Paul Gould. Paul was involved in Cru. He received a master's from TST, studying under J.P. Moreland. He then received a PhD in Philosophy from Purdue U. He taught Apologetics at Southwestern Baptist Theological Seminary, and at Oklahoma Baptist U. and as a visiting professor at TEDS. He now teaches at Palm Beach Atlantic U. He is the founder of the Two Tasks Institute and is a popular lecturer on college campuses. He is active in the EPS and has written and edited a number of books. His book *Cultural Apologetics*, was recognized in the annual book survey of CT.

Justin and Kristen Gravitt. Justin, who was active with the Navs at Miami, became the director of the Navs. He and his wife Kristen served with a government school at Lampang, a large city in northern Thailand for four years. After returning to the States Justin has served as a director for Innovation and Advancement for the Navs.

John Grossmann. John was the son of David Grossmann, a noted judge in Cincinnati. He was involved in IV. He earned the MDiv and the MTh from TEDS. He is the lead pastor of the Grace EFCA church in Cincinnati. He has served as the head of the Greater Cincinnati EFCA Ministerial Council. He serves on the Tenure Board of TEDS.

Tom Grossmann. Tom, John's brother, was also active in IV. Tom earned his JD from UC College of Law. He has served as Hamilton County's assistant prosecutor and has also been on Mason City's council. His wife has served as the mayor of Mason. Tom has served as chair of the Warren County Republican Party.

Nijay Gupta. Nijay's parents, who are Hindu, emigrated from India to the US in 1972. His father was an ophthalmologist in Ashland, OH. Neil, his brother who is four years older, came to Miami and was converted to Christ through Cru. Nijay followed him to Miami and was in turn converted through his brother. He became active with Cru, going on four mission trips to Macedonia. He also helped Ryan Massey at OBF with middle school youth in 1999–2000. He graduated as a Public Relations major. He attended GCTS and worked for Hendrickson Publishers in 2005–2006. He earned the PhD in NT at the U. of Durham. He has taught at a number of schools including Portland Seminary and most recently Northern Seminary. He puts out a popular blog, and has written many books on the NT. He edited the *Bulletin for Biblical Research* from 2020 to 2022.

Darryl Handy. After graduating from TEDS, Darryl planted a church in western North Carolina. He has served as a pastor at Mission Community Church in Sylva, as well as Blue Ridge Community Church in Cullowhee, ministering to the students of Western Carolina U.

Bethany (Hanke) Hoang. Bethany was active with Cru. She went to Princeton Theological Seminary where she earned a MDiv in Missional and Systematic Theology. She married Anthony Hoang, a graduate of the

U. of Virginia. Bethany served for ten years as the director of the International Justice Mission's IJM Institute. She has written *Deepening the Soul for Justice* and *The Justice Calling: Where Passion Meets Perseverance*, a book written with Kristen Deede Johnson that was a 2017 CT Book Award winner.

David Henderson. David was an atheist who was converted to Christ through Cru. After graduating from GCTS, he became in 1997 the lead pastor of the Covenant (Presbyterian) Church in West Lafayette, ministering to students of Purdue U.

Roger Hershey. Roger, who was a cheerleader at Penn State U., became a member of Cru at Miami in 1980. Roger also served as an elder at OBF. He was the director of Cru until 1997. He then became the Midwest Regional director for Cru from 1997 to 2002, after which he returned to State College. He and Roxanne then moved b ack to Indiana.

Randy Hildreth. Randy was the son of the superintendent of schools. He joined the youth fellowship that Dale Burke organized After graduating from Miami, he attended TEDS. He then served as a pastor of a church in south Florida. He and Elizabeth then went to Jos, Nigeria, where he served as a chaplain for the mission school. When the Islamic Boko Haram launched attacks in the area, the Hildreths returned to the States. Randy is pastoring Bay Point Christian Church in St. Petersburg, FL.

Larry Hoop. Larry was active in IV and then went on the staff of IV. He graduated from TEDS *summa cum laude* with an M. Div. in Church History and Pastoral Ministry. He also earned a D.Min. in Rural Ministry from Covenant Theological Seminary. After serving for many years in Iowa with his wife Debbie at a church of the Presbyterian Church in America, Larry returned to southern Ohio where he has pastored a church in rural West Union. He has been active on PCA's Administrative Committee.

Ann (Hunsinger) Hinman. Ann was active with Cru and became a Cru staff member. She met and married George Hinman, a grad of Brown U. Together they served in the Boston area from 1988 to 1993, ministering to students from Brandeis, Harvard and MIT. After graduating from GCTS. George became an assistant minister from 2004 to 2008 at the Bel Air Presbyterian Church in LA, a church that had been attended by the

Reagans. He is the senior pastor of the University Presbyterian Church in Seattle ministering to the students at the U. of Washington.

Ross and Mary Hunter. Ross's parents, Truman and Mary Dodd Hunter were pillars of the Oxford Presbyterian Church. Ross and Mary became involved with the youth ministry at OBF. Graduating from MBI, they have served in Ecuador among the Quichua Indians in the high Andes under various mission boards, most recently with Pioneers. Ross has promoted seminary training among the Quichuas and is pursuing a PhD at CIU. Ross and Mary have also aided the many Venezuelans who have flooded into Ecuador.

Jonathan Hunter. Jonathan, the son of Ross and Mary, was active at OBF. After graduating from MBI, he and his wife Maggie worked with the youth of missionary families in Costa Rica under United World Mission. After graduating *summa cum laude* from the Charlotte branch of GCTS, Jonathan was accepted into the PhD program at the University of St. Andrews in Scotland.

Dave and Deborah Iverson. Dave, a grad in Journalism and Broadcasting from the U. of North Dakota, came as the first Cru staff member at Miami, and joined the speakers' rotation when we were at Presser Hall. He later left to serve as a broadcaster with AIA in California, and then moved to Seattle in 1981. He served as a radio broadcaster with a company owned by the Latter-Day Saints. He then started his own broadcasting company that served universities in Washington, Oregon, and Hawaii. Finally, he began a gourmet culinary tour company. Deborah worked with a large commercial print company.

Mark and Jennifer Jensen After graduating in 1995 from Miami, Mark and his wife Jen both studied at TST under J. P. Moreland. Mark and Jen received their PhDs in Philosophy from Notre Dame. After teaching at Calvin College, Mark joined the Philosophy Dept. of the Air Force Academy in 2010. Mark received the "Outstanding Educator Award" of the Academy in 2013. Jen teaches at the U. of Colorado branch in Colorado Springs.

Bill and Carol Jones. Bill and Carol were the first couple married by Dale Burke. After attending TEDS, Bill was involved with the EFCA in church plants (2005 to 2008) and as an EFCA pastor (2008 to 2017). Since 2017 he has served as the director of training for Reach Global, serving in five countries in Latin America, Asia and Africa.

Tom Kidd. Tom was active in IV. He graduated Phi Beta Kappa with a degree in Political Science. After graduating from the law school at OSU, he spent a decade as a public prosecutor. He then went into private law practice in West Chester. Active in Republican politics, Tom has done work for the Alliance Defending Freedom and the Home School Legal Defense Association.

Kyle Killian. Kyle was the son of an education professor. He received his PhD.in Psychology from Syracuse U., and taught at the U. of Houston and then with his wife Anna Agathangelou at York U. He is a professor with Capella U. and researches the phenomenon of vicarious resilience. Kyle also trains Chinese psychotherapists in couple and family therapy at Ling Yu International Psychological Training.

Peter and Robin Kim. Peter's father, an immigrant from Korea, taught at Marshall U. in West Virginia. While at Miami Peter worked with children at OBF and was active in IV. After receiving his MD in Family Medicine at OSU, Peter has practiced medicine at Indianapolis. His philanthropic work with the poor has been noted by the Indianapolis press.

Rudy and Laurie Klaas. Rudy and Laurie were active in IV. They attended a World Missions series at OBF taught by elder Ralph Gutowski. Rudy and Laurie have been serving with WBT in Senegal, West Africa. Rudy has also worked with the government of South Sudan.

Ron Knopf. An engineer who graduated from OSU, Ron was a plant manager for Ford Motor Company in Cincinnati. Ron served as an elder at OBF. Ford then sent Ron and his family to Chongqing (formerly known as Chunking), a major city of 30 million in southern China to build a factory for Ford. He was so successful that Ford asked him to extend his stay to build even more factories there.

Steve Kurtz. After Miami, Steve and his wife Jennifer graduated from MBI. He then served as a missionary to Romania, and then as a professor and dean of the Evangelical Theological Seminary in Osijek, Croatia. Upon returning to the States, he became the pastor of Central Presbyterian Church of Fort Smith, AR.

Steve Lambacher. Steve was a *summa cum laude* graduate in History from Ohio U. He earned an MA in American History with a minor in Ancient History. He served with the Navs in Korea for two years. He then earned an MA in English as a Second Language at Ball State U. He married Kimiko, one of his students from Japan. Steve earned a PhD in Cognitive Science from Chukyo U. He has been teaching at Aoyama Gakuin U. in a suburb of Tokyo.

Jason Larson. Jason was a grad of Gordon C. Jason was hearing impaired but was able to read lips. He earned his MA in Ancient History, and then the MLS at the U. of Kentucky. He served as the archivist for Harvard's Children Hospital. After earning the PhD in Religious Studies at the Syracuse U., he taught at Bates C. He is now teaching at the Hotchkiss School in western Connecticut, one of the most prestigious private high schools in the nation.

Martha (Lee) Conrad. Martha was involved in Cru and joined its staff. After her marriage to Duane Conrad, a grad of Purdue, she and her husband served as the leaders of Cru in Germany from 1976. They were instrumental in the conversion of Carsten Thiede, a NT textual scholar, who made the claim that Magdalen papyri of Matthew could be dated to the first century, a claim that was not accepted by other scholars. After the reunification of Germany, the Conrads turned over leadership of the Cru ministry to Germans.

Mark Lindsey. Mark was involved with IV. He and his future wife Sumita helped in the children's ministry at OBF. After earning his MD.at OSU, Mark is now in Columbus, practicing as a specialist in Colon and Rectal Surgery.

Peggy Lowry. Peggy was the daughter of a professor of Aeronautical Engineering at the U. of Virginia. She was active in IV and served as a Sunday school teacher at OBF. After joining the staff of IV, she went under OMF in 1981 as a missionary teacher to Indonesia. She taught English and Drama at Petra Christian U., then from 1987 at Maranatha U. in Bandug, from 2001 at Sanata Dharma U. in Jogjakarta, and from 2007 until her retirement at the Christian U. of Indonesia in Jakarta. She focused on student evangelism and discipleship, working closely with Perkantas, the Indonesian movement associated with IFES.

Baron and Beth Luechauer. Baron's father was an air force pilot who flew in the movie Top Gun. Baron and Beth were active with Cru. The Luechauers served with Cru in (North) Macedonia, where they trained national staff, and help to send national missionaries to other countries in central Europe, including Bulgaria and Romania. After 10 years in Macedonia, the Luechauers moved to Birmingham, England, to serve with Cru's UK Agape ministry.

Scott Luley. With a PhD in Marketing from Penn State U., Scott became an instructor at Miami (1974 to 1976). Then he shocked his colleagues and his parents by leaving academia to become a staff member of Cru. He first served at Purdue U. (1977 to 1980), then as a national field director of Cru Global at Dallas (1980 to 1991). Together with Stan Oakes he helped to develop the Faculty Commons, Cru's network of about 10.000 Christian faculty at 900 colleges and universities. Scott spent 24 years (1991 to 2015) ministering to the faculty and students of Princeton U. From 2016 until his retirement in 2020 Scott and Jan took their highly effective ministry to international grad students to the U. of N. Carolina.

Kirk MacGregor. Kirk graduated as a *summa cum laude* Mathematics and Statistics major. He earned the Highest Honors in Apologetics at Biola U., and then a PhD in Religious Studies from the U. of Iowa. After many temporary stints at numerous colleges, Kirk became the chair of the Dept. of Philosophy and Religion at McPherson C. He is a prolific author and has written most notably a biography of Luis de Molina, the Jesuit philosopher who proposed the concept of "Middle Knowledge," which has been embraced by the evangelical philosopher William Lane Craig. Kirk is an active member of EPS and ETS.

David Mahan. David's father was the director of the Natural Museum in Cleveland. David was a History major. He was active in Cru and joined its staff, serving at different colleges in Virginia and New England. He became the director of Cru at Yale U, and co-founded the Rivendell Institute to minister to the faculty and grad students at Yale. David earned a PhD in Divinity (literature and poetry) at the U. of Cambridge and serves as an adjunct lecturer at Yale Divinity School and at the Institute of Sacred Music. He is a cofounder of the Consortium of Christian Study Centers.

Ron Mahurin. Ron earned his PhD in Political Science and taught this subject at Gordon C. Ron became the vice-president of the Council for Christian Colleges and Universities in Washington, DC, and served as the provost of Houghton C. He then served as a vice-president of Stamats, before joining Design Group International.

Cliff Mansley Jr. Cliff's father was a calligrapher as were he and his sister Holly. Cliff was active with IV. After graduating from GCTS, Cliff pastored a Presbyterian Church in Pittsburgh. He became the founding pastor of the New Creation Church in 2007 in Joplin, Missouri. In 2011 when the town was hit by a devastating tornado, the costliest tornado in US history, Cliff and his congregation worked tirelessly to help the community recover. In 2019 Cliff became the pastor of Grace Community Church in Surprise, a community of retirees in Arizona

James Marcum. Jim after graduating from Miami earned a PhD in Physiology from the U. of Cincinnati. He did a postdoc at MIT, and earned a PhD in Philosophy from Boston C. He taught for ten years at Harvard's Medical School before moving to Baylor U. where he teaches medical ethics in the Philosophy Dept. He is the author of *Thomas Kuhn's Revolutions: A Historical and an Evolutionary Philosophy of Science.*

Daniel Master. Daniel's father taught the OT at the Philadelphia School of the Bible, which Daniel attended. Daniel earned his MA in Ancient History. He then earned a PhD in Near Eastern Languages and Civilizations from Harvard U Since 2005 he has been professor of Archaeology at Wheaton. He worked at the excavations at Ashkelon for about 25 years. In 2007 he succeeded his mentor, Larry Stager of Harvard, as the field director of the Ashkelon excavations which were completed in 2016. He then began new excavations at Tel Shimron, the largest tel in the Jezreel Valley, funded by the Museum of the Bible. Daniel edited the *Oxford Encyclopedia of the Bible and Archaeology.*

Doug Matthews. Doug earned his PhD in Psychology and taught at the U. of Memphis and at Baylor U. Doug served as the head of the Psychology Department of Nanyang Technological U. in Singapore (2009 to 2014). Since 2014 he has been the chair of the Psychology Dept. at the U. of Wisconsin at Eau Claire.

Michael (Mickey) Maudlin and Karen (Grimshaw) Maudlin. Mickey and Karen were both active in IV. When Karen went to Wheaton C. to pursue a master's in psychology, Mickey worked in a Christian bookstore. He obtained a master's from Wheaton C. in Theological Studies. He worked at InterVarsity Press as an editor (1983 to 1989). Mickey then joined CT and worked as its Book Editor and Managing Editor before becoming its Editorial Vice-President (1989 to 2002). In 2002 he joined HarperCollins, one of the largest publishers, becoming an Executive Editor and Senior VicePresident, specializing in religious books. Karen became a clinical psychologist (PsyD Chicago School of Prof. Psy.) and later trained and became an executive coach and consultant for global leaders. She has been involved in a number of ministries, including the National Prayer Breakfast, Telemachus, as well as being an adjunct teacher at Wheaton C. As Karen has a number of counseling centers in the area, Mickey still resides in Wheaton and commutes to his office in San Francisco!

Mark McCloskey. Mark was active in Cru and served on its staff. He was Cru's regional director for N. Dakota, S. Dakota, and Minnesota. He earned the MA and MDiv from Bethel Seminary, and the PhD in Leadership from the U. of South Florida. He joined the faculty of Bethel Seminary in 1998 and became the Dean of the Center for Transformational Leadership at Bethel. Mark serves on the boards of the Christian Legal Society, of the Urban Leadership Academy, and of Love Inc.

Greg McMahon. A grad of the U. of Kansas, Greg earned his MA in Ancient History. He earned his PhD writing on ancient Hittite religious texts at the U. of Chicago under Harry Hoffner. He served as a professor of History at the U. of New Hampshire. Greg excavated in central Turkey for 25 years and is the coeditor of *The Oxford Handbook of Ancient Anatolia*. He has been cited as an outstanding teacher by the university. Greg has served as an advisor to the IV chapter. His wife Mindy teaches the harp and is the choir director at their church.

Brian Mennecke. Brian earned a MBA and a MA. He then earned the PhD from Indiana U. in Management Information Systems. After teaching at East Carolina U. Brian is now an associate professor of Management Information Systems at Iowa State U.

Matthew Miller. Matt was active with Cru and went as a missionary to Russia in 1990 and 1991. From 1997 to 2008 Matt worked in Moscow, teaching at the Russian-American Christian U. After earning an MA from Wheaton C. and the PhD. rom the U. of Minnesota, Matt joined the faculty of U. of Northwestern in St. Paul, where he serves as the chair of the Dept. of History and the chair of the Dept of World Languages. He published the book *John R, Mott, the American YMCA and Revolutionary Russia*.

Tim Muelhoff. Tim, a grad of Eastern Michigan U. served with Cru at Miami. He then received an MA and PhD in Communications from the U. of North Carolina. He is a professor of Communication Studies at Biola U. He and his wife Noreen have been popular speakers at conferences on Christian marriage for forty years. Tim has authored and co-authored a number of books on marriage, communication and persuasion published by InterVarsity Press. Tim's *Eyes to See* was cited by CT.

Margaret (Mundell) Cottle. Margaret, the daughter of a Chemistry professor, became a physician. She married a doctor, Canadian Robin Cottle. At OBF Robin was on the worship team. The Cottles served a short term at the Rift Valley Academy in Kenya. After Robin earned a degree in ophthalmology in Halifax, the Cottles moved to Vancouver. Margaret has been an active spokesperson of Focus on the Family's pro-life movement. She has served on the board of the Euthanasia Prevention Coalition and on the Christian Advocacy Society of Greater Vancouver.

Eva Mwanika. Eva graduated from the U. of Nairobi in Kenya, earned her MA in Ancient History. She pursued biblical languages at GCTS, then studied Arabic in Morocco and Hebrew in Israel. She is completing a PhD. to the United Nations. She has worked with the UN's Peacebuilding Commission.

Kenneth Newhouse. Ken was involved in IV. After recovering from a horrific auto accident, Ken went on to earn his MD at Yale Medical School. He has been living in Pocatello, Idaho, where he specializes in Orthopedics and Sports Medicine.

Julie Park. Julie, who is of Korean descent, was a grad of Vanderbilt U., where she was active in IV. She did her PhD at UCLA, where she wrote her dissertation on an unnamed Christian group (which was IV), as it went through the changes wrought by Proposition 209, which did away with ethnic factors in Affirmative Action. As a result, the numbers of Blacks and Hispanics plummeted while those of Asian Americans rose in elite schools such as Berkeley and UCLA. Her dissertation was published as *When Diversity Drops: Race, Religion and Affirmative Action in Higher Education*. Julie taught in the Dept. of Educational Leadership before moving on to the U. of Maryland. She has served as a witness for Harvard in a case in which Asian Americans accused Harvard of unfairly favoring other groups which kept the numbers of Asian Americans unfairly low. Ironically Julie herself was one of the Asian American applicants who was rejected by Harvard! Her book *Race on Campus: Debunking Myths with Data* was published by Harvard in 2018.

Wood Parker. Wood, a grad of Auburn U., was on the staff of the NROTC program at Miami, where he earned an MA in International Relations and National Security Studies. Wood served as an assistant to the Secretary of the Navy. In 1990 he commanded a destroyer, which ran aground during a storm in the Gulf of Mexico. This ended his 20-year career as a naval officer. He then went into the consulting business and became a vice-president of Northrup Grumman. He led the divestiture of The Advisory Services Division from Grumman as an independent company worth 1.65 billion dollars. He and his wife Emmy have made numerous trips to Haiti on humanitarian missions.

Wes and Sue Pastor. A grad of OSU, Wes earned the MBA from Miami and taught accounting courses. He served as an elder at OBF and was involved with the Navs. He attended DTS and in 1985 transferred to WTS, where he finished his seminary degree. He later earned the MTh from the U. of Wales. The Pastors moved in 1991 to Burlington to reach students at the U. of Vermont. In 1992 Wes started Christ Memorial Church. With a congregation of 350, it is now the largest Baptist church in the state. In 2000 with the counsel of George Hill, Wes launched NETS (New England Training and Sending Center). NETS first sent out Don Willeman to develop Christ Redeemer Church in Hanover, NH, to minister to the students of Dartmouth C. As of 2021 the couples trained by NETS have established or revitalized churches throughout New England (including nine in Vermont, three in Maine, three in New Hampshire, three in Massachusetts, and one in Connecticut) as well as one in Cameroon, West Africa, and one at Abu Dhabi in the United Arab Emirates.

Jerry Pattengale. Jerry graduated from Marion College (later Indiana Wesleyan University). After earning an MA from Wheaton College, he earned the PhD from Miami and taught at Azusa Pacific University. He played a role in the development of the Scriptorium, and a major role in the development of the Museum of the Bible (see chapters 44 and 45). He also served as an administrator at Indiana Wesleyan University and has served on many boards including *Christianity Today* and the Religious News Service.

Brett Payne. Brett graduated from GCTS with an MA in Church History and then received a master's in music from the Southern Baptist Theological Seminary. He served as a worship pastor in churches in California, Kentucky, and Pennsylvania. He is now a pastor of Cross Point in Downington, Pennsylvania where he also serves as a spiritual life coach.

Michael (Mick) Pechan Mick, who was from Wisconsin, earned his PhD in Physics from Iowa State U. Mick taught for many years at Miami, doing research on magnetic physics. He became the chair of the Physics Dept. and served as an elder at OBF. After his term as chair ended, Mick assumed a position as the Program Manager, Experimental Condensed Matter Physics of the Dept. of Energy in charge of disbursing 50 million dollars of research funds. His wife Kathy has a counseling service.

Sarah (Pechan) Driver. Sarah, a daughter of the Pechans, attended Miami and was active in IV. She was a journalism major who spent part of her senior year in Guatemala. She earned an MSc in Social Policy and Development at the London School of Economics. She also spent some time at The Carter Center in Atlanta. She taught at the George Washington Academy in Casablanca, Morocco. She married Cory Driver, a grad of Purdue U., who served in the Peace Corps in Morocco. Living in Rabat, Cory did research on the Jews of Morocco for his PhD at Emory U., while Sarah directed a project funded by the US government that focused on gender equality in the workplace. Cory earned a MDiv from Luther Seminary while working for the Lutherans in the Midwest.

Christine (Pellegrini) Ferch. Christine, the daughter of OBFers Mike and Joanne Pellegrini, graduated from OSU. She served in Nepal with Operation Mopbilization Nepal from 2010 to 2014, Through AIDS Link Nepal she and coworkers helped raise up local believers to be advocates for those infected with HIV at area hospitals, opened a Crisis Care Center for those needing a place to stay while promoting the education of several dozen children impacted by HIV. They ran a monthly support group meeting for local families, and trained churches and villages to destigmatize HIV. Christine co-wrote a Life Skills curriculum for Nepali schools that covered topics of identity and community from a biblical perspective. She met and married a co-worker, Mark Ferch. Mark and Christine are active in a church in Columbus, reaching out to OSU students.

Christian and Lisa Pettitt. The son of OBFers Dick and Ruth, Christian was active with Cru and as student went on a mission trip to Albania. He then joined the staff of Cru. He and his wife Lisa spent a year (2000 to 2001) at the U. of Leiden. They were assigned to Miami (2001 to 2013) and were involved in spring and summer projects in the US and in England, Switzerland, and Montenegro. He became the associate Director for Leadership with 26 staff teams in the Midwest. After 2016 he served as the city director for Cru in Indianapolis reaching out to young adults.

Vince and Karen (Bush) Purpero. Vince made the wooden cross that hung in the front of OBF. He was a member of Miami's football team. Karen is a trained classical pianist. They were both active in Cru. Vince has ministered to youth in Florida, Italy, Germany and North Carolina. Karen has used her musical gifts to present Christ. Vince served as the national director for the high school ministries of AIA. Vince has also coached various local sports teams.

James Read. A Canadian and Salvation Army officer, Jim after earning a PhD in Philosophy from UCLA, came to Miami as a visiting professor in the Philosophy Dept. Upon returning to Canada Jim taught at Booth University College in Winnipeg, Manitoba. He is the founder and the executive director of the Salvation Army's Ethics Centre.

Joshua Reitano. Josh was active with Cru and joined its staff, serving in Leiden, the Netherlands. He received the MA in Comparative Religion at Miami, and then the MDiv from Princeton Theological Seminary. He served as an assistant pastor at the North Cincinnati Community Church. He then became the founder and lead pastor of the New City Presbyterian Church in Norwood (a neighborhood of Cincinnati), which has grown to about 600 members, the largest Presbyterian Church in America congregation in Ohio.

EXCURSUS T: NOTABLE OBF ALUMNI

Andy Rhodenbaugh. Andy, the son of OBFers Tim and Becky, was a track star who joined the staff of AIA. He married Reisha, another track athlete. They minister to the athletes of Georgia State U. in Atlanta.

Moses Rumano. Moses was a grad student in the School of Education from Zimbabwe (former Southern Rhodesia), a country which was ruled ruthlessly by the dictator Moses Mugabe, which caused runaway inflation and made life there quite precarious. OBF raised the funds to bring members of his family to the US. After earning his PhD., Moses became a professor of Education at Malone U.

Doug Rumford. Doug attended GCTS, where he graduated *summa cum laude* and served as his class's valedictorian. He received a DMin degree from Fuller Theological Seminary. After pastoring Presbyterian churches in Fairfield, CT, Fresno, CA, and Kansas City, MO, Doug was called to be the senior pastor of the large Trinity United Presbyterian Church in Santa Ana, California. He is the author of several books including *What About Heaven and Hell?*, *What About spiritual Warfare?* and *What About Unanswered Prayers?*

Eric Russ. Eric was a tall Black man, who came from a criminal family background in Cleveland, and who hated whites. Upon entering Miami, he beat up some white students. But then at a retreat for Black students sponsored by Cru, Eric committed his life to Christ and was transformed. He joined the staff of Cru and graduated from GCTS, where he met his wife, Sarah. They served a short term in Uganda. Eric then established the Mack Avenue Community Church, a highly successful multiethnic and multi-service church in a crime ridden area of Detroit. Eric then pursued a PhD in NT at the University of Aberdeen in Scotland. After obtaining the PhD Eric is serving at Christ Covenant Church and also teaching as an adjunct at the Charlotte Reformed Theological Seminary.

Bill Schmidt. Bill was active in IV and was a political activist. He has served as an instructor in English to the military at Abu Dhabi in the United Arab Emirates, and more recently in the Kingdom of Jordan.

Floyd Sebald. Floyd was active in Cru, and served on the staff of Cru at Northern Arizona U. He earned an MS in Forest Management and Silviculture. He served with Cru for twenty-two years in Mongolia, including twelve years as the national director. He also taught at the National

University of Mongolia and advised the government on issues of forestry. Upon his return to the States Floyd became the director of the First Presbyterian Church in Colorado Springs.

Robert and Patrice Shebeck. Bob and Patrice served under Global Ministries in France. Bob served as the pastor of the United Protestant Church of the Annunciation in the heart of Paris. Patrice served as a Protestant chaplain at a hospital and nursing homes in Paris. Upon returning to the States Bob became the Assistant Vice President and Marketing Director of the Board of Church Extension of Disciples of Christ Inc. in Indianapolis.

Paul Sheneman. After receiving his PhD in English Paul first taught at Belhaven C. in Mississippi, where he experienced a number of panic attacks. After therapy and recovery, Paul then became a successful professor of English at Warner U. and then at Webber International U., both in Florida. He has written scholarly articles on Chaucer and Piers Plowman.

Jeff and Melinda Smith. Jeff and Melinda were active with IV. They served as missionaries in Uzbekistan before that country expelled all the missionaries. After earning a master's in teaching English as a Second Language from the U. of Findlay, Jeff joined the faculty of Ohio Northern U., where he serves as the director of Global Initiatives.

David and Maggie Smith. Dave and his wife Maggie (Aho) were active in IV. After earning his PhD in Psychology from OSU, Dave became the director of Psychology at the Cincinnati Children's Center (1990 to 2010). Since 2010, he has served as the senior director of Psychology at the Lifeway Counseling Centers.

Mark and Megan Smith. Mark and his wife Megan were active with the Navs. Mark served as the director of the Navs at Miami from 2007 to 2014. Together with the Jarvis the Smiths trained a number of future directors of other campuses. In 2014, the Smiths moved to Orlando to begin a thriving Navs chapter of 75 to 100 students at the U. of Central Florida, one of the largest universities in the US. In 2020, Mark passed on the leadership of the chapter to others and prepared to go overseas to Croatia, but this was stymied by the pandemic. In 2021 he then prepared to go to Austria, but a diving accident prevented an overseas assignment.

Mark was assigned to work in the Cincinnati area with the Navs at the U. of Cincinnati, Xavier, and Northern Kentucky U.

Kent and Linda Stephens. Kent and Linda were grads of Ball State U. Kent succeeded Barney Ford as the second IV staff at Miami. He then served as a regional director for IV. He established a consulting firm Quest Global in Dublin, a suburb of Columbus. Since 2010 he has served on the board of directors of IFES and as its vice-chairman.

Dennis and Ellen Stokes. A grad of Penn State, where he was a member of the marching band, Dennis served as the director of the Navs at Miami. In 2001 he moved to the Navs headquarters at Glen Eyrie where he served as the national director of Leadership Services, developing leaders and influencers. He trained hundreds of Navs who went to the countries of the former Soviet Union.

Matt Stonecypher. Matt was active in IV and helped in the children's ministry at OBF. He earned the Doctor of Veterinary Medicine degree from OSU. Matt now works at an animal clinic in Xenia.

Susan Swieringa. Susan, a grad of Wheaton C., earned her MA in Botany. She was one of the earliest missionaries from OBF. She went to the Philippines under International Missions (later named Christar) and served many years as the assistant principal of Faith Academy, a school for missionary children in the Philippines. She also helped start a church in the slums of Manila. Upon returning to the States Susan became a vice-president of Christar.

Dustin Swinehart. Dustin was an outstanding soccer player for Miami, scoring a record thirty-two goals. He became the leading scorer for the professional Charlotte Eagles, a team of Christian players who played in the second division of the United Soccer League. He won many honors during his soccer career. Upon retiring from the sport, he began Project 658, an organization ministering to the poor of Charlotte. He then returned to the Charlotte Eagles in 2020 to become their Director of Community Relations.

Bob and Barb Thompson. Bob and Barb were active with Cru and were married by Dr. Bill Wilson. After attending TEDS Bob served with Cru at Northwestern U., Northern Arizona U. and Arizona State U. He then served as the senior pastor of Desert View Baptist Church in Gilbert before establishing Elijah's Cave Ministries in 1999 at Tempe to minister to the international students at Arizona State U.

Lisa Toland. Lisa, a grad of Indiana Wesleyan U., earned the MA in European History. After graduate studies at the U. of Oxford, where her research centered on seventeeth and eighteenth-century British history, Lisa then returned to her alma mater. She is the director of the John Wesley Honors C. at Indiana Wesleyan U.

Jim Toy. Jim was active with Cru and served as a regional director for Cru for Washington, Oregon and Idaho. After attending TEDS, he served as a pastor in Lebanon, OH and then as the Discipleship and Small Groups Pastor at the large Cincinnati Vineyard Church. He now serves as a volunteer at the Crossroads Mason Church.

Ben Voth. Ben served as an elder at OBF. Ben thought about becoming a minister. Instead, he earned a PhD in Communications. He taught that subject at Miami and coached award-winning debate teams. He was an outspoken Christian witness at the university. One of his Jewish students, who was hired at the Holocaust Museum in DC, recommended Ben as a speaking coach for Holocaust survivors. He is now a professor of Communications and Public Affairs and director of Speech and Debate at the Southern Methodist U. He is an advisor to the George Bush Presidential Library and the Calvin Coolidge Presidential Foundation. His book, *The Rhetoric of Genocide* won the American Forensic Association's top book award.

Brandon Walker. A grad of Longwood C., Brandon earned the MA in Ancient History. His computer skills were indispensable to me as I planned the annual conference of the ETS in 2005. Brandon served as a teacher missionary in Malawi and Mozambique and married a coworker from South Africa. He earned a PhD in NT from the U. of Nottingham but was unable to secure a teaching position. He has done some teaching as an adjunct at Regent U. Brandon is working as a cyber security engineer for the military.

Stan Wallace. Stan was active in Cru. Stan earned an MA and PhD in Philosophy from TST. At first, he served with Cru in their student ministry and then their faculty ministry. He began Cru's Academic Initiative. Then from 2003 to 2010 he became IV's national director of its faculty ministry. He also began the Emerging Scholars Network to help prepare grad students to become professors. He joined Global Scholars in 2010 and now serves as its president. Global Scholars has placed 316 Christian professors in universities in sixty-six nations.

Charley Warner. Charley majored in Russian at Miami, where he was involved with Cru. He took further studies at Wheaton C. His wife Cheryl is the daughter of noted Christian musician Dick Anthony. Charley has taken graduate studies in Russian history in England. Charley taught for many years at a seminary in Odessa in the Ukraine. The Warners then made their base in Vienna. After a few years residing at Wheaton, the Warners returned to a city near Kyiv. Charley plays an important role as the liaison between numerous seminaries in the former countries of the Soviet Union and in eastern Europe. He teaches at a seminary in Armenia and provided contacts for OBF's partnership with the seminary and churches in Armenia. Some of his Ukrainian students have served as missionaries in Central Asia. The Warners left Ukraine shortly before the Russian invasion, but returned in 2023 to their home near the capital.

Mike Weaver. Mike was active in IV. He graduated from Luther Seminary in Minnesota and has served as the pastor of Lutheran churches in the Columbus area. He is currently a pastor at St. Luke Lutheran Church in Gahanna. Mike also serves as a Leadership and Influencer coach.

Joe and Diane Webb. The Webbs attended OBF when we first began. They were members of IV but joined Cru staff. Joe served with Cru at Boston U. and became the director of Cru in New England. He then became the director of the Here's Life campaign in Europe, which involved fifty thousand Bible study groups. After returning to the States, he formed a missions consulting organization, Global Village. Joe earned the MA in Missiology from Fuller Theological Seminary and then became the school's vice president for Advancement. He is the president of Joe B Webb and Associates, an organization that counsels non-governmental organizations.

Tom Weiner. Tom, a grad of the U. of Texas, served with the Navs at Miami. He had studied Japanese and hoped to serve in Japan. Instead he became the director of the Navs at the U. of Hawaii, a chapter that was started by Greg and Emily Bryan, Navs from Miami. He has taken students from Hawaii to Japan on mission trips.

Barrett and Audrey Wells. Barrett and his wife Audrey were active with the Navs. Back when Miami's football team was known as the "Redskins" rather than the "Redhawks," Barrett played the role of the Indian mascot. Barrett graduated *magna cum laude* with a BA in Applied Sciences. He served as a quality control engineer with many firms including Honeywell Aerospace and Space Avionics. While working in Romania, Barrett and Audrey served as "tent missionaries." He is active at Grace Chapel in West Liberty and with the Gideons.

Ellen (Wheeler) and Bob Hargraves. Ellen was active in IV. She met and married Bob Hargraves, a former submarine sailor. They then served for eighteen years under the Africa Inland Mission as agricultural missionaries in Kenya. In 2003, they relocated in Fort Myers, Florida, where they have worked with ECHO, an organization that promotes sustainable farming throughout the world. They have returned frequently to Kenya.

Tolivar Wills. Tolivar, a grad of Wittenberg U., served with AIA at Miami. After graduating from GCTS, Tolivar, who is Black, served as an assistant pastor at a Presbyterian Church in New Haven, establishing a church in the poor Black neighborhood of New Haven. He is now the lead pastor of Ponce Presbyterian Church in Atlanta.

Robert Winn. Bob was a grad of Cedarville U. who earned his MA in Ancient History. He then earned his PhD in Early Church History at the Catholic U. of America, specializing in ancient Armenian texts. Bob is the chair of the History Department of Northwestern C. in Iowa. He is the author of *Eusebius of Emesa* and *Christianity in the Roman Empire*.

Rich Zeigler. Rich was active with IV. He is on the staff of IV's Graduate & Faculty Ministries, reaching out to international graduate students at Vanderbilt U. In 2012 Vanderbilt "derecognized" IV and other religious groups, denying them access to campus buildings. Despite this, IV and other groups are still flourishing. The largest is the Asian American Christian Fellowship affiliated with IV.

Richard Zimmerman. Rick, who was active with Cru, graduated with a BS.in Chemistry. He received his MD from OSU and also received the MPH (Master of Public Health) in Epidemiology from the U. of Minnesota. He earned the MA in Bioethics from Trinity International University. He has authored more than 175 papers on immunization and on vaccine preventable diseases and is a professor in the Department of Family Medicine at the University of Pittsburgh Medical School. He is the vice chairman for Preventative Medicine Research. He has served on the CDC's Advisory Committee on Immunization Practices. He also serves as the chairman of the board of the international student ministry in Pittsburgh.

Excursus U

List of Publications

BOOKS:

1. ***Composition and Corroboration in Classical and Biblical Studies.*** (An International Library of Philosophy and Theology.) Philadelphia: PA Presbyterian and Reformed Pub., 1966.

2. ***Greece and Babylon: Early Contacts between the Aegean and the Near East.*** (Baker Studies in Biblical Archaeology.) Grand Rapids, MI: Baker Book House, 1967.

3. ***Mandaic Incantation Texts.*** (American Oriental Series.) New Haven, CT: American Oriental Society, 1967.

    Reprint Edition: Piscataway, NJ: Gorgias Press, 2005.

4. ***Gnostic Ethics and Mandaean Origins.*** (Harvard Theological Studies.) Cambridge, MA: Harvard University Press, 1970.

    a. British Edition: London, UK: Oxford University Press, 1970.

    b. Reprint Edition: Piscataway, NJ: Gorgias Press, 2004.

5. ***The Stones and the Scriptures.*** (Evangelical Perspectives.) Philadelphia, PA: J. B. Lippincott, 1972.

    a. British Edition: London, UK: InterVarsity Press, 1973.

b. Spanish Edition: *Las Excavaciones y las Escrituras.* El Paso, TX: Casa Bautista, 1977.

c. Reprint Edition: Grand Rapids, MI: Baker Book House, 1981.

6. *Pre-Christian Gnosticism.* London, UK: Tyndale Press, 1973.

   a. US Edition: Grand Rapids, MI: Wm. B. Eerdmans Pub., 1973.

   b. Second Edition: Grand Rapids, MI: Baker Book House, 1983.

   c. Reprint Edition: Eugene, OR: Wipf & Stock, 2003.

7. With D. J. Wiseman. *Archaeology and the Bible.* (Contemporary Evangelical Perspectives.) Grand Rapids, MI: Zondervan, 1979.

   a. British Edition: London/Glasgow, UK: Pickering & Inglis, 1980.

   b. Japanese Edition: *Seisho to Kokogaku.* Tokyo, Japan: Inochi no Kotoba, 1985.

8. *The Archaeology of New Testament Cities in Western Asia Minor.* Grand Rapids, MI: Baker Book House, 1980.

   a. British Edition: London, UK: Pickering & Inglis, 1980.

   b. *New Testament Cities in Western Asia Minor.* Grand Rapids, MI Baker Book House, 1987.

   c. Paperback Edition: Grand Rapids, MI: Baker Book House, 1998

   d. Korean Edition: *Ich'ŏjin ttang.* Korea: Ch'o P'an, Seoul, Korea: Christian Literature Crusade, 1998.

   e. Reprint Edition: Eugene, OR: Wipf and Stock, 2003.

   f. Japanese Edition: *Sho-Ajia no Kodai Toshi.* Tokyo, Japan: Shinkyo Shuppansha, 2010.

9. *The Scriptures and Archaeology.* (Bueermann-Champion Lectures.) Portland, OR: Western Conservative Baptist Seminary, 1980.

   Reprint Edition: Eugene, OR: Wipf and Stock, 2013.

10. *The World of the First Christians.* Tring, UK: Lion Pub., 1981.

    a. British Paperback Edition: Tring, UK: Lion Pub., 1982.

    b. Canadian Edition: Toronto, Canada: Fitzhenry & Whiteside, 1981.

    c. Australian Edition: Sutherland, Australia: Albatross Books, 1981.

d. US Edition: *Harper's World of the New Testament.* San Francisco, CA: Harper & Row, 1981.

e. Norwegian Edition: *De Forste Kristnes Verden.* Oslo, Norway: Lunde Forlag og Bokhandel, 1981.

f. Swedish Edition: *De första Kristnas värld.* Örebro, Sweden: Svensk Bokförlaget Libris, 1981.

g. German Edition: *Die Welt der ersten Christen.* Wuppertal, Germany: R. Brockhaus Verlag, 1981.

h. Dutch Edition: *De wereld van de eerste christenen.* The Hague, Netherlands: J. N. Voorhoeve, 1981.

i. Finnish Edition: *Ensimmäisten kristittyjen masilma.* Vantaa, Finland: Raamatun Tietokirja, 1983.

j. Italian Edition: *Il mondo dei primi cristiani.* Torino, Italy: Claudiana, 1983.

k. Croatian Edition: *Svijet Prvih Kršcana.* Zagreb, Croatia: Duhovna Stvarnost, 1985.

l. Spanish Edition: *El mundo de los primeros cristianos.* Mexico City, Mexico: Editorial Trillas, 1985.

11. *Foes from the Northern Frontier.* (Baker Studies in Biblical Archaeology.) Grand Rapids, MI: Baker Book House, 1982.

    Reprint Edition: Eugene, OR: Wipf and Stock Publishers, 2003.

12. Co-editor with Jerry Vardaman. *Christos, Chronos, and Kairos: Nativity and Chronological Studies Presented to Jack Finegan.* Winona Lake, IN: Eisenbrauns, 1989.

13. *Persia and the Bible.* Grand Rapids, MI: Baker Book House, 1990.

    a. Paperback edition, 1997.

    b. Korean Edition: *Paereushiah wa Songyong.* Seoul, Korea: Christian Literature Crusade, 2010.

    c. Farsi Edition: *Iran va Adiān bāstāni.* Tehran, Iran: Qoqnoos, 2011.

14. Co-author with R. Clouse and R. Pierard. *The Two Kingdoms: The Church and Culture throughout the Ages.* Chicago, IL: Moody Press, 1993.

a. ***The Story of the Church.*** Chicago, IL: Moody Press, 2002. An abridged illustrated version.

   b. Portuguese Edition: ***Dois Reinas.*** São Paulo, Brazil, Brazil: Editora Cultura Cristã, 2003.

15. Co-editor with G. Mattingly and A. Hoerth. ***Peoples of the Old Testament World.*** Grand Rapids, MI: Baker Book House, 1994.

    a. Recognized as one of the two "Best Popular Books on Archaeology" published in 1993–1994 by the *Biblical Archaeology Review*.

    b. British Edition: Cambridge. UK: Lutterworth Press, 1998.

    c. Paperback Edition: Grand Rapids, MI: Baker Book House, 1998.

    d. Korean Edition: ***Godae Keundong Munhwa: B.C. 3,000 nyunkyung-B.C. 323.*** Seoul, Korea: Christian Literature Crusade, 2012. Korea Christian Best Book Award, 2013.

16. Editor, ***Africa and Africans in Antiquity.*** East Lansing, MI: Michigan State University Press, 2001.

17. ***Africa and the Bible.*** Grand Rapids, MI: Baker Book House, 2004. In 2005 cited by *Christianity Today* as the best book on the Bible.

18. Co-edited with Marvin R. Wilson, ***Dictionary of Daily Life in Biblical and Post-Biblical Antiquity I: A–Da.*** Peabody, MA: Hendrickson, 2014.

19. Co-edited with Marvin R. Wilson, ***Dictionary of Daily Life in Biblical and Post-Biblical Antiquity II: De–H.*** Peabody, MA: Hendrickson, 2015.

20. Co-edited with Marvin R. Wilson, ***Dictionary of Daily Life in Biblical and Post-Biblical Antiquity III: I–N.*** Peabody, MA: Hendrickson, 2016.

21. Co-edited with Marvin R. Wilson, ***Dictionary of Daily Life in Biblical and Post-Biblical Antiquity IV: O–Z.*** Peabody, MA: Hendrickson, 2016

22. Co-edited with Marvin R. Wilson, ***Dictionary of Daily Life in Biblical and Post-Biblical Antiquity: Complete in One Volume, A–Z.*** Peabody, MA: Hendrickson, 2017

EXCURSUS U: LIST OF PUBLICATIONS

CHAPTERS:

1. "The Greek Words in Daniel in the Light of Greek Influence in the Near East," *New Perspectives on the Old Testament*, ed. J. B. Payne. Waco, TX: Word Books, 1970. Pp. 170–200.

2. "Cultic Prostitution—A Case Study in Cultural Diffusion," *Orient and Occident* (Cyrus H. Gordon Festschrift), ed. H. Hoffner. (Alter Orient und Altes Testament.) Kevelaer, Germany: Butzon und Bercker, 1973. Pp. 213–22.

3. "The Archaeological Confirmation of Suspect Elements in the Classical and the Biblical Traditions." *The Law and the Prophets* (O. T. Allis Festschrift), ed. J. Skilton et al. Nutley, NJ: Presbyterian & Reformed Pub., 1974. Pp. 54–70.

4. "Some Alleged Evidences for Pre-Christian Gnosticism," *New Dimensions in New Testament Studies*, ed. R. N. Longenecker and M. Tenney. Grand Rapids. MI: Zondervan, 1975. Pp. 46–70.

5. "Concord, Conflict, and Community," *Evangelicals and Jews in Conversation on Scripture, Theology, and History*, ed. M. H. Tanenbaum, M. R. Wilson, & A. J. Rudin. Grand Rapids, MI: Baker Book House, 1978. Pp. 154–96.

6. "*The Apocalypse of Adam*, Mithraism and Pre-Christian Gnosticism," *Études Mithriaques, Textes et Mémoires*, ed. J. Duchesne-Guillemin. (Acta Iranica.) Teheran, Iran-Liège, Belgium: Bibliothèque Pahlavi, 1978. IV, pp. 537–63.

7. "Two Reformers Compared: Solon of Athens and Nehemiah of Jerusalem," *The Bible World: Essays in Honor of Cyrus H. Gordon*, ed. G. Rendsburg, Ruth Adler, Milton Arfa, and Nathan H. Winter. New York, NY: KTAV, 1980. Pp. 269–92.

8. "Jewish Gnosticism? The Prologue of John, Mandaean Parallels, and the Trimorphic Protennoia," *Studies in Gnosticism and Hellenistic Religions* (Gilles Quispel Festschrift), ed. R. Van Den Broek and M. J. Vermaseren. Leiden, Netherlands: E. J. Brill, 1981. Pp. 467–97.

9. "Nehemiah, A Model Leader," *A Spectrum of Thought: Essays in Honor of Dennis F. Kinlaw*, ed. Michael L. Peterson. Wilmore, KY: Francis Asbury Pub., 1982. Pp. 171–80.

10. "Ramsay's Views on Archaeology in Asia Minor Reviewed," *The New Testament Student and His Field*, ed. J. H. Skilton and C. A. Ladley. Phillipsburg, NJ: Presbyterian and Reformed Pub., 1982. Pp. 27–40.

11. "Babylon," *Major Cities of the Biblical World*, ed. R. K. Harrison. Nashville, TN: Thomas Nelson, 1985. Pp. 32–48.

12. "Post-Biblical Traditions about Ezra and Nehemiah," *A Tribute to Gleason Archer*, ed. W. Kaiser and R. Youngblood. Chicago, IL: Moody Press. 1986. Pp. 167–76.

13. "Magic or Miracle? Demons, Diseases and Exorcisms," *The Miracles of Jesus*, ed. D. Wenham and C. Blomberg. (Gospel Perspectives VI.) Sheffield, UK: JSOT Press, 1986. Pp. 89–183.

    Italian Version: "Magia o Miracolo? Malattie, Demoni ed Esorcismi," *Studi di Teologia* 11 (1988) 53–144.

14. "The Magi Episode," *Christos, Chronos, and Kairos: Nativity and Chronological studies Presented to Jack Finegan*, ed. Jerry Vardaman and Edwin M. Yamauchi. Winona Lake, IN: Eisenbrauns, 1989. Pp. 15–39.

15. "Archaeology and the Gospels: Discoveries and Publications of the Past Decade (1977–1987)," *The Gospels Today*, ed. J. H. Skilton. Philadelphia, PA: Skilton House, 1990. Pp. 1–12.

16. "Persians," *Peoples of the Old Testament*, ed. A. Hoerth, G. Mattingly and E. Yamauchi. Grand Rapids, MI: Baker Book House, 1994. Pp. 107–24.

17. "The Present Status of Old Testament Historiography," *Faith, Tradition, and History: Old Testament Historiography in Its Near Eastern Context*, ed. D. Baker, J. Hoffmeier, and A. Millard. Winona Lake, IN: Eisenbrauns, 1994. Pp. 1–36.

18. "Jesus outside the New Testament: What Is the Evidence?" *Jesus under Fire*, ed. M. J. Wilkins and J. P. Moreland. Grand Rapids, MI: Zondervan, 1995. Pp. 207–29

19. "Gnosticism and Early Christianity," *Hellenization Revisited*, ed. W. Helleman. Lanham, MD: University Press of America, 1994. Pp. 29–61

EXCURSUS U: LIST OF PUBLICATIONS

20. "The Archaeological Background of Daniel," *Vital Old Testament Issues*, ed. Roy B. Zuck. Grand Rapids, MI: Kregel, 1996. Pp. 160–70.

21. "Cambyses in Egypt," *Go to the Land I Will Show You: Studies in Honor of Dwight W. Young*, ed. J. Coleson and V. H. Matthews. Winona Lake, IN: Eisenbrauns, 1996. Pp. 371–92.

22. "The Issue of Pre-Christian Gnosticism Reviewed in the Light of the Nag Hammadi Texts," *The Nag Hammadi Library after Fifty Years*, ed. John Turner and Anne McGuire. Leiden, Netherlands: Brill, 1997. Pp. 72–88.

23. "Greece and Babylon Revisited," *To Understand the Scriptures: Essays in Honor of William H. Shea*, ed. David Merling. Berrien Springs, MI: Institute of Archaeology/Horn Archaeological Museum, 1997. Pp. 127–35.

24. "Herodotus--Historian or Liar," *Crossing Boundaries and Linking Horizons: Studies in Honor of Michael C. Astour*, ed. G. D. Young, M. W. Chavalas, and R. E. Averbeck. Bethesda, MD: CDL Press, 1997. Pp. 599–614.

25. "Life, Death, and the Afterlife in the Ancient Near East," *Life in the Face of Death: The Resurrection Message of the New Testament*, ed. by R. N. Longenecker. Grand Rapids, MI: Eerdmans, 1998. Pp. 21–50.

26. "An Ancient Historian's View of Christianity," *Professors Who Believe: The Spiritual Journeys of Christian Faculty*, ed. Paul M. Anderson. Downers Grove, IL: InterVarsity Press, 1998. Pp. 192–99.

27. "The Romans and Meroe in Nubia," *Itali-Africa: Bridging Continents and Cultures*, ed. Sante Matteo. Stony Brook, NY: Forum Italicum Publishing, 2001. Pp. 38–46.

28. "The Eastern Jewish Diaspora under the Babylonians," *Mesopotamia and the Bible*, ed. M. W. Chavalas and K. L. Younger, Jr. Grand Rapids, MI: Baker Academic, 2002. Pp. 356–77.

29. "Athletics in the Ancient Near East," *Daily Life in the Ancient Near East*, ed. R. Averbeck, M. Chavalas, and D. Weisberg. Bethesda, MD: CDL Press, 2003. Pp. 491–500.

30. "Exilic and Post-Exilic Period: Current Developments," *Giving the Sense: Understanding and Using Old Testament Historical Texts*

(Eugene H. Merrill Festschrift), ed. by D. M. Howard, Jr., and M. A. Grisanti. Grand Rapids. MI: Kregel, 2003. Pp. 201–14.

31. "Homer and Archaeology: Minimalists and Maximalists in Classical Context," *The Future of Biblical Archaeology*, ed. J. K. Hoffmeier and A. R. Millard. Grand Rapids, MI: Eerdmans, 2004. Pp. 69–90.

32. "Elchasaites, Manichaeans and Mandaeans in the Light of the Cologne Mani Codex," *Beyond the Jordan: Studies in Honor of W. Harold Mare*, ed. Glenn A. Carnagey, Sr. Eugene, OR: Wipf and Stock, 2005. Pp. 49–60.

33. "Why the Ethiopian Eunuch Was Not from Ethiopia," *Interpreting the New Testament Text: An Introduction to the Art and Science of Exegesis* (Harold W. Hoehner Festschrift), ed. B. Fanning and D. Bock. Wheaton, IL: Crossway Books, 2006. Pp. 351–366.

34. "Did Persian Zoroastrianism Influence Judaism?" *Israel: Ancient Kingdom or Late Invention?*, ed. Daniel I. Block. Nashville, TN: B & H Academic, 2008. Pp. 282–297.

35. "The Reconstruction of Jewish Communities During the Persian Empire," *Tough-Minded Christianity: Honoring the Legacy of John W. Montgomery*, ed; William Dembski and Thomas Shirrmacher. Nashville, TN: B & H Academic, 2008. Pp. 350–374.

36. "A Model Leader: Leadership in Nehemiah," in *Biblical Leadership: Theology for the Everyday Leader*, ed. Benjamin R. Forrest and Chet Roden. Grand Rapids, MI: Kregel Academic, 2017. Pp. 266–76.

37. "Did Christianity Copy Earlier Pagan Resurrection Stories?" *The Harvest Handbook of Apologetics*, ed. Joseph M. Holden. Eugene, OR: Harvest House, 2018. Pp. 149–156.

38. "In Praise of a Venerable Scribe, A Bibliographic Tribute to Alan R. Millard," *Write That They May Read: Studies in Literacy and Textualization in the Ancient Near East and in the Hebrew Scriptures: Essays in Honour of Alan R. Millard*, ed. Daniel I. Block, David C. Deuel, Paul J.N. Lawrence, and C. John Collins. Eugene, OR: Wipf and Stock, 2020. Pp. 395–417.

39. "The Philistine Giant Goliath," *The Legacy and Current State of Japanese Hebrew Bible and Ancient Near Eastern Studies: Essays*

in Honor of David Toshio Tsumura, ed. Kaz Hayashi and Masashi Tamura. Louvain, Belgium: Peeters, forthcoming.

ARTICLES IN REFERENCE WORKS:

1. "Descent of Ishtar," ***The Biblical World: A Dictionary of Biblical Archaeology***, ed. by C. Pfeiffer. Grand Rapids, MI: Baker Book House, 1966. Pp. 196–200.

2. "Culture," ***Baker's Dictionary of Christian Ethics***, ed. by C. F. H. Henry. Grand Rapids, MI: Baker Book House, 1973. Pp. 158–59.

3. "Gnosticism," ***The New International Dictionary of the Christian Church***, ed. by J. D. Douglas. Grand Rapids, MI: Zondervan Pub., 1974. Pp. 416–18.

4. "Darius the Persian" p. 425, "Dead Sea Scrolls" pp. 434–42, "Education" pp. 493–97, "Machaerus" p. 1064, "Nabonidus" pp. 1170–71, "Nebuzaradan" p. 1191, "Nergal-sharezer" p. 1198, "Palestine" pp. 1259–73, "Patriarchal Age" pp. 1287–91, "Rabsaris" p. 1437, "Rezin" p. 1468, "Solomon, Song of" pp. 1608–10, "Tatnai" p. 1663, "Theudas" p. 1699, "Tammuz" p. 707, ***Wycliffe Bible Encyclopedia***, ed. by C. F. Pfeiffer, H. F. Vos and J. Rea. Chicago, IL: Moody Press, 1975.

5. "Fertility Cults," ***The Zondervan Pictorial Encyclopedia of the Bible***, ed. by M. C. Tenney. Grand Rapids, MI: Zondervan Pub., 1974. II, pp. 531–532.

6. "Hermetic Literature" p. 408, "Mandaeism" p. 563, ***Supplementary Volume, The Interpreter's Dictionary of the Bible***, ed. by V. Furnish et al. Nashville, TN: Abingdon Press, 1976.

7. "The Religion of the Romans" pp. 46–47, "Manichaeans" pp. 48–49, "The Gnostics" pp. 98–100, ***Eerdmans' Handbook to the History of Christianity***, ed. by T. Dowley. Grand Rapids, MI: Wm. B. Eerdmans, 1977.

8. "Archaeology and the New Testament," ***The Expositor's Bible Commentary***, ed. by F. E. Gaebelein. Grand Rapids, MI: Zondervan Pub., 1979. I, pp. 645–69.

9. "Agrapha" pp. 69–71, "Apocryphal Gospels" pp. 181–88, "Archaeology of Palestine and Syria" pp. 270–82, ***The International Standard***

EXCURSUS U: LIST OF PUBLICATIONS

Bible Encyclopedia, Vol. I, ed. by G. W. Bromiley. Rev. edition; Grand Rapids, MI: Wm. B. Eerdmans, 1979.

10. "Prostitution," *The Illustrated Bible Dictionary*, ed. by N. Hillyer. Leicester, UK: Inter-Varsity Press, 1980. Vol. III, p. 1289.

11. Forty entries discussing 75 Hebrew words, *Theological Wordbook of the Old Testament*, ed. by R. L. Harris, G. L. Archer & B. K. Waltke. Chicago, IL: Moody Press, 1981. Pp. 158, 261, 263–70, 274–76, 282, 284–86, 302–04, 310, 314–21, 332–33, 343–45, 349–51, 381, 401–03, 828–29.

12. "The Gnostics," "The Mandaeans" p. 110, "The Manichaeans" p. 113, *The World's Religions*, ed. by R. P. Beaver et al. Tring, UK: Lion Pub., 1982.

13. "Prostitution," *New Bible Dictionary*, ed. by J. Douglas and N. Hillyer. Rev. edition; Leicester, UK: InterVarsity Press, 1982. P. 988.

14. "Aramaic" pp. 38–41, "Archaeology in Israel and Jordan Since 1948" pp. 60–66, "Bactria" pp. 87–90, "Chaldea, Chaldeans" pp. 123–25, "Cyrus" pp. 145–46, "Darius" pp. 149–53, "Ecbatana" pp. 167–68, "Ekron" p. 173, "Etana" p. 187, "Evil-Merodach" p. 188, "Habiru" pp. 223–24, "Jebusites" pp. 256–57, "Joppa" pp. 271–73, "Kassites" pp. 276–78, "Marriage" pp. 300–02, "Medes" pp. 304–06, "Nabopolassar" pp. 326–27, "Nebuchadnezzar" pp. 332–34, "Nippur" pp. 339–41, "Oaths" pp. 343–44, "Pasargadae" pp. 354–56, "Patara" pp. 356–57, "Prostitution, Cultic" pp. 369–71, "Qarqar" pp. 375–77, "Qumran New Testament Fragments" pp. 379–81, "Shinar" p. 411, "Shishak" pp. 412–13, "Solomon" pp. 419–22, "Susa" pp. 426–30, "Tell Arpachiyah" p. 438, "Tell Nagila" p. 442, Tell Qasile" pp. 442–43, "Tell Sheikh Ahmed el-'Areini" p. 443, "Tepe Gawra" pp. 446–47, "Tepe Sialk" p. 447, "Tiglath-Pileser" pp. 451–53, "Ummah" p. 461, "Urartu" pp. 463–65, "Vultures, Stele of" pp. 469–70, "Zarephath" p. 433, "Ziusudra" p. 485, *The New International Dictionary of Biblical Archaeology*, ed. by E. M. Blaiklock and R. K. Harrison. Grand Rapids, MI: Zondervan, 1983.

15. "Jerusalem," *Young's Bible Dictionary*, ed. by G. Douglas Young. Wheaton, IL: Tyndale House, 1984. Pp. 333–40.

EXCURSUS U: LIST OF PUBLICATIONS

16. "Notes on Ezra, Nehemiah, Esther," *The NIV Study Bible*, ed. by Kenneth Barker. Grand Rapids, IL: Zondervan Pub., 1985. Pp. 670–730.

17. "Logia" pp. 152–54, "Meremoth" p. 324, "Nabonidus" pp. 468–70, "Obelisk" pp. 577–78, "Palace" pp. 629–32, "Parbar" p. 662, "Perseus" pp. 775–76, "Pyramid" p. 1060, *The International Standard Bible Encyclopedia, III*, ed. by G.W. Bromiley. Grand Rapids, IL: Eerdmans, 1986.

18. "Religions of the Biblical World: Persia," *The International Standard Bible Encyclopedia*, ed. by G. W. Bromiley. Grand Rapids, MI: Eerdmans, 1988. IV, pp. 123–29.

19. "Gnosticism" pp. 272–74, "History-of-Religions School" pp. 308–309, "Zoroastrianism and Christianity" pp. 735–36, *New Dictionary of Christian Theology*, ed. by S. B. Ferguson and D. F. Wright. Leicester, UK: InterVarsity Press, 1988.

20. "Ignatius of Antioch" pp. 35–38, "Justin Martyr" pp. 39–42, *Great Leaders of the Christian Church*, ed. by J. D. Woodbridge. Chicago, IL: Moody Press, 1988.

21. "Archaeology," *Baker Encyclopedia of the Bible*, ed. by W. A. Elwell. Grand Rapids, IL: Baker Book House, 1988. I, pp. 148–56.

22. "Ezra, Nehemiah," *The Expositor's Bible Commentary*, ed. F. E. Gaebelein Grand Rapids, IL: Zondervan, 1988. IV, pp. 563–771

23. "Jews in the New Testament" pp. 794–95, "Library" pp. 879–91, and "Nineveh" pp. 1024–25, *Layman's Bible Dictionary*, ed. by T. Butler. Nashville, TN: Holman, 1991.

24. "Synagogue," *Dictionary of Jesus and the Gospels*, ed. by J. B. Green, S. McKnight & I. H. Marshall. Downers Grove, IL: InterVarsity Press, 1992. Pp. 781–84.

25. "Ahasuerus" I, p. 105, "Assos" I, p. 503, "Astyages" I, pp. 507–08, "Herodotus" III, pp. 180–81, "Myra" IV, pp. 939–40, "Troas" VI, pp. 666–67, and "Tyrannos" VI, p. 686, *The Anchor Bible Dictionary*, ed. by D. N. Freedman. Nashville, TN: Abingdon, 1992.

26. "Archaeology and the Bible," *The Oxford Companion to the Bible*, ed. by B. M. Metzger & M. D. Coogan. New York, NY: Oxford University, 1993. Pp. 46–54.

27. "Gnosticism" pp. 350–54, "Hellenism" pp. 383–88, *Dictionary of Paul and His Letters*, ed. by G. Hawthorne & R. Martin. Downers Grove, IL: InterVarsity Press, 1993.

28. "Pergamum Library," *Encyclopedia of Library History*, ed. by W. A. Wiegand and D. G. Davis. New York, NY: Garland Pub., 1994. Pp. 491–92.

29. "Nebuchadnezzar" pp. 132–35, "Cyrus" pp. 136–40, "Darius" pp. 455–59, "Xerxes" pp. 702–06, *World Leaders Edition I*, ed. by A. Commire. Waterford, CT: Gale Research, 1994.

30. "Ezra and Nehemiah," *Zondervan NIV Bible Commentary I: Old Testament*, ed. by K. L. Barker and J. Kohlenberger III. Grand Rapids, MI: Zondervan, 1994. Pp. 680–725.

31. "yehûdî" II, pp. 415–17, "yḥṣ" II, pp. 437–39, "Cyrus" IV, pp. 493–95, *New International Dictionary of Old Testament Theology and Exegesis*, ed. by Willem A. VanGemeren. Grand Rapids, MI: Zondervan, 1997.

32. "Herodotus" pp. 528–29, "Josephus" pp. 627–28 in *Encyclopedia of Historians and Historical Writing*, ed. by Kelly Boyd. London, UK & Chicago, IL: Fitzroy Dearborn, 1999.

33. "Gnosticism" pp. 414–18, and (with B. Chilton), "Synagogues" pp. 1145–53, in *Dictionary of New Testament Background*, ed. by C. A. Evans and S. E. Porter. Downers Grove, IL: InterVarsity Press, 2000.

34. "Achaemenian Dynasty" I, pp. 183–85, "Astyages" I, p. 306, "Cyaxares" II, p. 452, "Kassites" II, pp. 702–03, "Manichaeanism" II, pp. 759–60, "Zurvanism" III, pp. 1171–72, *Encyclopedia of the Ancient World*, ed. by T. J. Sienkewicz. Pasadena, CA: Salem Press, 2002.

35. "Gnosticism" pp. 406–10, "Synagogues" pp. 1049–52, in *The IVP Dictionary of the New Testament*, ed. by D. G. Reid. Downers Grove, IL: InterVarsity Press, 2004.

36. "Ezra and Nehemiah, Books of," in *Dictionary of the Old Testament: Historical Books*, ed. by Bill T. Arnold and H. G. M. Williamson. Downers Grove, IL: InterVarsity Press, 2005. Pp. 284–95.

37. "Josephus," in *New Dictionary of Christian Apologetics*, ed. by Campbell Campbell-Jack and Gavin J. McGrath. Leicester, UK: InterVarsity Press, 2006. Pp. 373–74.

38. "Magic, Sorcery," in *The Encyclopedia of the Historical Jesus*, ed. Craig Evans. London, UK: Routledge, 2008. Pp. 383–84.

39. "Susa," "Vashti," in *Dictionary of the Old Testament: Wisdom, Poetry & Writings*, ed. Tremper Longman III and Peter Enns. Downers Grove, IL: IVP Academic, 2008. Pp. 781–83, 825–28.

40. "Ezra and Nehemiah," in *Zondervan Illustrated Bible Backgrounds Commentary*, ed. John H. Walton. Grand Rapids, MI: Zondervan, 2009. III, pp. 394–467.

41. "Ezra and Nehemiah," in *The Expositor's Bible Commentary*, Revised Edition, ed. Tremper Longman III and David E. Garland. Grand Rapids, MI: Zondervan, 2010. IV, pp, 337–568.

42. "Notes on Ezra and Nehemiah" in *NIV Cultural Backgrounds Bible*, ed. J. Walton and C. Keener. Grand Rapids. MI: Zondervan, 2016. Pp, 762–98.

43. "Notes on Ezra and Nehemiah" in *NKJC Cultural Backgrounds Bible*, ed. J. Walton and C. Keener, Grand Rapids, MI: Zondervan, 2017. Pp,790–827.

44. "Abortion" pp. 7–10; "Adultery" pp. 18–26; "Age & the Aged" pp. 27–35; "Agriculture"*[1] pp. 36–42; "Alcoholic Beverages" pp. 43–52; "Animal Husbandry"* pp. 53–59; "Aphrodisiacs & Erotic Spells" pp. 60–66; "Aqueducts & Water Supply" pp. 67–74; "Archives" pp. 75–81; "Art"* pp. 91–99; "Athletics" pp. 109–117; "Banquets"* pp. 127–135; "Calendars" pp. 236–252; "Celibacy" pp. 253–261; "Census"* pp. 262–271; "Ceramics & Pottery"* pp. 272–279; "Childbirth & Children"* pp. 280–289; "Cities"* pp. 290–305; "Citizens & Aliens" pp. 306–321; "Clothing"* pp. 322–336; "Communications & Messengers" pp. 337–357; "Contraception & Control of Births" pp. 358–366; "Cosmetics"* pp. 367–373; "Demons" pp. 410–427; "Dentistry & Teeth" pp. 428–446; "Diseases & Plagues"* pp. 447–468; "Divination & Sortition" pp. 469–496; "Divorce" pp. 497–518; "Dogs" pp. 519–535; "Drama & Theaters" pp. 547–572; "Dreams" pp. 573–598; "Education"[2] pp. 632–668; "Eunuchs" pp.

---

1. * = co-authored articles with the late R. K. Harrison (d. 1993). I updated his bibliographies and added sections to his articles on the Ancient Near Eastern World, Greco-Roman World, Jewish World and Christian World.

2. Marvin R. Wilson wrote the sections on the Old Testament, New Testament, and the Jewish World; I wrote the sections on the Near Eastern World, Greco-Roman World, and Christian World.

669–677; "Food Consumption"* pp. 688–713; "Food Production"* pp. 714–733; "Horses" pp. 817–824; "Human Sacrifice" pp. 825–848; "Infanticide & Exposure" pp. 865–875; "Insects" pp. 886–904; "Laundry & Fullers"* pp. 959–970; "Libraries & Books" pp. 1001–1053; "Marriage" pp. 1065–1093; "Medicine & Physicians"* pp. 1094–1117; "Milk & Milk Products"[3] pp. 1193–1207; "Mourning & Weeping"[4] pp. 1232–1261; "Nursing & Wet Nurses"[5] 1303–1328; "Palaces" pp. 1342–1364; "Sanitation" pp. 1477–1504; "Taxation"* pp. 1550–1560; "Textiles"* pp. 1561–1577; "Wild Animals & Hunting" pp. 1761–1786, in *Dictionary of Daily Life in Biblical and Post-Biblical Antiquity*, ed. Edwin M. Yamauchi and Marvin R. Wilson. Peabody, MA: Hendrickson, 2017. (note: *=co-authored articles)

Abbreviations

AHR	*American Historical Review*
Arc	*Archaeology*
BA	*Biblical Archaeology*
BAR	*Biblical Archaeology Reviw*
BETS	*Bulletin of the Evangelical Theological Society*
BSac	*Bibliotheca Sacra*
CSR	*Christian Scholars Review*
CT	*Christianity Today*
FH	*Fides et Historia*
JAOS	*Journal of the American Oriental Society*
JASA	*Journal of the American Scientific Affiliation*
JECS	*Journal of Early Christian Studies*

---

3. Marvin R. Wilson wrote the sections on the Old Testament, New Testament, and the Jewish World; I wrote the sections on the Near Eastern World, Greco-Roman World, and Christian World.

4. Marvin R. Wilson wrote the sections on the Old Testament, New Testament, and the Jewish World; I wrote the sections on the Near Eastern World, Greco-Roman World, and Christian World.

5. Craig S. Keener wrote the sections on the Old Testament and the New Testament; I wrote the sections on the Near Eastern World, Greco-Roman World, Jewish World, and Christian World

JETS	Journal of the Evangelical Theological Society
JLH	Journal of Library History
NEASB	Near Eastern Archaeological Socirty Bulletin
SecCen	Second Century
Then	Themelios
TSFB	Theological Students Fellowship Bulletin
TynBul	Tyndale Bulletin
WTJ	Westminster Theological Journal

ARTICLES IN JOURNALS:

1. "Cultic Clues in Canticles?" *BETS* 4 (1961) 80–88.
2. "The Sapiential Septuagint," *BETS* 5 (1962) 109–15.
3. "Qumran and Colosse," *BSac* 121 (1964) 141–52.
4. "Tammuz and the Bible," *Journal of Biblical Literature* 81 (1965) 283–90.
5. "Abraham and Mesopotamia," *The Way* (June 1965) 1–5.
6. "Joseph in Egypt," *The Way* (Sept. 1965) 28–36.
7. "Aramaic Magic Bowls," *JAOS* 85 (1965) 511–23.
8. "Do the Bible's Critics Use a Double Standard?" *CT* 10 (Nov. 19, 1965) 179–82.

    8a. Reprinted in: *Focus* 2 (1969) 21–27.

9. "The Daily Bread Motif in Antiquity," *WTJ* 28 (1966) 145–56.
10. "The Present Status of Mandaean Studies," *Journal of Near Eastern Studies* 25 (1966) 88–96.
11. "Additional Notes on Tammuz," *Journal of Semitic Studies* 11 (1966) 10–15.
12. "Slaves of God," *BETS* 9 (1966) 31–49.
13. "The Teacher of Righteousness from Qumran and Jesus of Nazareth," *CT* 10 (May 13, 1966) 816–18.

    13a. Spanish version, "Cristo y los Essenios," in **Quién es Cristo hoy?** Buenos Aires, Argentina: Ediciones Certeza, 1970. Pp. 35–48.

14. "Anthropomorphism in Ancient Religions," *BSac* 125 (1968) 29–44.
15. "A Mandaic Magic Bowl from the Yale Babylonian Collection," *Berytus* 17 (1967) 49–63.
16. "Stones, Scripts, and Scholars," *CT* 13 (Feb. 14, 1969), 432–34, 436–37.
17. "Anthropomorphism in Hellenism and in Judaism," *BSac* 127 (1970) 212–20.
18. "The Gnostics and History," *JETS* 14 (1971) 29–40.
19. "Historical Notes on the Trial and Crucifixion of Jesus Christ," *CT* 15 (Apr. 9, 1971) 6–11.
20. "Historical Notes on the (In)comparable Christ," *CT* 16 (Oct. 22, 1971) 7–11.

    20a. Revised and expanded as a pamphlet: ***Jesus, Zoroaster, Buddha, Socrates, Muhammad***. Downers Grove. IL: InterVarsity Press, 1972.

    20b. Revised and reprinted as: ***What's so Special about Jesus?*** Richmond, Vancouver, Canada: Digory Designs, 1999.

21. "Christianity and Cultural Differences," *CT* 16 (June 23, 1972) 5–8.

    21a. revised and reprinted as: "Go Ye Therefore and *Insult* All Nations," *Perspective Digest* 1.2 (1996), 14–21.

22. "How the Early Church Responded to Social Problems," *CT* 17 (Nov. 24, 1972) 6–8.
23. "Homer, History, and Archaeology," *NEASB* 3 (1973) 21–42.
24. "Immanuel Velikovsky's Catastrophic History," *JASA* 25 (1973) 134–39.
25. "Easter–Myth, Hallucination, or History?" *CT* 18 (March 15, 1974) 4–7; (March 29, 1974) 12–14, 16.

    25a. reprinted in *Impact* 21 (Feb.–March 1997)

26. "Greek, Hebrew, Aramaic or Syriac?—A Critique of the Claims of G. M. Lamsa," *BSac* 131 (1974) 320–31.
27. "A Decade and a Half of Archaeology in Israel and in Jordan," *Journal of the American Academy of Religion* 42 (1974) 710–26.

28. "Problems of Radiocarbon Dating and of Cultural Diffusion in Pre-History," *JASA* 27 (1975) 25–31.
29. "The Achaemenid Capitals," *NEASB* 8 (1976) 5–81.
30. "Meshech, Tubal, and Company," *JETS* 19 (1976) 239–47.
31. "Look at What They're Digging Up!" *Decision* 18 (Oct. 1977) 4–5.
32. "Critical Comments on the Search for Noah's Ark," *NEASB* 10 (1977) 5–27.
33. "The Greco-Roman World: A Bibliographical and Review Article," *JETS* 20 (1977) 157–64.
34. "The Word from Nag Hammadi," *CT* 13 (Jan. 13, 1978) 19–22.
35. "Is That an Ark on Ararat?" *Eternity* 28 (Feb. 1978) 27–32.
36. "Cultural Aspects of Marriage in the Ancient World," *BSac* 135 (1978) 241–52.
37. "Nehemiah: Master of Business Administration," *His* 39 (Jan. 1979) 8–10.

   37a. Reprinted: *Youth Leader* 36 (1979) 8–9.

   37b. Chinese version in *Ne Da Ren*, ed. P. Chang and E. Poon. Hong Kong, China: Christian Witness Press, 1985. Pp. 71–76.

38. "Tells, Digs, and Buried Treasure," *Evangelical Newsletter* 6.7 (April 6, 1979) 4.
39. "Pre–Christian Gnosticism in the Nag Hammadi Texts?" *Church History* 48 (1979) 129–41.
40. "Documents from Old Testament Times," *WTJ* 41.1 (1978) 1–32.
41. "The Descent of Ishtar, the Fall of Sophia, and the Jewish Roots of Gnosticism," *TynBul* 29 (1978) 140–71.
42–44. "Archaeology and the Scriptures: Archaeology and the Patriarchs, From the Sojourn in Egypt to the United Monarchy, and The Divided Kingdoms," *The Seminary Journal* 25 (1974) 163–84, 185–213, 215–41.
45. "Recent Archaeological Work in the New Testament Cities of Western Anatolia," *NEASB* 13 (1979) 37–116.
46. "The Archaeological Background of Daniel," *BSac* 137.1 (1980) 3–16.

46a. reprinted in *Vital Old Testament Issues*, ed. by Roy B. Zuck. Grand Rapids, MI: Kregel, 1996. Pp. 160–70.

47. "The Archaeological Background of Esther," *BSac* 137.2 (1980) 99–117.

48. "The Archaeological Background of Ezra," *BSac* 137.3 (1980) 195–211.

49. "The Reverse Order of Ezra/Nehemiah Reconsidered," *Them* 5.3 (1980) 7–13.

50. "Hermeneutical Issues in the Book of Daniel," *JETS* 23 (1980) 13–21.

51. "Was Nehemiah the Cupbearer a Eunuch?" *Zeitschrift für die alttestamentliche Wissenschaft* 92.1 (1980) 132–42.

52. "The Archaeological Background of Nehemiah," *BSac* 137.4 (1980) 291–309.

53. "Ancient Ecologies and the Biblical Perspective," *JASA* 32.4 (1980) 193–203.

54. "Josephus and the Scriptures," *FH* 13 (1980) 42–63.

55. "Josephus: First-Century War Correspondent," *Eternity* 32.4 (Apr. 1980) 35–39.

56. "Daniel and Contacts between the Aegean and the Near East before Alexander," *Evangelical Quarterly* 53.1 (1981) 37–47.

57. "Unearthing Ebla's Ancient Secrets," *CT* 25 (May 8, 1981) 18–21.

58. "The Crucifixion and Docetic Christology," *Concordia Theological Quarterly* 46.1 (1982) 1–20.

59. "The Scythians: Invading Hordes from the Russian Steppes," *BA* 46.2 (1983) 90–99.

60. "Magic in the Biblical World," *TynBul* 34 (1983) 169–200.

61. "The Proofs, Problems and Promises of Biblical Archaeology," *JASA* 36.3 (1984) 129–38.

61a. reprinted in *The Evangelical Review of Theology* 9.2 (April 1985147–138.

62. "Palaces in the Biblical Word," *NEASB* 23 (1984) 35–67.

63. "Pre–Christian Gnosticism, the New Testament and Nag Hammadi in Recent Debate," *Them* 10.1 (1984) 22–27.
64. "Sociology, Scripture and the Supernatural," *JETS* 27.2 (1984) 169–92.
65. "Obelisks and Pyramids," *NEASB* 24 (1985) 111–15.
66. "History and Hermeneutics," *Evangelical Journal* 5.2 (1987) 55–66.
67. "The Nag Hammadi Library," *JLH* 22 (1987) 425–41.
68. "Erasmus's Contributions to New Testament Scholarship," *FH* 19.3 (1987) 6–24.
69. "Gnosticism: Has Nag–Hammadi Changed Our View?" *Evangel: The British Evangelical Review* 8 (1990) 4–7.
70. "Christians and the Jewish Revolts against Rome," *FH* 23 (1991) 11–30.
71. "Mordecai, the Persepolis Tablets, and the Susa Excavations," *Vetus Testamentum* 42 (1992) 272–75.
72. "The Archaeology of Biblical Africa: Cyrene in Libya," *Archaeology in the Biblical World* 2 (1992) 6–18.
73. Interview with Timothy Jones, "Scrolls Hype," *CT* 37 (Oct. 4, 1993) 28–31.
74. "Metal Sources and Metallurgy in the Biblical World," *Perspectives on Science and Christian Faith* 45 (1993) 252–59.
75. "Hellenistic Bactria and Buddhism," *Humanitas* 18.3 (1995) 5–10.
76. "On the Road with Paul: The Ease and Dangers of Travel in the Ancient World," *Christian History* 14.3 (1995) 16–19.
77. "Cyrus H. Gordon and the Ubiquity of Magic in the Pre–Modern World," *BA* 59 (1996) 51–55.
78. "Afrocentric Biblical Interpretation," *JETS* 39 (1996) 397–409.
79. "Adaptation and Assimilation in Asia," *Stulos Theological Journal* 4.2 (1996) 103–126.
80. "'God and the Shah': Church and State in Sasanid Persia," *FH* 30 (1998) 80–99.
81. "Zarathustras laere og Det Gamle Testamente," (Danish "Zoroaster's Teaching and the Old Testament," *Tel* 4 (1999) 8–9.

82. "Martin Bernal's *Black Athena* Reviewed," *Journal of Ancient Civilizations* 14 (1999) 145–52.
83. "Attitudes Toward the Aged in Antiquity," *NEASB* 45 (2000) 1–9.
84. "Mandaic Incantations: Lead Rolls and Magic Bowls," *Aram* 11 & 12 (1999–2000) 253–68.
85. "Banquets in the Biblical World," *Proceedings of the Eastern Great Lakes and Midwest Biblical Society* 22 (2002) 147–57.
86. "The Reconstruction of Jewish Communities during the Persian Empire." *The Journal of the Historical Society* 4 (2004) 1–25.
87. "Historic Homer: Did It Happen?" *BAR* 33.2 (2007) 28–37, 76.
88. "Scripture as Talisman, Specimen and Dragoman." *JETS* 50 (2007) 3–30.
89. "The Scythians—Who Were They and Why Did Paul Include Them in Colossians 3:11?" *Priscilla Papers* 21.4 (2007) 13–17.
90. "The Curse of Ham," *Criswell Theological Review* 6.2 (2009) 45–60.
91. "Akhenaten, Moses and Monotheism," *NEASB* 55 (2010) 1–15

Reviews

1. W. Taylour, *The Mycenaeans* in *JAOS* 85 (1965) 415–18.
2. U. Cassuto, *The Documentary Hypothesis* in *JAOS* 85 (1965) 582–83.
3. R. Collin, *Evolution* in *JASA* 17 (1965) 123–24.
4. E. Speiser, *Genesis* in *JASA* 18 (1966) 57.
5. J. Myers, *I Chronicles* and *II Chronicles* in *Eternity* 17 (May 1966) 44.
6. H. Schonfield, *The Passover Plot* in *Gordon Review* 10 (1967) 150–60.

    6a. reprinted in *JASA* 21 (1969) 27–32.

    6b. reprinted in *Christianity for the Tough-Minded*, ed. J. W. Montgomery. Minneapolis, MN: Bethany Fellowship, 1975. Pp. 261–71.

7. C. Glock, *To Comfort and to Challenge* in *CT* 11 (Sept. 15, 1967) 1206.
8. J. Myers, *Invitation to the Old Testament* in *Eternity* 19 (Jan. 1968) 45.

9. K. Kitchen, *Ancient Orient and Old Testament* in *JASA* 20 (1968) 94.
10. W. Albright, *Historical Analogy and Early Biblical Tradition* in *Arch* 22 (1969) 78, 80.
11. D. Kidner, *Genesis* in *Eternity* 20 (July 1969) 47-48.
12. J. Bottéro et al., *The Near East* in *Arch* 22 (1969) 156.
13. E. Sollberger, *The Babylonian Legend of the Flood* in *Arch* 22 (1969) 156, 159.
14. A. Salonen, *Agricultura Mesopotamica nach sumerisch-akkadischen Quellen* in *AHR* 74 (1969) 1589.
15. O. Dalton, *The Treasure of the Oxus* in *JAOS* 90 (1970) 340-43.
16. W. McCullough, *Jewish and Mandaean Incantation Texts* in *Journal of Near Eastern Studies* 29 (1970) 141-44.
17. J. Finegan, *The Archaeology of the New Testament* in *CT* 14 (June 5, 1970) 31-32.
18. H. Camping, "The Biblical Calendar of History" in *JASA* 22 (1970) 99-101.
19. J. Allegro, *The Sacred Mushroom and the Cross* in *Eternity* 22 (Nov. 1971) 54-55.
20. D. Freedman & J. Greenfield, ed., *New Directions in Biblical Archaeology* in *WTJ* 33 (1971) 199-202.
21. R. Longenecker, *The Christology of Early Jewish Christianity* in *CT* 15 (Aug. 27, 1971) 29.
22. H. Cohn, *The Trial and Death of Jesus* in *CT* 15 (Sept. 10, 1971) 22-23.
23. J. Isaac, *Jesus and Israel* in *CT* 15 (Sept. 24, 1971) 32-33.
24. J. Sanders, ed., *Near Eastern Archeology in the Twentieth Century* in *CT* 16 (Oct. 22, 1971) 26-27.
25. W. Wilson, *The Execution of Jesus* in *CSR* l (1971) 385-89.
26. D. Baly & A. Tushingham, *Atlas of the Biblical World* in *CT* 16 (March 17, 1972) 17-18.
27. E. Goodenough, *Jewish Symbols in the Greco-Roman Period* XIII in *Arch* 25 (1972) 318.

28. H. Orlinsky, *Understanding the Bible through History & Archaeology* in *The Review of Books and Religion* 2 (Jan. 1973) 10.

29. W. LaSor, *The Dead Sea Scrolls and the New Testament* in CT 17 (Sept. 28, 1973) 34–35.

30. "Archaeological Evidence for the Philistines," rev. of E. Hindson, *The Philistines and the Old Testament* in WTJ 35 (1973) 315–23.

31. "Biblical Backgrounds," rev. of J. Lewis, *Historical Backgrounds of Bible History* in WTJ 36 (1973) 82–89.

32. D. Courville, *The Exodus Problem and Its Ramifications* in JASA 25 (1973) 160–61.

33. J. Daniélou, *Gospel Message and Hellenistic Culture* in CT 18 (Apr. 12, 1974) 36, 38–40.

34. "A Secret Gospel of Jesus as 'Magus'?": rev. of M. Smith, *Clement of Alexandria and a Secret Gospel of Mark* and *The Secret Gospel* in CSR 4 (1975) 233–51.

35. C. Andresen, Einführung in die Christliche Archäologie in AHR 80 (1975) 77–78.

36. "'Chariots' Is Just So Much Humbug," rev. of E. von Däniken, *Chariots of Gods?* and *Gods from Outer Space* in Eternity 25 (Jan. 1974) 34–35.

    36a. Reprinted in *The Christian Reader* 12 (June–Aug. 1974) 11–14.

37. M. Hengel, *Judaism and Hellenism* in CT 20 (Dec. 19, 1975) 321–22.

38. M. Avi-Yonah and I. Shatzman, eds., *Illustrated Encyclopedia of the Classical World* in CT 20 (June 4, 1976) 36.

39. G. Jeremias et al., eds., *Tradition und Glaube* in WTJ 39 (1976) 161–67.

40. E. Havelock, *Origins of Western Literacy* in JLH 13 (1978) 66–68.

41. E.-M. Laperrousaz, *Qoumrân: L'établissement Essénien des bords de la Mer Morte* in AHR 83 (1978) 135–36.

42. E. Lohse, *The New Testament Environment* in Them 4 (1978) 35–36.

43. J. M. Robinson, ed., *The Nag Hammadi Library in English* in CT 23 (Oct. 6, 1978) 35–40, 42–43.

44. E. Pagels, *The Gnostic Gospels* in Eternity 31 (Sept. 1980) 66–67, 69.

45. M. Magnusson, *Archaeology of the Bible* in FH 12 (1980) 150–52.

46. K. Kitchen, *The Bible in Its World* in CSR 10 (1980) 80–81.

47. S. Sandmel, *Philo of Alexandria* in JETS 23.3 (1980) 264–65.

48. R. Macuch, K. Rudolph & E. Segelberg, *Zur Sprache und Literatur der Mandäer* in JAOS 100 (1980) 79–82.

49. R. M. Grant, *Eusebius as Church Historian* in AHR 86 (1981) 1079–80.

50. P. Perkins, *The Gnostic Dialogue* in CSR 11 (1982) 171.

51. A. J. Heisserer, *Alexander the Great and the Greeks* in JLH 17.2 (1982) 193–95.

52. F. Reichmann, *The Sources of Western Literacy: The Middle Eastern Civilizations* in JLH 17.4 (1982) 479–81.

53. C. A. Raschke, *The Interruption of Eternity* in JASA 35.2 (1983) 111–12.

54. M. J. Gorman, *Abortion and the Early Church* in Eternity 34.6 (1983) 37–38.

55. E. P. Sanders, ed., *Jewish and Christian Self-Definition I: The Shaping of Christianity in the Second and Third Centuries* in JETS 26.2 (1983) 228–29.

56. E. Yarshater, ed., *The Cambridge History of Iran III: The Seleucid, Parthian and Sasanian Periods* in AHR 89 (1984) 1055–56.

57. G. Widengren, ed., *Der Mandäismus* in JAOS 105 (1985) 345–46.

58. C. H. Roberts & T. C. Skeat, *The Birth of the Codex* in JLH 20.2 (1985) 202–204.

59–60. John G. Gammie, *Daniel* and W. Sibley Towner *Daniel* in TSFB 9.1 (Sept.–Oct. 1985) 22, 24–25.

61. S. R. F. Price, *Rituals and Power: The Roman Imperial Cult in Asia Minor* in AHR 90 (1985) 1173.

62. R. Cameron, ed., *The Other Gospels* in SecCent 5.1 (1985–86) 49–51.

63. J. Baldwin, *Esther: An Introduction and Commentary* in JETS 28.4 (1985) 491.

64–65. R. E. Brown, *Recent Discoveries and the Biblical World* and G. Báez-Camargo, *Archaeological Commentary on the Bible* in CSR 14.4 (1985) 375–78.

66. J. A. Davis, *Wisdom and Spirit* in TSFB 10 (Sept.–Oct. 1986) 33.

67. W. H. C. Frend, *The Rise of Christianity* in CSR 16.1 (1986) 66–70.

68. S. H. Ali Al-Khalifa & M. Rice, ed., *Bahrain through the Ages: The Archaeology* in NEASB 28 (1987) 78–83.

69. L. Bier, *Sarvistan: A Study in Early Iranian Architecture* in NEASB 28 (1987) 83–84

70. P. A. Porter, *Metaphors and Monsters* in JAOS 107.3 (1987) 552–53.

71. C. Tuckett, *Nag Hammadi and the Gospel Tradition* in Them 13.2 (1988) 64–65.

72. A. K. Bowman, *Egypt after the Pharaohs: 322 BC—AD 642* in Libraries & Culture 23.1 (1988), 83–85.

73. I. Kikawada and A. Quinn, *Before Abraham Was* in JAOS 108.2 (1988) 310–11.

74. N. S. Fujita, *A Crack in the Jar* in BA 52 (1989) 54–55.

75. J. Harpur, *Great Events of Bible Times* in BAR 16.1 (1990) 12.

76. D. Wilber, *Persepolis* in BA 53 (1990) 236–37.

77. J. Walvoord, *Armageddon, Oil and the Middle East Crisis* in CT 35.5 (1991) 50–51.

78. R. A. Horsley, *Jesus and the Spiral of Violence* in FH 23 (1991) 111–13.

79. H. C. Kee, *Knowing the Truth: A Sociological Approach to New Testament Interpretation* in Them 17.1 (1991) 31.

80. E. Ferguson, ed., *Encyclopedia of Early Christianity* in FH 23 (1991) 80–87.

81. J. Bottéro, *Mesopotamia: Writing, Reasoning, and the Gods* in NEASB 37 (1992) 61–62.

82. M. Dandamaev, *A Political History of the Achaemenid Empire* in Bibliotheca Orientalis 49 (1992) 455–56.

83. L. Stadelman, *Love and Politics: A New Commentary on the Song of Songs* in NEASB 38 (1993) 61–62.

84. R. Charron, *Concordance des textes de Nag Hammadi: Le Codex VII* in *JECS* 2 (1994) 107–09.

85. S. H. Moffett, *A History of Christianity in Asia I: Beginnings to 1500* in *AHR* 99 (1994) 617.

86. L. H. Schiffman and M. D. Swartz, *Hebrew and Aramaic Incantation Texts from the Cairo Genizah* in *Critical Review of Books in Religion*. Atlanta: Scholars Press, 1994. Pp. 439–40.

87. K. Armstrong, *A History of God* in *The Historian* 57 (1995) 192–93.

88. L. H. Feldman, *Jew and Gentile in the Ancient World* in *FH* 26 (1994) 72–74.

89. J. J. Buckley, *The Scroll of Exalted Kingship: Diwan Malkuta 'Laita* in *JAOS* 115 (1995) 526–27.

90. H.-J. Klimkeit, *Gnosis on the Silk Road* in *NEASB* 39–40 (1995) 132–33.

91. R. W. Ferrier, *The Arts of Persia* in *NEASB* 39–40 (1995) 133–35.

92. P. Cherix, *Concordance des Textes de Nag Hammadi, Le Codex VI* in *JECS* 5 (1997) 120–21.

93. G. L. Kelm and A. Mazar, *Timna: A Biblical City in the Sorek Valley* in *BAR* 23.6 (1997) 68 & 70.

94. B. A. Pearson, ed., *Nag Hammadi Codex VII* in *JECS* 5 (1997) 587–88.

95. Bruce Kuklick, *Puritans in Babylon: The Ancient Near East and American Intellectual Life* in *Libraries & Culture* 32.4 (1997), 481–82.

96. P. L. Maier, *A Skeleton in God's Closet* in *NEASB* 41 (1996) 87–88.

97. R. E. Brown, *The Death of the Messiah* in *NEASB* 41 (1996) 88–90.

98. Jan Assmann, *Moses the Egyptian: The Memory of Egypt in Western Monotheism* in *FH* 27 (1997) 103–104.

99. J. J. Collins, *Daniel* in *JETS* 46 (1998) 124–25.

100. J. Bottero, *Mesopotamia: Writing, Reasoning and the Gods* in *NEASB* 43 (1998) 66–67.

101. J. Hoffmeier, *Israel in Egypt*, in *Review of Biblical Literature* (May 2001) web version.

102. E. Stern, *Archaeology of the Bible II: The Assyrian, Babylonian and Persian Periods* in *Bulletin for Biblical Research* 13 (2003) 297–98.

103. V. P. Long, D. W. Baker and G. J. Wenham, eds., *Windows into Old Testament History* in *NEASB* 48 (2003) 65–66.

104. J. F. Bowman, *Ancient Israel and Ancient Greece* in *JETS* 47 (2004) 153–54.

105. P. Briant, *From Cyrus to Alexander: A History of the Persian Empire* in *NEASB* 49 (2004) 61–62.

106. J. J. Buckley, *The Mandaeans: Ancient Texts and Modern People* in *JAOS* 124 (2004) 136–37.

107. F. Rochberg, *The Heavenly Writing: Divination, Horoscopy, and Astronomy in Mesopotamian Culture* in *The Historian* 68.2 (2006) 398–99.

108. E. Alvstad, *Reading the Dream Text: A Nexus Between Dreams and Texts in the Rabbinic Literature of Late Antiquity* in *NEASB* 56 (2011) 56–57.

109. K. C. Way, *Donkeys in the Biblical World: Ceremony and Symbol* in *Bulletin for Biblical Research* 22.4 (2012) 567–68.

110. J. Alvarez-Mon and M. B. Garrison, eds., *Elam and Persia* in *JAOS* 133.1 (2013) 36–37.

111. Aida B. Spencer, *I Timothy* in *JETS* 58.1 (2015) 194–97.

Excursus V

Biographical Listings

1. Bio-Bibliographies de 134 Savants (Act1a Iranica 20)
2. The Blue Book: Leaders of the English-Speaking World
3. Contemporary Authors, vol. 45–48
4. Dictionary of International Biography, 12th–17th ed.
5. Directory of American Scholars, 5th–7th ed.
6. Media Personnel Directory, 1st ed.
7. Men and Women of Distinction, 1st–2nd ed.
8. Men of Achievement, 3rd–8th ed.
9. The International Authors Who's Who, 8th–9th ed.
10. International Scholars Directory, 1st ed.
11. International Who's Who of Community Service., 1st ed.
12. International Who's Who of Intellectuals, 1st–3rd ed.
13. Who's Who in America, 62nd ed.
14. Who's Who in American Education, 8th ed.
15. Who's Who in Biblical Studies and Archaeology, 1st ed.
16. Who's Who in the East, 13th ed.
17. Who's Who in the Midwest, 14th–24th ed.
18. Who's Who in Religion, 2nd ed.

19. Who's Who in Theology and Science, 1st ed.
20. Who's Who in the World, 25th ed.
21. Albert Nelson Marquis Lifetime Achievement Award, 2019

www.ingramcontent.com/pod-product-compliance
Lightning Source LLC
Chambersburg PA
CBHW070802020526
44116CB00030B/977